The Indian Yearbook of Comparative Law 2016

AF793220

The Indian Yearbook of Comparative Law 2016

Edited by
Mahendra Pal Singh

OXFORD
UNIVERSITY PRESS

OXFORD
UNIVERSITY PRESS

Oxford University Press is a department of the University of Oxford.
It furthers the University's objective of excellence in research, scholarship,
and education by publishing worldwide. Oxford is a registered trademark of
Oxford University Press in the UK and in certain other countries.

Published in India by
Oxford University Press
2/11 Ground Floor, Ansari Road, Daryaganj, New Delhi 110 002, India

© Oxford University Press 2017

The moral rights of the authors have been asserted.

First Edition published in 2017

All rights reserved. No part of this publication may be reproduced, stored in a retrieval system, or transmitted, in any form or by any means, without the prior permission in writing of Oxford University Press, or as expressly permitted by law, by licence, or under terms agreed with the appropriate reprographics rights organization. Enquiries concerning reproduction outside the scope of the above should be sent to the Rights Department, Oxford University Press, at the address above.

You must not circulate this work in any other form
and you must impose this same condition on any acquirer.

ISBN-13: 978-0-19-948213-9
ISBN-10: 0-19-948213-6

Typeset in Adobe Garamond Pro 11/13
by Tranistics Data Technologies, New Delhi 110 044
Printed in India by Replika Press Pvt. Ltd

In the memory of
Professor P.K. Tripathi
and
Professor Parmanand Singh

Advisory Board

1. A.K. Sikri, Judge, Supreme Court of India
2. Anne Peters, Director, Max Planck Institute for Comparative Public Law and International Law, Heidelberg, Germany
3. Armin von Bogdandy, Max Planck Institute for Comparative Public Law and International Law, Heidelberg, Germany
4. Cheryl Saunders, University of Melbourne, Australia
5. Domenico Amirante, University of Naples II, Italy
6. Georg Nolte, Humboldt University of Berlin, Germany
7. Han Dayuan, Renmin University of China Law School, China
8. Jose Serna, National University of Mexico
9. Mark Tushnet, William Cromwell Professor of Law, Harvard Law School, USA
10. Martin Loughlin, London School of Economics and Political Science, UK
11. Qianfan Zhang, Peking University, China
12. Ruma Pal, Former Judge, Supreme Court of India
13. Upendra Baxi, Emeritus Professor of Law, University of Warwick, UK, and University of Delhi, India
14. Werner Menski, Emeritus Professor, School of Oriental and African Studies, UK
15. Yash Ghai, Emeritus Professor, University of Hong Kong

Contents

PART III PUBLIC LAW

SECTION A CONSTITUTIONAL LAW

SECTION B HUMAN RIGHTS

SECTION C ENVIRONMENTAL LAW

Tables and Figures

Tables

Figures

Preface

Comparative law as a subject of legal studies in the universities in India was unknown until the early part of 1960s when I studied for my bachelors and masters degrees in law. Although at the bachelor's level I studied Roman law and at master's level subjects like English and Indian legal history, constitutional law of USA and Switzerland, constitutional law of Australia and Canada, and English and US administrative law as one unit each. But no mention was ever made either by any of my professors or by any colleague that such study constituted or could be called comparative law because in all probability the term had not yet entered the vocabulary of legal studies in the universities in our country. It is only towards the middle of the 1960s that for the first time I heard comparative law had been introduced as one of the mandatory courses in legal studies at the bachelor's level by the Bar Council of India. But I found no mention of it in the syllabus of the university where I taught before I moved to the University of Delhi in 1970, where I found it included among the elective subjects in the final year of the three-year LLB course. Later in several other universities I found it included in the course on jurisprudence. But it never caught popular imagination amongst the legal studies at the universities even though some monographs were produced on it for the guidance of the students. Perhaps the best amongst them was the one prepared by Professor Rahmatullah Khan for the Indian Law Institute, New Delhi, in 1971 under the title *An Introduction to the Study of Comparative Law* based on a report prepared by Professor C.J. Hamson of the University of Cambridge after a seminar directed by him at the institute. Among others, the monograph recommended doing comparative law in reference to our neighbouring countries which we are currently doing in the comparative public law course in LLM.

But in spite of these developments even at the University of Delhi, comparative law was not a popular option and very few, and often no one, opted for it. It is only after some exposure to German public law, especially administrative law, in the early 1980s that I decided to teach this course. In the beginning, students were somewhat sceptic about the course, but within a few years it became quite a popular course, even though I made it more demanding than other courses by introducing the requirement of writing and presenting a paper in small groups. I continued to offer this course until my retirement from the university in 2005. Later when I moved to the West Bengal National University of Juridical Sciences, Kolkata, I initiated it there too as an elective course, initially in the tenth semester of bachelor's course, which was later extended to sixth and eighth semesters as well as to LLM. After the University Grants Commission introduced a one-year LLM course in 2013 with a mandatory course on comparative public law, I was asked by the current vice chancellor of National Law University, Delhi, Professor Ranbir Singh, to conduct this course which I have continued to do since then with the addition of a seminar course on comparative law in the other semester.

At this point, let me admit my ignorance of the scope of the subject that I did not refer to Professor Tripathi's pioneering work in comparative public law titled 'Foreign Precedents and Constitutional Law' published in 1957 in *Columbia Law Review*, 57: 319–47, even though I had read it and included among his publications in the festschrift for him under the title 'Comparative Constitutional Law' in 1989, revised for the second edition in 2011. Subsequently, I realized that the paper has been referred to in almost every important work on comparative public law. That paper and its antiquity must be a lesson and inspiration to every student of law to do that kind of research and get it published in one of the most prestigious legal journals internationally.

It is in the course of teaching the mandatory course to LLM that towards the end of 2015 the students initiated the proposal to start a journal in comparative law which in course of discussion was finally converted into the *Indian Yearbook of Comparative Law*. But in view of the short duration of the LLM course during which students must complete multiple assignments within fixed deadlines, they could not sustain their initial enthusiasm. However, as the need was felt to have at least one publication in a year in the country on this important and growing discipline in legal studies, I, along with my colleague Dr Niraj Kumar and then the successive research associates comprising initially Dinesh Singh followed by Kanika Gauba, decided to take the responsibility of bringing out the *Yearbook*. After Kanika handed over the charge to Akhilendra Pratap Singh, he too committed himself to the production of the *Yearbook* at the earliest. Believing that the educative role of the *Yearbook* will remain incomplete without the involvement of students, bachelor's-degree course students were also invited to participate in the publication of the

Yearbook, who could not fulfil their promise of contributing papers jointly or otherwise, but a few of them assisted in editing the contributions received for the *Yearbook*. Experience has taught me that running a periodical either in the form of a journal or under any other title, including a yearbook, is not possible in a law school unless students actively participate in its production or undertake the responsibility of organizing and running it. Hoping that the students at National Law University, Delhi, will come forward not only to share but to undertake the responsibility of ensuring the regular publication of the *Yearbook* with required and successively improved standards, they will respond to my call enthusiastically and undertake the responsibility of timely and successively improved contents of the *Yearbook* in their own interest, interest of their institution and the legal education, and learning generally in the country and abroad. I am sure academic colleagues in this and other universities in the country and abroad will continue to give their full support to this venture in future as they have done in this maiden attempt. Strategically, besides its location in the capital of the country, National Law University, Delhi, has the unique advantage of having Professor Ranbir Singh as its founding vice chancellor, who has unparallel ability to provide excellent opportunity for research and learning in all disciplines of law and related disciplines. We must exploit this opportunity to the maximum possible extent.

Finally, I trust my academic colleagues in this and other institutions in the country and abroad that they will progressively continue to give their full support to this venture by their academic contributions and other suggestions in future as they have done in this maiden attempt. On behalf of the editorial team of the *Yearbook* and my own, I express my sincere gratitude to them for either agreeing to be a member of the advisory board or contributor of a paper, or both.

With that hope and expectation I dedicate this maiden volume of the *Yearbook* to the memory of Professor P.K. Tripathi, whom I consider the initiator amongst us of comparative public law, and recognized and acknowledged as such internationally, and also to our colleague Professor Parmanand Singh who continued to pursue scholarship and its imparting to students until a few months prior to his breathing last on 20 February this year. I hope their spirit will continue to inspire us in the pursuit of scholarship partly reflected in the *Yearbook*.

Mahendra Pal Singh
New Delhi, India
8 March 2017

Introduction

This excellent volume (so painstakingly assembled by Professor M.P. Singh) charts out, inter alia, comparative jurisprudence of the European Union (EU) and India, though there are important contributions also to other comparative regions. More generally, it is a welcome addition to the slender literature on comparative constitutional law. The work extends the domains of comparative legal studies in several directions and regions. It deals, for example, with comparative law and jurisprudence (both in the sense of adjudicatory decisions and high comparative legal theory) of ethnicity, affirmative action, environmentalism, and legal pluralism. It also has contributions more specifically concerned with the human rights law and jurisprudence, especially concerning people living with disabilities; it is of importance to acknowledge the value addition by way of a section on private law and corporate law/governance and environmental law domains. A comparative analysis of human rights law and jurisprudence is also emergent in this fine work. This is, indeed, a rewarding collection useful for comparative law learning, teaching, and research.

What to compare and how to do so have been the staple diet of comparativists. Having been taught at Berkeley by Professor Albert Eherenzwig (as early as 1964), I believe that we should talk about comparative law and jurisprudence, rather than merely of comparative law as such. And comparison should, at any rate, go beyond (what dear Albert used to name as) common law and civil law 'orbits', even if this means comparing the incomparable. The present collection, however, finds responsible ways of comparing the EU and India as systematic units of meaningful comparison.

This signifies, in my view, a step forward in the practice of doing comparative law and jurisprudence. In the apt words of Philipp Dann, Maxim Bönnemann, and Tanja Herklotz, underlying the comparative method, 'the purpose of the comparison is central—as is being mindful of certain methodological guidelines … the careful *translation* of notions, the sensible selection of *functional equivalents*, and finally the particular concern and reference to the *contexts* of the instruments or entities being compared.'

One moves differently when comparing metanorms as providing a singular *grundnorm* for legal orders. Professor M.P. Singh, for example, says that the metanorm of 'social justice' is common both to the EU and India. No doubt it is, but there is no agreement concerning which metanorm shall be the grundnorm; for example, Professor Phillip Dann proposed (in the discussion) that development and equality should be regarded as central, while many German colleagues accentuated 'human dignity' as central to Germany's basic law. It would now be foolhardy for anyone to propose any basic norm for India or to say what the doctrine of basic structure essentially means except for saying how infinite are the ways of doing demosprudence or exercising demosprudential adjudicative leadership.[1]

Long ago, Dean Roscoe Pound—concluding a very long chapter 34 on comparative civil procedure (in his germinal work on jurisprudence)—said, 'Laws are easily made instruments of dictators. Law, by which a reasoned technique is applied to laws to achieve an ideal relation among men, is the arch-enemy of dictators.'[2] The very idea of law as an 'arch enemy' of tyrannical political and social orders is very appealing; and so is the distinction between 'laws' and the 'law' (a distinction Jeremy Bentham made between *a* law and *the* law, of course, a long time ago).

Pound, of course, wrote at the height of the Cold War but his words are equally crucial to this era of a New Cold War. Frankly, comparative law discipline has its own teleology: namely, resistance to old-fashioned tyranny or to deploy a newfangled phrase 'authoritarian statism'. However, any value-free (or neutral) method of comparative law and jurisprudence eschews explicit telos. Hope is notably articulated by Professor Markus Kotzur: 'Even though comparison has to be aware of their mostly culturally particular origins, it can help to "universalize" legal standards.' And yet (as Moiz Tundawala and Salmoli Choudhuri demonstrate in their study of Babashaeb Ambedkar) reading telos in comparative studies of law and jurisprudence is a contested arena: do we find any satisfactory reason for discarding the 'slave' category and adopting instead the 'dalit' as the principal tool of equality movements and constitutional jurisprudence?

At another level, one may say that all constitutions are concerned with justice, liberty, equality, fraternity, and subsistence as core values. One may also want to say that the 'postcolonial'[3] constitutions[4] are concerned with four core ideas, even concepts: governance and rights, development and justice. And these concepts are always in conflict: this, in part, helps us to understand and analyse the salience of judicial review power and process. Comparative studies in constitutional law entail (to use a phrase-regime of Paul Ricœur) a 'clash of interpretation'.[5]

The 'we-ness' of those wielding constitutional laws making and changing power contrasts with the 'we-ness' of those who chose to wield *influence*.[6] A very important step in comparative reflexive method was indicated (at the Indo-German conference, which in part this volume covers) by Professor Jörg Luther, who reminded us that 'what we can do depends very much on who are'. As academics, we wield no power but seek to influence power; and the distinction, while important, does tell us when and where that often people with power are not easily influenced by what we (the comparativists) chose to say. How to become the masters of influence so that we can impact power is the enduring question that informs the modern secular theology of all teaching and research.

The issue of cultural diversity preoccupies comparative studies. Trade and commerce can, of course, foster cultural diversity; but global business also can restrict this. It is this interplay that we should consider closely. The question that ought to engage all comparativists is whether unity in diversity is the constitutional nomos, is unity in perversity the nomos of free trade?

Comparative law (like all throughways) moves across two Western holy trinities: Hobbes, Locke, and Rousseau, on the one hand, and Marx, Freud, and Nietzsche, on the other, or the masters of order, on the one hand, and the master of suspicion, on the other. It is here that both progressive and regressive Eurocentrism indwells. Are they two sides of the same coin? Or, can the 'progressive' be kept apart from the 'regressive' Eurocentrism, and indeed comparative law and jurisprudence?

To this difficult question we must add another: in the Anthropocene era now upon us, is thinking about 'sustainable development' (SD) all that we have? As I have often said, one can think SD only by way of unsustainable thought! Anthropocene law and justice take us all in the direction not of sustainable development but of sustainable degrowth. More poignantly put, should we continue to think out of the box or do we smash the box itself in the Anthropocene?[7] Or, to put the matter less dramatically, what may comparative law and jurisprudence offer as salvation from the problematic of extinction of all forms of life on this planet?

In this short introduction, I have resisted the temptation of touching the riches of valued contributions from other comparative law regions or other areas centred on specific, and specialized, human rights issues. Certainly, the comparative method needs to be extended further to new areas such as environmental regulation, disability jurisprudence, corporate governance, and human rights. And we do not here have domain-specific problem merely; one also moves to the new questions of methods and ends of comparison.

My abstinence, I need add, does not arise from the *habitus* of progressive or regressive Eurocentrism! But an introduction or the introduction to a book, by its very nature, remains always a fragment, not a finished project. All of us need to learn afresh this distinction and we ought not to lose the value of fragments in the pursuit of finished products. Comparative law and jurisprudence is a series of tales of many cities, which are in turn conflicted narratives of many an imaginary and imagined fragments.

This welcome work contains many happy surprises: comparative law and jurisprudence always excites our capabilities to wonder and (as Max Weber had said about religion) to be astonished.

Upendra Baxi

Notes and References

1. Upendra Baxi. 2016. 'Demosprudence and Socially Responsible/Response-Able Criticism: The NJAC Decision and Beyond', *NUJS Law Review*, 9(3–4).
2. See Roscoe Pound. 1959. *Jurisprudence*, vol. V, p. 715. Minnesota: West Publishing Co.
3. I have used the term 'postcolonialism' as the stage of being liberated from the social consciousness and organization of the Empire. Such liberation is, indeed, worthy of aspiration but never complete, so pervasive are historic effects and impacts. Carelessly used, the term 'postcolonial' masks authoritarian statism or centralized despotism, which comes close to the states of colonization and the empire. Further, the term 'postcolonialism' misleads insofar as it eschews neocolonialism. Kwame Nkrumah presciently described the passage of colonialism into neocolonialism, which was 'exploitation without redress' and 'power without accountability'. See Kwame Nkrumah. 1965. *Neo-Colonialism, the Last Stage of Imperialism*, trans. Dominic Tweedie. London: Thomas Nelson. The question that arises is: is comparative law, both as a method and as a substantive discipline, neocolonial or postcolonial?
4. Upendra Baxi. 2000. 'Constitutionalism as a Site for State Formative Practices', *Cardozo Law Review*', 21(4): 1183–210.
5. See Paul Ricœur. 2007. *The Conflict of Interpretations: A Study in Hermeneutics*. Northwestern University Press.
6. I am much influenced, in drawing this distinction, by Lewis Coser. 1956. *The Functions of Social Conflict*. New York: The Free Press.
7. See Will Steffen, Jacques Grinevald, Paul Crutzen, and John Mcneill. 2011. 'The Anthropocene: Conceptual and Historical Perspectives', *Philosophical Transactions of the Royal Society*, 369(1938): 842–67, esp. p. 843. And see Upendra Baxi. 2016. 'Towards Climate Justice Theory?' *Journal of Human Rights and the Environment*, 7(1): 7–31.

Abbreviations

AA	Air (Prevention and Control of Pollution) Act
AHPPL	Adani-Hazira Port Private Limited
ALL	Administration Litigation Law
AMDAL	Analisis Mengenai Dampak Lingkungan
B-BBEEAA	Broad-Based Black Economic Empowerment Amendment Act
BBEE	Black Based Economic Empowerment
CBEF	County Budget Forum
CCI	Competition Commission of India
CCP	Chinese Communist Party
CDFEU	Charter of Fundamental Rights of the European Union
CEDAW	Convention on the Elimination of All Forms of Discrimination Against Women
CFI	Court of First Instance
CGA	County Governments Act, 2012
CHT	Chittagong Hill Tracts
CII	Confederation of Indian Industries
CJEU	Court of Justice of the European Union
CoE	Committee of Experts
CRPD	Convention on the Rights of Persons with Disabilities
CSDS	Centre for the Study of Developing Societies
CSR	Corporate Social Responsibility
DEIAA	District Environment Impact Assessment Authority
DM	District magistrate
DPSP	Directive Principles of State Policy
EAC	Expert Appraisal Committee
ECHR	European Convention of Human Rights
ECJ	European Court of Justice
ECSR	European Committee of Social Rights
ECT	Environment Court and Tribunal

EIA	Environmental Impact Assessment
EITI	Extractive Industries Transparency Initiative
ELMA	Environmental Laws (Management) Act
EMA	Environmental Management
EPA	Environment Protection Act
ESC	European Social Charter
ESV	Enlightened Shareholder Value
EU	European Union
FATA	Federally Administered Tribal Areas
FRA	Fundamental Rights Agency, Forest Rights Act
FRC	Family-run Company
GDP	Gross Domestic Product
GEL	General Environmental Legislation
HKCC	HKFE Clearing Corporation Limited
HKEx	Hong Kong Exchanges and Clearing Limited
HKFE	Hong Kong Futures Exchange
HKMA	Hong Kong Monetary Authority
HKSA	Hong Kong Society of Accountants
HKSCC	Hong Kong Securities Clearing Company Limited
IAPP	International Association on Public Participation
IBP	International Budget Partnership
ICCPR	International Covenant on Civil and Political Rights
ICSI	Institute of Company Secretaries of India
IDA	International Disability Alliance
IFA	Indian Forest Act
ILO	International Labour Organization
IMF	International Monetary Fund
KLGRP	Kenya Local Government Reform Programme
LAC	Legal Affairs Commission
LAO	Legal Affairs Office
LEC	Land and Environment Court
LEL	Local Environmental Legislation
LL	Law on Legislation
LPG	Local People's Government
MCA	Ministry of Corporate Affairs
MI	Mental Illness
MMR	Maternal Mortality Ratio
MOEF	Ministry of Environment and Forests
MP	Member of Parliament
MQM	Mohajir Qaumi Movement

NASSCOM	National Association of Software and Services Companies
NATO	North Atlantic Treaty Organization
NCC	National Constitutional Conference
NCST	National Commission for Scheduled Tribes
NEMA	National Environment Management Authority
NGT	National Green Tribunal
NPC	National People's Congress
NPCSC	National People's Congress Standing Committee
NTA	National Taxpayers' Association
NWFP	North-West Frontier Province
OBC	Other Backward Classes
OECD	Organisation for Economic Co-operation and Development
OHCHR	Office of the United Nations High Commissioner for Human Rights
PCB	Pollution Control Board
PCJSS	Parbattya Chattagram Jana Samhati Samiti
PEL	Provincial Environmental Legislation
PLC	Politics and Law Commission
PLIA	Public Liability Insurance Act
PSC	Politburo Standing Committee
PWD	Persons with Disabilities
REC	Ratified Environmental Convention
RESC	Revised European Social Charter
SAARC	South Asian Association for Regional Cooperation
SAARCSC	SAARC Social Charter
SC	Scheduled Caste
SCCLR	Standing Committee on Company Law Reform
SEA	Strategic Environmental Assessment
SEAC	State Expert Appraisal Committee
SEBI	Securities and Exchange Board of India
SEHK	Stock Exchange of Hong Kong
SEIAA	State-level Environment Impact Assessment Agency
SEL	Sector Environmental Legislation
SEMA	State Environment Management Authority
SEOCH	SEHK Options Clearing House Limited
SFC	Securities and Futures Commission
SFCO	Securities and Futures Commission Ordinance
SPC	Supreme People's Court
SRI	Socially Responsible Investing
SSS	Security, Self-government and Social Justice

ST	Scheduled Tribe
TEU	Treaty on European Union
TFEU	Treaty on the Functioning of the European Union
TISA	The Institute for Social Accountability
TOR	Terms of Reference
UN	United Nations
UNCEDAW	United Nations Committee on the Elimination of Discrimination against Women
UNESCO	United Nations Educational, Scientific and Cultural Organization
WA	Water (Prevention and Control of Pollution) Act
WCAR	World Conference Against Racism
WHO	World Health Organization
WPA	Wildlife Protection Act
WTO	World Trade Organization

PART I

COMPARATIVE LAW

GENERAL THEMES

1

Of Apples and Mangoes

Comparing the European Union and India

Philipp Dann, Maxim Bönnemann, and *Tanja Herklotz*

I Introduction

This chapter suggests a new field of comparative constitutional studies: comparisons between the European Union (EU)[1] and India. It suggests that there is a wealth of fascinating topics in which these two legal and constitutional systems could be compared with mutual benefit, such as social rights, religious freedom, democracy, federal structures, and the role of courts—as well as economic law (internal market, competition law) or environmental regulations. While in some of these areas, the EU seems to have more experience, in others India clearly brings more expertise, giving the comparative field a truly dialogical nature.

Yet, such comparisons have rarely been made. While comparative studies of both systems (EU and India) with that of the US are well established and numerous, this cannot be said about comparative endeavours between the EU and India. This is all the more astonishing since a brief reflection on their societal structure, ideological self-understanding, and constitutional framework suggests that Europe and India might actually share more similarities than the US and India do. So, what are the reasons for this gap in comparative attention and research? Are we perceiving that these polities are too far apart to be compared or to offer valuable insights—in other words as incomparable as apples and mangoes, sour and sweet?

This chapter will proceed in two steps. It will first examine in a more general way methodological rules for case selection in comparative law that might be relevant for an EU–India comparison (section II). Against this background, it will then study more closely arguments potentially impeding a comparison between the EU and India—and turn them into research questions for future comparison (section III).

The chapter hopes to instigate and encourage more scholarship and exchange between Indians and Europeans—and to break open Eurocentric orientations in European scholarship, as well as US fixations within Indian academia.

II Case Selection in Comparative Legal Studies

When engaging in a comparative endeavour, the question of case selection is a preliminary one. In particular, if the comparison enters new and less familiar ground, asking which units can meaningfully be compared is surely the first step and precedes the description of the law in its context and the analysis.[2] Must the units of comparison be very similar or very different? How many units should be compared? And to what extent is the case selection dependent on the aim of the comparison and the broader methodological approach?

II.1 General Considerations for Case Selection

Very basic advice surely is to compare legal systems that are neither too similar, as such a comparison would be uninteresting, nor too different, as that would lead to comparisons between 'apples and oranges',[3] or in our case apples and mangoes. Put differently: 'There is no point in comparing what is identical, and little point in comparing what has nothing in common.'[4]

John Stuart Mill has already distinguished between comparisons that look at very different cases in order to explain a common variable ('method of agreement') or very similar cases that differ in only one causal condition in order to explain a variable that the two units do not share ('method of difference').[5] Consequently, the decision whether to select similar or different units depends on the purpose of the comparative enquiry.[6] Such enquiries could, on the one hand, establish *similarities* in development, arguments, structures, and results in spite of substantial general differences between the systems under consideration.[7] On the other hand, they could establish certain *differences* in spite of substantial similarities between the systems under consideration and thereby unearth what was hidden from view.[8]

That the goal and purpose of comparison are central for determining which legal orders to consider also applies to comparative constitutional studies. Vicky Jackson, for example, identifies three potential goals in comparative constitutional law scholarship: (a) to develop a better intellectual understanding of one or more other systems; (b) to enhance the capacity for self-reflection; and (c) to normatively evaluate 'best practices'.[9] The problem of case selection is rather tricky and especially relevant with regard to the 'best practices' goal.[10] But the question of case selection is also closely linked to the broader methodological approaches (which again depend on the purpose of the research). Depending on whether the nature of the methodological approach is classificatory, historical, normative, functional, or contextual, the techniques of pursuing the comparison may range from a detailed analysis of one or a few foreign constitutions to large-N statistical analyses of particular phenomena.[11]

According to Ran Hirschl,[12] methodological considerations in case selection are more important in some cases than others. They play a subordinate role in free-standing single country studies or when the comparative referencing is aimed at self-reflection. They are, however, of crucial importance in comparative research aimed at generating thick concepts and thinking tools through multifaceted descriptions as well as in studies that draw upon a controlled comparison and aim at theory building through causal inference.[13] For these latter enquiries, Hirschl outlines five very different principles of research design in comparative constitutional law: (a) the 'most similar cases' principle, (b) the 'most different cases' principle, (c) the 'prototypical cases' principle, (d) the 'most difficult cases' principle, and (e) the 'outlier cases' principle.[14]

For a comparison between the EU and India, these are helpful guidelines. They militate not against such a comparison generally but rather advise us to be clear about the concrete purpose of the comparison.

II.2 Vertical Comparison as an Impediment?

One particular problem of case selection and a potential objection against a comparison between India and the EU might be the fact that India is a state and the EU is not. Due to the unique legal character of the EU such a comparative enterprise might face the objection that it lacks a *tertium comparationis* around which a meaningful inquiry can be built. Indeed, the EU has often been described as something of a structure *sui generis*; it is not a typical international organization anymore but also, it is clearly not a nation-state.[15] Formulated in general terms, the underlying assumption behind such objections is that comparative enterprises have to be conducted horizontally, for example, among legal systems that belong to the same level (national legal systems with other national legal systems, regional systems with other regional systems, the legal system of one international organization with that of another international organization). But is such self-limitation of comparative constitutional law to horizontal inquiries plausible?

A closer look reveals that comparative constitutional scholarship has already begun to change its reference points from a horizontal to a vertical comparison in different legal contexts (although the phrase to compare 'vertically' is still rarely used).[16] Put simply, vertical comparisons refer to inquiries into legal systems that operate at different levels of authority. This can be, for instance, a comparison of a legal instrument of an international organization with that of a nation state,[17] of national constitutional law with transnational law,[18] or of supranational with national federal systems.[19] Likewise, inquiries into 'migration' and the 'borrowing' of legal concepts may be undertaken not only along horizontal lines but also in a cross-level fashion.[20]

One legal context where cross-level legal comparison has become a routine operation is the EU. Being a federal and multilayered legal system in which the different layers may collide, overlap, and mutually influence each other, it has become impossible to understand this structure fully without taking into account all legal levels. At the level of practice, think only of the EU's most prominent legal actor, the Court of Justice of the European Union (CJEU). In many cases, the 'pretext' to interpreting EU law is a comparison of the respective provisions with member states' laws.[21] Similarly, a comparison between certain areas of EU law and the domestic legal level has become a standard feature of many comparative works in the European context.[22]

But also beyond Europe, cross-level legal analysis has become a rather usual type of analysis since hardly any legal order is untouched by the influences of international law anymore. The increasing number of international institutions and transnational regulatory bodies may serve as an example here. The governance activities of those institutions not only affect more and more areas of life but also increasingly limit the freedom of individuals in constraining ways. Thinking about legal standards concerning the procedures and accountability of international institutions will almost necessarily go along with a vertical comparison of the respective legal standards at the domestic level.[23] In sum, there is no doubt that the overall field of comparative constitutional law still plays out in a world of nation states. Yet, vertical comparative law has become an integral part of the field's steady transnationalization.

In conclusion, we might say that the vertical nature of a comparison is no formal obstacle. There is no ontological barrier, no 'nature' of an entity standing in the way. In fact, we will see later that the caveat of formal difference (nation state versus international organization) actually appears less convincing when we take a closer look at the specific case of the EU and India. What is more important and ultimately decisive for the case selection, however, is the purpose of comparison and the function of the instruments being compared. This leads to a number of general methodological considerations that are relevant for a large number of comparisons—but which we consider especially relevant for a vertical comparison of India and the EU.

II.3 Three Methodological Guidelines

First, vertical comparisons have to take into account what has been labelled with regard to the EU 'the problem of translation'.[24] While large parts of our constitutional vocabulary still revolve around the idea of nation states one has to be cautious in applying this vocabulary in legal contexts beyond the state. In other words, not all analytical or normative concepts can easily be shifted from one level of analysis to another.[25] For instance, the notion of a 'constitution' has historically evolved in the national context. This does not mean that using it for the EU foundational treaties and comparing them to national constitutions, that is, 'translating' the notion from a domestic into a supranational key, is impossible. But the 'translation' has to be done carefully for the context and a comparative yardstick should be chosen with sensitivity to the (otherwise relevant) differences between the domestic and the supranational levels.

Secondly, when comparing the EU and India there are good reasons to engage *functional* methods, even though those methods have to be handled with care. Why is that so? Comparing the EU and India means comparing two entities that are different in many respects. While it is important to keep doctrinal, epistemic, or institutional differences between the two different units in mind, those differences must certainly not mean the end of comparative law. In fact, horizontal comparative inquiries, too, face the problem of large differences between two systems (for instance capitalist and socialist, or religious and secular systems). In this regard, it has been a useful strategy to structure the comparison not along the lines of institutions that are seemingly the same, but along functional equivalents. The comparative 'entry point' is thus to ask how two different systems respond to a similar societal need. However, functional methods have to be handled with care. With few exceptions, societal problems and needs are not universal but contingent and context-specific. Moreover, functionalism has been forcefully criticized for focusing on similarities not on differences. This is an important critique since any presumption of similitude may indeed always lead to overly simplistic homogenization and marginalization of heterodox or subaltern practice.[26] Functionalism thus may serve as an appropriate method for Indo-European comparisons, but only as long as we remain sensitive to its pitfalls.[27]

Finally, structuring a comparative inquiry along functional equivalents is a fruitful starting point, but only as long as it is supplemented by contextual analysis. In particular in constitutional law, both the questions of what constitutes a societal need and what role the law plays are deeply embedded in political, economic, and cultural contexts.[28] Naturally, contextual differences play an important role in horizontal constellations too. However, there are some particularities with regard to supranational constitutional structures that should be kept in mind when comparing them to national constitutions. Take as an example the symbolic dimension of constitutions. Supranational constitutions are often perceived as technocratic and 'far away' from society whereas national constitutions can build on rich symbolic resources and are embedded in popular political imaginations (founding myths, revolution, collective autonomy, etc.).[29] These differences in terms of symbolic functions may play an important role when evaluating whether a constitution is perceived as legitimate or how a constitution is lived in practice. Yet, analysing those structures of beliefs behind a constitution cannot be done by functional analysis alone but has to be supplemented by relying on neighbouring disciplines such as political science, postcolonial theory, or cultural studies.

In sum, we can say that the methodological rules on case selection do not bar any comparison between the EU and India. Rather, they underline that the purpose of the comparison is central—as is being mindful of certain methodological guidelines that we just mentioned: the careful '*translation*' of notions, the sensible selection of *functional equivalents* and finally the particular concern and reference to the *contexts* of the instruments or entities being compared.

III Comparing the EU and India

Against this background, we can now turn to the concrete consideration of a comparison between the EU and India. Since the purpose of each comparison might be different, we will focus here on understanding the contexts and basic structures of the EU and India, which might be seen as limitations to their comparison. As we go along, however, likely arguments against an EU–India comparison actually turn into fascinating research questions.

III.1 Substantive and Sociological Similarities: Constitutional State Nations in India and the EU

We have already explained that the largely formal argument against the EU–India comparison (the EU is not a state, while India is a state) is not convincing. At this point, we would like to make the substantive point that the description itself is not convincing—neither of the EU nor of India.

We conceive of the EU not as an international organization that follows an international law rationale but as a separate polity resting on legal foundations that are autonomous from member state law. While the predecessors of the EU, the European Coal and Steel Community (1951) and the European Economic Community (1958), were created in the form of a classical international law agreement, soon thereafter the European Economic Community underwent a legal process that transformed the union into a structure that resembles many elements of national constitutions.[30] At the beginning of this constitutionalization stand two ground-breaking decisions of the CJEU. First, the court held that (in contrast to public international law) EU law has direct effect in EU member states. This means that individuals can invoke EU law directly in front of the member states' courts (doctrine of direct effect).[31] Secondly, in cases where EU law and member state law collide, the former trumps the latter (doctrine of supremacy).[32] Both decisions unfold their impact and important role for Europe's constitutionalization if some other features of the EU are taken into account.

Much like at the national level, the legal architecture of the EU is marked by a complex institutional design and several layers of law. Unlike in international organizations, decision-making is not concentrated in the exclusive realm of member states, but divided between the council (representing member states) and a directly elected parliament with far reaching competences. Moreover, all actions by EU institutions can be reviewed and annulled by the European Court of Justice if they violate EU law or fundamental rights or do not fall within the scope of the union's competences. Finally, Europe's two basic treaties contain many provisions that are similar to national constitutions. The Treaty on European Union (TEU) and the Treaty on the Functioning of the European Union (TFEU), which stand at the top of the EU's legal system, define the power and competences of the Union's institutions, as well as decision-making procedures, citizenship, and EU citizens' fundamental rights. A second thick and immensely detailed layer of law consists of regulations, directives, and decisions that are directly applicable in all member states. Taken together, all of these features not only set apart the Union from regular international organizations but have also turned the

Union into a legal system that is an object of comparison in its own right. In sum, the EU functions today more like a federal system than an international organization and is hence already formally not so dissimilar from India, as we will now see.

Just as it would be a mistake to characterize the EU as a typical international organization, it is equally misleading to depict India as a classical nation state. Thinking about the comparability of India and the EU depends not least on the analytical lens through which we look at both units. If we change our perspective slightly, the aforementioned dichotomy might appear in a different light. To do so, we suggest relying on an analytical category, developed by Stepan, Linz, and Yadav, labelled the *state–nation* model.[33]

The state–nation model has been developed in order to describe countries that are 'politically robustly multinational'. In contrast to states like Japan, France, or Germany, which (at least until recently or in their self-perception) still match the idea of a homogenous nation state, other states are marked by an immense cultural and linguistic heterogeneity. These latter states in fact consist of many different nations within one state and are consequently not nation states but rather state-nations. The most important features of these state-nations are their high degree of cultural diversity, which is territorially based, the multiple identities one finds within these entities, and two or more official languages.[34] All of these features are mirrored in India's constitutional system, which accommodates and guards those identities.[35] For Stepan, Linz, and Yadav, India is an example par excellence for their concept of a state-nation; in the light of India's diversity attempting to organize it in a similar fashion to the homogeneous nation state has not been an option. Another author who has pointedly captured this point is Sunil Khilnani, who observed:

> Nehru's regime was able to install a layered pluralistic definition of Indianness, one which he saw as the end culmination of a millennia of historical mixing and cultural fusion. Unlike German or Italian nationalism which saw the state as the response or result of the struggle towards a common ethnic identity, Nehru felt that Indian nationalism and an Indian identity could only emerge within the territorial and institutional framework of a state. This Nehruvian model protected and celebrated linguistic, religious and cultural differences, rather than imposing a uniform Indianness.[36]

The success story of developing this 'layered Indianness' is in many ways unique. But if we turn or eyes to Europe we find some astonishing parallels. Both the EU and India are continents rather than countries in this sense. In the EU 510 million inhabitants live in 28 member states. India consists of 29 states and seven union territories and is inhabited by 1.2 billion people.

Both legal systems operate with a multitude of languages, 23 in India and 24 in the EU. Both policies accommodate a variety of different religions, in each case one majority religion (Hinduism in India and Christianity in the EU) and several minority religions. Both the Indian constitution[37]as well as the European Treaties[38] emphasize respect for cultural and religious diversity as well as for regional identities.[39] These regional identities remain strong in both policies: Statistics show that a large number of citizens have a 'dual identity'—42 per cent of Indians identify with the Indian nation *as well as* with their particular state and 52 per cent of EU citizens define themselves by their nationality *and* as Europeans.[40] The 'deep cultural diversity' that Stepan, Linz, and Yadav attest to India in the sense that significant groups (especially in the Kashmir Valley, Mizoram and Nagaland, or Punjab) advance claims of independence in the name of nationalism and self-determination,[41] finds its parallels in the striving for independence of some EU member states with the UK's referendum to leave the Union being the most prominent example.

III.2 Role of Law, Constitutionalism, Legal Pluralism

There is another aspect, however, that might complicate the comparison between Indian and EU constitutional law and that is the role of law most generally in both societies. Law is more than a mere set of rules and norms. Comparative constitutional inquiries also have to delve into legal cultures and cultures of legality, or in Upendra Baxi's words: 'Behind every written constitution lies an unwritten one, which enacts the conventions and usages, the protocols and accoutrements of power that resist linguistic codification.'[42] In many postcolonial societies, India included, there is a scepticism about the role of law, as postcolonial legality is perceived in many cases as a continuation of colonialism's repressive legacy. The role of law here is often characterized by a contradiction between governance and justice.[43]

Another important difference concerning the role of law lies in the very notion of law, which might be quite different in India and the EU. In India, indigenous and local normative systems often fulfil functions of law. Religious communities as well as tribal groups are granted freedom in governing their lives according to their 'personal laws'. Many people organize their lives according to justice systems that have little or no connection to state law or state legal institutions, such as courts or state administration. Legal pluralism is hence an important feature of the Indian legal system and a wide gap exists between the law in books and the law as practised on the ground.[44] While this lived law on the ground has featured prominently in legal anthropology, one might question how far it serves comparative law scholars.

At first glance, these elements of a surely complex multifaceted role of law in India could stand in the way of a comparison with the EU legal system, which is traditionally depicted as being guided by the rule of law, based on rationality and the monopoly of state law. But this depiction has to be questioned. It is more grounded in popular imaginations as in the empirical analysis of law or its 'reality'.[45] Recent crises (like the migration crisis, fiscal crisis, etc.) show that the political can trump the rule of law in Europe as well. Furthermore, legal pluralism is no longer such a distant and strange phenomenon for Europeans either. The changing demographics as a result of massive migration have brought up the topic of religion based laws in Europe as well and scholars have begun to question the assumption that the Western legal systems are solely composed of state law.[46]

At the same time, constitutional law and constitutionalism in India are not only characterized by scepticism but also contain a long tradition and use a language of emancipation and struggle. Law also plays an important role in compensating for state failure and defective institutions. In particular courts play a central role and obviously do so with the language of law to mediate within societies, to bridge quests for justice on the one side and low state capacity on the other side.[47] The judiciary in general has been central in formulating and advancing an agenda of social justice with the help of social action litigation that also forms the basis of an affirmative culture of constitutionalism.

III.3 Constitutional Structures and Fields of Comparison

India's and Europe's shared experience of organizing the diversity of state nations on a continental scale reverberates in the constitutional structure and is based on similar constitutional values in both polities. These invite Indo-European comparisons in at least five entry areas.

First, and following most directly from the foregoing description of the sociological diversity, both constitutional systems deal with such diversity within a system of democracy, based on the concept of individual equality. Democracy and collective self-determination are fundamental values in both India and the EU, and are operationalized through their constitutions.[48] Elections, multiparty systems, protections for intermediary social organizations (trade unions, religious groups, civil society organizations, etc.), and many other aspects are regulated by law. This might be more obvious with regard to India than to the EU, which introduced direct elections to its parliament only in 1979 and is still an emerging democracy. But the EU today is clearly a democratic system in its own right. Nevertheless, in this respect, it would be of tremendous value for European scholars to better understand the Indian experiences of organizing democratic self-determination in the face of such—and sometimes—overwhelming social diversity. Democracy as a collective structure rests in both constitutional systems on the idea of equality of all citizens. Ensuring such equality is a major task in both polities—and an equally fascinating field of comparison.[49]

Secondly, both constitutional systems are organized along federal lines. Like in India, legislative competences and the exercise of public authority in the EU are divided between the Union on the one hand and the different member states on the other. Naturally, multilayered structures of governance are a key feature to every federal system. But if we zoom a little bit more into the federal experiences of both continents, there is more that each can learn from the other. Unlike in the US, both federal systems are embedded in a multinational setting that is marked by significant regional differences in terms of power, identity, language, and culture. In both Europe and India, the regional level plays an important role with regard to the attachment of the citizens' identities. In India's constitutional structure of federalism, this is captured by the idea of an 'asymmetric federalism'; the federation's different sub-units are granted different rights and they enjoy different degrees of self-governance.[50] Europe's federal model can also be characterized as asymmetric federalism, when we take into account the flexible structures of, for example, the Euro zone, the Schengen visa regime, or its policing laws.[51] Likewise, scenarios of European disintegration push for new comparative research.[52] In the light of the fiscal and banking crisis, Great Britain's vote to leave the EU, and increasing attention being paid to models such as a 'two-speed' Europe,[53] the EU might move more towards (and learn from) the Indian model of carefully balancing differences in terms of population size and cultural identities in the member states.

A third area in which the EU and India seem to have much more in common than the two states respectively share with the US, is fundamental rights. With regard to rights and rights adjudication, both India and the EU put a stronger emphasis on dignity and hence give the idea of rights a different horizon and grounding than US jurisprudence does.[54] More obvious is the EU–Indian connection with regard to social and economic rights. These are non-existent in the US constitutional system but play a profound and characteristic role for India and almost equally for the EU and its member states.[55]

A fourth field in which a comparison is especially fruitful concerns the ambit of secularism and religious freedom. In particular, against the background of the current increased religious diversification in the EU through immigration, this is an area in which Europeans can learn a lot from India's experience with secularism in a multireligious context. European courts are currently challenged and have not yet found a coherent position in accommodating religious freedom and equality. Whereas Christian symbols have been treated with a certain religion-friendly attitude, rights to religious freedom have been defined more narrowly when it came to Muslim claims for collective autonomy and religious identity.[56] In the subcontinent, on the other hand, the coexistence of multiple religions is the foundation on which Indian secularism is built.[57] The Indian concept of secularism contrasts sharply with, for instance, the US–American understanding of a strict divide between church and state and the assumption that religion can be distilled from the public sphere.[58] While American secularism was developed in the context of a single religion society, Indian secularism meets the needs of a society with deep religious diversity while complying with the principles of freedom and equality.[59] It is concerned as much with interreligious domination as it is with intrareligious domination.[60] It allows the state to intervene in religions in specific situations, both in a supporting way (that is, granting aid to religious educational institutions or exempting Sikhs from mandatory helmet laws to accommodate the wearing of religiously required turbans) and in a restrictive manner (that is, forbidding practices that deny equal dignity such as untouchability in Hinduism).[61]

Finally, an area where a comparison might be especially productive is economic law. For decades, economic policy in India was marked by a thick regulatory environment and embedded in the idea of social revolution.[62] It was only after the ideological shift in 1991 that India's economic sector underwent a process of liberalization and privatization. India's experience with regulating its economic sector and achieving a balance between liberalization and community interest is thus relatively young, both at the level of legislation and judicial review.[63] By contrast, the EU has begun as and still is fundamentally a project of economic integration and has an extensive legal structure aimed at progressively realizing an internal market. A good illustration of an area in which Indo-European comparisons could be highly productive is competition law. After having introduced a new competition law, the Competition Commission of India started to enforce the act only in 2009. Already at the level of legislation, some parts of the act have been inspired by EU competition law. For Indian lawyers, it would thus be a promising comparative enterprise to delve into the long-standing jurisprudence of the European Court of Justice on competition and merger control when it comes to further interpreting and enforcing the Indian Competition Act in the future.

IV Conclusion

When one starts thinking about it, the comparison between the EU and India becomes a somewhat obvious field of research, one that is challenging but surely productive—for self-reflection on each system as well as to test and formulate thick doctrinal concepts or even to work on theories and explanation based on causal inferences.

But then again, with few exceptions,[64] little has been done here. Are there perhaps social and epistemic rather than intellectual impediments? From a sociological standpoint, it is true that numerous Indian scholars live and work in the US and that they share English as a language. Despite the fact that there are almost twice as many non-resident Indians (NRI) living in the EU[65] it seems that the US is way ahead of the EU with regard to employing academics of Indian origin. Indeed, comparatively few Indian legal scholars work in (continental) Europe, and even fewer European legal academics work in India. In addition, the public and academic discourse on EU law is often not led in English, but in the languages of the respective member states.

Also, European legal scholarship has long been (and might still be) shaped by a certain fixation on the Global North.[66] In contrast to area studies or anthropology, scholarship in the legal departments as well as the syllabuses of comparative law courses have long tended to limit themselves to studying the legal systems of Europe and North America. The Global South has only recently begun to feature in legal academic work.[67] Furthermore, law faculties at European universities have also not been particularly known for taking interdisciplinary approaches like, for instance, cooperating with South Asia studies or anthropology. To be sure, the fact that India has long been a blind spot for European legal academics is mirrored by the fact that the EU has also hardly been on the Indian academic radar.

It is about time that these impediments were overcome and that we delved into the rich potential of EU–India comparisons—in the area of constitutional law but also in many other fields. The new Indian Yearbook of Comparative Law might be exactly the right forum to present respective studies.

Notes and References

1. When we suggest comparing the EU and India, it is important to note that with respect to Europe, we do not mean comparing European national systems (such as that of France, Italy, etc.) to India—but the EU itself. This presupposes a certain understanding of the EU, which we will explain in more detail in section III.1. It suffices to say here that we conceive the EU as an autonomous constitutional system.

2. G. Dannemann. 2006. 'Comparative Law: Study of Similarities of Differences?' in M. Reimann and R. Zimmermann (eds), *The Oxford Handbook of Comparative Law*. Oxford and New York: Oxford University Press.
3. Mathias Siems. 2014. *Comparative Law*, p. 16. Cambridge: Cambridge University Press.
4. Dannemann, 'Comparative Law', p. 384.
5. J.S. Mill. 2006 [1843]. 'Of the Four Methods of Experimental Inquiry', in A. Sica, *Comparative Methods in the Social Sciences*, pp. 105–23. London: SAGE Publications.
6. Dannemann, 'Comparative Law', p. 385.
7. Dannemann, 'Comparative Law', p. 406.
8. Dannemann, 'Comparative Law', p. 406.
9. V. Jackson. 2012. 'Comparative Constitutional Law: Methodologies', in M. Rosenfeld and A. Sajó (eds), *The Oxford Handbook of Comparative Constitutional Law*, pp. 54–75, esp. p. 70. Oxford and New York: Oxford University Press.
10. Jackson, 'Comparative Constitutional Law', p. 70.
11. Jackson, 'Comparative Constitutional Law', p. 55 et seq.
12. R. Hirschl. 2005. 'The Question of Case Selection in Comparative Constitutional Law', *The American Journal of Comparative Law*, 53(1): 125–55.
13. Hirschl, 'The Question of Case Selection', p. 131.
14. Hirschl, 'The Question of Case Selection', p. 133 et seq.
15. J.H.H. Weiler and U. Haltern. 1996. 'The Autonomy of the Community Legal Order: Through the Looking Glass', *Harvard International Law Journal*, 37: 411–48.
16. See H.F. Zacher (ed.). 1978. 'Einleitung: Horizontaler und vertikaler Sozialrechtsvergleich', in *Sozialrechtsvergleich im Bezugsrahmen internationalen und supranationalen Rechts*, p. 9 et seq. Berlin: Duncker and Humblot; A. Momirov and A. Naudé-Fourie. 2009. 'Vertical Comparative Law Methods: Tools for Conceptualizing the International Rule of Law', *Erasmus Law Review*, 2(3): 291–311; A. Peters. 2015. 'Immune against Constitutionalisation?' in A. Peters, E. Lagrange, S. Oeter, and C. Tomuschat (eds), *Immunities in the Age of Global Constitutionalism*, pp. 1–19, esp. p. 5. Leiden: Brill Nijhoff; J.B. Wiener. 2001. 'Something Borrowed for Something Blue: Legal Transplants and the Evolution of Global Environmental Law', *Ecology Law Quarterly*, 27(4): 1295–371; and R. Scarciglia. 2014. 'Methodological Pluralism and Legal Comparison', in R. Scarciglia and W. Menski (eds), *Islamic Symbols in European Courts*, pp. 21–34, esp. p. 31. Padova: Cedam-Kluwer.
17. B. Fassbender. 1998. 'The United Nations Charter as Constitution of the International Community', *Columbia Journal of International Law*, 36: 529–619; and P. Dann. 2013. *The Law of Development Cooperation: A Comparative Analysis of the World Bank, the EU and Germany*. Cambridge: Cambridge University Press.
18. P. Zumbansen. 2012. 'Transnational Comparisons: Theory and Practice of Comparative Law as a Critique of Global Governance', in M. Adams and

J. Bomhoff (eds), *Practice and Theory in Comparative Law*, pp. 186–211. Cambridge: Cambridge University Press.

19. M. Cappeletti, M. Seccombe, and J.H Weiler (eds). 1986. *Integration through Law: Europe and the American Federal Experience*, vol. 1. Berlin and New York: Walter de Gruyter; and Kalypso Nicolaidis and Robert Howse (eds), *The Federal Vision: Legitimacy and Levels of Governance in the United States and the European Union*. Oxford and New York: Oxford University Press.
20. Wiener, 'Something Borrowed'.
21. K. Lenaerts. 2003. 'Interlocking Legal Orders in the European Union and Comparative Law', *International and Comparative Law Quarterly*, 52(4): 873–906, esp. p. 896.
22. R. Dehousse. 1994. 'Comparing National and EC Law: The Problem of the Level of Analysis', *American Journal of Comparative Law*, 42(4): 761–81; Christoph Schönberger. 2006. *Unionsbürger: Europas föderales Bürgerrecht in vergleichender Sicht*. Tübingen: Mohr Siebeck; Christoph Möllers. 2005. *Gewaltengliederung: Legitimation und Dogmatik im nationalen und internationalen Rechtsvergleich*. Tübingen: Mohr Siebeck; and Philipp Dann. 2004. *Parlamente im Exekutivföderalismus. Eine Studie zum Verhältnis von föderaler Ordnung und parlamentarischer Demokratie in der Europäischen Union*. Heidelberg: Springer.
23. See A.N. Fourie. 2009. *The World Bank Inspection Panel and Quasi-Judicial Oversight: In Search of the 'Judicial Spirit' in Public International Law*. Utrecht: Eleven International Publishing. Fourie compares the judicial oversight mechanism of the World Bank to the US, the EU, and South Africa.
24. J.H.H. Weiler. 1999. 'European Democracy and Its Critics: Polity and System', in *The Constitution of Europe: 'Do the New Clothes Have an Emperor?' and Other Essays on European Integration*, pp. 264–76, esp. pp. 268–9. Cambridge: Cambridge University Press.
25. Dehousse, 'Comparing National and EC Law', p. 774.
26. J. Schacherreiter. 2016. 'Postcolonial Theory and Comparative Law', *Verfassung und Recht in Übersee (VRÜ)/Law and Politics in Africa, Asia, and Latin America*, 49(3): 291–312. M. Bönnemann and L. Jung. 2017. 'Critical Legal Studies and Comparative Constitutional Law', in R. Grote, F. Lachenmann, and R. Wolfrum (eds), Max Planck Encyclopedia of Comparative Constitutional Law, Oxford: Oxford University Press.
27. C. Saunders. 2009. 'Towards a Global Constitutional Gene Pool', *National Taiwan University Law Review*, 4: 1–38. This work favours a critical and cautious use of functionalism in comparative constitutional law.
28. G. Frankenberg. 2006. 'Comparing Constitutions: Ideas, Ideals, and Ideology—Toward a Layered Narrative', *International Journal of Constitutional Law*, 4(3): 439–59.
29. U. Haltern. 2003. 'Pathos and Patina: The Failure and Promise of Constitutionalism in the European Imagination', *European Law Journal*, 9(1): 14–44.

30. J.H.H. Weiler. 1991. 'The Transformation of Europe', *Yale Law Journal*, 100(8): 2403–83.
31. Case 26/62 *Van Gend en Loos v Nederlandse Administratie der Belastingen* [1963] ECR 1.
32. Case 6/64 *Flaminio Costa v E.N.E.L.* [1964] ECR 585.
33. Alfred Stepan, Juan J. Linz, and Yogendra Yadav. 2011. *Crafting State-Nations: Indian and Other Multinational Democracies*. Baltimore: The Johns Hopkins University Press.
34. Stepan et al., *Crafting State-Nations*, chapter 1.
35. Think of the structure of asymmetric federalism (Articles 73 and 162 of the Constitution of India) and the special provisions for the state of Jammu and Kashmir (Article 370) as well as for the states of Andhra Pradesh, Arunachal Pradesh, Assam, Goa, Mizoram, Manipur, Nagaland, and Sikkim (Article 371) and the protection of linguistic and religious diversity [Articles 29, 30, 51A(e) and (f)].
36. Sunil Khilnani. 1998. *The Idea of India*, p. 166. New Delhi: Penguin Books.
37. Articles 29, 30, 51A(e) and (f) of the Constitution of India.
38. Articles 3(3) and 4(2) TEU.
39. For a critical comparison, see J. Tripathy and S. Padmanabhan (eds). 2013. *The Democratic Predicament*. London and New York: Routledge.
40. For India, see Stepan et al. *Crafting State-Nations*, pp. 60–1, drawing on a survey on 'Subjective National Identity' carried out by the Centre for the Study of Developing Societies (CSDS) in 2005: 34 per cent of the respondents regarded themselves as 'only Indian' and 12 per cent identified only with their respective state. In the EU, only 2 per cent of the citizens regard themselves as Europeans and 38 per cent define themselves only by their nationality (statistics from 2015). European Commission. 2015. *Standard Eurobarometer, 83: Citizenship*, http://ec.europa.eu/public_opinion/archives/eb/eb83/eb83_citizen_en.pdf, accessed 9 October 2016.
41. Stepan et al. *Crafting State-Nations*, p. 1.
42. U. Baxi. 2012. 'Postcolonial Legality', *Verfassung und Recht in Übersee (VRÜ)/ Law and Politics in Africa, Asia, and Latin America*, 45(2): 178–94, esp. p. 180.
43. Baxi, 'Postcolonial Legality', p. 185.
44. Werner Menski. 2000. *Comparative Law in a Global Context: The Legal Systems of Asia and Africa*, p. 143. London: Platinum.
45. Teemu Ruskola. 2013. *Legal Orientalism*, p. 30 et seq. Cambridge: Harvard University Press.
46. Patrick Glenn. 2010. *Legal Traditions of the World*, p. 2. Oxford: Oxford University Press, stating that 'Western law is traditional law'.
47. N. Robinson. 2009. 'Judicial Architecture and Capacity', in S. Choudry, M. Khosla, and P.B. Mehta (eds), *The Oxford Handbook of the Indian Constitution*, pp. 330–48. Oxford: Oxford University Press.
48. For the EU, see Christopher Lord and Harris Erika. 2006. *Democracy in the New Europe*. Basingstoke: Palgrave Macmillan. For India, see U.S. Mehta. 2010. 'Constitutionalism', in N.G. Jayal and B. Mehta (eds), *The Oxford Companion to Politics in India*, pp. 15–27. Oxford: Oxford University Press.

49. K. Tarunabh. 2016. 'Equality', in S. Choudhry, M. Khosla, and P.B. Mehta (eds), *The Oxford Handbook of the Indian Constitution*, pp. 699–719. Oxford: Oxford University Press.
50. See L. Tillin. 2016. 'Asymmetric Federalism', in S. Choudhry, M. Khosla, and P.B. Mehta (eds), *The Oxford Handbook of the Indian Constitution*, pp. 540–95. Oxford: Oxford University Press; and Madhav Khosla. 2012. *The Indian Constitution*, p. 74 et seq. Oxford: Oxford University Press. For more critical information on this concept see L. Tillin. 2006. 'United in Diversity? Asymmetry in Indian Federalism', *The Journal of Federalism*, 37: 45–67.
51. D. Thym. 2005. '"United in Diversity": The Integration of Enhanced Cooperation into the European Constitutional Order', *German Law Journal*, 6: 1731–48. For a recent account of the European Union's asymmetric federalism see G. Martinico, The Asymmetric Bet of Europe, Verfassungsblog, 12 March 2017, available at http://verfassungsblog.de/the-asymmetric-bet-of-europe/, accessed 21 July 2017.
52. On this topic, see H. Vollaard. 2014. 'Explaining European Disintegration', *Journal of Common Market Studies*, 52(5): 1142–59; P.C. Schmitter. 2012. 'European Disintegration? A Way Forward', *Journal of Democracy*, 23(4): 39–48; and J. Hayward and R. Wurzel (eds). 2012. *European Disunion: Between Sovereignty and Solidarity*. London: Palgrave Macmillan.
53. Jean-Claude Piris. 2011. *The Future of Europe: Towards a Two-Speed EU?* Cambridge: Cambridge University Press.
54. In the Indian constitution, dignity is mentioned in the preamble, in Articles 39(f) and 51A(e). The Indian Supreme Court draws on dignity in its jurisprudence on social rights; see, for instance: *Francins Coralie Mullin v The Administrator*, 1981 AIR 746 and *Olga Tellis & Ors v Bombay Municipal Corporation*, 1986 AIR 180. The EU's Charter of Fundamental Rights, which is applicable for the EU through Article 6(1) TEU, mentions human dignity in its preamble as well as in Articles 1, 25, and 31.
55. For India, see G. Bhatia. 2016. 'Directive Principles of State Policy', in S. Choudhry, M. Khosla, and P.B. Mehta (eds), *The Oxford Handbook of the Indian Constitution*, pp. 644–61. Oxford: Oxford University Press; S. Shankar and P.B. Mehta. 2008. 'Courts and Socioeconomic Rights in India', in V. Gauri and D. Brinks (eds), pp. 146–82. *Courting Social Justice*. New York: Cambridge University Press. For Europe, see Gráinne De Búrca and Bruno de Witte (eds), Larissa Ogertschnig (asc. ed.). 2005. *Social Rights in Europe*. Oxford: Oxford University Press.
56. P. Danchin. 2011. 'Islam in the Secular Nomos of the European Court of Human Rights', *Michigan Journal of International Law*, 32: 663–747.
57. R. Bhargava. 2011. 'Should Europe Learn from Indian Secularism?', *India Seminar*, no. 621, http://www.india-seminar.com/2011/621/621_rajeev_bhargava.htm, accessed 16 October 2016.
58. Gary J. Jacobsohn. 2003. *The Wheel of Law: India's Secularism in Comparative Constitutional Context*, pp. xii, xiii. Princeton and Oxford: Princeton University Press.

59. Bhargava, 'Should Europe Learn from Indian Secularism?'.
60. Bhargava, 'Should Europe Learn from Indian Secularism?'.
61. Bhargava, 'Should Europe Learn from Indian Secularism?'.
62. From the perspective of constitutional law, see A. Fischer. 2007. 'Which Road to Social Revolution? Liberalization and Constitutional Reform', Working Paper 34, in India, Heidelberg Papers in South Asian and Comparative Politics series.
63. For two recent analyses of the role of the Supreme Court in India's liberalization process, see the interesting contributions by M. Mate. 2016. 'Globalization, Rights, and Judicial Review in the Supreme Court of India', *Washington International Law Journal*, 25(3): 643–71; and P. Gupta. 2014. 'Judicial Constructions: Modernity, Economic Liberalization, and the Urban Poor in India', *Fordham Urban Law Journal*, 42: 25–90.
64. S. Shastri. 1993–4. 'Lessons for the European Community from the Indian Experience with Federalism', *Hastings International and Comparative Law Rev*iew, 17: 633–63; P. Dann. 2011. 'Federal Democracy in India and the European Union: Towards Transcontinental Comparison of Constitutional Law', *Verfassung und Recht in Übersee (VRÜ)/Law and Politics in Africa, Asia, and Latin America*, 44(2): 160–76; A. Wankhede. 2016. 'Data Protection in India and the EU: Insights in Recent Trends and Issues in the Protection of Personal Data', *European Data Protection Law Review*, 2: 70–9; and T. Allen. 2007. 'Property as a Fundamental Right in India, Europe and South Africa', *Asia Pacific Law Rev*iew, 15: 193–218.
65. In the US, 3,443,063 NRIs live and 6,300,000 in Europe (1,451,862 of those in the UK), http://nriol.com/indiandiaspora/statistics-indians-abroad.asp, accessed 9 October 2016.
66. See W. Menski. 2016. 'Still Asking for the Moon? Opening Windows of Opportunity for Better Justice in India', *Verfassung und Recht in Übersee (VRÜ)/Law and Politics in Africa, Asia, and Latin America*, 49(2): 125–47, esp. p. 128.
67. See, for instance, M. Hailbronner. 2016. 'Overcoming Obstacles to North-South Dialogue: Transformative Constitutionalism and the Fight against Poverty and Institutional Failure', *Verfassung und Recht in Übersee (VRÜ)/Law and Politics in Africa, Asia, and Latin America*, 49(3): 253–62; D. Bonilla Maldonado (ed.). 2013. *Constitutionalism of the Global South*. New York: Cambridge University Press; and D. Amirante. 2012. 'Nation Building through Constitutionalism: Lessons from the Indian Experience', *Hong Kong Law Journal*, 42(1): 23–42.

2

Legal Cultures in Comparative Perspective

Markus Kotzur

I Introduction: Comparison Matters in Comparative Matters[1]

Antonin Scalia, late justice of the US Supreme Court and influential member of the Court's conservative wing, was not only famous for his originalist[2] and textualist approaches to constitutional law but also well known as both astute and tart-tongued critic of law comparison. He argued:

> If there was any thought absolutely foreign to the founders of our country, surely it was the notion that we Americans should be governed the way Europeans are.... What reason is there to believe that other dispositions of a foreign country are so obviously suitable to the morals and manners of our people that they can be judicially imposed through constitutional adjudication? Is it really an appropriate function of judges to say which are and which are not?[3]

Scalia, by resorting to 'We, The People's' self-determined sovereignty, introduced a valid democratic argument and nevertheless drew a rather distorted picture of the comparative lawyer whose task is neither to anti-democratically impose 'morals and manners' of the '*others*' on '*us*' nor to arbitrarily select rules from a '*foreign*' legal system that could be applied one-to-one to '*ours*'. Law comparison[4] proves to be a more *complex* and *reflective* toolkit for 'finding the law'.[5]

Far from simply seeking blueprints of fixed solutions—let's do it like the others!—the comparative lawyer is in constant search of a *matrix* that allows her to weigh, to probe, and to critically reconsider her own arguments against the background of experiences that others have made or solutions that others have found.[6] Law comparison is not based on (scientific) curiosity as an end in itself; it is not an idle glass bead game with the foreign, the unknown, or, even more exciting, the exotic.[7] Comparison shall reflect the 'own' in the light of the 'other' and help to get to know oneself better, one's own legal system and one's own legal culture: discover yourself by understanding others![8] Consequently, to simply copy-paste a rule from another legal system or restate a judgement of a foreign Court has nothing to do with serious comparative work meeting scientific standards. It would both misconceive the cultural heterogeneity of the legal world and ignore a political community's own *legal identity* as *cultural identity*.[9] Meaningful comparative work may not limit itself to the idea of comparing 'the laws' (that is to say written norms, legal texts or, with specific importance in common law systems,[10] judgements) but it has, in a broader sense, to encompass a more sensitive *comparison of cultures*.[11] Whoever wants to undertake the endeavour of this *holistic comparison*[12] must necessarily descend from the ivory tower of pure legal thought without losing themselves in the narrow world of law-school-comparison all too often limiting itself to rather fruitless *semantic exercises*. Analytically skilled and dogmatically trained lawyers tend to explain the world before they have described it. For the comparative lawyer, however, 'Mapping first',[13] 'description before explanation', should be the *epistemic creed*. A shift from comparative constitutional law *stricto sensu* to a more generous notion of comparative constitutional studies is the obvious consequence.[14]

Comparative intentions, in other words, have to meet the real world and thus to undergo a reality check. In this real world, pluralism qualifies as an *essential structure* of modern democracies.[15] Consequently, laws and constitutional regimes are equally pluralist in nature.[16] They face *cultural pluralism* and have to deal with cultural diversity—even within the nation state let alone beyond. In such a culturally diverse real world, law depends on its contexts.[17] It is embedded in culture; it lives in a certain cultural ambiance;[18] it itself is an 'emanation of culture' (P. Häberle 1982). That has, of course, methodological consequences. Comparative and transdisciplinary openness are twin siblings. 'Many of the tools necessary to engage in the systematic study of constitutionalism across polities can be found in the social sciences in general, and political sciences particular', is a key position in R. Hirschl's recent study on comparative constitutional law.[19] The 'comparative turn' and what some describe as the 'empirical turn'[20] in legal studies—others envisage a 'new legal realism'[21]—might very well go hand in hand. So, any comparative interdisciplinary study of constitutional systems is confronted with the classic universalism versus cultural relativism (or particularism) dichotomy[22] and has to take into account the relevant theoretical conceptualizations. It has, for example, to follow recent developments in the cultural sciences,[23] to refer back to theories of contestatory practices as developed by the political sciences,[24] or to consider the postcolonial studies movement.[25] It goes—as to the letter approach—without saying that the 'Global North' has to be very well aware of the 'Global South' critique.[26] For some time now influential voices in public international law and international politics have attempted to overcome the Eurocentric visions of their field.[27] Many more aspects requiring cultural sensitivity and intercultural discourse[28] could be added. Nevertheless, one can conclude at this point with a *final twist*.

Even though comparison has to be aware of their mostly culturally particular origins, it can help to 'universalize' legal standards.[29] The comparative method, as stated above, is not limited to the comparison of legal texts, but extends to broader cultural, economic, political, social, etc. contexts. Comparing these contexts (by describing, by mapping, for example) is a first step in universalizing their contents. It should be emphasized at this point that universality itself is more a process than a static a-historic idea(l), rather a cultural product of real-world interaction—political, scientific, philosophical, most importantly communicative interaction—than pure Platonic heritage. Universality has, admittedly, always been a principle of European Constitutionalism and based upon the Platonic (or anti-Platonic) tradition of European philosophy, but the very idea of universality reaches far beyond the cultural boundaries of Europe.[30] Its origins might be European: the concept itself—aiming at universal needs, threats, vulnerabilities, etc.—is a global one. To figure out what best serves these needs, what best fights these threats and what best addresses these vulnerabilities, requires worldwide law comparison including microstates, developing countries, and reform or transformation democracies, that is to say societies in transition from a totalitarian past to a democratic future.[31] All the differences between the legal systems and all the asymmetries as to the status of (political, social, economic, etc.) development have to be considered carefully.[32] Without any doubt, the awareness *of* and *for* these different, asymmetrical and therefore particular structures limits the possibilities of comparison, but at the very same time—maybe paradoxically—gives the outcome a certain universal drive. In this regard 'comparative matters' really do matter. In particular, the European and public international lawyer is invited to put legal cultures in a comparative perspective in order to see what common legal principles (see Article 6 III TEU) can be discovered or universal legal standards can be developed at the end of the day. In the following, three different but—given their 'common' cultural underpinnings and overtones—interdependent fields of reference are briefly discussed. The ongoing controversies they create and the up-to-date relevance they display stand for their global legal importance and their intrinsic comparative momentum: *religious cultures* or *mutatis mutandis* cultures of religions (II); a *culture of solidarity*—often desired but not all that often realized (III); and finally *(cosmopolitan) citizenship* as cultural promise and educational aim (IV).

However, these frames of reference will not be used to conceptualize a new or at least refined stand-alone theory of law comparison.[33] They will not even be seen as examples to further develop the methodology of comparative (constitutional) law in detail.[34] The chapter's much more limited yet nonetheless ambitious intention is to draw the reader's attention to describing real world phenomena and mapping the global legal landscape. The chapter aims to create context-awareness, to tell stories of cultural ambiances, and, most importantly, to dare to identify crossovers (instead of getting stuck in dichotomies) between the local and the global, between the culturally particular (or relative) and the universal. This is undertaken in a world of 'in-betweens' and with the mindset of a public international lawyer who is always, as Article 38 I lit. c ICJ-Statute states, searching for 'general principles of law recognized by civilized nations'. The success of such an endeavour depends on comparing problems first and not solutions. All in all, it depends on what Anne-Marie Slaughter characterized a long time ago as the essential feature of law comparison: 'a process of collective judicial deliberation on a set of common problems.'[35]

II Religious Cultures: Universal Standards

II.1 The Historical Development

The freedom of religion creates manifold opportunities to deliberate on a set of common problems the solutions for which have yet to be found. One might feel inclined to start the discussions with France's recent debate over the burkini ban[36]—but without wanting to downplay the heated controversies of the present, we might be better served to look back a bit further to the past. The guarantee of religious freedom is a core feature of modern constitutionalism and human rights guarantees since the aftermath of the American and the French Revolutions.[37] The modern constitutional state has always been confronted with and often challenged by a *world of believers.* Notwithstanding such sometimes fruitful, sometimes violent controversies, the constitutional State displayed a rather positive attitude towards diverse emanations of religious beliefs and it did so even where state and religion were strictly separated, for example in the US.[38] The reason for such a 'benevolent distance' is a cultural one. A political community's cultural identity is to an important extent shaped by the religious identities of the citizens it is composed of. This starts with religious holidays[39] and ends with in 'God we trust' on the one-dollar-bill. Andy yet, in times of the Islamic State,[40] jihadist terrorism, and an increasing Islamophobia[41] at the expense of moderate Muslims worldwide, religions, are all too easily misrepresented as danger[42] rather than being situated in the context of freedom of thought and freedom of conscience as an essential part of a free human being's identity. Religious diversity, once distorted into radical forms, no longer seems to go hand in hand with the constitutional state.[43]

The sober public international lawyer, when starting these discussions, should remember the significant role which religion and religions play in the evolution of public international law. Up until the sixteenth century, the pre-modern paradigm of a so-called 'res publica Christiana'[44] had determined the mutual relations of political entities and political powers according to a universal notion of Catholicism under the guidance of the Roman Catholic church. The discovery of the New World had already challenged this notion. The Protestant reformation and the religious wars in consequence thereof put a definite end to it.[45] Regardless of whether or not the Peace of Westphalia can be qualified as the beginning of modern statehood and, in parallel, modern public international law,[46] it clearly displays an early 'constitutional moment' (B. Ackermann)[47] for the modern international community and organized a 'ground of coexistence for Christians of different confessional persuasions': cuius regio, eius religio being the famous Latin leitmotif.[48] The origin of post-1648 public international law can accordingly be described along two different but interdependent 'religious' narratives. The first narrative tells the story of overcoming religious determination in order to clear the way for a secular, enlightened modernity. It is the 'from-a-distance' story. The second narrative tells the story of making religious pluralism constitutive for the international legal system. It is the 'diversity-as-an-asset' story. After 1945, this has also become a guiding theme of the United Nations and backed-up by the 'international bill of rights'.[49] The wording used in the Preamble of the UN Charter does not leave any room for misunderstandings: 'to practice tolerance and live together in peace with one another as good neighbours'. When nowadays a 'no tolerance' story becomes more and more attractive, one has to distinguish carefully between necessary 'no tolerance' for violence and inacceptable 'no tolerance' for minority religions.

II.2 The International Community's Religious Textbook

Never forget: religious tolerance is the Charter's unequivocal demand. Today, a variety of public international law treaties and declarations, in particular human rights treaties, follow this programmatic model. Read together, all these texts, whether binding or non-binding, resemble something like a textbook of global ethical standards of religious freedom and tolerance. The textbook's content might very well be conceived as the result of far-reaching holistic comparative attempts which have been described above. Within the nation states and in regional contexts a set of values or—less empathic—attitudes towards religions, backed up by constitutional guarantees emerge and spill over onto the global plane.[50] The reason for such a spill-over-effect might not in fact be that these values are indeed shared across all cultures, but rather, that across all cultures the threats and challenges underpinning the creation of these values in the first place are identified as being the same.

Keeping that in mind, one should get back to the UN Charter's Preamble: it reaffirms its 'faith in fundamental human rights, in the dignity and worth of the human person'. The 'Friendly Relations Declarations'[51] re-emphasizes the aim of living together in peace and practicing tolerance as good neighbours in its Preamble, too. The Universal Declaration on Human Rights,[52] issued by the General Assembly in 1948, states in Article 26 II on education: 'Education shall be directed to the full development of the human personality and to the strengthening of respect for human rights and fundamental freedoms. It shall promote understanding, tolerance and friendship among all nations, racial or religious groups, and shall further the activities of the United Nations for the maintenance of peace.' The systematic context plays an important role: religious freedom is linked to the maintenance of peace and thus has a universal intent. If we recall the recent war against the Islamic State and the acts of violence IS terrorists claim for their project, the importance of such a nexus becomes depressingly evident.

Article 13 Nr. 1 of the International Covenant on Economic, Social and Cultural Rights, now in form of binding law (the enforcement of which is another story), repeats the request:

> The States Parties to the present Covenant recognize the right of everyone to education. They agree that education shall be directed to the full development of the human personality and the sense of its dignity, and shall strengthen the respect for human rights and fundamental freedoms. They further agree that education shall enable all persons to participate effectively in a free society, promote understanding, tolerance and friendship among all nations and all racial, ethnic or religious groups, and further the activities of the United Nations for the maintenance of peace.

Religious tolerance is once more seen as an indispensable prerequisite for international peace. Article 18 I of the International Covenant on Civil and Political Rights enshrines religious freedom as a core human right: 'Everyone shall have the right to freedom of thought, conscience and religion. This right shall include freedom to have or to adopt a religion or belief of his choice, and freedom, either individually or in community with others and in public or private, to manifest his religion or belief in worship, observance, practice and teaching.'

Another significant text has been drafted by the 1959 Declaration of the Rights of the Child.[53] Principle 10 of the declaration states: 'The child shall be protected from practices which may foster racial, religious and any other form of discrimination. He shall be brought up in a spirit of understanding, tolerance, friendship among peoples, peace and universal brotherhood, and in full consciousness that his energy and talents should be devoted to the service of his fellow men.' A 'spirit of tolerance' is furthermore pointed out in the Preamble of the Convention on the Rights of the Child.[54] The UN General Assembly 'Declaration on the Elimination of All Forms of Intolerance and of Discrimination Based on Religion or Belief'[55] obviously qualifies as one of the most important international law documents on religious tolerance. Already in the emphatic opening lines, the General Assembly expresses its conviction 'that freedom of religion and belief should also contribute to the attainment of the goals of world peace, social justice and friendship among peoples and to the elimination of ideologies or practices of colonialism and racial discrimination'. The text then introduces the consideration 'that it is essential to promote understanding, tolerance and respect in matters relating to freedom of religion and belief and to ensure that the use of religion or belief for ends inconsistent with the Charter of the United Nations, other relevant instruments of the United Nations and the purposes and principles of the present Declaration is inadmissible'.

II.3 The Textbook's Universal Reading and Understanding

Without doubt, the 'textbook' as introduced so far uses language centred on universality and inspired by value. However, will the textbook's reading and understanding be as universal? Can it live up to its promises and the expectations it raises? What is universal exists and prevails everywhere. It has a certain relation, extension, and applicability to more or less everything. Universality therefore 'should be looked for, not in abstract theoretical "principles" or other a-historical judgement or vision, but in concrete experience', which is to say: 'normative authority, in so far as it exists for man, resides in historical particularity'.[56]

These historical particularities could be traced back to Greek and Roman antiquity, or as concerns recent history to the eighteenth century. E. de Vattel had framed a 'humankind-oriented' concept of a 'société des nations'.[57] However, the strong focus on the human being as an individual at the same time questioned whether universality could be a source of normativity. Fundamental dichotomies emerged from the universal-individual model: universality versus particularity, universality of values versus relativity of values, universality versus diversity.[58] The impressive intellectual level of the philosophical universality-particularity debate aside, a black-and-white scheme of the universal and the particular individual is not an adequate means of explaining today's theory and practice, especially of human rights protection.[59] Human rights are both universal and individual in nature. They are based upon the universal notion of human dignity and the particular realization thereof in a particular legal culture at a particular moment in time.[60]

II.4 The European Momentum

So, what then might turn out to be the specific European momentum? Europe can be portrayed as 'united in diversity'. Notwithstanding all its recent crises (public debts crisis,[61] refugee crisis) and the Brexit shock,[62] the Union remains a rather unique model for political unity without relying on the cultural unity of a nation. This European identity-shaping rationale of 'cultural pluralism' can be seen behind numerous legal provisions such as Article 2 TEU, Article 5 Sec. 3 TEU (principle of subsidiarity), or Article 6 Sec. 3 TEU (general principles of law being common to the Member States). Texts like these provide proof that democratic as well as cultural forms of pluralism can coexist on the European plane at the very same time. To some extent, European governance can be described as 'diversity management'. This also holds true for the freedom of religion. Already the Preamble of the TEU emphasizes not explicitly the Judeo-Christian[63] but 'the cultural, religious and humanist inheritance of Europe, from which have developed the universal values of the inviolable and inalienable rights of the human person, freedom, democracy, equality and the rule of law'.[64] Following that 'inspiration', which shall guide the whole European integration process, Article 10 TFEU requests that the Union, when 'defining and implementing its policies and activities', shall 'aim to combat discrimination based on sex, racial or ethnic origin, religion or belief, disability, age or sexual orientation'.[65]

Religion is relevant in more or less all fields of Union policies. This is made quite clear by Article 13 TFEU:

> In formulating and implementing the Union's agriculture, fisheries, transport, internal market, research and technological development and space policies, the Union and the Member States shall, since animals are sentient beings, pay full regard to the welfare requirements of animals, while respecting the legislative or administrative provisions and customs of the Member States relating in particular to religious rites, cultural traditions and regional heritage.[66]

Moreover, the fight against religious discrimination ranks among the most relevant aims and purposes not only of the market-driven but also the policy-oriented and human rights-based integration processes, see Article 19 Sec. 1 TFEU:

> Without prejudice to the other provisions of the Treaties and within the limits of the powers conferred by them upon the Union, the Council, acting unanimously in accordance with a special legislative procedure and after obtaining the consent of the European Parliament, may take appropriate action to combat discrimination based on sex, racial or ethnic origin, religion or belief, disability, age or sexual orientation.

The institutional dimension of religion and the collective exercise thereof is present in Article 17 TFEU: 'The Union respects and does not prejudice the status under national law of churches and religious associations or communities in the Member States.'[67]

The Charter of Fundamental Rights of the European Union (EU) guarantees manifold dimensions of religious freedom and religious equality as a human right.[68] The classic guarantee can be found in Article 10 I: 'Everyone has the right to freedom of thought, conscience and religion. This right includes freedom to change religion or belief and freedom, either alone or in community with others and in public or in private, to manifest religion or belief, in worship, teaching, practice and observance.' Article 14 III of the Charter enshrines the parental right of religious education: 'The freedom to found educational establishments with due respect for democratic principles and the right of parents to ensure the education and teaching of their children in conformity with their religious, philosophical and pedagogical convictions shall be respected, in accordance with the national laws governing the exercise of such freedom and right.' Corresponding to Article 10 TFEU, Article 21 I of the Charter forbids religious discrimination: 'Any discrimination based on any ground such as sex, race, colour, ethnic or social origin, genetic features, language, religion or belief, political or any other opinion, membership of a national minority, property, birth, disability, age or sexual orientation shall be prohibited.' Finally, the 'unity in diversity' motto of the EU is re-emphasized by Article 22: 'The Union shall respect cultural, religious and linguistic diversity.' This respect—which should be 'informed' respect—requires comparative knowledge and knowledge acquired by comparative work as well.[69]

Beyond the EU, all Member States of the Council of Europe are bound by the European Convention on Human Rights.[70] Article 9 of the Convention combines the freedoms of thought, conscience and religion. Religious discrimination is prohibited by Article 14 of the Convention: 'The enjoyment of the rights and freedoms set forth in this Convention shall be secured without discrimination on any ground such as sex, race, colour, language, religion, political or other opinion, national or social origin, association with a national minority, property, birth or other status.'[71] All these guarantees on the regional European plane are to some extent culturally particular concretizations of universal human rights standards. Yet at the same time they themselves gave (and give) rise to universalized religious freedom on the global plane. This, indeed, might be seen as the 'universalistic paradox' which law comparison is at once based on and can overcome.[72] The same conclusion can be drawn from the way(s) the European and other legal (constitutional) orders deal with 'solidarity'.

III A Culture of Solidarity: A Universal Desire

III.1 Solidarity and Integration

To shed light on what might compose or endanger a culture of solidarity, the EU is a regional example with—again—universal implications and expectations. They start with the narrative of 'ever deepening integration' in an 'ever closer Union'. For quite a long time, this narrative expressed the European polity's integrationist creed (far beyond the initial market integration[73]) and was shared by many Euro-optimist Union citizens: 'We, the citizens of Europe!'[74] Such optimistic beliefs, however, seem to have fallen out of fashion somewhat. Along with the recent crises-driven Eurosceptic challenges of this narrative, the fundamental principles and values (see Article 2 TEU)[75] it is based upon have also been called into question. In particular it is solidarity that is at stake: when the financial crisis divides rescue policy supporters from Grexit advocates; or when the refugee crisis provokes strong tendencies of re-nationalization in sovereignty-centred 'splendid isolation'. Unsurprisingly (or perhaps surprisingly?), Donald Trump is following the same populist path in his 2016 Presidential campaign. Is the willingness or reluctance towards burden-sharing the litmus test for European and many other forms of (regional) integration in times of solidarity crises? Since solidarity itself is both a contentious and contested[76] idea, the conflicts might reach even further and ground even deeper. Keeping all these uncertainties, ambiguities and complexities in mind, the numerous references to solidarity in the Lisbon treaty leave the comparative lawyer with somewhat uneasy feelings and raise some critical question: which overall expectations, moral obligations, political assumptions, and normative force can be attributed to what the Union's primary law calls 'solidarity'?

III.2 The (Universal) Concept of Solidarity

The concept of solidarity, whilst dating back to the French Revolution's programmatic leitmotif 'Liberté, Égalité, Fraternité'[77] and being enshrined as early as 1804 in the 'Code Civil', is comparatively young. It was the French sociologist Émile Durkheim who, based on sociological facts, provided a first comprehensive scientific elaboration.[78] Many other scholars followed, so in modern sociology Talcott Parsons, in the field of law in general Leon Duguit and in the field of public international law in particular Georges Scelle.[79] These scientists not only tried to 'translate' the all too often neglected revolutionary ideal of 'fraternité'—Anthony Giddens by the way found it amazing how little scholarly attention has been paid to establishing a precise meaning for solidarity[80]—into modern-day language[81] but also focused on conceptualizing solidarity as a mode of organizing a polity and, where such a polity transcends the nation state, as a mode of fostering transnational cooperation. Conceived in these terms, solidarity reaches far beyond certain moral obligations which the individual might have towards the other members of her or his polity in cases of necessity/emergency[82]—though prevailing tendencies to restrict solidarity either to the private sphere (family, friends, colleagues, etc.), smaller political entities (neighbourhoods, municipalities, etc.), or the national 'Schicksalsgemeinschaft'[83] should not be underestimated. Not only has the refugee crisis taught the lesson that—besides a common migration policy which would be urgently needed and require some comparative effort given the EU Member States' quite diverse migration policies[84]—belonging has a strong emotional impact on solidarity, it has also shown that many would disagree with the description of the European demos as a 'People composed of Others' (J. Weiler 1991).

Constitutional law and theory have nevertheless established some tradition to conceive solidarity as program and/or principle and paved the way for shifting the solidarity paradigm from the domestic/regional to the global plane.[85] Notwithstanding this transnational progress of ideas as well as ideals, Kirsten Schmalenbach, Sonja Puntscher Riekmann, and Doris Wydra rightfully outline in their research proposal for the Salzburg Centre of European Union Studies, that the notion 'solidarity'—rather 'lavishly if not inflationary' used in the Lisbon Treaty—is ambiguous in its content: solidarity can simply be a 'moral orientation' of pre-legal nature or amount to a 'legal duty'.[86] It can be used in a purely descriptive or decisively normative way. Going even further, it can programmatically and purposefully be used as a means of policymaking, constitution building and social engineering. Different concepts of society might go hand in hand with different notions of solidarity: for example, the Christian ideal of charity or, in the Islamic world, the principle of Zakat, both demanding that a fair share of one's wealth be given to the poor and the needy.[87] After 1789, as already stated, solidarity's predecessor 'fraternité' was conceived as a political, philosophical, and legal concept within post-revolutionary France.[88] In the age of constitutionalism, many other European legal and political idea(l)s followed the French example. Public international law took to the scene later, but it did so on similar terms.

In his influential studies on solidarity, K. Wellens refers to the conceptual foundation of solidarity in public international law as laid down by Michel Virally some 40 years prior: solidarity was first a simple notion, then a political and finally a legal principle in public international law.[89] The principle, having, as A. Peters puts it, a 'strong ethical underpinning', is undoubtedly 'value-driven'.[90] This, however, is true for many if not all legal principles—human dignity first and foremost—and does not establish a verdict against (binding) legal quality. Another feature which solidarity shares with many principles of public international law is its multifunctionality and its multilayered character, resisting any essentialist definition and requiring instead context-sensitive interpretations.[91] Malcom Ross convincingly argues that solidarity is 'persistent by diverse presence' in EU law.

Solidarity can be perceived as a prerequisite for integration, it needs to be contextualized with democracy, subsidiarity, loyalty, sustainability and citizenship. It is concretized in the human rights context as the social right to something.[92] Going beyond Europe, the Indian Constitution gives striking examples which the European comparative lawyer must study carefully.[93] Solidarity, again within and beyond Europe, is interpreted as a means of reconciling competition-based market integration and social welfare orientation. More generally, solidarity as a legal principle contains within it a *negative* and a positive component. Negative solidarity constitutes the mere response to certain dangers or events, whereas positive solidarity creates, consequent upon the previous negative notion, joint rights and obligations.[94] Solidarity operates as a principle to achieve common goals; sometimes it imposes common, sometimes it imposes differentiated obligations or responsibilities: it encompasses procedural and operational, substantive and normative elements, values and legal obligations (and/or entitlements).[95]

III.3 Legal Substantiations of Solidarity within the EU and Beyond

This becomes very clear when focusing on the law of the EU as a form of regional public international law with a specific constitutional quality. Article 2 TEU, addressing the Union's basic values, declares that these values derive from a society upholding, among others, the principle of solidarity.[96] Beyond plain economic interdependence, a political community needs a more demanding 'bonum commune' orientation which not only reflects the different national notions of their 'common good' but also has a clear focus on a common European 'bonum commune'.[97] Beyond that, the bonum-commune ideal might—in today's globalized world more so than ever before—even require a Kantian focus on humankind as such. Consequently, Article 3 TEU ranks bonum-commune solidarity among the Union's aims and purposes, promoting cooperative solidarity among the Member States (para 3) and in the global realm (para 5).[98] In the intergovernmental field of the common foreign and security policy,[99] 'mutual political solidarity' is a prerequisite for of the capacity to act at all, see Articles 24(2) and 24(3) TEU. Not surprisingly, solidarity and loyalty are of (and stem from) the same spirit, as Article 24(3) TEU refers to a 'spirit of loyalty and mutual solidarity'—emphasized again in the voting procedure (Article 31 TEU).

The mutual defence clause enshrined in Article 42 (7) TEU can—like the collective self-defence option in Article 51 UN Charter—also be seen as an expression of solidarity ('mutual aid and assistance') but is, of course, much more narrowly formulated.[100] In a broader sense, all policies in the area of freedom, security, and justice are based upon the principle of solidarity, which thus becomes a constitutional element within the EU's cooperative architecture [Articles 67(2), 80 TFEU].[101] Not only within times of crisis and beyond the Monetary Union, economic integration also requires solidarity when grave difficulties arise (Articles 122 TFEU and 143 TFEU).[102] A 'spirit of solidarity' is present in the field of energy policies as well.[103] Most obviously, terrorist attacks, and natural or man-made disasters require 'solidarity' (Article 222 TFEU).

When 196 (1) TFEU obliges the Union to 'encourage cooperation between Member States in order to improve the effectiveness of systems for preventing and protecting against natural or man-made disasters', it implicitly presupposes a 'spirit of solidarity' between the cooperating entities.[104] In that regard, Article 222(1) TFEU is more forthright still. Stating that 'the Union and its Member States act jointly in a spirit of solidarity', the wording discloses a 'supranational intent' of the solidarity clause clearly going beyond merely intergovernmental obligations.[105] The Union's legal architecture corresponds with this 'supranational intent'. It displays a multilayered structure of overlapping 'constitutional regimes' often referred to as 'multilevel constitutionalism'[106] or 'constitutional pluralism'.[107] This multilayered structure sees human relationships (as well as order building mechanisms necessary for human relationships in freedom, peace, and security) as no longer dependent on just one legal system but on a mixed texture of multiple legal orders. This order has to take into account that different (and differentiated) sets of norms do exist on the subnational, the national, and the regional plane—overall framed by public international law or other relevant transnational regimes. In their interplay they can only be fully conceived through a comparative lens.

In EU law as well as in public international law, finding out the relevant meaning and normative relevance of solidarity might become easier if one focuses on the nexus between solidarity and other paradigmatic (or even constitutional) principles of the relevant legal orders—another comparative endeavour. One example that holds true in particular for the law of international or supranational organizations might be the following: loyalty has to be clearly distinguished from solidarity,[108] but loyalty without a minimum degree of solidarity would be theoretically inconceivable and practically impossible. Even more inseparably intertwined are solidarity and legitimacy. The successful integration of any polity, national, regional, or global depends on what J.H.H. Weiler in his famous essay 'The Transformation of Europe' has called 'social legitimacy': 'What becomes crucial for the integration process is the social legitimacy of the new integrated polity despite the loss of total control over the integrated policy areas by each polity.'[109]

One further nexus or systematic context is particularly apparent: solidarity has a human rights basis not only with reference to 'solidarity rights' but also when focusing on the human rights based 'responsibility to protect'.[110] In this regard, the EU can learn via comparison from the international community in its project of promoting human rights, democracy and the rule of laws in its external policies, can learn. UN General Assembly Resolution 59/193 on the 'Promotion of a democratic and equitable international order' states under number 4 lit. f: 'Solidarity, as a fundamental value, by virtue of which global challenges must be managed in a way that distributes costs and burdens fairly, in accordance with basic principles of equity and social justice, and ensures that those who suffer or benefit the least receive help from those who benefit the most.' The Declaration expressly contextualizes solidarity with equity and social justice. Last but not least, solidarity can be seen as 'a way of rationalizing collective responses towards a range of new threats'.[111]

The way EU law uses solidarity qualifies the concept as a constitutional paradigm. Within a broader context of citizenship and loyalty, it frames the duties of membership, and within the context of human rights displays clear universal tendencies. In its most extensive—and most idealistic—reading solidarity addresses the needs and aspirations of humankind as such[112] and requires 'a humanization of International Law' in general. The European paradigm is universalized. In a more limited, that is to say integration-oriented reading, solidarity—though it might sound paradox—is both a prerequisite for and a means of integration. As the great European Jacques Delors said: 'Solidarity mechanisms are not based on pure generosity but on enlightened self-interest.' Whenever EU citizens hear the voices of irresponsible populists trying to destroy the European project, they should never forget that they live in and have to fight for an age of enlightenment. Saying this, the last field of reference has to be addressed: the enlightened citizen as nucleus of a political community and the universal expectations which the notion of citizenship might raise.

IV Cosmopolitan Citizenship: A Cultural Promise and Educational Aim

IV.1 Empowerment for the People

Citizenship and fundamental human rights—as demonstrated above in the context of the freedom of religion, conscience and thought—rank among the most important paradigms of political modernity. Both involve a certain legal status of the individual versus the state and both require a certain degree of 'empowerment' without which the individual would lack the capacity to participate politically and democratically. The readiness to participate, however, distinguishes the citoyen from the bourgeois (see section IV.2). The political citizen who wants to be active and to act responsibly needs to be empowered (or enabled) by knowledge, by information and, most importantly, by education; whoever actively desires to exercise her or his human rights depends on the same prerequisites—the capacity to act. Given this needs-based scenario, citizenship and education form what could be called a 'genuine relationship'. Citizenship as a capacity—also implying responsibility, ethical standards, and respect for the other (especially minorities)—depends on education and is, at the same time, an educational aim of any living democracy.[113] In other words: citizenship and—if at all possible—cosmopolitan citizenship[114] are universal educational aims.

IV.2 The Traditional Distinction between Citoyen and Bourgeois

But this raises the fundamental question: who and what are the citizens that build the political bond of 'We, the People'? A first potential answer is not a legal one. 'There is no more dynamic social figure in modern history than the Citizen,' Ralf Dahrendorf wrote in a famous 1974 article.[115] The modern 'citoyen' is to a very important extent the common child of the American and the French Revolutions. Both revolutions, strongly influenced by enlightenment idea(l)s, sought to create what can be described as the substance of citizenship and participatory democracy: '[T]he equilibrium of equality and liberty.'[116]

The Declaration of Independence illustrates the political notion of active citizenship inherent in the democratic principle: 'Governments are instituted among Men,[117] deriving their just powers from the consent of the governed.' Despite its title, the 1789 Declaration of the Rights of Man and the Citizen does not explicitly define a concept of the citizen or citizenship as political status. However, it refers to citizens as those 'who participate in the formation of the general will', 'who form the Nation, in the sense of being the moral title holders of sovereignty'.[118] The august title of 'citoyen', an 'active citizen', was bestowed on enlightened and emancipated individuals endowed with civil as well as political rights. The right to vote became the most important means of political participation.[119]

To this day, the citoyen is defined by the ability (and the corresponding responsibility) to take part in the political decision-making processes of his or her political community, whereas the bourgeois is characterized by his or her 'autonomy as a private subject (especially as owner of the means of production and entrepreneur), free from any State intervention'.[120] The bourgeois enjoys the 'right to be let alone'; the citoyen is expected to serve the common good. When conceptualized as a responsible political participant, as a *homo politicus*, the citoyen becomes the institutional counterpart of rationality—the 'crystallization of rationality into a social role'.[121] However, modernity and post-modernity[122] have lost the Enlightenment's unshakeable confidence in rationality. They brought about not only fractures and distortions but also drew a fragmented picture of the twenty-first century's postmodern citizen living both at home and in the global village. The Hobbesian 'homo homini lupus', whose evil nature needs to be restrained by public authority, encounters and counteracts the Lockean rationalist, who may enter into the social contract with his free and equal fellow citizens. This holds true for the local, national or regional as well as for the international plane. Being a cosmopolitan does not make the citizen a better human being per se. The citizen can be a self-interested consumer or a political actor (both altruistic and/or interest-driven)—even the missionary activist—concerned about freedom, security and justice (that is to say, about political unity.) The citizen might be a private egoist or a public-spirited altruist (or vice versa and even both at the same time); educated and responsible, or ignorant and irresponsible. Most likely, the real citizen is a bit of all these. She comprises fragmented political, religious, cultural, and social identities.[123]

What follows from this real-world picture for the citoyen as nucleus of political unity? H. Heller, in his 1927 treatise on sovereignty, gave a classic answer that is still valid today. Even though only a small minority of citizens participates in the daily plebiscite, the completely indifferent individual, the 'sleeping citizen', still has his share in order-building: whatever s/he does or fails to do is regulated by the laws of the political community and has an impact.[124] All these actions or non-actions test, confirm, or question those laws. None of the actions are irrelevant, in particular not in an egalitarian democracy. Heller's sleeping citizen thus is continuously relevant for a(ny) concept of citizenship.

IV.3 A Concept of Citizenship

Citizenship involves 'numerous political, historical, social, and cultural overtones' that engender significant 'diversity in the make up' of citizen-based legal entities.[125] From a jurisprudential point of view, what these entities have in common is the transformation of political ideas into a legal status that substantially defines the bond between the individual and the political community.[126] The status, however, need not be static; it qualifies as the foundation of a legally structured process of community building. Citizenship thus creates a Rechtsgemeinschaft, a community under law. As Dahrendorf remarked, citizenship 'makes those who belong a part of the system of rules which protects them from each other and (from) outsiders'.[127] Belonging is expressed in the legal language of rights and duties. However, it is also expressed by the perception of the self and the other—individually and collectively—that is to say, by consciousness as a prerequisite for identity.[128]

One important reference point for the political pattern of identity is societal self-organization (in a democratic society, the self-organization of the free and the equal). At its core are interdependent patterns of participation and communication, of cultural practices and religious beliefs (see above), of 'national consciousness' and 'multicultural sensibility'.[129] It is often said that a citizen perceives the identity of the polity as part of his own identity. This equation, however, must not be mistaken for a holistic or totalitarian concept of citizenship. The community is a heterogeneous amalgamation of imaginations, institutionalizations, and organizations with multiple and fragmented identities. The growing internal and external complexity of communities is paralleled by a growing number of reference points for identity—amongst them the Nation, the Union and maybe the 'Cosmopolitan'.[130] The consequent distinction between a national and a citizen amounts to a 'conceptual decoupling of nationality from citizenship' and to the 'conception of a polity the demos of which, its membership, is understood in the first place in civic and political rather than ethno-cultural terms'.[131] These political terms can be described by the means of commitment, shared values, responsibility for the public good, mutual rights, duties, and social responsibility. All these means work on different levels—for example, the family, the workplace, local municipalities, regional communities, federal states, the nation state, the European community, or at the outermost the global community. The relevant identities as a member of are multiple, as is belonging.

IV.4 Citizenship and Right to Education

Both, the citoyen and the bourgeois are vested with rights: the former particularly with rights of participation, the latter particularly with the 'right to be let alone'. The interdependent dimensions of human rights can be defined as a *status negativus*, *status positivus*, and *status activus* (G. Jellinek). Citizenship is based on this threefold status. Fundamental (and thus universal) human rights should be enjoyed by any person as such, whereas particular citizenship rights are selectively granted to those who belong to a correspondingly particular political community. The status of citizenship, however, can strengthen the status of basic human rights.[132] This is not as contradictory as it might sound. The privileged status of citizenship is a status of inclusion and exclusion as to a specific political community. At the same time, citizenship, due to its implicit reference to humanity and a human rights universe, describes a process of overcoming the inclusion/exclusion dichotomy. The citoyen can become active on the global plane. However, he or she can only become active, if at the same time protected and enabled by their relevant political community which means being empowered by education.[133] The comparative lawyer might think strictly of legal education,[134] but in this regard the notion of education is to be cast much wider.

A right to education is enshrined in Article 26 of the Universal Declaration of Human Rights, a soft law document.[135] Articles 14[136] and also—beyond education in a narrow sense—Article 15[137] of the International Covenant on Civil and Political Rights transform the Declaration's soft-law promise into binding treaty law. As early as 1960, the UNESCO Convention against Discrimination in Education was drafted; the 1981 Convention on all Forms of Discrimination against Women reaffirms this non-discrimination guarantee. In Europe, Article 2 of the first Protocol to the 1950 European

Convention on Human Rights should also be mentioned.[138] The particular relevance of education for the active citizen has been, at least implicitly, recognized in Article 1(a) of the UESCO's 1974 Recommendation concerning Education for International Understanding, Co-operation and Peace and Education relating to Human Rights and Fundamental Freedoms, which describes education as 'the entire process of social life by means of which individuals and social groups learn to develop consciously within, and for the benefit of, the national and international communities, the whole of their personal capabilities, attitudes, aptitudes and knowledge'.[139]

IV.5 Rights and Duties

Citizenship entails not only rights and freedoms but also duties, responsibilities, and obligations of the citoyen. In modern constitutional terms, the vertical dimension of duties towards the political community is most prominently expressed by the obligation to serve on juries, to pay taxes, and to perform military or social service. Few constitutions mandate that citizens vote; in other words: oblige them to—at least intermittently—become, or at least behave as, citoyens.[140] The horizontal dimension of duties towards fellow citizens is chiefly expressed by balancing human rights and freedoms, by the horizontal effect of human rights provisions, and by implicit social dimensions of human rights. However, the twofold notion of the citizen as 'selfish' bourgeois and 'altruistic' citoyen is still valid and is reflected on the national as well as the supranational plane. Here as well as there, citizenship is composed of rights and duties. Here as well as there, active citizenship requires the capacity to act—that is to say the sufficiently capable, well-educated and enlightened (national, Union, or cosmopolitan) citizen. Here as well as, there comparison matters.

V Concluding Remarks

Enlightenment arose like a golden thread and common theme in all three fields of reference. The age-of-enlightenment lawyer practices enlightened law comparison. Her or his comparative work is much more than a (semantic) means of interpretation. It certainly does not intend to impose the 'foreign' on the 'own'. On the contrary, it is ambitious to reflect the 'own' in light of the 'foreign'. That process of reflection might produce some insightful outcomes. The 'own' and the 'foreign' might, for example, turn out to have more in common than one had expected before. Maybe, the 'own' and the 'common' appear to be (expectedly) different, at least culturally particular, but one discovers ways to meaningfully translate the 'foreign' into the 'own' and by way of translation to enrich the own. And even though there might remain substantial fields where such a translation simply does not work, one might nevertheless gain more insights into how to distinguish what should become universal and what should (could) stay different, relative, or particular. Law comparison can help both to universalize legal standards and to provide a rationale for why legal standards should be universalized. Its starting point and its end (aim) are the same: intercultural communication. The newly published Indian Journal on 'comparative matters' establishes a most important scientific forum for discourses and dialogues between cultures. Congratulations and ad multos annos.

Notes and References

1. The title's implicit *double entendre* of R. Hirschl. 2014. *Comparative Matters: The Renaissance of Comparative Constitutional Law*. Oxford: Oxford University Press.
2. J.M. Lynch. 1999. *Negotiating the Constitution. The Earliest Debates over Original Intent*. New York: Cornell University Press.
3. A. Scalia. 2004. 'Foreign Legal Authority in the Federal Courts', Keynote Address to the Annual Meeting of the American Society of International Law, 31 March–3 April, in 98 Am. Soc'y Int'l L. Proc. 305, S. 310.
4. A German classic is E. Rabel. 1967. 'Aufgabe und Notwendigkeit der Rechtsvergleichung', reprinted in H.G. Leser (ed.), *Ernst Rabel Gesammelte Aufsätze*, vol. III, pp. 1–21. Tübingen: J.C.B. Mohr 1967. Asked what the purpose of law comparison was, he gave the stunningly simple but at the same time sophisticated answer: '*Der Name ihres Ziels heißt einfach: Erkenntnis*' (The purpose simply is: gaining knowledge).
5. B. Markesinis (ed.). 1997. *Law Making, Law Finding and Law Shaping: The Diverse Influences*. Oxford: Oxford University Press.
6. Constitutionalism in Europe, the Americas, or in Asia should thus be engaged in a permanent dialogue on constitutionalism; for Asian example, see A.H.Y. Chen (ed.). 2014. *Constitutionalism in Asia in the Early Twenty-first Century*. Cambridge: Cambridge University Press.
7. Ch. Schönberger. 2010. '*Verfassungsvergleich heute: Der schwierige abschied vom ptolemäischen weltbild*', *VRÜ*, 43: 6–7.
8. Schönberger, '*Verfassungsvergleich heute*'.
9. For further relevant discussions, see F. Cownie. 2004. *Legal Academics: Cultures and Identities*. Oxford and Portland: Hart Publishing.
10. See in this context also M.P. Singh. 1985. *German Administrative Law in a Common Law Perspective*. Berlin: Springer-Verlag.
11. A classic of such an approach is P. Häberle. 1982. *Verfassungslehre als Kulturwissenschaft*, 1st ed. p. 33, 2nd ed. 1998, p. 463f.; later, R. Wahl. 2000.

Verfassungsvergleichung als Kulturvergleichung, in FS H. Quaritsch, pp. 163ff., 173ff.; furthermore C. Varga (ed.). 1992. *Comparative Legal Culture*. Dartmouth and New York: The New York University Press; and H.W. Ehrmann. 1976. *Comparative Legal Cultures*. Englewood Cliffs: Prentice Hall.

12. R. Hirschl. 2014. *Comparative Matters: The Renaissance of Comparative Constitutional Law*. Oxford: Oxford University Press: '[T]hat for historical, analytical, and methodological reasons, maintaining the disciplinary divide between comparative constitutional law and other closely relates disciplines that study various aspects of the same constitutional phenomena artificially and unnecessarily limits our horizons' (p. 13).
13. See also S. Douglas-Scott. 2013. *Law after Modernity*. Oxford and Portland: Hart Publishing.
14. Douglas-Scott, *Law after Modernity*, p. 151.
15. E. Fraenkel. 1965. *Der pluralismus als strukturelement der freiheitlich-rechtsstaatlichen demokratie, verhandlungen des 45. Deutschen juristentags, Bd. 2 B*; P. Häberle. 1980. *Die verfassung des pluralismus: Studien zur verfassungstheorie der offenen gesellschaft*; Häberle, *Verfassungslehre als Kulturwissenschaft*, 2nd ed. 1998, p. 134; R. Bellamy. 1999. *Liberalism and Pluralism: Towards a Politics of Compromise*. New York: Routledge; G. McLennan. 1995. *Pluralism*. Buckingham: The Open University Press; and, recently, J. Williams (ed.). 2015. *Ethics, Diversity, and World Politics. Saving Pluralism from Itself?* Oxford: Oxford University Press.
16. N. Walker. 2002. 'The Idea of Constitutional Pluralism', *Modern Law Review*, 65: 317.
17. For an early and programmatic law in context approach, see P. Häberle. 1979. *Kommentierte Verfassungsrechtsprechung*, p. 44ff; recently A. Voßkuhle and T. Wischmeyer. 2015. '*Der Jurist im Kontext: Peter Häberle zum 80 Geburtstag*', *Jahrbuch des Öffentlichen Rechts*, 63: 401–28.
18. This concept is, in particular, pursued in the field of human rights law; see F. Lenzerini. 2014. *The Culturalization of Human Rights Law*. Oxford: Oxford University Press; see also U. Baxi. 2012. *The Future of Human Rights*. New Delhi: Oxford University Press; and U. Baxi. 2007. *Human Rights in a Posthuman World*. New Delhi: Oxford University Press.
19. R. Hirschl. 2014. *Comparative Matters: The Renaissance of Comparative Constitutional Law*. Oxford: Oxford University Press.
20. G. Shaffer. 2012. 'The Empirical Turn in International Legal Scholarship', *American Journal of International Law*, 106: 1–46, esp. p. 1.
21. S. Macaulay, E. Mertz, and T.W. Mitchell (eds). 2016. *The New Legal Realism: Translating Law-And-Society for Today's Legal Practice*. New York: Cambridge University Press.
22. R. Hirschl. 2014. *Comparative Matters: The Renaissance of Comparative Constitutional Law*, p. 192. Oxford: Oxford University Press.
23. See, for example, S. Hall. 2016. *Cultural Studies 1983: A Theoretical History*, eds J. Daryl Slack and L. Grossberg. North Carolina: Duke University Press.

24. A. Wiener. 2008. *The Invisible Constitution of Politics: Contested Norms and International Encounters*. Cambridge: Cambridge University Press; and A. Wiener. 2014. *A Theory of Contestation*. Heidelberg, New York, Dordrecht, and London: Springer.
25. P. Nayar. 2015. *The Postcolonial Studies Dictionary*. United Kingdom: Wiley.
26. R. Hirschl. 2014. *Comparative Matters: The Renaissance of Comparative Constitutional Law*, p. 205. Oxford: Oxford University Press.
27. Z.G. Capan. 2015. Decentering IR: Excavating Stories of International Relations. Erfurt: Universitätsbibliothek Erfurt; and J.M. Hobson. 2012. *The Eurocentric Conception of World Politics: Western International Theory 1760–2010*. Cambridge: Cambridge University Press.
28. M. Gotti and C. Williams (eds). 2010. *Legal Discourse across Languages and Cultures*. Bern: Peter Lang; V.K. Bhatia, C.N. Candlin, and P. Evangelisti Allori. 2008. *Language, Culture and the Law: The Formulation of Legal Concepts across Systems and Cultures*. To find a 'common language' can, from a practice-oriented point of view, be a very difficult task for a Euro-Asian dialogue; see M. Timoteo. 2015. 'Law and Language: Issues Related to Legal Translation and Interpretation of Chinese Rules on Tortious Liability of Environmental Pollution', *China-EU Law Journal*, 4: 121.
29. A 'global intellectual history' might be a useful mean to support such an endeavour: S. Moyn and A. Sartori (eds). 2013. *Global Intellectual History*. New York: Columbia University Press.
30. S. Heselhaus. 2011. 'Universality of International Law in the 20th Century', in T. Marauhn and H. Steiger (eds), *Universality and Continuity in International Law*, p. 471; and B. Simma. 2009. 'Universality of International Law from the Perspective of a Practitioner', *EJIL*, 20: 265–97.
31. For example, J.O. Frosini and F. Biagi (eds), 2015. *Political and Constitutional Transitions in North Africa: Actors and Factors*. London: Routledge.
32. See also R. Grote. 2001. '*Rechtskreise im öffentlichen Recht*', *AöR*, 126: S. 10f., 14ff.
33. J. Husa. 2015. *A New Introduction to Comparative Law*. Oxford and Portland: Hart Publishing; and U. Kischel. 2015. *Rechtsvergleichung*. Munich: C.H. Beck.
34. See, from a German point of view, P. Häberle. 1992. *Rechtsvergleichung im Kraftfeld des Verfassungsstaates*; S. Bär. 2004. '*Verfassungsvergleichung und reflexive Methode: Interkulturelle und intersubjektive Kompetenz*', *ZaöRV*, 64: 735; A. Tschentscher. 2007. '*Dialektische Rechtsvergleichung: zur Methode der Komparatistik im öffentlichen Recht*', *JZ*, p. 807; from an EU law perspective, P. Pescatore. 1980. '*Le recours, dans la jurisprudence de la Cour de justice des Communautés européennes, à des normes déduites de la comparaison des droits des États membres*', *Revue internationale de droit comparé*, 32(2): 337–59; and A. Vespaziani. 2004. '*Die Europäische Verfassungslehre im Wandel zur post-ontologischen Rechtsvergleichung*', in Liber Amicorum P. Häberle, pp. 455–79. Tübingen: Mohr Siebeck.
35. Anne-MarieSlaughter. 1994. *A Typology of Transjudicial Communication*, 29 U. Rich. L. Rev. 99, 119.

36. On 28 August 2016, the online edition of the *Guardian* (https://www.theguardian.com/world/2016/aug/28/french-mayors-burkini-ban-court-ruling) reported that a 'majority of mayors who have banned burkinis in about 30 French coastal resorts are refusing to lift the restrictions despite the country's highest administrative court ruling that the bans are illegal, leaving the state facing a dilemma about how to react.'
37. F.B. Cross. 2014. *Constitutions and Religious Freedom*. Cambridge: Cambridge University Press.
38. H. Goerlich. 2014. *Zur zugewandten Säkularität: Beiträge auf dem Weg dahin: Ausgewählte Schriften*, eds L. Jaeckel, M. Kotzur, and R. Zimmermann. Berlin: Duncker & Humlot.
39. P. Häberle. 1987. *Feiertagsgarantien als kulturelle Identitätselemente des Verfassungsstaates*. Berlin: Duncker & Humblot.
40. A. Gerges. 2016. *ISIS: A History*. New Jersey: Princeton University Press.
41. S.R. Arjana. 2015. *Muslims in the Western Imagination*. New York: Oxford University Press.
42. As to the discussion in Germany, U. Sacksofsky and C. Möllers. 2009. '*Religiöse Freiheit als Gefahr*', in *VVDStRL*, 68: 7 and 42, respectively.
43. See V. Bader. 2003. 'Religious Diversity and Democratic Institutional Pluralism', in *Political Theory*, 31(8): 265–94, esp. p. 265.
44. H. Rudolph. 2011. '*Res publica Christiana and "corpus mysticum"*: Some Remarks on Their Meaning in the Political Thought of Leibniz', in *Zeitschrift für Geschichte der Philosophie und der Wissenschaften*, 43: 24–35, esp. p. 24.
45. H.J. Berman. 2003. *Law and Revolution*, vol. II: *The Impact of the Protestant Reformations on the Western Legal Tradition*, p. 61 et passim. Cambridge, MA: Harvard University Press. Volume I of Berman's work, published in 1983, deals with the formation of western legal tradition in general.
46. Public international law scholarship very often speaks of a 'Westphalian system of international law' and emphasizes: 'Wetsphalia evolved a new image of coordinated states within its territorial sphere'. See R.A. Falk. 1969. 'The Interplay of Westphalia and Charter Conceptions of International Legal Order', in C.E. Black and R.A. Falk (eds), *The Future of the International Legal Order*, vol. 1: *Trends and Patterns*, pp. 32 at 43. New Jersey: Princeton University Press. A critical perspective is taken by D. Kennedy. 1988. 'A New Stream of International Law Scholarship', *Wisconsin International Law*, 7(1): 12–28.
47. B. Ackerman. 1989. 'Constitutional Politics/Constitutional Law', *Yale Law Journal*, 99(3): 453–547; Ackerman. 1997. 'The Rise of World Constitutionalism', *Vanderbilt Law Review*, 83: 770–97; Ackerman. 1991. *We the People: Foundations*. Harvard: Cambridge University Press; Ackerman. 1998. *We the People: Transformations*. Harvard: Cambridge University Press. For a critical account of Ackerman's theory, see J. Klarmann. 1992. 'Constitutional Fact/Constitutional Fiction: A Critique of Bruce Ackermann's Theory of Constitutional Moments', *Stanford Law Review*, 44: 759.
48. C. Taylor. 2007. *A Secular Age*, p. 32. Cambridge, MA: Harvard University Press.

49. C.N.J. Roberts. 2015. *The Contentious History of the International Bill of Human Rights*. New York: Cambridge University Press.
50. E. de Wet. 2006. 'The Emergence of International and Regional Value Systems as a Manifestation of the Emerging International Constitutional Order', *Leiden Journal of International Law*, 19: 611–32.
51. GA Res. 2625 (XXV) vom 24. Oktober 1970.
52. B. Fassbender. 2009. '*Die Menschenrechtserklärung der Vereinten Nationen von 1948: Eine Einführung in ihre Entstehung, Bedeutung und Wirkung*', in ders (Hrsg.), *Menschenrechtserklärung: Neuübersetzung, Synopse, Erläuterung, Materialien*, p. 1.
53. G.A. res. 1386 (XIV), 14 U.N. GAOR Supp. (No. 16) at 19, U.N. Doc. A/4354.
54. Adopted and opened for signature, ratification, and accession by General Assembly resolution 44/25 (20 November 1989). The convention entered into force on 2 September 1990.
55. Proclaimed by General Assembly resolution 36/55 of 25 November 1981. For further important details, see M.J. Roca. 2007. *Der Toleranzbegriff im internationalen Recht, Festschrift Ch. Starck*, pp. 905–8.
56. C.G. Ryn. 1992–3. 'Universality and History: The Concrete as Normative', in *Humanitas*, 6(1, Fall/Winter).
57. C.W. Jenks. 1958. *The Common Law of Mankind*, S. 19 et passim. New York: Frederick A. Praeger.
58. M.-C. Foblets. 2013. *Legal Approaches to Cultural Diversity*. Leiden and Boston: Martinus Nijhoff Publishers.
59. See L. Kühnhardt. 1987. *Die Universalität der Menschenrechte*. Munich: Olzog; furthermore, A.B. Fields and W.-D. Narr. 1992. 'Human Rights as a Holistic Concept', *Human Rights Quarterly*, 14: p. 1ff.; R. Higgins. 1994. *Problems and Process*, S. 96ff. Oxford University Press; P. Alston. 1994. 'The UN's Human Rights Record: From San Francisco to Vienna and Beyond', *Human Rights Quarterly*, 16: 375ff, 380f, 382ff.
60. See in this context UN Doc. A/Conf. 157/22 of July 6 1993: 'The World Conference on Human Rights reaffirms the solemn commitment of all States to fulfil their obligations to promote universal respect for, and observance of, all human rights and fundamental freedoms for all in accordance with the Charter of the United Nations, other instruments relating to human rights, and international law. The universal nature of these rights and freedoms is beyond question.'
61. A. Steinbach. 2016. 'The Lender of Last Resort in the Eurozone', *Common Market Law Review*, 53: 361–83.
62. S. Peers. 2016. *Brexit. The Legal Framework for the Withdrawal from the EU or Renegotiation of EU Membership*. Oxford: Hart Publishing.
63. H. Goerlich, W. Huber, and K. Lehmann. 2004. *Verfassung ohne gottesbezug? Zu einer aktuellen europäischen kontroverse*. Leipzig: Evangelische Verlagsanstalt.

64. See, for example, P. Häberle. 1994. *Europäische rechtskultur*. Baden-Baden: Nomos; and M. Stolleis. 1997. *Europa: Seine historischen wurzeln und seine künftige verfassung*. Tartu: Tartu Ülikooli Kirjastus.
65. In general, S. Baer. 2001. '*Recht gegen fremdenfeindlichkeit und andere ausgrenzungen*', *ZRP*, 34: 500–4, esp. p. 500.
66. M. Kotzur, in R. Geiger, D.-E. Khan, and M. Kotzur (eds). 2015. *European Union Treaties: A Commentary*, Art. 10 TFEU, paras 1 and 2. C.H. Beck.
67. C. Walter. 2006. *Religionsverfassungsrecht*. Tübingen: Mohr Siebeck; P. Häberle and M. Kotzur. 2016. *Europäische verfassungslehre*, 8th ed., p. 847. Nomos.
68. For the following, see M. Kotzur, in *European Union Treaties*, Charter of the Fundamental Rights of the European Union, Introduction, p. 1063.
69. See also G. Frankenberg. 1985. 'Critical Comparisons: Re-thinking Comparative Law', *Harvard International Law Journal*, 26(2): 411–56, esp. p. 411.
70. The Convention is not only the oldest but so far also the effective instrument of regional human rights protection: B. Rainey, E. Wicks, and C. Ovey (eds). 2014. *Jacobs, White and Ovey: The European Convention on Human Rights*, 6th ed. Oxford: Oxford University Press; and S. Greer. 2006. *The European Convention on Human Rights: Achievements, Problems and Prospects*. Cambridge: Cambridge University Press.
71. Manifold guarantees of religious freedom, pluralism, and tolerance can also be found in regional law beyond Europe. This is not only true for the Jewish and Christian West but also, of course, to a lesser extent, for Islamic countries. The 2004 Arab Charter on Human Rights develops its human rights scheme 'pursuant to the eternal principles of brotherhood, equality and tolerance among all human beings which were firmly established by the Islamic Shari'a and other divinely-revealed religions'. A translation (as well as introduction) provided by M. Amin Al-Midani and M. Cabanettes (revised by S.M. Akram) can be found in the Boston University's *International Law Journal*, 24 (2004), p. 147. If the promise of tolerance is taken seriously, the limitation to the 'the Islamic Shari'a' has to be questioned.
72. See also M. Herdegen. 2012. 'Legal Cultures between Self-assertion and Universal Standards', in W. Gephart (ed.), *Rechtsanalyse als Kulturforschung*, pp. 181–91. Frankfurt am Main.
73. An interesting comparative perspective in that regard is R. Broemel and L. Xie. 2015. 'Concepts of Economic Freedoms in China and the EU: A Methodological Approach', *China-EU Law Journal*, 4: 1.
74. M. Kotzur. 2009. 'We, the Citizens of Europe: European Union Citizenship', in M.S. Greve and M. Zöller (eds), *Citizenship in America and Europe: Beyond the Nation-State?*, p. 71. AEI Press.
75. R. Geiger, in: *European Union Treaties*, Art. 2 TEU para 1 et subsequent.
76. A. Wiener. 2004. 'Contested Compliance: Interventions on the Normative Structure of World Politics', *European Journal of International Relations*, 10: 189–234; and Wiener, *A Theory of Contestation*.

77. P. Häberle. 1990. '1789 als teil der geschichte, gegenwart und zukunft des verfassungsstaates', *JöR*, 37: 35–64, esp. p. 35.
78. É. Durkheim. 1893. *De la division du travail social*. Paris: Les Presses universitaires de France; see A.V. Bogdandy. 2010. 'Opening Address', in R. Wolfrum and C. Kojima (eds), *Solidarity: A Structural Principle of International Law*, p. 1. Heidelberg: Springer.
79. Durkheim, *De la division*; and Bogdandy, 'Opening Address'.
80. A. Giddens. 2007. *Europe in the Global Age*, p. 112. Cambridge: Polity Press.
81. H. Krüger. 1971. '*Brüderlichkeit: Das dritte, fast vergessene Ideal der Demokratie*', in *Festschrift Maunz*, p. 249.
82. U. Haltern. 2009. '*Finalität*', in V. Bogdandy and J. Bast (eds), *Europäisches Verfassungsrecht*, 2nd ed., pp. 279–323. Springer; with reference to ICJ, case C-184/99, Grzelczyk, para 44.
83. D. Senghaas. 1992. '*Weltinnenpolitik: Ansätze für ein konzept*', in *Europaarchiv*, pp. 643–52 speaks of a global Schicksalsgemeinschaft; see p. 646 and subsequent.
84. P.J. Cardwell. 2016. 'Rethinking Law and New Governance in the European Union: The Case of Migration Management', *European Law Review*, 41: 362–78; and A. Geddes. 2015. 'Temporary and Circular Migration in the Construction of European Migration Governance', *Cambridge Review of International Affairs*, 28: 571–88. Going beyond Europe, see P. Pasquali. 2015. 'Borders of Migration: A Comparative Legal Perspective between EU and China', *China-EU Law Journal*, 4: 223–42.
85. K. Wellens. 2005. 'Solidarity as a Constitutional Principle: 1st Expanding Role and Inherent Limitations', in R.St.J. Macdonald and D.M. Johnston (eds), *Towards World Constitutionalism: Issues in the Legal Ordering of the World Community*, pp. 775–807. Leiden: Martinus Nijhoff Publishers; K. Wellens, 'Revisiting Solidarity as a (Re-)Emerging Constitutional Principle: Some Further Reflections', in *Solidarity*, p. 3; see, in this context, also A. de Julios-Campuzano. 2008. 'Legal Cultures and Globalization', *Archiv für Rechts- und Sozialphilosophie*, 94(4): 498–511.
86. See http://www.uni-salzburg.at/portal/page?_pageid=465,1835853&_dad=portal&_schema=PORTAL, accessed 15 April 2014.
87. D. Campanelli. 2012. 'Solidarity, Principle of', in *MPEIL*, para 5; in general, U. Volkmann. 1998. *Solidarität: Programm und Prinzip der Verfassung*, p. 52.
88. Campanelli, 'Solidarity', para 5; and Volkmann, *Solidarität*, p. 52.
89. Wellens, 'Revisiting Solidarity', p. 4; M. Virally. 1968. '*Le rôle des "principes" dans le développement du droit international*', in *Recueil d'études de droit international en hommage à Paul Guggenheim*, pp. 531–554, esp. pp. 542–3. Genève: Tribune; more generally, J.E. Viñuales. 2012. 'The Secret of Tomorrow: International Organization through the Eyes of Michel Virally', *European Journal of International Law*, 23: 543–64.
90. A. Peters. 2006. 'Compensatory Constitutionalism: The Function and Potential of Fundamental International Norms and Structures', *Leiden Journal of International Law*, 19(3): 579–610, esp. p. 601.

91. R. Wolfrum. 2006. 'Solidarity amongst States: An Emerging Structural Principle of Public International Law', in P.-M. Dupuy (ed.), *Völkerrecht als Weltordnung: Festschrift für Christian Tomuschat*, p. 1087.
92. See S. Deva (ed.). 2016. *Socio-economic Rights in Emerging Free Markets: Comparative Insights from India and China*. London: Routledge.
93. V.N. Shukla. 2013. *The Constitution of India*. Eastern Book Company.
94. Wellens, 'Revisiting Solidarity', p. 4.
95. Wolfrum, 'Solidarity amongst States', p. 1087; and Wellens, 'Revisiting Solidarity', p. 13.
96. Ch. Mandry. 2009. *Europa als Wertegemeinschaft*.
97. On the current debate, see the examples discussed in A. Héritier (ed.). 2002. *Common Goods: Reinventing European and International Governance*. Lanham, Md: Rowman & Littlefield Publishers.
98. A.V. Bogdandy, '*Grundprinzipien*', in *Europäisches Verfassungsrecht*, p. 13; furthermore M. Lais. 2007. *Das Solidaritätsprinzip im europäischen verfassungsverbund*.
99. K. Smith. 2008. *European Union Foreign Policy in a Changing World*. 2nd ed. Polity Press.
100. S. Myrdal and M. Rhinard. 2010. 'The European Union's Solidarity Clause: Empty Letter or Effective Tool?' UI Occasional Papers No. 2, p. 1; and J. Wouters, S. Bijlmakers, and K. Meuwissen. 2012. 'The EU as a Multilateral Security Actor after Lisbon: Constitutional and Institutional Aspects', Working Paper No. 80, Leuven Centre for Global Governance Studies, February, p. 9.
101. Kotzur, in *European Union Treaties*, Art. 80 TFEU para 1.
102. See, for example, U. Häde. 2009. *Die Wirtschafts-und Währungsunion im Vertrag von Lissabon, EuR*, p. 200; Häde. 2009. *Haushaltsdisziplin und Solidarität im Zeichen der Finanzkrise, EuZW*, p. 399.
103. J.F. Braun. 2011. 'EU Energy Policy under the Treaty of Lisbon Rules: Between a New Policy and Business as Usual', in *Politics and Institutions*, EPIN Working Papers, No. 31/2011.
104. For the general scope of EU disaster preparedness, disaster response, and civil protection, see also the Statements of the Commission, for example, COM (2010) 600 final.
105. Myrdal and Rhinard, 'The European Union's Solidarity Clause', p. 6.
106. I. Pernice. 2009. 'The Treaty of Lisbon: Multilevel Constitutionalism in Action', *Columbia Journal of European Law*, 15: 349; and Pernice. 1999. 'Multilevel Constitutionalism and the Treaty of Amsterdam: European Constitution-Making Revisited?' *CMLR*, 36: 703–50.
107. N. Walker. 2002. 'The Idea of Constitutional Pluralism', 65 MLR, p. 317; M. Maduro. 2001. 'Contrapunctual Law: Europe's Constitutional Pluralism in Action', in N. Walker (ed.), *Sovereignty in Transition*, p. 21. Oxford: Hart Publishing.
108. A. Hatje. 2001. *Loyalität als Rechtsprinzip der EU*, p. 16. Baden-Baden: Nomos.

109. J.H.H. Weiler. 1991. 'The Transformation of Europe', *Yale Law Journal*, 100: S. 2403 ff., at 2471.
110. 'Report of the International Law Commission on Intervention and State Sovereignty (ICISS), The Responsibility to Protect', 2001; UN Doc. GA/Res. 60/1 (2005 World Summit and Outcome); C. Stahn. 2007. 'Responsibility to Protect. Political Rhetoric or Emerging Legal Norm', *AJIL*, 101: 99; and A.V. Arnauld. 2009. 'Souveränität und die responsibility to protect', in *Die Friedenswarte*, 84: 11.
111. T. Konstantinides. 2011. 'Civil Protection in Europe and the Lisbon "Solidarity Clause": A Genuine Legal Concept or a Paper Exercise', Uppsala Faculty of Law Working Paper No. 3, p. 7.
112. Already a classic is C.W. Jenks. 1958. *The Common Law of Mankind*. London; A.A. Cançado Trindade. 2010. *International Law for Humankind: Towards a New Jus Gentium*. Martinus Nijhoff Publishers.
113. P. Häberle. 2009. 'Bürgerschaft durch bildung als europäische aufgabe', in L. Michael and M. Kotzur (eds), *Verfassungsvergleichung in europa-und weltbürgerlicher Absicht*, p. 161. Berlin: Duncker & Humbolt.
114. P. Kemp. 2010. *Citizen of the World: An Cosmopolitan Ideal for the 21st Century*. Humanity Books.
115. R. Dahrendorf. 1994. 'Citizenship and Beyond: The Social Dynamics of an Idea', in B.S. Turner and P. Hamilton (eds), *Citizenship: Critical Concepts*, vol. II, p. 292. London and New York: Routledge.
116. Dahrendorf, 'Citizenship and Beyond', p. 292.
117. And women(!), we have to add.
118. F. Borella. 1987. '*Nationalité et citoyenneté en droit français*', in Colas (ed.), *L'Etat de droit: Travaux de la mission de la modernisation de l'Etat*, p. 35. The English translation provided for by B. Guiguet. 1998. 'Citizenship and Nationality: Tracing the French Roots of the Distinction', in M. La Torre (ed.), *European Citizenship: An Institutional Challenge*, pp. 95–111, esp. pp. 95, 98. The Hague: Clair Law International.
119. M. Troper, 'The Concept of Citizenship in the Period of the French Revolution', in La Torre (ed.), *European Citizenship*, pp. 27, 29.
120. M. La Torre. 1995. *Citizenship: A European Wager*, vol. 8, *Ratio Juris*, p. 113; R. Smend. 1968. '*Bürger und Bourgeois im deutschen Staatsrecht*', in *Staatsrechtliche Abhandlungen*, 2nd ed.; distinguishing between the 'sittlich an den Staat gebundenen Bürger' (citoyen) and the 'rechenhafter Egoist der kapitalistischen Zeit' (bourgeois). See also U.K. Preuß. 2002. '*Der EU-Staatsbürger: Bourgeois oder Citoyen*', in G. Winter (ed.), *Das Öffentliche Heute*, p. 179.
121. Dahrendorf, 'Citizenship and Beyond', pp. 292, 294.
122. Steven Best and Douglas Kellner. 1997. *The Postmodern Turn*. New York: Guilford Press; and Zygmunt Bauman. 1992. *Intimations of Postmodernity*. Routledge.
123. See also J.T. Checkel and P.J. Katzenstein (eds). 2009. *European Identity*. Cambridge: Cambridge University Press.

124. H. Heller. 1971 [1927]. '*Die Souveränität*', in *Gesammelte Schriften*, vol. II, pp. 31, 108–9; furthermore, W. Berka. 1996. '*Bürgerverantwortung im demokratischen Verfassungsstaat*', *VVDStRL*, 55: 48–58.
125. S. O'Leary. 1996. *European Union Citizenship: The Options for Reform*, p. 12, London: Institute for Public Policy Research.
126. J.D. Galloway. 1998. 'Citizenship: A Jurisprudential Paradox', in La Torre (ed.), *European Citizenship*, pp. 65, 68.
127. Dahrendorf, 'Citizenship and Beyond', p. 292.
128. See Häberle and Kotzur, *Europäische Verfassungslehre*; Häberle, *Verfassungslehre als Kulturwissenschaft*, 2nd ed., p. 624; and Y.N. Soysal. 1994. *Limits of Citizenship: Migrants and Postnational Membership in Europe*. Chicago: University of Chicago.
129. J. Habermas. 1992. Citizenship and National Identity: Some Reflections on the Future of Europe, Praxis International, 1992, vol. 12, p. 1.
130. J.H.H. Weiler. 1999. 'To Be a European Citizen: Eros und Civilization', in *The Constitution of Europe: "Do the New Clothes Have an Emperor?" And Other Essays on European Integration*, p. 324. Cambridge: Cambridge University Press; and see J.H.H. Weiler. 1999. 'Epilogue, The European Courts of Justice: Beyond "Beyond Doctrine" or the Legitimacy Crisis of European Constitutionalism', in A.-M. Slaughter, A.S. Sweet, and J.H.H. Weiler (eds), *The European Courts and National Courts*, S. 365 ff., 377 f.; and Weiler, *The Constitution of Europe*, p. 238.
131. Weiler, 'To Be a European Citizen', pp. 324, 344.
132. This, however, raises controversial discussions. See O'Leary, *European Union Citizenship*, p. 69.
133. D. Evrigenis. 1981. '*Der Europäische gerichtshof für menschenrechte und das recht auf bildung*', *EuGRZ*, S. 637ff; K. Halvorsen. 1990. 'Notes on the Realisation of the Human Right to Education', *Human Rights Quarterly*, 12: S. 341ff. J. Delbrück. 1992. 'The Right to Education as an International Human Right', *German Yearbook of International Law*, 35: S. 475ff; and K.D. Beiter, 2006. *The Protection of the Right to Education by International Law*. Leiden: Brill.
134. The *China-EU Law Journal*, 3(2014, 1 and 2) devoted a special issue to legal education in a comparative perspective.
135. J. Morsink. 2000. *A Review of the Universal Declaration of Human Rights: Drafting, Origins and Intent*. Philadelphia: University of Pennsylvania Press.
136. 'Each State Party to the present Covenant which, at the time of becoming a Party, has not been able to secure in its metropolitan territory or other territories under its jurisdiction compulsory primary education, free of charge, undertakes, within two years, to work out and adopt a detailed plan of action for the progressive implementation, within a reasonable number of years, to be fixed in the plan, of the principle of compulsory education free of charge for all.'

137. "1. The States Parties to the present Covenant recognize the right of everyone: (a) To take part in cultural life; (b) To enjoy the benefits of scientific progress and its applications; [...].'
138. See also Delbrück, 'The Right to Education', p. 92.
139. For the quote see Beiter, *The Protection of the Right to Education by International Law.*
140. Which includes respect for others, in particular minorities, see G. Alfredsson. 2001. 'Human Rights Education and Minority Rights', in United Nations Educational, Scientific and Cultural Organization and Intercenter (eds), *The Right to Education of Vulnerable Groups Whilst Respecting Their Cultural Identity*, p. 125; and Minority Rights Group (ed.). 1994. *Education Rights and Minorities*, 1994.

3

Democracy, Privatization, and the Rise of Non-state Regulatory Power

George Katrougalos

Globalization entails a gradual demise of the time-honoured concept of state sovereignty, in tandem with a trend of privatization of traditionally public functions of the state, including the most regal of all regulation. In earlier work[1] I have tried to show that the basic limitative constitutional rule of these trends is the democratic principle and, especially in Europe, the social state principle. I am presenting briefly this argument in section I, before investigating if it is possible to use the same criteria for checking transnational private regulation (in section II).

I Constitutional Limitations of Privatization at the National Level

The reaction to the recent economic crisis has put into question the common wisdom of the neoliberal economic orthodoxy that 'steering, not rowing' is the exclusive role of the state. The new nationalizations and the emergency powers afforded to governments both in USA and in Europe clearly showed that the state 'has not just taken over the rowing but is frantically bailing out the boat'.[2]

This should not surprise us. The frontiers between the public and private spheres have always been—at least since the beginning of the last century—blurred and porous. Initially, the strict separation of the classical liberal state and market has been fundamentally altered by the direct involvement of the government and public enterprises to the economic activity. Moreover, in Europe—in contrast with the USA—the introduction of constitutional social rights imposed new, positive obligations on public power.

I.1 USA and Europe: An Ocean Apart?[3]

The roots of the divergence between Europe and USA—or, more generally, the Anglo-Saxon world—extend backwards to the eighteenth century, and the intrinsic difference between the American and French Revolutions: the first aimed at political independence as an end in itself, whereas the second aimed primarily at a different social and legal order, and only when this proved unfeasible under the 'ancien régime' the monarchy was overthrown.[4] It is illustrative that, already in 1793, Robespierre had proposed to the Convention a Bill of Rights which recognized as legally enforceable the rights to work and to social assistance and which treated the right to property not as a natural or absolute right, but as one limited by the law and the needs of other people.[5]

Still, it was the nineteenth century that shaped definitively the European legal concept of property and social rights, as a response to the great 'social question' of this century: how could the market and the representative, democratic[6] system be made compatible with the extension of political and social rights, without a socialist revolution?[7]

On the contrary, this question has not been posed in the USA, at least not in the same terms. During all the nineteenth century the social tensions there had not acquired an explosive character, as the vastness of the country's resources and its 'new, open frontiers' provided land and opportunities in a scale unknown in the Old Continent.[8] In the words of Tocqueville:[9] 'Why is it that in America, the land par excellence of democracy, no one makes the outcry against property in general that often echoes through Europe? Is it needed to explain? It is because there are no proletarians in America. Everyone, having some possession to defend, recognizes the right to property in principle.'[10]

More generally, human rights in liberal thought are conceived as inherent to human nature and inalienable, possessed at birth, and not granted by either society or state. The role of the government was not to establish these rights, since they preceded it, but simply to respect them and guarantee their free exercise.[11] Social rights, as individual or collective claims towards the state, could never be conceived as prior to society, because their role was precisely to compensate societal risks and alleviate extreme inequalities produced by the functioning of the market.

Besides, the primacy of the right to property over the other two fundamental rights of liberalism (freedom and equality) prohibited the introduction of any kinds of claims that could limit its exercise. Hamilton's remark regarding American judges, that 'in the universe behind their hats liberty was the opportunity to acquire property',[12] was valid universally for the most part of the nineteenth century, up to the point of recognition of social rights.

The recognition of social rights implied a passage to a new type of polity: from the liberal state of the nineteenth century to the social state. In the latter, instead of the watertight separation of the political and economic spheres of early liberalism, social rights and nationalizations introduced mechanisms of political intervention in the socio-economic process, as a corrective mechanism for the risks and failures that the 'invisible hand' of the market could not prevent. In this way, they implied the re-politicization of the market, in the opposite direction of the French revolution of 1789, which separated the realms of state and economy.[13]

In this model, the state, instead of regulating the market only on the basis of norms that derive from the private law of contract, property, and tort,[14] uses, in addition 'political power to supersede, supplement or modify operations of the economic system in order to achieve results, which the economic system would not achieve on its own … guided by other values than those determined by open market forces'.[15] As R. Aron has remarked, in Europe 'the concept of State and law is not anymore merely negative, but also positive, in the sense that the law is considered to be not only the juridical foundation but also the source of the material conditions for its fulfillment.'[16] On the contrary, the functions of the liberal state are essentially negative. They consist of the removal of arbitrary legal impediments and not of the provision of positive means for the exercise of rights and liberties. Consequently, there is an eclipse of positive or affirmative rights, even as guarantees of traditional liberties.[17]

This fundamental division of European, 'social' and Anglo-American 'liberal' states cannot be reduced only to the legal differences between the common law and continental legal traditions.[18] It reflects much more profound political, moral and societal choices.[19] This happens because one of the functions of constitution is to ensure social integration, by presupposing and promising the common values that constitute the foundations of the political community.[20] This is a two-directional process, because the constitution crystallizes already embedded social values and also contributes to their consolidation to an objective system, which can have normative repercussions. Thus the normative and axiological elements are closely and mutually underpinned.

The recent empirical studies of Alberto Alesina reaffirm the deep clash of values between Europe and America[21] with regard to the redistributive functions of the state. In the former, in the words of Abbe Sieyès, the citizens feel that they have the right to demand from the state everything it can do for them.[22] In the latter, the belief that individual talent and effort determine income, that all have a right to enjoy the fruits of their effort, in tandem with the traditional mistrust towards the state, results in a much more individualistic, Lockean *Weltanschauung* and especially a fundamentally different conceptualization of equality. As Slaughter remarks, the American concept of equality tolerates a lot of inequality, as it focuses on starting points and not on endpoints. The idea that everybody is created equal, but opportunity and individual effort can make a difference, is deeply embedded in the American imagination.[23] That is why many poor people are for tax cuts for the wealthier, hoping that one day they will be rich, too.[24]

It is true that the 'general welfare constitution' introduced by F.D. Roosevelt in his 1934 address to Congress, announcing the formation of the Social Security Act of 1935, seemed to take America to the European understanding of rights. Under the New Deal conception, the social rights were 'the modern substance' of the traditional liberties.[25] Even in 1944 Roosevelt proclaimed 'a second Bill of Rights' containing the rights to education, job, adequate medical care, and 'a decent home', 'under which a new basis of security and prosperity can be established for all—regardless of station or race or creed'.[26] However, the New Deal was just a parenthesis, which could not overcome the racially motivated so-called 'Southern Veto'.[27]

Hence, the 'Social State' can be used as *terminus technicus*, in order to differentiate European welfare states from Anglo-Saxon liberal states.[28] In this sense, the terms 'Welfare State' and 'Social State' are not interchangeable: the first one is descriptive and denotes the universal type of state which emerged in all developed countries in the twentieth century, as a response to functional necessities of the modern capitalist economy. On the other hand, the 'Social State' is a normative, prescriptive principle, which defines a specific polity, a subcategory of the welfare state in the former sense, where the state has the constitutional obligation to assume interventionist functions in the economic and social spheres.[29] In this sense, the USA or Australia are 'welfare states' but not 'social states' because their social policy has no constitutional foundation. On the contrary, countries like India or South Africa, although lacking the basic infrastructure of a mature welfare state, they can be considered as 'social' ones, due to their constitutional arrangements regarding the protection of social rights. This is true also for the majority of Latin American countries.[30]

Along these lines, Habermas[31] distinguishes two opposite 'thrusts' of the 'juridification' of the political system: the first is related to the foundation of the liberal state, through the differentiation of the economy from the politics and the guarantee of personal freedom and property. The recognition of constitutional social rights, on the contrary, results in a new de-differentiation of the political and economic spheres: '[A] life-world which was at first placed at the disposal of the market ... little by little makes good its claims.'[32]

I.2 Globalization and Privatization

Nowadays there is, once again, a reverse trend. The constraints of the state's regulatory capacity and the removal of barriers to market access are part of the broader process of globalization, as a driving force of both denationalization and extraterritoriality. There is an evolving 'disaggregation' of the state[33] through the transfer of public functions both 'upwards' to international or transnational entities (EU, WTO) and 'downwards', through the decentralization of the decision-making either to lower state levels (devolution) or by new blends of public and private power at all levels of government.[34]

Consequently, states no longer have a real monopoly on the policies they implement. In this new, globalizing environment, the greater mobility of capital entails polycentric relationships between the public/private and national/international/transnational spheres. Even functions traditionally believed to be exclusively public and belonging to the hard core of state, such as the public defence or the penitentiary system, are gradually privatized. Therefore, the public-private divide should not be conceived anymore in a binary logic. There is not a dichotomy but rather a continuum in the axis of public–private. In this sense, privatization is the movement on this axis towards the private 'end', through the shifting of a public function or the transfer of public wealth to private sector.

However, only apparently the public space is shrinking and the private sector is expanding. Actually, what is happening is not the 'retraction' of government but a new way of governance where the private actors have more substantial (and often democratically unchecked) power, with discretionary authority over public resources.[35] In other words, the withdrawal of the state is partial, as the deregulation of traditional functions is replaced by a new regulatory project in which 'the state's role has merely shifted away from redistribution toward the legitimization and enforcement of market outcomes'.[36]

This remodelling of the 'public' sphere of politics is not politically neutral, as it constitutes a transfer of power from public to private actors and, at least in Europe, a major ideological shift from the dominant Keynesian policies towards the new economic orthodoxy of market liberalization, unfettered competition and austerity. Private and public sectors are not functionally equivalent. There are some roles, as, for instance, redistribution, that only the state can fulfil. The latter has simultaneously the constitutional authority and the institutional legitimacy to arbitrate the conflicting social interests, as well as the adequate fiscal and administrative instruments to organize transfers of resources. In the words of Lord Beveridge in a letter to Roy Harrod: '[W]hile I want to preserve freedom of enterprise, there are some things I am sure which the state must do, because only the state can do them.'[37]

Globalization creates a new regulatory arena, in which public and private parties compete, interact and bargain. In this framework, public law faces two challenges: First, how to extend public law remedies to newly privatized areas, in order to maintain accountability, quality, and equality of provision for services and respect of other public values[38] and second, to delimit the areas where privatization is constitutionally forbidden. The definition of governmental functions that cannot be privatized can no longer be essentialist, as if there were a sacrosanct, immutable core of state functions immune from historical change. There is no such thing as a natural law defining public functions. The dividing line of private and public is always historically determined. The exact demarcation of the frontiers between private and public will be inevitably a political matter of ideological hegemony between competing social interests,[39] juridically based on two fundamental principles: democracy and social state. This of course is the case in polities where the latter is recognized. This is one of the major differences between the European and the Anglo-American legal orders.[40]

In this sense, the social state principle imposes at least the obligation for the existence of a public 'market-free' pillar of social security. On the other hand, the democratic principle, imposes on the government an exclusive 'duty to govern'[41] in some areas of the state that are still part of a '*domainereservé*'.[42] Along this line, the American Office of Management and Budget defines as 'inherently governmental' all activities intimately 'related to the public interest, which require the exercise of substantial discretion in applying government authority and/or making decisions for the government. Inherently, governmental activities normally fall into two categories: the exercise of sovereign government authority or the establishment of procedures and processes related to the oversight of monetary transactions or entitlements.'[43]

II The Application of Democratic Principle to Transnational Private Regulation

II.1 Regulation in the Global Administrative Space

Global administrative space is increasingly occupied by transnational private regulators and hybrid bodies involving states, international or interstate organizations, which are not under the control of the nation states. Because of this trend, global governance implies an increased recourse to informality, as 'many institutions, procedures and instruments escape the grasp of established legal concepts'.[44] Regulation is not imposed only by 'hard law'. Legal subjects can also be conditioned by instruments without deontic operators (for example, statistical data contained in PISA reports).[45] The same goes for private standard-setting function, that has initially been adopted either as international soft law, which has then been redeployed by international organizations and implemented later through hard law at international, regional, or state level, as it happened with the Codex Alimentarius.[46]

As a result, transnational regulation is very hard to define as either predominantly public or private and the public–private distinction seems to be even more elusive on the international and transnational level than on the national one. Hence, the global arena constitutes 'a battlefield ... in the hands of multiple political, institutional and economic actors, who struggle, interact and bargain. It's a place and an instrument of conflict in itself, resulting from the moves of different players',[47] who 'coordinate through hierarchy, cooperation and/or competition'.[48]

Prima facie, the democratic principle does not seem to apply in this environment. Key issues are, indeed, removed from the domestic, or any other, political agenda through 'deliberate technocratic depoliticization'[49] on ground of improving efficiency and neutrality. The insulation of the Central Banks, for instance, from the political decisions of the legislatures is one of the most indicative examples. It is very doubtful if this trend has enhanced the epistemic quality of decision making[50] or it has just degenerated important political decisions into 'pervasive bureaucratic micromanagement'.[51] There is hardly any neutral, value-free technical choice or Pareto optimality of 'one best way'. Any expert decision is founded on political criteria and has redistributive effects, which should be politically challenged in terms of their fairness and appropriateness.

Efficiency alone, or any Pareto-optimal technocratic solutions, legitimised by output considerations, cannot be accepted as equivalents to democracy, not only because of their inconsistency with the normative character of the principle but also primarily because they are based on an unsound cyclical foundation: in order to identify optimal results, one should first define the public goods and values related to them and their teleology. How can this possibly be founded on non-political or technical fundaments?

The of Law is also not a substitute for democratic decisions. The judicial accountability mechanisms may, instead, lead to a *juridification* of global governance, narrowing further the space for democratic decision-making,[52] as it is clearly illustrated by the WTO's recent evolution. This does not so much establish a *juristocracy*, but rather isolates further the political decision-making from nationally accountable institutions: we cannot have equation of control by law and control by democratic politics, especially when 'law' itself (that is, the global regulation) is not democratically instituted[53]. Therefore, by the introduction of elements of rule of law, such as, for instance, an improvement in transparency or introduction of some forms of consultation, one might get, at best, what Stewart calls '*administrative law lite*',[54] not democracy.

Neither exists at supranational level any essential mechanisms of checks and balances, despite the presence of a legion of competing actors. The transnationalization processes, at least at the level of the transnational economy, are politically one-dimensioned: neo-liberal orthodoxy for deregulation of financial and social rules as a necessary precondition to efficiency and economic growth has become the prevailing ideology of global governance, through not only the direct interventions of the World Bank and the International Monetary Fund, but also the free-trade treaties of WTO.[55] Moreover, rule-conforming behaviour is not produced only by 'legal' instruments but also by 'policy' documents or other 'soft law' means. This 'rule-oriented landscape'[56] does not merely affect internal economic policies but results in the supersession of the national public values of administrative and constitutional law by an ideologically global setup of very different nature.

It corresponds to a supranational economic constitution, based on a coherent set of constituent principles such as monetary stability, open markets, freedom of contract and liability.[57] This 'policy coherence' is far away from the Keynesian compromise of social states. In this sense, there is a latent revision of the fundamental principles regulating domestic economic activity, without direct public consent and under minimal political control.

At the domestic level, the freedom of market actors has been controlled by public regulation for reasons of general interest. Whereas the conciliation of democracy and capitalism became possible in last century's welfare state by the democratic, political control of national markets, something similar has never been established at the level of international transactions. The inexistence of a democratic regulation of the international markets at the ecumenical level does not only mean the inability of political power to rein in private global players. It signifies also a progressive upset of the domestic balance between markets and state that is creating an internal democracy deficit. Hence, the crucial normative dilemma for transnational regulation turns to be the choice between recognition of some overarching principles of constitutional character (especially rule of law and democratic principle) or the acknowledgment of a fully open-ended pluralist global order.

It is clear that at the present state of international affairs a coherent, hierarchically structured transnational order cannot exist. Therefore, many scholars consider that the post-national realm constitutes a 'hierarchy'[58]. Before this assertion and the impossibility to normatively reconcile the conflicting demands of accountability of national, international, and global audiences, it is often advised that we should look for pragmatic and pluralist solutions.[59]

Along this line, others argue that instead of seeking an impossible hierarchical 'constitutional' settlement of the issue of democratic governance, we should opt for a pluralist, hierarchical model, more adequate to the context of the global space. An additional argument for pluralism is that even without overarching principles, the actors involved in global governance are expected to keep each other in check through mutual contestation.[60] Vertical accountability will be combined with horizontal accountability 'inter-institutional accountability',[61] in order to ensure factual mechanisms of control. However, this pattern does not fulfil the same function as democracy, because the result of concurring and opposing forces does not necessarily keep power under democratic control.

The separation of powers in the state checks and balances powers that have the support of popular sovereignty. This is not the case with transnational entities, which can easily be captured by special interests. In this sense, the fragmentation of global regulatory regimes could result in a feudal equilibrium, favouring the strongest political or economic actor. Thus, Benvenisti and Downs remark that 'powerful states labor to maintain and even actively promote fragmentation because it enables them to preserve their dominance in an era in which hierarchy is increasingly viewed as illegitimate, and to opportunistically break the rules without seriously jeopardizing the system they have created'.[62]

It is, nevertheless, undeniable that designing a global constitutional frame, destined to embrace universal substantive and procedural principles, would be an impossible project, not only due to the lack of a global demos but also because of the vast multitude of prevalent conflicting values in various parts of the world, especially outside the Western world. Still, this divergence and the development of a plurality of governance loci does not infer impossibility of the recognition of global overarching principles, emerging from the common constitutional tradition of nation states and the need of legitimization of the transnational order.[63]

As we cannot have a global constitutionalism based either on a universal Grundnorm or on a generally accepted rule of recognition, our constitutional arrangements will inevitably be pluralistic. This does not preclude the recognition of some common constitutional 'jusgentium'. In this line, Kumm's proposal for a 'cosmopolitan constitutionalism' does not seek to construct hierarchies between different levels of law but puts forward the affirmation of some fundamental overarching norms, such as rule of law and democracy, that are meant to direct the solution of conflicts.[64]

I share the idea of constitutional pluralism, which 'is not monist and allows for the possibility of conflict not ultimately resolved by the law, but it includes common constitutional principles that provide a framework that allows for the constructive engagement of different sites of authority with one another'.[65] I have, however, a different understanding of the democratic principle, as a foundational value of constitutionalism. Kumm's paradigm 'takes as basic a commitment to rights-based public reason and interprets acts by the democratic legislator as an attempt to spell out what that abstract commitment to rights amounts to under the circumstances addressed by the legislative act'.[66]

I still consider that the liberal element of democracy remains very weak if is dissociated from its republican counterpart and above all from the idea of self-government.[67] Self-government presupposes the existence of a demo, but not necessarily of a traditional, national pre-political 'Volk', within state boundaries. Demos, in my understanding, is a public body constituted by a political decision, on the basis of an overlapping consensus over some basic supporting values and choices, capable of reaching majoritarian decisions, after an informed open discourse. In this framework 'public reason', in contrast to pure reason, is a product basically of conflicts of interests, rather than of conflicts of arguments. It should be clear that in the foreseeable future, any feasible supranational demos would be possible only as a federation of national *demoi*, which would make the international democracy to be rather a demoi-cracy.[68]

Further on, what I consider as a basic problem for a liberal, 'rights-based public reason' as a constitutive material for a cosmopolitan constitutionalism that integrates national and international law, is the asymmetrical character of national and international legal orders. They are not based on the same fundamental principles, with more striking difference the complete lack of the social state principle at supranational level. In its absence, globalization is resulting to a completely different conceptualization of rights than in national social states. Therefore, for 'the capture of the international jurisgenerative process by states, in particular the state's executive branches' is not as much the core concern as politically unchecked economic power that redefines traditional concepts of constitutional law.

II.2 Democratic Principles at the Transnational Level

For all the aforementioned reasons, the basic priority is to impose democratic limitations on the development of global space. Teubner, better than others, has shown that the basic constitutive function of transnational regimes was to promote the institutional conditions for their autonomy vis-à-vis the national states.

> To dismantle such nation-state boundaries has become the primary constitutional aim of transnational regimes. Today's global constitutionalism thus aims to accomplish two things: to break down the close structural coupling between the function systems and nation-state politics and law and to enable function specific communications to become globally interconnected.... It has produced not only specific political regulations but also fundamental constitutional principles. In the economy these have aimed at giving global corporations unlimited options for action, abolishing government shareholdings in corporations, combating trade protectionism and freeing business corporations from political regulation.... *Limitative constitutional norms are now needed, rather than constitutive ones.*[69]

Hence, the main issue for the emerging global constitutionalism is to democratically control the transnational economic power. Now that globalization 'gets in the way of national democracy',[70] the re-politicization and re-democratization of the global economic relations, even if they acquire a private or semi-private form, is imperative. By neglecting to face the challenge as it is, we risk bypassing the basic political problem posed by globalization, what Rodrik calls the 'Globalization Trilemma': From the tension between national democracy and global markets stem three options: We cannot have (a) hyperglobalization, (b) democracy, and (c) national sovereignty all at once, although we can have any pair of them. In this sense, the possible political outcomes are: (a) to have 1 and 3 by restricting national democratic legitimacy, or (b) to have 2 and 3, by limiting globalization, or (c) to have 1 and 2, that is, 'globalize democracy' by moving the forum of democracy from national to global level.[71]

Globalization is inevitable, but not linear. It can be shaped and transformed by political rules, although not by extrapolation of the nation-state model of democracy but rather along two principal directions: (a) by introducing limitative procedures for the incorporation of transnational regulation at national level and (b) by constituting democratic decision-making and enhancing accountability at transnational level. In this sense, rules and standards should be constructed at the transnational level so as to ensure the optimal provision of global public goods, such as climate or environmental protection,[72] after deliberation in horizontal networks between national demoi or more partial stakeholders.

This horizontal dimension is what distinguishes a global democracy both from a national democracy and a federation, where the relationship between a unitary state and a federal unit are basically vertical. But deliberation and horizontal networking cannot translate themselves into authoritative decisions, without final approval of their outcome by the self-governing demoi, or the entities of the international law acting upon delegation of the latter.

Hence, in the present state of affairs, the basic yardstick for qualifying the democratic quality of transnational policies is their impact on national democracies.[73] Yet, the actual asymmetry between capacities for political action and social participation at national and transnational levels results in a disjunction between global socioeconomic and political processes, on the one hand, and local processes of democratic participation, on the other.[74] The governance of global space is especially democratically deficient when it comes to private regulatory mechanisms.[75] For example, procedural mechanisms such as the Basel II, which may be used primarily by organized business and financial interests, may result in an even greater disregard of weaker and more vulnerable groups. In other contexts, there is the danger of bias and capture, as stronger and better organized actors exert greater sway in the informal, opaque, negotiation-driven networks of transnational decision making than more weakly organized general societal interests.

Therefore, parallel to any measures aimed at remedying the existing democratic deficit of institutions of global governance, it is even more important to introduce political and juridical means for containment of unchecked intrusion of transnational rules into national legal orders, without an explicit previous popular consent. In this sense, it will be necessary to centralize regulation,[76] not in the sense of recreating control monopoly of national governments, but so as to ensure a democratic oversight on diffused regulatory strategies.[77] Such oversight may be deemed higher in the case of sensitive areas, as core labour standards,[78] or in transnational regimes that involve the privatization of functions that traditionally have been regulated within the public sphere.[79]

The establishment of procedures and devises for containment of superimposition of norms lacking democratic legitimacy is not unfeasible or unrealistic.

For instance, it has been suggested that the outcome of the WTO's Doha Round of negotiations and any consequential treaties should be the object of a referendum at national level.[80] Empirical research shows that in almost all jurisdictions the ex post legislative scrutiny of negotiated rules of WTO's Uruguay Round Agreements clearly was largely perfunctory.[81] In view of the united logic of unleashed markets, the national demoi do not have any substantial influence and their citizens have the reason to feel politically dispossessed.

Besides the reconfirmation of the democratic character of constitutional settlements, similar procedures could contribute to the gradual formation of a global, or at least regional, public space, as the related political issues would be discussed horizontally in all involved countries. The creation of a similar public discourse arena, overlapping and complementing the national ones, is a functional prerequisite for the emergence of an eventual cosmopolitan deliberative democracy and a global demoi, in the sense of 'demoicracy' described earlier.[82]

Finally, another dimension of unequal power relations created by global governance is the 'attenuation of sovereign equality' of poorer and developing countries. The existing international legal order remains broadly irresponsive to the concerns of developing countries and their people.[83] Problems of democratic accountability may occur either in the absence of efficient control mechanisms or due to 'substantive disregard, in exercise of power that unjustly harms or treats some of those affected'.[84] As Stewart remarks: '[T]he appearance of procedural legitimacy may veil and further entrench that disregard [as] the problem is [not so much lack of accountability but] rather disproportionate accountability to ... well organized economic interests, to the detriment of less cohesive societal interests.'[85]

Shifts in quota shares of developing and to under-represented countries, such as India, are already under discussion in the IMF, but the reform is far from remedying the existing inequalities.[86] Of even greater importance would be the reintroduction of some form of minority blocking mechanism for a panel or Appellate Body decision in WTO, preventing that decision from becoming binding WTO law.

In hybrid, semi-public institutions, the creation or expansion of participation rights could be an alternative solution. In some cases where the addressees of transnational regulation could be delimited and specified with accuracy, one could claim that they constitute, in a minimal sense, a specific micro-demoi, although not the kind of demos we have become accustomed to in national democracies.[87] Along this line, held envisions a quasi-federal political structure in which all those affected by a particular issue have a right to participate in decisions on it, combined with the principle of subsidiarity.[88]

However, it is not easy to establish international structures of democratic participation as thick and representative as those at the national level. Providing groups or diffusing of societal representative interests with participation prior to decision-making, for example, by granting them voting membership in a collegial authority or rights of questioning decisions, enhances the democratic function of transnational institutions only to the extent that a majority of the stakeholders could be efficiently and fairly represented.

But even in case global bodies purport to provide representation, there exists the danger of bias and co-option in the selection process to the detriment of less cohesive societal interests. Besides, hierarchies of social power operate in civil society no less than in other political spaces. Civil society is itself a site of struggles to be heard and its inadequate representation can reproduce or even enlarge structural inequalities and arbitrary privileges connected with class, gender, nationality, race, religion, urban versus rural location, and so on.[89] There is evidence, for instance, that NGOs working as monitors of non-governmental systems of labour standards in Central America have unduly supplanted the trade unions in discussing wages and working conditions with factory managers, a process that objectively helped companies in not letting workers union organize and enforce collective agreements or public regulation.

As Weiler suggests, at the supranational level 'democracy can be measured by the closeness, responsiveness, representativeness, and accountability of the governors to the governed'.[90] Hence, the core of the democratic principle, in the sense that there must be an ultimate link between the decision making and the will of the people can and should be promoted also at the international level.

Notes and References

1. G. Katrougalos. 2010. 'Constitutional Limitations of Privatization in USA and Europe: A Theoretical and Comparative Perspective', *Constellations*, 17(3): 407–25; and G. Katrougalos. 2010. 'Constitutional Limitations of Social Security Privatisation', *European Journal of Social Security*, 12(1): 16–40.
2. J. Black. 2008. 'The Credit Crunch and the Constitution', Paper for the IACL Conference, 'The Regulatory State: Constitutional Implications', 14–15 November, http://constitution-iacl.eventbrite.com.
3. G. Katrougalos. 2008. 'European "Social States" and the USA: An Ocean Apart?' *European Constitutional Law Review*, 4: 225–50.
4. D. Grimm. 2005. 'The Protective Function of the State', in G. Nolte (ed.), *European and US Constitutionalism*, p. 139. Cambridge and New York: Cambridge University Press.

5. These articles had as follow [M. Robespierre. 1793. *Textes Choisis*, p. 138. Paris: Éditions Sociales]:

> Art. 9: The right of property cannot harm the security, the freedom, the existence or the property of other citizens. Art. 10. Every property that violates this principle is essentially illegal and immoral. Art. 11. The society is obliged to ensure the existence of all its members, either by giving work to them, or by providing to those who cannot work the means to survive. Art. 12. The assistance to the miserable is the debt of the rich toward the poor. The law will determine how this duty is going to be paid.

However, the Constitution of the Convention (24 June 1793), despite adopting in its Declaration of Rights some of these propositions, especially in Articles 21 (right to work and to public assistance) and 22 (right to education), was merely referring to them as 'a sacred debt of the society'.

6. In the UK, the most democratically developed country of this century, only 1.8 per cent of the population had electoral rights before the Reform Act of 1832 and just 2.7 per cent after it. In 1867 and 1884, the respective figures have been 6.4 and 12.1 per cent. F. Zakaria. 2003. *The Future of Freedom*, p. 80. New York and London: Norton & Co.
7. U. Preuss. 1985. 'The Concept of Rights in the Welfare State', in G. Teubner (ed.), *Dilemmas of Law in the Welfare State*, p. 152. Berlin and New York: W. de Gruyter.
8. During the nineteenth century, the US government passed a number of legislative acts (Homestead Act 1862, Timber Culture Act 1873, Dessert Land Act 1887) in order to provide dozens of millions of acres of public land to farmers and to settlers of the 'new frontiers', creating, thus, millions of new property holders. It was only in 1890 the US Census Bureau has officially announced the end of the American frontier. J. Rifkin. 2004. *The European Dream*, p. 151. New York: Tarcher/Penguin.
9. A. de Tocqueville. 1988. *Democracy in America*, trans. G. Lawrence, p. 238. New York: Harper. Cf. F.D. Roosevelt who has said, quoting Jefferson, that America had no paupers, as 'most of the labor class possessed property'. See F.D. Roosevelt. 1938. 'New Conditions Impose New Requirements upon Government and Those Who Conduct Government', Campaign Address, 1932, in *The Public Papers of Franklin Roosevelt*, San Francisco.
10. Naturally, even the American nineteenth century was not entirely idyllic and 'pauper-free'. This is shown by many dramatic incidents of class warfare, such as the violent strike against the Pennsylvania Railroad in 1877 or the industrial war at Andrew Carnegie's Homestead steel plant in 1890. J. Beatty. 2007. *Age of Betrayal: The Triumph of Money in America, 1865–1900*. Harvard: A. Knopf.
11. B. Binoche. 1989. *Critiques des droits de l'homme*, p. 4. Paris.
12. C.A. Reich. 1964. 'The New Property', *Yale Law Journal*, 5: 733–87, esp. p. 772.
13. J. Habermas. 1985. 'Law as Medium and Law as Institution', in *Dilemmas of Law in the Welfare State*, p. 220; cf. S. Rokkan. 1974. 'Cities, States and Nations', in S. Rokkan and S.N. Eisentat (eds), *Building States and Nations*, vol. 1: *Models and Data Resources*, p. 73. London: SAGE Publications.

14. Cf. F.A. Hayek. 1980. *Law, Legislation and Liberty: A New Statement of the Liberal Principles of Justice and Political Economy*, p. 141. London: Routledge.
15. T.H. Marshall. 1975. *Social Policy*, p. 15. London: Routledge. Marshall was referring to the social policy in general, but his description defines very elusively also the basic functions of the social state principle.
16. R. Aron. 1972. *Etudes Politiques*, p. 242. Paris: Gallimard.
17. *Harris v MacRae*, 448 US 297 (1980), *Deshaney v Winnebago County Department of Social Services*, 489 US 189 (1989).
18. K. Dyson. 1980. *The State Tradition in Western Europe*. Oxford: Martin Robertson; cf. O. Kahn-Freund. 1978. 'Common Law and Civil Law: Imaginary and Real Obstacles to Assimilation', in Mauro Cappelleti (ed.), *New Perspectives for a Common Law of Europe*. London: Sijmoff.
19. Cf. B. Markezinis. 2001. 'Unity or Division: The Search for Similarities in Contemporary European Law', *Current Legal Problems*, 51: 591–617, esp. p. 612.
20. N. Walker. 2006. 'European Constitutionalism in the State Constitutional Tradition', *Current Legal Problems*, 57: 51–63; D. Grimm. 2005. 'Integration by Constitution', *ICON*, 3: 193–208; cf. R. Smend, 1956. 'Integrationslehre', in *Handwörterbuch der Sozialwissenschaften*, 5: 299–302.
21. A. Alesina and M. Angeletos. 1983. 'Fairness and Redistribution: US versus Europe', Harvard Institute of Economic Research Working Papers, Institute of Economic Research, Harvard.
22. '*Il suffit de dire que les citoyens en commun ont droit à tout ce que l'Etat peut faire en leur faveur.*' Abba Sieyès. 1939. '*Des droits de l'homme et du citoyen*', lu les 20 et 21 juillet 1789 au comité de la Constitution, p. 70. Hermann.
23. A.-M. Slaughter. 2007. *The Idea That Is America*, pp. 80, 105. Cambridge: Basic Books.
24. According to the World Values Survey, 71 per cent of Americans versus 40 per cent of Europeans believe that the poor could become rich if they just tried hard enough. See Alesina and Angeletos, 'Fairness and Redistribution'.
25. W. Forbath. 2001. 'Constitutional Welfare Rights: A History, Critique and Reconstruction', *Fordham Law Review*, 69: 1833, who, additionally remarks that 'This was a conceptual revolution. Even Holmes, in his dissenting opinion in Lokhner was agreeing with the majority that a Constitution is not intended to embody a particular economic theory, whether of paternalism and the organic relation of the citizen to the state or of laisser faire' [198 US 45 (1905) at 75].
26. Speech of 11 January 1944; see C. Sunstein. 2004. *The Second Bill of Rights: FDR's Unfinished Revolution and Why We Need It More Than Ever*. New York: Basic Books.
27. Half of the Southern Democratic senators have voted against FDR welfare legislation. See J. Weiss. 1983. *Farewell to the Party of Lincoln: Black Politics in the Age of FDR.* Princeton: Princeton University Press.
28. Sometimes the term 'social welfare states' is used instead. A. Sajó. 2005. 'Social Rights: A Wide Agenda', *European Constitutional Law Review* 1(1): 38–43.

29. On the varieties of American and European versions of economic constitution, see also T. Heller. 1996. 'Comments on the Economic Constitution of the European Community', in F. Snyder (ed.), *Constitutional Dimensions of European Economic Integration*, p. 149. London: Kluwer Law International. Cf. G. Katrougalos. 1998. *Constitution, Law and Rights in the Welfare State ... and Beyond*, p. 56. Athens: A. Sakkoulas.
30. Cf. S.E. Hendrix. 1995. 'Property Law Innovation in Latin America with Recommendations', 18 B.C. 1, Int'l & Comp. L. Rev. 7.
31. Habermas, 'Law as Medium and Law as Institution', p. 203.
32. Habermas, 'Law as Medium and Law as Institution', p. 205.
33. A.M. Slaughter. 1997. 'The Real New World Order', *Foreign Affairs*, 76: 183–94.
34. J. Black. 'Decentring Regulation: Understanding the Role of Regulation and Self-regulation in a "Post-regulatory" World', *Current Legal Problems*, 54(1): 103–46.
35. All 'concessions of public services', in the European legal terminology or 'delegation of public functions', in the American one, have this characteristic. G. Metzger. 2003. 'Privatization as Delegation', *Columbia Law Review*, 103: 1367–406.
36. T. Prosser. 1998. 'Public Service Law, Privatization's Unexpected Offspring', *Current Legal Problems*, 51: 393.
37. Letter of 15 September 1944, *The Beveridge Papers*, Archives Section, British Library of Political and Economic Science, London School of Economics and Political Science, London.
38. Cf. C. Harlow, D. Dyzenhaus, M. Hunt, and G. Huscroft (eds). 2009. *The Hidden Path of the State and the Publicisation of Private Law: A Simple Common Lawyer: Essays in Honour of Michael Taggart*, p. 75. Oxford and Portland: Hart.
39. P. Kosonen. 1987. 'From Collectivity to Individualism in the Welfare State?' *Acta Sociologica*, 30: 281–93.
40. Katrougalos, 'European "Social States" and the USA', p. 225.
41. P. Verkuil. 2007. *Outsourcing Sovereignty, Why Privatization of Government Functions Threatens Democracy and What We Can Do About It.* Cambridge: Cambridge University Press; and J. Freeman and M. Minow (eds). 2009. *Government by Contract: Outsourcing and American Democracy.* Cambridge: Harvard University Press.
42. Cf. J.A. Kämmerer. 1996. '*Verfassungsstaat auf Diät*', *Juristische Zeitung*, p. 1042; C. Gramm. 2004. *Privatisierung und notwendige Staatsaufgaben.* Berlin; I. Ewald. 2004. *Privatisierung Staatlicher Aufgaben.* Brühl: Rheinland; R. Thérion. 2002. *La privatisation des entreprises publiques dans une économie de marché aspects juridiquesBruxelles*, p. 387. Bruylant-LGDJ.
43. US Office of Management and Budget. 2003. Circular No. A-76, revised; originally issued in 1983, section B.1.a. Washington, DC.
44. A. von Bogdandy, P. Dann, and M. Goldmann. 2009. 'Developing the Publicness of Public International Law: Towards a Legal Framework for Global Governance Activities', *German Law Journal*, 11: 1376.
45. A. von Bogdandy. 2004. 'Globalization and Europe: How to Square Democracy and Globalization', *European Journal of International Law*, 15: 885, cf. K.W.

Abbott and D. Snidal. 2000. 'Hard and Soft Law in International Governance', *International Organization*, 54: 421.
46. J. Kurtz. 2007. 'A Look behind the Mirror: Standardization, Institutions and the WTO SPS and TBT Agreements', *University of New South Wales Law Journal*, 30: 504, http://www.austlii.edu.au/au/journals/UNSWLJ/2007/31.pdf.
47. G. Napolitano. 2012. 'Conflicts in Administrative Law: Struggles, Games and Negotiations between Political, Institutional and Economic Actors', Paper for the IRPA-NYU JMC seminar on 'Toward a Multipolar Administrative Law A Theoretical Perspective', 9–10 September, New York.
48. F. Cafaggi. 2006. 'Rethinking Private Regulation in the European Regulatory Space', Working Paper LAW No. 2006/13.
49. A.-M. Slaughter. 2001. 'The Accountability of Government Networks', *Indiana Journal of Global Legal Studies*, 8: 349.
50. R.O. Keohane, S. Macedo, and A. Moravcsik. 2009. 'Democracy-enhancing Multilateralism', in *International Organization*, 63(Winter): 1–31, esp. p. 26.
51. M. Shapiro. 2001. 'Administrative Law Unbounded: Reflections on Government and Governance', *Indiana Journal of Global Legal Studies*, 8: 369–77.
52. Cf. C. Harlow. 2006. 'Global Administrative Law: The Quest for Principles and Values', *European Journal of International Law*, 17: 187–214; and B. Zangl and M. Zürn. 2004. *Verrechtlichung: Bausteinfür Global Governance?* Bonn: Dietz.
53. Cf. M. Shapiro. 2005. '"Deliberative", "Independent" Technocracy v. Democratic Politics: Will the Globe Echo the E.U.?' *Law and Contemporary Problems*, 68(63): 341.
54. R.B. Stewart, 'U.S. Administrative Law: A Model for Global Administrative Law?' *Law and Contemporary* Problems, 68(63): 63–108.
55. Cf. D. Nicol. 2010. *The Constitutional Protection of Capitalism*. Oxford and Portland: Hart Publishing.
56. J. Jackson. 2006. *Sovereignty: The WTO and Changing Fundamentals of International Law*. Cambridge: Cambridge University Press.
57. E.U. Petersmann. 2001. 'European and International Constitutional Law: Time for Promoting 'Cosmopolitan Democracy in the WTO', in G. de Burca and J. Scott (eds), *The EU and the WTO: Legal and Constitutional Issues*, pp. 81–110, esp. p. 88. Oxford; cf. B. Hoekman and M. Kostecki. 2001. *The Political Economy of the World Trading System*. Oxford: Oxford University Press.
58. Etymologically speaking, instead of 'heterarchy' one should use the term 'polyarchy'. The former means in Greek not lack of hierarchy, but a hierarchy imposed from above, by an external or alien factor (heteros, έτερος, is 'other' in Greek).
59. N. Krisch. 2006. 'The Pluralism of Global Administrative Law', *The European Journal of International Law*, 17: 245–48.
60. B. Kingsbury. 2005. 'Omnilateralism and Partial International Communities: Contributions of the Emerging Global Administrative Law', *Journal of International Law and Diplomacy*, 104: 98. Cf. Krisch, 'The Pluralism of Global Administrative Law', p. 247.

61. G. O'Donnell. 1999. 'Horizontal Accountability in New Democracies', in Andreas Schedler, Larry Diamond, and Marc F. Plattnereds (eds), *The Self-restraining State, Power and Accountability in New Democracies*, p. 29. Boulder: Lynne Rienner.
62. E. Benvenisti and G.W. Downs. 2007–8. 'The Empire's New Clothes. Political Economy and the Fragmentation of International Law', *Stanford Law Review*, 60: 595–631. See also the remarks of Keohane and Nye on the now obsolete 'club model' of international governance in the framework of international organizations. R.O. Keohane and J.S. Nye, Jr., 'The Club Model of Multilateral Cooperation and Problems of Democratic Legitimacy', Paper for the American Political Science Convention, Washington, DC, 31 August–3 September 2000, http:www.ksg.harvard.edu/cbg/trade/keohane.htm. See also C. Barfield. 2001. 'Free Trade, Sovereignty, Democracy: The Future of the World Trade Organization', *American Enterprise Institute Press*.
63. R. Hülsse. 2008. 'Even Clubs Can't Do without Legitimacy: Why the Anti-money Laundering Blacklist Was Suspended', *Regulation and Governance*, 459.
64. M. Kumm. 2009. 'The Cosmopolitan Turn in Constitutionalism: On the Relationship between National Constitutional Law and Constitutionalism beyond the State', in J.L. Dunoff and J.P. Trachtman (eds), *Ruling the World? Constitutionalism, International Law and Global Government*. Cambridge: Cambridge University Press. In this sense of 'constitutionalization' beyond the state, see also M.P. Maduro. 2006. 'From Constitutions to Constitutionalism: A Constitutional Approach for Global Governance', in D. Lewis (ed.), *Global Governance and the Quest for Justice*. Oxford, Hart Publishing; A.C. Bogdandy. 2006. 'Constitutionalism in International Law: Comment on a Proposal from Germany', *Harvard International Law Journal*, 47: 223–42; A.C. Bogdandy. 2004. 'Globalization and Europe: How to Square Democracy and Globalization', *European Journal of International Law*, 15: 885,J. Klabbers, A. Peters, and Geir Ulfstein. 2009. *The Constitutionalization of International Law*. Oxford: Oxford University Press; E.-U. Petersmann. 2006. 'Multilevel Trade Governance in the WTO Requires Multilevel Constitutionalism', in Christian Joerges and Ernst-Ulrich Petersmann (eds), *Constitutionalism, Multilevel Trade Governance and Social Regulation*, p. 5. Oxford: Hart Publishing.
65. Kumm, 'The Cosmopolitan Turn'.
66. Kumm, 'The Cosmopolitan Turn'.
67. Cf. D. Miller. 2009. 'Democracy's Domain', *Philosophy and Public Affairs*, 37(3): 201–28.
68. Cf. K. Nicolaïdis. 2003. 'Our European Demoï-cracy: Is This Constitution a Third Way for Europe?' in K. Nicolaides and S Weatherill (eds), *Whose Europe? National Models and the Constitution of the European Union*, European Studies at Oxford Series. Oxford University Press; and F. Cheneval and F. Schimmelfennig. 2011. 'The Case for Demoicracy in the EU', Paper presented at EUSA Conference Boston, March, http://euce.org/eusa/2011/papers/8h_cheneval.pdf.

69. G. Teubner. 2012. *Constitutional Fragments: Societal Constitutionalism and Globalization*, pp. 76–78. Oxford University Press; emphasis added.
70. D. Rodrik. 2011. *The Globalization Paradox: Democracy and the Future of the World*. New York: W.W. Norton & Co.
71. Rodrik, *The Globalization Paradox*.
72. D. Bodansky. 2006. 'What's in a Concept? Global Public Goods, International Law, and Legitimacy', *European Journal of International Law*, 23(3): 651–68. Also see D.C. Esty. 2006. 'Good Governance at the Supranational Scale: Globalizing Administrative Law', *Yale Law Journal*, 115: 1490–562.
73. Cf. A.M. Slaughter. 2004. *A New World Order*. Princeton: Princeton University Press.
74. Cf. J. Habermas. 2012. 'The Crisis of the European Union in the Light of a Constitutionalization of International Law', *European Journal of International Law*, 2(23): 335–48.
75. L.A. Dickinson. 2005. 'Government for Hire: Privatizing Foreign Affairs and the Problem of Accountability under International Law', *William and Mary Law Review*, 47(1): 135–237. Also See J.A. Scholte. 2001. 'Civil Society and Democracy in Global Governance', Centre for Study Globalization Regionalization Working Paper No. 65.
76. Cf. J. Black. 2001. 'Decentring Regulation: Understanding the Role of Regulation and Private Regulation in a Postregulatory World', *Current Legal Problems*, 54: 103ff.; and J. Black. 2008. 'Constructing and Contesting Legitimacy and Accountability in Polycentric Regulatory Regimes', in *Regulation and Governance*, 2: 137–64.
77. Cf. S. Benhabib. 2004. *The Rights of Others*. Cambridge: Cambridge University Press.
78. T. Macdonald and K. Macdonald. 2006. 'Non-electoral Accountability in Global Politics: Strengthening Democratic Control within the Global Garment Industry', *European Journal of International Law*, 17(1): 89–119, esp. p. 91. Cf. J. Salzman. 2000. 'Labor Rights, Globalization and Institutions: The Role and Influence of the Organization for Economic Cooperation and Development', *Michigan Journal of International Law*, 21:769–805.
79. J. Freeman. 1999. 'Private Parties, Public Functions and the New Administrative Law', in D. Dyzenhaus (ed.), *Recrafting the Rule of Law*, p. 331. Oxford: Hart Publishing.
80. Howse R. 'How to Begin to Think about the "Democratic Deficit" at the WTO', in *Recrafting the Rule of Law*.
81. J. Jackson and A. Sykes (eds). 1997. *Implementing the Uruguay Round*. Oxford; cf. Howse, 'How to Begin to Think About the "Democratic Deficit" at the WTO'; and M. Fakhri. 2001. 'Reconstruing WTO Legitimacy Debates', *Notre Dame Journal of International and Comparative Law*, 2: 64.
82. J. Cohen and C.F. Sabel. 2005. 'Global Democracy', *New York University Journal of International Law and Politics*, 37: 763–97. Cf.J. Delbrück. 2003.

'Exercising Public Authority beyond the State: Transnational Democracy and/ or Alternative Legitimation Strategies?' *Indiana Journal of Global Legal Studies*, 10(1): 29–43; and R. Falk and A. Strauss. 2000. 'On the Creation of a Global Peoples Assembly: Legitimacy and the Power of Popular Sovereignty', *Stanford Journal of International Law*, 36: 191–220.

83. B.S. Chimni. 2004. 'International Institutions Today: An Imperial Global State in the Making', *European Journal of International Law*, 15(1): 1–37; cf. B.S. Chimni. 2005. 'Co-option and Resistance: Two Faces of Global Administrative Law', *Institute of International Law and Justice*, 16; N. Krisch. 2005. 'International Law in Times of Hegemony: Unequal Power and the Shaping of the International Legal Order', *European Journal of International Law*, 16: 369.
84. R.B. Stewart. 'Accountability, Participation, and the Problem of Disregard in Global Regulatory Governance', International Legal Theory Colloquium, http://iilj.org/courses/2008IILJColloqium.asp.
85. Stewart, 'Accountability', pp. 12, 56.
86. G. Napolitano. 2010. 'The Two Ways of Global Governance after the Financial Crisis Multilateralism', Jean Monnet Working Paper 10/13, 19 September.
87. D. Curtin and L. Senden. 2010. *Public Accountability of Transnational Private Regulation Chimera or Reality?* Amsterdam: Centre for European Law and Governance.
88. D. Held. 1995. *Democracy and the Global Order*. Cambridge: Polity Press; and D. Held. 2004. 'Democratic Accountability and Effectiveness from a Cosmopolitan Perspective', *Government & Opposition*, 39: 382–83.
89. Scholte, 'Civil Society'.
90. J.H.H. Weiler. 1999. 'To Be a European Citizen: Eros und Civilization', in *The Constitution of Europe: "Do the New Clothes Have an Emperor?" And Other Essays on European Integration*, p. 81. Cambridge University Press. Cf. J. H. H. Weiler and I. Motoc. 2003. 'Taking Democracy Seriously: The Normative Challenges to the International Legal System', in S. Griller (ed.), *International Economic Governance and Non-Economic Concerns: New Challenges for the International Legal Order*, pp. 68–9. Wien: Springer.

4

Ambedkar's Liberty Concept in Comparative Constitutional Thought

*Moiz Tundawala and Salmoli Choudhuri**

I Introduction

By dedicating his 1873 treatise *Gulamgiri* (Slavery) to the 'good people of the United States as a token of admiration for their sublime disinterested and self-sacrificing devotion in the cause of Negro slavery',[1] the militant anti-caste leader Jyotiba Phule sought to draw inspiration from the experience of the Civil War in that country for the struggle of Sudra emancipation from 'the trammels of Brahmin thraldom'[2] in India. This struggle reached a pivotal juncture on 29 November 1948 when the Constituent Assembly of independent India under the supervision of Dr B.R. Ambedkar, a revolutionary constitutionalist from the Mahar community of Dalits,[3] abolished the practice of untouchability and forbade its practice in all forms.[4] If constitutional concepts migrated freely across jurisdictions, those flowing from the anti-caste movement ought to occupy a prominent place in the globalizing grammar of modern constitutionalism just as have the ones associated with the Western constitutional discourse on anti-slavery. But proceedings of the 2001 World Conference against Racism (WCAR) at Durban show that this has unfortunately not turned out to be the case. Here Dalits were compelled to use a language specific to race in order to internationalize the issue of caste discrimination.[5] This seems paradoxical since contrary to an influential strand in colonial anthropology that equated caste with race owing to an apparently common emphasis on skin colour and phenotype, it was Ambedkar who showed that the hierarchical caste system owed its origin to custom subsequently codified in the *Dharmashastra* and not in ethnology, as a result of which it could not be treated as a synonym for race.[6] However, over a period of time, it was race as a concept which came to be hegemonic in international fora and the Dalit resort to it at Durban was the only progressive option available to them under the circumstances.[7] More so as issues of caste and untouchability were deemed to be oddities peculiar to the South Asian subcontinent, both by the international public as well as the Indian government.[8] While the former may have been motivated by the belief that a universal framework was not appropriate here since these concerns were remnants of a deviant history local to South Asia alone, the latter was positively invested in furthering the logic of postcolonial difference whereby such social questions strictly pertained to the spiritual domain over which none but the nationalist elite could exercise sovereign authority. As a consequence, given their presupposed particularity caste and untouchability failed to command the attention of international comparative scholars as independent pedagogical categories. On the other hand, race and slavery, in spite of having their own Anglo-American and West European historical context, could produce legal and constitutional concepts which came to be seen as transhistorical and transcontextual enough to be generalizable to the rest of the world. This in a way corroborates the critical 'one-way traffic' thesis in comparative constitutional studies, which asserts that the inbuilt biases within the discipline make it predominantly oriented towards mapping constitutional transfers from the global North to the global South while spending very little time or effort in considering alternative possibilities which may encompass hitherto ignored regions as sources of constitutional concepts with transnational appeal.[9]

We believe that it is not fruitful to merely lament over or derive rhetorical purchase from this asymmetry of the comparative enterprise. Neither are we interested in setting up a new universal from the South to rival its dominant paradigms. Rather, in our understanding it would be possible to draw up a fresh approach to comparison cognizant of a wider variety of theoretical and practical experiences by probing the contours of the framing of universals in comparative constitutional studies and destabilizing some of their key presuppositions on account of what they effectively end up excluding. This paper pursues such an agenda by comparing Ambedkar's constitutional thought on liberty with its competing conceptualizations in European political traditions. It shows that unlike the figure of the slave which has been central to the imagination of liberty in its three most powerful formations—negative, positive, and republican—for Ambedkar it was the figure of the untouchable that defined his concept of what we would call 'liberty as non-oppression'. By doing so, this paper would complicate the universalist paradigm which relies upon the figure of the slave to conceptualize liberty no matter how so contested otherwise. This complication is neither particularistic by nature, in that Ambedkar's account is not relevant merely for the South Asian case of caste, nor is it suggestive of a simple replacement of the slave by the untouchable as a new universal paradigm of liberty conceptualization fit for all constitutional circumstances everywhere else in the world. Both these propositions would run us into discomforting difficulties. Instead what we are interested in doing through the example of Ambedkar is to take cautious steps towards a comparative methodology that does not treat universal and particular as oppositional categories, is aware of the critical intimacy which they are likely to share, and practices de-contextualization and re-contextualization without taking them as fixed pre-givens in terms of content, but rather always as objects of agential construction. What this amounts to in respect of comparative constitutional discourse on liberty is that the complimentary yet unstable categories of universal and particular within which it is framed are as much subjects of comparative enquiry as are the different conceptualizations of liberty themselves.

This essay is divided into three parts. Part one shall set up the figure of the slave as the ultimate *tertiumcomparationis* for the three rival conceptions of negative, positive, and republican liberty in European constitutional thought; that is, howsoever antagonistic with one another their respective proponents might present themselves as, what unites them is a common foundational engagement with slavery in respect to which their formulations on liberty are made. In part two, we move to Ambedkar's reluctance in relying upon the figure of the slave when conceptualizing liberty and instead basing it on the figure of the untouchable. So even while thinking deeply about liberty, he did not associate his account with what was most fundamental in the extant Western literature on the concept, and instead chose to politicize an almost defunct Indic tradition of Buddhism, which enabled him to conceive of liberty as non-oppression. Finally, in part three we will bring this discussion on liberty in conversation with interdisciplinary scholarship exploring the relationship between universalism and particularism. Our contention would be that comparativist approaches which are either exclusively universal or particular, or accommodative of particularities in an otherwise hegemonic universal framework are not productive. By reading Ambedkar as an exemplary comparativist on the liberty concept, we would suggest that a better way to do activist comparison is to contemporanize different time-spaces whereby these two categories are not only rendered unsettled but newer possibilities are opened up for bringing them in critical alignment.

II Part One

Liberty as a concept has a long genealogy in the Western history of ideas, and is therefore hard to put within strict definitional constraints. It may be described as a contested concept with at least three predominant rival conceptualizations—negative, positive, and republican—which have withstood the vicissitudes of time. Although these distinctions have their roots in the ancient world and its transition to modernity, we would like to begin with Isaiah Berlin's mid-twentieth century classification of negative and positive liberty which has come to acquire canonical status in the literature.[10] Following Hobbes, Locke and Bentham, Berlin stated negative liberty to mean non-interference or non-coercion of a person's movement and will by others.[11] In contrast, following the thought tradition of Hegel, Green and Bosanquet he understood positive liberty as self-mastery, self-realization, and self-perfection. That is the ability to autonomously pursue one's genuine life goals.[12] While there may be a disagreement as to whether negative liberty shares with positive liberty an urge to probe obstacles interior to the self such as passions of the soul and effects of internalized social norms,[13] what categorically sets the two apart is the latter's perfectionist emphasis on fulfilling the essence of human nature, howsoever divergently it may have come to be defined. Different positive liberty theorists usually do so by drawing a distinction between a lower empirical self and a higher ideal self—a dangerous step whose authoritarian and anti-pluralist implications have historically been blamed for destructions wrought by political ideologies such as official communism, Nazism, Fascism and even nationalism as a result of which their accounts get condemned by someone like Berlin[14] although they have gone on to make substantive revisions to deal with such objections.[15] It is not necessary for us to entangle ourselves in this debate any further, but rather move to a third concept of republican liberty which although claiming to be the oldest in the liberty tradition, has recently been revived by philosophers such as Quentin Skinner and Philip Pettit as a response to the limitations of the earlier two versions.[16]

Claiming to combine what is valuable in negative and positive traditions of liberty, it stresses upon absence of mastery by others or non-domination as the core of the republican variety. This view of liberty is negative to the extent that it cherishes a certain form of absence, but an absence defined in terms of domination rather than interference.[17] Domination eludes to the positive dimension of liberty in that it is associated with the issue of mastery, but instead of stressing upon self-mastery, republican liberty chooses to emphasise non-mastery by others as necessary and sufficient for its realization.[18]

Without getting into the merits and demerits of negative, positive, and republican liberty, we would like to briefly attend to the three forms of liberal, communitarian, and republican constitutionalism that have been perceived as emerging from these three accounts respectively. Crudely put, liberal constitutionalism cast in its most familiar Lockean rendition seeks protection for the so-called natural rights of individuals, including the right to private property, by limiting the intervention of external agencies in general and the state in particular. Parallel to the variety in theories of positive liberty, communitarian constitutionalism also seems to cover a wide range of institutional and societal possibilities, which, even if sharing a family resemblance, need not necessarily be compatible with one another. If we arbitrarily pick up on the Rousseauvian account as an influential statement in this thought tradition, it would be immediately clear that self-mastery can be attained only under arrangements where the General Will can be said to reign supreme rather than those where individualistic rights trump collective constitutional aspirations. Republican constitutionalism, as has been discerned in the Italian-Atlantic imagination of Cicero and Machiavelli, seeks to translate non-domination in constitutional terms by harping upon mixed constitutionalism and a contestatory citizenry as core features instead of sticking to the communitarian privileging of a popular majoritarian sovereignty.

These formulations on liberty and constitutionalism are no doubt irreconcilable, yet we would like to argue that on a closer scrutiny there is one aspect which unites them all, that being an engagement with the figure of the slave as their paradigmatic case of an unfree person. The expression liberty etymologically derives from the Latin word *libertas* meaning free men who are 'in their own power' as opposed to being 'under the power of someone else'.[19] Those living under the latter condition were referred to as slaves in the context of ancient Rome for the reason that they were subject to the arbitrary will of their masters. In other words, what was being suggested was that a person who is a slave is not free. It is precisely this tradition of thinking about liberty, wholly dependent on the figure of the slave for its articulation, that has inspired Republican theorists across times, for what else besides the condition of slavery can better signify the disdain for dominion or domination by others which they all share. We notice that republicanism travelled to the common law world in the medieval period instigating a similar love for liberty there, on occasions even managing to pose existential challenges to the monarchical system, which had to find a counter-revolutionary ally in the Hobbesian account of negative liberty to deal with this resistance. In order to establish that people living under monarchy continued to enjoy natural and civil liberties, Hobbes preferred a freedom of action approach to liberty which could be hindered only by physical impediments of the sort experienced by a slave in chains.[20] The negative liberty tradition grew subsequently under Locke and Bentham to also include within it nonphysical sources of unfreedom such as the coercion of a person's will, but an insistence on actual interference as the only possible instance of non-liberty meant that it nevertheless remained comfortable with a non-interfering benevolent master.[21] Proponents of positive liberty sought to present an idealized state of self-mastery as the only comprehensive negation of slavery in all forms. Thus, it can be seen that the figure of the slave plays a pivotal role as an aversive model in all the three narratives sketched before, even if there is disagreement with respect to its precise definition. In the language of comparative studies, it can be described as a pre-comparative *tertium,* which is commonly assumed yet only implicitly acknowledged in the comparative enterprise.[22] To be sure, there have been other subjectivities like serfs and vassals under feudalism, labourers under capitalism, women and children under patriarchy, and indigenous and colonized populations in modern states, which have featured prominently in the liberty discourse, but the figurative hold of slavery in the Western tradition of political thought has been such that their condition has generally been analogized with that of the slave.

III Part Two

That the idea of liberty travelled from Europe to other parts of the world in the post-Enlightenment period is hardly disputable, even if there may have arisen different practices around its reception. More intriguing is how the figure of the slave has also managed to travel along with it to become an influential component in the imagination of those who spoke or wrote about freedom. This is not to ignore non-European histories of slavery and cultures of resistance surrounding them, but to simply point to the way in which the Western conceptualization of the slave has ended up serving as a dominant stimulant in liberty discourses elsewhere. Two examples which immediately come to mind may be cited: Franz Fanon's critical use of Hegel's master–slave dialectic while thinking about the emancipation of Blacks;[23] popular use of the Persian expression *azadi* for freedom in India during the colonial movement, and even more recently, as contrasted with the unacceptable subjugated position of the people described in terms of *ghulami* or slavery. The same was true for Phule as we noticed in the introduction to this essay. In this part, our contention would be that something interesting happens to the figure of the slave in Ambedkar's constitutional thought on liberty, so much so that it makes coherent sense only if we replace the condition of slavery with untouchability as his paradigm case of unfreedom.

We are not suggesting that Ambedkar consistently distinguished between the slave and the untouchable all throughout his intellectual career. Two other possibilities of conceptually interlinking untouchability with slavery also featured in his work. The first is where he treated untouchability merely as a synonym for slavery. Consider this. In his Evidence before the Southborough Committee, Ambedkar submitted that '[i]f one agrees with the definition of slave as given by Plato, who defines him as one who accepts from another the purposes which control his conduct, the untouchables are really slaves'.[24] Second is where everybody under the caste system is considered a slave to it. Ambedkar wrote:

> The Caste system has two aspects. In one of its aspects, it divides men into separate communities. In its second aspect, it places these communities in a graded order one above the other in social status ... this gradation, this scaling of castes, makes it impossible to organize a common front against the Caste System. If a caste claims the right to inter-dine and inter-marry with another caste placed above it, it is frozen, instantly it is told by mischief-mongers, and there are many Brahmins amongst such mischief-mongers, that it will have to concede inter-dining and inter-marriage with castes below it! All are slaves of the Caste System. But all the slaves are not equal in status.[25]

If Ambedkar had really settled for such an equation of untouchability with slavery, we might not have come across the several paradoxes in his constitutional thought, which cannot be explained by a singular preference for either negative, positive, or republican liberty, along with its concomitant forms of constitutionalism discussed in part one. Let us enlist at least four of them.

First, Upendra Baxi reads Ambedkar as suggesting that the caste system is a 'dominance without hegemony' supported by the lawless laws of the Hindus.[26] In Ranajit Guha's original use of the expression which Baxi simply borrowed, dominance referred to a state of affairs where coercion outweighed persuasion that is one characterized by the absence of negative liberties.[27] This reading is corroborated by Ambedkar's endorsement of freedom of occupation, inter-caste marriages, and cessation of other caste-based coercive practices. But at the same time, instead of merely stopping at ameliorative measures to address these restrictions or aligning himself with progressive Hindu reformers of his age who spoke about elimination of untouchability by keeping *varnashram dharma* intact, he emphatically spoke in favour of annihilation of caste and social endosmosis.[28]

Second, Ambedkar's view of nationalism grounded in the construction of a social homogeneity led him to argue in favour of India's partition and propose a strong centrist imperium for the independent union.[29] But this did not prevent him from standing up for seemingly divisive constitutional mechanisms such as separate electorates and reservations, as also fervently practicing a politics of Dalit minoritarianism.

Third, in the Constituent Assembly, Ambedkar came across as denouncing 'bloody methods of revolution' as well as Gandhian style 'civil disobedience, non-violence and *satyagraha*' as a 'grammar of anarchy' and exhorted society to 'hold fast to constitutional methods of achieving...social and economic objectives'.[30] But those like Pratap Bhanu Mehta, who want to reduce him to an advocate of a liberal constitutional morality,[31] would be surprised to come across gestures of defiance such as going to the floor of Parliament and suggesting that the Constitution must be burnt since it did not suit anybody and that he was merely a hack who wrote it much against his will.[32] This is to merely add to the more well-known act of public dissensus, that being his conversion to Buddhism in a mass ceremony along with five hundred thousand followers two months before his death.[33]

Fourth, combining Marx and Buddha, Ambedkar acknowledged that private property was a source of sorrow[34] and called for its abolition through nationalization of basic industries including agriculture.[35] Yet we find in his practical engagements with the property question, instances such as these. In the Bombay Legislative Assembly, he vehemently argued in favour of regularizing *watan* lands owned by *Mahar*s to bring them under the regime of private property.[36] Secondly, in *Kameshwar Singh v State of Bihar*,[37] he argued against zamindari abolition without payment of just compensation to erstwhile landowners.

Fifth, Ambedkar is considered as one of the first to have perceptibly understood the inter-linkages between the violence of patriarchy and the caste system.[38] But at the same time, we also find in him as a legislator during the Hindu Code Bill debate, a reluctance to continue with customs relating to property inheritance favourable to women.[39]

These paradoxes suggest that Ambedkar's position on liberty does not fit any of its rival accounts in totality. Let us deal with each conception of liberty individually and illustrate how it falls short of helping us understand his constitutional thought coherently.

Taking negative liberty first, Ambedkar's arch enemy was not the state but the extant Hindu society, and so he could not have found much utility in a tradition of liberty which espoused that the state ought to keep away from intervening in an autonomously operating social sphere. One may nevertheless read him as proposing that the injunction of non-interference in the Indian context applied to society rather than the state, insofar as it prohibited things such as freedom of occupation and inter-caste marriages. But such a position is ruled out since he did not confine his targeting only to a gamut of coercive practices but rather the entirety of the caste order itself. What is more, the problem for him was not that the caste system was a dominance without hegemony; it was in fact hegemony supported by the consent of *dvijas* (that is, the twice born or the first four castes) situated at different rungs in a graded system of inequality. If at all, the caste system can be said to be dominance in Guha's sense only as regards the untouchables who were explicitly or implicitly coerced rather than persuaded to fall in line with its prescriptions. Even then, the negative liberty tradition could not have excited Ambedkar much, since he considered the caste system to be inextricably linked with the problem of untouchability, which meant that mere removal of coercive practices against the untouchables would not cure the larger problem with the caste system. In the same way as Republicans find it impossible to conceive of a free slave, Ambedkar found it unfathomable to think of a caste system with no untouchability. For this reason, we agree with Chris Bayly that Ambedkar was counter-liberal, in so far as liberalism is aligned with the negative liberty tradition.[40]

There is much in Ambedkar's thinking on nationalism, state socialism, and Buddhism which gives an impression of simply being influenced by various strands in the positive liberty tradition. But such an easy association must be avoided, for his thinking posed a fundamental objection to this line of thought. Ambedkar's interest in Buddhism shows that his conceptions of individual and collective selfhood could not have been grounded in an ontology of substances—that is, it could not have possessed a determinate and concrete essence worth preserving.[41] Furthermore, unlike those who privileged self-mastery as opposed to being a slave, Ambedkar could not have normativized Brahminism in opposition to untouchability.[42] As a result, in his constitutional project of citizenship, the social value thus far associated with the elite was not presented as an aspiration generalizable to the masses. Coupled with this, as is clear from a careful look at our paradoxes, he was as anxious about this tradition's anti-pluralist and authoritarian implications as had been proponents of negative liberty. No doubt Ambedkar was antagonistically predisposed to communism and Gandhism, since he saw them as ideologies challenging the very legitimacy of the nation-state project which he valued; but this did not in any way prevent him from deconstructing majoritarian communal rule masquerading as nationalism.[43] This explains his support for and participation in different forms of constitutional politics which favoured political minorities and his radical revision of orthodox Buddhism as a religion for the minor.[44] Similarly, his advocacy for abolition of private property did not lead him to ignore the dictatorial potential which such projects had been capable of unleashing in recent history. He, therefore, demanded a non-violent abolition without any bloodshed, which in constitutional terms got translated into a rather liberal sounding formula of 'no acquisition without public purpose and just compensation'.[45] To add to this, he did not entirely share the Marxian hostility for private property, since the more basic fight for the stigmatized untouchables was to first make space for themselves in capitalist modernity even if this be through the mediating language of universal bourgeois rights.[46]

Ambedkar has often been situated in the republican constitutionalist tradition and not without justification. We find in his work for the Constituent Assembly a deep concern for institutionalizing political power in such a way that it is not monopolized by any particular party or organ of government.[47] Perhaps his discomfort with anti-pluralist and authoritarian tendencies in communitarian constitutionalism could effectively be addressed by the contestatory role for the citizenry envisaged under republican constitutionalism. But such an assessment holds provided we resort to its critical agonistic versions which look beyond formal categories such as individual citizenship and unitary body politic, to appreciate the wide disparities separating socio-economic elites from subalterns in all walks of life, and being open enough to make them relevant for radical politics of recognition and redistribution.[48] Furthermore, Ambedkar's selection of Buddhism as a civic religion for his community of Dalits would seem dangerous from a secular republican perspective based on the public private distinction. However, from his point of view, the caste system was in its core a religious problem requiring a religious solution, and could not have been dealt with by legal means alone.[49] In fact, instead of merely seeking to connect his conception of constitutional morality to the literature on procedural and direct democracy, it might also be productive to draw affinities with his formulation of Buddha's *dhamma* and idealization of the sangha as a model for the political community of the nation to emulate. Never the less, in spite of these qualifications, Ambedkar's constitutional corpus comes across as broadly resonant with the republican liberty tradition, at least much more so than it is with either of the previous two accounts. But if non-domination was indeed his central driving motivation, Ambedkar would have left untinkered woman friendly customs on property inheritance in his Hindu Code Bill. For him, given their intrinsic interlinkages in the Indian context, the only workable solution to the violence of patriarchy was the elimination of caste root and branch. In our understanding, what separates Ambedkar from republican liberty decisively is that he could not have approached an institution like caste, with its hierarchy and graded inequality, through a binary prism of domination and non-domination. Untouchables did not have to deal merely with one identifiable master; it was a larger network comprising caste Hindus, even Muslims and British, which contributed to their systemic subordination.[50]

Ambedkar's constitutional thought thus cannot be confined to any of the three rival conceptions of liberty. But is it not possible to read him as a pragmatist who drew upon whatever suited his purpose from these accounts? If this were the case, he would have managed to reconcile what we believe, following the likes of Berlin[51] and Skinner, have been historically and conceptually irreconcilable. But our clinching contention in this regard is that more than the competing stipulations contained in the negative, positive and republican liberty traditions, Ambedkar's major discomfort was actually with the figure of the slave in which all of them were grounded, and his critical intervention was to have managed to displace it by the figure of the untouchable while thinking about liberty. It is not that he believed India to have lacked a culture of slavery; rather, at several places he asserted that it was an important legal institution among the *savarnas* which got corrupted by graded inequalities of the caste system. In fact, he opined that if this were the only problem confronting the Hindus, 'it would have had at least one beneficial effect. It would have been a levelling force. The foundation of caste would have been destroyed.'[52]

Although not entirely consistent all throughout, we have been able to find the following points which makes it amply clear how he distinguished the case of the untouchable from that of the slave. First, unlike untouchability, slavery was not obligatory. This implied that slavery was simply permissible and it was never mandatory for a master to hold another as his slave. However, as Ambedkar poignantly observed, 'an Untouchable has no option. Once he is born an Untouchable, he is subject to all the disabilities of an Untouchable.'[53] The possibility of emancipation is, therefore, never present in the case of an untouchable. Second, whereas slavery was a de-jure and therefore a direct practice of discrimination, untouchability was merely a de-facto and therefore, an indirect one. Thus, Ambedkar suggested that although a slave was aware of his/her position of unfreedom in society, an untouchable was always deliberately kept unconscious of it.[54] He believed that it is this deception that added to the robustness of the caste system. Third, in spite of both being illiberal social orders, slavery was better than untouchability on account of the fact that a master, either for his own benefit or out of benevolence, in the former system was likely to take care of his slaves' material and intellectual development.[55] Fourth, citing Hindu religion as the source of untouchability, Ambedkar noted that 'Legally the slave was not a freeman. Yet, socially he had all the freedom necessary for the growth of his personality. Legally the Untouchable is a freeman. Yet, socially he has no freedom for the growth of his personality.'[56] Fifth and most importantly, in Ambedkar's words,

> [T]he serf and the slave were permitted to have physical contact, from which the Depressed Classes are debarred. What is worse that this enforced servility and bar to human intercourse, due to their untouchability, involves, not merely the possibility of discrimination in public life, but actually works out as a positive denial of all equality of opportunity and the denial of those most elementary of civic rights on which all human existence depends.[57]

These differences between the figures of the slave and untouchable read with our previous discussion clearly shows that none of the three accounts of negative, positive and republican liberty could have by themselves served Ambedkar's fashioning of a legal and political project for Dalit emancipation. Here, one may argue like Ananya Vajpeyi that more than liberty, it was the concept of social equality which framed his response to the question of untouchability.[58] That Ambedkar's thinking on liberty was integrated with his love for equality and fraternity is evident,[59] but this does not suffice to establish a lexical priority for the latter two over the former. Further we believe that it is more generative to study the liberty concept by locating it within a 'constellation of satellite concepts' rather than confining it to precise definitional demarcations. Having made these caveats, we would now venture to assert that there is something distinct that liberty could bring to the table for Ambedkar when grounded in the figure of the untouchable. It enabled clear thinking about liberation from oppression—a social concern which preoccupied him the most, without being constrained by limitations of non-interference, self-mastery, and non-domination. Critically for Ambedkar, unlike categories of interference and domination, untouchability could not be stripped down to a legal definition. In his words, 'Untouchability is a social concept which has become embodied in a custom and as custom varies so does untouchability.'[60] As a result we submit that it makes a lot of sense to use oppression which is a non-jural expression to describe the experience of untouchability in all its variegated manifestations. In order to talk about liberation from the oppression of untouchability, we would be well served in looking at Ambedkar's re-interpretation of the Indic discourse on *Nibbana,* the hegemonic versions of which, particularly during the anti-colonial movement, situated it within a transcendental framework of individual renunciation. Traditionally, this conception of liberty was conceived as other-worldly, but as modernity took roots in India, it was imaginatively refashioned as a this-worldly phenomenon by Hindu social reformers culminating in the figure of Mohandas Gandhi. This-worldly liberty in a transcendental framework of the individual renouncing society meant that a person could continue to engage in this world and yet be not of it.[61] Ambedkar was definitely this-worldly in orientation but had very little tolerance for the hegemonic transcendental framework of individual renunciation, which was in his understanding not only a Brahmanical vice but also something for which orthodox Buddhists could be held guilty.[62] At base, what he was interested in was not the liberation of individuals which would have naturally kept the oppressive social structure of caste intact. In order to deal with untouchability, nothing apart from a collective liberationary mobilization of Dalits would have served his purpose. It is this conception of liberty as non-oppression grounded in the figure of the untouchable that Ambedkar sought to generalize with varying degrees of success in his career as a constitutionalist.

IV Part Three

Our engagement with Ambedkar on liberty for the purpose of comparison should make it clear that we are *not* interested here in critiquing disciplinary conventions of comparative constitutional studies from the point of view of post-colonial difference which seems to have colonized most global South perspectives in academia today. Ambedkar, as is well known, was for the longest time, not taken seriously enough in India by its nationalists for his offensively radical anti-Hindu position, its Marxists for his liberalism and obsession with caste, and its Subaltern scholars for his arch-modernism and uncritical statism. There has been a recent surge of attention in his corpus largely due to the democratic successes of Dalit politics. But even then, he has been refashioned in consonance with the preferences of established ideological camps, either as a de-radicalized quasi-Hindu nationalist, a Marxian theorist of class, or someone whose politics could simply be situated on the side of subaltern heterogeneity finally deemed reconcilable enough with nationalist homogeneity. This is not to say that ideology can be eliminated from discourse, but simply to point to the fact that concerns of autonomy from the West never racked his imagination in the same way as they might have done to many of his illustrious contemporaries. So our questioning of the way in which concepts such as liberty or the figure of the slave come to be framed in comparative constitutional thought is by no means aligned to a celebration of particularity otherwise suffering epistemic neglect at the hands of universal metanarratives. We are broadly familiar with the terms of the Watson-Legrand debate on universality and particularity in comparative law but do not find them illuminating after a point.

We believe that universality and particularity cannot be pitted in opposition with one another and are therefore interested in a third approach in inter-disciplinary comparative studies which claims to reckon with both of them seriously as complementary analytical categories. But our difficulty with proponents of this approach in comparative law such as Günter Frankenberg and Ran Hirschl is their tendency to treat universality and particularity almost as fixed pre-givens, thereby presenting an untrue lopsided picture of the way in which constitutional transfers really pan out.[63] Take Hirschl for instance, who while criticizing proponents of universalism and particularism for overstating their respective cases, gives examples of specific constitutional areas such as basic rights where particularistic concerns of context were less powerful as opposed to other areas like polity-specific aspirational goals and organic features of respective constitutions where idiosyncrasies and contingencies became more relevant.[64] Similarly Frankenberg, although sympathetic to processes of global decontextualization and subsequent recontextualization in local settings, ultimately seems to fall prey to the 'one way traffic' thesis.[65] His global warehouse of constitutional ideas acts as a universal mediator where particular concepts are reified, formalized and idealized before they are ready for transfer.[66] Even though he may admit that this is merely an imaginative construct, the determinate way in which it comes to be defined, effectively ends up privileging only those constitutional ideas which germinate in the global North. No wonder that he brackets off Article 17 of the Indian Constitution as an oddity rooted in at most a South Asia specific history of untouchability, thereby having no potential for decontextualization and recontextualization.[67]

The likes of Hirschl and Frankenberg are led astray by their inability to appreciate that universality and particularity do not have static stipulative definitions which would enable us to treat them as strictly segregable categories. As can be seen from our discussion of the concept of liberty and its grounding in figures of the slave and the untouchable, it is not so easy to identify what counts as universal and particular in a comparative enterprise. Not only can traces of one be found in the other, but at times the two are so radically dispossessed of their claimed characteristics that the entire distinction between them gets destabilized. The figure of the slave which universally frames the European discourse on liberty becomes in Ambedkar only a particularity which although shared by India did not help him formulate a conception of liberty relevant for his emancipatory project. Taking cue from an Indic metaphor, we liken European liberty frameworks which claim global hegemony in comparative discourses to the 'oilman's oxen'. In the same way as the oilman's oxen are tied to a pole and made to move in circles around it, we believe that European concepts of liberty have for long been tied to the silent pre-comparative tertium of the slave. It is because of such a historically rigid attachment that negative, positive and republican frameworks of liberty failed to transcend their limitations of origin. This is precisely what Ambedkar was able to show us. However, it is not our intention to classify the slave as empirically particular for all constitutional context since it has continued to remain crucial in shaping liberty discourses across traditions beyond Europe, just as the historical component in the figure of the slave has been recalcitrant towards framing European liberty concepts as universal. Reading Ambedkar as a comparativist, we inferred that the figure of the slave was eventually displaced by that of the untouchable, on the basis of which he was able to formulate liberty as non-oppression. The empirical untouchable may indeed be a peculiarity produced by the Hindu caste system, but this does not condemn its figuration and the resultant conceptual possibility opened up to a perennial life of particularity. At the same time, we do not believe that there is any point in thinking of the untouchable as a new universal that can somehow replace the slave in liberty discourse, as it might come to be perceived in another context as characterized by the same sort of limitations as was the case with the latter for Ambedkar. All we are saying here is that there is nothing intrinsic to untouchability and liberty as non-oppression which may hinder their cross constitutional generalization, provided they are permitted as tenuous a relationship to specific histories of origin as so often happens to be the case with concepts travelling from the global North to the global South.

Thus, our conclusion is that the relationship between universality and particularity is messier than what most comparativists would have us believe. It would be generative to treat both as constituting a dyad,[68] with each element capable of bearing different constructions on different occasions depending upon the political orientation of the comparativist. Ambedkar's investment in activist comparison led him to a method which has helpfully been termed as contemporanization, that is the bringing together of materials from a diversity of time-spaces into encounter with one another for the purpose of transforming the contemporary.[69] He could by no stretch of imagination be called a disciplinary postcolonial critic, but instead a theoretician and practitioner interested in building new concepts based on different legal and historical sources across traditions. For him, like the historical particularity of slavery, untouchability was a particular Dalit experience, emancipation from which necessitated the mobilization of a universal liberty concept alongside an equally universal Buddhist liberation theology, but only after both were sufficiently modified to speak to his concerns—the former by being decoupled from the figure of the slave, and the latter by being dissociated from its culture of transcendental individual renunciation. These corrective interventions we have shown enabled him to arrive at the concept of liberty as non-oppression, which if nothing else, has at least been able to galvanize Dalits as a subjectivity in resistance movements which have, from time to time challenged the might of hegemonic socio-political consensus in various spheres of life.

There is no reason why Ambedkar's constitutional thought on liberty cannot be more widely contemporanized across the globe. Illustratively, his perceptive appreciation of the caste system as a social rather than ethnological phenomenon coheres very well with the contemporary identification of disciplinary interlinkages between biology and sociology. It is common in critical studies today to probe the way in which various markers of the human body have come to be constructed, with race, gender and even sex now being viewed in sociological rather than strictly biological terms.[70] The graded inequalities and cultures of ghettoization within which Ambedkar's figure of the untouchable was situated are also endemic to racism in different parts of the world. Even if slavery as a legal institution may no longer be officially in vogue, its lingering effects and pernicious indirect manifestations at various junctures should have brought the figures of the former slave and untouchable in convivial conversation with one another as everyday survivors of racism and caste system respectively. There is much in India's constitutional policy on reservations substantially drafted by Ambedkar that can and has contributed to discussions pertaining to affirmative action programmes elsewhere. Perhaps the reason for its comparative robustness is testimony to his insistence on politicizing the social problem of caste, which is not how the question of race is constitutionally perceived say in the United States. This may possibly explain why the relatively benign discourse on affirmative action there has not been able to progress beyond debates over 'colour blindness' and diversity. Further, Ambedkarite discussions on touchability and untouchability also resonate with feminist politics encouraging women entry in temples, mosques, and shrines, at least in South Asia if not elsewhere. His understanding of caste as rooted in religion and therefore requiring a solution in religion can be connected with Muslim feminists who read the problem of patriarchy in similar terms and proceed to enunciate radically creative non-patriarchal interpretations of Islam, sometimes even daring to blame the Qur'an itself for its sexist readings.[71] Finally, since the figure of the untouchable has not been set up here as a new universal for all liberty based movements, we do not mind the possibility of its displacement by another figure if need arises. The same can be said for Ambedkar's conception of liberty as non-oppression. Unlike rival accounts of European liberty, we are not making the ambitious normative claim that all assertions of liberty ought to have something to do with oppression in order to properly qualify as liberty claims. There may be non-oppressive contexts for which negative, positive, republican or even another freshly developed conception of liberty may be more relevant. What needs also to be admitted is that there may emerge situations for which liberty as non-oppression might need to be thought about without invoking the figure of the untouchable. In Ambedkar's time, Dalit political alliances with other groups such as Muslims, Sudras and Adivasis could not fructify, and he was left with no option but to fashion a minoritarian politics for his community. Today, when Dalits choose to or are compelled by circumstances to go it alone, the pursuit of liberty as non-oppression grounded in the figure of the untouchable continues to inspire, but when the coming together on a common platform with other oppressed communities becomes possible, we are not entirely clear about its utility as a basis for liberty claims, for such a majoritarian politics may be united not by a commonly shared experience of untouchability, but rather by a common oppressor as adversary.[72] Liberty as non-oppression should thus remain open ended enough so that it can be drawn upon for a broad range of libratory causes even where the figure of the untouchable is not seen as integral to discourse formation. This may be done perhaps by conceiving the oppressed person as an empty signifier which bears no definite content, and is therefore free to represent different subjectivities in different contexts, without needing to analogize itself to the untouchable.

Notes and References

* We would like to thank Professor Ishwara Bhat for providing us a working space at WB NUJS. Our deepest gratitude to Professor Mahendra Pal Singh, without whose guidance and inspirational motivation this paper could not have been written.

1. Jotirao Govindraw Fule. 1873. *Slavery*. Pune: Poona City Press.
2. Fule, *Slavery*.
3. Dalits referred to the group of untouchables formally outside the fourfold caste system, also known as Atisudras and Panchamas. However, no distinction was

commonly made between the fourth caste of Sudras and Atisudras when Phule wrote *Gulamgiri*.

4. 'Constituent Assembly of India, Vol. VII', http://parliamentofindia.nic.in/ls/debates/vol7p15.htm.
5. See Kalpana Kannabiran. 2012. Tools of Justice, pp. 150–1. New Delhi: Routledge.
6. B.R. Ambedkar, 'Castes in India: Their Mechanism, Genesis and Development', http://www.columbia.edu/itc/mealac/pritchett/00ambedkar/txt_ambedkar_castes.html.
7. See Nivedita Menon. 2011. 'Caste on the International Stage', *Economic and Political Weekly*, 46(3): 15.
8. Menon, 'Caste on the International Stage'.
9. Upendra Baxi. 2013. '"Ordering" Constitutional Transfers: A View from India', in Günter Frankenberg (ed.), *Order from Transfer: Comparative Constitutional Design and Legal Culture*, pp. 189–209. London: Edward Elgar Publishing.
10. Henry Hardy (ed.). 2002. *Isaiah Berlin Liberty: Incorporating Four Essays on Liberty*. Oxford: Oxford University Press.
11. In specific terms, to use his words, it was the answer to be obtained by enquiring 'what is the *area* in which a person or a group is or should *be left* to do or be what he is *able* to *without interference* by other persons?' He asserted: 'by being free, I mean not being interfered by others' and that 'the area of interference should be as small as possible'; Hardy, *Isaiah Berlin Liberty*, p. 169.
12. In order to understand what positive liberty was all about, Berlin suggested that the following question be posed: 'What or who is the *source of control* or *interference* that can determine the person to do or be this or that?' Hardy, *Isaiah Berlin Liberty*, p. 169.
13. We have in mind thinkers such as Plato, Mill, Marx, and Freud.
14. Hardy, *Isaiah Berlin Liberty*.
15. See Charles Taylor. 1989. 'Hegel's Ambiguous Legacy for Modern Liberalism', *Cardozo Law Review*, 10: 857–70; and Joseph Raz. 1986. *The Morality of Freedom*, pp. 1–16. Oxford: Clarendon Press.
16. Quentin Skinner. 2008. *Hobbes and Republican Liberty*. Cambridge: Cambridge University Press; and Philip Pettit. 2002. *Republicanism: A Theory of Freedom and Government*. Oxford: Oxford University Press. See also Quentin Skinner. 2002. 'A Third Concept of Liberty', *Proceedings of the British Academy*, 117: 237–68.
17. Skinner, *Hobbes and Republican Liberty*; and Pettit, *Republicanism*.
18. Skinner, *Hobbes and Republican Liberty*; and Pettit, *Republicanism*.
19. Skinner, *Hobbes and Republican Liberty*, p. x.
20. Thomas Hobbes, *Leviathan*, pp. 124–5, http://socserv2.socsci.mcmaster.ca/econ/ugcm/3ll3/hobbes/Leviathan.pdf.
21. Hardy, *Isaiah Berlin Liberty*.
22. Arindam Chakrabarti and Ralph Weber (eds). 2016. *Comparative Philosophy without Borders*, p. 7. Chennai: Bloomsbury.
23. Frantz Fanon. 2008 [1952]. *Black Skin, White Masks*, trans. Charles Lam Markmann. London: Pluto Press.

24. Vasant Moon (ed.). 2014 [1979]. *Dr. Babasaheb Ambedkar Writings and Speeches*, vol. 1, p. 255. Delhi: Dr Ambedkar Foundation.
25. Moon, *Dr. Babasaheb Ambedkar Writings and Speeches*, vol. 1, p. 72.
26. Upendra Baxi. 1995. 'Emancipation as Justice: Babasaheb Ambedkar's Legacy and Vision', in Upendra Baxi and Bhikhu Parekh (eds), *Crisis and Change in Contemporary India*, p. 143. New Delhi: SAGE Publications.
27. Ranajit Guha. 1998. *Dominance without Hegemony: History and Power in Colonial India*, p. xii. New Delhi: Oxford University Press.
28. Aakash Singh. 2014. 'Gandhi and Ambedkar: Irreconcilable Differences?' *International Journal of Hindu Studies*, 18(3): 416, 432. For an explanation of social endosmosis, see Moon, *Dr. Babasaheb Ambedkar Writings and Speeches*, vol. 1, p. 57.
29. Shabnum Tejani. 2013. 'The Necessary Conditions for Democracy: B.R. Ambedkar on Nationalism, Minorities and Pakistan', *Economic and Political Weekly*, 48(50): 111–9.
30. 'Constituent Assembly of India, Vol. VII'.
31. Pratap Bhanu Mehta, 'What Is Constitutional Morality?' http://www.indiaseminar.com/2010/615/615_pratap_bhanu_mehta.htm.
32. Dhananjay Keer. 1962. *Dr. Ambedkar: Life and Mission*, p. 447. Bombay: Popular Prakashan.
33. See generally, Sangharakshita, 1986. *Ambedkar and Buddhism*, esp. ch. 7. Cambridge: Windhorse Publication.
34. Moon, *Dr. Babasaheb Ambedkar Writings and Speeches*, vol. 3, pp. 441–62.
35. Moon, *Dr. Babasaheb Ambedkar Writings and Speeches*, vol. 1, pp. 381–452.
36. For discussion on Ambedkar's engagement with watan lands, see Anupama Rao. 2009. *The Caste Question: Dalits and the Politics in Modern India*, pp. 63–117. London: University of California Press.
37. 1962 AIR 1166 (22 February 1962).
38. Sharmila Rege. 2013. *Against the Madness of Manu*, pp. 14–56. Delhi: Navayana Publication; and Eleanor Newbigin. 2013. *The Hindu Family and the Emergence of Modern India*, pp. 170–2. Cambridge: Cambridge University Press.
39. Newbigin, *The Hindu Family*, p. 177.
40. Christopher Bayly. 2011. *Recovering Liberties: Indian Thought in the Age of Liberalism and Empire*, p. 277. Cambridge: Cambridge University Press.
41. The phrase 'ontology of substances' is borrowed from Hans Lindahl who used it in the context of Carl Schmitt's constitutional theory. See Hans Lindahl. 2008. 'Constituent Power and Reflexive Identity', in Martin Loughlin and Neil Walker (eds), *The Paradox of Constitutionalism*. Oxford: Oxford University Press.
42. This stance was utterly different from that of his contemporaries like Rabindranath Tagore and Mohandas Gandhi who normativized Brahmin and Sudra values respectively; see Ashis Nandy. 2010. *Bonfire of Creeds*. Oxford: Oxford University Press.
43. Moon, *Dr. Babasaheb Ambedkar Writings and Speeches*, vol. 9.

44. See Ajay Skaria. 2015. 'Ambedkar, Marx and the Buddhist Question', *South Asia: Journal of South Asian Studies*, 38(3): 450–65.
45. Moon, *Dr. Babasaheb Ambedkar Writings and Speeches*, vol. 3, pp. 441–62.
46. Anupama Rao. 2013. 'Revisiting Interwar Thought: Stigma, Labour, and the Immanence of Caste-Class', in Cosimo Zene (ed.), *The Political Philosophies of Antonio Gramsci and B.R. Ambedkar: Itineraries of Dalits and Subalterns*, p. 54. Oxford: Routledge.
47. In his last speech before the Constituent Assembly of India, Ambedkar stated:

> [I]n India, Bhakti or what may be called the path of devotion or hero-worship, plays a part in its politics unequalled in magnitude by the part it plays in the politics of any other country in the world. Bhakti in religion may be a road to the salvation of the soul. But in politics, Bhakti or hero-worship is a sure road to degradation and to eventual dictatorship.

See 'Constituent Assembly of India, Vol. VII'.
48. Shruti Kapila. 2014. 'Global Intellectual History and the Indian Political', in M. McMohan Darrin and Samuel Moyn (eds), *Rethinking Modern European Intellectual History*, pp. 267–71. Oxford: Oxford University Press. For difficulties with mainstream republican accounts, see John P. McCormick. 2011. *Machiavellian Democracy*, pp. 141–69. Cambridge: Cambridge University Press.
49. Moon, *Dr. Babasaheb Ambedkar Writings and Speeches*, vol. 5, p. 93.
50. Moon, *Dr. Babasaheb Ambedkar Writings and Speeches*, vol. 2, pp. 504–5 and vol. 12, pp.75–154.
51. Hardy, *Isaiah Berlin Liberty*, p. 42; Skinner, 'A Third Concept of Liberty', p. 241.
52. Moon, *Dr. Babasaheb Ambedkar Writings and Speeches*, vol. 3, p. 107–8.
53. Moon, *Dr. Babasaheb Ambedkar Writings and Speeches*, vol. 5, p. 15.
54. Moon, *Dr. Babasaheb Ambedkar Writings and Speeches*, vol. 5, p. 15.
55. Moon, *Dr. Babasaheb Ambedkar Writings and Speeches*, vol. 5, p. 16.
56. Moon, *Dr. Babasaheb Ambedkar Writings and Speeches*, vol. 5, pp. 91, 93.
57. Moon, *Dr. Babasaheb Ambedkar Writings and Speeches*, vol. 2, pp. 503.
58. Ananya Vajpeyi. 2012. *Righteous Republic: The Political Foundations of Modern India*, p. 212. Harvard: Harvard University Press. It is to Berlin that an emphasis on maintaining analytical clarity while dealing with the concept of liberty can be traced in Hardy, *Isaiah Berlin Liberty*, p. 72.
59. 'Constituent Assembly of India, Vol. VII'.
60. Moon, *Dr. Babasaheb Ambedkar Writings and Speeches*, vol. 5, p. 229.
61. Mithi Mukherjee. 2009. *India in the Shadows of the Empire*, pp. 151–80. New Delhi: Oxford University Press; and J. Barton Scott. 2016. *Spiritual Despots: Modern Hinduism and the Geneologies of Self-Rule*, p. 146. Chicago: University of Chicago Press.
62. Moon, *Dr. Babasaheb Ambedkar Writings and Speeches*, vol. 11, pp. 233–8.

63. Refer to Günter Frankenberg. 2010. 'Constitutional Transfer: The IKEA Theory Revisited', *International Journal of Constitutional Law*, 8: 563; and Ran Hirschl. 2014. *Comparative Matters: The Renaissance of Comparative Constitutional Law*. Oxford: Oxford University Press.
64. Hirschl, *Comparative Matters*, p. 203.
65. Frankenberg, 'Constitutional Transfer'.
66. Frankenberg, 'Constitutional Transfer', p. 5.
67. Frankenberg, 'Constitutional Transfer', p. 6.
68. We borrow this idea from Andrew Sartori. 2008. *Bengal in Global Concept History: Culturalism in the Age of Capital*, p. 9. Chicago and London: The University of Chicago Press.
69. Prathama Banerjee, Aditya Nigam, and Rakesh Pandey. 2016. 'The Work of Theory', *Economic and Political Weekly*, 51 (37): 42–50.
70. Judith Butler. 2006. *Gender Trouble: Feminism and the Subversion of Identity*. New York and London: Routledge.
71. See Aysha Hidayatullah. 2014. *Feminist Edges of the Qur'an*. Oxford: Oxford University Press.
72. Although Kancha Ilaiah talks about the possibility of dalitizing the nation. See Kancha Ilaiah (ed.). 2010. 'Towards Dalitization of the Nation', in *The Weapon of the Other: Dalitbahujan Writings and the Remaking of Indian Nationalist Thought*, pp. 81–104. Noida: Pearson.

PART II

PRIVATE LAW

5

The Stakeholder Approach towards Directors' Duties under Indian Company Law

A Comparative Analysis

Mihir Naniwadekar and Umakanth Varottil

I Introduction

An existential (but problematic) question in company law relates to the very purpose for which companies are incorporated and managed. Are companies to be run solely for the purpose of maximizing the profits of the shareholders? Does the law insist upon protecting—or even recognizing—the interests of non-shareholder constituencies? Do the directors of a company owe any duties to act in the interests of anyone other than shareholders? Theoretically speaking, these thorny questions have been the subject matter of rival claims. On the one hand, the shareholder theory visualizes the shareholders as owners of the firms, thereby requiring companies to be run in a manner that maximizes their value. On the other hand, the stakeholder theory adopts a broader perspective and requires companies to be managed on a sustainable and inclusive basis so as to consider the interests of non-shareholder constituencies such as employees, creditors, consumers, the environment, and the community in general. It is generally believed that while Anglo-American jurisdictions tend to be shareholder centric in nature, other jurisdictions in Europe and Asia embrace the stakeholder theory to varying degrees.[1]

This debate plays out more specifically in the context of duties owed by directors of companies. In common law, although directors legally owe their duties to the company (being a separate legal personality) and are required to act in the best interests of the company, this effectively means that in a solvent company they are to consider the interests of the members as a whole (as opposed to individual members).[2] Indeed, common law has often recognized that the directors of a company may have duties relating to non-shareholder constituencies in specific contexts. For instance, directors of a company have a duty to consider the interests of creditors during insolvency.[3] Although the matter is not devoid of controversy, it is arguable that while the directors do not owe a duty to the company's creditors, in discharging their duty to an insolvent company they ought to keep in mind the interests of the creditors, which displace shareholders' interests at that stage.[4]

Recognizing that common law does not cast any general duty upon directors towards non-shareholder constituencies, legislatures have sought to formulate a tolerable solution to what they perceive as a gap in existing common law. The British Parliament engaged in one such legislative intervention by adopting the 'enlightened shareholder value' (ESV) model through Section 172 of the UK Companies Act 2006 (the '2006 Act'). Briefly, this requires directors to have regard to non-shareholder interests *as a means* of enhancing shareholder value over the long term.[5] Although this is a hybrid approach that adopts features of both the shareholder and stakeholder theories, in the event of a conflict among various interests, it has a stated preference for shareholder interest thereby creating a distinct hierarchy. Another approach was taken by the Indian Parliament through Section 166(2) of the Companies Act, 2013 (the '2013 Act'), which appears at first glance to cast a duty on directors to treat non-shareholder interests as an end in itself. In other words, Section 166(2) follows the pluralist approach by placing all interests (whether of shareholders or other stakeholders) on par without creating any hierarchy and as being valid in their own right (without necessarily constituting a means to enhancing shareholder value).[6] This approach stays true to the stakeholder model in corporate law.

In this article, we examine the nature and content of the duty cast under Section 166(2) of the 2013 Act in India. We consider the implications of the duty on the scheme of the law generally, and how it is likely to impact other settled principles. We also examine some of the difficult questions emanating from Section 166(2). How do directors resolve conflicts among various stakeholder interests? How do non-shareholder constituencies obtain the benefit of these directors' duties? How should Indian courts rationalize and apply the provisions of Section 166(2)? In looking at these questions, we also draw on the experiences from similar debates in other jurisdictions, principally the United Kingdom (UK). We believe that analysing Section 166(2) in the context of the comparative developments in the UK will be helpful in several ways. First, both India and the UK have engaged in codification exercises when it comes to directors' duties in general, and those relating to non-shareholder constituencies in particular. Second, one can make up for the lack of clarity in legislative debates in the enactment of Section 166(2) in India by examining the rather detailed legislative efforts and consultations that preceded Section 172 in the UK. Such a comparative analysis will shed light on the purpose, scope and meaning of Section 166(2), which is an important exercise given that the provision is likely to receive judicial attention in the near future.

Our principal thesis in this article is that while Section 166(2) of the 2013 Act in India at a superficial level extensively encompasses the interests of non-shareholder constituencies in the context of directors' duties and textually adheres to the pluralist stakeholder approach, a detailed analysis based on an interpretation of the Section and the possible difficulties that may arise in its implementation substantially restrict the rights of stakeholders in Indian companies. Moreover, while the stated preference of the Indian Parliament veers towards the pluralist approach that recognizes the interests of shareholders and non-shareholder constituencies with equal weight, the functioning the Companies Act as well as principles of common law relating to directors' duties makes the Indian situation not altogether different from the ESV model followed in the UK. Proponents of the stakeholder theory in India must do better than to declare victory with the enactment of Section 166(2). Arguably, the magnanimity of its verbiage and rhetoric in favour of stakeholders merely pays lip service to them and obscures any real teeth or legal ammunition available to non-shareholder constituencies to assert those rights as a matter of law.

This introduction apart, we begin in the second section of this article with a broad outline of the shareholder-versus-stakeholder debate in the corporate law literature and an examination of the position of stakeholders under law (both in India and the UK) prior to the codification exercise. The third section examines the language of Section 166(2) as enacted, and also looks at the intentions of the legislature in introducing the provision in its present form. We also take a brief detour into the provisions of Section 172 of the 2006 Act in the UK to examine the similarities and differences in the statutory scheme in the two jurisdictions. The fourth section attempts to look at some of the problems that may arise in applying the language of Section 166(2). In particular, we look at the question of conflicts between the interests of various stakeholders inter se, and conflicts between stakeholders on the one hand and shareholders on the other. We also examine whether the recognition of the directors' duties to consider non-stakeholder interests would in any manner affect any broader principles of law. We conclude by offering some brief remarks on how one could interpret the relevant provisions going ahead.

II The Background: Shareholders and Stakeholders

An underlying theory behind the company law of most common-law jurisdictions is that the managerial powers of the board arise out of delegation from the shareholders.[7] This delegation is now also seen as having constitutional—and not just agency—character; yet, the role of directors was traditionally seen as promoting the interests of the shareholders.[8] The question of whether that is all there is to the role of directors has risen to prominence recently. Should directors consider only shareholder interests, or should they also consider 'stakeholder' interests? The question is not a new one,[9] yet modern developments and attempts at legislative reformulations in recent years have thrust it into prime focus.

To be sure, the shareholder primacy approach does not mean that directors must refrain from considering the interests of other stakeholders: directors are not prevented from taking into account the interests of other stakeholders, as long as they do this as a means to the end of maximizing shareholder wealth in the long term. Prior to the codification of directors' duties, company law in both India and the UK did recognize stakeholder interests to varying extents.

Beginning with India, at the time of independence the colonial law was unequivocal in its zeal to protect shareholders so as to enable companies to attract capital.[10] Corporate law did not play any role at all in taking cognizance of the interests of non-shareholder constituencies. This position continued immediately following independence, but the change in philosophy began taking shape in the 1960s with amendments to the Companies Act, 1956 (the predecessor of the 2013 legislation).[11] Consistent with the country's journey through years of socialism, the role of company law in India has extended beyond the mere protection of shareholders.[12] It encompasses the protection of employees, creditors, consumers, and society. For instance, employees obtained certain special rights under company law, such as preferential payment for dues in case of winding up of a company,[13] and also the right to be heard in case of significant proceedings involving a company such as in a scheme of arrangement (merger, demerger, or other corporate restructuring)[14] or in a winding up[15] of the company.

As far as creditors are concerned, while company law does provide them with the standard rights and remedies,[16] other special laws confer further corporate law rights such as the ability of the creditors to convert their loans into equity of the debtor company and, more specifically from a corporate governance standpoint, to appoint nominee directors on boards of debtor companies.[17] These rights are seemingly provided to protect the interests of the creditors. Building upon the element of 'public interest', affected parties may exercise remedies in case the affairs of a company are carried out in a manner prejudicial to public interest,[18] or if a scheme of arrangement[19] is not in consonance with public interest.[20] For example, while according its sanction to a merger, demerger, or corporate restructuring that is carried out through a scheme of arrangement, the court must take into consideration the effect of such a transaction on public interest.[21] Hence, Indian company law (both under common law as well as statute) did recognize stakeholder interests even before the codification of directors' duties was effected in 2013.

Moving to the UK, the seemingly shareholder-centric approach adopted in that jurisdiction did leave sufficient room to cater to stakeholder interests. At one level, English courts have been understood to interpret the 'interests of the company' as synonymous with the interests of the shareholders as a collective body (rather than individual shareholders).[22] Less clear is the answer to the question whether the interests of the shareholders are to be considered in the short term or on a long-term basis.[23] While the realization of short-term value to shareholders will narrow the focus on their interests, a long-term sustainable view of shareholder interests will naturally require the directors to consider the interests of other stakeholders such as employees, creditors, and consumers.[24] There is, however, some level of clarity that the law has rarely insisted upon realization of short-term profits to shareholders.[25] The long-term view of shareholders is consistent with the ESV model.

Moreover, common law as well as statute have recognized the interests of specific stakeholders such as creditors and employees. As already discussed,[26] directors must take cognizance of the interests of creditors (whose interests represent those of the company) in case of insolvency. There are also instances of stakeholder interests being considered in specific factual scenarios. For instance, in *Parke v Daily News*, the Court considered whether it was legitimate for a company to pay gratuitous compensation to an employee who has been dismissed. An action by a shareholder challenging such gratuitous payment to the employees was allowed.[27] The Supreme Court of India considering a somewhat similar issue arrived at a different conclusion: it emphatically considered that it was within the proper purpose of the company to consider employee interests, and upheld the payments of ex gratia sums to employees.[28] Statutorily, Section 309 of the Companies Act 1985 in the UK provided that directors had a duty to consider the interests of employees, although the employees did not have a remedy against the directors for breach of such a duty.[29] Hence, while the interests of stakeholders did receive recognition under English law, there was nothing to suggest that these interests were to be considered on par with that of shareholders. In that sense, the preexisting position appears similar ESV model rather than a pluralist approach.[30]

Apart from legal developments, it is also worth noting that the ideas of corporate social responsibility (CSR) and socially responsible investing (SRI) gained traction towards the end of the twentieth century.[31] The interests and preferences of institutional investors altered the manner in which boards and managements began viewing stakeholders.[32] To that extent, the ethical preferences of shareholders began driving greater recognition of stakeholder interests.

All of these developments indicate that stakeholder interests did receive a fair bit of attention in the UK even prior to the reforms that led to the enactment of the 2006 Act. Although stakeholders did not necessarily possess legally enforceable rights against corporate boards, directors did owe duties (to the company) to consider stakeholder interests. Hence, some commentators have argued that the ESV model did exist even prior to the 2006 Act, and that Section 172 merely codifies the preexisting position, and does not create any new rights to stakeholders.[33]

After highlighting that stakeholder interests were recognized both in India and in the UK prior to recent legal reforms, we now analyse the specific statutory duties imposed on directors with respect to the interests of stakeholders in both these jurisdictions.

III The Language and Legislative Intent: Breaking Down the Statutory Duties

Starting with the statutory reforms in India, Section 166(2) of the 2013 Act reads:

> A director of a company shall act in good faith in order to promote the objects of the company for the benefit of its members as a whole, and in the best interests of the company, its employees, the shareholders, the community and for the protection of environment.

The journey of this provision from its original draft form to the finally enacted version is itself illuminating. The genesis of this provision can be found in Clause 147(2) of the Companies Bill, 2008, which remained unchanged in the Companies Bill, 2009. The clause in these Bills was based on the recommendations of the Irani Committee Report.[34] The provision as originally inserted did not make reference to non-shareholder constituencies. The Irani Committee Report did not categorically indicate that the intent at that time was anything other than a codification of existing common law; at the same time, the Committee did make a reference to the duties of directors to the interest of employees and potentially other stakeholders. After finding that international practice (especially the UK) considers a wide spectrum of directors' duties, the Irani Committee Report in the relevant part states:[35]

> 18.3 Certain basic duties should be spelt out in the Act itself such as
>
> (a) duty of care and diligence;
> (b) exercise of powers in good faith, i.e., discharge of duties in the best interest of the company, no improper use of position and information to gain an advantage for themselves or someone else;
> (c) duty to have regard to the interest of the employees, etc.

Interestingly, the Committee does not appear to have spelt out in detail as to which stakeholders other than the employees would benefit from the duty. Further, the Committee did mention that there was a duty of exercise of powers in good faith in the best interest of the company. At the same time, the duty recommended with respect to employees and other possible stakeholders was not one of acting in good faith to promote their interests: it was simply a duty to 'have regard to the interest of the employees, etc.' In the event, Clause 147 of the 2008 and 2009 Bills did not spell out specifically any duty in relation to non-shareholder interests. Clause 147(2) simply stated:

> A director of a company shall act in good faith in order to promote the objects of the company for the benefit of its members as a whole, and in the best interest of the company.

The introduction of the phrase 'a director ... shall act ... in the best interest of *its employees, the community and the environment*...' can be traced to the corresponding provision in the Companies Bill, 2011 (which eventually took shape in the form of the 2013 Act). The 2011 Bill is the result of deliberations by a Parliamentary Standing Committee on Finance, and the rationale for the introduction of this phrase can be gleaned from the Standing Committee Report.[36] The Standing Committee noted that the Institute of Company Secretaries of India ('ICSI'), the professional body regulating company secretaries, had recommended that a specific reference be inserted for a duty of directors towards shareholders, employees, environment and community.[37] This suggestion was forwarded to the Ministry of Corporate Affairs. The Ministry accepted the suggestion; in addition to accepting the suggestion, the Ministry also noted that an appropriate provision was required to be made by way of an enabling clause allowing directors to consider non-shareholder interests particularly in view of the proposed voluntary CSR norms also sought to be introduced.[38] The Ministry therefore recommended the insertion of the clause as it presently stands. It needs to be clarified that the Ministry does not appear to have considered the clause merely as an enabling provision for CSR norms; in other words, the Ministry appears to have considered the provision as something more than simply enabling directors to consider non-shareholder interests. This is evident from at least two factors: first, the specific wordings were inserted on the suggestion of the Ministry, which could easily have chosen different wordings if the intent was a mere enabling provision (for example, 'having regard to' stakeholder interests); secondly, the Ministry did make reference to 'enabling' CSR, but also specifically accepted the recommendations of the ICSI. The ICSI had clearly envisaged the clause as being in the nature of a positive duty on the directors, *requiring* directors to consider stakeholder interests and not merely as being in the nature of an enabling provision *allowing* directors to do so. The Ministry's recommendation was seconded by the Standing Committee, which noted: 'The Committee welcome the proposed changes with regard to the duties of a director to promote the objects of the company in the best interests of its employees, the community and the environment as well, particularly in the backdrop of Corporate Social Responsibility, which is proposed to be included in this statute…'[39]

This discussion indicates that the language of Section 166(2) was a well-considered one and inserted to cast a positive duty on directors; and was not merely an enabling provision as such. The legislative policy seems to be specifically to adopt the pluralist model; and the language chosen thus seems to deliberately shy away from the ESV model.[40]

The Committee's concluding remark on this issue reproduced earlier is of some interest: the Committee seems to read the clause as casting a duty to act in good faith for the promotion of the objects of the company in the interest of the shareholders and other stakeholders. Thus, the duty is seen as one of good faith to promote the objects of the company. The objects of the company are to be promoted in the best interest of the shareholders and other stakeholders. Thus, there is no independent duty to the stakeholders. The plain language of Section 166(2) however could be construed as meaning that there is a duty to act in good faith, (a) in order to promote the objects of the company for the benefit of its members as a whole, and (b) in the best interests of the company, its employees, the shareholders, the community and for the protection of environment. In other words, the text of Section 166(2) seems to leave open the interpretation that there are two duties of good faith; first, to act in good faith in order to promote the objects for the benefit of the members as a whole, and secondly, in addition, to act in good faith in the best interests of stakeholders. The Standing Committee however seems to have considered the clause as resulting in a duty to act in good faith to promote the objects of the company in the interests of the company and all stakeholders. On the Committee's view, there is no independent duty to act in the best interests of the stakeholders: the duty is simply one of promoting the objects. The objects are to be promoted in the best interests of the company as well as the stakeholders. It is not clear that the Committee's view is borne out by the language of the clause; in particular, the clause seems to be distinctly in two parts. This is clear from the separate references to 'for the benefit of its members as a whole' and 'and in the best interest of the company…'. The Committee's view will make one of those parts redundant. The point is not merely linguistic: whether there is one single duty or two separate duties will be of relevance in attempting to analyse how to resolve conflicts between the interests of shareholders and stakeholders.[41] It will also be of relevance in determining the nature and content of the duties and the types of conduct which will satisfy the thresholds set by the clause. We return to these aspects later.

The relevance of these discussions becomes clearer from an examination of the corresponding English provision. The debates in the UK point ultimately to a choice by Parliament in the 2006 Act to adopt the ESV model rather than the pluralist approach. We now briefly examine the relevant debates at the time of enactment of the 2006 Act in the UK, before comparing the language of Section 166(2) of the 2013 Act with the language of Section 172 of the 2006 Act. We also briefly examine the significance of another provision in the 2006 Act specifying to whom the relevant duties in Section 172 are owed. In particular, Section 170(1) of the 2006 Act clearly states that the duties are owed to the company.

A minor point is in order here: as we have seen,[42] it is not as if the common law barred directors from taking into account non-shareholder interests. In the words of Bowen LJ, 'law does not say that there are to be no cakes and ale, but that there are to be no cakes and ale except such as are required for the benefit of the company'.[43] Again, the common law did not equate shareholder interests with short-termism: directors could well have the discretion even in common law to consider stakeholder interests as a means of promoting long-term shareholder value.[44] However, the 2006 Act converts that discretion to consider stakeholder interests into a duty to do so.

The common law prior to legislative reformulations cast a duty of loyalty on directors, which included a duty to act in good faith in the best interests of the company. The test was a subjective one. The classic formulation is in *Re Smith & Fawcett*:[45] '[Directors] must exercise their discretion bona fide in what they consider—not what a court may consider—is in the interest of the company....'[46] In 1998, when thoughts were given to enacting a new companies statute in England, the UK Department of Trade and Industry constituted a committee, the Company Law Review Steering Group ('CLRSG') for formulating proposals for reform. The CLRSG saw the question of whose interests the company law ought to protect as being central to any debate on reform of English law.[47] The CLRSG labeled the two competing principles as 'shareholder value approach' and 'pluralist approach'. Ultimately, the CLRSG adopted the ESV model as a hybrid. It expressly rejected the pluralist approach on the grounds that such an approach would require complete reformulation of the entire law on directors' duties, and was not desirable or practicable. The UK government adopted the ESV approach, which made its way to Section 172. Ultimately, Section 172 was enacted to read as follows:

> (1) A director of a company must act in a way that he considers, in good faith, would be most likely to promote the success of the company for the benefit of its members as a whole, and in doing so have regard (amongst other matters) to—
>
> (a) the likely consequences of any decision in the long term,
> (b) the interests of the company's employees,
> (c) the need to foster the company's business relationships with suppliers, customers and others,
> (d) the impact of the company's operations on the community and the environment,
> (e) the desirability of the company maintaining a reputation for high standards of business conduct, and
> (f) the need to act fairly between the members of the company.

The ESV model in the UK thus asserts that the directors are to act in shareholder interests, but in doing so to have regard to certain enumerated stakeholder interests. As one author notes:

> Under this conception, attention to traditional 'stakeholder' interests such as effect of corporate operations on the environment, employees or local

> communities, is seen as a *means of* generating long-term shareholder wealth and improving portfolio—and firm-level risk assessment. Enlightened shareholder value thus emphasizes the benefits to *shareholders* that can result from focusing corporate management on areas of shared shareholder and stakeholder concern while recognizing the very real challenges posed by the diversity of shareholder and stakeholder interests.[48]

At the same time, it is clear that stakeholders do not have an independent cause of action against either the company or the directors that enable them to assert their rights.[49] Moreover, the ESV approach is designed to be clearly hierarchical in that in case of conflict between various interests, the directors must prioritize shareholders' interests, which is the paramount goal.[50] Such a tiered approach is also borne out by the language of Section 172 of the 2006 Act, which imposes an obligation on the directors 'to promote the success of the company for the benefit of its members as a whole', but in doing so only to 'have regard to' the interests of the other stakeholders. While the success of the company for the benefits of members is the ultimate goal, having regard to stakeholder interests is only a means to achieving that end.

Finally, in comparing the position in India and the UK, we have already seen that Indian law does not adopt the 'have regard to' approach or a hierarchical approach (that puts shareholder interest on top), but rather casts a positive duty on directors to cater to the interests of shareholders and other stakeholders in equal measure. Nor is there is a specific provision in India clarifying that the duty is owed to the company, leaving open the question of whether there is an enforceable right given to any of the stakeholders to bring an action for breach of duty. However, in the UK, shareholder interests continue to be paramount, and it is clear that directors owe their duties only to the company (and not directly to shareholders or other stakeholders). At first blush, the textual analyses of the statutory provisions in India and the UK suggest a great deal of disparity in the treatment of stakeholders as beneficiaries of directors' duties. While India appears to have adopted the pluralist approach (that was expressly rejected in the UK), the UK has expressly resorted to the ESV model (that India seems to have distanced itself from). On that count, India seems to have granted better protection to stakeholders in comparison with the UK.

However, if we were to dig deeper into the legalities of the enforcement of directors' duties and other operational matters regarding the assertion of rights by stakeholders, an altogether different picture emerges. Despite the textual disparity between Indian and English law in the directors' duties to uphold stakeholder interests, we find that a deeper analysis suggests that the two regimes are not entirely far apart. Several issues relating to the inability of stakeholders to assert their rights and take advantage of a seemingly beneficial regime brings the law in India somewhat closer to English law than it appears at first blush. We examine these matters in the following section.

IV The Problems: Potential Issues Arising in Implementation

The scope and effectiveness of Section 166 of the 2013 Act in India ought to be really tested in its functioning and implementation. In doing so, it is clear that a number of problems emerge. Stakeholder interests are not as wide-ranging as the text of the provisions would suggest. This is because stakeholders are devoid of remedies in case directors breach their duty to act in their interests. The common remedies of derivative action and class action are available only to shareholders and not to other stakeholders. Moreover, the nature of the directors' duties themselves is fuzzy and incapable of clear enforcement. The pluralistic approach towards the stakeholder theory reveals several shortcomings that make Section 166 operate more by way of rhetoric than legally enforceable rights to stakeholders. To that extent, Section 166 of the 2013 Act in India does no better in protecting stakeholder interests than Section 172 of the 2006 Act in the UK, thereby reducing the dissimilarities in the operation of the two provisions.

IV.1 The Lack of Enforcement Powers

The first question that confronts us on a plain reading of Section 166 is: to whom are these duties owed? How are they enforceable? A rather straightforward argument would be one based on a literal meaning of the words used. The argument would be that Section 166 states in terms that the directors must act in good faith to promote the objects of the company, and must also act in good faith in the best interests of the stakeholders. Thus, Section 166 casts a specific obligation to act in good faith in the best interests of the stakeholders. This, coupled with the omission of a provision similar to the English Section 170(1) (that clarifies that the duties are owed to the company), suggests that duties are owed to each individual stakeholders too. It could then be further argued that as the duty is owed to the stakeholders, there would be nothing to bar a civil claim raised by the stakeholders, for instance.

We respectfully submit that such an argument would be entirely misconceived. We support our position by beginning with a brief discussion on duties and remedies under general law, and then proceed to consider the remedies of stakeholders under company law.

The answer to the question of whether a statutory provision gives rise to a civil action depends 'on a consideration of the whole Act and the circumstances, including the pre-existing law, in which it was enacted….'[51] If one were to examine the Section 166 from this angle, it is evident that the provisions cannot be realistically interpreted to give a right of action to all stakeholders.

First, the text is not all that clear. As we noted in the previous section, the Standing Committee in its concluding remarks seems to have read the clause in a different manner: the committee mentions that the duty is one of promoting the objects of the company, and stakeholder interests are to be necessarily taken into account in promoting the objects. The duty is however still only of promoting the objects.

Second, the categories of stakeholders mentioned in the clause are fairly vague; and at least in respect of some categories, it is clear that there is no 'injured party' except for the larger public interest. For instance, the only easily ascertainable category of stakeholders is 'employees'.[52] It is evident that Parliament could not have intended that a right to sue accrues independently to stakeholders as vague as 'the community' and 'the environment'. Generally speaking, the editors of Winfield note, 'where there is no [limited, identifiable] class, it is inherently unlikely that Parliament would have intended a duty, sounding in damages, to the public as a whole in the absence of plain words….'[53]

Third, any such wide understanding of to whom the duty is owed would throw much of the modern law of negligence into disarray. The law of negligence identifies three approaches to the question of determination of 'duty of care'. The first is the 'tripartite test': (a) is the harm foreseeable? (b) is there sufficient proximity between the parties? and (c) would the imposition of a duty of care be fair, just and reasonable?[54] The second approach involves asking whether there is an 'assumption of responsibility'.[55] Third, there is an incremental approach of expanding the categories of duty of care by drawing analogies from existing, settled categories.[56] It is evident that none of these approaches readily accommodates a broad idea of a duty of care to all stakeholders. It would be a rather surprising result if Section 166 were then to be interpreted as brushing away at a stroke the entire basis of the modern law on when there is a duty of care in tort.

Finally, there is nothing particularly odd or incoherent with saying that the law casts a duty that is owed by the directors to one person (the company), which involves taking into consideration the interests of third persons (stakeholders). Company law itself provides for a similar case: duties owed by the directors to consider the interests of existing creditors.[57] Insofar as existing creditors are concerned, duties are owed to them through the company. The creditors' interests are protected by proceedings in the name of the company to which ratification by the shareholders is no defence.[58] Thus, no individual creditor can bring any claim against the company: proceedings are brought in the name of the company itself. This is analogous to the principle whereby, ordinarily, shareholders cannot bring a claim in respect of the company's losses against a third party: the claim must be brought by the company. To that extent, Section 166 is consistent with English law whereby in case of a breach of directors' duties, it is only the company that is entitled to bring an action, and neither shareholders nor other stakeholders can directly seek remedies against the directors.[59]

Thus, conceptually, there is nothing extraordinary with saying that the duties under Section 166 are owed to the *company*. This is a well-established principle of company law,[60] and Section 166 does nothing to alter that position.

This still leaves open the point of enforcement. Insofar as creditors' interests are concerned, that aspect becomes relevant mainly during insolvency, and the liquidator is empowered to bring the necessary proceedings in the name of the company.[61] Shareholders enjoy the benefit of bringing a derivative action in exceptional cases. But how can the law ensure that stakeholder interests are protected? If the company is the one that can bring an action, but refuses to do so (which is especially likely in a case where the interests of the majority shareholder and the stakeholders are in conflict), what is the value to be attached to the pluralist approach?[62] Here, we examine two possible actions under Indian law that may be brought by persons other than the company (operating through the board of directors). We begin with class actions (that have been statutorily recognized under the 2013 Act) and then consider derivative actions (that, although not statutorily recognized, are possible under common law).

Could there be a case for instituting a class action, for example? The class action provisions are contained in Section 245 of the 2013 Act. That provision entitles members or depositors to file a class action if they are of the view that the management or conduct of the affairs of the company are being conducted in a manner prejudicial to the interests of the company or its members or depositors. The interests of stakeholders are not mentioned here.[63] However, can members argue that a class action is nonetheless possible, because directors have breached a duty that is owed to the company, and this breach is prejudicial to the interests of the company? It seems that this is not what is intended in the scheme of class actions, which seem to be premised in damage to a class of members. The class action procedure does not seem to be intended to agitate the interests of members of a class other than the suing class. The specific reference to 'interests of the company or its members and depositors' appears to indicate that interests of other stakeholders were not in the legislature's contemplation in crafting the class action remedy. Subsection (10) provides that subject to compliance with the other subsections, a class action may be filed by a person or association representing 'the persons affected by the act or omission, specified in subsection (1)'. As noted above, the act or omission specified in subsection (1) does not contemplate the lack of consideration of interests of persons other than member and depositors.

Hence, not only is the availability of the class action remedy limited to members (and depositors), but it appears that they cannot assuage the rights of other stakeholders in bringing those actions.[64] Hence, the class action remedy is unavailable to stakeholders in ensuring the enforcement of directors' duties of which they are the ultimate beneficiaries.

Another possible suggestion, which could perhaps be made if one were anxious to provide some remedy to stakeholders, would be for the initiation of a derivative action against breaching directors to challenge an action that is against stakeholder interests. Since the directors owe a duty to the company, such a derivative action can be brought on behalf of the company with the benefit of the action flowing to the company (and not to the initiating party). A threshold question is: who can bring a derivative action? Can stakeholders bring a derivative action against errant directors? The answer to these questions is rather straightforward in that the law recognizes that only shareholders can bring derivative actions on behalf of the company against directors who have breached their duties. This is so under Indian law where derivative actions can be brought under common law due to the lack of their express recognition under the 2013 Act.[65] This position is concomitant with that in the UK where derivative action is codified under the 2006 Act and available only to shareholders.[66]

This then raises the question of whether a person wearing the hat of a shareholder can agitate questions that pertain to the interests of non-shareholder constituencies: does a shareholder have the standing to make claims when her direct interests are not affected?[67] A possible answer is to say that once the duty is owed to the company and the company does not take steps to enforce this duty, as a derivative action, the shareholder certainly can do so: she need not prove that any duty was directly owed to her at all. Ultimately, the duty is owed to the company and breach necessarily results in legal injury to the company; apart from that, the remedy from the derivative action flows to the company. The ordinary derivative action can typically be categorized under the 'fraud on the minority' exception to *Foss v Harbottle*.[68] A derivative action by the shareholder to enforce a duty to consider stakeholder interests is hard to justify under any of the existing exceptions to the rule; but in principle, the development of an analogous exception cannot be ruled out.[69] It is however clear that ultimately the fruits of a derivative action enure to the benefit of the company. The action is 'derivative' in order to protect the real interests of the company, which cannot protect itself if (say) the wrongdoers are in control. This entire logic breaks down when considering stakeholder interests. Unless the law is expanded—and this would necessarily involve the legislative creation of an entirely new remedy—to encapsulate stakeholder remedies through shareholder derivative actions, the current law is quite unsatisfactory in enabling shareholders to seek remedies for breach of directors' duties to act in the interests of stakeholders. Here again, analogous positions emanate from both India as well as the UK.

In these circumstances, a more efficacious remedy may well be necessary. This could potentially be found in the provisions of Section 241 of the 2013 Act. Can the failure to take into account the interests of stakeholders result in a claim under the oppression and mismanagement provisions? The very fact that directors are in breach could also be relevant to regulatory sanctions. For instance, under Section 241(2), the central government is entitled to apply to the National Company Law Tribunal (NCLT) for appropriate orders under the oppression and mismanagement chapter, if the central government is of the opinion that the affairs of the company are being conducted in a manner prejudicial to the public interest. Failing to consider stakeholder interests is conceivably something that would fall within the scope of this clause. At the same time, oppression and mismanagement provisions are generally meant to be remedies for minority shareholders, and it remains to be seen whether they are an appropriate avenue for assuaging stakeholder interests in case of breach of directors' duties.[70]

In all, regardless of the specific approaches followed towards stakeholder empowerment either in India or the UK, the statutory provisions that impose directors' duties to consider the interests of non-shareholder constituencies are not capable of being enforced by their ultimate beneficiaries. To that extent, one may question whether the beneficial provisions contained in Section 166(2) of the 2013 Act in India and Section 172 of the 2006 Act in India carry any legal wherewithal, or if they are simply aspirational in drawing attention to the interests of stakeholders that boards may not afford to ignore.

IV.2 Scope of the Directors' Duties

We now turn to the content of the duty itself. The words used by Parliament suggest that the duty on directors is to 'act in good faith in order to promote the objects of the company for the benefit of its members as a whole, and in the best interests of the company, its employees, the shareholders, the community and for the protection of environment....'

The first question that arises is whether the 'good faith' qualification applies only to the first part of the clause (that is, to the words 'in order to promote the objects of the company for the benefit of its members as a whole') or whether the qualification applies to the second part as well. The difference is not merely semantic: if the good faith qualification applies only to the first part, that would mean that the second part is an objective test. In other words, is it the case that (a) directors must act in good faith in order to promote the objects of the company as a whole, and (b) directors must act in the best interests of the company, its employees, the shareholders, the community and for the protection of environment? Or is it instead the case that (a) directors must act in good faith in order to promote the interests of the company as a whole and (b) directors must act in good faith in the best interests of the company, its employees, the shareholders, the community and for the protection of environment? In the first interpretation, the 'good faith' qualifier operates only with respect to promoting the objects of the company as a whole, while in the second it also extents to acting in the interests of stakeholders.

It is submitted that the language is capable of both meanings; but the provision ought not to be construed as giving rise to a duty of objectively acting in the best interests of stakeholders. The section must be read as meaning that there is a duty on directors to act in order to promote the objects of the company as a whole and to act in the best interests of the company and the stakeholders; however, this duty is to be assessed not by an objective test of what the best interests are. Rather, it would be sufficient in the directors subjectively believe in good faith that they are acting in the interests of all stakeholders. This again does not make the provision meaningless: there is a positive duty on directors to actively consider the interests of stakeholders. If an objective interpretation were preferred, directors would be under a duty to objectively act in the best interests of all the stakeholders. It would often be impossible for directors to be objectively right about whether to prefer the interests of shareholders or employees, for instance. The objective interpretation will also not sit comfortably with the legislative history and Parliamentary materials, including the Standing Committee's views.

In sum, therefore, it seems that the best interpretation of the clause is to consider that it casts a duty on directors that is owed to the company. What directors *could* have done under common law, they *must* do now. To effectively discharge this duty, directors must act in order to promote the objects of the company, in the best interests of the company as well as other stakeholders. However, the principle in *Smith & Fawcett*[71] continues to apply while discharging the duty.

In passing, it is also worth noting that a subjective duty imposed on the directors coupled with a pluralist approach towards stakeholders' interest may turn out to be a recipe for failure. The pluralist approach is confronted with several problems.[72] Due to the subject nature of the duty, directors could be faced with several choices. For instance, in case of conflict between the interests of shareholders and stakeholder, or among various types of stakeholders, whose interests they ought to prefer. This leaves with directors with substantial (and somewhat untrammeled) discretion.[73] More dangerously, the opportunity available to the directors to balance various competing interests may be utilized to foster their own self-interest, and leave them with little accountability to anyone.[74] All of these could potentially have the effect of substantially diluting the interests of stakeholders.

The subjective nature of the directors' duties regarding stakeholder interests is similar to the one that ensues in the UK where the position is stated rather expressly. As previously discussed, directors in English companies only need to 'have regard' to stakeholders' interests while discharging their duties.[75] More pertinently, if the common law that preceded the 2006 Companies Act made the relevant directors' duties subjective, that position has not altered under statute. Section 172 expressly provides that a director 'must act *in the way he considers*, in good faith, would be most likely to promote the success of the company....' It is clear that directors enjoy a great deal of discretion in that it is for the directors rather than for the courts to decide whether and how the various stakeholders' interests are to be considered when directors discharge their duties.[76] For this reason, even if a shareholder derivative action were possible, it would be an onerous task on the part of the claimant to demonstrate the breach of directors' duties as the situation is dependent upon the subjective opinion of the relevant director, which can be defensible in a number of ways.[77] A claim, if at all, may lie only if the director acted so egregiously as to have failed to act in good faith.[78] This may not be easy to establish for a claimant.

In sum, both in India as well as the UK, there could be difficulties in the implementation and enforcement of directors' duties under Section 166(2) of the 2013 Act and Section 172 of the 2006 Act respectively. In both jurisdictions, stakeholders do not enjoy meaningful remedies in case of breach of directors' duties that require them to take care of stakeholder interests. Mechanisms such as derivative actions and class actions are woefully inadequate. While shareholders, in theory, could espouse the claims of stakeholders, we are not sanguine that there is reason for them to do so. Even if they do, we do not expect them to succeed as it would incongruous for shareholders to pursue claims on behalf of stakeholders. In any event, the high degree of subjectivity in the duties imposed on directors not only compound the problems of stakeholders, but it also confers a great amount of discretion to directors that they could potentially use to act in their own interest. Both the pluralist approach in India and the ESV approach in the UK suffer from similar problems when it comes to such implementation matters. Hence, we conclude in this section that despite the perceived dissimilarities of the approaches followed in the two jurisdictions relating to directors' duties to consider stakeholder interests, in the end the ability of the stakeholders to address their concerns remain more or less the same in both. To that extent, stakeholder power in India is not as extensive as it is made out to be.

V Conclusion

Section 166(2) is likely to be considered by courts and tribunals sooner rather than later. However, as far as tackling the problems in the existing provision are concerned (some of which we have pointed out above), it seems that a well-thought-out legislative reconsideration would be more appropriate than fashioning ad hoc judicial responses. As we have seen, providing real ammunition to stakeholders on the basis of the existing provision is likely to be a double-edged sword: any innovative approach by the judiciary is likely to have repercussions on the entire scheme of the common law which are better addressed by legislative rather than judicial measures. The question of what remedies are to be provided to stakeholders must be one which needs to be squarely addressed in any legislative reformulation of the provisions.

Meanwhile, courts and tribunals will have to ensure that the provision does not become a shield for directors from all accountability. In other words, it will be for the judiciary to ensure that the provision does not become a means of excuse to the director who acts in neither the shareholders' nor the stakeholders' interests. If a director claims the she acted in good faith to balance the interests of shareholders and stakeholders, that claim must be scrutinized through properly manageable judicial standards. Evolving those standards of scrutiny—perhaps by incrementally developing on the common law standards of scrutiny of the actions of directors—is likely to be the most important challenge the judiciary will have to address in deciding cases involving the application of Section 166(2).

We do not suggest that courts or tribunals should substitute the judgment of directors with their own judgment. However, a case may well be made out that a purposive reading of the provisions compels courts to proactively satisfy themselves that the judgment of the directors was actually held in good faith, and was based on relevant materials and considerations.

Notes and References

1. For a discussion on the competing theories and the relevant literature, see Andrew Keay. 2010. 'Stakeholder Theory in Corporate Law: Has It Got What It Takes?' *Richmond Journal of Global Law & Business*, 9(3): 249; and Sarah Kiarie. 2006. 'At Crossroads: Shareholder Value, Stakeholder Value and Enlightened Shareholder Value: Which Road Should the United Kingdom Take?' *ICCLR*, 17: 329.
2. This principle was effectively summed up by the UK Company Law Review Steering Group when it said, while considering a possible statutory formulation of a duty to promote the success of the company: 'what is in view is not the individual interests of members, but their interests as members of an association with the purposes and the mutual arrangements embodied in the constitution....' Company Law Review Steering Group. 2000. *Modern Company Law for a Competitive Economy: Developing the Framework*, para 3.51. Department of Trade and Industry.
3. For a duty to consider the interests of creditors, see generally, *Liquidator of West Mercia Safetywear Ltd v Dodd* (1988) 4 BCC 30; *Facia Footwear Ltd (In Administration) v Hinchliffe* [1998] 1 BCLC 218; *Re Pantone 485 Ltd* [2002] 1 BCLC 266; *Gwyer v London Wharf (Limehouse) Ltd* [2003] 2 BCLC 153; [2002] EWHC 2748; *Re MDA Investment Management Ltd* [2004] BPIR 75; and [2003] EWHC 227 (Ch).
4. *Kuwait Asia Bank EC v National Mutual Life Nominees Ltd* [1991] 1 AC 187; and *Yukong Line Ltd v Rendsburg Investments Corporation (No. 2)* [1998] 1 WLR 294.
5. Deryn Fisher. 2009. 'The Enlightened Shareholder: leaving Stakeholders in the Dark: Will Section 172(1) of the Companies Act 2006 Make Directors Consider the Impact of Their Decisions on Third Parties?' *ICCLR*, 20: 10; Andrew Keay. 2007. 'Tackling the Issue of the Corporate Objective: An Analysis of the United Kingdom's "Enlightened Shareholder Value Approach"', *Sydney Law Review*, 29: 577; and Virginia Harper Ho. 2010. '"Enlightened Shareholder Value": Corporate Governance Beyond the Shareholder-Stakeholder Divide', *Journal of Corporation Law*, 36: 59.
6. See Umakanth Varottil. 2016. 'The Evolution of Corporate Law in Post-colonial India: From Transplant to Autochthony', *American University International Law Review*, 31: 253–325.
7. Reinier Kraakman, John Armour, Paul Davies, Luca Enriques, Henry Hansmann, Gerard Hertig, Klaus Hopt, Hideki Kanda, Mariana Pargendler, Wolf-Georg Ringe, and Edward Rock. 2009. *The Anatomy of Corporate Law*, 2nd ed., pp. 12–14. Oxford: Oxford University Press.
8. See generally, for a broad outline, Paul Davies. 2005. 'Enlightened Shareholder Value and the New Responsibilities of Directors', Inaugural W.E. Hearn Lecture, University of Melbourne Law School. Davies also clarifies that directors' duties to act in 'the interests of the company' identifies the company with one or more groups of people who, in the case of a solvent company, ought to be its members

(or shareholders). Paul Davies. 2000. 'Shareholder Value, Company Law and Securities Markets Law', pp. 6–7, available at http://ssrn.com/abstract=250324.

9. The question was in a sense central to the Berle-Dodd debate that occurred decades ago. A.A. Berle, Jr. 1931. 'Corporate Powers as Powers in Trust', *Harvard Law Review*, 44: 1049; E. Merrick Dodd, Jr. 1932. 'For Whom Are Corporate Managers Trustees?' *Harvard Law Review*, 45: 1145 (with Berle arguing that companies must have responsibilities only to shareholders, and Dodd arguing that companies must be responsible to other constituencies such as employees, customers, and the general public).
10. Varottil, 'The Evolution of Corporate Law'.
11. Varottil, 'The Evolution of Corporate Law'.
12. See Tarun Khanna and Krishna Palepu. 2004. 'Globalization and Convergence in Corporate Governance: Evidence from Infosys and the Indian Software Industry', *Journal of International Business Studies*, 35: 484 (laying out the debate in the context of protection of employees using the stakeholder theory).
13. Companies Act, 1956, s. 529-A.
14. Companies Act 1956, s. 391. See *In Re, River Steam Navigation Co. Ltd* (1967) 2 Comp LJ 106 (Cal.) (holding that in considering any scheme proposed, the court will also consider its effects on workers or employees); *In Re Hathisingh Manufacturing Co. Ltd* (1976) 46 Comp Cas 59 (Guj) and *Bhartiya Kamgar Sena v Geoffrey Manners & Co Ltd* (1992) 73 Comp Cas 122 (Bom) (approving the proposition that while sanctioning a scheme of arrangement the court should consider not merely the interests of the shareholders and creditors but also the wider interests of the workmen and of the community).
15. Companies Act, 1956, s. 443. See *National Textile Workers' Union v Ramakrishnan (P.R.)* A.I.R. 1983 SC 75 (holding that a court can hear the employee if it determines the employee should be heard to administer justice).
16. Companies Act, 1956, s. 439(1)(b) (stating that these include the right to initiate a winding up of the company, which is a customary company law right conferred on creditors in most jurisdictions).
17. See, for example, State Bank of India Act, 1955, s. 35A.
18. Companies Act, 1956, s. 397(2).
19. See Jennifer Payne. 2011. 'Schemes of Arrangement, Takeovers and Minority Shareholder Protection', *Journal of Corporate Law Studies*, 11: 67 (mergers, demergers, and other forms of corporate restructuring are usually effected through a scheme of arrangement that not only requires the approval of different classes of shareholders and creditors, but also the sanction of the relevant court of law).
20. Companies Act, 1956, s. 394(1), proviso.
21. *Hindustan Lever Employees' Union v Hindustan Lever Ltd* AIR 1995 SC 470.
22. See *Brady v Brady* (1987) 3 BCC 535; Elaine Lynch. 2012. 'Section 172: a ground-breaking reform of director's duties, or the emperor's new clothes?' *Compensation Law*, 196, 33: 196; and Daniel Attenborough. 2007. 'Recent Developments in Australian Corporate Law and Their Implications for Directors' Duties: Lessons To Be Learned from the UK Perspective', *ICCLR*, 18: 313.

23. *Provident International Corporation v International Leasing Corp Ltd [1969] 1 NSWR 424 at 440; Paramount Communications Inc v Time Inc 571 A. 2d 1140 (Del, 1989)*; *Harlowe's Nominees Pty Ltd v Woodside (Lakes Entrance) Oil NL* (1968) 121 CLR 483; *Teck Corporation Ltd v Millar* (1973) 33 DLR (3d) 288 (BCSC); *People's Department Stores Inc v Wise* [2004] SCC 68; and *Lonrho Ltd v Shell Petroleum Co Ltd* [1980] 1 WLR 627 (HL). Keay summarizes the principle emerging from these cases by saying, 'while directors are to manage their companies with shareholders in mind, they do have a reasonably wide discretion in the factors which they may consider in deciding what is going to benefit the company'. Keay, 'Tackling the Issue of the Corporate Objective', p. 581.
24. Generally, it is understood that directors are not required to prefer short-term shareholder interests. Illustratively, even if a company makes adequate profits, it may well choose not to distribute them entirely as dividend. Directors may well choose to retain the funds within the company or use them for purposes other than distribution, with the goal of long-term wealth creation, which might benefit other stakeholders as well. There is also no obligation to maximize immediate profits at the cost of long-term interests. Keay, 'Tackling the Issue of the Corporate Objective', p. 577. Also see, for a useful summary, Corporations and Markets Advisory Committee. 2006. *The Social Responsibility of Corporations*, pp. 84–9.
25. Exceptional situations include the extensively debated ruling of a US court in *Dodge v Ford Motor Co* 170 NW 668 (1919) (Michigan), or where a company is up for sale and the principal duty of the directors is to realize the best possible price for shareholders (*Heron International Ltd v Lord Grade* [1983] BCLC 244 [Court of Appeal]).
26. See notes 3 and 4 in this chapter.
27. In a note commenting on this decision, Professor Pennington foreshadowed the modern debate: 'The other question of policy is whether it is satisfactory that directors should be required by law to manage the company's affairs solely with a view to the financial benefit of shareholders. Are there not other interests which deserve recognition?' R.R. Pennington. 1962. 'Terminal Compensation for Employees of Companies in Liquidation', *Modern Law Review*, 25: 715.
28. *Shahzada Nand & Sons v CIT*, AIR 1977 SC 1182. The Court held (at para 4):

> 'It is obvious that no business can prosper unless the employees engaged in it are satisfied and contented and they feel a sense of involvement and identification and this can be best secured by giving them a stake in the business and allowing them to share in the profits… What is the requirement of commercial expediency must be judged not in the light of the 19th Century laissez faire doctrine which regarded man as an economic being concerned only to protect and advance his self-interest but in the context of current socio-economic thinking which places the general interest of the community above the personal interest of the individual and believes that a business or undertaking is the product of the combined efforts of the employer and the employees….'

29. Lynch, 'Section 172', pp. 198–9.

30. Lynch, 'Section 172', pp. 198–9.
31. Kiarie, 'At Crossroads', p. 336.
32. Fisher, 'The Enlightened Shareholder', p. 14.
33. Attenborough, 'Recent Developments in Australian Corporate Law', p. 318; Lynch, 'Section 172', pp. 202–3; and Rachel C. Tate, 'Section 172 CA 2006: The Ticket to Stakeholder Value or Simply Tokenism?' available at https://www.abdn.ac.uk/law/documents/Section172CA2006-thetickettostakeholdervalueorsimplytokenism.pdf.
34. Report of the Expert Committee on Company Law, May 2005 (Irani Committee Report), available at http://reports.mca.gov.in/Reports/23-Irani%20committee%20report%20of%20the%20expert%20committee%20on%20Company%20law,2005.pdf.
35. Irani Committee Report, part 3, chapter IV, 'Management and Board Governance, Duties and Responsibilities of Directors', paras 18.1–18.3, pp. 43–4.
36. Twenty-first Report, Standing Committee on Finance (2009–2010) (Fifteenth Lok Sabha), 'The Companies Bill, 2009' (Ministry of Corporate Affairs), Lok Sabha Secretariat, New Delhi, 31 August 2010, available at http://www.prsindia.org/uploads/media/Companies%20Bill%202009.pdf.
37. 'The Companies Bill, 2009', para. 11.77.
38. 'The Companies Bill, 2009', para. 11.78.
39. 'The Companies Bill, 2009', para 11.80.
40. It is also interesting to note that around the time the Standing Committee was deliberating upon these issues, business associations in India were also moving towards a pluralist approach. Illustratively, one may consider the recommendations of the Murthy Committee constituted by the National Association of Software and Services Companies (NASSCOM), a premier trade body of the Indian IT/BPO industry. The Committee was constituted to make recommendations in the aftermath of the Satyam scandal which had emerged by then, where a leading Indian IT company had admitted to large-scale irregularities. The Murthy Committee also leans towards a pluralist approach towards directors' duties; and in exploring the interests of non-shareholder parties, it considers not just stakeholders such as employees and customers, but also vendors and even competitors. See NASCOMM. 2010. 'Corporate Governance and Ethics Report', available at http://survey.nasscom.in/sites/default/files/upload/66719/Corporate_Governance_Report.pdf.
41. The point that there may be two duties does not detract from the proposition, discussed later, that both the duties are of good faith.
42. See Section II in this chapter.
43. *Hutton v West Cork Railway* (1883) 23 Ch D 645, at 673.
44. This is the position adopted by courts not just in England but also in jurisdictions such as Australia and Delaware, *Provident International Corporation v International Leasing Corp Ltd* [1969] 1 NSWR 424 at 440 (Helsham J); *Paramount Communications Inc v Time Inc* 571 A. 2d 1140 (Del, 1989).
45. [1942] Ch 304 (CA).

46. [1942] Ch 304 (CA), p. 306.
47. 'The Company Law Review Steering Group, Modern Company Law for a Competitive Economy: The Strategic Framework', http://www.berr.gov.uk/files/file23279.pdf.
48. Harper Ho, "Enlightened Shareholder Value", p. 62; emphasis in original.
49. Tate, 'Section 172 CA 2006'.
50. See Christopher M. Bruner. 2013. *Corporate Governance in the Common-Law World: The Political Foundations of Shareholder Power*, pp. 34, 44. Cambridge University Press.
51. *Cutler v Wandsworth Stadium* [1949] AC 3398 at 407.
52. Companies Act, 2013. 'Creditors' as a category of stakeholders are conspicuous by their absence in the statutory provision, and hence are not stated beneficiaries thereof. In the UK too, while Section 172(1) of the 2006 does not expressly include creditors as a beneficiary of the provision, Section 172(3) preserves the interests of creditors under general law (which presumably encompasses insolvency law). Derek French, Stephen Mayson, and Christopher Ryan. 2014. *Mayson, French & Ryan on Company Law*, p. 483. Oxford University Press.
53. W.V.H. Rogers. 2010. *Winfield & Jolowicz on Tort*, 18th ed., p. 387. Sweet & Maxwell. They give the example of *Mid Kent Holdings v General Utilities* [1997] 1 WLR 14, where a literal interpretation of Section 93A the (UK) Fair Trading Act 1973 would have led to what is termed as an 'extraordinary' result 'of allowing any of the whole population to bring proceedings to enforce an undertaking to the Minister'. It is submitted that an interpretation of Section 166 giving a cause of action to members of the 'community' would be no less extraordinary.
54. *Caparo Industries v Dickman* [1990] 2 AC 605.
55. *Customs & Excise Commissioners v Barclays* [2006] UKHL 28.
56. Rogers, *Winfield & Jolowicz on Tort*, p. 161.
57. Lord Templeman's statement in *Winkworth v Edward Baron Development Co.* [1986] 1 WLR 1512 that a company owes a duty to future and present creditors to preserve its assets, is presumably limited to the context of a company which is unlikely to remain solvent. See Goode. 2005. *Principles of Corporate Insolvency*, 3rd ed., p. 522. Sweet & Maxwell.
58. *Miller v Bain* [2002] 1 BCLC 266; and DD Prentice, 'Creditors Interests and Directors Duties' (1990) 10 OJLS 275.
59. An extensive body of literature affirms this point in the context of Section 172 of the 2006 Act in the UK. This is more so because Section 170(3) expressly states that directors' duties are owed to the company. Kiarie, 'At Crossroads', p. 331; Tate, 'Section 172 CA 2006'; Andrew Keay. 2010. 'The Duty to Promote the Success of the Company: Is It Fit for Purpose?', p. 13, available at http://ssrn.com/abstract=1662411; Martin Gelter and Genevieve Helleringer. 2015. 'Lift Not the Painted Veil! To Whom Are Directors' Duties Really Owed?' *Illinois Law Review*, p. 1095; Lynch, 'Section 172', p. 200; and Ahmed Al-Hawamdeh, Iris H.-Y. Chiu, Marc Goergen, Chris Mallin, and Eve Mitleton-Kelly. 2013.

'The Interpretation of the Director's Duty under Section 172 Companies Act 2006: Insights from Complexity Theory', *Journal of Business Law*, 4: 417–33, esp. p. 420.

60. In *Percival v Wright* [1902] 2 Ch421 it was established that directors owed their duties to the company and not directly to shareholders.
61. It must be pointed out that loss suffered by individual creditors is not recoverable directly. Analogous to principles barring direct claims by shareholders in respect of breaches to the company, the loss to creditors is 'a reflection of the loss to the company', and the liquidator can recover this in the name of the company. Any recovery will go to increase the general pool of assets available in liquidation. See *Johnson v Gore Wood & Co.*, [2002] 2 AC 1; and Goode, *Principles of Corporate Insolvency*, pp. 522–3.
62. Employees may have a right to sue under applicable labour laws; other stakeholders may have some specific remedies: that, however, does not answer the question in principle regarding the enforcement of directors' duties in company law, of which stakeholders are the ultimate beneficiaries.
63. However, it may be worth noting that the remedy of class action is available to depositors, who are certain specific types of creditors of the company. It is not available to other types of creditors or to other stakeholders.
64. From a comparative perspective, this issue is immaterial in the UK context as no such statutory class action mechanism is available under the 2006 Act.
65. For a detailed analysis of the law on derivative actions in India, see Vikramaditya Khanna and Umakanth Varottil. 2012. 'The Rarity of Derivative Actions in India: Reasons and Consequences', in Dan W. Puchniak, Harald Baum, and Michael Ewing-Chow. 2012. *The Derivative Action in Asia: A Comparative and Functional Approach*. Cambridge University Press.
66. See Keay, 'Stakeholder Theory in Corporate Law', p. 294, noting, however, that certain other jurisdictions such as Canada and Singapore do recognize the rights of persons other than shareholders to initiate a derivate action, subject to the discretion of the court.
67. Some commentators have suggested possible grounds on which shareholders may initiate derivative actions for breaches of directors' duties to take into account stakeholder interests. For example, (a) shareholders may sue on the ground that their long-term interests are affected, (b) shareholders may have dual capacities, for instance, as employees, or where shareholders are living in the community where the carries out company operations, and (c) affected stakeholders may acquire shares so as to become shareholders and obtain the *locus standi* to initiate derivative actions. See Keay, 'The Duty to Promote the Success of the Company', p. 27; and Tate, 'Section 172 CA 2006'.
68. (1843) 2 Har 461.Under this exception, shareholders initiating a derivative action must show that majority shareholders or controllers obtained a benefit from wrongful conduct at the expense of the company, which suffers some loss or detriment. This continues to be the standard under common law in India. See Khanna and Varottil, 'The Rarity of Derivative Actions in India', p. 385.

69. The multiple derivative action is one such analogous development. Arad Reisberg. 2009. 'Multiple Derivative Actions', *Law Quarterly Review*, 125: 209. However, a derivative action by the shareholder to safeguard the interests of stakeholders is a far wider proposition.
70. It is also the case that remedies for oppression and mismanagement are granted only when specified grounds are satisfied. A mere breach of directors' duties, with nothing more, may not necessarily satisfy the requirements of oppression and mismanagement, thereby leaving stakeholders in the lurch.
71. [1942] Ch 304 (CA).
72. For this reason, the approach was jettisoned in the UK in favour of the ESV approach.
73. See Vikramaditya Khanna and Umakanth Varottil. 2016. 'Board Independence in India: From Form to Function?' in Dan W. Puchniak, Harald Baum, and Luke Nottage (eds), *Independent Directors in Asia: A Historical, Contextual and Comparative Approach*, p. 26. Cambridge University Press.
74. Keay, 'The Duty to Promote the Success of the Company', p. 18; Mark Arnold and Marcus Haywood. 2013. 'Duty to Promote the Success of the Company', in Simon Mortimore QC (ed.), *Company Directors: Duties, Liabilities, and Remedies*, p. 257. Oxford University Press. It is to avoid such a situation that the UK adopted the ESV approach that will make boards accountable to at least one constituency, namely, shareholders.
75. Companies Act 2006, s. 172(1).
76. See Keay, 'Stakeholder Theory in Corporate Law', p. 287.
77. Lynch, 'Section 172', p. 201.
78. See Keay, 'Stakeholder Theory in Corporate Law', p. 287.

6

Corporate Governance of Family-run Companies

Comparison of India and Hong Kong

Swati Deva

I Introduction

Corporate governance, as the phrase suggests, is the process by which a corporation is governed. The governance process includes managers/directors and the shareholders/owners of the company. In the process of such governance, the purpose is to act for the best interest of the company as well as its members. Good corporate governance not only requires efficiency, it also requires independence, transparency, and accountability, at the same time.

The family-run companies (FRCs) raise some interesting issues as regards to corporate governance. The initial management of an FRC usually remains in the hands of the owners. Therefore, the interest of the company, its members, and the management run hand in hand. However, with time, as the business and the family grows, not all the family members may make to the board, which may give rise to resentment. Also, a growing company needs external and additional expertise, for which the management duties may be delegated to professional managers, non-executive directors, etc.

The agency theory argues that salaried directors may not share the same goals as the owners. In FRCs, directors would like to be independent and make professional business decisions, keeping in mind the interest of the company as a whole. At the same time, the owners would like to keep control over the business and would like the management to act within the powers provided to the board by the articles of association. This may lead to mismanagement and loss of investors' trust. Therefore, FRCs' corporate governance needs a very efficient and sustainable system in place. As Tricker rightly puts:

> Throughout the life cycle of the family company ... it is vital that the corporate governance framework is appropriate to the stage of development. The corporate governance policies and board-level practices need to reflect the scale and complexity of the company's activities, determining the relationships between shareholders, directors and management. The structure and composition of the board should reflect the stage of the maturity of the company and its business. Similarly, board-level information, board appraisal and director development need to be appropriate.[1]

Corporate governance took a centre stage in the later part of the last century, especially after the failure of some big corporations, a few of them involved with fraud. These raised not only a call for corporate responsibility but also accountability, and as a result, in the UK a committee was created under the chairmanship of Sir Adrian Cadbury in the year 1992. The Report of the Committee on the Financial Aspects of Corporate Governance (Cadbury report) was the first major report on corporate governance and received international attention.

The Cadbury report was published more than two decades ago and it only dealt with financial aspects. However, some of the issues raised in it still hold good. Its opening paragraph says: 'The country's economy depends on the drive and efficiency of its companies. Thus, the effectiveness with which their boards discharge their responsibilities determines Britain's competitive position. They must be free to drive their companies forward, but exercise that freedom within a framework of effective accountability. This is the essence of any system of good corporate governance' (para 1.1). Since the Cadbury report there have been many developments, research, and amendments of various rules and regulations all over the world.

At the international level, the Organisation for Economic Co-operation and Development (OECD) also suggested five principles which may be followed by various institutions around the world. These principles are discussed in detail in the later part of the chapter. However, it would be apt to mention here that these principles influenced many corporate governance codes around the world, including that of Hong Kong and India. To date, the OECD principles constitute the only internationally accepted body of governance principles that address the entire corporate governance framework: the legal, institutional, and regulatory practices that create the context within which companies operate.[2]

Some of the developments in Hong Kong and India were very much influenced by the Cadbury report and the OECD Principles. This chapter would first discuss the corporate governance and legal environment in Hong Kong and India, highlighting some of the reforms undertaken in the recent past. As FRCs give rise to unique corporate governance issues and challenges, the chapter would describe some of the common challenges both the countries are facing, with a couple of recent examples. In the last part of the chapter, the author would suggest some of the steps which may be taken to overcome these challenges.

II Corporate Governance in HK

Family-controlled businesses are a norm in Hong Kong. Most of the major businesses are owned and controlled by families. The Corporate Governance Working Group of the Hong Kong Society of Accountants has published two reports on the topic (in 1995 and 1997). The findings showed that family businesses are the predominant form of listed companies in Hong Kong. It was noted that almost 90 per cent of listed companies have a major shareholder who by himself or with family members owns 25 per cent or more of the share capital. In such a business set-up there is less of agency cost as ownership and control remains in the same hands.

Hong Kong's history as a former British dependent territory, the concentration of its company ownership at the family level, the long tradition of laissez-faire government policy, and the region's strong desire to maintain its status as a major financial centre in Asia, have shaped the environment of corporate governance today, and will continue to impact its evolution in the future.[3]

The primary legislation dealing with companies and corporate governance is the Companies Ordinance. This law was first enacted in 1865 and was based on the UK's Companies Act 1862. The Ordinance was continuously revised, updated and changed in the past. However, despite the revisions, it became necessary to bring a major reform in the law and thus, in 2014 a new Companies Ordinance was adopted. This Ordinance provides the basic regulatory framework under which all companies in Hong Kong, both private and public, function. Also, there are certain regulatory bodies dealing with corporate governance, such as, the Securities and Futures Commission (SFC), Hong Kong Exchanges and Clearing Limited (HKEx), Hong Kong Monetary Authority (HKMA), Stock Exchange of Hong Kong (SEHK), Hong Kong Society of Accountants (HKSA), etc.

Also, the government here mostly adopts the 'positive non-intervention' policy, which in turn has supported the progress of commercial enterprises. The economy is based on free enterprise, free trade, and a free market. This kind of free business environment and ownership and control of companies remaining in the same hands, has given rise to much criticism of FRCs' corporate governance. Thus, in the past couple of decades, corporate governance has been in focus and many developments have taken place in this area. These developments are discussed as follows:

- **Corporate governance review:** A comprehensive review of corporate governance was undertaken in the year 2000 to identify and plug any gaps in Hong Kong's corporate governance regime. The Standing Committee on Company Law Reform (SCCLR) was given the task to undertake an overall review of corporate governance. Three sub-committees were established under the SCCLR to consider the specific areas of directors, shareholders, and corporate reporting to take the review forward. One of the issues to be considered was 'in the case of many companies listed on the SEHK, a single dominant shareholder or single group of persons controls the company. This may be the significant shareholder or a person connected with the "controlling" shareholder….' The sub-committees produced two reports in the year 2001 and 2013 and the implementation of their recommendations necessitated the participation of different bodies, including the government, the SFC, HKEx, and the HKSA.
- **Recommendations of SCCLR:** SCCLR issued its Final Recommendations in January 2014, arising from the Corporate Governance Review Phase II. Some of those were:
    - On proposals relating to directors: a set of 'Non-statutory Guidelines on Directors' Duties' were drawn to help company directors to better understand their roles. It included the general legal position on self-dealing by directors, as well as proposals on shareholders' approval for significant transactions involving directors. To address the increasing public concern over the directors' remuneration, SCCLR recommended that listed companies should disclose individual director's remuneration packages by name in their annual financial statements. The Code of Best Practice (of the Listing Rules) should contain a

requirement that a listed company should disclose the arrangements made to train its directors in view of the importance of directors' qualifications and training.

- o On proposals relating to Shareholders: SCCLR adopted in its Final Recommendations the proposals on self-dealing by controlling shareholders in the Consultation Paper and that 'controlling shareholders' should be defined for the purpose of connected transactions using the same criterion as that under the Listing Rules for 'substantial shareholder', that is, a person controlling 10 per cent or more of the voting power at any general meeting of the company. The SCCLR also adopted the proposals in the Consultation Paper to enhance the effectiveness and transparency of company general meetings.

- **Corporate governance code:** The principal regulator of Hong Kong's securities and futures markets is the SFC, which is an independent statutory body established in 1989 by the Securities and Futures Commission Ordinance (SFCO). The SFCO and nine other securities and futures related ordinances were consolidated into the Securities and Futures Ordinance, which came into operation on 1 April 2003. HKEx is a recognized exchange controller under the SFO. It owns and operates the only stock exchange and futures exchange in Hong Kong and their related clearing houses, namely, Hong Kong Securities Clearing Company Limited (HKSCC), HKFE Clearing Corporation Limited (HKCC), and the SEHK Options Clearing House Limited (SEOCH). The Corporate Governance Code is a non-statutory document under the Listing Rules of the HKEx (Appendix 14). This Code sets out the principles of good corporate governance, and two levels of recommendations: (a) code provisions; and (b) recommended best practices. Issuers are expected to comply with, but may choose to deviate from, the code provisions. The recommended best practices are for guidance only. Issuers may also devise their own code on corporate governance on the terms they consider appropriate. On the principle of Board Composition, it provides: The board should have a balance of skills, experience, and diversity of perspectives appropriate to the requirements of the issuer's business. It should ensure that changes to its composition can be managed without undue disruption. It should include a balanced composition of executive and non-executive directors (including independent non-executive directors) so that there is a strong independent element on the board, which can effectively exercise independent judgement. Non-executive directors should be of sufficient calibre and number for their views to carry weight.

Despite the regulation on business and FRCs, corporate governance in these companies have posed various challenges, which are discussed later.

III Corporate Governance in India

The Indian corporate environment is also influenced by the British rule in India. The establishment of the East India Company and its trading in India for over a century laid down the foundation of the modern company law. Once the East India Company ceased business in India, British merchants who wanted to set up operations in India appointed managing agents who, in turn, not only provided capital, managerial labour, and share ownership, but also technical, social, and other benefits.[4]

Starting as simple commission agents, the agency houses over the years began offering many other services, such as banking, bill broking, ship owning, freight, insurance, etc. With the strengthening of colonial rule, the agency houses evolved into the managing-agency system that in a way pioneered the growth of modern corporations of India. This was helped by the passing of the Joint Stock Companies Act in 1850 and its subsequent amendment in 1857 to provide for limited liability.[5]

That led to the growth of large businesses and as these agencies were mostly owned and managed by families, thus begun the establishment of the FRCs in India. Most of the large businesses were managed by families and there was hardly any government regulation. In fact, some of these large businesses had helped the government in financing the pre- and post-Independence activities and thus, the linkage helped the businesses bargain for certain privileges. This led to economic concentration in limited hands and also abuse of managerial power over shareholders. That led to the need to regulate the private sector. The first law regulating corporations in India was the Companies Act, passed in 1956. This law was passed to consolidate and amend the law relating to companies and certain other associations.

However, even with the passing of the law and other guidelines, corporate governance was never referred to as an independent issue. In fact, most of the large businesses were managed at the whims and will of the owners of the company, with a lot of political and other support from outside, leading to corruption and malpractices. That resulted in poor management and also failure of some large corporations, as well as frauds on a lot of investors. Therefore, with the growing need for regulatory checks and better corporate governance environment, it became necessary to enact a new regulatory framework.

The government has realized that markets and investors take notice of well-managed companies, respond positively to them, and reward such companies, with higher valuations. A common feature of such companies is that they have systems in place, which allow sufficient freedom to the boards and management to take decisions towards the progress of their companies and to innovate, while remaining within a framework of effective accountability. Keeping this in mind and getting influenced by some of the recent developments on the international level, such as the Commonwealth Association for Corporate Governance Guidelines 1999, OECD Principles on Corporate Governance 1999, The Euro shareholders Corporate Governance Guidelines 2000, etc., the Indian government was encouraged to develop its own corporate governance principles.

The first institutional initiative on corporate governance in India was taken by the Confederation of Indian Industries (CII) in 1996 when it set up a national task force to develop and promote a code for corporate governance for Indian companies. Later, in the year 2013, the new Companies Act received the assent of the President and became the present law-governing companies in India. These changes and some of the other regulatory bodies including the Securities and Exchange Board of India (SEBI), the Ministry of Corporate Affairs (MCA), the Company Law Board, the Reserve Bank of India, etc., changed the way corporate governance is dealt with in India now. Some of the other developments are discussed as follows:

- **Report of the Kumar Mangalam Birla Committee on Corporate Governance (Birla Report):** SEBI appointed the Committee on Corporate Governance in 1999 under the Chairmanship of Shri Kumar Mangalam Birla, member SEBI Board, to promote and raise the standards of Corporate Governance. The Committee identified the three key constituents of corporate governance as the Shareholders, the Board of Directors, and the Management and attempted to identify in respect of each of these constituents, their roles and responsibilities as also their rights in the context of good corporate governance. Fundamental to this examination and permeating throughout this exercise was the recognition of the three key aspects of corporate governance, namely; accountability, transparency, and equality of treatment for all stakeholders. The Committee recommended that the board of a company have an optimum combination of executive and non-executive directors with not less than 50 per cent of the board comprising the non-executive directors. The number of independent directors (independence being as defined in the foregoing paragraph) would depend on the nature of the chairman of the board. In case a company has a non-executive chairman, at least one-third of the board should comprise of independent directors and in case a company has an executive chairman, at least half of board should be independent. This is a mandatory recommendation.

- **Clause 49:** In the year 2000, SEBI adopted the recommendation of the Birla Report in its Listing Agreement. Accordingly, a new Clause 49 of corporate governance was inserted into the listing agreement of the Stock Exchange to ensure the compliance with corporate governance codes by Indian companies. This clause has been revised and amended time and again, and more recently in 2014. This listing agreement is for all listed companies to agree to make provisions for corporate governance. It provides for special composition of Board, with not less than 50 per cent of the board of directors comprising non-executive directors. There is a provision for director's remuneration, disclosures, and code of conduct. The agreement also asks to set up a qualified and independent audit committee, with details of their powers and role as a committee. It further provides for a detailed compliance report on corporate governance in the annual reports of the company.
- **Other committee:** The SEBI appointed a committee under the chairmanship of Mr Narayan Murthy, to evaluate the adequacy of existing corporate governance practices and further improve these practices, in 2003. The committee recommended that there shall be no nominee directors. Where an institution wishes to appoint a director on the board, such appointment should be made by the shareholders. An institutional director, so appointed, shall have the same responsibilities and shall be subject to the same liabilities as any other director. The nominee of the government on public sector companies shall be similarly elected and shall be subject to the same responsibilities and liabilities as other directors.
- **Corporate governance voluntary guidelines:** Keeping in mind that the subject of corporate governance may go well beyond the law and that there are inherent limitations in enforcing many aspects of corporate governance through legislative or regulatory means, the MCA considered necessary that a set of voluntary guidelines called 'Corporate Governance—Voluntary Guidelines 2009', are prepared and disseminated for consideration and adoption by corporates. These guidelines provide for a set of good practices which may be voluntarily adopted by the Public companies. Private companies, particularly the bigger ones, may also like to adopt these guidelines. The guidelines are not intended to be a substitute for or additions to the existing laws, but are recommendatory in nature.

But corporate governance extends beyond corporate law. Its fundamental objective is not mere fulfilment of the requirements of law but in ensuring commitment of the board in managing the company in a transparent manner for maximizing long-term shareholder value (Birla report). In FRCs this commitment is vital to the efficient and steady growth of the business. However, FRCs have their own share of challenges, which are highlighted later in the chapter.

IV Company Law

The main legislation dealing with companies and corporate governance in Hong Kong is the Companies Ordinance (Cap 622). As mentioned earlier, this law has recently been revised to keep pace with the changes in the business environment. The Companies Ordinance, along with the Corporate Governance Code, under the Listing Rules of the HKEx, has laid down a strong foundation for the development of corporate governance system in Hong Kong. Similarly, in India the primary legislation of Companies Act, 2013 has been remodelled to cover the developments in the corporate world. Some of the provisions which specifically deal with corporate governance have been highlighted below:

- **Companies ordinance:** Part 10 of the new Companies Ordinance deals with directors and company secretaries, and it is in this part mainly that certain provisions have been made to accommodate corporate governance principles. For example, it lays down specific restrictions on the number of directors and their qualifications, etc. Section 465 lays down the duty to exercise reasonable care, skill, and diligence for the director, a breach of which may result in civil liability. Further, section 478 provides that if a director appoints an alternate director to act on his behalf, then that director is vicariously liable for acts of the alternate. These are some of the provisions in the law that is a step towards integrating the law with the principles of corporate governance. The Ordinance has also given more powers to the shareholders and now even 5 per cent of the members can make decisions like:
    - Make an application to the Court for an order restraining the giving of financial assistance (sec 286).
    - Request the directors to call a general meeting (sec 566).

Further, according to section 388, directors must prepare a directors' report every year. Schedule 5 of the Ordinance provides for the contents of a director's report, which requires directors to include a business review that consists of—(a) a fair review of the company's business; (b) a description of the principal risks and uncertainties facing the company; (c) particulars of important events affecting the company that have occurred since the end of the financial year; and (d) an indication of likely future development in the company's business. The Ordinance lays down stricter duties on auditors to work diligently as well. Section 406(2) lays down that if a company's auditor is of the opinion that the information in a directors' report for a financial year is not consistent with the financial statements for the financial year, the auditor, (a) must state that opinion in the auditor's report; and (b) may bring that opinion to the members' attention at a general meeting.

- **Companies Act 2013:** The new Companies Act in India has added certain provisions in the law, which specifically deals with matters relating to corporate governance. For example:
    - In Chapter IX on accounts of companies, section 134 lays responsibility over the board of directors to make sure that all the statements are in order. Interestingly, section 135 provides that every company having a net worth of rupees five-hundred crore or more, or a turnover of rupees one-thousand crore or more, or a net profit of rupees five crore or more during any financial year shall constitute a Corporate Social Responsibility Committee of the Board consisting of three or more directors, out of which at least one director shall be an independent director.
    - In Chapter X on audit and auditors, section 144 provides for certain services which an auditor must not render to the company.
    - In Chapter XI on appointment and qualifications of directors, section 149 provides that every listed public company shall have at least one-third of the total number of directors as independent directors. Section 166 lays down the duties of directors, including the duty to act with due and reasonable care, skill, and diligence and to exercise independent judgment. Section 172 has added a punishment of fine, for the company and every officer of the company, for contravening any of the provisions of this chapter.
    - In Chapter XII on meetings of the board and its powers, section 177 provides that the board of directors of every listed company shall constitute an audit committee. This committee shall consist of at least three directors with majority being independent directors and the majority of members, including its chairperson, shall have the ability to read and understand financial statements. Section 180

provides for certain restrictions on the powers of the board. This part also provides for the duty of disclosure and accountability of directors towards the company (section 184). Sections 194 and 195 lay down prohibition on forward dealings in securities and insider trading of securities, respectively, by directors.

- In Chapter XIII on appointment and remuneration of managerial personnel, section 197 lays down limits on the overall maximum managerial remuneration and managerial remuneration in case of absence or inadequacy of profits of a public company.
- Chapter XIV lays down provisions for conducting inspection, inquiry, and investigation of companies' affairs. Section 211 provides for the establishment of Serious Fraud Investigation Office to investigate frauds relating to a company.
- Chapter XXIX on miscellaneous matters provides for punishment.

These are some of the provisions which are intended to integrate corporate governance principles into the written law.

V Challenges

The main challenge for any FRC is to keep family members united and their interest aligned over the years, and to attract outside investors and retain qualified professionals. The concentration of power discourages investors and reduces the company's value. This challenge gets more complex as the family and the business grows. Therefore, it is very important for every FRC to not only have a strong and transparent corporate governance policy but to implement it efficiently and equitably.

Cadbury sums up the three requisites for family firms to manage the impacts of growth successfully: They need to be able to recruit and retain the very best people for the business, they need to be able to develop a culture of trust and transparency, and they need to define logical and efficient organizational structures.[6]

Atop many of Hong Kong's largest companies are aging entrepreneurs who began making fortunes in the 1950s and 1960s, at the height of the post-war boom. Now that these magnates are in their twilight years, the question of their succession is coming to light—and often being settled with ugly court battles, including mothers suing their children and brothers ousting brothers. In the past few years, a number of legal disputes have erupted over the distribution of money and power in multibillion-dollar family businesses.

No amount of law or regulations can do anything to help the business of an FRC if the members themselves do not step up to the challenge and take control of the situation. One example in Hong Kong is of the Kwok brothers. Kwok Tak Seng established the business of property in Hong Kong in 1958 with two partners. Later the business grew and became a public listed company. It is one of the largest and most successful property businesses in Hong Kong, known as the Sun Hung Kai Properties. In 1990, after the senior Kwok's death, his elder son Wilson Kwok took over the business. He was the chairman and the chief executive of the company.

Everything was going very well till 1997 when Wilson was kidnapped for a ransom. It is said that after his return he suffered some mental problems (which he has denied). In the year 2008, his mother (a majority shareholder) replaced him as the chairman and appointed his two younger brothers, Thomas and Raymond, to take over the control of the business. All of this brought negative publicity for the company, showed the weakness in corporate governance and resulted in loss of investors' trust.

In 2012, the co-chairmen brothers and three others were accused of giving bribes in exchange for information on land sales between 2005 and 2007. The trial, which lasted more than three months, highlighted the close ties between some of Hong Kong's most powerful businessmen and government. Their company is one of the world's most valuable real estate companies. However, the brothers' arrest caused its shares to plunge to a 14-year low, erasing billions in market value.

Thomas stepped down as co-chairman and co-managing director at Sun Hung Kai after he was sentenced in 2014. Thomas's brother Raymond was also arrested but later acquitted of all charges. He has since been running the group as chairman. Thomas's resignation did little to restore the company's image. He publicly stated that he would rather learn to ride a bike and study theology than return to his office while on bail. But critics suspect he may still influence the group, by acting as a consultant or appointing close relatives to the board. His son Adam became an executive director in 2014. Recently, the current chairman's younger son, was named executive director. Another cousin became an alternative director to the chairman. Fortunately, however, among all these controversies the company has done well in business.

Similarly, in India, Dhirubhai Ambani, the founder of Reliance Industries, started the business as a textiles company, which grew to become one of India's biggest conglomerates. His two sons, Mukesh and Anil, inherited the empire in 2002, after his death. A rift developed over the following years between the brothers over their inheritance and the management of the group, and they ended up parting ways and dividing the family business. In 2005, a demerger of the Reliance Empire was approved, brokered by their mother (a majority shareholder).

However, the family drama did not end here. Soon the brothers were out in the open, battling court cases. At the heart of the dispute was a 2005 contract which gave Mukesh the rights to India's gas supply and handed his brother the power plants, which needed the gas to generate the country's energy. The legal battle over the terms of this contract was estimated to have already soaked up £20 million in legal fees, but the cost to the country was being measured in much more than just money.

During this demerger and afterwards, many accusations and counter accusations were made between the brothers, including mismanagement, conflict of interest, and the directors of the company being not independent, etc. In 2010, the mother brokered a peace agreement between the brothers. They agreed to draft a non-compete agreement and resolved their disputes in an amicable way.

In the wake of controversies like these, the main question is whether changes in law or signing agreements (Clause 49) make any difference to how the corporation would eventually be run. This is specially so in the case of FRCs, where emotions and personal feuds may overtake the interests of other stakeholders, including that of the company. The challenge for any FRC is to not let the family feuds affect the day to day business and to make sure that there is a system in place where personal matters can be resolved amicably, without interfering with the business or grabbing any negative media attention.

VI Step Forward

Good corporate governance leads to various benefits, including: stability and long-term sustainability for investors; stability and growth for the enterprise; acquisition and retention of talent; reduction in risks, mismanagement and corruption; reputation and recognition; and higher firm valuation.[7]

The OECD Principles on Corporate Governance describe the kind of corporate governance framework a company may adopt. Following is a brief look at this framework:

- It should promote transparent and fair markets, and the efficient allocation of resources. It should be consistent with the rule of law and support effective supervision and enforcement.

- It should protect and facilitate the exercise of shareholders' rights and ensure the equitable treatment of all shareholders, including minority and foreign shareholders. All shareholders should have the opportunity to obtain effective redress for violation of their rights.
- It should provide sound incentives throughout the investment chain and provide for stock markets to function in a way that contributes to good corporate governance.
- It should recognize the rights of stakeholders established by law or through mutual agreements and encourage active cooperation between corporations and stakeholders in creating wealth, jobs, and the sustainability of financially sound enterprises.
- It should ensure that timely and accurate disclosure is made on all material matters regarding the corporation, including the financial situation, performance, ownership, and governance of the company.
- It should ensure the strategic guidance of the company, the effective monitoring of management by the board, and the board's accountability to the company and the shareholders.

Every FRC should protect and facilitate the exercise of shareholders' rights, and create investment opportunities. It is vital for the business to create an environment of transparency, stability, and good governance. This can only be achieved by creating such a relationship between family managers and non-family professionals that it creates a well-functioning management team and leads the company to success.

> The question arises as to how to develop a theory of good governance that may protect the interests of both stakeholders and shareholders. The answer lies in the 'balance' or 'conciliation' of interests. A fair and balanced stakeholder perspective results in the long-term maximization of shareholder value. There is no inherent economic conflict between shareholders and stakeholders over time, with the result that maximizing shareholder value will maximize the benefits to all stakeholders.[8]

The owner family members must understand that the business does not exist in isolation nor does it function only on the whims and will of the family who founded it. A strong business needs a strong team of professionals, experts, and enthusiastic employees. The interest of the business is to involve the interest of all the stakeholders. Also, they must recognize that their own personal and family issues must not hinder the efficiency of the management, otherwise it leads to chaos, loss of business, and mistrust among the stakeholders.

Similarly, if directors are trained and made to understand that their role is not of just being an executive, but their duty is to design, install, maintain, and refine the prudent control systems of their company,[9] the result might be very different than just laying down rules and company policies. Good managers should not just focus on profit; they should be able to focus on growth of the company and increasing its wealth generating capacity in a healthy way, which must last it for a long-term. Directors must also be involved with the business as owners/family members. They should not feel that they are salaried employees who have no role in business decisions. This requires a transparent system of management and well-defined roles.

For directors, it is suggested, that there could be director development activities/workshops where they can be given training and updates on the social, legal, and economic changes, etc. These development programs can be run either at a state/government level and/or company level where the owner directors and independent directors, all can be given the same kind of information and training in order for them to function in unison.

It is also suggested that every FRC should have a family council or a forum where they can express their grievances, discuss their concerns, and resolve their conflicts. These councils may have some of the older family members (men and women) and some independent outsiders. They can act as facilitators, mediators, or even counsellors for other members. Even in the early stages of a family firm, it is wise to have some sort of forum where the views of family members regarding the business and its development can be expressed.[10]

Most of the FRCs face the problem of personal feuds and resentment between senior and junior family members. A family council can provide a platform where all the members can be brought together and resolve their issues face to face. Such a council may involve other shareholders, professional managers, or even auditors, etc., depending on the severity and need of the issues. Many family issues get aggravated because of lack of timely response. A family council can provide a formal/informal set-up where the family members may share their views, ideas, or resentments.

These councils can meet formally three to four times in a year, and should have a system of being requested to meet in between too. There should be an informal procedure to conduct the proceedings in such councils so that every member feels comfortable to talk about their concerns. No minutes should be kept of such proceedings, except any formal decisions made by the members, which need to be implemented in the future. For every council meeting, only members who have issues to raise and resolve must be present, and all proceedings should be kept confidential. Any person who is not a family member should only be allowed to attend the meeting if all the concerned members agree.

Any decisions taken in such council meetings, which would have any long-term or short-term effect on the interest of the company, shall be discussed with the board. The board here must also consist of family members, professionals, non-executive directors, etc. The advantages of a formal governance structure are that there is a defined structure with defined channels for decision-making and clear lines of responsibility; the board can tackle areas that may be sensitive from a family point of view but which nonetheless need to be dealt with; and the appointment of non-executive directors would encourage external shareholder participation.[11]

In fact, OECD also recognizes some of the governance challenges for family-owned businesses as well, such as keeping peace in the family for interpersonal, social, and business reasons; presence of outside, non-family shareholders, etc. Solutions used include mechanisms to:

- Separate functions of ownership, control, and management.
- Create family offices to clarify boundaries between the family's and company's accounts.
- Develop the skills and knowledge of heirs so they can become responsible owners, as they assume various roles as an owner, director or an employee (chapter 5, para 3.4).

The International Finance Corporation, in its Family Business Governance Handbook, provides for certain solution at the senior management level. It states that ensuring that the family-owned company has the right senior managers is a process that should start early, even as early as during the founder(s) stage of the family business. Some of the steps of this process are:

- Analysing the organizational structure and contrasting the current and optimal roles and responsibilities (compared to peer companies) of each senior manager.
- Designing a formal organizational structure that clearly defines the roles and responsibilities of all senior managers. This should be based on the company's current and future business operations' needs.
- Evaluating the skills and qualifications of the current senior management based on the new organizational structure.
- Replacing and/or hiring senior managers.

- Decentralizing the decision-making process and approval levels as necessary. Decision-making powers should be linked to the roles/ responsibilities of managers and not to their ties to the family.
- Establishing a clear family employment policy and making its content available to all family members.
- Developing an internal training program that allows skilled employees to be prepared for taking on senior assignments in the future.
- Establishing a remuneration system that provides the right incentives to all managers depending on their performance and not their ties to the family (p. 47).

Even for the government, there are certain recommended steps which can be taken to further improve the corporate governance environment. Governments should ensure that there is a system in place where large companies will not be able to register their businesses if they do not have any principle/code on corporate governance. Every FRC must show a family council/committee/forum structure before they can commence business. Government should also introduce incentives for companies which have a good corporate governance record. Governments cannot be a silent spectator to the mismanagement and then the failure of these large companies, especially when the efficient working of the economy is dependent on such large businesses. The legal and regulatory framework should ensure that the stakeholders' interests are protected and there is no exploitation of rights.

Therefore, it can very well be said that to survive and thrive in today's competitive and globalized economies it is vital for every business to refer to the corporate governance guidelines by various institutions, such as the OECD principles, Clause 49 of the listing agreement or other institutional corporate governance codes. Every company needs to take its corporate governance responsibility very seriously, for the sake of its business as well as its stakeholders.

Therefore, just to reiterate, it is suggested that an FRC must have an efficient management team, involving owners, non-executive directors, etc., with a transparent, independent and responsible system. There should be an independent family council to deal with matters which may affect the business of the company. However, these councils must act for the benefit of the company as a whole and in tune with the management of the company. Good corporate governance not only requires a strong and efficient legal framework, it also requires participation and commitment of the corporate members to act in the best interest of the company. In an FRC this participation and commitment comes with an added responsibility of not letting the family feuds or personal resentment come in the way of progress of the business.

Notes and References

1. Bob Tricker and Robert Ian. 2012. *Corporate Governance: Principles, Policies, and Practices*. Oxford: Oxford University Press.
2. Gordon Jones. 2012. *Corporate Governance and Compliance in Hong Kong*. Hong Kong: LexisNexis.
3. Standard & Poor. 2002. 'Corporate Governance in Hong Kong', http://www.legco.gov.hk/yr01-02/english/panels/fa/papers/fa0724cb1-2513-1e.pdf.
4. Praveen B. Malla. 2010. *Corporate Governance: History, Evolution and India Story*. New Delhi and London: Routledge.
5. Banik, Gupta, and Bhaumik (eds). 2015. *Corporate Governance, Responsibility and Sustainability: Initiatives in Emerging Economies*. New York: Palgrave Macmillan.
6. Sir Adrian Cadbury. 2000. *Family Firms and their Governance: Creating Tomorrow's company from Today's*. London: Egon Zehnder International.
7. Priyanka K. Sharma. 2015. *Corporate Governance Practices in India: A Synthesis of Theories, Practices, and Cases*. Houndmills, Basingstoke Hampshire, New York: Palgrave Macmillan.
8. Singh, in Roger Blanpain, William Bromwich, Olga Rymkevich, and Iacopo Senatori (eds). 2011. *Rethinking Corporate Governance: From Shareholder Value to Stakeholder Value*. Wolters Kluwer, Law & Business.
9. Alireza Tourani-Rad and Coral Ingley. 2011. *Handbook on Emerging Issues in Corporate Governance*. Singapore, Hackensack, and New Jersey: World Scientific.
10. Christine A. Mallin. 2013. *Corporate Governance*. Oxford: Oxford University Press.
11. Mallin, *Corporate Governance*.

Additional References

Books

Boubaker, Sabri, DucKhuong Nguyen (eds.). 2014. *Corporate Governance In Emerging Markets: Theories, Practices and Cases*. Heidelberg, New York: Springer.

Nordberg, Donald. 2011. *Corporate Governance: Principles and Issues*. London: SAGE.

Malik, Fredmund F. 2012. *Richtige Corporate Governance*. Frankfurt: Campus-Verlag.

Sarkar, Jayati, Subrata Sarkar. 2012. *Corporate Governance in India*. Thousand Oaks, Calif: SAGE Publications.

Lethbridge, David G., Ng Sek Hong (eds.). 2000. *The Business Environment in Hong Kong*.New York: Oxford University Press.

Goo, SH, Anne Carver. 2003. *Corporate Governance: the Hong Kong Debate*. Hong Kong: Sweet & Maxwell Asia. Fernando, AC. 2009. *Corporate Governance: Principles, Policies and Practices*. Pearson Education India.

Articles

Claessens, S, S. Djankov and LHP Lang. 2000. 'The separation of ownership and control in East Asian Corporations', *Journal of Financial Economics*, 58(1–2): 81–112.

Tsui, J and FA Gul. 2000. 'Corporate governance and financial transparencies in the Hong Kong Special Administrative Region of the People's Republic of China', Second Asian Roundtable on Corporate Governance, Organization for Economic Co-operation and Development.

South China Morning Post. 2000. 'Family control and the Asian crisis. Business Post'.

Websites

'Companies Registry—Standing Committee on Company Law Reform: Consultation Papers and Reports.' http://www.cr.gov.hk/en/standing/consultation.htm, accessed 28 July 2016.

'HKEx: Introduction to Regulatory Framework.' https://www.hkex.com.hk/eng/rulesreg/regintro/introreg.htm, accessed 28 July 2016.

'Conventus Law: India—Legal Framework Governing Corporate Governance.' http://www.conventuslaw.com/archive/legal-framework-governing-corporate-governance-in-india/, accessed 12 Aug 2016.

'OECD. G20/OECD Principles of Corporate Governance. Paris.' http://dx.doi.org/10.1787/9789264236882-en. 2015, accessed 14 July 2017.

'Can Mrs Ambani sort out her sons' £10 billion feud?'http://www.independent.co.uk/news/world/asia/can-mrs-ambani-sort-out-her-sons-16310bn-feud-1812276.html, accessed 15 August 2016.

https://www.hkex.com.hk/eng/rulesreg/listrules/mbrules/documents/appendix_14.pdf.

A Qualitative Study of Corporate Governance: Boards of Directors in Hong Kong Family-Owned Companies. http://libproject.hkbu.edu.hk/trsimage/hp/09011129.pdf, accessed 14 July 2017.

http://www.gcgf.org/wps/wcm/connect/6a9001004f9f5979933cff0098cb14b9/FamilyBusinessGovernance_Handbook_English.pdf?MOD=AJPERES.

'Governance Challenges for Family-owned Businesses,' https://www.oecd.org/daf/ca/corporategovernanceprinciples/43654301.pdf, accessed 14 July 2017.

'Indian Family-managed Companies—the Corporate Governance Conundrum,' http://unpan1.un.org/intradoc/groups/public/documents/apcity/unpan033971.pdf, accessed 14 July 2017.

'Hong Kong's Feuding Families,' http://blogs.wsj.com/hong-kong/2011/01/27/hong-kongs-feuding-families/, accessed 15 August 2016.

Shigufta Hena Uzma., Embedding Corporate Governance and Corporate Social Responsibility in Emerging Countries. http://www.emeraldinsight.com/doi/abs/10.1108/IJLMA-04-2015-0015. 2016, accessed 14 July 2017.

http://www.ecgi.org/codes/documents/cadbury.pdf.

http://www.sebi.gov.in/commreport/corpgov.html, accessed 2 August 2016.

'Who are the Kwok brothers?' http://www.bbc.com/news/business-17752115, accessed 3 August 2016.

'Sun Hung Kai's Struggle to Restore Investor Confidence,' http://www.ft.com/cms/s/0/c558abcc-54dc-11e6-befd-2fc0c26b3c60.html#axzz4GKWD6pvJ, accessed 4 August 2016.

'Hong Kong tycoon Thomas Kwok found guilty of corruption.' http://www.bbc.com/news/business-30545341, accessed 5 August 2016.

'Unhealthy rivalry clouds Ambani family business in India,' http://www.thenational.ae/business/industry-insights/economics/unhealthy-rivalry-clouds-ambani-family-business-in-india, accessed 5 August 2016.

PART III

PUBLIC LAW

SECTION A

CONSTITUTIONAL LAW

7

Constitutionalism

African Perspectives

Yash Ghai

I Introduction

One of the most interesting articles on constitutionalism was written by Hastings Okoth-Ogendo for a conference celebrating the 200th anniversary of the US's constitution, with the title, 'Constitutions without Constitutionalism: Reflections on an African Political Paradox'. Presented in 1988, it was printed in various books or journals. It became one of the most frequently cited articles on the subject of constitutionalism. He managed to inject light and heat into a topic which had generally been regarded as somewhat boring. Partly because of his interesting perspectives, constitutionalism today is perhaps the most popular topic in comparative constitution studies, attracting lawyers as well as social scientists. In a recent publication, *Constitutionalism in Asia in the Early Twenty-First Century* (2014), distinguished Asian constitutional scholar Albert Chen opens the book with an introductory essay, 'The Achievement of Constitutionalism in Asia: Moving beyond "Constitutions without Constitutionalism"'. In his first footnote, he refers to Okoth-Ogendo's famous article. Chen was not the first author to recognize the relevance of 'constitutions without constitutionalism' beyond

Africa; Vlad Perju noted the same point in 2012 in an essay on constitutional transplants, in his comment on 'constitutional text that lacks political and cultural traction'.[1] Having studied a fair sample of articles paying homage to Okoth-Ogendo, I am left with the impression that the authors quoting him have not fully understood him.[2] For this Okoth-Ogendo might himself be responsible for he did not clarify in which contexts his paradox would apply—a point I will return to soon.

Frequent references to his 'paradox' are owed in part to the growing international interest in constitutionalism as a result of the massive ideological reordering in numerous countries all over the world, motivated by the end of the Cold War and the decline of communism, particularly in Europe, and resolution of bilateral or national conflicts. A large number of constitutions, inclining towards forms of democracy, liberalism, and market, have created an unusual interest in the normally tedious subject of constitutions. The international community (for which read the West) have participated in the making of several constitutions; there has been considerable interstate borrowing, and certain norms drawn from international agreements are now considered essential. The partial liberalization of the Chinese economy and some opening up of the political space, however limited, have stimulated much theorizing on the nature and orientation of constitutionalism.[3] International lawyers have also shown some interest in constitutions because of the international norms that are deemed to be desirable, if not compulsory, in national constitutions. And the borrowing of judicial precedents from the superior courts of similarly oriented constitutions has aroused the curiosity of both constitutional and international lawyers in comparative 'constitutionalism'.

I.1 'Constitutions without Constitutionalism'

Okoth-Ogendo did not specify clearly what he meant by 'constitutions without constitutionalism'. A constitution can be without 'constitutionalism' in at least two ways. The more obvious meaning is when the constitution does not aim for 'constitutionalism' (as with military or one-party constitutions or, as is sometimes put, one leader constitutions). The second meaning refers to constitutions which promise human rights, democracy, fair trials, but little is done to implement them—indeed much is done to negate them. Both of these scenarios have been found in abundance in Africa. My understanding is that Okoth-Ogendo had both these instances in mind. He put his thesis more broadly, as follows: 'commitment to the idea of the constitution but rejection of the classical notation of constitutionalism'.[4] He and some scholars have argued that most African 'leaders' have valued constitutions solely for their significance internationally: conferring sovereignty on the state and immunity for its head, not sovereignty of its citizens. Albert Chen uses the notion in the second sense:

> Just as in the daily life of individuals, it is relatively easy to say something or make a promise, but more difficult to translate what is said or promised into action and reality, so in the political and legal life of nations, it is relatively easy to make a constitution, but more difficult to put it into practice, to implement it and be governed by it—which is what 'constitutionalism' is about.[5]

He also associates constitutionalism with Western ideas, theories and institutions of constitutions—'transplanted in the course of the last two centuries'. His study is in the transplantation of constitutions, making a distinction between 'pristine constitutions' (western) and 'secondary constitutions', and concludes that the former are more likely to succeed. Indeed, he says that 'even in the early twenty-first century, constitutionalism is still a work in progress in many parts of the world, particularly in Asia, Africa, and Latin America.'[6]

I now turn to a discussion of what I call the context of the origin and the understanding of the classical concept of constitutionalism. I will then return to contemporary issues, starting with three essays on constitutionalism by East African scholars, Okoth-Ogendo, Issa Shivji, and Yash Ghai. This, I hope, will help us to locate the issues nearer home for those not in the West. After that I will return to the nature of the new constitutions of Kenya, its neighbours, and South Africa (often described as 'transformative constitutions') to consider the utility or otherwise of 'constitutionalism' within its classical meaning.

II Classical Concept of Constitutionalism

It is best to turn to Charles McIlwain for an understanding of constitutionalism. In the older days (that is, when I was young) it connoted limitations on powers of the government. In *Constitutionalism: Ancient and Modern*, McIlwain, then a distinguished professor of politics at Harvard, discusses first the origin of the 'constitution', drawing on the politically advanced ideas of the American rebels. He quotes with approval Thomas Paine's explanation:

> That there is a fundamental difference between a people's government and that people's constitution, whether the government happens to be entrusted to a king or a representative assembly. That this constitution is 'antecedent' to the government. That it defines the authority which the people commit to its government, and in so doing thereby limits it. That any exercise of authority beyond these limits by any government is an exercise of 'power without right'. That in any state in which the distinction is not actually observed

> between the constitution and the government there is in reality no constitution, because the will of the government has no check upon it, and that state is in fact a despotism.

He emphasized Paine's dictum 'that a constitution is not the act of government but of a people constituting a government'.[7] He stated that the government cannot exercise any powers not granted in the constitution, which McIlwain summarized as, 'All constitutional government is by definition limited government'. Its powers are 'fundamental', that is, they cannot be altered by ordinary legal process. McIlwain noted that one element of good governance missing from Paine's account was the 'element of judicial review'.

McIlwain noted that 'in all its successive phases, constitutionalism has one essential quality: it is a legal limitation on government; it is the antithesis of arbitrary rule; its opposite is despotic government, the government of will instead of law. In modern times the growth of political responsibility has been added....' Constitutionalism is also tied, tentatively, to the mode of adoption of the constitution. McIlwain goes on to say, 'And if it be true, the consequence is that the forms and limits followed by this "constituting" become the embodiment of a "a constitution" superior in character to any acts of any "government" it creates'. He reiterates, 'the most persistent, and the most lasting of the essentials of true constitutionalism still remains what it has been always been from the beginning, the limitation of government by law. Constitutional limitations, if not the most important part of our constitutionalism, are beyond doubt the most ancient'.[8]

McIlwain makes clear that his primary interest is in what he calls 'our Anglo-Saxon' traditions (and examines the growth of ideas of governance), but in his discussion of other European nations, he makes clear that similar developments were taking place. He notes that 'the medieval constitutionalism disclosed by the English historical materials was no monopoly of England or of Englishmen, but a datum with which the historian must reckon no matter with what particular European constitutional system he is immediately concerned'.[9] The French Declaration of the Rights of Man and Citizen in 1789 endorses constitutionalism in the sense outlined by McIlwain, with the rights of man and restrictions on what the state can do. Article 16 even says, 'Any society in which the guarantee of rights is not assured nor the separation of powers defined, has no constitution at all'.

McIlwain makes a few observations that make sense of the contemporary discussions on constitutionalism, or at least of why the notions of constitutionalism seem to be changing, expanding, or modified.[10] The first point, already noted above, is that the notion of constitutionalism is not restricted to Anglo/US values or traditions (though it has been fairly influential, as in

France after the revolution). Secondly, circumstances keep on changing and with it, priorities, values, or context (for example, whether the concern is with freedom or security). Writing as Hitler's army was taking over Europe and, at home, killing Jews, Gypsies, and gays, McIlwain's book/lectures were a plea for preserving liberties in Europe and America. He was only too conscious of the dangers of sacrificing liberties when the government stirs the public with danger of threats from abroad (of terrorism, for example). He cautioned his audience as follows, 'Constitutional history is usually the record of a series of oscillations. At one time, private right is the chief concern of the citizens; at another the prevention of disorder that threatens to become anarchy.... When the rights of government are unduly stressed, the rights of individuals are threatened; when the latter are overemphasized, government becomes too weak to keep order'.[11] Okoth-Ogendo showed well how soon after independence African governments talked of the threats to the integrity of their states as well as their plans for development as justification for authoritarianism when not long previously they had demanded independence and human rights for the people from the colonists.

Over time, the somewhat limited elements of constitutionalism as outlined by McIlwain expanded to include a clear notion of democracy and, something that McIlwain did not consider part of constitutionalism—the separation of powers. In fact, he considered it antagonistic to constitutionalism. MacIlwain wrote (worried about the excessive power of judicial review),

> But to insist thus on the indispensability of legal limits to governmental power and the safeguarding of these limits by an independent court is not to advocate the enfeebling of what government itself. Among all the modern fallacies that have obscured the true teachings of constitutional history, few are worse than the extreme doctrine of the separation of powers and the indiscriminate use of the phrase 'checks and balances'.[12]

In this regard, he was among the US scholars who have denigrated judicial review, on the basis that it undermines democracy. Judicial review has also been attacked as against the separation of powers. There is clearly a dilemma here ('solved' by the US Supreme Court in *Marbury v Madison* early in the history of the US Constitution). Today this dilemma is resolved by the constitution itself in the definition of the functions and responsibilities of the judiciary.[13]

II.1 Separation of Powers and Judicial Review

Twenty-four years after McIlwain's book, the requirements of constitutionalism had expanded somewhat as stated by the distinguished British scholar, Stanley de Smith. He offered the following account of constitutionalism,

> A contemporary liberal democrat, if asked to lay down a set of minimum standards, may be very willing to concede that constitutionalism is practised in a country where the government is genuinely accountable to an entity or organ distinct from itself, where elections are freely held on a wide franchise at frequent intervals, where political groups are free to organize in opposition to the government in office and where there are effective legal guarantees of fundamental liberties enforced by an independent judiciary; and he may not easily be persuaded to identify constitutionalism in a country where any of these conditions is lacking.[14]

A non-English academic might add to de Smith's list a written constitution, with special entrenchment of provisions dealing with the invalidity of laws that violate the constitution, the entrenchment of the constitution itself, and the duty of courts to declare invalid laws that are inconsistent with the constitution.

Though McIlwain has a historical account of constitutionalism, it is more about chronology or sequences than explanation of the circumstances (or ideology) which led to the adoption of the specific characteristics of constitutionalism (in the style of Karl Marx or Max Weber). There is little account of the changes in social relations or in the economy or political alliances that might explain the relative importance of constitutionalism or its form. Moreover, constitutions were rather brief, and dealt principally with institutions of the state and their power. The underlying circumstances, values, and the role of the state have changed greatly since the birth of constitutionalism. Their implications for constitutionalism are considered after the review of the essays by Okoth-Ogendo, Shivji, and Ghai.

III Three Essays

The three essays are closely connected. They were written as part of celebrations of the 200th anniversary of the US constitution organized by the American Council of Learned Societies. The essay by Okoth-Ogendo appeared twice, once in a book edited by the American Council,[15] and, earlier, in a book edited by Issa Shivji.[16] Shivji's essay appeared in the African volume. My essay appeared in the American Council book. The title of Okoth-Ogendo's essay is 'Constitutions Without Constitutionalism: Reflections on an African Paradox', Shivji's, 'State and Constitutionalism: A New Democratic Perspective', and mine, 'The Theory of the State in the Third World and the Problematic of Constitutionalism'.

The juxtaposition of these essays was of particular interest for me: both Okoth-Ogendo and Shivji were my students at Dar es Salaam in the late

1960s; both extremely bright and imaginative, but holding diverse, indeed conflicting, views on the role of law in society and development. And Okoth-Ogendo's opening lines in his famous essay is a reference to Patrick McAuslan and my book *Public Law and Political Change in Kenya* (1970).[17] Both Okoth-Ogendo and Shivji made copious references to my other writings (pupils' homage to their teacher—though, I am happy to say, not always in agreement with me). On ideology, I was somewhat between Okoth-Ogendo (liberal theory) and Issa (Marxist theory), though tending towards Marxist theory the more I reflected on what was happening in Africa—and reading Issa's writings. My vacillation between liberalism and Marxism was well captured in my chapter, 'Legal Radicalism, Professionalism and Social Action: Reflections on Teaching Law in Dar es Salaam' in a book edited by Shivji, *Limits of Legal Radicalism* (1986; Issa's own contribution was titled 'Within and Beyond Legal Radicalism'). Since those exciting times, I have taught in numerous universities, some among the most distinguished in the world, but I have met few students as bright, sharp, and of such inquiring minds as Okoth-Ogendo and Shivji. It was my good fortune to be tutored by them, operating from opposite ends of the ideological debates on development and justice.[18]

III.1 Okoth-Ogendo: 'Constitutions without Constitutionalism: Reflections on an African Political Paradox'

Okoth-Ogendo's main thesis is set out in the form of a paradox: the commitment of African governments to the idea of the constitution and 'an equally emphatic rejection of the classical notion of constitutionalism'. In order to explain the paradox, he examines the theory of the constitution as organized power; the constitution as a power map and the making of it as pre-eminently a political process—which points have been ignored by scholars. States accept and establish constitutions for particular purposes, not just 'a simple reproduction of some basic principles which particular societies may have found operational'.[19] The motives which have compelled African elites to adopt constitutions are the realisation that without the constitution 'the polity can have no legitimate or sovereign existence'. The second concept is of the constitution as a basic law, not as something sacrosanct, but that 'does entail … minimum and perhaps popular observance of the rules contained in the constitution'. One might say it is opportunistic; choosing those bits that serve the political elite but rejecting what does not suit it. The justification of what constitutionalists might say is expediency, is presented by the elite as more in tune with the realities of African states. Okoth-Ogendo cites Nyerere (one of the more intellectual, and, one can say, more honest, of African leaders) as follows:

> We refuse to adopt the institutions of other countries even where they have served those countries well because it is our conditions that have to be served by our institutions. We refuse to put ourselves in a strait-jacket of constitutional devices—even of our own making. The constitution of Tanzania must serve the people of Tanzania. We do not intend that the people of Tanzania should serve the constitution.[20]

Okoth-Ogendo concludes that 'a purely instrumental view' of what constitutions are for, and one which is evident in Nyerere's position has, therefore, been one in which the state elites have found themselves searching for the 'formal means by which to preserve the integrity of the "constituted polity" without being embroiled in a maze of constitutional law whose function, in classical theory, is to control and supervise constitutionality.'[21] Okoth-Ogendo argued that the strength of the colonial state lay not in constitutional mandates but the structure and powers of the bureaucracy. '[C]ontrol and coercion rather than management and persuasion were the hallmarks of colonial legal order'.[22] The traditions of the judiciary were more resonant of this colonial approach than of the rule of law. He also argued that independence constitutions were more geared towards conflict (among political parties and communities) than peace. The bureaucracy acquired a stronger status and powers than in the colonial period, and operated without the rule of law or impartiality practised by the British bureaucracy in the UK. Over course of time it established a relationship with the political class to plunder the resources of the state. Okoth-Ogendo makes another important point that the bureaucracy did more than accede to colonial administrative power; its role was expanded, particularly as regards the management of the economy.

Independent constitutions were for the most part in the mould of British or Western constitutions, whose hallmark was 'a remarkable distrust of centralized power' and 'where laws or state acts in violation of the constitution were unconstitutional'.[23] Post-independence amendments or replacements approximated to the colonial model (in spirit, if not in structure or detail). Okoth-Ogendo discusses in considerable detail some key elements of the new constitutional orders—familiar I am sure to Kenyans and citizens of other African states. He summarizes the 'actual process of subverting' the constitutional order as follows, 'The most notorious was the *coup d'etat* that did not merely involve "opting" out of the basic law but often its total abrogation. Another form was a cavalier disregard of constitutional niceties and processes such as the postponement of election ... the declaration of no contest against certain election candidates.... The more interesting for our purposes was the move by state elites in a number of African countries to *politicise* the constitution; initially, by declaring it a liability, and subsequently by converting it into an instrument of political warfare'.[24]

Among the devices for politicization, Okoth-Ogendo lists the extension of the powers of the chief executive to appoint and dismiss holders of all public offices, even 'constitutional' offices like judges and the attorneys-general; restricting public appointments to members of the ruling party (this tendency led in a number of countries to formal one party states); expanding the coercive power of the state to derogate from the Bill of Rights, and to ensure that the constitution conforms to the rest of the legal order (as for example our present president Uhuru Kenyatta tried to do in respect of security officers and their powers). He concludes, 'A run to amend the constitution whenever a political crisis emerged or was apprehended, therefore, became increasingly attractive as a method of re-establishing equilibrium within the body politic.... Thus the coercive orientation of the legal order continued to be enhanced even as the essence of constitutionalism was being drained' from the reconstituted power map.[25] The consequences are an imperial presidency, the immunity of the holder of that office, removal of restrictions on the number of terms a person may hold the office, and the high degree of paranoia which tends to surround the exercise of executive power. These developments result in the 'shrinking' of the political arena.[26]

Okoth-Ogendo did not set out his understanding of constitutionalism as such, though one can infer from his critique of post-colonial constitutional arrangements what he meant by it. For example, he preferred the 'constitutional order' to be an arbiter in the power process, and regretted that the order became instead ' a most crucial element of and for the appropriation of power; the Constitution lost most of its claims to being the basic law of the land'. It is also clear that he regarded administrative law as protecting the rights of the people against unfair or unlawful acts or decisions of state officials and regretted restrictions on civil rights like processions and marches. His detailed critique of 'imperial presidency' as undermining the separation of powers, and the legal immunity of the president as negating the rule of law, provides further guidance on his conception of constitutionalism. His commitment to democracy is implicit in his discussion of the centrality of the role of political parties to public participation and the broadening of policy options. He writes, 'In Africa, however, the reconstitution of the independence power maps has recast political parties into very different instruments. Instead of expanding the arena of politics ... political parties have been used to shrink it'.[27] Okoth-Ogendo's position is undoubtedly liberal in the older sense of the term—a believer in human rights above all. His constitutionalism is based on both rights and democracy. But he was not an activist when some academics (among others) struggled for constitutional reforms nor did he contribute to any of the several books and booklets arguing for reform.

Okoth-Ogendo explains the lack of constitutionalism in Africa by reference to its poor socio-economic conditions—and the consequent greed of the elite for accumulation of wealth, in dubious ways. I would perhaps put the same idea somewhat differently—the poverty of Africans is the result of the greed and selfishness of its 'leaders' —of which few countries provide more convincing evidence than Kenya. Looking to the future, he said that constitutionalism will be feasible only when there is prosperity in the country. 'Constitutionalism being the end product of social, economic, cultural, and political progress can only become a tradition it forms part of the shared history of the people'.[28]

Okoth-Ogendo's conclusion is not very comforting to those who struggled for constitutional reform and pushed through, despite some damage in the process, the CKRC draft constitution as the 2010 Constitution—a constitution replete with values of constitutionalism, but not those alone since a major theme of the constitution is social justice for the present and future generations and redressing past injustices in matters pertaining to land. It has also to be said that Okoth-Ogendo worked hard for the achievement of the CKRC and Bomas drafts constitutions, despite his failing health. It would be imprudent to dismiss the Okoth-Ogendo thesis regarding the emergence of constitutionalism out of hand—the fortunes of the 2010 Constitution will be a good test. Unfortunately, Okoth-Ogendo will not be with us to share the outcome.

III.2 Issa Shivji: 'State and Constitutionalism: A New Democratic Perspective'

Shivji's engagement with constitutionalism is informed by a different hypothesis from that of Okoth-Ogendo. Nor does he subscribe to Okoth-Ogendo's view that corruption would cease and constitutionalism prevail once a country achieves a level of affluence. His interest is not in liberalism, but in neo-colonialism and imperialism. Shivji says (as the foundation of his approach), 'It is clear that endemic underdevelopment is integrally related to the role that these economies play in the international economic order dominated by imperialist countries'. Another difference is that Okoth-Ogendo's framework of analysis is the nation (dominated by state sovereignty) and Shivji's concern is with the state or 'statism' as he calls it (in the context of domination by global forces). Shivji says that social scientists question the relevance of the liberal democratic model, preferring a different democratic model from that of Western liberalism. The basis of his discussion of constitutionalism is significantly different from that of Okoth-Ogendo. He aims to 'recast constitutional issues and concerns within a different conceptual framework of constitutionalism guided by a new democratic perspective'.[29]

Shivji begins by categorizing the colonial state as despotic, its legal order inconsistent with constitutionalism, a statement with which Okoth-Ogendo would have had no problem, as he would not with Shivji's account of the resurgence of the colonial order through 'amendments, modifications or overthrow' of the constitution. His analysis of reasons given by the new political elite for the erosion of constitutionalism (for example, individual human rights and the separation of powers) are similar to Okoth-Ogendo's—principally about the imperative of 'developmentalism'. Like Okoth-Ogendo he concludes that the result was 'an authoritarian neo-colonial state'. So far, both seem to agree on the meaning of constitutionalism, though neither defines it as such, just passing references. Shivji has a more detailed analysis of the characteristics and methods of the colonial/neo-colonial state than Okoth-Ogendo; however, they agree that it rules by coercion rather than consent. But unlike Okoth-Ogendo who is satisfied with the liberal or 'bourgeois' definition of constitutionalism, Shivji sets out to redefine it, consistent with his notions of a fair and just political order.

So, what is this constitutional order? To start with, Shivji does not accept Okoth-Ogendo's explanation that constitutionalism will only be respected once Africa achieves development, which Shivji understands as bourgeois development or constitutionalism. The constitutionalism that Shivji is looking for would deal with the present socio-economic conditions. As he explains, 'The process of "underdevelopment and poverty" are in this view, not an earlier condition of a society moving toward development but rather an integral condition produced by the same single process in the development of the dominant countries on the one hand, and imperialist domination of the third world on the other.' He attributes the authoritarian state in Africa to the integration of the African political economy in the world capitalist system, and the way it articulates with social and political forces.[30]

Shivji sets out at considerable length how Africa gets out of this bind, based on national independence and anti-imperialist struggles. An important element of independence is the liberation of minorities from their oppression by the state, reflected in the 'intense uneven and unequal development' of their regions. He advocates national integration not through assimilation but through the recognition of diversity. The second element is democratic governance; he argues that the western democratic forms, including the parliamentary Westminster system, have failed in Africa because that is rule from the top. What Africa needs is direct democracy, with initiatives coming from below, and constant accountability to the people organized in different groups. The third element is a vibrant role for autonomous civil organizations. He says, 'The crucial structure or medium through which the society "confronts" the state is precisely its autonomous organisations which may express varied vertical and horizontal interests within itself cutting across class and cultural boundaries'. The fourth element is the right 'to the integrity of the person', including through respect for human rights now well acknowledged internationally, as ways of influencing policies through, for example, the right of petition. These four elements (suitably developed) provide 'us with some pointers and guidelines to attempt a new conceptual framework for the concept of constitutionalism' which he attempts to draw in the rest of the chapter—certainly much broader than, as he notes, 'twin pillars of limited *government* and individual fundamental freedoms/rights'.[31]

Okoth-Ogendo sees liberal constitutionalism as covering a critical but limited area; but Shivji's constitutionalism is broader and covers most of the constitution.

In the book which includes these and other articles, Shivji, as editor, tries to weave the threads (spun by the several distinguished African scholars and activists who contributed) together, and notes frankly that the traditional notion of constitutionalism implied and to some extent explained by Okoth-Ogendo had greater support from the contributors than Shivji's own approach. I will return to his reflections after the next section, which is about my chapter.

III.3 Yash Ghai: 'The Theory of the State in the Third World and the Problematic of Constitutionalism'

My chapter focuses on the nature of the state, principally in Africa, and tries to demonstrate how its dynamics makes it improbable that constitutionalism (à la McIlwain) would be observed by the government. I state that my analysis is based on Marxism though I use the terminology of Max Weber to explain the reasons for the development of constitutionalism in Europe, tying it to relations between the growth of the market economy and the pre-eminence of constitutionalism or the rule of law. I argue that the relations between the state and economy/markets which led in Europe to constitutionalism ('legal-rational') were completely the reverse of the relations between the state and economy in Africa ('patrimonial')—and thus, far from constitutionalism being critical to the kind of economy that African governments preferred (based on a key role for the state, politicians, and bureaucrats), what was critical were/are the discretionary powers of the state over the economy. The 'entrepreneurs' in Europe were in the private sector, who wanted a reliable legal framework for their plans and contracts, while in Africa the 'entrepreneurs' were those who used the state mechanisms which they did not want fettered or questioned, and preferably were not accountable to a legal regime. This is what I said in my chapter,

> It is well known that the notion of the rule of law is associated with a mode of nomination and legitimation, the legal-rational, that Weber regarded as central to the development and functioning of the modern state. The authority of state actions is founded in the law, which also provides the basic framework for institutions and the operation of the state. No one is above the law, which is itself purposive and rational, the product of human deliberation.... The constitutions of most Third World countries promulgated on independence conformed to this pattern, establishing the supremacy of the constitution, the neutrality of the public service, and independence of the judiciary.
>
> Patrimonalism is a different form of domination. It is a form of personal rule, which does not tolerate opposition. Administration is based on the total power and discretion of the ruler. The bureaucracy is an extension of his household, and to which he delegates its powers. There is no clear separation between the private and public spheres of the ruler. He is above the law, as are his officials, and dispenses justice; petitions to him for clemency and generosity substitute for legal writs. The ideological superstructure of such domination is the goodness, generosity, and concern of the ruler for his people. He is the 'father of his people', 'the father of his nation'.

I clarify that the legal-rational model (as well as the accompanying ideology) is not completely superseded but co-exists with the patrimonial. The trend has fundamental implications for constitutionalism and the status and role of rules.

As regards the rule of law, I wrote:

> If the rule of law as an ideology is unimportant, it will come as no surprise that is it also unimportant in its substantive aspect. In most developing countries, whether the economic system is a species of capitalism or socialism, general norms play a secondary role. Both kinds of economy are essentially administered economies, where license is the king and discretion is the norm.... Capitalists seek the embrace of the governments, and concentration of state with capital is extensive and complex. Markets themselves are the creation of governments, whose leaders, not having a secure base of their own in production or distribution process, are fearful of the free play of economic forces. Multinationals accept that bargains have to be struck with the government and concessions negotiated. Key prices are regulated and controlled. The administered economy is incompatible with generalised norms operating

> autonomously. But more fundamentally, it is the character of the state and the nature of the process of accumulation in most Third World countries that undermine constitutionalism.

I did not necessarily see this state of affairs as permanent.

> Perhaps there is no straight route from colonial legality to constitutionalism; perhaps it must pass through a new process of state building.... In certain situations it may well be that the costs of suppression outweigh the gains from it. Circumstances may so change that the vested rights of the dominant class (and the interests of foreign states and capital) are better served through a democratic rather than an authoritarian polity. The forms of development generated through authoritarianism frequently give rise to their own contradictions, for instance, the development of a propertied and professional middle class that values democracy and human rights for pragmatic and ideological reasons.[32]

After all, Weber, although reluctant to commit himself to an evolutionary scheme, had envisaged the progression from patrimonialism to the rational–legal state, with the growing purposiveness and rationality of the law and state institutions. 'What we have been examining is the rapid emergence of a patrimonial state on the legal foundations of constitutionalist state, some transformations secured through the manipulation, trivialisation, and disregard of the law'.[33] To understand the dynamics and functions of constitutionalism, one has to uncover its social and economic bases, and thus transcend the formal boundaries of the law.

III.4 Brief Comparison of the Three Essays

I have already given some indication of the differences in the approach of the writers to constitutionalism. The biggest difference was between Okoth-Ogendo and Shivji. My approach and analysis were not significantly different from that of Okoth-Ogendo and had some resonances with Shivji (though of course his framework was global rather than national, as mine was). All three essays are more sociological and political than purely 'legal'. There is considerable agreement on some important issues, particularly on the nature of the colonial state, without a trace of constitutionalism (extensively illustrated in Ghai and McAuslan), and the predatory nature of its descendant the independent state.

While Okoth-Ogendo and Ghai conduct their discussion largely within the McIlwainian concept of constitutionalism, they introduce elements of its socio-economic background, and say a great deal more than McIlwain on the nature and dialectics of the state. Shivji has little time for McIlwain or his framework. For him, constitutionalism in that sense is merely an obstacle to the fundamental changes in the state and globally, necessary for justice to all. Shivji as such does not consider the virtues or drawbacks of the components of constitutionalism—but attacks the system associated with it (liberalism) without examining the working of the system and the precise role of constitutionalism—maybe they too were marginalized in the capitalist economies. Capitalism after all changed over time, and the original understanding of constitutionalism (once favourable) may no longer be so functional for current capitalism (as hinted by Okoth-Ogendo and me). And in Marxist societies also, the components of constitutionalism may not be without benefit to the people. In fact, looking at the record of communist states in Europe, one can see the advantages of a measure of restrictions on the executive.

III.5 The Spring of 'Constitutionalisms'

The McIlwain model seems to have dominated the approach of most authors who participated in the 200th anniversary of the US constitution. Editors of the Council of Learned Societies reached this conclusion after surveying the papers and discussions in the programme, stating in the Introduction to the primary book: 'The distillation of these varied and energetic discussions suggests an approximate definition of constitutionalism: it is a commitment to limitations on ordinary political power; it revolves around a political process, one that overlaps with democracy in seeking to balance state power and individual and collective rights; it draws on particular cultural and historical contexts from which it emanates; and it resides in public consciousness'.

Shivji, however, sets up his own version of constitutionalism, more directed to values, communities, and institutions, freeing them from old McIlwainian constraints. This is indeed a clever device, moving the debate to what he considers as key social issues. By attaching the concept constitutionalism to totally different social, economic, and political systems, not only does he challenge McIlwainian concepts and policies, but he opens up a new framework labelled 'constitutionalism'—of his own making. In this respect too, Shivji was quite innovative (though he did not attach a prefix to it, such as 'socialist constitutionalism').

Interestingly, Professor Jackton Ojwang, a leading constitutional scholar (now a member of Kenya's Supreme Court), at about the same time, coming from different political perspectives from those of Shivji, argued that there could be no one understanding of constitutionalism, when he compared the very different positions in Europe between the constitutions of market oriented states and those of socialist oriented states. Noting the firm conviction with which scholars from each camp spoke of their 'constitutionalism', he concluded that,

> To claim, therefore, that the notion of constitutionalism demands the same approach to government practice, always and everywhere, would not be consistent with reality. The one inference which might be made is that constitutionalism entails a spirit of "good" government. Such government must inevitably take into account the circumstances of each society. Subject to that condition, constitutionalism requires as objective an assessment as possible of the social, economic, and cultural characteristics of any given society and their incorporation into the practice of government.

His definition of 'constitutionalism' would therefore imply,

> a sensitivity to the basic orientation of the people; it requires reasonable consultation between government and people; it calls for fair procedures of government designation; it would demand a reasonable degree of accountability of government to the governed; it requires that the law-making process be responsive to the public needs; it calls for fair and effective adjudicatory procedures; it demands effective adjudicatory procedures; it demands effective management of public policy and administration, in the general interest of the people.[34]

Today, there is a proliferation of different kinds of constitutionalism—each with its own prefixes. In a short space of time I came across the following (the list is not complete by any means): democratic constitutionalism, political constitutionalism, judicial constitutionalism, illiberal constitutionalism (oxymoron no more?), new constitutionalism, contemporary constitutionalism, popular constitutionalism, corporatist constitutionalism, negative constitutionalism, Russian constitutionalism, Confucian constitutionalism, African constitutionalism, transformative constitutionalism, plurinational constitutionalism, feminist constitutionalism, secular constitutionalism, modern constitutionalism, aggregative constitutionalism, Sinicized Marxist constitutionalism—and, to crown it all, world constitutionalism. We have not yet seen the end of it.

We owe this multiplicity of 'isms' to the great renewal of interest in constitutions after the end of the cold war—and to some extent the convergence of the interests of some constitutional and political science scholars. Large parts of the world were released from the bondage of the west or the east (meaning Russia). But they could not have the constitutions they pleased—many might have preferred to continue with their 'dictatorial constitutionalism' were it not for two of the world's great 'democrats'—Reagan and Thatcher. States with 'dependent constitutionalism' had to shift to 'democratic constitutionalism'.

Many citizens living under 'dependent constitutionalism' began or intensified their demand for 'constitutionalism' in its comprehensive form. They wanted constitutions which were based on democracy and accountability, ('participatory constitutionalism'?), human rights, dignity, and gender equity, sharing of power, and social justice. Interest in constitutions increased when international lawyers began to take interest in constitutions (under the mistaken idea that constitutional bills of rights were owed to international law, forgetting that numerous constitutions innovated with human rights centuries ago). But it is true that the international community (for which read mostly western states/NGOs) played a not unimportant role in the making of constitutions in a number of states ('imposed constitutionalism')—which inevitably drew in US, Canadian, and European academics, often prolific writers, into offering their advice. Often foreign academics had better access to giving advice than local academics—and they were also more given to 'theory' than local academics. One knows what happens if US scholars get into the act. Perhaps for this reason, in the west the term 'constitutionalism' is used freely, to express the author's preference or the dominating orientation of the constitution ('political constitutionalism', 'pluriconstutionalism', 'feminist constitutionalism', 'judicial constitutionalism', etc). Whereas in Asia, Latin America, and Africa, the academics are also (sometimes more) interested in the mechanisms of decision making and enforcement of the constitution. In the west, which developed the concept of constitutionalism as a system to curb the power of the state and to increase the liberty of the people, it is increasingly giving way to a somewhat meaningless use of 'constitutionalism'. There is a real danger that scholars from developing countries might lose sight of 'constitutionalism' and its significance in their own study of western disquisitions.

One is reminded of Alice in Wonderland's anxious response to Humpty Dumpty's statement made—in rather a scornful tone: 'When I use a word, it means just what I choose it to mean—neither more nor less.' 'The question is', responded Alice, 'whether you can make words mean so many different things.' 'The question is', said Humpty Dumpty, 'which is to be master—that's all.' The difficulty here is that often what the 'ism' means is not explained. Consequently, it is not surprising that there is such an explosion of literature on constitutionalism, nor that there is now no common understanding of what constitutionalism means. I return later, briefly, to this issue.

III.6 Back to Africa

For the most part, when African and Asian scholars use the word 'constitutionalism', they mean its classical or McIlwainian sense. I believe the reason for this is that for a long time they have lived under authoritarian regimes (colonial as well as indigenous). I intend in conclusion to try to locate 'constitutionalism' within contemporary African contexts and constitutions. A number of leading African scholars have devoted their energies to elucidating the significance of constitutionalism—Ben Nwabueze, Mahmood Mamdani, Kwesi Prempah, Abdullahi Ahmed An-Nai'm, Charles Fombad, Jackton Ojwang, Oloko-Onyango, and others. Unfortunately, space allows only brief references to the work of Nwabueze, Ojwang, and An-Nai'm.

***Ben Nwabueze*:** African scholars have strongly supported constitutionalism in the traditional sense, as far back as 1973 when the distinguished Nigerian scholar Ben Nwabueze wrote his book *Constitutionalism in the Emergent States* (1973). By that time the euphoria of independence and with it rights, freedom and justice had worn off and the colonial type of state had re-established itself. Constitutionalism, he said, 'recognises the necessity of government but insists upon a limitation being put placed upon its powers'.[35] He went on to say, 'There are indeed many countries in the world with written constitutions but without constitutionalism'.[36] He reminded us of constitutions which 'consist to a large extent of nothing but lofty declarations of objectives and a description of the organs of government in terms that impose no enforceable legal restraints'.[37] Hence the need for constitutionalism. Nwabueze, a disciple of Stanley de Smith, endorsed forcefully all its ingredients: a written constitution which is the supreme law, government of limited powers, separation of powers, and judicial review—all reinforcing the democracy underlying such a regime ('the democratic control of mechanisms of popular representation and the responsibility of the government to the governed unquestionably increase the efficacy of any system of restraints upon government').[38] He sets out meticulously the ways in which some governments in Africa and Asia had managed to subvert constitutionalism despite the above elements (through incitement of racial conflicts, various forms of political coercion, declarations of emergencies, coups d'état, and secessions—working his way through a substantial part of the Commonwealth).

He wrote of constitutionalism with greater passion than any scholar I know. He was very ardent, even evangelical, about constitutionalism. He wrote with great passion about the need for freedom, and how that should be secured. Thirty-one years later, he was still deeply engaged with and committed to constitutionalism, the underlying theme of his monumental study in seven volumes of *Constitutional Democracy in Africa* (of which I have to confess I have only read the first five).

***Jackton Ojwang*:** Jackton Ojwang's earlier views were not supportive of 'western constitutionalism'. One of the most controversial themes of his work was the legitimacy of political parties in Africa. His general thesis was that the Western type of multiparty system had failed to establish either unity or stability. He argued that African states needed a one-party system to maintain law and order. A clear statement of his views as to the appropriateness of western conception of constitutionalism appears in his chapter, 'Constitutionalism in Classical Terms and in African Nationhood', in a book edited by Nasile Rembe and Evance Kalula (eds), *Constitutional Government and Human Rights in Africa* (1990). He argues that the western notion of constitutionalism cannot be adopted as such in Africa; instead, it must incorporate Africa's conditions of social, economic, political, and cultural dimensions, which present valid dimensions which must be incorporated in national schemes of constitutionalism. The same, he argued, necessitated the adjustment of the theory and practices of human rights. Apart from economic constraints, he considered cultural differences as of major consequences. More than once in his writings he summarized the views of the then president, Daniel Arap Moi as follows:[39]

> President Moi underlines the cultural base of intellectualism, suggesting in effect that the concept of a footloose intellectual would be either a rarity or of a contradiction in terms. He considers that the intellectual riches of the mind are a growth from the "rich cultural and philosophical heritage of [one's] own country". Thus, one claiming to be an intellectual without caring to understand one's genesis, without benefiting from the lesson of history, without appreciating the social, cultural and political conjuncture in which one finds oneself, without the haziest picture of one's bearings and one's interplay with the milieu obtaining, would not be a true intellectual and ought not to pass for an exemplar in Kenya [in Africa].

In the same vein, Professor Ojwang justified, in a number of papers, the establishment of the one-party political system in Africa. He argued that Africa did not have diversity in the economy which justified a multiparty system in liberal societies. Furthermore, he argued that in African states people did not have primary loyalty to the nation but to the tribe, and therefore a multiparty system would divide the people. He continued,

> It is unfortunate that lawyers and political scientists have not taken full note of the relatively long period during which the institutional basis of Western liberalism has been falling apart in Africa. Instead many of them have passed censorious judgments on the non-practice of these values, in this way placing themselves in a complacent and unconstructive intellectual posture and becoming unhelpful for any solution to the problems they see.[40]

In a sense, his position was not dissimilar to Okoth-Ogendo's position, except that at that time he was trying to explain, not justify, the African approach.

However, Ojwang gradually moved away from this position to one more liberal oriented, accepting many features of 'western constitutionalism'. This features very strongly in his latest published book, *Ascendant Judiciary in East Africa*. He does not offer a detailed explanation of the change in his views, but did hint in one or two articles that the economic and social circumstances—constituting the underlying basis of society in Kenya and Africa—have changed. The change in his own views appears most clearly in this recent book … and in his learned judgments in the Supreme Court.[41] He seems to have reconciled himself to the constitution most driven by 'constitutionalism' of any African constitution.

Abdullahi Ahmed An-Na'im: Thirty-three years after Nwabueze's first major study of constitutionalism, another distinguished African scholar, Abdullahi Ahmed An-Na'im, addresses the same issues (though with slightly different perspectives), bemoaning deficiencies in the realization of constitutionalism, but with a somewhat different approach to the solution.[42] An-Na'im has a particular interest in and great knowledge of Islam which he discusses at length in the context of constitutionalism, including adjustments in religious practices. Contextually of constitutionalism, he poses the following question:

> The question is how can people of different religious/cultural traditions, even if they all live in the same country, agree to accept the same normative system? In other words, tensions in the relationship between Islam and constitutionalism in Islam and constitutionalism in Islamic societies are simply specific manifestations of the broader problem of cultural legitimacy and contextual sustainability of constitutionalism in these countries.

While Ojwang, in his powerful defence of one-party rule and deviations from constitutionalism, concluded that culture must override constitutionalism, An-Na'aim explores, optimistically, the prospects of constitutionalism. He himself is committed to traditional constitutionalism, but realizes that that conditions in Africa may not be fully suitable. His concern is with creating conditions for the realisation of complete constitutionalism rather than ideological debate about it. He talks of an 'incremental process of constitutionalism in Africa', realizing the difficulties facing its complete implementation immediately.[43] Among the hurdles he outlines is dependence on outside assistance and the resulting 'western neo-colonial hegemony'. He says, 'The only way forward is through the practice of constitutionalism in order to empower civil society actors to hold governments legally and politically accountable to their own populations.... The main question for the book is how to make that happen in a sustainable way manner throughout the continent.'

He examines how that approach would work in African Islamic states, given the tension between the understandings of Shari'a and modern principles of constitutionalism and suggests that it might principally be through the reinterpretation of Shari'a to reformulate its relevance particularly in multicultural societies. He argues that that tensions within African countries (due, for example, to multiple ethnic groups) should not be taken as a reason why constitutionalism cannot function; on the contrary, it is the reason why it should be promoted. He justifies different conceptions of constitutionalism, seeing them as complementary approaches to an ideal 'to be adapted to different conditions of time and place, rather than as representing sharp dichotomies or categories'—and should be harmonized over time. He attempts to relate 'constitutionalism' to the country's circumstances, rather like Ojwang, but unlike Ojwang he is committed to traditional constitutionalism values: 'uphold the rule of law, enforce effective limitations on government powers, and the protection of fundamental rights'.[44] But my primary interest here is his analysis of what he calls 'the contingent role of Islam' which he claims can help to mediate between traditional understandings of Islam, on the one hand, and modern principles of constitutionalism on the other.[45]

He demonstrates the variability of Shari'a, dependent on the history/circumstances of the Muslim country, 'product of the history of their own societies'. Shari'a is, he says, a matter of interpretation of the Qur'an and Sunna, so it is neither divine nor immutable. Certain principles may be incompatible with constitutionalism but perhaps some accommodation may be possible. He points to the inadequacy of the Shari'a—it makes it difficult for the state to fulfil its essential domestic and international functions in the present increasingly global context. Referring to inequalities under Shari'a of women and non-Muslims, he says, 'While such aspects of Shari'a represented significant improvements on political and legal systems that prevailed throughout the pre-modern world, they are totally unacceptable from a constitutional point of view today'. But in practice there is a great push for the inequalities, presented as an essential aspect of Islam. However, if there were the will for constitutionalism, then the problem could be solved by reinterpretation (can one say that this is An-Na'im's weak point?). He considers that what is needed is a commitment to reform (which the custodians of Islam are not interested in). He says, 'issues must be framed in terms of historically conditioned forms of the relationship between Islam and the state, rather than a sharp dichotomy between total unity or categorical separation of religion and the state'.[46] He then explains the contingency of Islam to mean,

> the kinds of social, political and cultural changes and transformations associated with Islam cannot be reduced *solely* to either an 'African' or 'Islamic' agency or motivation. Moreover, to view the spread of Islam in a given context primarily in terms of its appeal as a religious ideology may draw on certain assumptions regarding the role of 'religion' for the society in question.... The concept of contingency means that a particular outcome can be simultaneously viewed as, on the one hand, local African, and Islamic, and on the other hand, religious, ideological, social, cultural, and/or political.[47]

And An-Na'im gives various instances of this, particularly from West Africa, but discusses also the special case of East Africa, quoting Pouwel's study: 'In coastal East Africa, with its long tradition of welcoming immigrants from great distances, cultural change was an inescapable fact of life'[48] and goes on to say that the local understanding and practice of Islam was not only influenced by African culture, but also exhibited elements of Asian influence that created a culture distinct from coastal East African culture. Others have commented that as Muslim traders went inland for trade purposes, they built good relations with communities there and adopted local customs, while some of the people there converted to Islam without losing much of their cultural heritage.[49]

IV Conclusion: Reflections on Constitutionalism in our Age[50]

An-Na'im's principal concern in his book was to explore the consistency of Islam with constitutionalism—and the answer was positive provided certain interpretations were adopted. Ojwang acknowledges that circumstances can change, making constitutionalism acceptable, indeed imperative. As I and others have argued, constitutionalism emerged in the West in certain economic circumstances, with the rise of capitalism. Recent writings on constitutionalism have taken a new turn, when everything is 'constitutionalism' but the question is what kind. The proliferation of the concept has made the concept somewhat meaningless.

In my own feeble way, I tried to distinguish 'constitutionalism' from 'constitution' thus:

> The constitution is a set of rules and institutions that regulate the governing of the country. Constitutionalism is an ideology based on certain values, procedures, and practices. At one level, the concept of constitution is very simple: it is a text that is the supreme law of the land. Constitutions have been a way of consolidating power—as is well illustrated by colonial constitutions, but they have the same tendency, indeed purpose, in other contexts. The necessity of constitutionalism was to balance this state power, often enormous, armed with

> the police and the army, by granting rights to citizens and obliging the state not to transgress these rights—an act of restraint. In contemporary period, while some rights still relate to restraint by the state, other rights (socio-economic rights as well those on equality) require the state to undertake positive action in favour of citizens. Thus, the concept of constitutionalism at first focused on the supremacy of the constitution, as a means to control the people. Later it was used to limit the power of the state but in due course some powers had to be returned to the state. In a paradoxical way, constitutionalism now requires an activist rather than a passive state. But the "activism" is not unregulated; the state is no longer distanced from the people—instead the people are the state.

Several contemporary constitutions illustrate this point. The new constitutions are based on different values, procedures, and institutions, with the emphasis on nation building, participatory democracy, sharing of state power and resources, a strong regime of rights, particularly social and economic rights with a view to eliminating poverty, and preventing corruption. Some have called this new type of constitution (of which South Africa and Kenya are examples) transformative constitutions. Klare describes transformative constitutionalism as 'a long-term project of constitutional enactment, interpretation, and enforcement committed to transforming a country's political and social institutions and power relationships in a democratic, participatory, and egalitarian direction.'[51] This depicts the constitution as having the desired effect of social justice. However, to restore social justice a creative jurisprudence of equality coupled with substantive interpretation of the content of socio-economic rights should be considered.

It is uncontested that constitutionalism as we use it in this chapter is of western derivation. Its fundamental principles have not changed, though safeguards against abuse of power have increased. Since the state in contemporary Africa owes so much to its creation by the west (making it more powerful than any 'state' before colonialism), it is not unreasonable to look to it for safeguards against the abuse of that power. Questions like the following are pertinent: does the state in the West and in Africa serve similar functions and have similar responsibilities? If so, do we need different structures and authority from that in the west? For example, the relationship between the state and society may be quite different in the two regimes. In the West, much social control emanates from civil society; this is unlikely to be the case in Africa where the state occupies space which in the West is occupied by society.

More broadly, what is the relationship between the state, economy, and society? Does it differ significantly in Africa from that in the west? In Europe, the idea of the state and nation coincided a long time ago, but the colonial state was, almost deliberately, designed as multi-ethnic. The idea of constitutionalism as we understand it is based on the experience of western states. Central to that is an agreement under which the people have delegated power to the government—in most cases, the agreement takes the form of a constitution. The constitution represents the form of government, the structure of civil society, and the relations between the state and citizens that have developed over a long historical experience that are broadly acceptable to the people (the elite and masses) of the country. The constitution does not so much create public power or the relations between citizens among themselves, or between them and the state, as reflected in historical compromises which have ensured a substantial measure of stability and predictability. In Africa, the constitutions have been regarded as the means for creating structures and powers of the state, and the limitations on them. They seldom represent any continuity in the development of public power. They may not, indeed do not, have much connection with the reality of the depository of power or its accountability to society. But we continue to repose faith, or pretend to, in the document called the constitution, in the face of overwhelming evidence that it is a piece of paper (or rather, pieces of paper—constitutions have become very long!). The constitution is not a self-operating or self-executing instrument. The real task of establishing constitutionalism lies in other spheres: politics, the judiciary, the rise of professionalism, civic associations, and enlightened leadership. Perhaps the emphasis on constitutions (to the point that a new constitution is called for not only in cases of regime change, but also government change) has in that sense done Africa a disservice, distracting attention from the real task of building constitutionalism.

Notes and References

1. Perju's essay is published in Michel Rosenfeld and Andras Sajo (eds). 2012. *The Oxford Handbook of Comparative Constitutional Law*, p. 1317. Oxford: Oxford University Press.
2. Without derogating from Okoth-Ogendo's imagination and ability to marry theory and practice, the great interest shown in the US and Europe in his 'constitutions without constitutionalism' thesis is because his article was published in the USA (the first time I came across this expression was in Ben Nwabueze's book, *Constitutionalism in the Emergent States* in 1973. In my experience, US scholars make singularly little effort to study African or Asian scholarship. I discuss Nwabueze's book later.
3. See for example, Stephanie Balme and Michael (eds), *Building Constitutionalism in China* (New York: Palgrave Macmillan, 2009) and Albert H.Y. Chen (ed.), *Constitutionalism in Asia in the Early Twenty-First Century* (Cambridge: Cambridge University Press, 2014).

4. Okoth-Ogendo. 1988. 'Constitutions without Constitutionalism: Reflections on an African Political Paradox', Paper presented at a conference celebrating the 200th anniversary of the US's constitution, p. 67.
5. Albert Chen. 2014. *Constitutionalism in Asia in the Early Twenty-First Century*, p. 1.
6. Chen, *Constitutionalism in Asia*, pp. 1, 2.
7. Charles McIlwain. 1940. *Constitutionalism: Ancient and Modern*, (Ithaca, NY: Cornell University Press) pp. 9, 20. The full text seems to be available on the Constitution Society website at http://www.constitution.org/cmt/mcilw/mcilw.htm.
8. McIlwain, *Constitutionalism*, pp. 21–2, 20, 20–1, 22.
9. McIlwain, *Constitutionalism*, p. 91.
10. McIlwain, *Constitutionalism*, pp. 137–9
11. McIlwain, *Constitutionalism*, p. 136.
12. For his fuller critique of judicial review, see McIlwain, *Constitutionalism*, pp. 141–3.
13. See Yash Ghai for a discussion of Kenya's 2010 Constitution on judicial review ('Dilemmas for the Judiciary' in *The Nairobi Law Monthly*, pp. 46–51, December 2015).
14. Stanley de Smith, *The New Commonwealth and its Constitutions* (London: Stevens and Sons, 1964, p. 106).
15. *Constitutionalism and Democracy: Transitions in the Contemporary World* (New York: Oxford University Press, 1993) pp. 65–82.
16. *State and Constitutionalism: An African Debate on Democracy* (Harare, Zimbabwe: SAPES Books, 1991).
17. (Nairobi: Oxford University Press, 1970) Okoth-Ogendo cites our critique of narrow legal studies, eschewing 'politics ... and concentrating instead on a broad survey of the text of the constitution, other relevant laws and the few cases that [had] arisen in the courts on the constitution' (Preface p. v). Consequently, not merely the books themselves, but constitutional law and lawyers tended to be almost irrelevant to much academic discussion of political and economic development in Africa. (Okoth-Ogendo, 'Constitutions without Constitutionalism', p. 65). Okoth-Ogendo adds that much of the political science literature coming out of Africa in the 1960s and 1970s 'was mainly concerned with leadership styles and roles, elections and electoral behaviour, political parties and political mobilisation, etc., and did not relate these to the structural parameters within which they operated'.
18. Neither Okoth-Ogendo nor Shivji was necessarily dogmatic. The latter found much that was acceptable in Nyerere's socialist policies despite eschewing Marxism, while the former made his peace with President Moi, despite his strong attack on the kind of policies associated with Moi, to the extent that some thought he almost became his admirer.
19. Okoth-Ogendo, 'Constitutions without Constitutionalism', p. 67.
20. Okoth-Ogendo, 'Constitutions without Constitutionalism', p. 68. Nyerere in a speech to Parliament in 1965 (as Tanzania moved to a one-party constitution), reproduced in R. Martin, *Personal Freedom and the Law in Tanzania*

(Nairobi: Oxford, 1974), p. 47. Nyerere put a similar idea in another statement that Africa needed a constitution that acts as an accelerator rather than as a brake.

21. Okoth-Ogendo, 'Constitutions without Constitutionalism', pp. 68–9.
22. Okoth-Ogendo, 'Constitutions without Constitutionalism', p. 69.
23. Okoth-Ogendo, 'Constitutions without Constitutionalism', p. 70.
24. Okoth-Ogendo, 'Constitutions without Constitutionalism', p. 72.
25. Okoth-Ogendo, 'Constitutions without Constitutionalism', pp. 72–3.
26. The reference here is perhaps to Nelson Kasfir, *The Shrinking Political Arena* (Berkeley: University of California, 1976).
27. Okoth-Ogendo, 'Constitutions without Constitutionalism', p. 75.
28. Okoth-Ogendo, 'Constitutions without Constitutionalism', p. 80.
29. Shivji in *State and Constitutionalism,* pp. 33, 27.
30. Shivji in *State and Constitutionalism,* pp. 31, 32.
31. Shivji in *State and Constitutionalism,* pp. 33, 35, 37, 39
32. Ghai in *The Theory of the State,* p. 196.
33. Ghai in *The Theory of the State,* p. 196.
34. J.B. Ojwang, *Constitutional Development in Kenya: Institutional Adaptation and Social Change*, (Nairobi: Acts Press, 1990), p. 215. I discuss later a possible change in his position.
35. Ben Nwabueze. 1973. *Constitutionalism in the Emergent States*, (London: Hurst) p. 1.
36. Nwabueze, *Constitutionalism in the Emergent States*, p. 2.
37. Nwabueze, *Constitutionalism in the Emergent States*, p. 2.
38. Nwabueze, *Constitutionalism in the Emergent States*, p. 11.
39. For example, 'Authochthony, Nationhood and Development: A Review Article', *African Urban Quarterly*, vol. 2, 454 at 456 (1987).
40. 'Liberal Values in African Constitutional Development' African Society of International and Comparative Law, *Proceedings of the Third Annual Conference* Arusha 2–5 April 1991, p. 19, esp. p. 27.
41. Ascendant Judiciary in East Africa: reconfiguring the balance of power in a democratizing constitutional order (Nairobi: Strathmore University Press, 2013). Among the cases in which he has been involved is *Speaker of the Senate v Attorney-General* Advisory Opinion No. 2 of 2013, http:kenyalaw.org/caselaw/cases/view/91815/.
42. My discussion of An-Na'im is based on his book, *African Constitutionalism and the Role of Islam* (Philadelphia: University of Philadelphia Press, 2006).
43. An-Na'im, *African Constitutionalism*, p. viii.
44. An-Na'im, *African Constitutionalism*, p. 3.
45. An-Na'im, *African Constitutionalism*, p. 99.
46. An-Na'im, *African Constitutionalism*, pp. 100, 105, 107.
47. An-Na'im, *African Constitutionalism*, p. 109.
48. Pouwel. 1987. *Horn and Crescent: Cultural Change and Traditional Islam on the East African Coast.*
49. An-Na'im, pp. 208–9.

50. This section draws on my three articles: 'Creating a New Constitutional Order: Kenya's Predicament' in Elizabeth Gachenga, Luis Francheschi, Migai Akech, and David Lutz (eds), *Governance, Institutions and the Human Conditions* (Nairobi: Strathmore University, 2009)—this book was dedicated to Okoth-Ogendo; 'Constitutions and constitutionalism: the fate of the 2010 constitution' in Godwin Murunga, Duncan Okello, and Anders Sjogren (eds), *Kenya: The Struggle for a New Constitutional Order* (London: Zed Books, 2014); Yash Ghai and Jill Cottrell, 'State and Constitutionalism in Post-Colonial Africa', in Abdul Paliwala, Christopher McCrudden, and Upendra Baxi (eds) *Law's Ethical, Global and Theoretical Contexts: Essays in Honour of William Twining* (Cambridge: Cambridge University Press, 2015).
51. *S* v *Makwanyane* 1995 (6) BCLR 665 (CC), para 262 (per Mahomed J); *Bato Star Fishing (Pty) Ltd v Minister of Environmental Affairs and Tourism and Others* 2004 (7) BCLR 687 (CC); *Minister of Finance and Another v Van Heerden* 2004 (11) BCLR 1125 (CC); *Rates Action Group v City of Cape Town* 2004 (12) BCLR 1328 (C), para 100.25, pp. 72–3.

8

Establishing Judicial Review in China

Impediments and Prospects

Qianfan Zhang

I Introduction

Judicial review is commonly viewed as a necessary ingredient for constitutionalism, without which the constitution can hardly be put to effective use in real life. Judicial review of the constitutionality of legislative acts is also seen as a necessary check against the majoritarian abuse of legislative power. However, for China, a country governed neither by democracy nor by rule of law for millennia, the absence of judicial review is not surprising. And it is not alone among the 'socialist camp' in rejecting judicial review. Leftist ideology in socialist countries typically hyperbolizes popular sovereignty in opposition to any institutional control, not least against a judiciary commonly viewed as part of an undemocratic 'elite' minority. Thus, the current Constitution, enacted in 1982, is completely silent on the issue of judicial review. It neither authorizes ordinary courts nor establishes a special institution to engage in judicial review. As a result, there has not been a single constitutional case, so to speak, since the establishment of the Communist regime in 1949,[1] despite the fact that numerous issues of constitutional significance occur on a daily basis.

The long constitutional dormancy was briefly interrupted in 2001, when the Supreme People's Court (SPC) historically cited a constitutional provision in its reply to a provincial high court. In retrospect, this was a somewhat extraordinary event, viewed in the context of an ambitious judicial reform initiated two years before which aimed to fundamentally transform the status and role of judges. But that precedent for the judicial application of the constitution was never followed, and was repealed by the SPC itself without providing a reason in 2008, when judicial reform suffered a setback under the control of Zhou Yongkang, the chief in charge of the political and judicial affairs in the Politburo, and the new SPC president, Wang Shengjun. While Zhou is now being charged with corruption and Wang left the SPC presidency, the judicial application of the Constitution has not found new hope.

Divided into six parts, this chapter analyses China's existing mechanism of reviewing the constitutionality and legality of legislation and its deficiencies. The second part describes the *Qi Yuling case* and the failure to maintain a judicial review mechanism. The third part discusses some of the constitutional cases, mostly on equality, that are dealt with without reference to the Constitution. The fourth and fifth parts explore the political and legal context of the existing review mechanism, in which the role of the judiciary is minimized, and the limitations that inhere in the legislative review mechanism. The final part discusses the theoretical and practical impediments to establishing judicial review in China, and proposes several reforms aimed to improve the mechanism for ensuring conformity to China's Constitution and the laws.

II Establishing Judicial Review?

II.1 The Qi Yuling Case of 2001

The case of *Qi Yuling v Chen Xiaoqi et al.* is now a desolate milestone in the constitutional history of China.[2] In 1990, Qi Yuling passed the entrance examination for specialized secondary professions (*zhongzhuan*) and was admitted by Jining Commercial School (Shandong province). But her admission letter was stolen by her classmate, Chen Xiaoqi, who then studied under her name and went on to take a good job in a bank upon graduation. Qi found out about the whole affair only a decade later, during which she had unsuccessfully sought to find a good job, owing to her lack of technical education. After she initiated litigation, the middle-level court of Tengzhou (Shangdong province) ordered the defendants to pay RMB¥35,000 for the emotional damage caused by the infringement of Qi's right to her name, which is protected by civil law, but the court declined to provide a remedy for the alleged violation of her right to education, which is protected in Article 46 of the 1982 Constitution.

During appeal, in an extremely succinct reply to the request of the Shandong High Court for judicial interpretation, the SPC held that the plaintiff's 'basic right to education as provided by the Constitution' was violated.[3] This was the first case in which the SPC explicitly cited a constitutional provision as the legal ground for a judicial decision or interpretation. The Shandong High Court went on to order the defendants to pay RMB¥100,000 for the loss that Qi suffered from the infringement of her constitutional right to education. The decision, often hailed as China's 'first constitutional case' since it formally 'judicializes' the Constitution,[4] shocked the legal community and generated a large body of academic literature debating the propriety of 'constitutional judicialization'.[5]

Despite minor technical problems, the first constitutional case did offer some bright hope, not only for the right to education specifically but also for the promotion of constitutionalism as a whole. Western experiences almost unanimously suggest that the words of a constitution do not count unless it is somehow 'judicialized'—in the US by ordinary courts, in France by the special Constitutional Council and in Germany by federal and state constitutional courts. Had it been allowed to develop under its own momentum, China's constitutionalism could have travelled along a similar path, and the *Qi Yuling* case might now have been known as China's *Marbury v Madison*.[6]

II.2 The Failure of 'Constitutional Judicialization'

Unfortunately, subsequent developments quashed the prospect of developing constitutionally enforceable rights. Chinese judges have not taken any steps to consolidate their power in the aftermath of the *Qi Yuling* case; on the contrary, they have chosen to avoid invoking the Constitution. Since 2001, there has not been a single 'constitutional case' to speak of. This is not to say that the People's Republic has not made any progress on constitutional issues. Indeed, in recent years there have been several cases on equality in which the plaintiffs won, either in or outside the courts, but none were decided on constitutional grounds.

More fundamentally, the judicial application of the Constitution has been viewed as a potential threat to the leadership of the Chinese Communist Party (CCP). It was rumoured that the SPC circulated an internal directive forbidding courts from following the *Qi Yuling* decision, which might have explained the de facto demise of the potential precedent. In any case, the new SPC president who assumed the post in 2007 seemed to be dissatisfied even with its dysfunctional existence and moved to explicitly delete the *Qi Yuling* case from the case book. In December 2008, the SPC published a document that officially voided the legal effect of several outdated judicial explanations, among which the *Qi Yuling* case was the only one voided without so even a brief explanation.[7] In retrospect, the demise of the *Qi Yuling* case came as no surprise. It was the product of Huang Songyou, the then progressive chief judge of the civil section of the SPC; he was under investigation for corruption by 2008,[8] and the constitutional progress he helped to initiate came to an end along with his judicial career.

The failure of the judicial experiment with constitutional review vividly illustrates the powerless and dependent status of China's judiciary and particularly that of individual judges. While rank-and-file judges are obliged to follow the direction of their court presidents, lower courts are obliged to follow the direction of higher courts, and the SPC is dominated by its president. The SPC president himself is but a cadre of middle rank in the power echelon of the party and is under the leadership of the Central Politics and Law Commission (PLC), the secretary of which used to be a member (among nine) of the Politburo Standing Committee (PSC) headed by the secretary-general of the CCP, the most powerful decision-making institution in China today. Such practice is *not* followed in the recent regime turnover, where the number of PSC members is reduced to seven, and the secretary of the Central PLC is no longer one of them. However, General Secretary Xi Jinping has established numerous 'groups' (*xiaozu*) within the ruling party, most of which are directly headed by himself. The most recent judicial reform is orchestrated by a group in charge of 'deepening reform' and the Central PLC.

In any case, the courts in China remain dependent on the political will of the ruling party, which apparently opposes the idea that the courts shall have anything to do with the Constitution. The SPC president, who is in charge of drafting and implementing plans for judicial reform, merely follows and executes the directive of the ruling party. Thus, when the president changes during a shift in the political leadership, so does the direction of judicial and constitutional reform. The recent Decision issued at the end of the Third Plenum of the 18th Congress of the CCP opened a new era for judicial reform and rehabilitated the professionalization reform initiated in 1999.[9] Indeed, it expressly highlights the importance of improving the procedure of constitutional application so as to strengthen the legal effect of the Constitution. But the Decision says nothing about the judicial role in implementing the Constitution, and it seems unlikely that the First Constitutional Case will be rehabilitated in the foreseeable future. The lack of institutional independence thus preordained the premature death of the judicially initiated experiment with constitutional review.

III Protecting Rights in Spite of the Constitution? Taking Equality as an Example

Despite its failure, the First Constitutional Case illustrates that the courts can be crucially important to the future of Chinese constitutional law. If the constitution is 'judicialized' through right to education, the judicialization may in turn bring the realization of this right as well as other rights stipulated in the Constitution to a new height. Most significantly, Article 33 of the Constitution explicitly dictates that 'all citizens are equal before law', and presumably also before the education laws. If this provision is directly enforceable, the Chinese courts *can* become the most effective organ for combating the now ubiquitous inequality and discrimination officially sanctioned, as is clearly demonstrated in the practices regarding education.[10] One can even hope that Article 33 (or similar provisions in future constitutions) might play a role as important as the Fourteenth Amendment has done in the US.

Indeed, since the *Qi Yuling* case, there have been several cases specifically based on the equality clause of Article 33. In the *Bank Employment Advertisement* case (2002),[11] the Chengdu Branch of the People's Bank of China put up an employment advertisement, which limited applicants to certain majors and educational qualifications. In addition to those, however, the bank also required the heights of male and female applicants to be above 168 cm and 155 cm, respectively. Jiang Tao, one of the male applicants and a law student at Sichuan University at that time, fell short of the height requirement. He alleged that the bank infringed his constitutionally guaranteed equal right to a public post. The court of the Wuhou district, Chengdu, decided that the employment practice was not an 'administrative act' (*xingzheng xingwei*) in the sense of exercising its administrative management functions as defined in law. Plus, the defendant bank had already revised its advertisement and deleted the height restrictions after the litigation was initiated and before the effective date of application. Thus, the court declined to judge against the bank. It should be pointed out that, unlike the *Qi Yulin* case, this case was litigated against the proper defendant—a state-owned bank.[12] The rationale given by the court with respect to the nature of the act was quite suspicious, since there is little reason to exclude the bank employment process from the purview of its 'administrative acts'.

Employment of civil servants in China is subject to a variety of discriminating limitations. Frequent complaints have been made against the criterion for excluding non-infectious hepatitis-B virus carriers, recently leading to a tragedy in which an applicant was rejected on the ground of committing manslaughter out of sheer fury. In the *Hepatitis-B Virus* Case (2004), the government of Anhui province was sued for maintaining such a restriction in admitting civil servants. The victim charged that such health criterion constituted discrimination in violation of Article 33 and his constitutionally protected interest in taking public post. The court of Wuhu city (Anhui) held the concrete decision of rejecting admissions invalid on the ground of 'insufficient evidence', but eschewed the constitutional grounds. In fact, the chief judge of the administrative section of Anhui High Court believed that constitutional equality is limited only to the application of relevant laws in the administrative process rather than legal classifications themselves.[13] Such a limited understanding, used to be taken for granted in the legal community and is still not uncommon among the Chinese officials, obviously serves as an impediment to a general application of the equality clause.

More recently, women have become active in vindicating their equal rights in employment practice. After the communists took over power, gender equality was a priority in policy agenda, and women were given early retirements out of consideration for their health conditions. Yet the implications of such gender policy changed over the years, and what used to mean a privilege may now be considered a disadvantage. Nowadays it is a settled practice for female employees in state-owned enterprises to retire at the age of fifty-five and their male counterparts at sixty, but earlier retirement meant to women a loss of job opportunities and a cut in wages. A woman employee who just reached the retirement age challenged the employment policy of China Construction Bank (Mount Pingding Branch), which is based on the State Council's Provisional Method for Allocating Old, Weak, Sick, and Handicapped Cadres, which has been in force since 1978. She argues that she is in excellent health condition and can perform her professional functions with competence; therefore, the early retirement policy violates both Article 33 of the Constitution and relevant provisions in labour law regarding gender equality. The dispute has been forwarded to the labour arbitration board of Mount Pingding city.

Since China lacks a mechanism for constitutional adjudication, all the cases of constitutional nature have been dealt with *not* by constitutional litigations, but by administrative litigations or other means. This is the most obvious and most fundamental limitation for the Chinese constitutional cause. At this stage, we can only hope that constitutional rights can find some protection in the administrative section of the Chinese courts through continuing improvements in the processes of administrative justice, which can hopefully provide a springboard for establishing a formal mechanism for constitutional adjudication. It does not seem optimistic that the Chinese judiciary will live up to that hope.

IV Ensuring Uniformity of Laws in a Unitary State

The procedure for constitutional review is, however, not completely absent in China. It only means that the review is not done or to be done by the courts, but by other institutions. Article 67 of the 1982 Constitution provides that the Standing Committee of the National People's Congress (NPCSC) has the authority to 'interpret the Constitution and supervise its implementation'. Thus, the Constitution provides for a legislative rather than judicial review. Unfortunately, the NPCSC has been woefully deficient in fulfilling its constitutional mandate. Since 1982, although it has interpreted many laws, including the Basic Law of Hong Kong, it has never interpreted a single provision of the Constitution despite a number of laws and regulations suspected to be in serious violation of the Constitution. In the landmark event which caused the death of Sun Zhigang in 2003, for example, the notorious Detention and Repatriation Method was publically challenged for violating the Constitution (Article 37 protecting personal freedom) and the Law on Legislation (or LL; Article 8 requiring the compulsory restriction of personal freedom to be authorized by law), but the NPCSC failed to take any action.[14]

Failure to interpret and implement the Constitution not only leaves the constitutional rights unenforced, but also reduces the uniformity of the entire legal system since the Constitution, according to its own Preamble, 'is the fundamental law of the state and has supreme legal authority'. In fact, due to judicial inaction and the lack of an alternative effective mechanism for interpreting and applying laws, laws enacted by the National People's Congress (NPC) and its Standing Committee are often left helpless before the encroachments of local regulations and practices, producing pervasive local protectionism. During the last three decades of reform, local authorities have gained freedom to provide for local interests, and conflicts between local and central legislation have become inevitable. The problem is especially acute for a giant country like China, where central and local legislative competences are not constitutionally delimited. Article 3 of the 1982 Constitution merely states a vague principle of 'giving full scope to the initiative and enthusiasm of the local authorities under the unified leadership of the central authorities', which provides little guidance for dividing the central and local functions. As a result, China's centre–local relationship has been trapped in a rather lawless state, in which conflict between legislation at different levels, commonly known as 'legislation fighting', has been both pervasive and perennial.

In 2000, the LL was enacted precisely to curb legislation fighting by specifying the order of legal norms and their law-making procedures, as well as the ways to resolve legislative conflict. In this sense it is the 'law of laws', with a prominent status next to the Constitution.[15] Unlike the Constitution of the

US, the LL does not provide an absolute principle of national supremacy but employs a complex ex post facto review procedure to resolve the conflicts between local regulations and national legislation that is below the level of administrative regulations. If a discrepancy occurs between a local rule and an administrative rule, or between administrative rules concerning a similar matter, a ruling shall be made by the State Council (Article 86.3). If a discrepancy occurs between a local regulation and an administrative rule concerning the same matter, then the process becomes more cumbersome: 'The State Council shall give its opinion; where the State Council deems that the local regulation should apply, in the local jurisdiction the local regulation shall be applied; where the State Council deems that the administrative rule should apply, it shall request the Standing Committee of the National People's Congress to make a ruling.'[16]

Since China lacks a centralized mechanism for reviewing the legality of legislation, the LL is at pains to define a complex hierarchy of reviewing authorities. Generally, a state institution has the authority to review legislation enacted by another situated one level below it in the constitutional hierarchy, and an enabling agency has the authority to directly invalidate delegated legislation beyond the scope of authorization or inconsistent with the objective of the enabling decision (Article 88.7). For example, while the NPC has the power to 'amend or withdraw any inappropriate law enacted by its Standing Committee' (Article 88.1) and to 'amend or withdraw any inappropriate administrative rule or local rule' (Article 88.3), the NPCSC has the power to invalidate, among other things, any administrative regulation that contravenes the Constitution or any law, and any local regulation that contravenes the Constitution or any law or administrative regulation (Article 88.2). Likewise, while the State Council has the authority to amend or invalidate an inappropriate departmental or provincial rule (Article 88.2), a provincial Local People's Government (LPG) has the power to amend or withdraw any inappropriate local rule enacted by the LPG at the next lower level (Article 88.6). To facilitate legislative review, an inferior agency is obliged to report its legislation within 30 days of its promulgation to its superior (Articles 88 and 89). This complex setup of cascading review aims to ensure the legality of legislation at all levels.

Finally, the LL grants to state institutions, social organizations, and individual citizens the right to request a review of legislative conflict. Unlike judicial review, which usually requires personal standing to initiate review procedures, China's legislative review process may be initiated by almost anyone. First, Article 90 provides that certain state institutions can request and initiate the review process by right, even though such a request has never been put forward since the promulgation of the LL in 2000. The State Council, the CMC, the SPC, the Supreme People's Procuratorate, a special committee of the NPCSC or a standing committee of a provincial LPC may all make written requests to the NPCSC for review if they deem that an administrative regulation or local regulation contravenes the Constitution or any law. The 'working office' of the NPCSC, the Legal Affairs Commission (LAC), distributes such requests to the relevant special committees of the NPC for review and comment, a process that may eventually lead to the NPCSC deliberating on and deciding the matter.

Second, a private citizen or social group may also make written proposals to the NPCSC for review if any of the above kinds of legislation is deemed to contravene the Constitution or any law, but their proposals will be 'studied' by the LAC and distributed to the relevant special committee for review and comments only 'where necessary' (LL, Article 90, para 2). So far, although hundreds and perhaps even thousands of such private requests have been made, none of them has been deemed 'necessary' enough to initiate the review process; even the request made by legal scholars to invalidate the egregious Detention and Repatriation Measures, which was repealed shortly afterwards by the State Council itself, failed to initiate the review process in the aftermath of the Sun Zhigang incident. In fact, although a special office has been created for 'regulatory review and record' in 2005 under the LAC, it has never even published the list of requests received, making it impossible to assess the number or nature of such requests. In any case, despite the minimal standing requirement, private individuals have never been able to trigger the seemingly well-designed albeit convoluted review process provided for by LL, while no public institution has ever even bothered to try.

V Limitations of the Law on Legislation

As the 'law of laws', yet seldom if ever used since its promulgation in China, LL suffers from several serious limitations. First, although its original purpose was to curb legislation fighting, it has done little to strengthen the uniformity of national legislation and to clarify the order of different norms below administrative regulations. In contrast to a federal system such as that of the US, where federal powers are limited to those granted in the Constitution but have supremacy vis-à-vis state and local legislation,[17] China's central legislation needs no constitutional grant; however, they are not supreme over local legislation in the complete sense—a departmental rule is not necessarily superior to a local regulation or rule, even if it is entirely consistent with national laws and regulations that in turn comply with the Constitution. Far from curbing legislation fights, LL runs the serious risk of encouraging conflict between legislative acts that sit below the level of administrative regulations. While it may accommodate local diversity and prevent 'cutting across the board with one knife' by departmental rules or decisions, it undermines legal uniformity as a basic requirement of the rule of law.

Second, it is not only impossible to decide a priori the rank of a departmental rule vis-à-vis a local regulation or rule, but it is also extremely difficult to apply the review mechanism in practice. If a conflict between a departmental rule and provincial regulation or rule occurs, a request for review will have to be submitted to the State Council, an extremely busy bureaucratic centre that has only one Legal Affairs Office (LAO) (*fazhiban*) to handle issues of legislative conflict, and this results in long delays in conflict resolution. Adding to that agony, if the State Council decides for its department against a provincial regulation, the matter will have to be appealed further to the NPCSC, which is preoccupied with its own legislative agenda.[18] This process is meant to both temper the natural inclination of the State Council toward its own departments, which would disqualify it as a neutral arbitrator in dispute resolution, and make up for any democratic deficiency inherent in a process where the national administration imposes its decisions on locally elected People's Congresses. In reality, however, it simply prolongs an already lengthy process and creates further delays.

On the whole, both the State Council and the NPCSC are preoccupied with their own administrative and legislative work and thus can hardly devote significant time to resolving pervasive legislation fighting in such a massive state as China or to processing the massive number of individual complaints that are made possible by the lack of a standing requirement. Timely resolution of legal conflicts requires a far more decentralized process, whereby impartial judicial institutions across the country are able to take up and speedily dispense with the local complaints.

This leads to the third and most important point: the conspicuous absence of courts in the entire review process. Indeed, LL completely leaves out the courts. This is consistent with the old version of Administration Litigation Law (ALL), which limits the scope of judicial review to 'concrete administrative acts' and does not extend to 'abstract administrative acts' such as laws, regulations (*fagui*), rules (*guizhang*), or any normative documents of general nature.[19] In fact, the courts are obliged to take laws and regulations as 'legal grounds' and rules as 'references' (*canzhao*) in adjudications (Article 51). Although the new version of ALL, revised in 2014, does not explicitly limit the scope of review to concrete as opposed to abstract administrative acts, it does exclude the jurisdiction over 'administrative regulations and rules or decisions and orders with general binding force developed and issued by administrative agencies' (Article 13, para 2).

A small breakthrough is made in Article 53 of ALL, which now allows citizens to challenge the legality of a normative document below the level of rules in litigation against a concrete administrative act. If the court finds such norm to be legally groundless, it shall not take that as the ground for holding the administrative act legal, and shall recommend a solution to the agency that enacted the norm (Article 64). Such a small step does not, however, change the overall characterization of China's courts as an inadequate and powerless institution for resolving the conflicts of laws.

That the courts play little role in resolving conflicts in legislation merely reinforces the impression that the review provided for in the LL is purely legislative—or more accurately, political rather than judicial in nature. Not only is the review of legislation directed to purely abstract norms with no requirements about personal standing—and is thus able to avoid the concrete cases and controversies normally associated with judicial review—but when review is conducted by a non-judicial institution without the guidance of any higher legal principles such as the supremacy of national legislation, legal criteria are completely absent. When the State Council or the NPCSC confronts a conflict between a departmental rule and a provincial regulation deemed to be of the same rank, what can possibly be the legal ground that predictably governs its ruling except ad hoc policy considerations? As a result, the legislative review contemplated in Article 90 of LL is nothing but ad hoc law-making by the reviewing agency, which does so at best with a vague idea of the relevant situation at the time of review. For other review systems in which the hierarchy of legal norms is well defined, such clear violations of higher norms as found in the Detention and Repatriation Measures can meaningfully be reviewed even without a concrete case, but they are best conducted by an impartial institution of a judicial nature since, as Chief Justice Marshall pointed out in *Marbury v Madison*: 'It is emphatically the province and duty of the judicial department to say what the law is.'[20] Unfortunately, the courts in China are excluded from this task, leaving the basic objective of curbing legislation fights unfulfilled.

Not surprising, then, that precisely two centuries after the *Marbury* decision, a similar case appeared in Luoyang, Henan province, but the very opposite result was reached. The case itself was simple enough: a seed company agreed with the plaintiff to provide an amount of corn seed but defaulted by selling the seed to other parties at market price. The dispute came to the Luoyang City Court in 2003, focusing on the amount of damages liable to the plaintiff. While the plaintiff insisted on payment of the market price according to the Seed Law enacted by the NPCSC, which would amount to damages of CNY¥700,000, the defendant, citing Article 36 of the Henan Provincial Regulation on Crop Seeds enacted by the provincial LPCSC, claimed that the 'government guidance price' should be the standard for calculating the damage, which would amount to CNY¥20,000. The assistant judge presiding over the case, Li Huijuan, found for the plaintiff, interpreting the Seed Law as having established the principle of applying a market price standard. Since the Henan Regulation was local legislation, which is below the level of national law in the legal hierarchy, its provision that conflicted with the Seed Law was null and void.[21]

The case did not even implicate any constitutional provisions as *Marbury* did, although the nature of the question was similar: does the court have *any* power to review abstract norms, if only to safeguard the supremacy of the Constitution and national laws? And the answer provided by the Luoyang court was commonsensical enough in any jurisdiction committed to rule of law: of course, the court, through the pivotal role of judicial review, is obliged to maintain a rational legal order, and reason dictates that a higher law be given effect, notwithstanding lower laws to the contrary. But the Henan provincial LPCSC reacted strongly against the decision and forced the City Court to renounce the judgment.[22] When the courts are unable to defend the law, local protectionism necessarily runs amuck, fatally damaging the uniformity of the entire legal system.

VI Impediments and Prospects

Both the *Qi Yuling* and the *Corn Seed* cases illustrate the necessity for establishing some form of judicial review in China. While the *Qi Yuling* case proves positively the importance of courts for protecting constitutional rights, the *Corn Seed* case shows negatively that the legal system will fall into disorder if courts are prevented from playing an effective role in enforcing the constitution and national laws. Repealing the legal effect of the SPC reply to the *Qi Yuling* case, thus foreclosing the judicial remedy to constitutional violations, merely leaves the Constitution unenforced. When the courts cannot apply the Constitution in adjudicating cases, the constitutional issues cannot adequately be dealt with. As the equality cases amply illustrated, the principle of administrative legality is no substitute for constitutionality, not to mention that the Chinese courts are severely handicapped in reviewing the legality of administrative acts.

On the theoretical ground, some argue that judicial review is impeded in China by a parliamentary system akin to that of the Westminster Hall. [23]

According to A.V. Dicey, the British do not accept judicial review because the House of Commons is thought to be the supreme legislator, whose legislative initiatives cannot be arrested by judges.[24] They further argue, citing populist critics in the US, that judicial review is undemocratic in the sense that it allows a few judges unaccountable to the populace to strike down, in the interest of elite minorities, legislations enacted by popularly elected representatives, hence the counter-majoritarian difficulty.[25] These arguments seem to make a point, but only superficially. To begin with, if Dicey's argument still holds true today, it is because the British legal system differs fundamentally from that of China since it does *not* have a written constitution as the 'higher law' in its legal system, so that the British judges have nothing against which to review the parliamentary legislation. As soon as the UK changes this feature of its legal system and enact any law higher than ordinary legislation, its judges will immediately confront the same question raised by Chief Justice Marshall over two centuries ago: if a law 'be in opposition to the constitution; if both the law and the constitution apply to a particular case … the court must determine which of these conflicting rules governs the case', and of course the only reasonable answer is that 'an act of the legislature, repugnant to the constitution, is void'.[26] Since the task of statutory interpretation and conflict resolution is traditionally relegated to the courts, judicial review will immediately come into being as a natural consequence of resolving any legal conflicts that might arise between the higher law and ordinary laws. Indeed, the British situation has already been changed in 1998, when the Human Rights Act incorporated the European Convention of Human Rights and empowered the British judges to review legislation and make declarations of any incompatibility with the Act. Although the House of Commons may choose to ignore such a declaration, it has in fact respected every judicial declaration the court has made so far, so that the declaratory scheme has already been categorized as a 'weak' form of judicial review.[27]

Although China's NPC, much like the British House of Commons, is the supreme body which elects the key positions in the state, including the judges, and to which all these positions are held accountable, China differs from the UK in a key aspect that it does have a written constitution, which defines itself in the Preamble as 'the fundamental law of the state' with 'supreme legal authority'. It further commands 'all state organs … must take the constitution as the fundamental standard of conduct'. Article 5 of the Constitution dictates explicitly that

> No laws or administrative or local regulations shall contravene the Constitution.
>
> All state organs … shall abide by the Constitution and the laws. All acts in violation of the Constitution or the laws must be investigated.

No organization or individual is privileged to be beyond the Constitution or the laws.

Here, 'all state organs' obviously include the NPC and its Standing Committee. It is certainly possible that the NPC or its Standing Committee enacts a law that contravenes the Constitution, so that it is necessary to establish a mechanism that reviews the constitutionality of laws. Neither the NPC nor its Standing Committee is suitable for such a vocation since they would violate the basic principle of impartiality by judging their own cases—the constitutionality of legislations they make. Unfortunately, Article 67 clause 1 of the Constitution does just that by authorizing the Standing Committee 'to interpret the Constitution and supervise its enforcement'. For reason just explained, however, this clause should not be interpreted as authorizing the Standing Committee to be the *sole* body capable of interpreting the Constitution. At least the Constitution never prohibits other state institutions to interpret the Constitution. Indeed, they are required, just as the NPC or its Standing Committee is, to 'take the constitution as the fundamental standard of conduct'. How do they take the Constitution as their 'fundamental standard of conduct' without even understanding and interpreting it, particularly on occasions where the Standing Committee fails to provide any interpretive guidance? And the Standing Committee has failed to do that ever since the Constitution was enacted in 1982. Thus far, it has never produced a single constitutional interpretation, a crucial task that Article 67 of the Constitution entrusts to it. Does that mean that the enforcement of the Constitution is entirely at the mercy of the Standing Committee, and should be left unenforced when it has failed to any take action? Is it not much more reasonable to interpret Article 67 as conferring only the interpretive power of last resort to the Standing Committee, while allowing other state institutions to make their own constitutional interpretations, as long as they do not contradict the Standing Committee interpretation, if there is one?

Since the Constitution characterizes itself as 'the fundamental law', and since the court is in charge of daily application and interpretation of laws, it seems only natural that the courts should have the authority to interpret the Constitution. More than that, the judicial interpretation of the Constitution should bind all state institutions other than the NPC and the Standing Committee. In other words, the judicial interpretation of the Constitution should be inferior only to that of the Standing Committee (and occasionally, to the NPC if it takes the initiative to apply the Constitution, a highly unlikely event). Indeed, this is precisely the way in which the normal interpretive business is conducted in China. In areas such as civil, criminal and procedural laws, the Standing Committee often issues official interpretations, which bind the courts and other state institutions to interpret and apply these laws. The same Article 67 in its Clause 4 authorizes the Standing Committee 'to interpret the laws' and this clause has never been interpreted as prohibiting, against the common sense, the courts to interpret laws. What is the rationale to interpret the two clauses of the same article to mean the opposite? True, the courts are not authorized to review the legality of, say, a regulation made by the State Council in implementing a law, but if the court finds that regulation to be inconsistent with either the Standing Committee interpretation or its own interpretation of a relevant law, then good policy counsels against applying the regulation, just as Judge Li Huijuan declined to apply the Henan provincial regulation in the *Corn Seed* case. Anyway, there is nothing in sound jurisprudence that prevents courts from interpreting and applying the Constitution as the fundamental law in adjudicating cases. Quite to the contrary, the Constitution binds courts just as any law does, and imposes upon them the duty to properly interpret and apply the fundamental law of the state to concrete cases.

Nor is the counter-majoritarian difficulty anything serious to worry about once the courts begin to apply the Constitution in China. The difficulty is felt acutely in the US, primarily because it has, in James Bryce's term, a 'rigid constitution'. Since the text of the US Constitution is difficult to amend, the Supreme Court has become the de facto supreme interpreter of the Constitution. In Chief Justice Hughes's perhaps exaggerated expression in his 1907 speech, 'We are under a Constitution, but the Constitution is what the judges say it is'.[28] During the New Deal, the Supreme Court even obviated the state democratic process of the heavy burden of constitutional amendment by changing its constitutional interpretation. As a result, the American constitutional dialogue is dominated by the Supreme Court, which in effect has the final say on what the Constitution means. Even if that is a serious difficulty with the constitutional process in the US, it is irrelevant to China since the 1982 Constitution is rather flexible, requiring only two-thirds majority of the NPC to amend the text, and has since been amended four times, adding such new principles as rule of law and respect for human rights and private property to the Constitution.[29] Even if the court errs in a constitutional interpretation, it can be overturned by the NPC amending the constitutional text. In most cases, however, it needs not even to go that far, since the judicial interpretation can easily be overridden by the Standing Committee interpretation if it chooses to act. If the court is authorized to interpret the Constitution in China, it is expected to engage itself in a healthy dialogue with the NPC and its Standing Committee, among other state institutions, rather than dominating the constitutional interpretation as in the US. And, even in the US, hardly anyone seriously challenges the legitimacy of judicial review per se and proposes its total abolition; but rather the debates focus on the proper functions of judicial review so as to make it fit congenially with democracy. As this article has shown, prohibiting judicial review raises the serious question whether the Constitution has any meaning at all without judicial review of legislation.

The alternative, legislative review mechanism, as laid out in LL, has proven to be ineffective for ensuring the supremacy of the Constitution and the laws in China. To make the words of the Constitution and the laws count, then, serious institutional reforms are in order to take place. A common proposal raised by China's legal community is to establish a constitutional committee to oversee the interpretation and implementation of the Constitution. It will be best, of course, if such committee can maintain an independent status, much like a court. Under the current dominant understanding, however, such an independent institution seems to be incompatible with the supremacy of the NPC, which supposedly represents the will of the nation through its legislation. Alternative arrangements are to place the constitutional committee as a special committee within the NPC or its Standing Committee. As an initial step, for example, the constitutional committee can be a working agency on behalf and under the direction of the NPCSC. Under such situation, the mechanism of constitutional review can be established even without amending the Constitution. The reviewing committee can simply deal with ordinary constitutional claims on daily basis, with the NPCSC acting as a rubber stamp and intervening only in politically important cases. The constitutional committee may become more formally independent when it gains more experience and reputation. So far, however, there has been no sign that even the modest constitutional design is within the purview of the ruling party.

Despite the setback of the *Qi Yuling* case as an experiment of 'judicializing' the Constitution, the role of courts cannot simply be cast aside. Even if constitutional issues are politically too 'sensitive' to be handled by courts, at least they should be sufficiently empowered to decide the *Corn Seed* case, that is, to review the legality of abstract norms and resolve the conflicts among legislations of different order. Otherwise the unitary 'socialist' state will be reduced by local protectionism of various sorts into a feudal fiefdom with a fragmented legal system. Whether any special institution is established for ensuring the constitutionality of legal acts, the existing mechanism of legal interpretation needs fundamental reform. Either courts shall be authorized to review the legality of regulations and rules of administrative nature, thus becoming a regular institution for resolving the conflict of laws, or a specialized judicial mechanism is to be established for reviewing the legal norms.[30] It is apparently more consistent with the order of things that the principle of legality in the ordinary sense be observed before introducing mechanism to ensure the constitutionality of all laws.

Till now, however, the same force that has handicapped China's rule of law has handicapped its constitutionalism. The lack of judicial review is far from a purely theoretical question as I have shown that nothing in the Chinese constitutional jurisprudence prevents courts from taking the Constitution seriously. Nor is the total absence of the Standing Committee interpretation, in spite of the constitutional mandate in Article 67, a pure accident. The NPC, its Standing Committee, and the courts all depend on the ruling Communist Party, which is yet to make up its mind to bind itself by the Constitution and laws, despite its high-pitch commitment to 'build a socialist state of rule of law' avowed in Article 5 of the Constitution. It is particularly difficult for a socialist state to establish rule of law and constitutionalism since the ruling party, with its totalitarian legacy, is above all limitations and refuses to be bound by the limits of law. In 2003, the same year that the *Corn Seed* case was decided, I wrote that China's rule of law is; limited by the ultimate political bottom line: a party that is essentially above the law'.[31] Very much the same can be said today about China's prospect of constitutionalism and judicial review.

Notes and References

1. The same can be said about the Republican regime that was defeated by the Communists and retreated to Taiwan in 1949. It enacted in 1949 the Constitution of the Republic of China, which is still effective in Taiwan. The Republic of China Constitution does authorize the Conference of Justices to engage in judicial review, but the mechanism has never had the chance to operate in mainland China during the barely two years when the constitution was effective.
2. *Guangming Daily*. 2001. 'Right to Education Is Not to be Violated: The Topic Introduced by the First Case on Violation of Right to Education', 4 September.
3. 'Reply regarding whether One who Violated the Constitutionally Protected Basic Right to Education of the Citizen should Bear Civil Obligation' (2001) *Judicial Interpretation* 25.
4. To be precise, this was not the 'first case' in which the Constitution was cited as ground for a judicial decision, since several local civil courts had done so in their judgments before; but it was the first time the SPC explicitly affirmed that constitutional provisions can be cited as independent grounds for judgment.
5. *Southern Weekend.* 2001. 'The Admission Theft Event Triggered the First Case of Constitutional Judicialisation', 16 August.

6. 137 US 5 (1803).
7. 'The Seventh Decision of the Supreme People's Court to Repeal Relevant Judicial Interpretations Released before 2007', 18 December 2008. Most of these judicial interpretations were voided either because their effective period had expired or because the circumstances in which they were enacted had changed.
8. He was charged for corruption and sentenced to life imprisonment. Zhu Yan, 'Disagreeing with the Trial Sentence, Huang Songyou Will Appeal', *New Beijing Daily*, 29 January 2010.
9. The CCP Decision on Several Important Issues Concerning Comprehensively Deepening the Reform.
10. To just give one example, the students who are residents in the major cities, especially Beijing and Shanghai, can be admitted by the best colleges located in these cities at grades that are as many as a hundred points lower than students from other places.
11. *Jiang Tao v People's Bank of China*, Chengdu Branch, see Zhang Qianfan. 2004. *Introduction to Studies of Constitutional Law* (*Xianfaxue Daolun*), pp. 503–4. Beijing: Law Press.
12. An earlier case encountered the same defendant standing problem as the Qi Yulin Case did. In the Restaurant Advertisement Case (2000), a private restaurant in Chengdu advertised that state servants could enjoy a deduction from the normal food price. Several law students at Sichuan University sued this practice on the ground of Article 33. The court in that case quite properly declined jurisdiction as the civil activities were to be governed by the General Principle of Civil Law (*Minfa Tongze*), not the Constitution.
13. Zhou Wei. 2004. *Study of Judical Remedies of Constitutional Fundamental Rights* (*Xianfa Jiben Quanli Sifa Jiuji Yanjiu*), p. 100. Beijing: China People's Public Security University.
14. Qianfan Zhang. 2012. *The Constitution of China: A Contextual Analysis*, pp. 75–80. London: Hart Publishing Co.
15. For a concise explanation of the Chinese legal structure, see Albert (Hongyi) Chen. 2011. *An Introduction to Legal System of the People's Republic of China*, Chapters 1 and 2. (4th edition) LexisNexis Butterworths.
16. LL, Art 86.2.
17. Constitution of the United States of America, Article 6.
18. Zhang, *The Constitution of China*, pp. 84–96.
19. Zhang, *The Constitution of China*, pp. 160–8.
20. *Marbury v Madison*, 5 US 137 (1803).
21. Guo Guosong. 2003. 'The Judge Stroke Struck? Down a Local Regulation: Is She Violating the Law or Vindicating the Law', *Southern Weekend*, 20 November.
22. Zhang, *The Constitution of China*, pp. 84–96.
23. Fei Shancheng. 1999. 'On the Choice of Constitutional Review Models in China', *Tribune of Political Science and Law*, vol. 2: 5–6.
24. A.V. Dicey. 1915. *Introduction to the Study of the Law of the Constitution* (8th ed.), p. 39. London: Macmillan.

25. For a critique, see Zhang Qianfan.2009. 'Judicial Review and Democracy: A Community of Contraries?', *Global Law Review*, vol. 1, pp. 58–66.
26. *Marbury v Madison*, 5 US 137, 178 (1803).
27. See Rivka Weill. 2014. 'The New Commonwealth Model of Constitutionalism Notwithstanding: On Judicial Review and Constitution-Making', *American Journal of Comparative Law,* vol. 62 p. 127.
28. Quoted in Craig R. Ducat. 2012. *Constitutional Interpretation: Rights of Individual,* vol. 2, p. xvi. Wadsworth.
29. There are exceptions, of course. The Liberal Democratic Party that has dominated the Japanese parliament since 1955, for example, attempted to amend the 1946 Constitution for several times, but it has not been able to muster the two-thirds majority requirement in order to amend the Constitution, so much so that the Constitution has never been amended in the past seventy years.
30. For details, see Zhang Qianfan. 2004. 'Establishing Review of Legal Norms in China: A Theory of Constitutional Revision', *Strategy and Management*, vol. 2, pp. 61–9.
31. Zhang Qianfan. Spring 2003. 'The People's Court in Transition: The Prospects of the Chinese Judicial Reform', *Journal of Contemporary China*, vol. 12, pp. 69–101.

9

Constitutionalizing Public Participation in Kenya

Jill Cottrell

I Introduction

The 2010 Constitution of Kenya took a major step away from representative democracy towards a democracy with ongoing public participation in decision-making as a major element. The main focus of this chapter is how, and how far, this aspect of the constitution has been implemented and institutionalized.

II Public Participation Generally

There is now a very considerable literature on public participation, whether in policymaking or in more specific, often local, decision-making. Among the issues raised are:

- The tensions between the need for expertise and the desirability (if that is accepted) of participation of the ordinary citizen.[1]
- Whether it is possible to have public participation involving genuine deliberation.

- Whether there is a tension between citizen involvement in decision-making and citizens holding decision-makers accountable.[2]

'Participation' used to be used to refer to what proportion of the population votes, and whether certain groups were excluded or withdrew. The usage discussed here raises the question of what is wrong with representative democracy. The latter tends to assume that citizens have preferences over policies that they think will advance their interests. They indicate their preferences to government by voting for parties and politicians whose programmes most closely match their preferences. Those elected respond as they make policies, and professional administrators carry out these policies, generating outcomes that advance public interests.[3]

In the Kenyan context, I would argue that this works even less well than the model assumes because of:

- the lack of true political parties with policies that form the basis for their election appeals, and benchmark by which they can be judged;
- the self-seeking orientation of many of those in public office;
- corruption that means that decisions are not made on the basis of what will benefit the electorate;
- the electoral system, based on single member, 'first past the post', constituencies, where many votes are 'wasted';
- the existence of some very small communities which can make very little impact on the elections; and
- the absence of democratically elected truly local authorities.[4]

In elaborating a policy, or in detailed planning to embrace participation, certain questions inevitably arise. Who may participate? On what sorts of matters? In what processes: law making, policymaking, budgeting, or administrative decisions—and in the work of what types of decision-making body? How do the members of the public participate? And how do public bodies encourage or ensure public participation. Indeed is participation compulsory, just made possible, or positively encouraged?

Beyond these issues is the question of what participation is. It is common to draw on the 'ladder of participation' concept: from non-participation (including being manipulated), through a form of tokenism such as being informed or being consulted, to 'citizens' power' envisaged—on ascending rungs—as partnership, delegated power, or citizen control.[5] This does serve to underline that a lot of what is called 'participation' is nothing of the sort, even if full citizen power, while valuable for local development projects, is neither practical nor perhaps desirable when it comes to national policymaking.

III Effective Participation: Developments in Other Countries

Public participation has been a growth area in many countries in recent years. It is unusual to have constitutional requirements.[6] But guidelines and even legislative frameworks have proliferated. The Italian region of Tuscany has legislation that embraces a right to participate, a single-person 'authority for the guarantee and promotion of participation', training programmes to develop a civic and participatory culture, and provision for groups within the community to ask for financial assistance with participation. Priority is to be given to participation of the vulnerable or disadvantaged, and exercises that involve development on land that will have significant potential impact on the landscape or environment, that facilitate gender-balanced participation, that adopt 'innovative forms of communication', and especially that permit the people to be involved in the final stages of the process.[7]

The Australian State of Queensland has developed guidelines for public participation comprising ten separate publications on community engagement, methods, and techniques, including on engaging with different sections of the community such as indigenous groups, persons with disability communities, lesbian and gay groups, and on evaluating community engagement.[8]

Many government agencies, and non-governmental organizations, have developed sets of values and principles and published guides to participation techniques.[9] The International Association on Public Participation sets out its core values, including the belief that those affected by a decision have a right to be involved in the decision-making process, the promise that the public's contribution will influence the decision, positively facilitating the involvement of those potentially affected by or interested in a decision, seeking input from participants in designing participation, providing participants with the information they need for meaningful participation and communicating to participants how their input affected the decision.[10]

IV The Kenyan Background

The push for a new constitution was itself a civil society-led, participatory movement during the 1990s. It was not so much a grassroots as a middle-class movement. As one of its most prominent leaders said, '[I]f the routes to the people are inaccessible, what is to be done in the meantime? Moreso, if the organisations of workers and peasants have been co-opted and taken over by the comprador class because of the betrayal by the leaders of these organisations, is it not the duty of the middle class to take the lead in the reform process?'[11]

During the 1990s, calls for popular participation were mainly focussed on the need for input into the constitution-making process. Participation was not a major theme of the draft constitution put forward in 1994 by the Law Society of Kenya, the Kenya Human Rights Commission, and the Kenya Section of the International Commission of Jurists.[12] The legislation that established an official constitution making process that began in 2000 emphasized representative democracy, though hinting at something more for the proposed new second tier of government (devolution). However, it went on to add 'ensuring the full participation of people in the management of public affairs'.

The relevant influences were less ancient Greece or even modern Switzerland than developments like the Rio Declaration on Environmental and Development of 1992. This included 'Principle 10', stressing that 'Environmental issues are best handled with the participation of all concerned citizens, at the relevant level', and the importance of access to information. The 1990s were the era of 'participatory poverty assessments',[13] 'participatory rural appraisal', and participatory techniques in development more broadly. Kenya had a longish history of use of these techniques.[14] The South African Constitution of 1996—which emphasizes 'participatory democracy', encouragement of the public to participate in policymaking and public involvement in the work of the legislature—was also a significant influence on the new Kenyan document.

The first products of the official Kenyan process, following on a period of broad public engagement, were a draft Constitution and accompanying Report in 2002.[15] The Constitution of Kenya Review Commission wrote:[16]

> The whole nation feels alienated from the government and structures of authority. People feel neglected, and victimised. They consider they have no control over their life or destiny. Outside elections, participation is almost non-existent….
>
> We have tried to place the people at the centre of the constitution—constantly emphasising people's participation; bringing power closer to them; giving them greater control over their everyday lives.

Their draft constitution spelled out a set of values that included 'Participation, openness and transparency in public life'.

That draft went to the National Constitutional Conference (NCC), which, in March 2004, produced a revised version. This did not entirely please the government of the day, which took it over, amended the law on the constitution-making process, amended the draft through Parliament, and submitted this to a referendum (in 2005). The result was a resounding 'No'—though mainly to do with ethnic loyalties and support or otherwise for the government than with the content of the document.

After election-related violence in 2007–8, the process was restarted (with a new body called the Committee of Experts or CoE). Its first draft, largely based on the 2004 draft, was revised in the light of public feedback and further reflection; the revised version was required to be sent to a parliamentary committee which made various changes; the CoE adopted some of the changes, rejected others, and made a few further amendments. This last version went to referendum, was approved, and promulgated on 27 August 2010. Interestingly, the parliamentary committee, though in many respects its changes were regressive, seems to have improved, by simplifying, the values—including participation.[17]

Early drafts were somewhat more emphatic, and even creative, in their approaches to public participation issues than the version finally adopted. The 2004 draft included an obligation on the state to take 'measures to promote and encourage civil society participation in decision-making …' under the freedom of association. And there were provisions about registering NGOs (important vehicles for participation) including registration only if really necessary, and an independent body to register, and, if essential, to deregister them.

The early draft provisions about participation of the public in the work of Parliament included a requirement that a committee of Parliament have responsibility to ensure participation in law making and other Parliamentary roles. And the usual 'explanatory memorandum' submitted to Parliament with all Bills was required to include recommendations for public participation in considering the law.

Another participation proposal at the NCC was that—when the government reported to international human rights monitoring bodies—it should also give notice to the public, and a chance to comment on the report, so that this reporting process became a national event involving public debate on the government's record.

Unfortunately, some distrust of civil society, as well as a certain conservatism and desire for a shorter document, seem to have motivated some developments in the later phases, and these provisions disappeared.

V The Constitution as Adopted

Participation of the people is one of the national values (Article 10)—these 'bind all State organs, State officers, public officers and all persons whenever any of them applies or interprets this Constitution, enacts, applies or interprets any law; or makes or implements public policy decisions'.

Public participation 'in the management, protection and conservation of the environment' must be encouraged by the state (Article 69). Public participation is also to be encouraged generally in issues of public finance

(Article 201). Particularly in connection with the distribution between the lower level of government (counties) of their share of revenue raised national, the Commission on Revenue Allocation (broad equivalent of India's Finance Commission) must 'invite the public, including professional bodies, to make submissions to it on the matter' [Article 217(2)(d)].

Parliament must positively facilitate public participation in its legislative and other work (Article 118). Similar provisions apply to county assemblies (Article 197). Anyone may present a petition to Parliament, asking for a law to be passed or for any other purpose (Article 119).

The Constitution picks up the participatory significance of devolution, and the objects of devolution include (Article 174):

> (c) to give powers of self-governance to the people and enhance the participation of the people in the exercise of the powers of the State and in making decisions affecting them;
>
> (d) to recognize the right of communities to manage their own affairs and to further their development.

The Constitution, unlike that of India or South Africa, does not require elected local government below the county (state or province). But among the county functions is 'Ensuring and coordinating the participation of communities and locations in governance at the local level and assisting communities and locations to develop the administrative capacity for the effective exercise of the functions and powers and participation in governance at the local level.'[18]

The human rights chapter includes rights that are key to effective public participation, including not only the standard freedoms of speech and expression, association, and assembly, but the right to information (for which enabling legislation has just been passed). The 'participation' of various groups that are or may be excluded is emphasized, including the youth (Article 55), minorities and marginalized groups (Article 56), and the elderly (Article 57).

V.1 International Law

The 2010 Constitution took a bold step, becoming a 'monist' country as opposed to the dualist tradition of most common law countries; ratified treaties are now 'part of the law of Kenya under this Constitution' (Article 2(6)). The implications would include the direct application of the International Covenant on Civil and Political Rights (ICCPR), Article 25, on the right of every citizen '(a) To take part in the conduct of public affairs, directly or through freely chosen representatives'. Of this, the South African

Constitutional Court said: '[T]he ICCPR guarantees not only the "right" but also the "opportunity" to take part in the conduct of public affairs. This imposes an obligation on states to take positive steps to ensure that their citizens have an opportunity to exercise their right to political participation.'[19]

But the UN Committee has observed: 'It is for the legal and constitutional system of the State party to provide for the modalities of such participation'.[20]

Kenya is a party to the ICCPR, the 'Women's Convention' (Convention on the Elimination of All Forms of Discrimination Against Women: CEDAW), the Convention on the Rights of the Child, the Disability Convention, as well as the African Charter on Human and People's Rights, and African Charter on the Rights and Welfare of the Child and the Maputo Protocol to the African Charter on the Rights of Women.

Some treaties are not phrased in terms that impose specific obligations on the state to do something, or grant a very specific right. In applying Article 2(6), the courts of Kenya may be called upon to decide whether such treaties are directly part of the law of Kenya. For example, States Parties to the Maputo Protocol undertaken to 'ensure the protection of women with disabilities and take specific measures commensurate with their physical, economic and social needs to facilitate ... their participation in decision-making.'

This does not clearly indicate what the State is expected to do. Nonetheless it might be used, if no such measures have been taken, or clearly inadequate measures have been adopted, to argue that certain groups have been excluded, contrary to the Constitution and the Protocol, from any participation.

The CoE originally included the right of the child 'to know of decisions affecting the child, express an opinion and have that opinion taken into account, taking into consideration the age and maturity of the child and the nature of the decision.' This was removed by the parliamentary committee, and not reintroduced by the CoE. Was this a deliberate choice not to include it in the Constitution—despite Article 4 of the African Charter on the Rights and Welfare of the Child? Or did the CoE consider that this provision was implied by Article 33 (the general 'freedom of expression, which includes—(a) freedom to seek, receive or impart information or ideas'), or by Article 53(2) on the best interests of the child?

The ILO is also a source of useful ideas and information, as well as obligations on participation. Kenya is not a party to the ILO Convention 169 on Indigenous Peoples. But it is to the Tripartite Consultation (International Labour Standards) Convention, 1976 (No. 144).[21] This requires state parties to 'operate procedures ... which ensure effective consultations between representatives of the government, of employers and of workers' about international labour standards. The ILO has gone further to encourage the concept of 'tripartite social dialogue' as 'a key instrument in promoting and achieving decent work, inclusive development and social cohesion'.[22]

Other treaties to which Kenya is a party and which urge or require public participation include the Convention on Biological Diversity, and its more specific Cartagena Protocol on Bio-safety, in which public participation figures prominently. The Convention for the Safeguarding of the Intangible Cultural Heritage (2003) obliges states parties to involve communities, groups and relevant nongovernmental organizations in identification of the various elements of their intangible cultural heritage (Article 11), and the active involvement of 'communities, groups and, where appropriate, individuals' in its management (Article 15).

Treaties may focus attention on participation of particular groups—true of the Biodiversity Convention, which emphasizes 'knowledge, innovations and practices of indigenous and local communities embodying traditional lifestyles relevant for the conservation and sustainable use of biological diversity' and 'the approval and involvement of the holders of such knowledge' [Article 8(j)].[23]

After the Constitution, the Treaty Making and Ratification Act, 2012, was enacted. This does envisage, in a rather imprecise way, public consultation. First, a Cabinet Secretary[24] must, when submitting a request to the Cabinet to approve ratification, supply various types of information including 'the views of the public on the ratification of the treaty'.[25] But the Act does not specify how those views are to be sought. Parliament, when discussing whether to approve ratification must ensure public participation in accordance with its own rules.[26] Those rules are themselves very limited in scope, just requiring public participation to be facilitated by the relevant committee and that the views and recommendations of the public are to be taken into account when the committee makes its report to the House;[27] treaty ratification is not mentioned.

V.2 International 'Non-law'

Only ratified treaties are part of Kenyans law, but softer law may inspire both decision-makers and courts. The UN Declaration on the Right to Development (1986) includes, 'States should encourage popular participation in all spheres as an important factor in development and in the full realization of all human rights' (Article 8.2). There is also a UN Declaration, providing that persons belonging to minorities have the 'right to participate effectively in decisions on the national and, where appropriate, regional level concerning the minority to which they belong or the regions in which they live, in a manner not incompatible with national legislation' (Article 2.3).[28]

The African Charter for Popular Participation in Development and Transformation (Arusha 1990)[29] includes the following interesting points:

- [P]opular participation begins and must be earnestly practiced at the family level, because home is the base for development. It must also be practised at the workplace, and in all organizations, and in all walks of life.
- African governments must adopt development strategies, approaches, and programmes, the content and parameters of which are in line with the interest and aspirations of the people and which incorporate, rather than alienate, African values and economic, social, cultural, political, and environmental realities.
- There is a need for 'the identification and elimination of laws and bureaucratic procedures that pose obstacles to people's participation'.

Kenya is a member of the Open Government Partnership. Eligibility is limited to countries with a 'minimum level of commitment to open government principles in four key areas (Fiscal Transparency, Access to Information, Income and Asset Disclosures, and Citizen Engagement)'.[30]

VI After the Constitution

The principle of participation caught the public imagination, and many ordinary people with limited knowledge of the Constitution are aware of the principle. It also seems to have appealed to government departments, and to legislators, and evidently to the donor community. Much legislation, and production of guidelines, has been the consequence, with some lack of coordination. It became clear that, while the Law Reform Commission had produced a model Bill for counties, the Ministry of Devolution was working on a major set of Guidelines for counties, and the Public Service Commission had produced a document called 'Guidelines for Public Participation in Policy Formulation'—obeying a directive in the Public Service (Values and Principles) Act, 2015.[31] None of these activities had been undertaken with reference to any of the others, and each was differently funded. At the same time the Ministry of Justice was embarking on a project to develop a policy and perhaps legislation.

A study of the three initiatives that had been proceeding in parallel showed that fundamentally all had the same concern: to advise on how to make participation effective, by ensuring that the right people are involved, that the public are properly informed—that they are told what the issues are, clearly, and given enough time to prepare, and time to make their views known.

Their views should be taken seriously, there should be feedback to the public, and there should be a process of monitoring and evaluation of public participation. There was fundamentally no conflict between the documents though there were differences of emphasis.[32]

VII Who?

An overview of national legislation shows a number of approaches in terms of who is to be involved. The phrase used may be 'public' or 'stakeholders', or perhaps 'community participation'. The Electoral Commission is required to 'observe the principle of public participation and the requirement for consultation with stakeholders' without any explanation of who the latter are and how it is to be done.[33] Basic education is to be conducted with regard to the 'inclusiveness of parents, communities, private sector and other stakeholders in development and management'.[34] In that Act the word 'stakeholders' is used in at least three different provisions which could have three different meanings—depending on the principle of *ejusdem generis*.[35] The Public Finance Management Act requires that at national and county level there are 'measures that allow the intended beneficiaries to participate in the design and management of the projects or public services' financed by grant from the exchequer.

The 'public' generally is used, for example, in the Public Finance Management Act. The Cabinet Secretary must ensure public participation in the budget process, specify annually in a circular about the budget process how participation is to take place, and make regulations dealing with the same issue. The accounting officer for the Parliamentary Service Commission and the chief registrar of the judiciary must ensure that the public are able to participate in budget preparation. The Act also uses the expression 'community participation' in connection with regulations, without any clarity as to whether this is different from public participation.

VIII How?

The Constitution says little about the methods by which participation takes place. But some methods have been identified, if not elaborated, in legislation at national and county levels. There is, of course, the time-honoured petition (in the Constitution, national legislation and parliamentary standing orders)—but no detail outside the legislative context. There is mention of referendums for amendment of the Constitution, while the County Governments Act 2012 (CGA) envisages the possibility of local referendums.

The American expression 'town hall meetings' has, rather oddly, made its way into Kenyan statute, in the County Governments Act (CGA), and at least one county Act[36]—but there is no definition.[37] Public meetings more generally are frequently referred to.[38] The Public Service (Values and Principles) Act envisages participation through citizens' fora (a concept developed in the CGA), village councils (under the CGA village elders are appointed not elected), or elected leaders. The CGA also refers to budget preparation and validation fora, but without any clarification. The same act refers to notice boards (as do county acts[39]). The 'citizens' fora' under the CGA are required to include faith-based organizations or groups and a ragbag list of other sorts of local groups.

Some county acts refer to the use of the internet and other new technologies,[40] while some refer to mass media including radio and television.[41]

Apart from these often rather unhelpful, perhaps sometimes restrictive, lists of methodologies, some of the legislation has tried to achieve *effective* participation. Some specifies that the public must be informed early enough,[42] and that enough time must be allowed for the various stages.[43] Some specifies that the public must be educated on the issues,[44] or that adequate information must be provided in a clear form, covering the issues on which input is being sought, and about the consultation process itself[45] or that it must be 'objective'.[46] Some legislation requires special arrangements to be made if necessary for those who cannot read, or persons with disability,[47] or generally that arrangements must be inclusive, and appropriate for target groups.

Some provisions require that the final decision-making must consider the views submitted[48] or take public input into account,[49] some that the view of the public must be publicized,[50] or that there must be feedback to the public.[51] Other elements in legislation include the need for adequate resources to be devoted to public participation,[52] that staff must be trained,[53] and that some officer or a unit must be charged with the responsibility to ensure that participation happens. The need for development of a 'culture of participation' is sometimes stressed.[54]

IX Guidance: Official and Civil Society

The enthusiasm of the community, and of donors, has produced a good deal of Guidelines on the how of participation. The Ministry of Devolution Guidelines for participation at the county level were eventually published.[55] The Commission on Revenue Allocation produced its own Guidelines on how the public should be involved in budget processes.[56] The county government of Makueni set out its own Public Participation Framework,[57] envisaging a six-tiered system of people's forums, from 3,455 quarterly village level forums with at least 100 members each, through the county electoral district, and the national electoral districts within the county to the county level (where the annual forum is to have 1,000 members).

NGOs have produced guidance for the citizens or for the government agencies, or indeed both, on the why and the how of participation, usually stressing the benefits of participation, something about methodology, and some principles.[58] The International Budget Partnership's (IBP) *Deliberating Budgets: How Public Deliberation Can Move Us Beyond the Public Participation Rhetoric* is directed at particularly the county level, arguing for an approach based on the principles of deliberative democracy to make participation much more effective.[59] The IBP has also produced a series on reading budget-related documents, directed at both public and legislators.[60]

X Preliminary Evaluation

These are early days for what has to be a major culture shift as well as a practical question of establishing the mechanics for effective participation. There are signs of far more public involvement than ever existed in the past. Initiatives have included the great strengthening of court users' committees,[61] the views of which can be channelled to the National Council on the Administration of Justice, and public participation in public procurement.[62]

Under the Constitution, all members of the judiciary already in post were to be 'vetted' for continued suitability. This took place in public only if the individual judge or magistrate wished (a few did). But the names of those to be vetted were published in advance and the public invited to submit what they knew. The Board noted in its reports that the public had shown willingness to participate, and they had had significant numbers of members of the public as witnesses at hearings.[63]

The vetting principle was extended, though not required by the Constitution, to the police.[64] The National Commission on Human Rights has reported that they had held public meetings to gauge the response to this exercise, and most people seemed unaware of when and how to make a contribution to the process.[65]

Openness in appointments has significantly increased. Some countries might be surprised at its extent: for example, lists of applicants for judicial posts made public, as is the list of those shortlisted, interviews to be in public as were the hearing in Parliament for the confirmation of the appointment of the Chief Justice and Deputy. This does not prevent secretive decisions by the Judicial Service Commission in shortlisting those for interview.[66]

The standard technique seems to be the public meeting, open to anyone, provided they can find their way there, and sometimes can talk their way into the venue.[67]

The author has observed a limited amount of public participation. In 2016 she attended a day of public consultation on the national medium term budget framework—the last of a three-day event. The event was announced in the press just a few days before and was held at the premises of a public body, in a rather obscure location—evidently many people had difficulty finding it. The event was well organized. Staff were welcoming and sign-up sheets were available. At lunch time water, tea and snacks were available for the public.

The day covered three groups of ministries/agencies. The platform party in each case included very senior public officials (up to Principal [Permanent] Secretary). The (very complex) issues were introduced at some length with PowerPoint presentations, and then commented on by experts from a public think tank. The sizeable hall was over half full, but it transpired that for at least one of the sessions there were as many public servants in the hall as members of the public.

Hardly anyone had been able to see the documents before the meeting. I had been unable to find them online. Copies were not available at the meeting. The length of the presentations in the first session, coupled with the fact that the meeting began at least forty minutes late, meant that only two or three members of the public were able to speak. The last session of the day was extended for about an hour to enable more people to speak. But very few were able to speak knowledgeably about the issues.

In terms of the time of senior individuals, in relation to the input that was forthcoming at the meeting, it was a major waste of public money.

Another participation context that has grave shortcomings is the legislative. At early stages, consultations with 'stakeholders' do frequently take place but these depend on contacts and perceptions of who can make a contribution. The wider public's opportunity often comes much later, and is seriously circumscribed. A press advertisement will announce that a Bill has been submitted to a Parliamentary committee and invite the public to attend a sitting of the committee or submit written memoranda—with perhaps six or seven days' notice. A particularly egregious example concerned a Bill amending various aspects of criminal procedural law, and some substantive law. A press advertisement appeared, in December 2014, before the public were even aware that the Bill existed. It gave notice that the relevant committee was meeting that very day, and the deadline for submissions was five days away. The government has recognized this issue, observing:

> Parliamentary calls for memoranda and invitations to public hearings are only published in newspapers as advertisements which only about 2% of the Kenyan population have access to. It would be more effective if other media such as radio and mobile phone, which 80% of Kenyans can access, are used.
>
> There is need for improved tracking of bills including the real-time changes made at various stages of the legislative process. Currently you can only track the process of the bill as opposed to the content.

It has undertaken to develop policy and law to 'prescribe sufficient time for release and feedback on parliamentary information', ensure that Parliament publishes committee on its website, and that 'the legislative process is transparent from drafting to enactment'.[68]

There are some less anecdotal studies of participation, mostly at county level, often focussing on budgetary processes. Various issues have arisen. Public meetings are often not well advertised, with some counties relying on the national press.[69] Documentation is often not shared with participants, and if shared is too technical for many to understand, is long, and only in English. The IBP commented:

> [M]ost national and county budget documents fall short of providing the information required to meet the standards for deliberation. Many lack basic information about how decisions are made and the descriptive information needed to discuss these decisions. Their most significant deficiency, however, is the lack of serious public justification for the choices they contain. For the public to debate these choices, they must know what the choices are, but also what the reasoning behind those choices is supposed to be.[70]

Sometimes only those who views are acceptable to the county authorities are invited (county assembly members are identified as being particularly prone to this fault).[71] 'The public opinions were managed in a way that only those who praised the establishment were given opportunity to speak'; 'Meetings were organized at inconvenient times for most people, for instance, during market days when people had other priorities to attend to hence low participation in the forums.'[72] The same report commented that insecurity inhibits attendance, and that livelihood issues are more pressing for many.[73]

Civic education is inadequate, with communities not knowing that they could participate or what was expected of them.[74] Sometimes the failure is that of the public to attend public meetings.[75] In another county, 'most of the projects had already been predetermined and the meetings were intended for information sharing'.[76] Feedback to the public is inadequate, and discourages later participation.[77]

The necessary culture change has not taken place in some counties where 'departments have not fully embraced public participation as a value and have not changed their practices to incorporate public views in decision-making. These departments avoid engaging communities even when it is critical and they could get support and facilitation.'[78]

Lack of communication within counties is an obstacle,[79] and 'competition between the county assemblies and county executives'. Administrators often lack the information needed to be effective, and some administrators refused to participate unless they were paid allowances.

'The County Government of Kitui was found to have developed a Community Level Infrastructure Development Program which supports village and ward level programs identified through ward level community committees under the ward development fund.'[80] But, this report continued, the involvement of County Assembly members in managing the programme creates problems. There may even be hostility on the part of members of Parliament (MPs) to popular mobilization at the ward level and even sabotage of planned meetings.[81] Again 'Despite adequate mobilization, most Members of the County Assembly failed to turn up for the community conversation citing busy schedules. This demonstrates an unwillingness to face the public.'[82]

Another issue noted has been poor interaction with civil society (often there was resentment because of civil society criticism). And the same report noted: 'There was no consideration given for People Living with Disabilities.'[83]

Another sort of culture is a hindrance to effective participation, well expressed by The Institute for Social Accountability (TISA):

> Civil society and county officials lamented that public participation has become an expensive affair primarily because citizens expected a token in order to attend public participation forums. The participants admitted that many people prefer Tullow Oil meetings due to possible transport reimbursements, concessions, scholarships, job prospects and other gifts that Tullow meetings avail.[84]

The TISA county budget study (April 2014 and June 2015) concluded that 'all counties had made considerable efforts to engage the public in the county planning and budget process'.[85] But the IBP's study of the workings of the county budget forums (CBEFs)[86] observed:

> While there has been a surge in the formation and operationalization of CBEFs across the country in the past 18 months, the evidence suggests that most CBEFs are barely functional. Our review of four CBEFs that appear to be above average in their degree of activity suggests that even these forums are falling

far short of their potential. Governors have shown only limited enthusiasm for CBEF, and non-state members are not playing their representative role. Until citizens organize themselves to demand more from their representatives in CBEF, and from the county budget process itself, it is hard to imagine this changing.[87]

Makueni county seems to have had some success. It has made considerable effort with civic education, producing a *Handbook for Civic Education: County Governance and Citizens' Participation*.[88] It has established effective public participation structures. The public has actively been participating in civic education, decision-making on development projects and in oversight of projects being implemented. Ironically, public involvement went to the extent of over 50,000 signatures being collected through citizen groups within two weeks seeking the dissolution of the county government because people were aggrieved by the lack of cooperation between the two arms of government.

The IBP has also analysed Kenya's performance in terms of national budget process openness. Its analysis for 2015 concluded:

- The Government of Kenya provides the public with limited budget information (with a score of 48 out of 100, slightly higher than the global average)
- The Government of Kenya is weak in providing the public with opportunities to engage in the budget process (with a score of 33 out of 100).[89]

Incidentally the scores they gave to India the same year were 46 and 19, respectively.[90]

One area of great potential importance is the extractive industries. Yet:

> Despite the fact that public participation is enshrined in the 2010 Constitution, it is not yet common practice to consult local communities in the decision-making of county government development projects or the county government's role in oil exploration. Apart from occasional visits by national Members of Parliament (MPs) and other county-level politicians, most local communities in Turkana have not yet had meaningful interaction with national and county level decision-makers.[91]

Another study, in connection with coal mining, found that 89.2 per cent of respondents had not heard of consultations. Far fewer women than men had been involved, because of the 'prevalent perception that mining is largely a masculine occupation'.[92]

So far Kenya has not joined the Extractive Industries Transparency Initiative (EITI).[93] However, the government has undertaken, in a new National Action Plan under the Open Government Partnership, to move towards compliance with the EITI, making 'information on decision-making and financial flows related to the extractive industries publicly accessible and usable'.[94]

XI Litigation

Lawyers were anxious to see how the Kenyan courts would respond to actions based on the failure to consult or engage with the public as the Constitution required. They were aware that in some countries failure to comply with statutory consultation requirements had led to administrative decisions being set aside,[95] and that in South Africa a provision—similar to that in the Kenyan Constitution—about participation in the business of Parliament had even led to legislation being declared unconstitutional.[96]

Kenya has yet to have its *Doctors for Life* case. In a challenge to the rushed 2014 amendments to the security laws mentioned earlier, the court held that there had been enough opportunity for public consultation.[97] This was a most regrettable decision: the court seems to have allowed itself to be convinced without real inquiry that there was urgency that precluded more consultation, and ignored the fact that invitations published in newspapers circulating mainly in Nairobi and giving a mere five days for submission on a Bill amending some 20 sections of a variety of statutes necessarily gave only a small section of the country time to be involved. The bodies that went to court had also worked extraordinarily hard over the five days allowed by Parliament, and seem to have shot themselves in the proverbial foot because the court took the fact that they had been able to submit comments show that there had been adequate consultation. However, the court did not reject the concept that legislation might be invalid for want of participation. Another court appears to have condoned the placing of advertisements about public meetings in the newspapers only one or two days before the meetings.[98]

In a more recent case, the court did hold that amendments to existing statute were unconstitutional not just because they were in conflict with the substance of the Constitution but because 'by introducing totally new and substantial amendments to the Judicial Service Act, 2011, on the floor of the House, Parliament not only set out to circumvent the constitutional requirements of public participation but, with due respect, mischievously short-circuited and circumvented the letter and the spirit of the Constitution'.[99]

A number of pieces of legislation at the county level have been held unconstitutional, for want of proper consultation, including some county

Finance Bills.[100] And subsidiary legislation in which there has been no consultation—as required by legislation and, by implication if not expressly, by the Constitution—has also been declared invalid.[101]

Other decisions have been set aside for lack of participation, including the renaming of a local post office,[102] a resolution of a county assembly to move the county seat,[103] and the initiation of impeachment of a county governor by the county assembly.[104]

And there have been some challenges to major infrastructure and extractive developments without adequate public participation. In one—concerning coal mining—the court said, 'the Attorney General, and Fenxi Mining Industry Company Limited are required to continue to engage with the local community and provide reasonable opportunities for public participation during the process of preparing an Environmental Impact Assessment and the process of Resettlement'.[105] Another case is before the courts about a major port development that will disrupt traditional lifestyles and economy in a world heritage site on the coast.[106]

The Supreme Court said:[107]

> [381]Public participation calls for the appreciation by State, Government and all stakeholders implicated in this appeal that the Kenyan citizenry is adult enough to understand what its rights are under Article 34. In the cases of establishment, licensing, promotion and protection of media freedom, public participation ensures that private 'sweet heart' deals, secret contracting processes, skewed sharing of benefits-generally a contract and investment regime enveloped in non-disclosure, do not happen. Thus, threats to both political stability and sustainable development are nipped in the bud by public participation.

The courts have begun to try to give guidance as to what is appropriate participation. The Kiambu County Finance Act case has often been quoted by other courts:[108]

> 75. It behoves Parliament in enacting legislation to ensure that the spirit of public participation is attained both quantitatively and qualitatively. It is not enough to simply 'tweet' messages as it were and leave it to those who care to scavenge for it. Parliament ought to do whatever is reasonable to ensure that as many Kenyans are aware of the intention to pass legislation. It is the duty of Parliament in such circumstances to exhort the people to participate in the process of the enactment of legislation by making use of as many fora as possible such as churches, mosques, temples, public barazas, national and vernacular radio broadcasting stations and other avenues where the public are known to converge to disseminate information with respect to the intended action.

> 76. In my view to huddle a few people in a 5 star hotel on one day cannot by any stretch of imagination be termed as public participation for the purposes of meeting constitutional and legislative threshold. Whereas the magnitude of the publicity required may depend from one action to another a one day newspaper advertisement in a country such as ours where a majority of the populace survive on less than a dollar per day and to whom newspapers are a luxury leave alone the level of illiteracy in some parts of this country may not suffice for the purposes of seeking public views and public participation.

The recently retired Chief Justice[109] made a point of expounding the concept when the opportunity presented itself. He observed that 'public participation calls for significant mental shifts in our mode of consultation, communication, learning, and accommodation of the views of ordinary Kenyans'.[110]

In the governor's impeachment case, GBM Kariuki J. said: 'The litany of activities presented by the County Assembly as constituting public participation were general in nature and were not specific enough as to the event of removal of the governor.'[111]

In another case Emukule J. said:

> The strategic logistics are even more important. There are gender issues, equal ear to women and youth groups, minorities and the marginalized. There are also individuals from the full range of economic, trade and commercial activities, hoteliers and industrial interests, not to mention ethnic, marginalized and religious backgrounds whose participation is necessary in the budgetary planning process. In other words if public participation does not include large sections of society, it may fail the test of legitimacy.[112]

The courts have resisted some attempts by business to use the participation requirements to thwart regulatory measures. Most striking was an effort by the tobacco industry to undermine efforts to implement the Framework Convention on Tobacco Control. The court was unimpressed: 'The petitioner and other stakeholders participated in various meetings of stakeholders and submitted their views. They participated in various meetings with committees of Parliament.'[113]

In another case the private veterinary profession tried to stop a government proposal to provide subsidized insemination services—using failure to carry out public participation as the reason. The judge said:

> My understanding of the concept of public participation as contemplated under Articles 10 and 174 of the Constitution is that the participation of the public in affairs that concern them should not be narrowly interpreted to mean

engagement of a section of people purporting to be professionals who are out to rip maximum profits out of services for which they are neither registered nor qualified to offer; the ultimate goal for public engagement as envisaged in the constitution is for the larger public benefit.[114]

XII Conclusion

Public participation offers some potential for a radically different style of governance. A great deal of effort is being poured into public participation, by public servants, NGOs, and academics. Not to mention Kenyan and donor money. There are undoubtedly problems of public service culture to be overcome. And further study and planning is needed to ensure that effective methods are used, with adequate preparation of officials and public, procedures for ensuring that public input is taken seriously, and feedback provided so that the public are aware whether and to what extent their input has had an impact. Almost certainly there needs to be a move away from the predominant mode of the public meetings described earlier. As an earlier report said, 'A single consultation meeting of hundreds of people in a ward does not constitute participation neither does it inspire confidence in the citizens.'[115]

Many challenges remain. And dilemmas: for example, the Advisory Committee on the Power of Mercy is currently collecting public views on the death penalty.[116] In writing a submission the author quoted from the leading author, Roger Hood:

> As all other research on attitudes shows, there is a large gap between the sort of 'off the top of the head opinion' which is tapped by opinion polls conducted on the telephone or in the street, and the complex weighing up of considerations that juries have to undertake. Most members of the public have been found to possess very limited knowledge about the circumstances in which murder takes place, the characteristics of murderers, and all aspects of capital punishment. Without such knowledge, their immediate opinions are a dubious basis on which to form policy.[117]

Kenya—like other countries—has a long way to go before it has the sort of deliberative democracy that would ensure that public debate reached the depth of understanding that would enable a thorough consideration of complex issues of this kind. One of the main NGOs engaged has recently commented on:

> [T]he lack of a framework to guide the process and low citizen awareness due to inadequate civic education. In Kenya's context barriers to public

participation also include: Low awareness by citizens of their political roles, rights and responsibilities and the channels through which they can exercise them; Absence of an implementation framework; Citizen apathy rooted in a mistrust of government, the absence of a sense of civic responsibility, or in other social, political or economic factors; Low appreciation of participatory governance by public officers; Traditional 'official secrets mentality' dominates the thinking and attitudes of public officers; The low confidence the public attaches to official participatory mechanisms due to the placement of kinship bonds above development bonds; Participatory frameworks are prone to elite capture and may be manipulated and further marginalizing vulnerable groups.[118]

One can only hope that the government is serious in its recently expressed intention 'to deepen openness and thereby ensure that the democratic dividend flowing from transparency is sustained'.[119]

Notes and References

1. Archon Fung. 2006. 'Democratizing the Policy Process', in Michael Moran, Martin Rein, and Robert E Goodin (eds), *The Oxford Handbook of Public Policy*, pp. 669–85, 669. New York: Oxford University Press.
2. Bofil Hamgard and Jenny M Lewis. 2014. 'Accountability and Citizen Participation', in Mark Bovens, Robert E Goodin and Thomas Schillemans (eds), *The Oxford Handbook of Public Accountability*, pp. 258–72, 266. New York: Oxford University Press.
3. Summary based on Fung, 'Democratizing the Policy Process', 671.
4. I have argued this in 'Public Participation: An Overview', in *Effective Citizens' Participation: Broadening Citizen's Opportunities sunder the Constitution of Kenya 2010* (edited by Steve Ouma Akoth), pp. 39–66, 39. Nairobi: Commission for the Implementation of the Constitution, 2015.
5. S. Arnstein. 1969. 'A ladder of citizen participation', 35 *Journal of the American Institute of Planners*, vol. 35, pp. 216–24. It is part of the framework of the chapter by Hamgard and Lewis, 'Accountability and Citizen Participation'.
6. Examples include Bolivia (2009), Ecuador (2006) and Thailand (2007 – since overthrown). See 'The Right to Public Participation in the Egyptian Constitution', http://www.tadamun.co/2013/12/05/the-right-to-public-participation-2/?lang=en#.WWuqTIiGM2w, accessed 16 July 2017.
7. 'Norms on the promotion of participation in the elaboration of regional and local policies' (2007 – revised 2013). For an account see Rodolfo Lewanski, 'Institutionalizing Deliberative Democracy: the "Tuscany laboratory"' (2013) 9(1) *Journal of Public Deliberation* Article 10http://www.publicdeliberation.net/cgi/viewcontent.cgi?article=1185&context=jpd, accessed 16 July 2017.
8. http://www.qld.gov.au/web/community-engagement/.

9. *Effective Engagement: Building Relationships with Community and Other Stakeholders; Book 3 The Engagement Toolkit* (Melbourne: Victorian Government Department of Sustainability and Environment, 2005) http://www.dse.vic.gov.au/effective-engagement/resources/download-effective-engagement, *Public Participation in Government Decision-making* (Melbourne: Victorian Auditor-General's Office, 2015) http://preview.tinyurl.com/VAGOPP *Health Canada Policy Toolkit for Public Involvement in Decision Making* (Ottawa: Health Canada, 2000) https://www.canada.ca/en/health-canada/corporate/about-health-canada/reports-publications/health-canada-policy-toolkit-public-involvement-decision-making.html, all accessed 16 July 2017.
10. 'International Association for Public Participation: IAP2 Core Values,' http://www.iap2.org/?page=A4, accessed 16 July 2017.
11. Willy Mutunga, 1999. *Constitution-Making from the Middle: Civil Society and Transition Politics in Kenya, 1992–1997,* p. 5. Nairobi and Harare: Sareat/MWENGO.
12. The Law Society is the professional body of all legal practitioners; the Kenya Human Rights Commission is a non-governmental body. For the text of the constitution draft see Mutunga, *Constitution-Making from the Middle*, 323.
13. See Andy Norton with others, *A rough guide to PPAs Participatory Poverty Assessment An introduction to theory and practice* Overseas Development Institute 2001 https://www.odi.org/publications/1747-rough-guide-ppas-participatory-poverty-assessment-introduction-theory-practice, accessed 16 July 2017.
14. See *Reflections on PRA and Participation in Kenya: Feedback from the Pathways to Participation consultative meetings July 1999,* Institute of Development Studies, Sussex in collaboration with the Participatory Methodologies Forum of Kenya (PAMFORK).
15. For accounts of the early stages of the process see Jill Cottrell and Yash Ghai, 2007. 'Constitution Making and Democratization in Kenya (2000–2005)', (14) *Democratization*, pp. 1–25, Makau Mutua, 2008. *Kenya's Quest for Democracy: Taming Leviathan.* Michigan: L Rienner Publishers, PLO Lumumba, 2008. *Kenya's Quest for a Constitution: The Postponed Promise,* Nairobi: Jomo Kenyatta Foundation.
16. *The People's Choice: The Report of the Constitution of Kenya Review Commission Short Version* (September 2002).
17. They removed 'ensuring full participation of women, persons with disabilities, marginalized communities, the youth, and all other citizens in the political, social and economic life of the nation' leaving a simple statement on participation.
18. Fourth Schedule Part 2 Item 14.
19. *Doctors for Life International v The Speaker of the National Assembly* Case CCT 12/05, [2006] ZACC 11 2006 (6) SA 416, para. 91.
20. *Marshall v Canada*, Communication No. 205/1986.
21. Ratified in 1990.

22. *National Tripartite Social Dialogue: An ILO guide for improved governance* (2013) http://www.ilo.org/wcmsp5/groups/public/—ed_dialogue/—dialogue/documents/publication/wcms_231193.pdf, accessed 16 July 2017.
23. And see 'Convention on Biological Diversity,' https://www.cbd.int/traditional/general.shtml, accessed 16 July 2017.
24. Minister—terminology changed in the 2010 Constitution.
25. S 7(m).
26. S 8(3).
27. Order 127 (3).
28. Declaration on the Rights of Persons Belonging to National or Ethnic, Religious and Linguistic Minorities, Adopted by General Assembly resolution 47/135 of 18 December 1992.
29. http://www.afrimap.org/english/images/treaty/file4239ac8e921ed.pdf.
30. 'Open Government Partnership: How to Join,' http://www.opengovpartnership.org/how-it-works/how-join, accessed 16 July 2017.
31. S 12.
32. The study—unpublished—was by the author.
33. Independent Electoral and Boundaries Commission Act s 26.
34. Basic Education Act s 4(l).
35. Namely that the meaning of a general phrase in a list is affected by the specific items in that list.
36. Meru County Public Participation Act (county legislation is in theory available at 'Kenya Law, County Acts 2015,' http://www.kenyalaw.org/kl/index.php?id=5193), accessed 16 July 2017.
37. Some descriptions would indicate that a town hall meeting is (i) informal, (ii) local—in the community—and (iii) focussed on a particular issue. See for example Kay Spearman, 2006. *Financial Management for Local Government, Volume 1* Earthscan, 254
38. For example, the Public Finance Management Act.
39. For example, of Meru County.
40. Meru and Machakos County Acts.
41. For example, Machakos and Elegyo/Marakwet County Acts.
42. For example, 'the public is given early and effective opportunities to participate and review action plans' in connection with noise and vibration mapping plans under the Environmental Management and Coordination (Noise and Excessive Vibration Pollution) (Control) Regulations, 2009, reg 24(3), under the Environmental Management and Co-Ordination Act (pre-Constitution legislation).
43. For example, 'the public is given early and effective opportunities to participate and review action plans' in connection with noise and vibration mapping plans under the Environmental Management and Coordination (Noise and Excessive Vibration Pollution) (Control) Regulations, 2009, reg 24(3), under the Environmental Management and Co-Ordination Act (pre-Constitution legislation).

44. Bio-safety Act s 54(1); Consumer Protection Act s 90(d).
45. Elegyo/Marakwet County Public Participation Act.
46. Meru County Public Participation Act.
47. Urban Areas and Cities Act, Second Schedule s 2(3)(b).
48. For example, the Fair Administrative Action Act, s 5(1)(b).
49. Noise and Excessive Vibration Pollution Control Regulation 24.
50. Elegyo/Marakwet County Act.
51. Noise and Vibration Regulation 243).
52. Machakos County Public Participation Act s 5(2)(d).
53. Machakos County Act.
54. For example, 'a culture of dialogue and participatory democratic governance at the institution' Basic Education Act s 59(j).
55. Ministry of Devolution and Planning & Council of Governors *County Public Participation Guidelines,* January 2016, http://www.devolutionplanning.go.ke/wp-content/uploads/2016/04/County-Public-Participation.pdf, accessed 16 July 2017.
56. 'Guidelines on Formation of the County Budget and Economic Forum' (Appended to Circular from Chair, March 2015) http://www.internationalbudget.org/wp-content/uploads/Signed-Circular-Cheserem-CRA-CBEF.pdf, accessed 16 July 2017.
57. 'Makueni County: Public Participation Framework,' http://www.makueni.go.ke/public-participation-framework, accessed 16 July 2017.
58. For example, Uraia (specializing in civic education); Uraia, 'What is Public Participation?', http://uraia.or.ke/wp-content/uploads/2016/11/Citizen-Participation-BOOKLET.pdf, Chrispine Oduor, 2014. *Handbook on County Planning, County Budgeting and Social Accountability,* Institute of Economic Affairs, http://uraia.or.ke/wp-content/uploads/2016/11/Brochure.pdf, TISA, 'Public Participation Framework in the County Assembly' (April 2015), http://www.tisa.or.ke/images/uploads/Public_Participation_Framework.pdf, all accessed 16 July 2017.
59. Jason Lakin and Mokeira Nyagaka, 'Deliberating Budgets' (February 2016), http://www.internationalbudget.org/wp-content/uploads/ibp-paper-public-deliberation-in-kenya-2016.pdf, accessed 16 July 2017, For 'deliberative democracy' see Amy Gutmann and Dennis Thompson, 2004. *Why Deliberative Democracy? p. 8.* Princeton University Press.
60. International Budget Partnership, January 2016, 'How to Read and Use a Budget Review and Outlook Paper', http://www.internationalbudget.org/wp-content/uploads/kenya-how-to-read-and-use-budget-review-outlook-paper-2015.pdf; Jason Lakin, February 2016, 'How to Read and Use a Budget Policy Statement and a County Fiscal Strategy Paper', http://www.internationalbudget.org/wp-content/uploads/kenya-how-to-read-and-use-budget-policy-statement-and-county-fiscal-strategy-paper-2016.pdf; Jason Lakin, May 2016,'Kenya: How to Read and Use the Budget Estimates', http://www.internationalbudget.org/wp-content/uploads/kenya-how-to-read-and-use-budget-estimates-2016.pdf, all accessed 17 July 2017.

61. An early study of these is the ICJ Kenya, 'International Commission of Jurists – Kenya Baseline Survey of the State of CUCs: Access to Justice and Public Participation in the Judicial Process: An Analysis of Court User Committees in Kenya', http://www.icj-kenya.org/dmdocuments/reports/cuc%20baseline%20report.pdf; see also a short paper by Justice Lenaola at the 2011 Judicial Colloquium: Issac Lenaola, 'Public Participation in Judicial Processes,' 2011. http://kenyalaw.org/kl/index.php?id=1934, accessed 17 July 2017. The first document appears to be unavailable.
62. For in interesting summary of comments from the Court Users' Committees, see *State of The Judiciary and the Administration of Justice Annual Report 2014–2015.* Nairobi: Judiciary. 159–167, http://www.judiciary.go.ke/portal/assets/filemanager_uploads/Downloads/STATE%20OF%20THE%20JUDICIARY%20REPORT%203.pdf, accessed 17 July 2017. On public participation in procurement see ICPAK [Institute of Certified Public Accountants of Kenya] 'Public participation in procurement in Kenya' in Steve Ouma Akoth(ed), 2015. *Effective Citizens' Participation: Broadening Citizen's Opportunities sunder the Constitution of Kenya 2010,* pp. 156–67. Nairobi: Commission for the Implementation of the Constitution.
63. See publications of the Board at http://www.jmvb.or.ke.
64. Conducted by the National Police Service Commission see http://www.npsc.go.ke/, accessed 17 July 2017.
65. Beryl Orao. 2015. 'Public Participation in the Police Vetting Process', http://hrd.knchr.org/Public-participation-in-the-police-vetting-process, accessed 15 May 2015.
66. At the time of writing, this secrecy is being challenged in court by the organization, Katiba Institute, with which the author is associated.
67. A meeting I attended concerned the approval of genetically modified cotton, and was held in a government training college. Some of the participants were farmers, and many were clearly not 'middle class'. Some complained it had taken an hour of persuasion to get them admitted to the college.
68. Kenya OGP Steering Committee, 'Open Government Partnership National Action Plan II, 2016–2018' 12–13, http://www.opengovpartnership.org/sites/default/files/Kenya_AP2_2016_0.pdf, accessed 17 July 2017.
69. *JIHUSISHE: Lessons in Participation in the County Budget* (The Institute for Social Accountability 2015) (funding particularly UK Government and OSIEA).
70. Jason Lakin and Mokeira Nyagaka, 'Deliberating Budgets', 17.
71. *Review of Status of Public Participation, and County Information Dissemination Frameworks A Case Study of Isiolo Kisumu Makueni and Turkana Counties* (Institute of Economic Affairs, 2015) p 14, http://uraia.or.ke/wp-content/uploads/2016/11/Review-of-status-of-Public-Participation-and-County-Information-Dissemination-Frameworks.pdf, accessed 17 Juy 2017.
72. *JIHUSISHE: Lessons in Participation in the County Budget,* 22.
73. *JIHUSISHE: Lessons in Participation in the County Budget,* 22.

74. *JIHUSISHE: Lessons in Participation in the County Budget,* 28.
75. *Review of Status of Public Participation,* 16.
76. *JIHUSISHE: Lessons in Participation in the County Budget,* 23.
77. *JIHUSISHE: Lessons in Participation in the County Budget,* 29.
78. *Review of Status of Public Participation,* 34.
79. *JIHUSISHE: Lessons in Participation in the County Budget,* 8.
80. *JIHUSISHE: Lessons in Participation in the County Budget,* 8.
81. *JIHUSISHE: Lessons in Participation in the County Budget,* 60.
82. *JIHUSISHE: Lessons in Participation in the County Budget,* 22.
83. *JIHUSISHE: Lessons in Participation in the County Budget,* 28.
84. P. 48. Tullow Oil is involved in oil prosecuting and industry development in Turkana county.
85. *JIHUSISHE: Lessons in Participation in the County Budget.*
86. Christine Kamau, 2015. 'Devolution in Kenya: The Establishment of County Budget and Economic Forums', http://www.internationalbudget.org/wp-content/uploads/devolution-in-kenya-establishment-of-cbef-nov-2015.pdf, accessed 17 July 2017.
87. P. v.
88. Department of Education and Civic Education Makueni County, 'A Handbook of Civic Education', http://www.globethics.net/gel/6188459/a-handbook-for-civic-education, accessed 17 July 2017.
89. International Budget Partnership, Kenya, April 2016, http://www.internationalbudget.org/opening-budgets/open-budget-initiative/open-budget-survey/country-info/?country=ke, accessed 17 July 2017.
90. International Budget Partnership, India, April 2016, http://www.internationalbudget.org/budget-work-by-country/findgroup/group-data/?country=in, accessed 17 July 2017.
91. Cordaid, 2015. *Oil Exploration in Kenya: Success Requires Consultation: Assessment of Community Perceptions of Oil Exploration in Turkana County, Kenya,* p. 22. https://www.cordaid.org/media/medialibrary/2015/09/Turkana_Baseline_Report_DEF-LR_Cordaid.pdf, accessed 17 July 2017.
92. Centre for Governance & Development, 2015. 'Re-thinking Gender Equality in the Extractive Sector in Kenya: A case study of Gender Dimensions and Implications on Coal Mining in Mui Basin, Kitui County', http://www.daogewe.org/index.php/publications/studies-1/25-mui-policy-brief-2015/file, accessed 17 July 2017.
93. EITI, 'Implementation Status', https://beta.eiti.org/, accessed 17 July 2017.
94. Kenya OGP Steering Committee, 'Open Government Partnership National Action Plan II, 2016–2018', 16.
95. A recent English example is *R (on the application of Joicey) v Northumberland County Council* [2014] EWHC 3657 (Admin) [2015] PTSR 622] where Cranston J said (para. 1), 'This judicial review raises an issue about the consequences when information which by law is to be accessible to members of the public is not available in a timely fashion to enable them to participate

effectively in democratic decision-making. I decide that a claimant in this position is entitled to have the decision quashed unless the decision-maker can demonstrate that it would inevitably have come to the same conclusion even if the information had been available.'

96. *Doctors for Life International v The Speaker National Assembly* (CCT12/05) [2006] ZACC 11.
97. *Coalition for Reform and Democracy(Cord), Kenya National Commission on Human Rights v Republic of Kenya* [2015] eKLR, http://kenyalaw.org/caselaw/cases/view/106083/, accessed 17 July 2017.
98. *Nairobi Metropolitan PSV Saccos Union Limited v County of Nairobi Government* [2013] eKLR, http://kenyalaw.org/caselaw/cases/view/93353/, accessed 24 July 2017. The judge promised 'I … find that there was adequate and appropriate public participation … but subject to what I shall say about the public advertisement in daily newspapers at the end of this judgment.'—but he said nothing.
99. *Law Society of Kenya v Attorney General & National Assembly* [2016] eKLR, http://kenyalaw.org/caselaw/cases/view/122379/, [250], accessed 17 July 2017.
100. *Robert N. Gakuru v Governor Kiambu County* [2014] eKLR, http://kenyalaw.org/caselaw/cases/view/97000/, accessed 17 July 2017.
101. *Keroche Breweries Limited v Attorney General* [2016] eKLR, http://kenyalaw.org/caselaw/cases/view/117414/, accessed 17 July 2017. The regulations were further in breach of the statute because they had never been laid before Parliament. The statute about the making of subsidiary legislation is the Statutory Instruments Act 2013 s. 5.
102. *Javan Oscar Buleemi (Suing as Secretary General Tiriki Union (EA) v Permanent Secretary, Ministry of Internal Security and Provincial Administration* [2015] eKLR, http://kenyalaw.org/caselaw/cases/view/110123/, accessed 17 July 2017.
103. *Sammy Ndung'u v Governor, Laikipia County* [2016] eKLR, http://kenyalaw.org/caselaw/cases/view/119505/, accessed 17 July 2017.
104. *Martin Nyaga Wambora v County Assembly of Embu* [2015] eKLR, http://kenyalaw.org/caselaw/cases/view/117084/, accessed 17 July 2017.
105. *In the Matter of the Mui Coal Basin Local Community* [2015] eKLR, http://kenyalaw.org/caselaw/cases/view/117704/, accessed 17 July 2017. The petition failed, so this statement seems to be by way of *obiter dictum*, not really part of the order. In view of the findings quoted earlier about the Mui coal project, it is to be hoped the judge was not over-optimistic.
106. The case is brought on behalf of Save Lamu—see https://www.savelamu.org/, accessed 17 July 2017.
107. *Communications Commission of Kenya v Royal Media Services Ltd.* Petition No. 14 of 2014.
108. *Robert N. Gakuru v Governor Kiambu County* [2014] eKLR.
109. Willy Mutunga (n 7).
110. *In the Matter of the National Land Commission* [2015], http://kenyalaw.org/caselaw/cases/view/116512/, eKLR Advisory Opinion Reference No. 2 of 2014 [356], accessed 17 July 2017.

111. Para 30.
112. *Diani Business Welfare Association v County Government of Kwale* [2015] eKLR, http://kenyalaw.org/caselaw/cases/view/114990/, [36], accessed 17 July 2017.
113. *British American Tobacco Kenya Ltd v Cabinet Secretary for the Ministry of Health* [2016] eKLR, http://kenyalaw.org/caselaw/cases/view/120311/, accessed 17 July 2017.
114. *Thuku Kirori v County Government of Murang'a* [2014] eKLR http://kenyalaw.org/caselaw/cases/view/98561/, accessed 17 July 2017.
115. Kenya Local Government Reform Programme (KLGRP) on the LASDAP Process quoted in *Budget Transparency and Citizen Participation in Counties in Kenya* A Guide by National Taxpayers Association (NTA) (2013).
116. The Committee advises the President (who may not act without their advice, though arguably may decline to act) on the use of the power to pardon, commute sentences etc. – Article 133.
117. Roger Hood, 1996. *The Death Penalty: A World-wide Perspective,* p. 218. Revised edition; Oxford: Clarendon Press.
118. TISA,'Request for Expression of Interest for Consultancies in Public Participation Policy Development TISA-PSDT-NCC' (2 August 2016) http://www.tisa.or.ke/images/uploads/EOI_Consultants_TISA-PSDT-AHADI.pdf, accessed 17 July 2017.
119. Kenya OGP Steering Committee, 'Open Government Partnership National Action Plan II, 2016–2018', 5.

10

Inclusive Constitutionalism and the Indigenous People of the Chittagong Hill Tracts in Bangladesh

Ridwanul Hoque

Moral or political inclusion is not the same thing as identity. There is an inescapable crudity in thinking that we cannot sympathise with the joys and miseries, with the predicaments and achievements, of others without actually seeing them as some kind of an extension of oneself. [...] As people capable of abstraction and reasoning, we should be able to respond humanely to the predicaments of others who simply are different and seen to be different. [...]

—Amartya Sen. 2001. 'Other People', British Academy Lecture, *Proceedings of the British Academy*, III, 7 November 2000, p. 333.

The founding fathers of the Constitution were conscious of and cognizant to the problem of the exploitation of the Tribals. They were anxious to preserve the tribal culture and their holdings.

—Supreme Court of India, *Samatha v State of Andhra Pradesh and Others*, AIR 1997 SC 3297, para 92.

I Introduction

We live in 'an age of diversity' that is, quite paradoxically, replete with a history of sufferings, 'actual and cultural genocide', conquest, penetration, and marginalization endured by indigenous peoples around the world.[1] The indigenous people in the Chittagong Hill Tracts (CHT) of Bangladesh are no exception.[2] They continue to live as a marginalized, excluded, and disadvantaged community in an otherwise plural society.[3] Various minorities in Bangladesh are often reported to have been victims of varying political, economic, and social discrimination. In particular, aboriginals and indigenous peoples of Bangladesh have suffered most, largely because of state-centric repressive and exclusionary policies that remain inspired by the politics of hegemonic identity.[4]

Although the Constitution of Bangladesh of 1972 ('Constitution') was premised upon the rule-of-law ethos, it nevertheless was deficient in inclusiveness. At its founding moment, Bangladesh did not take into account non-Bengali adivasi communities of the CHT, but rather clearly dismissed their demand for recognition. This constitutional exclusion in effect soon gave birth to long-standing hostilities. In the wake of mounting conflict in the CHT, a peace accord with the indigenous representatives was signed in 1997 with a clear commitment to uphold the indigenous rights of self-government and participation. Consequentially, a number of institutional changes like the regional self-government council were installed. Further, a 2011 constitutional amendment created a state duty to preserve the unique local culture and tradition of ethnic groups, although without using the terminology of 'indigenous people'. The most important demand of these people for their recognition as a distinct constitutional community, however, remains unfulfilled. Alongside good efforts, non-inclusive public policies and the settlers' distrust vis-à-vis the indigenous communities thus continued to exist, and the implementation of the CHT Peace Accord became eventually troublesome.

In the above backdrop and from the normative perspective of inclusive or pluralist constitutionalism, this chapter examines the governance-specialty of the CHT and its original peoples' claim for recognition of ethno-cultural separateness. It finds the constitutional non-inclusion of indigenous peoples to be a genetic defect in the Constitution, and argues that Bangladeshi constitutionalism is still deficient in inclusiveness. It is further argued that unless the country shifts more clearly to an accommodationist approach to these peoples' distinct identity, the peace in the CHT will likely remain elusive.

At the outset, two initial points need to be made clear. This chapter proceeds from a priori understanding that the indigenous peoples of Bangladesh are qualified as 'indigenous' according to international standards,[5] but does not deal with them except to a limited extent that it is needed for clarity. Secondly, the chapter remains concerned only with the cause of indigenous peoples of the CHT, leaving out from its ambit other similarly situated ethnic communities such as Garos of northeast Bangladesh.[6]

This chapter has seven parts. The next part discusses the concept of inclusive constitutionalism with specific reference to the normativity of including different ethnic nations within a given polity. The third part provides a brief background to the special administrative nature of the CHT, showing how indigenous autonomy and identity have or have not received protection during the colonial and post-colonial regimes. The fourth part is a trajectory of post-independence developments in Bangladesh that show a transition from exclusion to passive constitutional recognition of the indigenous peoples. Then follows an analysis of the judicial narrative in Bangladesh of the indigenous autonomy and self-government, while the sixth part briefly focuses on the utility of comparative experiences in managing ethnic diversities. The final part concludes the chapter.

II The Inclusiveness Virtue of Modern Constitutionalism

Recognition of indigenous peoples within the national constitutional framework seems to be a problem everywhere including in advanced democracies. Government policies and state institutions are often seen preoccupied with the notion of 'us *versus* them'. Judicial attitudes to the right of cultural identity of non-dominant peoples are also at variance: some courts are encouragingly inclusive[7] while others are insensitively hegemonic even despite their respective constitution's commitment to pluralist social structures.[8]

The inclusivity virtue of constitutionalism is based on a meta-normative rule-of-law framework. The rule of law in a diverse society requires and presupposes inclusive constitutionalism or constitutional pluralism that calls for the existence of a plurality of national identities as opposed to a unitary identity.[9] Inclusive constitutionalism thus seeks to ensure the political participation and representation of all peoples, and protect their civil-political, socio-cultural, and group rights against the usurpation by the majority.

It is difficult to define constitutionalism, if not a constitution that remains at the core of constitutionalism.[10] In a general sense, modern constitutionalism requires the state to assume a complete responsibility for those who are governed and thus refers to the state's duty to attain social justice and include all peoples in the governance system. As Walker puts it, constitutionalism 'came first and foremost to be defined in functional opposition to absolutism, as a guarantee of *limited* (by law) government as opposed to *unlimited* government'.[11] It thus requires, as Rosenfeld said, 'adherence to the rule of law, and the protection of fundamental rights'.[12] Plausible as they are, these narrations are not expressive *per se* of a state obligation to include 'the others' who do not belong to the dominant majority group.

Ghai, too, notes that 'the rule-of-law and constitutionalism' originally 'paid little attention to diversities among the people of the state', and were instead 'based on the assumption of the homogeneity of the people'.[13] As Walker rightly claims on another occasion, constitutionalism 'has been traditionally understood in unitary and hierarchical terms', with an empathic reference 'to a single, bounded, and ultimately indivisible' unit, that is, 'the state'.[14] That this state-centric idea of constitutionalism, overly reliant on the unity or indivisibility of the national identity, is incompatible with the modern notion of constitutionalism hardly needs stressing. The emergence of a 'new constitutional landscape' in today's 'post-modern globalized world' indeed compels us to reconstruct constitutionalism 'in non-unitary terms'.[15] Consequently, modern constitutionalism is inescapably inclusive of all peoples in the political governance, and cognitive of multi-ethnicity and national diversities.

Undeniably, however, whether modern constitutions are, or can really be, inclusive of indigenous peoples remains a practical question. Writing in 1995, James Tully argued that standard constitutional vocabularies are crafted in a way that they posit the question of diversity or inclusion as inimical to unity and indivisibility of the country concerned.[16] In his view, while toleration is practised, constitutional inclusion in the real sense of the term was still far-fetched.[17] Tully's pessimistic but pragmatic narration of the practices of constitutionalism[18] provides an important pointer to the global constitutional realism which, as indicated, sees constitutionalism through a unitary lens.[19]

Some constitutionalism scholars, inspired by a biased notion of unitary citizenship for the state durability, developed the theory of 'constitutional patriotism'[20] and thus proved right Tully's suspicions. Constitutional patriotism advocates argue that 'accommodation of sub-state nationalism will tend to undermine the viability of constitutional democracies'.[21] Integrationists and accommodation scholars dismiss the constitutional patriotists, arguing that inclusion of diverse nations constitutionally and as part of the polity will drive a divided society in the direction of a community based on principle and cohesion even in the absence of a common political identity.[22] Similarly, Rosenfeld and several other scholars came together portraying modern constitutionalism as a 'bridge between self and other' or as 'interplay between (dominant national) identity and diversity'.[23]

On the other hand, Ghai draws a picture of constitutionalism as necessarily accommodative of ethnicity or diversity, suggesting two distinct approaches that can be taken into account when designing a constitution.[24] First, one can pay attention to the concerns of minorities with regard to their political integration and participation, based on the notion of entitlements arising from individual citizenship but short of constitutional recognition of their distinct identity. For Ghai, this approach can be accommodated within the traditional view of constitutionalism or the rule of law. Second, which is Ghai's preferred approach, we can accord political or constitutional recognition to non-dominant communities, to provide them with a more solid basis for their participation in the polity. This approach presupposes a concept of constitutionalism that is inherently inclusive and hence distinct from its traditional facet. As Ghai continues to argue, this will require the change of the traditional notions of state sovereignty and hegemonic unitary nationality to the notions of sovereignty that is 'shared by communities' and 'nationality' that is based on multi-national identities.[25] What will also be necessary is the reorientation of our energy on the promotion of group and socio-economic rights of the diverse communities, as opposed to remaining disproportionately engaged with traditional fundamental rights of the individuals.[26]

In practical terms, too, the world has moved in recent years, though not in a remarkably greater extent, toward a framework of wider inclusion of the excluded communities within the 'nation states'.[27] For the constitutionalization of the value of inclusion, international standards provide a further normative impetus. International law today generally provides for a right of indigenous peoples to cultural autonomy and identity.[28] First and foremost, the international bill of rights recognise the right to self-determination of 'all peoples', a term which no doubt includes the indigenous peoples.[29] Moreover, specific international human rights instruments protect the rights of minorities and prohibit discrimination against them on the basis of race.[30] More specifically, two indigenous people-specific conventions of the International Labour Organization provide for state responsibilities in protecting the rights of indigenous peoples,[31] while the Declaration on the Rights of Indigenous Peoples 2007 establishes indigenous peoples' rights of self-determination and autonomy without external interference.[32] While there are debates over the binding effect of Declarations and although there are problems of implementation of even the binding instruments, they collectively express a widely-accepted norm that people of non-dominant identities should be accommodated in national governance.

III A Background of the Specialty of the Chittagong Hill Tracts

Of approximately 3 million indigenous people belonging to at least 54 different ethnic groups and speaking at least 35 different languages, about 0.7 million belong to the CHT in southeastern Bangladesh,[33] which comprises the Rangamati, Khagrachari, and Bandarban districts.[34]

Indigenous people of the CHT were an autonomous, culture-based community before their colonization by the British that in effect began in 1860 when the region was named as the 'Chittagong Hill Tracts' and placed as a separate district under the British colonial administration.[35] Even after this intervention of the British, the CHT remained largely autonomous and beyond the jurisdiction of the ordinary courts of judicature. Nor were all laws applicable in the CHT,[36] which had its own traditional justice system administered by courts of Rajas (circle chiefs) and their Headmen (*mauza* chiefs) and *Karbaris* (village chiefs) with respect to petty cases involving customs, usages, and institutions of three circles of Chakma, Mong, and Bohmong communities.[37]

The above legal indigeneity was recognized and entrenched in the Chittagong Hill Tracts Regulation 1900 (hereafter 'Regulation'),[38] which, along with the rules framed thereunder, sought to preserve the self-government and political participation of the indigenous people, by providing for a separate regime for civil, land, revenue, and judicial administration of the CHT. The Regulation, for example, imposed restrictions on land transfer[39] as well as on residence rights of non-indigenous people ('non-hillmen'), and preserved the administrative and judicial roles of *Rajas* or *mauza* headmen.[40] Subsequently, however, 'the British became concerned to isolate the region and its [peoples] from the rest of Bengal administratively and politically'.[41] They amended the Regulation, declaring the CHT a 'backward tract' to be administered as an 'excluded area'.[42]

After the independence of British India in 1947, the CHT was annexed to the newly established Pakistani state against the wishes and resistance of the indigenous people. Arguably, Pakistan thus had an uneasy relationship with, and a non-accommodationist attitude to, these people. The short-lived 1956 Constitution of Pakistan, however, retained the special administrative status of the CHT as an 'excluded area',[43] which meant that the provincial Dhaka government did not have any significant role in the region's governance and that not all laws were applicable there. Later the dominant Bengali interest groups began to demonstrate their rejection of the British policy of restrained non-indigenous residence in the region. This ultimately led the already desensitized central government to initiate deliberate Bengali in-migration to the CHT and the process of alienation of the indigenous land through the much criticized Kaptai hydro-power project.[44] This also led to a change of the status of the CHT to one of 'tribal area' in the 1962 Constitution of Pakistan. This change had the potential of a quasi-recognition of the indigenous people's autonomy, but the government's action was anything but sincerely inclusive. The 1962 Pakistani Constitution encouragingly provided that an area designated as 'tribal' could not be written off against the wishes of the people of the area concerned.[45] In a clear violation of this provision, the CHT was struck out of the list of tribal areas in 1964.[46] Curiously, however, the special administrative nature of the CHT under the 1900 Regulation continued to exist, but the region's constitutional de-recognition had damaging legal and policy implications.[47]

In the background of the above scenario, Bangladesh emerged as an independent nation in 1971 and adopted its Constitution in 1972 without expressly according to the CHT its special status. Regrettably, there has since been 'a persistent denial and systematic reluctance to acknowledge the plural and heterogeneous nature of [the Bangladeshi] society'.[48] There was once even an attempt during the second military regime in the 1980s to repeal the CHT Regulation altogether.[49] Ultimately, however, the Regulation survived and continued to exist as a valid law. This is, however, not to say that the absence of constitutional recognition of the indigenous people or of the special status of the CHT did not have any damaging implications. The constitutional silence, for example, led to a 2003 controversial decision by the High Court Division that the CHT Regulation was a 'dead law',[50] and to a 2010 decision that the CHT Regional Council was unconstitutional.[51] These two decisions, analysed below, indeed contradicted a series of decisions that directly or by implication affirmed the validity of the Regulation and the legal indigeneity of the indigenous peoples.[52] They now stand virtually reversed by a landmark decision of the Appellate Division of the Supreme Court in *Wagachara Tea Estate Ltd. v Muhammad Abu Taher and Others* (2014).[53]

The *Wagachara Tea Estate Ltd.* decision has in the clearest terms recognized the CHT's administrative specialty, and also has used the terminology of 'indigenous people' for the first time. For the Court, 'there is [an] implied [constitutional] recognition of special status of CHT which is completely distinct from [...] other parts of the Republic'. It further commented:

> There is no doubt that the Regulation of 1900 is a special law that applied to several parts of former British India [...] where indigenous peoples were inhabited. This piece of legislation was promulgated in accordance with the laws, customs and systems [pertaining] to the indigenous peoples of Chittagong Hill Districts. It not only retains the special legal and administrative status of the three districts, but also safeguards a wide body of customary laws on land, forest and other natural resources of the indigenous people residing in those districts.[54]

IV From Exclusion to Passive Recognition of the Indigenous People in Bangladesh

IV.1 Constitution-framing and the Exclusion of 'the Others'

Upon the emergence of Bangladesh, the CHT peoples' legitimate demand 'for political recognition and some form of autonomy' within the new State was refuted.[55] During the founding moment, the framers were indeed swayed by a feeling of a national homogeneity. At a general level, unlike the Indian and Pakistani constitutions, the Constitution of Bangladesh *per se* did not construct and recognise 'minorities' as a class for the purpose of protection. Until the 15th constitutional amendment of 2001, there was no mention at all of minorities or of cultural diversity.

In the Constituent Assembly, the only elected representative of the CHT, Manobendra Narayan Larma, expressed his dismay at the absence of a minority protection clause in the draft Constitution. Specifically, he raised an objection that the draft Constitution 'did not reflect the hopes and aspirations of the tribal population' of the CHT.[56] He proposed incorporating a clause in the fundamental rights chapter to give a recognition to autonomous status of the CHT 'so that the tribal population could establish its political, economic, social, and religious rights'.[57] To press their demand, a delegation of the indigenous people led by Mr Larma met Bangabandhu Sheikh Mujibur Rahman, the founding leader of the country, and demanded the following: (a) autonomy for the CHT with its own legislature, (b) constitutional protection of the 1900 Regulation, (c) continuation of the tribal chiefs' offices, and (d) the imposition of an embargo on in-migration of 'non-tribal people' into the CHT.[58]

These demands were impromptu rejected, because they were assumed to be against national sovereignty and the principle of Bengali nationalism. Regrettably, the founding leader of the country is rather reported to have asked the adivasis to assume the Bengali identity by shunning their own. This assimilative Bengali identity ideology is imputable to an aggressive majoritarianism arising from the war-time mandate in 1971 that ultimately came to 'subsume' and indeed 'delegitimize' all other identity claims.[59] Bangladesh thus began its troublesome constitutional journey arguably with an assimilative or integrational, and not accommodative[60] approach to the issues of indigenous autonomy and identity, embracing thereby 'constitutional patriotism'.[61]

Of the four demands from the indigenous people, the demand for substantive political autonomy with a separate legislature was too ambitious and was potentially a threat to the integrity of a just born state. The other three demands, which they had long been historically enjoying, were indeed quite rationale and hence could be accommodated without incurring any risk to the unitary sovereignty. Understandably, there was a valid reason, tied with the overarching need of nation building and managing complex international politics concerning the emergence of Bangladesh, to predicate the Constitution on the principle of Bangalee nationalism. The exclusion of marginalised indigenous communities, however, was a grave constitutional mistake. Clearly, there was a need, and no doubt an opportunity, to recognise the indigenous people's right to cultural identity in a meaningful way against the narrow, homogeneous identity markers in a heterogeneous or plurinational society.[62] Bangladesh is a country of rich pluralism—cultural, ethnic, religious, and political. As such, not addressing the issues of ethnic identity and linguistic distinction within the purview of national identity continued to be a significant issue of discontent in the later years.[63] A constitution in a diverse society should have a unifying or rallying power, able to strengthen the unity amidst diversity.[64] In the designing of the Bangladeshi Constitution this unifying attribute was missing.

The founding leaders thus un-pragmatically chose to entrench only the dominant Bengali nationalism, which was expressly declared to be a 'high ideal' of the Constitution.[65] They 'could not evaluate the blind spot' of this majoritarian nationalism that later turned out to be severely consequential.[66] As things began unfolding soon thereafter, the abrupt rejection of indigenous claims proved to be an organic defect in the country's otherwise democratic constitution. In South Asia, linguistic (or ethnic) nationalism has been one of the principal forces shaping constitutional developments for over sixty years.[67] That this is more so a case in Bangladesh became evident when Mr Larma established a political entity in 1972 with an armed wing (named as Shanti Bahinee/Peace Troops) in 1973 to fight for autonomy, if not secession, of the CHT and commenced a protracted insurgency.[68] The insurgency became intense in subsequent years, lingering for over 25 years. Arguably, the intensification of the CHT problem is mostly a consequence of the majoritarian imposition of a hegemonic national identity on the indigenous peoples.[69]

Although the Independence Constitution failed to adopt an inclusive approach, it had enacted several provisions aimed at establishing an exploitation-free society based on democratic principles and social justice.[70] It entrenched the principle of 'secularism', and provided for the right of 'every religious community or denomination' to establish, maintain, and manage its religious institutions.[71] Democracy is an essential feature of the constitution, and the state is duty-bound to ensure 'effective participation' by the people at all levels of administration through their elected representatives.[72] Importantly, the constitution establishes a substantive concept of legal equality of all citizens (art 27), with a provision for affirmative state actions. While the constitution prohibits discrimination among citizens and provides for the equality of opportunity for all citizens in public employment, it also makes it clear that these provisions shall not prevent 'the State from making special provision' 'for the advancement of any backward section of citizens', or 'for the purpose of securing their adequate representation in the service of the Republic'.[73] On the other hand, the constitutional possibility of imposing 'reasonable' restrictions on certain fundamental rights can be interpreted as lending support to any law limiting rights of the members of the political majority.[74] These provisions leave no doubt that the constitution supports, and indeed requires, affirmative actions in favour of various minority groups including the indigenous people.[75] The affirmative actions-enabling provisions could have been used to 'alleviate social discrimination' suffered by the indigenous communities of the CHT.[76] It, however, remains a different but curious question whether or to what extent Bangladesh has adopted any affirmative programmes for the indigenous peoples.

IV.2 Including the Excluded: The Peace Agreement and Other Structural Reform

Alongside formal legal inclusion of diverse ethno-cultural nationals, there might be informal inclusion of such groups within the concerned polity. As Sen poignantly tells us, 'the predicaments of others' can be mitigated through moral and political inclusion of non-dominant, marginalized or excluded peoples, without even invoking 'any great identity issue' in that inclusion.[77] This sort of indirect or tacit recognition of indigenous peoples is actually practised by some states such as Australia.

Although Bangladesh has not yet taken any systemic plan in the form of affirmative actions to improve the conditions of different minority or ethnic groups, the government has lately adopted a policy of indirect inclusion. A limited scheme of reserved seats for 'tribal' (*upajati*) students in universities and a 5 per cent quota for the inhabitants of the CHT (both 'tribal' and 'non-tribal') in civil public appointments were introduced in the late 1980s.

The process of dialogue with the indigenous peoples' representatives in effect started in the mid-70s with certain legal and institutional measures for the 'welfare' of the 'inhabitants' of the CHT having been initiated. These attempts continued amidst the continuing conflict in the region and the government's often repressive counter-insurgency actions. In January 1976, for example, the Chittagong Hill Tracts Development Board was established with a mandate to launch and implement development projects there,[78] with a policy of reserving 10 per cent development projects for indigenous contractors being introduced in 1983. Thereafter, in 1977, the first military regime began consulting the leaders of the CHT in search of a solution to the problem of insurgency. This process was revived later in the late 1980s.[79] Eventually, on 28 February 1989, Parliament enacted three statues with a view to recognising and protecting some form of self-government by the indigenous people. These laws provided for the introduction of a local district council in each of the CHT districts with majority indigenous representation.[80] They sought to give 22 counts of powers to those self-government bodies including power to appoint certain police officers and to approve or prohibit the transfer of tribal land (7 heads of powers were actually transferred).

A landmark policy intervention took place in 1997 when the government entered into a peace agreement, the Chittagong Hill Tracts Peace Accord, with the representative organization of indigenous communities in the CHT.[81] The Accord seemingly established peace by arriving at a seizure of armed belligerence, and by promising to establish indigenous peoples' right over the lands as well as their share in the governance of the state. The CHT Accord expressed the CHT-people's 'fullest and firm confidence in the sovereignty and integrity of Bangladesh', while aiming at 'the preservation of the character of the region' and the realization of its people's 'political, social, cultural, educational, and economic rights'.[82] Though a political instrument not backed or entrenched by any constitutional provision, the Accord can arguably be considered kind of a recognition of the indigenous autonomy, since it sought to increase in effect the indigenous self-rule through the regional and district councils as well as offices of circle chiefs and their deputies.

As expected, the CHT Accord prompted a number of legislative, administrative, and structural changes. In 1988, a separate CHT Affairs Ministry was created[83] and several laws amending the 1989 statues pertaining to the CHT district councils were enacted. Importantly, a special type of region-wide self-government body, namely the Chittagong Hill Tracts Regional Council (CHTRC), was also established.[84] Further later, in 2001, a land disputes settlement commission was established to deal with what by now had become the most complicated issue of land ownerships by the indigenous people.[85] Apart from their demand of constitutional recognition, a major concern for the indigenous people for many years has been to establish their right to collective ownership over land that remained ever-challenged and is until this day not protected through any meaningful remedies.[86]

The breadth of hopes that the Peace Accord had brought forth, however, soon began to shrink. The success of the Accord was marred by problems of implementation, and the conflict, albeit in a new form, continued to exist.[87] The problems of its implementation or the reasons for its inefficacy can be attributed, among other factors, to the absence of inclusive constitutionalism in Bangladesh both in terms of the lack of an entrenched recognition of the indigenous identity and the prevalence of 'cultural hegemony of Bengalis' in the name of 'the supremacy of the national state'.[88] Beginning in 2000s in particular, interested political quarters and Bengali settlers began to increasingly question the legitimacy and constitutionality of the Peace Accord and the consequential legal arrangements, by invoking the 'unitary', 'sovereignty', and 'equality' vocabularies.

As one informed commentator presciently observed in 2004, despite the above good efforts and structural reform, 'the overall political situation in the country' probably suggested that 'formal acceptance' of many of the indigenous peoples' demands on political, economic, and cultural matters, including their constitutional recognition as indigenous peoples, was 'still a long way away'.[89] A reflection of this apprehension is to be found in the new Article 23A of the Constitution, enacted through the 15th amendment.[90] Before the enactment of this new clause, indigenous leaders were consulted, albeit inadequately, and they once again strongly raised the demand of constitutional recognition of indigenous identity. Article 23A, however, emerged as a much lesser good in a sheer frustration of their expectation. This provision makes it a fundamental principle of state policy that the State shall take steps to 'protect and develop the unique local culture and tradition of the *tribes*, *minor races*, ethnic *sects* and communities'.[91] The use of these terminologies to refer to the people who have long been demanding for their recognition as 'indigenous' or 'aboriginals' is incompatible with the concept of human dignity and inclusive governance.[92] By the standards of international law, there is no doubt that the marginalized ethnic communities in Bangladesh qualify to be called 'indigenous'.[93] The government did not take into consideration the force of this international normative appeal, nor did it use the chance to make the Constitution an accommodationist instrument in a better way. By terms of the amended Article 6, the collective nationality of 'the people of Bangladesh' is still 'Bangalee'.

On a positive note, the recent arrangement, however deficient it might be, can be seen as an expression of plurality-consciousness from the top policymakers. When compared with the previous scenario of no recognition at all of indigenous peoples or the uncertain promise of constitutional affirmative actions, Article 23A seems to offer for the first time some kind of 'explicit' constitutional recognition of the excluded social groups.[94] This is however nothing like a truly fuller recognition of ethnic separateness of the indigenous people. Given the political reality and the culture of constitutional amendments, the 15th amendment's provision of an ethnic groups-specific state policy and the restoration of 'secularism' can nonetheless be seen as an 'attempt at inclusion'.[95] As Menski insightfully commented, 'avoidance of precariousness for the various minorities of Bangladesh has now been written into the basic structure of the revised Constitution'.[96] Menski takes these changes as 'an acknowledgement' that 'the integration and dutiful protection of the various concerned minority groups' is now 'a constitutional duty of the nation'.[97] The discharge of this duty would remain an onerous yet constitutional responsibility for the government.

V The Judicial Narrative of Indigenous Autonomy

As seen above, Bangladeshi constitutionalism is still exclusionary of identities of various ethnic groups. In the case of CHT, the absence of constitutional recognition of its special administrative status and its people's distinct identity has been of negative implications for the realization of indigenous rights.[98] This constitutional exclusion, coupled with the absence of an express constitutional backing for various post-Accord pro-indigenous reforms culminated in a successful legal challenge to the CHT Regional Council in *Mohammad Badiuzzaman v Bangladesh* (2010), analysed ahead.[99] First, it is convenient to briefly locate the trajectory of the judicial narrative of indigenous autonomy or self-determination that seemingly influenced the *Badiuzzaman* decision.

Way back in 1989, the Appellate Division in *Anwar Hossain Chowdhury v Bangladesh* declared the unitary-ness of the country as an unamendable basic structure of the Constitution.[100] Justice Shahabudin Ahmed, a majority judge, held:

> As to the unitary character of the State it is clear that in view of the *homogeneity of her people having same language, culture, tradition and way of life within a small territory* the state has been so organized as a unitary state by its founding fathers leaving no scope for devolution of executive, legislative and judicial powers on different regions to turn [it] into [a Federation] ultimately.[101]

To see the Bangladeshi State, which has historically been a culturally and religiously pluralist society, as homogeneous in terms of language, culture, and life-style seems to be a prejudiced idea. At its best, this obiter about the homogeneity of the Bangladeshi society was a historical blunder. However, both this obiter and the ruling that essential constitutional features including Bangladesh's unitary nature are unamendable were misapplied by courts on several occasions. In *Bikram Kishore Chakma v Land Appeal Board*

(2000), for example, the High Court Division held that the CHT could not claim a special status under the 'unitary' Constitution to exclude the application of an Act of Parliament.[102] The petitioner unsuccessfully argued that disputes relating to land in the CHT had to be resolved only in accordance with the CHT Regulation. Based on a blind reliance on the above obiter of Ahmed J, the *Chakma* Court held that all laws should by that very fact be applicable in the CHT, thereby implausibly rejecting the idea of special legal treatment of indigenous people. In a 2003 case, *Rangamati Food Products Ltd v Commissioner of Customs,* the HCD once again misapplied, indeed extremely, the notion of unitary sovereignty to find the Regulation to be an invalid law.[103] At issue was whether a tax law was applicable in the CHT so as to diminish special tax benefits claimed by a CHT-based company, an issue that is inextricably linked with the notion of inclusive constitutionalism based on a substantive concept of constitutional equality. By invoking their perceived notion of national unitary sovereignty, both courts dismissed the idea of 'extra privileges' under the Constitution for 'the hill districts'.[104]

Promisingly, however, the top courts have generally upheld the validity of the Regulation and endorsed the indigeneity of different peoples of the CHT and the normativity of their participation in their own social or cultural affairs.[105] Although the judiciary has not yet authoritatively pronounced on their identity, the indigenous peoples' distinctness has been recently clearly acknowledged by the Appellate Division in *Wagachara Tea Estate Ltd.* (2014).[106] By unequivocally endorsing the specialty of the Regulation, this decision has now effectively reversed the force of the above two HCD-decisions as well as of the *Badiuzzaman* decision.[107] Its most recent decision in this regard in *Bangladesh v Rangamati Food Products Ltd* held that the HCD was wrong in holding that the CHT Regulation was a dead law.[108] It is nevertheless profitable to analyse the *Badiuzzaman* judgment for a better understanding of the judicial narrative of ethno-cultural diversity and indigenous autonomy in Bangladesh.

In *Badiuzzaman,* a Bangalee settler in the CHT challenged the constitutionality of the Peace Accord and the Regional Council in 2000.[109] When this challenge was awaiting a hearing, a Dhaka-based lawyer, also an active member of a political party, brought an abstract constitutional petition in 2007 on similar grounds and praying for almost identical remedies.[110] Both petitioners invoked the principle of constitutional equality and the unitary character of the State. Deciding the two petitions jointly, the HCD declared the CHT Regional Council unconstitutional for violating the State's unitary character and for not being a local government within the meaning of the Constitution.[111] The court also struck down certain statutory provisions on the ground that they were discriminatory against non-indigenous citizens, an approach that is even more problematic from the perspective of inclusive constitutionalism. One such provision was the common section 6 of three amending Acts of 1998 concerning the three Hill Districts Councils, by virtue of which the Circle Chiefs could certify a person as a 'non-tribal' resident.[112] Another provision the court invalidated was the one that required a non-tribal person to be both a permanent resident of, and owning land in, the CHT for being eligible to vote in the elections of district councils. For the court, these provisions contravened, among others, the constitutional equality to be enjoyed by all citizens of the country.[113]

Interestingly, the court refused to invalidate the Peace Accord and the arrangement relating to the settlement of land disputes in the CHT, which it saw as acts of political expediency and wisdom. As it said, the court was cognizant of the limitations of its 'authority, expertise, and ability' to resolve such an admixture of social, economic, and political issues as were the Peace Accord and the land-issue.[114] Displaying a radical departure from this sound view of judicial role via-à-vis politically charged problems, however, the court indeed negated the core of that Accord by striking down the consequential laws providing for indigenous self-government.[115] The reasoning advanced was largely a technical one, that is, that those statutory provisions were incompatible with the scheme of the constitution. In this part of the chapter, we remain concerned mainly with the judicial invalidation of the CHTRC alone.

The 1997 Peace Accord, envisaging certain exclusive privileges and rights for the indigenous people, was a high-level policy issue. Despite the fact that its implementation became problematic, the Accord was a notable success in ending the decades-long conflict in the CHT. The CHTRC was one of two new institutions innovated pursuant to the Accord, which was not only a paradigmatic improvement in the style of indigenous people's participation, but also was a means of tacitly recognising their separate cultural and political identity. From the normative perspective of inclusive constitutionalism and in light of the specific political contexts, it seems that the court failed to properly appreciate the much-needed political solution that culminated in a special body like the CHTRC and the empowerment of district councils composed predominantly of members of indigenous groups.

Although the court showed some measure of sensitization about the need for a continuing peace process with regard to the CHT-problem, it 'never mentioned the distinct ethnic origin' of the indigenous peoples.[116] In invalidating the CHTRC, it had rather over-read the basic-structure doctrine to find this self-government body as an affront to the State's unitary character.

Focusing on the regional aspect of the CHTRC, the court found the Council's constitutive Act of 1998 to have 'the potential to eventually claim the status of a federating unit for the CHT, thereby, destroying the very fabric of a unitary Republic'.[117] In its view, with the establishment of the CHTRC and the consolidation of indigenous self-governance through district councils in 1998, the government's hitherto practised 'integrationist approach' became 'replaced by a rival approach [that] recognizes the right of tribal people[s] as distinct peoples.'.[118] The court ultimately found this 'paradigm shift' to be not 'correspond[ing] to [their] understanding of the concept of "autonomy" [within] the existing constitutional framework' of Bangladesh.[119]

It is abundantly clear, therefore, that the court invoked notions of 'autonomy' and 'self-determination' that are unduly conservative on the question of inclusiveness. For it, autonomy is 'an essential component of democracy', which can be viewed 'primarily as ensuring and protecting basic rights' as complemented by the state's limited capacity to intervene with the 'autonomous community'.[120] Yet the Court was unwilling to see 'autonomy' as anything more than that. According to a modern parlance of the term, 'indigenous self-determination' is about ensuring good democratic governance that requires responsiveness by the state and participation of the indigenous people in its affairs.[121] Today, the 'dominant principle of self-determination' is that of non-secessionist or 'internal self-determination' that, depending on the needs of the given society, may be based on devolution, federalism, power-sharing, or individual and group rights protections.[122] In its analysis, the *Badiuzzaman* court failed to appreciate that indigenous self-determination in a unitary State such as Bangladesh can be achieved through 'a range of possibilities of institutional re-ordering other than the creation of new states,'[123] or without undermining state sovereignty'.[124] The CHTRC and the transfer to the CHT district councils of certain indigenous-specific powers are definitely innovations of the type that is within the fold of a unitary constitutional order.

The *Badiuzzaman Case* was built on a narrow concept of constitutional equality. The petitioners argued that the CHTRC and the new model of enhanced indigenous participation through the district councils could alternatively be seen as constitutional affirmative actions. Dismissing this argument, the court claimed that there were no objective standards to determine the 'backwardness' of the indigenous people warranting such affirmative actions,[125] and that positive constitutional discrimination in favour of any group must not at the same time be discriminatory against other groups.[126] Needless to say, the court again resorted to an understanding of indigenous autonomy through a lens of majoritarian, hegemonic citizenship. Constitutional inclusion of ethnic minorities is in effect an issue of active citizenship, that is, the issue of realisation of one's self and 'not the extension of the self to others'.[127]

It should be noted here that the above obiter on the value of affirmative state actions now stands reversed in the Appellate Division's decision in *Wagachara Tea Estate Ltd*, which however did not specifically mention *Badiuzzaman*. The Appellate Division held as follows:

> There is no doubt that the citizens of three hill districts are backward people. These provisions embody the concept of making special provisions for the weaker backward section of the citizens by taking such measures as are necessary for [the] removal of economic inequalities and rectifying discriminations resulting from State actions between unequal in society. This may be achieved by special laws or by direct regulation of transactions by forbidding certain transactions. It also means that those who have been deprived [of] their property by unconstitutional actions should be [given back] their property.[128]

Indigenous autonomy, which is necessarily country-specific, emphasizes the implementation of indigenous group rights, which are rooted 'not just in claims to protect culture, but also in claims to economic and social equality and political participation'.[129] For durable peace in the CHT, political negotiations, legislative actions, judicial decisions, or constitutional designing should essentially take the distribution of political power more seriously. This will also require the political majority to involve in the redressal of past injustices suffered by, especially, the excluded minority.

The *Badiuzzaman case* was decided at a time when the erosions in the trust and confidence of the indigenous peoples had already turned from bad to worse, and when the implementation of the CHT Peace Accord was almost in limbo. That decision was no doubt of consequences for a political environment in which all groups or citizens can live together despite diversities and differences.[130]

VI Inclusive Constitutionalism for 'the Indigenous': A Comparative Approach

The problems of managing issues of ethnic diversity today are quite ubiquitous. Everywhere, indigenous peoples are claiming the right to manage their own affairs through distinctive community government. In South Asia, too, both this claim and the 'challenges to national identity and territory' are fairly identical among several nations.[131] As Adeney has argued, those countries of South Asia, such as Sri Lanka and Pakistan, which have not accommodated their non-dominant groups, have witnessed high levels of conflict.[132] This observation is also true of Nepal whose intensely negotiated new Constitution of 2015 has after many experimentations adopted an inclusionary approach to ethno-national communities aimed at an inclusion of them in the affairs of the state.[133]

Among the South Asian states, India has been the most accommodative constitutionalism in terms of managing ethnic or religious diversities.[134] Although it still has problems of ethnic conflicts, the country offers certain constitutional and political tools of better managing ethnic diversities that 'Bangladesh can and should learn'.[135] Indian founding constitutional pluralism recognized 'the right of cultural collectivities'[136] and guaranteed inclusion of different peoples including the indigenous people, providing for their cultural autonomy.[137] In addition to the famous positive discrimination clause, directive principles of the Indian Constitution mandate the protection of social, economic, and educational interests of the 'tribals'.[138] Importantly, regions dominated by indigenous people have been granted constitutional power to prevent alienation of land and to limit in-migration of non-indigenous people, which furthers the objective of preserving indigeneity of those regions.[139]

When adopting its own constitution, Bangladesh did not consider the above practice of inclusive constitutional designing from its most important neighbouring country, India, or from any other country. Nor have its courts followed indigenous-specific comparative jurisprudence effectively. In *Badiuzzaman,* for example, a constricted unitary view of state sovereignty led to the rejection of comparative experiences of liberal indigenous self-governance schemes from the United Kingdom, Italy, Spain, and China. These jurisdictions were refused to be considered on the ground that they were all federal and not unitary states.[140] It was unclear why was it necessary for a state to be 'federal' to effectively deal with the issues of indigenous autonomy or self-governance. First, autonomy to indigenous communities can be granted as a means of accommodating ethnic diversity or greater self-government in unitary states as is the case, for example, in Nicaragua.[141] Second, even in a federal state, a federating unit may have ethnic minority problems similar in nature to those in a unitary state. Consider, for example, the case of majority Bengali-dominated West Bengal in India that has established in 2011 an autonomous self-government system, wider in its extent, for the indigenous people in the Darjeeling District.[142] The West Bengal experience is the closest to the case of CHT in terms of the claim of autonomy, peace accord, and the majoritarian national identity. Yet this and other regional experiences from India[143] went largely missing in the Bangladeshi judicial or executive discourses on indigenous autonomy.

Recent Indian developments, especially with regard to the problem of ethnic conflicts in its north-eastern states bordering with Bangladesh, show that a new relationship between different ethnic groups and the Indian state authorities is graduating toward a solid base.[144] The Indian experience including the case of Wes Bengal 'basically shows that there is no viable long-term scope for tribal self-determination that would carve out a new nation station'.[145] Bangladesh, too, is not definitely going to give up its sovereignty over the territory of the CHT, whereas the indigenous leaders are not in reality claiming a complete regional autonomy but rather a better share for the indigenous people in the affairs of the state.

VII Conclusion

This chapter has shown that despite the nation's pluralist legal-constitutional order, Bangladesh's constitutionalism is not inclusive enough. Constitutional exclusion of different ethnic groups including the indigenous people of the CHT at the founding moment of Bangladesh, which was based on a majoritarian Bengali nationalism and inspired by constitutional patriotism, constituted a genetic defect in its Constitution. As seen above, this exclusion later proved quite damaging for peace and good governance of the country. Discourses about ethno-cultural diversities in Bangladesh still remain largely tainted by colonial understandings of identity, self-autonomy, and territorial chauvinism. As such, the genetic constitutional defect has still not been fully removed despite certain recent pro-indigenous legal and administrative reforms.

While the recent constitutional provision for a state duty to protect ethnic minority groups as well as restoring secularism and installing Bangladeshi nationalism along with Bengali nationalism should prove instrumental for the indigenous rights, constitutional arrangements are still not satisfactorily in line with the notion of inclusive constitutionalism. For example, the constitution does not expressly recognize the cultural, linguistic, and ethnic separateness of the indigenous people, while the top-level policymakers are seemingly inimical even to using the term 'indigenous people'. On the other hand, although the Supreme Court has in varying ways recognized the indigeneity of these people, it has yet to become robust enough on the issue of their constitutional inclusion and recognition. The recent judgment of the Appellate Division that there is an implied constitutional recognition of the special administrative status of the CHT should thus be considered the beginning of a shift towards a specific identity recognition of the indigenous peoples.

The lack of constitutional recognition of 'the Indigenous' is indeed an anti-thesis to the rule of law, and is generative of varying forms of human rights implications. Inclusive constitutionalism denotes an idea of inclusive rule-of-law that emphasizes a functional connection between the culturally diverse peoples and the 'nation state' of which they are constitutive members.[146] Such a functional inclusion often has a positive impact on the realization of indigenous rights as well as on the relationship between indigenous and settler communities.[147] In the Bangladeshi context too, a clear constitutional recognition would prove critical for the realization of human dignity and value of the indigenous people, and, importantly, for an environment of living together in the CHT. As described in passing above, a conflict-like situation is still persisting in the CHT despite the 1997 peace agreement and several other structural reforms. This situation can fairly be imputed to the absence of inclusive constitutionalism in Bangladesh. It is, therefore, argued that unless the Bangladeshi constitutionalism shifts more clearly to an accommodationist approach to ethno-national diversities based on a liberal idea of national unity, the lasting peace in the CHT will likely remain problematic.

Notes and References

1. See S. Wiessner, 1999. 'Rights and Status of Indigenous Peoples: A Global Comparative and International Legal Analysis', *Harvard Human Rights Journal*, 12: 57–128.
2. In this chapter, I use the term 'indigenous' interchangeably with *adivasis* ('the ancient/original inhabitants'), to refer to the first peoples of the CHT. The government and policy/legal instruments increasingly tend to dismiss both terms but instead prefer 'tribes' or 'tribal people'. Peter Dawson. 2015. 'On Self-determination and Constitutional Recognition', *Indigenous Law Bulletin*, 8(16): 1–4. The indigenous people themselves like to be called 'Jumma people' ('high landers'), on which see van Schendel, W. 1992. 'The Invention of the "Jummas": State Formation and Ethnicity in Southeastern Bangladesh', *Modern Asian Studies*, 26(1): pp. 95–128. On the politics of taxonomy of indigeneity, see Roy, *Juridical Pluralism*, below n 37, fn 4.
3. On this, from among a large body of literature, see generally Subir Bhaumik, Meghna Guhathakurta, and S.B. Ray Chaudhury. 1997. *Living on the Edge: Essays on the Chittagong Hill Tracts*. Kathmandu: South Asia Forum for Human Rights; Richard A. Gray, 1994. 'Genocide in the Chittagong Hill Tracts of Bangladesh', *Reference Services Review*, 22(4): pp. 59–79; and Tone Bleie, 2005. *Tribal Peoples, Nationalism and the Human Rights Challenge: The Adivasis of Bangladesh*. Dhaka: University Press Limited.

4. See Prashanta Tripura, 2014. 'Indigenous Peoples under the Legal and Policy Frameworks of Bangladesh', in Mong S. Chowdhury (ed.), *Survival under Threat: Human Rights Situation of Indigenous Peoples in Bangladesh*, pp. 28–38. Chiang Mai, Thailand: Asia Indigenous Peoples Pact and Kapaeeng Foundation.
5. See Ahmed, below n 93 and the accompanying text.
6. Indigenous peoples of the plains are generally known as 'aboriginals' or 'adivasi'. s. 97 of the East Bengal State Acquisition and Tenancy Act, 1950 (Act XX of 1950) that restricts the sale of lands of 'aboriginal castes and tribes' to anyone other than an aboriginal. On Garos, see Ellen Bal, 2007. 'Becoming the Garos of Bangladesh: Policies of Exclusion and the Ethnicisation of a "Tribal" Minority', *South Asia: Journal of South Asian Studies*, 30(3): pp. 439–55; M.R. Ullah, 2010. *The Garo Community: A Marginal Community of Bangladesh.* Dhaka: University Grants Commission.
7. The Indian Supreme Court provides an example. See, e.g., *Kailas and Others v State of Maharashtra* (2011) 1 SCR 94, in which it held (at paras 34–9): 'Among the ... disadvantaged groups, the most disadvantaged and marginalized in India are the Adivasis (STs), who, ..., are the descendants of the original inhabitants of India, ... It is time now to undo the historical injustice [done] to them.' See also *Samatha v State of Andhra Pradesh and Others*, AIR 1997 SC 3297, para 92.
8. The US Supreme Court is often critiqued for this. See, however, its recent decision in *the United States v Bryant* 579 U.S. (2016) (13 June 2016), endorsing the sovereignty of tribal courts and emphasising the need for tribal jurisdiction to tackle the crisis of sexual and domestic violence against Native women.
9. The term constitutional pluralism is used here to refer to pluralist constitutionalism based on multiple intra-state national identities, and not in a supranational context as used, for example, in the European Union. On constitutional pluralism within national legal orders see Alec S. Sweet, 2009. 'Constitutionalism, Legal Pluralism, and International Regimes', *Indiana Journal of Global Legal Studies*, 16(2): pp. 621–45, esp. pp. 631–5. See also Kamala Sankaran, 2013. 'Dealing with Difference: Experiments in Constitutional Pluralism', in P.I. Bhat (ed.), *Constitutionalism and Constitutional Pluralism*. New Delhi: LexisNexis, 287–95 (showing indigenous autonomy and religious family law systems in India as aspects of constitutional pluralism); and Stephen Tierney, 2004. *Constitutional Law and National Pluralism*. Oxford: Oxford University Press.
10. There exists a sheer volume of literature on constitutionalism, and I therefore refrain from citing sources. For our purpose here, a useful source is Yash Ghai, 2013. 'Constitutionalism and the Challenge of Ethnic Diversity', in R.L. Nelson, J.J. Heckman, and L. Cabatingan (eds), *Global Perspectives on the Rule of Law*, pp. 279–302. London: Routledge.
11. Neil Walker, 2010. 'Constitutionalism and the Incompleteness of Democracy: An Iterative Relationship', *Netherland Journal of Legal Philosophy*, 3: 206–33, esp. p. 209 (emphasis in original).

12. Michel Rosenfeld (ed.), 1994. 'Modern Constitutionalism as Interplay between Identity and Diversity', in *Constitutionalism, Identity, Difference, and Legitimacy*, pp. 3–38, esp. p. 3. Durham: Duke University Press.
13. Ghai, 'Constitutionalism and the Challenge of Ethnic Diversity', p. 279.
14. Neil Walker, 2012. 'Constitutionalism and Pluralism in Global Context', in M. Avbelj and J. Komarek (eds), *Constitutional Pluralism in the European Union and Beyond.* Oxford: Hart Publishing, pp. 17–38, esp. p. 17. Walker's remark is equally true in a national setting.
15. Walker, 'Constitutionalism and Pluralism in Global Context', pp. 17–18.
16. James Tully, 1995. *Strange Multiplicity: Constitutionalism in an Age of Diversity.* Cambridge: Cambridge University Press (asking, at p. 1, the question of 'Can a modern constitution recognize and accommodate cultural diversity?').
17. Tully, *Strange Multiplicity: Constitutionalism in an Age of Diversity.* See also M. Seidman, 2004. 'Out of Bounds', *Ohio State Law Journal*, 65: pp. 1329–39 (arguing that the test for true inclusion is whether we are willing to protect groups with whom we disagree).
18. Tully, however, is essentially a constitutional pluralist in the sense that he was for a constitution with an attitude of accommodating cultural and ethnic differences. For a brief critique of Tully, see M.Milde, 1998. 'Critical Notice of James Tully', *Canadian Journal of Philosophy*, 28(1): pp. 119–43.
19. On theoretical exposition of the so-called identity politics see Charles Taylor, 1994. 'The Politics of Recognition', in A. Gutmann (ed.), *Multiculturalism: Examining the Politics of Recognition.* Princeton: Princeton University Press, pp. 25–73; Will Kymlica. 1995. *Multicultural Citizenship: A Liberal Theory of Minority Rights.* Oxford: Oxford University Press; and Avril Bell, 2014. *Relating Indigenous and Settler Identities: Beyond Domination.* London: Palgrave Macmillan, esp. pp. 139–72.
20. On which see generally J. Habermas, 1988. 'The European Nation-State: On the Past and Future of Sovereignty and Citizenship', in C. Cronin and P. De Greiff (eds), *The Inclusion of the Other: Studies in Political Theory.* Cambridge, MA: MIT Press; J.W. Muller, 2007. *Constitutional Patriotism.* Princeton: Princeton University Press; J.W. Muller, and K.L. Scheppele. 2008. 'Constitutional Patriotism: An Introduction', *International Journal of Constitutional Law*, 6: pp. 67–71.
21. A. Schwartz, 2011. 'Patriotism or Integrity? Constitutional Community in Divided Societies', *Oxford Journal of Legal Studies*, 31(3): 503–26, esp. p. 503.
22. Schwartz, 'Patriotism or Integrity?', p. 503. See also Kymlica, *Multicultural Citizenship* (arguing that objections to recognizing minority cultural rights and identities on the ground of national unity can be answered). On various aspects of 'accommodation' see G. Mahajan, (ed.). 2001. *Accommodating Diversity: Ideas and Institutional Practices.* New Delhi: Oxford University Press.
23. Rosenfeld, 'Modern Constitutionalism', p. 3.
24. Ghai, 'Constitutionalism and the Challenge of Ethnic Diversity', p. 279.
25. Ghai, 'Constitutionalism and the Challenge of Ethnic Diversity', p. 279.

26. Ghai, 'Constitutionalism and the Challenge of Ethnic Diversity', p. 279.
27. Some constitutions such as the one of India took an accommodationist approach to ethnic diversities way back in the 1950s or even before. The major three states facing the issue of indigenous identity, the USA, Canada, and New Zealand, have constitutionally recognised aboriginal peoples. In New Zealand, the *Maori Representation Act 1867* introduced the voting rights for Maoris and reserved parliamentary seats for them. See also s. 35 of Canada's *Constitution Act 1982* that 'recognized and affirmed' the 'existing aboriginal and treaty rights of the aboriginal peoples of Canada'.
28. It is beyond the scope of this chapter to provide a detailed analysis of this aspect. But see Wiessner, 'Rights and Status of Indigenous Peoples'; P. Thornberry, 2002. *Indigenous Peoples and Human Rights.* Manchester: Manchester University Press; and J.K. Das. 2001. *Human Rights and Indigenous Peoples.* New Delhi: APH Publishing, esp. pp. 105–7.
29. See the common Article 1 of the International Covenant on Economic, Social and Cultural Rights 1966, and the International Covenant on Civil and Cultural Rights 1966. This right incorporates the right to 'freely determine their political status and freely pursue their economic, social and cultural development'.
30. See, for example, the International Convention on the Elimination of All Forms of Racial Discrimination 1969, and the Declaration on the Rights of Persons Belonging to National or Ethnic, Religious or Linguistic Minorities 1993 [GA Res 47/135, annex, 47 U.N. GAOR Supp. (No. 49) at 210].
31. See the ILO Convention No. 107 concerning Indigenous and Tribal Peoples 1957, and the ILO Convention 169 on Indigenous and Tribal Peoples 1989.
32. United Nations GA Res 61/295, UN Doc A/RES/47/1 (2007), Article 3. See also the Declaration's preamble that affirms that the superiority claim by any people over others is 'legally invalid' and 'socially unjust.' Bangladesh did not sign the Declaration. Dawson, 'On Self-determination and Constitutional Recognition'.
33. In addition, there were 650,000 Bangalee settlers according to an account of 2001 census. A disagreement persists as to the number of ethnic groups within the CHT (which according to some are 13) and also about the size of its population. See Raja D. Roy, *The ILO Convention on Indigenous and Tribal Populations, 1957 and the Laws of Bangladesh: A Comparative Review.* Dhaka: ILO Country Office in Dhaka, esp. pp. 7–10. See also the International Work Group for Indigenous Affairs: http://www.iwgia.org/regions/asia/bangladesh, accessed 17 July 2017.
34. Since 1860 the Chittagong Hill Tracts remained as one special District until 1981-1983 when it was divided into these three districts.
35. By virtue of the Act XXII of 1860 (repealed by the Scheduled Districts Act 1874). The CHT, however, was first annexed by the East-India Company as their tributary in 1787, although recognizing its quasi-independent status.
36. See, for example, s. 4 of the Chittagong Hill Tracts Regulation 1900.

37. Chittagong Hill Tracts Regulation, 1900, s. 8. See further Ridwanul Hoque, 2014. 'Courts and the Adjudication System in Bangladesh: In Quest of Viable Reforms', in J.R. Yeh, and Wen-Chen Chang (eds), *Asian Courts in Context.* Cambridge: Cambridge University Press, pp. 447–86. On customary laws and the adjudication system in the CHT, see Raja D. Roy, 2004. 'Challenges for Juridical Pluralism and Customary Laws of Indigenous Peoples: The Case of the Chittagong Hill Tracts, Bangladesh', *Arizona Journal of International and Comparative Law*, 21(1): pp. 113–82; Raja D. Roy, 2005. *Traditional Customary Laws and Indigenous Peoples in Asia*. London: Minority Rights Group International. The Circle-system was introduced by the Government of Bengal in 1881. See Sidhartha Chakma, 1986. *On the Chittagong Hill Tracts* (Prosongo Parbattya Chattagram). Calcutta: Nath, esp pp. 3–13.
38. Bengal Regulation I of 1900.
39. See especially rule 34 of the Rules for the Administration of the Chittagong Hill Tracts.
40. See, for example, rule 38, Rules for the Administration of the Chittagong Hill Tracts. (providing that the Circle-Chiefs would form an Advisory Council to the Deputy Commissioner to assist and advise him on all matters concerning the administration of their respective circles). See also s. 16 of the Regulation, and rule 38B (repealed in 1949) that provided for constitution of indigenous police force.
41. Shapan Adnan, 2008. 'Contestations Regarding Identity, Nationalism and Citizenship During the Struggles of the Indigenous Peoples of the Chittagong Hill Tracts of Bangladesh', *International Review of Modern Sociology*, 34(1): pp. 27–45.
42. These designations were kept in the Government of India Act 1919, the Government of India Act 1935 (s. 91), and the Government of India (Excluded and Partially Excluded Areas) Order 1936.
43. Article 103 of the Constitution of the Islamic Republic of Pakistan 1956 (read with Articles 1 and 201).
44. To facilitate this, the Chittagong Hill Tracts (Land Acquisition) Regulation 1958 was enacted. See Shapan Adnan, 2004. *Migration, Land Alienation and Ethnic Conflict. Causes of Poverty in the Chittagong Hill Tracts of Bangladesh.* Dhaka: Research and Advisory Services.
45. Article 223 of the Constitution of Pakistan 1962, to be read with arts 222 and 242(2) (which provided a list of special/tribal areas).
46. Via the Constitution (First Amendment) Act 1963 (effective 10 January 1964). See also Roy, above n 37.
47. See, for example, *Mustafa Ansari v Deputy Commissioner, Chittagong Hill Tracts and Another* (1965) 17 DLR (Dacca) 553, in which the then Dhaka High Court declared unconstitutional the government's power under r. 51 of the CHT Rules to expel from the District any person 'who [was] not a native' if they were found to be undesirable for the peace and good administration of the district.
48. Adnan, *Contestations*, in this chapter n 41, p. 27. See also Anna Tsing, 2001. 'Who Speaks for the Nation? Nationalist Rhetoric and the Challenge of

Cultural Pluralism in Bangladesh', in W. van Schendel and Erik-Jan Zürcher (eds), *Identity Politics in Central Asia and the Muslim World: Nationalism, Ethnicity and Labour in the Twentieth Century*. London and New York: I.B. Tauris, pp. 107–47.

49. See the Hill Districts (Repeal and Application of Laws and Special Provisions) Act 1989 (Act No XVI of 1989) (not put into effect).
50. *Rangamati Food Products Ltd.*, as in n. 103 below, at 534. Soon after this judgment, Parliament amended the Regulation via Act No. 38 of 2003, making it clear that the instrument remained a valid law all along. Further notably, the government in 2006 appealed this decision to the Appellate Division that stayed the operation of the judgment (CPLA 696 of 2006; a leave was granted on 15 November 2007). Recently, the Appellate Division in *Bangladesh* v *Rangamati Food Products Ltd.* (Civ. Appeal. No. 8 of 2008, decision of 22 November 2016) overruled the HCD's decision that the CHT Regulation 1900 was a dead law.
51. See the *Badiuzzaman Case*, below n. 99.
52. See *Shewe Hla Pru v Commissioner of Chittagong* (1992) 44 DLR (HCD) 539; *Aung Shwe Prue Chowdhury v Kyaw Sain Prue Chowdhury & Others* (1998) 18 BLD (AD) 33; *Sampriti Chakma v Commissioner of Customs & Others* (2000) 5 BLC (AD) 29; *Rajkumari Unika Devi v Bangladesh* (2004) 9 BLC (AD) 181; *Bikram Kishore Chakma v Land Appeal Board* (2001) 6 BLC 437 (22 May 2000); *Bangladesh Forest Industries Development Corporation and Others v Sheikh Abdul Jabbar* (2001) 53 DLR (HCD) 488; and *Abu Taher v Land Appeal Board* (2003) 8 BLC (HCD) 453.
53. Civil Appeal No. 147 of 2007 (judgement 2 December 2014), *per* S.K. Sinha J. The judgment is available at: http://supremecourt.gov.bd/resources/documents/450020_Civil_Appeal_No.147_of_2004.doc.pdf, accessed 12 August 2016.
54. Civil Appeal No. 147 of 2007 (judgement 2 December 2014), *per* S.K. Sinha J., p. 4. The judgment is available at: http://supremecourt.gov.bd/resources/documents/450020_Civil_Appeal_No.147_of_2004.doc.pdf, accessed 12 August 2016.
55. Helena Whall, 2005. 'Indigenous Self-determination in the Commonwealth of Nations', in Barbara A. Hocking, (ed.), *Unfinished Constitutional Business? Rethinking Indigenous Self-Determination*. Canberra: Aboriginal Studies Press, pp. 1–31, esp. p. 24.
56. See Rokeya Chowdhury, 2014. 'The Doctrine of Basic Structure in Bangladesh: From 'Calf-Path' to *Matryoshka* Dolls', *Bangladesh Journal of Law*, 14(1&2): 43–88, esp. p. 75 (citing Mr Larma's speech in the Constituent Assembly Debates (1972), 2[13]: p. 536).
57. Chowdhury, 'The Doctrine of Basic Structure in Bangladesh: From 'Calf-Path' to *Matryoshka* Dolls'.
58. See Borhan U. Khan and M.M. Rahman, 2012. *Protection of Minorities: Regimes, Norms and Issues in South Asia*. Newcastle upon Tyne: Cambridge Scholars Publishing, esp. ch. 5.3, pp. 72–83.

59. See L. Yasmin, 2014. 'The Tyranny of the Majority in Bangladesh: The Case of the Chittagong Hill Tracts', *Nationalism and Ethnic Politics*, 20: pp. 116–32.
60. The 'integration' approach to diverse identities seeks to promote one single public national identity, and is often considered the key 'to political stability, public unity, and the transcendence of group-based chauvinism', while the 'accommodation' approach seeks to promote dual or multiple public identities based on the principle of equality with institutional respect for a 'deep' diversity. See J. McGarry, B. O'Leary, and R. Simeon, 2008. 'Integration or Accommodation? The Enduring Debate in Conflict Regulation', in S. Choudhry (ed.), *Constitutional Design for Divided Societies: Integration or Accommodation*? Oxford: Oxford University Press, pp. 41–88, esp. p. 41.
61. Bangladesh's snobbish and abrupt denial of indigenous identity can be called a resistant approach to the management of ethnic conflict and diversity. Interestingly, immediately after the denial of constitutional integration, the government in 1972 ratified the ILO Convention No. 107 concerning Indigenous and Tribal Peoples, 1957. This has been interpreted as an indication, at least in theory, of the government's acknowledgement of the existence of the indigenous people and their rights under international law. See Tripura, in this chapter n 4, at 30.
62. See Arpeeta S. Mizan, 2015. *Need for a Right to Cultural Identity: The Dialectics of Narrow Identity Markers and Identity Crisis in Heterogeneous States*. Unpublished LLM Paper, Harvard Law School, Harvard University, May 2015.
63. As the Chairman of the Constitution Drafting Committee has recently acknowledged, albeit apologetically, the adoption of Bangalee nationalism 'led to smaller ethnic communities, in particular those living in the Chittagong Hill Tracts, feeling excluded'. See Kamal Hossain, 2013. *Bangladesh: Quest for Freedom and Justice*. Dhaka: University Press Limited, p. 141.
64. H.P. Lee, 2001. 'A Unifying Constitution for a Diverse Nation', *University of New South Wales Law Journal*, 24(3): pp. 605–10.
65. The Constitution of Bangladesh, art 6.
66. Chowdhury, in this chapter n 56, at 79, fn 242.
67. Sujit Choudhry, 2009. 'Managing Linguistic nationalism through constitutional design: Lessons from South Asia', *International Journal of Constitutional Law*, 7(4): pp. 577–618 (arguing that it is possible to manage linguistic nationalism through constitutional design and that the cost of getting official-language policy wrong can be very high).
68. On this see further Selina Haq and Ehsanul Haque, 1990. *Disintegration Process in Action: The Case of South Asia*. Dhaka: Bangladesh Institute of Law and International Affairs; Amena Mohsin, 2002. *The Politics of Nationalism: The Case of the Chittagong Hill Tracts, Bangladesh*. Dhaka: University Press Limited; S.A. Ahsan and B. Chakma,1989. 'Problems of National Integration in Bangladesh: The Chittagong Hill Tracts', *Asian Survey*, 29(10): pp. 959–70; Mahfuzul Haque, 1997. *Ethnic Insurgency and National Integration: A Study of*

Selected Ethnic Problems in South Asia. New Delhi: Lancer Books; Aftab Ahmed, 1993. 'Ethnicity and Insurgency in the Chittagong Hill Tracts Region: A Study of the Crisis of Political Integration in Bangladesh', *Journal of Commonwealth and Comparative Politics*, 31(3): pp. 32–66.

69. See Panday and Jamil, below n. 87, at 1053. On the identity politics in Bangladesh see, among others, Mohsin, *The Politics of Nationalism*, in this chapter n 68. See also Lamia Karim, 1998. 'Pushed to the Margins: Adivasi Peoples in Bangladesh and the case of Kalpana Chakma', *Contemporary South Asia*, 7(3): pp. 301–16.
70. See the Constitution of Bangladesh, preamble, and Article 19(2).
71. See the Constitution of Bangladesh, preamble, and, Ariticles 12 and 41(1)(b).
72. See the Constitution of Bangladesh, preamble, and Article 11. See also *Anwar Hosssain Chowdhury*, below n. 100.
73. Constitution of Bangladesh, preamble, and, Article 28, Clause 4, and Article 29, Clause 3(a).
74. The Appellate Division in *Wagachara Tea Estate Ltd.*, in this chapter n 53, seems to endorse this proposition.
75. Based on these provisions, the Appellate Division (in *Wagachara Tea Estate Ltd.*, at 13) held that '[i]t is, therefore, not [a] sound argument that under the scheme of the Constitution there is no scope to provide special status to [the CHT]. It is also not [a] correct view that all laws [of] the country [are] to be applicable to the three hill districts'.
76. See N.W. Barber, 2010. *The Constitutional State*. New York: Oxford University Press, at 53 ('On occasion, political equality requires legal inequalities. .... [P] ositive discrimination ... [seeks] to ensure that all members of the community can enter into the institution of citizenship to the greatest extent possible').
77. Amartya Sen, 2001. 'Other People'. British Academy Lecture, 7 November 2000. *Proceedings of the British Academy*, III: 319–35, esp. pp. 333, 335.
78. See the Chittagong Hill Tracts Development Board Ordinance 1976 (Ordinance No. LXXVII of 1976), now repealed by the Chittagong Hill Tracts Development Board Act 2014 (Act VIII of 2014), section 6 of which says that tribal people shall be preferred while appointing the chairperson of the Board. The 2014 Act also gives the CHT Regional Council a coordinating role.
79. See Ahmed, 'Ethnicity and Insurgency', pp. 52–3. See also Moudud Ahmed, 2002. *South Asia: Crisis of Development – the Case of Bangladesh*. Dhaka: University Press Limited.
80. The Bandarban Hill District Council Act 1989 (Act No. XXI of 1989); the Khagrachari Hill District Council Act 1989 (Act No. XX of 1989); and the Rangamati Hill District Council Act, 1989 (Act No. XIX of 1989) (all effective from 6 March 1989).
81. Signed on 2 December 1997 between the Government and the Parbatya Chattagram Jana Sanghati Samity (PCJSS) (Chittagong Hill Tracts Peoples' Solidarity Party). An English version of the Accord is available at https://

peaceaccords.nd.edu/sites/default/files/accords/Chittagong_Hill_Tracts_Peace_Accord.pdf, accessed 30 July 2016.

82. See especially the preamble and Part 1, clause 1, of the Accord, where both parties agreed that the CHT was a 'tribals-inhabited region' and that this character needed to be protected. The Accord no doubt thus supplied further legitimacy to the CHT Regulation 1900.
83. Moreover, a rehabilitation commission to help return and rehabilitate the refugees who took refuge in Tripura, India during the CHT conflict was established in 1997 (reconstituted in 2009).
84. See the Chittagong Hill Tracts Regional Council Act 1998 (Act No. XII of 1998), which too partially endorsed the region's special status by recognizing it as a 'tribals-inhabited area'.
85. See the Chittagong Hill Tracts Land-Disputes Resolution Commission Act 2001 (Act No. LIII of 2001), as amended in 2016.
86. R. Chowdhury, 2012. *Land Dispute Resolution in the Chittagong Hill Tracts: Caught between Liberalism and Legal Pluralism*. Unpublished LLM Thesis, Montreal, McGill University School of Law; Guro Mjanger, 2008. 'The Land Is Not Ours: Alienation of Land Rights of the Jumma in the Chittagong Hill Tracts, Bangladesh', unpublished Master's Research Paper. The Hague: Institute of Social Studies. See further Rajkumari C. Roy, 2000. *Land Rights of the Indigenous Peoples of the Chittagong Hill Tracts, Bangladesh*, Document No. 99. Copenhagen: International Work Group for Indigenous Affairs.
87. There is a large body of literature on this now. See generally Raja D. Roy, 2007. 'The Discordant Accord: Challenges in the Implementation of the Chittagong Hill Tracts Accord of 1997', in Miek Boltjes (ed.), *Implementing Negotiated Agreements: The Real Challenge to Intrastate Peace*. The Hague: TMC Asser Press, pp. 115–46; Pranab K. Panday, and I. Jamil. 2009. 'Conflict in the Chittagong Hill Tracts of Bangladesh: An Unimplemented Accord and Continued Violence', *Asian Survey*, 49(6): pp. 1052–70; and Abdullah A. Faruque, 2014. *Implementation of the Chittagong Hill Tracts Peace Accord: Challenges and Human Rights Issues*. Dhaka: National Human Rights Commission, Bangladesh.
88. See Yasmin, in this chapter n 59, at 116.
89. Roy, *Juridical Pluralism*, in this chapter n 37, at fn 4.
90. The Constitution (Fifteenth Amendment) Act 2011 (Act XIV of 2011), s. 14.
91. The Constitution of Bangladesh, art 23A (emphasis is of the author).
92. See also Tripura, in this chapter n 4, at 30–1.
93. See Kawser Ahmed, 2010. 'Defining "Indigenous" in Bangladesh: International Law in Domestic Context', *International Journal on Minority and Group Rights*, 17: pp. 47–73.
94. Tripura, in this chapter n 4, at 31.
95. Werner F. Menski. 2015. 'Bangladesh in 2015: Challenges of the *Iccher Ghuri* for Learning to Live Together', *University of Asia Pacific Journal of Law and Policy*, 1(1): 9–32, esp. p. 23.
96. Menski, 'Bangladesh in 2015', p. 23.

97. Menski, 'Bangladesh in 2015', p. 23. Menski thinks that the new inclusive provision of Article 23A is now something that should not be reneged on. In his words, 'negative reactions of many [...], for example, indicate in my view clear-cut lack of understanding about the current geopolitical dynamics and the complexity and historical depth of the pluralist challenges faced by the nation of Bangladesh'. Menski, 'Bangladesh in 2015', at 22–3.
98. Roy, *Juridical Pluralism*, in this chapter n 37, at 119–20.
99. (2010) 7 LG (HCD) 208. In 1999 there was another challenge: *Shamsuddin Ahmed v Government of Bangladesh and Others*, WP No. 4113 of 1999 (WP is Writ Petition).
100. (1989) 1 BLD (Special) 1.
101. *Ibid.*, at 145, per Shahabuddin Ahmed J.
102. (2001) 6 BLC 437, 443 (22 May 2000).
103. (2005) 10 BLC 525 (13 May 2003).
104. *Ibid.*, at 533. It also advised that it was a high time for the government to 'apply [in the CHT] all other laws of the country' (at para 15). A similar view was in *Chakma,* in this chapter n 102, at 446.
105. See *Rajkumari Unika Devi,* in this chapter n 52 (recognizing and applying as 'local law' indigenous customs of the Mong people to determine the question of succession of Chiefship of their Circle); *Aung Shwe Prue Chowdhury,* in this chapter n 52 ('the susceptibilities of the tribal people should not be ignored': per Mustafa Kamal J, at 43). See also *Aberchai Mog and others v Joint District Judge, Khagrachari and Others* (2014) 19 BLC (HCD) 358 (directing the concerned authorities to resolve a property dispute according to Marma customary succession law and in consultation with the Marma Circle Chief and the Headman).
106. As in n 53 in this chapter.
107. The Appellate Division approvingly cited the innovations brought forth by the Chittagong Hill Tracts Regional Council Act 1998, which the *Badiuzzaman* Court (in this chapter n 99) had struck down.
108. See earlier n 50.
109. *Badiuzzaman,* in this chapter n 99. Pursuant to a petition for leave to appeal against this judgment, the Appellate Division of the Supreme Court, on 11 March 2011, stayed the effectiveness of the HCD's decision.
110. *Md. Tajul Islam v Bangladesh and Others,* WP No. 6451 of 2007. As the issues surrounding this case unfolded, it became apparent that behind the scene was a political party. I have elsewhere analysed this political aspect of these two challenges in Ridwanul Hoque, 2015. 'The Judicialization of Politics in Bangladesh: Pragmatism, Legitimacy, and Consequences', in M. Tushnet and M. Khosla (eds), *Unstable Constitutionalism: Law and Politics in South Asia.* New York: Cambridge University Press, pp. 261–90, esp. pp. 275–7.
111. *Badiuzzaman,* in this chapter n 99, at 230. The Court refuted that the Regional Council was not a local government body. Rather, it said that it was a local government body of the type established beyond the pale of the Constitution, because the CHT was not declared an 'administrative unit' that was a

precondition for the establishment of such a body under Articles 59 and 60. It is unclear why the Court adjudged the CHTRC incompatible with the state's unitary character instead of confining its reasoning to this ground alone.

112. See, for example, section 6 of the Rangamati Hill District Council (Amendment) Act 1998.
113. *Badiuzzaman,* in this chapter n 99, 237–8. Compare with the Indian case of *Manchegowda and others v State of Karnataka and others,* 1984 (3) SCC 301, concerning the constitutionality of an Act prohibiting transfer of land of the tribal grantees in Karnataka, in which the Supreme Court held that such a special law to the exclusion of other communities was not incompatible with the constitutional equality provision.
114. *Badiuzzaman,* n 99, 238, 219.
115. In the Court's view, 'the CHT peace process to be sustainable must be informed by concerted innovative efforts at constant evaluation and reinvention'. Having said this, the Court set out to frame certain in-exhaustive guidelines for the policy-makers to follow. The Court reasoned that the type of intervention it made was 'necessary' to make the ongoing peace process ultimately fruitful. *Badiuzzaman,* above n 99, 238.
116. Chowdhury, *Land Dispute Resolution in the Chittagong Hill Tracts* 78.
117. *Badiuzzaman,* in this chapter n 99, at 235, para. 41 (citing opinions of Justice Ahmed and Justice Chowdhury from *Anwar Hossain Chowdhury* (in this chapter n 100) to strengthen its view that such a regional local body would destroy Bangladesh's unitary character).
118. *Badiuzzaman,* n 99, 228.
119. *Badiuzzaman,* n 99, 229.
120. *Badiuzzaman,* n 99, 236.
121. Helena, 'Indigenous Self-determination in the Commonwealth of Nations', 3.
122. Brendan O'Duffy, 2003. 'Self-Determination and Conflict Regulation in Sri Lanka, Northern Ireland, and Beyond'. A paper read in the International Centre for Ethnic Studies, Colombo, 8 May 2003. Available at: http://tamilnation.co/selfdetermination/tamileelam/0305duffy.htm, accessed 30 July 2016.
123. S.J. Anaya, 2002. 'The Contours of Self-determination and its Implementation: Implications of Developments Concerning Indigenous Peoples', in G. Alfredsson and M. Stravropoulou (eds), *Justice Pending: Indigenous Peoples and Other Good Causes: Essays in Honour of Erica-Irene Daes.* The Hague: Martinus Nijhoff, pp. 5–14, esp. p. 12.
124. Dawson, 'On Self-determination and Constitutional Recognition'. It should be of relevance to note here that an idea of self-determination as necessarily incompatible with the state sovereignty made Bangladesh to refrain from voting for the UN Declaration on Indigenous Rights. Moreover, in the negotiations leading to the Declaration, Bangladesh claimed that while it would not disagree that the right to self-determination included the right of indigenous communities to respect and preserve their identities, there was no indigenous/non-indigenous dichotomy in Bangladesh. See Helena, 'Indigenous Self-determination in the Commonwealth of Nations', 24.

125. In so holding, it even ignored a legislative recognition that the people of the CHT were such an un-advanced society. See the preamble to the Act No. XII of 1998, cited in n. 107 in this chapter.
126. *Badiuzzaman*, in this chapter n 99, pp. 236–7.
127. M. Lake, 1996. 'The Meaning of "Self" in Claims for Self-government: Re-claiming Citizenship for Women and Indigenous People in Australia', in C. Arup and L.A. Marks (eds), *Cross Currents: Internationalism, National Identity and Law*. Special Issue of *Law in Context*, 14(1): pp. 9–23, esp. p. 12.
128. *Wagachara Tea Estate Ltd*, in this chapter n 53, at 15.
129. Sujit Choudhry, 2012. 'Group Rights in Comparative Constitutional Law', in M. Rosenfeld and A. Sajo (eds), *The Oxford Handbook of Comparative Constitutional Law*. Oxford: Oxford University Press, pp. 1099-1123, at 1109. See also Hocking, in this chapter n 55.
130. In the aftermath of this decision, for example, the PCJSS threatened that it would begin a non-cooperation movement if the Peace Accord was not implemented. On the other hand, the government on 7 January 2015 allegedly imposed a restriction that a meeting by any person/organization, whether local or foreign, with any members of *upajati* ('ethnic minority') would have to be in the presence of the administration and the military. See *the Prothom Alo*, Dhaka, 16 February 2015. There are, however, certain positive developments. In 2014, for example, the government entered into a memorandum of understanding with the three Hill District Councils to allow the latter authority to control the management, supervision, and coordination of the secondary educational institutes in the CHT. See *the Dhaka Tribune*, Dhaka, 27 May 2014, p. 4.
131. Menski, 'Bangladesh in 2015', p. 21.
132. Katharine Adeney, 2015. 'A Move to Majoritarian Nationalism? Challenges of Representation in South Asia', *Representation*, 51(1): pp. 7–21.
133. See Yash Ghai, 2011. 'Ethnic Identity, Participation and Social Justice: A Constitution for New Nepal?' *International Journal on Minority and Group Rights*, 18: pp. 309–34, esp. p. 309. On the problematic history of this transition, see Mara Malagodi, 2012. *Constitutional Nationalism and Legal Exclusion: Equality, Identity Politics, and Democracy in Nepal*, 1990–2007. New Delhi: Oxford University Press.
134. Adeney, above n. 132.
135. Menski, 'Bangladesh in 2015', p. 21. On India's management of ethnic conflict or diversity issue, see generally Gurpreet Mahajan, 2005. 'Indian Exceptionalism or Indian Model: Negotiating Cultural Diversity and Minority Rights in a Democratic Nation-State', in Will Kymlicka and Baogang He (eds), *Multiculturalism in Asia*. Oxford: Oxford University Press, pp. 288–313.
136. Z. Hasan, 2015. 'Tokenism or Empowerment? Policies and Institutions for Disadvantaged Communities', in Wendy Doniger and Martha C. Nussbaum (eds), *Pluralism and Democracy in India: Debating the Hindu Right*. Oxford: Oxford University Press, pp. 174–90, esp. p. 175. See also D. Stuligross and A. Varshney. 2002. 'Ethnic Diversities, Constitutional Designs, and Public

Policies in India', in A. Reynolds (ed.), *The Architecture of Democracy: Constitutional Design, Conflict Management, and Democracy.* New York: Oxford University Press, pp. 429–87; and Sankaran, in this chapter n 9.

137. See the Constitution of India, arts. 298 and 244(1), and paras. 5-6 of the Fifth Schedule. See also Articles 46, 244A, and 332. The Indian constitutional pluralism was acknowledged in *Samatha v State of Andhra Pradesh and others*, AIR 1997 SC 3297, para. 92.
138. Articles 38, 39, and 46 of the Indian Constitution.
139. Choudhry, *Group Rights*, in this chapter n 128, at 1108.
140. It is interesting that the more successful jurisdictions of Canada and New Zealand, or even the most relevant case of India, were not cited in *Badiuzzaman*. But see *Wagachara Tea Estate Ltd*, in this chapter n 53, in which the Appellate Division cited in passing an Indian Supreme Court decision.
141. There are autonomous regimes in the multi-ethnic Nicaraguan Atlantic Coast regions. See the Nicaraguan Constitution of 1987, Articles 5, 89, 180, and 181. See C. Binder, 2013. 'Autonomy as Means to Accommodate Cultural Diversity? The Case of Indigenous Peoples', in P.I. Bhat (ed), *Constitutionalism*, in this chapter n 9, at 343–53, esp. p. 353. See especially C. Binder, 2004. 'Indigenous Peoples in Domestic Jurisdictions: The Case of Nicaragua', in J. Castellino and N. Walsh, (eds.), *Indigenous Peoples and Human Rights Law*. The Hague: Martinus Nijhoff, pp. 249–67.
142. Such a self-government body was first established in 1988 via the Darjeeling Gorkha Hill Council Act 1988 (West Bengal). A tripartite Accord was later signed on 6 December 2005 to replace that system by a more participatory one. Accordingly, the Gorkhaland Territorial Administration Act 2011 established a regionally autonomous administration.
143. In the Indian north-eastern states, nine autonomous district councils have been established as a form of indigenous self-government. See, among others, Das, *Human Rights and Indigenous Peoples*, pp. 105–7.
144. Menski, 'Bangladesh in 2015', p. 21 (citing the developments especially from Manipur).
145. Menski, 'Bangladesh in 2015', p. 21.
146. See Duncan Iveson, Paul Patton, and Will Sanders (eds), 2000. *Political Theory and the Rights of Indigenous Peoples*. Cambridge: Cambridge University Press; M. Weller, (ed.), 2010. *Political Participation of Minorities: A Commentary on International Standards and Practice*. Oxford: Oxford University Press.
147. For arguments of this line, see M. Davies, and Z. Lemezina, 2010. 'Indigenous Australians and the Preamble: Towards a More Inclusive Constitution or Entrenching Marginalisation?' *University of New South Wales Law Journal*, 33(2): pp. 239–66.

11

A Comparative Study of Constitutional Policies Relating to Ethnic Pluralism in SAARC Countries

P. Ishwara Bhat and Aratrika Choudhuri

I Introduction

Ethnic pluralism has emerged as a cornerstone of the edifice of socio-economic and geopolitical dynamics of South Asian nations. John S. Furnivall famously characterized Southeast Asian societies as 'plural societies', which house heterogeneous social orders coexisting, yet not comingling, in one political unit.[1] With the proliferation of sectarian and communal violence, majoritarian hegemony in trade and politics, and increasing religious intolerance and fanaticism, the ruling regimes of these states have sought to bridge these gaps in deeply divided democracies.[2] Transcending *plurality*, which merely denotes an empirical conjugation of a number of social groups, religious denominations, cultural sects, and public spaces, to proceed towards *pluralism* that involves a normative *interaction* between these agents in an open social process; the South Asian Association for Regional Cooperation (SAARC) countries have fashioned unique constitutional and political frameworks to tackle divisive and separatist tendencies.[3]

SAARC, comprising India, Pakistan, Bangladesh, Nepal, Sri Lanka, Bhutan, Maldives, and Afghanistan, exhibits coexistence of diverse and overlapping ethnic groups, pluralistic in religion, religious subsect, language, ethnicity, caste, and region. In the contexts of minorities of these South Asian states, an endeavour is made in this chapter to present an overview of extant ethnic pluralism of different states and outline the national policies towards the protection of the minority ethnic groups. This chapter seeks to undertake a comparative analysis of SAARC nations for gaining a more wholesome perspective of the prospects and limits of constitutional policy of ethnic pluralism, the effects of differences in ethno-linguistic and historical traditions on modern constitutional approaches towards minority rights, and the mobilization of judicial and constitutional resolutions to political polarization. To this end, the chapter shall focus on the historical institutionalization of state relations with the majority and minority groups, the modes of nation-building adopted for consolidation of ethno-religious heterogeneity and the impact of constitutional policies on multifarious paradigms of state formation and ethnic pluralism. It shall appraise the dynamics of ethnic identities and movements in South Asian states in a comparative framework, by evaluating the state of security (security of identity, land, customs, economic interests, forest rights), self-government (opportunity to have own patterns of governments, right to self-determination about territory and rights and governance) and social justice (justice in social relations, by ensuring backwardness arising out of geographical and other exclusions are properly compensated by providing for affirmative action), fulfilment of assured constitutional ideals (equality, religious freedom, liberty, etc.) and policy choices of the state (approaches of isolation, assimilation, integration), etc.[4]

II Ethnic Pluralism and Constitutional Policies: Delineating Epistemology

Modern political theory has sought to define multiculturalism through a spectrum of numerous lens, depending upon the choice of intellectual theorization (for example, individualism, communitarianism), the nature of the group (for example, refugees, immigrant groups, indigenous peoples) and the policy adopted towards such diversity (for example, isolation, assimilation, integration), etc.[5] The discourse on ethnic pluralism and minority rights is beset with two major issues: determining the rights and status of ethnic minorities in such diverse societies, and the nature of responsibilities that democratic citizenship would impose on them.[6] The differences in treatment and identification of minorities in different countries, can be traced back to historical differences of cultural heritage, ideology, philosophy and distinct patterns of group behaviour.[7] For instance, the history of the Indian subcontinent prior to British colonization demonstrates that as compared to the path of *extermination*, followed by Europeans in encounters with non-European peoples, isolation had never been an alternative in interaction between tribals and non-tribals in India. Instead, selective incorporation was followed, similar to patterns of assimilation.[8] Thus the Indian tribal hierarchy had, even before colonial rule, traditionally exhibited far greater overlap and coexistence of different modes of resource use, which materially distinguishes the Indian experience from the European and the new world paradigm of homo-hierarchies.[9]

The strain wrought by the conflicting forces of majoritarian hegemony and minority rebellion have manifested in secessionist movements across the SAARC countries—right from India (facing widespread separatist revolts in Kashmir, the north-east), Pakistan (seceding Bangladesh and beset with Baluch and Pashtun ethno-secessionist movements), Sri Lanka (braving age-old strife between the majority Sinhalese and minority Tamils), Bangladesh (facing ethnic counter-mobilization of the minority tribal of Chittagong Hills Tract), Afghanistan (burdened with unfettered influx of Pashtun families and resettlement of ethnic Punjabis), Nepal (witnessing violent ethnic clashes between majority Drukpas and minority Nepalese), and Bhutan (suffering spill-over effects from Nepalese ethnic conflict), to Maldives (facing internal security threats sponsored by external divisive forces).[10]

In this context, constitutions in plural societies serve as repositories of government structures which guarantee minority representation as well as implementing modes of accountability which may be activated where minority rights and/or concerns are adversely affected.[11] The choices array themselves in the following options—first, a pluralistic society may choose a broad and general individual rights regime centred on non-discrimination, where the focus is on living a shared life in the common domain as equal citizens with equal rights; secondly, the society may grant precedence to rights of the ethnic minorities over and above general human rights, which may relate to, for instance, religious, cultural and linguistic freedom, educational rights, participatory rights in relation to shaping local and national policy; thirdly, it may choose to create positive government obligations rather than enforceable rights, which may include the creation of separate courts, reconciliation programs or dispute resolution mechanisms to protect cultural practices; affirmative action programs; and lastly, where the ethno-religious cleavages revolve on a geospatial axis, it may choose to accord a measure of internal self-determination to the minorities, such as federalism, cooperative federalism, and confederation.[12]

International human rights norms, which have a great bearing upon municipal law, have laid emphasis on integrated development of indigenous communities. For instance, the International Convention on the Elimination of All Forms of Racial Discrimination, 1965 condemns race based discrimination and promotes understanding among all races.[13] As per International Covenant on Civil and Political Rights 1966, ethnic, religious or linguistic minorities shall not be denied the right, in community with the other members of their group, to enjoy their own culture, to profess and practice their own religion, or to use their own language.[14] The International Labour Organization (ILO) Recommendation concerning protection and integration of indigenous and other tribal and semi-tribal populations 1957 elaborates about their right to land reserve for shifting cultivation and for other purposes, about special measures for their recruitment and fair conditions of employment and for social security.[15] The Declaration of San Jose on Ethno-Development adopted by the United Nations Educational, Scientific and Cultural Organization (UNESCO) in 1982 conceptualizes ethno-development as an extension and consideration of the elements of a culture, through strengthening the independent decision making capacity of a culturally distinct society to direct its own development and exercise self-determination, at whatever level, which implies an equitable and independent share of power.[16]

Thus, it is possible to infer that an enduring problem for constitutional design and democratic practice within a pluralistic, multi-ethnic, and multicultural society is the way to address the aspirations, issues, identities, demands, fears and the very voices of the minority groups, in relation to threats to their autonomy and status in representative democracies.[17] The resolution of ethnic conflict is essential not only to stem secessionist movements and to preserve national security, but also to fulfil the potential of democracies for creating safe spaces for all groups to discuss and deliberate their issues freely without fear of backlash.[18] Rendering legal protection to the minority groups and endowing them with an all-inclusive citizenship are the first steps for any democratic state to earn their goodwill and solidarity, and to solidify their commitment to the state.[19]

III Comparing Demographic Profiles: With Special Focus on Ethnic Pluralism

This section presents an overview of the demographic profile of SAARC countries, replete with analysis of census data and national policies towards inclusion or exclusion of ethnic groups in mainstream population.

III.1 India

There are over 600 tribes spread over different states and union territories identified as Scheduled Tribes (STs).[20] About 75 primitive tribal groups live in 17 states and union territories; 8.2 per cent of the total population of the country (1.3 billion) is living in 15 per cent of the country's area including forests, hills, plains and inaccessible areas.[21] The literacy rate among tribals (47.10 per cent) is far below the overall population's literacy rate (65.38 per cent).[22] About 87 per cent of the main workers from these communities are engaged in primary sector activities.[23] A majority of STs continue to live below the poverty line, suffer from malnutrition and disease and are vulnerable to displacement.[24] From the perspective of demographics, India demonstrates considerable diversity in all axes of classification: linguistics, tribes, castes, and religion.

III.2 Sri Lanka

Sri Lanka has a plural society. According to the recent 2012 census, the Sinhalese now make up 74.9 per cent of the population, and are concentrated in the densely populated south-west and central parts of the island.[25] The Sri Lanka Tamils, who live predominantly in the north and east of the island, form the largest minority group at 11.1 per cent (according to the 2012 Census) of the population. [26] The Moors, descendants of Arab traders that settled in Sri Lanka and married local women, form the third largest ethnic group at 9.3 per cent of the population. There are also Indian Tamils who form a distinct ethnic group comprising 4.1 per cent of the population. Smaller minorities include the Malays who descend from South East Asian settlers, and the Burghers, who are descendants of European colonists. Minority and indigenous groups include Sri Lankan Tamils (12.7 per cent; 1981), Indian Tamil (5.5 per cent; 1981) Muslims (7.4 per cent; 1981), Veddhas 2,000 (1981 Census), and Burghers (0.3 per cent; 1981).[27]

III.3 Pakistan

The pluralist character of society in Pakistan draws upon the existence of four historical ethno-linguistic communities: Punjabi, Sindhi, Pakhtun, and Baluch. Urdu and Gujarati-speaking migrants from India who came to Pakistan after partition and settled largely in the province of Sindh emerged as a distinct community more than a quarter of a century after the bulk of migration took place in the late 1940s and early 1950s. All these communities have their distinct linguistic, historical and geographical identities which have become an essential part of their political expression in an organizational, electoral or agitation context.[28] Within the larger ethno-regional communities, subregional groups have struggled to project their separate identities, such as the Siraiki-speaking community in southern Punjab and adjoining areas of Sindh, the Hindko-speaking people in the North-West Frontier Province (NWFP) and the Brahui of Baluchistan, along with a sprinkling of smaller groups across the country.[29]

Punjabis are the largest ethnic minority group. Pashtuns (Pakhtuns) make up the second largest group and Sindhi are the third largest ethnic group. Saraikis (a transitional group between Punjabis and Sindhis) make up 10.53 per cent of the total population. The remaining large groups include the Muhajirs and the Baloch people, which make up 7.57 per cent and 3.57 per cent of the total population, respectively. Hindkowans and the Brahui, and the various peoples of the Gilgit–Baltistan, constitute roughly 4.66 per cent of the total population.[30]

III.4 Bangladesh

In Bangladesh, about 3 million of the country's 160 million people belong to 45 indigenous, or tribal, groups. The majority of indigenous people are Buddhists and animists.[31] Bengali and ethnic minority Christians live in communities across the country, including Barisal City, Gournadi in Barisal District, Baniarchar in Gopalganj, Monipuripara in Dhaka, Christianpara in Mohakhal, Nagori in Gazipur, and Khulna City. There also are small populations of Shia Muslims, Sikhs, Bahais, animists, and Ahmadis. Estimates of their numbers varied from a few thousand to 100,000 adherents per group.

In Bangladesh 27 different ethnic groups are officially recognized, though different indigenous organizations claim the number as up to 45.[32] They are residing both in the Chittagong Hill Tracts and in the plain lands.[33] The Chittagong Hill Tracts (CHT) is the homeland of at least 13 different communities, of which Chakmas form the largest group followed by Marma and Tripura.[34] The Chakmas are accounting for over half of the ethnic population of CHT and professes Buddhism. The Marmas are also Buddhists (with some animist beliefs). The Tipuras are Hindus. The Christian Missionaries have converted the Lusai, Pankho, Bom, and Mizo to Christianity. The Mru, Sak, and Khyang follow animism. Tanchangya and Brong are the subgroups of Chakma and Tripura. Mandi, Santal, Khasi, Monipuri, Paharia, Rakhaine, Rajbangshi, Koch, Oraon, Hajong, Mahat, Munda, etc., are the important plain land ethnic groups practicing a wide diversity of beliefs and languages.[35]

III.5 Afghanistan

Much akin to other decolonized states, Afghanistan is comprised of a patchwork of several ethno-linguistic groups and collective indigenous identities.[36] No single ethnic majority is discernible in Afghanistan, since there are two ethnicities composing at least a quarter of the population, and as many as five composing at least 5 per cent. The four major ethnicities of the country are Pashtuns, Tajiks, Hazaras, and Uzbeks.

The population of Afghanistan is around 32 million as of 2015. The nation is composed of a multi-ethnic and multilingual society, reflecting its location astride historic trade and invasion routes between Central Asia, Southern Asia, and Western Asia.[37] The largest ethnic group among Afghanistan's population is the Pashtuns, followed by Tajiks, Hazaras, Uzbeks, Aimaks, Turkmen, Baloch, and others. Excluding urban populations in the principal cities, most Afghans are organized into tribal and other kinship-based groups, who follow their own traditional customs, for instance, Pashtunwali.

III.6 Nepal

The population of Nepal is estimated to be 26,494,504 people based on the 2011 Census. Nepalese or Nepali people are citizens of Nepal. The country is home to people of many different national origins. As a result, Nepalese do not equate their nationality with ethnicity, but with citizenship and allegiance.[38] Although citizens make up the majority of Nepalese, non-citizen residents, dual citizeners, and expatriates may also claim a Nepalese identity. Nepalese are descendants of migrants from parts of India, Kashmir, Tibet, and parts of Burma and Yunnan, and much further traces origin to Central Asia, along with indigenous peoples. Nepal is multicultural and multi-ethnic country. Kathmandu Valley, in the middle hill region, constitutes a small fraction of the nation's area but is the most densely populated, with almost 5 per cent of the nation's population.

III.7 Bhutan

As of 1 January 2016, the population of Bhutan was estimated to be 781,168 people. The philosophy of 'One Nation, One People', propounded by His Majesty, is now firmly entrenched in both spirit and letter of the Constitution.[39] The Bhutanese Nepali minority following Hinduism constitutes an important ethnic minority, which has engaged in continual dialogue with the Bhutanese government for affirmation of their citizenship rights, instead of relegation to immigrant status.[40]

An estimated 650,000 Nepali-speaking people live mainly in the southern belt of Bhutan and are relatively recent immigrants to the area. They comprise a combination of caste and ethnic groups, including Bahun, Chhetri, Gurung, Limbu, Newar, Rai, and Tamang. Effectively, however, they form a single community bound together by the common Nepali tongue and the Hindu religion.[41]

III.8 Maldives

The contemporary homogeneous mixture of Sinhalese, Dravidian, Arab, Australasian, and African ethnicity in Maldives results from historical changes in regional hegemony over marine trade routes. Clarence Maloney, an anthropologist who conducted fieldwork in Maldives in the 1970s, determined that an early Dravidian-speaking substratum of population from Kerala in India had settled in the islands, leaving its legacy in the language and place names.[42] This group was subsequently displaced by Dhivehi speakers who arrived from Sri Lanka and whose language became the official one. Arabs compose the last main group to arrive beginning in the ninth century.[43] However, a rapidly disappearing endogamous subgroup of persons of African origin called the Ravare or Giraavaru also existed. The only distinct ethnic minority is found in Male among the trading community of Indians, who settled there in the 1800s.[44] Several hundred in number, they are also a religious minority, belonging to the Shia branch of Islam.

IV Inferences from Comparative Historical Conspectus

IV.1 India

From ancient times, the indigenous communities dwelling in forests and far-flung places in India exhibited their inclination and determination to maintain their ethnic and cultural identity and protection of their land and economic interests.[45] The kingdoms of Gondwana, the Bhil principalities, the Santhal Parganas, the Mina chieftains, and the traditional political systems of hill tribes of the Northeast were long-standing political and communitarian bases for expressing and effectuating the social will.[46]

With the advent of the British and their infiltration into tribal areas, new types of conflicts were experienced. The British adopted a double-edged policy of diverting the tribal anger against the moneylenders, contractors, forest officials and the police by allowing a free hand for the exploiters.[47] There were series of tribal mutinies and prolonged unrests against the British. The Santhal Rebellion of 1855 against land grabbing zamindars and moneylenders,[48] the Dhanbad tribal unrest in 1869 and 1870 against arbitrary enhancement of rent by zamindars and restriction on forest rights,[49] the revolts in Andhra Pradesh (1862, 1867–8), in Kandh (1837–56), and Keonjar (1867–8, 1891) in Odisha, in Bastar in Chhatisgarh (1911) as expressions of mass movements for autonomy, non-exploitation and reform exhibited inclination for security of their rights.

The policy of reserving seats in national and state legislatures on the basis of communal electorate system had initiated the idea of political empowerment through state action. All these tended towards acceptance of the policy of protective segregation, empowerment and development. In the Constituent Assembly, the policy chosen was for security of the land, natural resources, tradition and customs of the tribal communities, non-interference with their native self-governance institutions, and integrated tribal development for social justice. The formation of ethnicity based states in North-East (seven sisters), Jharkhand, Chhattisgarh, and Uttarakhand had indirect support to the policy of security, self-government and social justice.[50]

IV.2 Sri Lanka

Sri Lanka's ethnic pluralism had impact upon a rich tradition of both indigenous laws and transplanted laws. On an overall perspective, it is still feasible to trace these laws to Buddhist origins as well, especially among the Sinhalese, and Hindu law, among the Tamils, as well as religious law among Muslims and Christians.[51]

Sri Lanka received its independence from Great Britain in 1948. At the outset, it should be noted that the Tamil community had not participated in the drafting, nor in the adoption, of any of the post-Independence constitutions.[52] The Tamils therefore continue to claim that they have, therefore, never relinquished sovereignty over their traditional homelands. In essence, the Tamils claim the right to the international legal principle of self-determination. Conflict discourse and homeland claims in Sri Lanka have depended on primordial versions of 'Tamil' and 'Sinhalese' histories. Typically, the Tamils and Sinhalese are represented by their respective communities as two distinct linguistic and cultural groups, which have existed on the island since ancient times. Recognition of Tamil as one of the national languages, creation of Provincial Councils to accommodate local diversities, devolution of legislative powers to local bodies in the matter of land allotments, development works and welfare and recognition of land based rights of ethnic communities are some of the prominent developments emerged through constitutional amendments.

IV.3 Pakistan

The role of partition in 1947 in determining the nature of pluralism in Pakistan was crucial.[53] The ethnically pluralist character of Pakistan society was destined to face grave challenges from the very beginning her independence in 1947, in so far as it was not reflected in the emergent patterns of unitary—as opposed to federalist—currents of thought and practice.[54] The increasingly exclusivist modes of representation of the Muslim majority in elected assemblies constantly kept the minority communities of Hindus, Christians, Ahmadis, Buddhists, Parsis and others on their toes.[55] In 2002, the government of President Musharraf faced serious challenges to the prevalent patterns of authority in terms of demand for opening up the state system to the rule of public representatives at the federal and provincial levels, on the one hand, and the elimination of obstacles to proper representation of religious minorities in the elected legislatures, on the other.[56]

While the ethnic communities of Pakistan tried to grapple with the issue of developing a national consensus on the way their proper representation in the political and administrative fields could be secured, the 1970s saw the emergence of a new ethnic community of *mohajirs*. The sense of alienation among the mohajirs, who belonged to an erstwhile privileged group of immigrants from India, added to the ethnic mosaic of Pakistan. The country experienced the phenomenon of ethnicity-in-making as the mohajirs developed a separate ethno-linguistic identity, a distinct political party (Mohajir Qaumi Movement or MQM) and an all-encompassing political strategy for safeguarding their economic and political interests.[57]

IV.4 Bangladesh

Indigenous peoples remain among the most persecuted of all minorities, facing discrimination not only on the basis of their religion and ethnicity but also because of their indigenous identity and their socio-economic status.[58] In the CHT, the indigenous peoples took up arms in defence of their rights in 1976. In December 1997, the civil war ended with a 'Peace' Accord between the Government of Bangladesh and the Parbattya Chattagram Jana Samhati Samiti (PCJSS, United People's Party of CHT), which led the resistance movement. The Accord recognizes the CHT as a "tribal inhabited" region, its traditional governance system and the role of its chiefs, and provides building blocks for indigenous self-determination. The CHT Accord, however, remains largely unimplemented which has resulted in continued widespread human rights violations, violent conflicts and military control.[59] A 2011 amendment to the constitution refers to the indigenous peoples of Bangladesh as 'tribes', 'minor races' and 'ethnic sects and communities'. Bangladesh has ratified ILO Convention No. 107 on Indigenous and Tribal Populations but abstained when the UN Declaration on the Rights of Indigenous Peoples was up for voting in the General Assembly in 2007.

IV.5 Afghanistan

The creation of the Durrani monarchy in 1747 triggered a dramatic turning point in the history of the vast region wedged between the river Oxus and Indus, when the ethnic group, called 'Pashtun' constituted an overwhelming majority. The ethnic diversity of Afghanistan has led it to 'one of the major dynamics of civil war in the country'.[60] In the past, ethnic conflicts had acquired dangerous sectarian and regional dimensions and gradually transformed itself into an ethnic conflict between the Pashtun, who feared loss of power and control, and the Uzbek–Tajik coalition from the North who had gained greater political influence in Kabul, which had been traditionally dominated by the Pashtun elite.[61] Due to the lack of democratic outlets for resolution of differences, these factions were led into deep conflict, undermining national unity.

The rise of the Taliban movement, which sought reunification of the country through military conquest and established a highly centralized state apparatus run by a rigid theocratic line, also had Pashtun ethnic undertones.[62] The rights of the minorities were entirely relegated to the background, owing to the aggressive state pursuit of military objectives. However, with the ushering in of the new constitution and elections for the parliament and provincial councils, Afghanistan's political system is transforming into a more democratic and representative system.

IV.6 Nepal

Post 1768, after the gradual consolidation of smaller principalities into a unified kingdom under King Prithvi Narayan Shah's rule, the extant social fabric wove the four varnas of the traditional Hindu caste system and the 36 indigenous Buddhist, Hindu and animist tribes, with the 'Hindu great tradition', without denigrating the integrity of local cultures.[63] The Constitution of 1990 ensconced the idea of a pluralistic democracy by defining the Adhirajya as a multi-ethnic, multilingual, democratic, Hindu, and constitutional monarchical kingdom.[64] While many indigenous peoples in Nepal are not Hindus, the epistemological schema of the 1990 constitution, especially the Directive Principles of State Policy,[65] evinced Nepal's commitment to promote 'healthy and cordial social relations amongst the various religions, castes, tribes, communities and linguistic groups',[66] and to conserve 'their languages, literatures, scripts, arts and cultures'[67] for the first time.

However, the historical neglect of the Madhesis by the Pahade-dominated ruling regimes, the sudden infusion of land resettlement programs and developmental projects without appropriate implementation of integrationist strategies,[68] the absence of appropriate state mechanisms for tackling with separatist tendencies espousing a *pahadi hatao* agenda, the rapid acculturation of indigenous peoples without concomitant socio-economic emancipation, have all contributed to ethnic conflict and violence in Nepal.

IV.7 Bhutan

Historically, Bhutan remains one of the very few nation states successfully insulated from foreign invasion and British imperialism.[69] Despite some engagement with the British for the sake of healthy international relations, a combination of isolation-oriented geopolitical policies and Bhutanese monarchical refusal of foreign cultural influence, aided the 'Kingdom of the Dragon' to be 'the last physically isolated state in the modern world'.[70]

The 1950s marked the beginnings of modernization, under the third Druk Gyalpo Jigme Dorji Wangchuk's regime, concomitant with land reform, abolition of slavery, separation of executive from the judiciary, legal reform, and establishment of modern infrastructure.[71] The creation of the National Assembly in 1953 entailed the formation of a national platform for elected representatives, representatives of the monk body, and high civil servants directly appointed by the king, to decide on legislative matters together. Coupled with the Forest Act of 1969, the Land Act of 1979 envisaged to facilitate modernization by establishing state ownership over land and forest resources, such as trees growing on private land.[72]

In early 1996 nearly 100,000 people from Bhutan—nearly one-sixth of the total population of Bhutan and the large majority of them Nepali speakers, were residing in refugee camps in Nepal. Their exclusion from the dominant political-constitutional discourse, especially by legislations such as the 1985 Citizenship Act, which denied citizenship to many ethnic minorities, and by governmental measures such as eviction from land with little or no compensation, seriously hindered implementation of integrationist policies.[73] Further the insurrection led by southerners against imposition of Driglam Namza, an ancient code of social etiquette practised by the dominant Ngalop ethnic group, has also led to significant expulsion of over 100,000 Lhotshampas, who subsequently sought asylum in Nepal.[74] This exodus also precipitated government programmes encouraging intra-state migration from northern to southern Bhutan.

IV.8 Maldives

The Maldives was a caste society well into the 1920s. Modernization efforts however, have helped make Maldives more homogeneous in the early 1990s.

Traditionally, a significant gap has existed between the elite living on Male and the remainder of the population inhabiting the outer islands—those atolls distant from Male.[75] President Gayoom's development philosophy has centred on decreasing this gap by raising the standard of living among the 75 per cent of Maldivians who live in the outer atolls as well as making the Maldives more self-sufficient. Fortunately, social tensions that might have affected these two distinct societies were lessened by the isolation of the outer islands.[76] Ethnically, Maldives people consist of a homogenous mixture of Sinhalese, Dravidian, Arabs, Australasian, and Africans.[77]

The passion of the indigenous communities to assert their identity, autonomy, and freedom from exploitation; the colonial policy of drawing lines of non-intervention and self-governance; inter-country migration creating ethnic conflicts and calling for fair resolution; recognition of land based rights of ethnic communities; the concern for conservation of their social customs, traditions, language, and religion; and the need for affirmative action for their support are the broad themes arising from common experiences of SAARC nations.

V Constitutional Policy Choices and the State–Tribe Relationship: Comparative Exegesis

V.1 India

The Indian Constitution provides an elaborate normative framework for safeguarding ethnic pluralism through security of basic rights, land, natural resources, social custom, and identity; self-governance opportunities at grass root level for their autonomous development; and social justice for overall development and welfare of the tribes. Article 244 and 244A of the constitution envisage protections to the Tribes population as elaborated in the Fifth and Sixth Schedules to the Constitution. Para 5(2) of the Fifth Schedule provides that the governor may make regulations for the peace and good government of any area in a state which is for the time being a scheduled area. Providing effective protection to the tribes to their landed rights is the spirit of this provision.[78] Under Para 3 (1) of the Sixth Schedule, the district councils and regional councils, which consist of members of tribal communities, has the power to make laws on (a) the allotment, occupation, or use or the setting apart of land other than any land which is a reserved forest, for the purposes of agriculture or grazing or for residential or other non-agricultural purposes or for any other purposes likely to promote the interests of the inhabitants of any village or town subject to compulsory acquisition of any land for public purposes in accordance with law, (b) the management of forest not being reserved forest, (c) the use of canal or water course for the purpose of agriculture, and (d) the regulation of the practice of jhum cultivation.

Both are in line with international legal policies.[79] The judicial approach in an early case on the implication of (a) was restrictive as it did not bring transfer within its ambit.[80] In contrast, the legislations made by states of Bihar, Andhra Pradesh, Maharashtra, Kerala, Karnataka, Madhya Pradesh, and Odisha prohibited transfer of land by tribal to non-tribal and restored the alienated land back to the tribal.[81] Judiciary also supported the legislative policies through pro-tribes approach.[82]

In the matter of self-government as a feature of tribal development policy, constitutional provisions are explicit. The formation of an autonomous state within the state of Assam consisting of tribal areas with a special body to act as the legislature and council of ministers is also contemplated [Article 244A]. In the Fifth Schedule areas Tribes Advisory Councils are prevalent whose advice to the Governor in the matter of allotment of land to STs, the regulation of the money lending business, and the development of welfare schemes are crucial. Under Article 371-A the central laws will not affect the social customs of Nagaland unless its Legislative Assembly allows it through resolution.[83] The Panchayat Extension to Scheduled Area Act, 1996 enacted under Article 243 M aims to centre stage the functioning of gram sabhas by making it competent to preserve the traditions, customs, and cultural identity of the community; to plan for social and economic development; to restore land to the tribal; to provide control over moneylenders, forest produce, natural resources; and to supervise mining and land acquisition proceeding.

The third strand of constitutional policy on ethnic pluralism is the comprehensive goal of social justice. Guarantee of equality before the law and equal protection of the laws under Article 14, prohibition of discrimination on grounds of race, religion, caste, sex, and place of birth under Article 15 and 16, special measures for STs under Article 15 (4), 15 (5) and 16 (4), (4A) and (4B), protection of cultural and language rights under Articles 29 and 30, and the directive for amelioration of weaker sections including STs under Article 46 are the basic principles and policies for social justice and human dignity. Under Article 330 and 332, the reservation of seats in the Lok Sabha and state legislative assemblies for scheduled castes (SCs) and STs in proportion to the percentage of their population is contemplated. Under Article 338-A National Commission for Scheduled Tribes has extensive duties to inquire, investigate, recommend for remedies, and discharge such other functions for the welfare and development of the STs. Judicial approach in the matter of protective discrimination benefitting SCs and STs is one of the supportive factors to the cause of their amelioration.

V.2 Sri Lanka

The latest Constitution of 1978, amended several times over the years, has immensely broadened the scope of protection of the rights of minorities—which, first, places them on an equal footing along with the rest of the population as far as their right to equal treatment and the equal protection of the laws is concerned;[84] and secondly, there is an express and clear prohibition against discriminatory treatment of citizens on the grounds of race, religion, language, caste, sex, political opinion, place of birth, or any one of such grounds.[85] While the positive rights like freedom of thought and conscience and religion,[86] speech and expression,[87] peaceful assembly,[88] association,[89] the right to manifest their religious beliefs in diverse ways,[90] enjoy and promote their own cultures and use their own languages,[91] the right to engage in lawful occupations, professions, trades, or business,[92] enable them to the full realization of their human personality along with the rest of the citizenry, restrictions on these rights in order to promote racial and religious harmony are oriented towards social harmony.[93] The objectives in the Preamble to the effect that just social, economic, and cultural order shall be attained in order to promote unity of Sri Lanka also direct towards ethnically harmonious society.

In order to deal with the communal disharmony ensuing the declaration of Sinhala as the 'only' official language and the agency of the Indo-Sri Lanka Accord (1987), the 13th Amendment (Article 18) granting official status to the Tamil language was introduced by the Sri Lankan Legislature. After the 16th Amendment (1988), Sinhala and Tamil became the languages of administration in Sri Lanka.[94]

The latest constitution firmly ensconces the traditions of ethnic accommodation in the legal arena by resorting to devolution of power.[95] Land is a devolved subject and state land within a region is vested in Provincial Councils so as to accord priority to persons first of the district and then of the region in future land settlement schemes.[96] As per Ninth Schedule, List I, Appendix II, alienation of land shall be by the President on the basis of advice of the Regional Council; distribution of land shall be on the criteria of landlessness, low income position and background of agricultural profession; the distribution of all allotments of such land in inter-regional projects will be on the basis of national ethnic ratio.[97] It shall not disturb very significantly the demographic pattern of the province and shall be in accordance with the principle of ensuring community cohesiveness in human settlements. The Sri Lankan constitution is truly emulative of a strong commitment towards constitutive nation-building and multiethnic pluralism and harmony.

V.3 Pakistan

The 1973 Constitution of Pakistan enshrines the distinct and semi-autonomous status of the Federally Administered Tribal Areas (FATA).[98] Article 1 defines the territories of the Pakistani federation, distinguishing between provinces and FATA. The main operative provisions are contained in Article 247, which reaffirms and defines the distinct status of the FATA. In *Chaudhari Manzoor Elahi v Federation of Pakistan*,[99] it was held that Article 247(2) required that the jurisdiction of superior courts (the High Courts and the Supreme Court) be excluded in matters concerned with FATA. At this point, one should note that the Preamble of the Constitution declares that fundamental rights—including equality of status, of opportunity and before law; social, economic and political justice; as well as freedom of thought, expression, belief, faith, worship and association (subject to law and public morality)—shall be accorded to *all* citizens. A series of provisions of general application guarantee these fundamental rights and more. The supremacy of these rights over '[a]ny law, or any custom or usage having the force of law, in so far as it is inconsistent with the rights conferred' is affirmed in Article 8.

The unfortunate effect of excluding the jurisdiction of superior courts from FATA is apparent. On the one hand, a gamut of constitutional rights is guaranteed to every citizen. Yet by virtue of another set of constitutional provisions, enforcement of these rights is denied to inhabitants of FATA. Conscious of the potential negative impacts of his decision, Anwarul Haq J. interpreted Article 247(7) restrictively. The jurisdiction of the Supreme Court and High Courts was excluded from FATA only in matters exclusively concerned with FATA.

However, in 2001, the military Government of Pakistan created the FATA Reforms Committee to review, in collaboration with a special committee of the NWFP Government, the region's legal and political organization. Though criticized as unrepresentative, these committees presented formal proposals for legislative reform, some of which the Government of Pakistan has since publicly endorsed, but has not yet implemented.

V.4 Bangladesh

The Constitution of Bangladesh does not recognize any minority and, therefore, allows no special protection or promotion for them.[100] However, Part III of the Constitution dealing with fundamental rights guarantees to every citizens, among other things, equality before law,[101] safeguard against discrimination on grounds of religion, race, caste, sex, or place of birth,[102] equality of opportunity in public employment,[103] the freedom of association,[104] the freedom of thought, conscience, and speech,[105] and the freedom of religion.[106]

The Bangladesh government has undertaken a slew of affirmative action programmes for securing peace and cessation of conflict. Chief among these are establishment of a Special Affairs Division particularly for plain lands indigenous peoples; the signing of the CHT Peace Accord with the PCJSS as a solution of the CHT problem through political and peaceful means; the amendment of CHT Regulation in 2003 for establishment of a separate district judge court in CHT; and continuing the quota reservation for 'tribal' people in the government jobs and educational institutions[107]. In keeping with the Government's ratification of a number of international human rights treaties and conventions,[108] which have a fundamental bearing on the indigenous peoples- such as the CHT Peace Accord that ended more than two decades of armed struggle for self-determination and paves the way for the peace, development, and representation of the Jumma people. This philosophy of ethnic accommodation is reflected in the recent 2012 decision of the Supreme Court of Bangladesh where it upheld the application of social customs of the CHT community for resolution of the succession dispute within the Marma community—who are ethnically non-Bengali Buddhists, and do not possess written succession law—over Hindu Dayabhaga law, thus affirming the sanctity of social customary practice and law.[109] Further, the CHT Regulations of 1900 and 1958 consolidate rights of the indigenous peoples to occupation and extraction in the common lands, and their rights to homestead lands, the extraction of sun-grass, the right to herd, and the rights to *Jum*, and so on.

V.5 Afghanistan

Constitutionally, Article 47 requires the state to devise effective programs for fostering knowledge, culture, literature, and arts. Article 23 secures the 'natural right' to life, and prohibits unlawful deprivation of the same. Article 33 furthermore effectuates political participation by guaranteeing electoral rights of every Afghan citizen.[110] Article 22 forbids discrimination and favouritism, attributing equal rights and responsibilities to all Afghan citizens. Article 4 explicitly enshrines national sovereignty and enlists the tribes which constitute its ethnic fabric.[111] It mentions that the 'nation of Afghanistan shall be comprised of Pashtun, Tajik, Hazara, Uzbek, Turkman, Baluch, Pachaie, Nuristani, Aymaq, Arab, Qirghiz, Qizilbash, Gujur, Brahwui, and other tribes' while simultaneously providing that 'the word Afghan shall apply to every citizen of Afghanistan.' This indicates an inclusive connotation of national sovereignty in the constitutional epistemology of Afghanistan.

While there is no special provision recognizing minorities, usually the Hazaras, Hindus, and Sikhs are regarded as such.[112] Article 16 ensconces Pashto and Dari as the official languages of the state. However, it provides that in areas where the majority of the people speak in any one of Uzbeki, Turkmani, Pachaie, Nuristani, Baluchi, or Pamiri languages, such language shall be the third official language, the usage of which shall be regulated by law. Coupled with a mandate on the state to design and apply effective programs to foster and develop all languages of Afghanistan, this provision evinces a patently pro-diversity constitutional approach towards state affirmation of linguistic and ethnic pluralism.[113]

V.6 Nepal

Article 3 of the 2015 Constitution recognizes Nepal as a multi-ethnic, multilingual, multireligious, multicultural state. As prescribed by Article 4, the policy of secularism adopted by Nepal is avowedly different from the Western approach—it manifests the state's commitment to 'protection of religion and culture being practiced since ancient times and religious and cultural freedom'.[114]

Article 17 enlists the fundamental freedoms of life, of opinion and expression, of assembly, association, and movement. The formalistic conception of equality is guaranteed through Article 24, which forbids untouchability or discrimination in any private or public place on grounds of caste, ethnicity, origin, community, et al. This Article also explicitly asserts that no racial discrimination in any sphere shall be tolerated.

The wide freedoms granted under Article 26 to profess, practice, and preserve his/her religion according to his/her faith, and to religious denominations to maintain their autonomy in functioning, evince a clear constitutional commitment to upholding rights of religious minorities.[115] Furthermore, Article 47, in facilitating the right to social justice, provides that the Dalits, Adibasi, Janajati, Adibasi Janajati, Madhesi, Tharu, minority groups, the oppressed and the citizens of backward regions, and economically poor Khas Arya shall have the right to employment in state structures on the basis of the principle of inclusion. To fully realize the potential of these mandates, the Directive Principles embodied in provisions such as Article 51(j) delineate several measures for ensuring continuing national integration. In 2015, the extensive Madhesi agitation demanding for constitutional amendment for proportionately inclusive representation and determination of electoral constituencies had resulted in constitutional amendment.[116]

V.7 Bhutan

The Constitution of Bhutan has a focus on a harmonious state–citizen relationship.[117] The philosophy of "One Nation, One People", propounded by

His Majesty, is now firmly entrenched in both the spirit and the letter of the Constitution.[118]

Article 1(4) of the Constitution safeguards internal and national territorial integrity and by mandating that alteration of the territorial units of Dzongkhags (districts), Gewogs (Counties) and Thromdes (municipalities) cannot be altered without the consent of at least three-fourths of the total number of members of Parliament.[119] The recognition of Dzongkha as the national language does not undermine or prohibit use of other extant languages and dialects such as Tshangla,[120] Mangdephka,[121] Lhotsamkha,[122] et al, which are in fact explicitly preserved through Article 4.[123]

Article 7(15) adds that all persons are equal before the law and are entitled to equal and effective protection of the law and shall not be discriminated against on the grounds of race, sex, language, religion, politics, or other status. However, only Buddhists and Hindus are allowed to form organizations to function legally in the country. The Religious Organizations Act of 2007—the only legislation that provides for the formation of religious groups—says that its main intent is to 'benefit the religious institutions and protect the spiritual heritage of Bhutan,' which is Mahayana Buddhism.[124]

V.8 Maldives

The Maldivian constitution and legal framework grant the right to vote and opportunity to contest elections only to Muslim citizens and specifically to adherents of Sunni Islam, thus excluding the Christian minority and other religious groups.

Scholars have noted that the constitution fails to provide basic guarantees of rights and freedoms in the country for non-Muslims and also violates internationally accepted human rights standards and norms.[125] Article 9, Section D states that 'a non-Muslim may not become a citizen of the Maldives.' By denying citizenship to some people on the basis of their religion, the country is violating religious minorities' freedom of worship, whilst also establishing several other precepts which threaten the freedom of religion.[126] The new constitution favours Sunni Islam over other forms of Islam, establishes certain aspects of Shari'a law in the Maldives and limits the freedom of expression and thought to 'manners' which are 'not contrary to a tenet of Islam'.[127]

VI Conclusion

The SAARC countries being rich repositories of indigenous communities have responded to the problem of multi-ethnic communities in a responsible and commendable manner. Amidst varieties of approaches for constitutional management of ethnic pluralism, an integrated approach of security, self-government, and social justice (SSS) has emerged as a cardinal value in these countries. The level of their success has much revolved around the issue how far they could satisfy the claims of territoriality for larger ethnic communities, protection of their economic resources—land, forest, water—and safeguarding of their identity and culture along with a space for their self-governance and succour of social justice policy in an integrated way. The emergence of such a criterion is a product of history and an outcome of social movement and common experience that the otherwise vulnerable community would be lagging behind other communities in the absence of the triple S.

The SSS evinces deep human rights commitment, approach of multiculturalism, democratic participation, and sustainable economic and all-round development. None of the SAARC countries has embraced the policies of suppression, forced assimilation, or merciless extermination as deliberate policy. As decolonized democracies and carrying the burden of the heavy past, their movement was not a straight-line march in the background of undulating topography. Depending upon maturity of development and intensity of social movement, their attainment of goal has varied. But the acceptance of the grand path seems to be the general lesson especially when we look to the fact that Sri Lanka, Bangladesh, and Nepal ultimately traversed the avenue after initial deviation. Racial harmony is the essential condition of this approach, although similarities and dissimilarities in mechanisms and strategies persist amidst the SAARC nations in the method of its implementation.

Amidst the federal systems of India, Pakistan, Afghanistan, and Nepal special protection of ethnic minorities through territoriality principle and geographical location have similar approaches. Partnership of federal and state governments in administering, funding, and supporting the ethnic pockets is visible in both India and Pakistan. The fact that while federalism can provide some solution, it is not a guarantor of perfect solution regarding smaller ethnic communities or tribes spread over larger geographical areas is emerging from the Nepal experience about dealing with Madhesis. Coexistence of multitude ethnic communities without any one in majority position is the experience of Afghanistan.

Amidst the unitary nations the disadvantage of the absence of diverse geographical base for different ethnic minorities has been a point of trouble. For Sri Lanka, which faced severe ethnic conflicts, the Thirteenth Amendment which provided for devolution of power, creation of Regional Council and land security to satisfy ethnic ratio became a path breaking approach. The changed public policy with regard to CHT in Bangladesh has a parallel. How Bhutan is resolving the issue of Nepali migrants is a question that may attract a similar answer. Depending upon arrangement for federalism and local administration, the pattern of administration of tribal areas also varies.

All the three components of the triple S are mutually complementary and survive by flourish of all. As the Indian and Pakistan experience shows their coexistence and robust functioning with an approach of combination is a great tower of strength for the indigenous communities. While security gives external support, self-governance builds up internal strength, and social justice is an upgrading causative factor. Sri Lanka, Bhutan, Nepal, and Bangladesh are heading towards recognition of the importance of this integrated approach. Maldives represents cosmopolitan approach towards minorities while Afghan policy towards multitude of ethnic minorities aligns with the axis of equality and equity.

In all the SAARC country constitutions ethnic right is intertwined with language rights and religious freedom. Composite culture emerging from this phenomenon is a source of great strength for social harmony as people unite on one or other plank and overcome the cleavages. Prevention of loss of indigenous languages should be part of the agenda of security.

The SSS receives predominant human right influence both in conceptualization and implementation. The societal responses to legal and constitutional frameworks embracing pluralism evince a growing constitutional culture that espouses human and group rights, and is committed to sustaining ethnic-religious pluralism within the national order. Over the years, the SSS approach has gained credentials, viability and social acceptance. All the organs of government have contributed for such a position.

Notes and References

1. John S. Furnivall. 1948. *Colonial Policy and Practice: A Comparative Study of Burma and Netherlands India.* Cambridge: Cambridge University Press.
2. See Stanley J. Tambiah. 1997. *Leveling Crowds: Ethnonationalist Conflicts and Collective Violence in South Asia* (vol. 10.) Oakland: University of California Press.
3. See Daniel H. Levine. 2009. 'Pluralism as Challenges and Opportunity' in F. Hagopian (ed.), *Religious Pluralism, Democracy, and the Catholic Church in Latin America.* Indiana: University of Notre Dame Press.
4. See P. Ishwara Bhat. 2009. *Law and Social Transformation in India*, pp. 405–51. Lucknow: Eastern Book Co.
5. Bhat. *Law and Social Transformation in India*, pp. 58–63.
6. See Will Kymlicka and Wayne Norman. 2000. 'Citizenship in Culturally Diverse Societies: Issues, Contexts, Concepts' in *Citizenship in Diverse Societies.* Oxford: Oxford University Press.
7. Will Kymlicka. 1995. *Multicultural Citizenship: A Liberal Theory of Minority Rights.* Oxford: Clarendon Press.
8. See Rudolf C. Heredia. 2002. 'Interrogating Integration: The Counter-Cultural Tribal Other', *Economic and Political Weekly*, 37(52): p. 5177.
9. Heredia, 'Interrogating Integration'.

10. See Urmila Phadnis, 1989, 2001. *Ethnicity and Nation-Building in South Asia.* New Delhi: SAGE India Publications.
11. Li-Ann Thio. 2005. *Managing Babel: The International Legal Protection Of Minorities In The Twentieth Century.* Leiden: Martinus Nijhoff Publishers.
12. This involves two elements: first, power-sharing, which 'denotes the participation of representatives of all significant communal groups in political decision making, especially at the executive level;' second, group autonomy entails giving groups 'authority to run their own internal affairs, especially in the areas of education and culture.' Arend Lijphart, 2004. 'Constitutional Design for Divided Societies', *Journal of Democracy*, vol. 15: 96, 97.
13. See Theodor Meron, 1985. 'The meaning and reach of the international convention on the elimination of all forms of racial discrimination.' 79.2 *The American JIL* pp. 283–318.
14. Article 27, International Covenant on Civil and Political Rights 1966.
15. ILO, *Recommendation Concerning the Protection and Integration of Indigenous and Other Tribal and Semi-Tribal Populations in Independent Countries (No. 104),* Adopted in the 40th ILC Session, Geneva (June 26, 1957).
16. See Peter Poole. 2003. 'Cultural mapping and indigenous peoples.' *A Report for UNESCO.*
17. Francesco Mauro and Preston D. Hardison. 2000. 'Traditional knowledge of indigenous and local communities: international debate and policy initiatives.' 10.5 *Ecological Applications* pp. 1263–9.
18. Mauro and Hardison, 'Traditional Knowledge'.
19. Li-Ann Thio. 2010. 'Constitutional Accommodation Of The Rights Of Ethnic And Religious Minorities In Plural Democracies: Lessons And Cautionary Tales From South-East Asia.' 22 *Pace Int'l L. Rev.* 43.
20. Total number of ethnic groups in India exceed 2000.
21. *India, 2006*, p. 872. New Delhi: Publications Division.
22. *India, 2006*, p. 872.
23. *India, 2006*, p. 872.
24. See Marc Galanter. 1984. *Competing Equalities: Law and Backward Classes In India.* New Delhi: Oxford University Press.
25. See https://www.cia.gov/library/publications/the-world-factbook/geos/print/country/countrypdf_ce.pdf.
26. See https://www.cia.gov/library/publications/the-world-factbook/geos/print/country/countrypdf_ce.pdf.
27. The World Factbook – Sri Lanka.
28. See Ian Talbot. 2009. *Pakistan: A Modern History.* London: C. Hurst & Co.
29. See Ian Talbot. 2009. *Pakistan: A Modern History.* London: C. Hurst & Co.
30. The World Factbook- Pakistan.
31. *See* William van Schendel. 2009. *A History of Bangladesh.* Cambridge: Cambridge University Press.
32. 'Solidarity 2005' (International Indigenous Peoples Day publication of Bangladesh Indigenous Peoples Forum) published the list of 45 ethnic groups.

33. *See* Syed Masud Ahmed. 2001. 'Differing health and health-seeking behavior, ethnic minorities of the Chittagong Hill Tracts, Bangladesh.' 13.2 *Asia-Pacific Journal of Public Health*, pp. 100–8.
34. *See* Syed Masud Ahmed. 2001. 'Differing health and health-seeking behavior, ethnic minorities of the Chittagong Hill Tracts, Bangladesh.' 13.2 *Asia-Pacific Journal of Public Health*. pp. 100–8.
35. *See* Tania Rahman. 2010. 'A multilingual language-in-education policy for indigenous minorities in Bangladesh: Challenges and possibilities.' 11.4 *Current Issues in Language Planning*, pp. 341–59.
36. Vartan Gregorian. 1969. *The Emergence of Modern Afghanistan: Politics of Reform and Modernization, 1880–1946*. Stanford: Stanford University Press.
37. Pierre Centlivres and Micheline Centlivres-Demont. 2000. 'State, national awareness and levels of identity in Afghanistan from monarchy to Islamic state.' *Central Asian Survey*. 19.3–4, pp. 416–25.
38. John Whelpton. 2005. *A History of Nepal*. Cambridge: Cambridge University Press.
39. On 1 January 1974, during a public gathering at Sisboo, His Majesty said: 'You, the citizens of Southern Bhutan must never regard yourselves as aliens, because you and your forbearers also, were born and raised in Bhutan and as such, all of you are Bhutanese [...] All of us must remain united as one people and one nation and forge ahead together.'
40. See Nirmala Das. 1974. *The Dragon Country: The General History of Bhutan*. New Delhi: Orient Longman.
41. See George van Driem, 'Bhutan's endangered languages documentation programme under the Dzongkha Development Authority: The three rare gems'. *First International Seminar on Bhutan Studies, Thimphu*. 2004.
42. See, for example, Clarence Maloney. 1976. 'The Maldives: New stresses in an old nation.' *Asian Survey* 16.7 pp. 654–71.
43. See, for example, Clarence Maloney. 1976. 'The Maldives: New stresses in an old nation.' *Asian Survey* 16.7 pp. 654–71.
44. See, for example, Clarence Maloney. 1976. 'The Maldives: New stresses in an old nation.' *Asian Survey* 16.7 pp. 654–71.
45. Iain Chambers and Lidia Curti. 1996. *The Post-colonial Question: Common Skies, Divided Horizons*. Abingdon: Psychology Press.
46. R.C. Verma. Supra n 3, pp. 15 to 34.
47. Ross Mallick. 1998. *Development, Ethnicity and Human Rights in South Asia*. New Delhi: Sage Publications.
48. W. J. Culshaw and W. G. Archer. 1945.'The Santal Rebellion.' *Man in India* 25.4, pp. 218–239.
49. W. J. Culshaw and W. G. Archer. 1945.'The Santal Rebellion.' *Man in India* 25.4, p. 48.
50. Joseph E. Schwartzberg and Robert Stoddard. 'Evolving Ethnicity in South Asia With Particular Reference to India' (1995) *The Challenge Of Ethnic Conflict To National And International Order in The 1990s: Geographic Perspectives: A Conference Report*.

51. *See* Benjamin Perrin. 2004. 'Terrorism, Secession & Multinational Constitutions: The Challenge Of Sri Lanka,' 16 *Sri Lanka JIL* p. 175.
52. *See* Masaji Chiba. 1993. 'Legal Pluralism In Sri Lankan Society Toward A General Theory Of Non-Western Law,' 33 J. Legal Pluralism & Unofficial L. p. 197.
53. The constitution-making process involved consultation of minority groups. See Hamid Khan, 2001. *Constitutional and Political History of Pakistan* (2nd edition) Karachi: Oxford University Press, p. 52.
54. The constitution making process involved consultation of minority groups. See Hamid Khan, 2001. *Constitutional and Political History of Pakistan* (2nd edition) Karachi: Oxford University Press, p. 52.
55. Iftikhar H. Malik 'The state and civil society in Pakistan: From crisis to crisis' (1996) Asian Survey 36.7, 673–90.
56. Iftikhar H. Malik 'The state and civil society in Pakistan: From crisis to crisis' (1996) Asian Survey 36.7, 673–90.
57. Mohammad Waseem. 1998. 'Ethnic conflict in Pakistan: the case of the Mohajir Qaumi Movement.' in *Regional Security, Ethnicity and Governance.*
58. See Saleem Samad. 1999. 'State of Minorities in Bangladesh.' In S. Banarjee (ed), *Shrinking Space: Minority Rights in South Asia,* pp. 75–96.
59. See Livia Holden. 2015. *Legal Pluralism and Governance in South Asia and Diasporas,* Abingdon: Routledge.
60. See MS Azhar and others. 2012. 'Ethnic Factor in Afghanistan,' *Journal of Political Studies.*
61. See Thomas Barfield. 2010. *Afghanistan: A cultural and political history.* New Jersey: Princeton University Press.
62. See Thomas H. Johnson and M. Chris Mason. 2008. 'Understanding the Taliban and insurgency in Afghanistan.' *Orbis* 51.1 pp. 71–89.
63. H.P. Bhattarai, 2004. 'Cultural Diversity and Pluralism in Nepal: Emerging Issues and the Search for a New Paradigm.' 31 *Contributions to Nepalese Studies* 2, pp. 293–340.
64. Article 4, the 1990 Constitution.
65. (which were non-enforceable but nevertheless considered to be fundamental to governance, Art 24(2), 1990 constitution.)
66. Art. 26(2), 1990 Constitution.
67. Art. 26(2), 1990 Constitution.
68. See Mary Des Chene, et al. 1998. *Selves in time and place: Identities, experience, and history in Nepal.* Maryland: Rowman & Littlefield Publishers.
69. See Michael Hutt, 1996. 'Ethnic nationalism, refugees, and Bhutan.' *Journal of Refugee Studies* 9.4 pp. 397–420.
70. K.J. Holsti, 1982. 'From Isolation to Dependence: Bhutan. 1958–62.' in *Why Nations Realign: Foreign Policy Restructuring in the Postwar World.* Abingdon: Routledge.
71. See Karma Phuntsho. 2013. *The History of Bhutan.* New Delhi: Random House India.

72. *See* Lam Dorji, Edward L. Webb, and Ganesh P. Shivakoti. 2006. 'Forest property rights under nationalized forest management in Bhutan.' *Environmental Conservation,* 33.02: pp. 141–7.
73. Michael Hutt. 2004. 'Unbecoming citizens: culture, nationhood, and the flight of refugees from Bhutan.' *Refugee Survey Quarterly* 23.3.
74. Dhurba Rizal. 2004. 'The unknown refugee crisis: Expulsion of the ethnic Lhotsampa from Bhutan.' *Asian Ethnicity* 5.2: 151–77.
75. See Francis Robinson. 1989. *The Cambridge Encyclopedia of India, Pakistan, Bangladesh, Sri Lanka, Nepal, Bhutan, and the Maldives.* No. REF-954.052 ROB. CIMMYT.
76. See Francis Robinson. 1989. *The Cambridge Encyclopedia of India, Pakistan, Bangladesh, Sri Lanka, Nepal, Bhutan, and the Maldives.* No. REF-954.052 ROB. CIMMYT.
77. Christopher HB. Reynolds. 1978. 'Linguistic strands in the Maldives.' *Language and Civilization Change in South Asia,* pp. 155–166. Leiden: Brill.
78. *Samata v State of AP,* 1997 2 SCJ 539, para 49.
79. Article 15 of the ILO Convention Concerning Indigenous and Tribal Peoples in Independent Countries, 1989, Agenda 21 of Rio Declaration, Article 26–28 of the UN Declaration on the Rights of Indigenous Peoples 1994 recognizes their right to own, develop, control, and use the lands and territories, including the total environment.
80. *District Council of U.K. and J. Hills, Shillong v Sitimon Sawian* AIR 1972 SC 787.
81. Chota Nagpur Tenancy Act, 1908; the Santhal Pargana Tenancy (Supplementary Provisions) Act, 1959 and the Bihar Scheduled Areas Regulations, 1969; Gujarat Amendments to Bombay Land Revenue Code, 1879; The Maharashtra Land Revenue Code and Tenancy Laws (Amendment) Act, 1974 and Maharashtra (Restoration of Lands to Scheduled Tribes) Act, 1974; The Kerala Land Reforms Act, 1963; The Kerala Scheduled Tribes (Restriction of Transfer of Land and Regulation of Alienation of Lands), Act, 1975; Karnataka Scheduled Castes and Scheduled Tribes (Prohibition of Transfer of Certain Lands) Act (2 of 1979).
82. *P. Rami Reddy v State of Andhra Pradesh* (1988) 3 SCC 433: (AIR 1988 SC 1626); the Court observed, 'It is absolutely necessary to create conditions for peace and maintain peace and prevent the new non-tribals from settling down in the scheduled area. If the alienations are permitted to the non-tribals there is a danger of large-scale exploitation by the new non-tribals again with the result peace will be disturbed in that area.'; *State of Madhya Pradesh v Babu Lal* (1977) (2) SCC 435; *Amrendra Pratap Singh v Tej Bahadur Prajapati* AIR 2004 SC 3782: 'The tribals need to be settled, need to be taken care of by the protective arm of the law, and be saved from falling prey to unscrupulous device so that they may prosper and by an evolutionary process join the mainstream of the society.'
83. In *State of Nagaland v Ratan Singh,* (1966) 3 SCR 830 the Naga Rules of Administration of Justice 1937 was preferred to that of Civil Procedure code 1908.

84. Constitution of Sri Lanka, Article 12(1).
85. Constitution of Sri Lanka, Article 12(2).
86. Constitution of Sri Lanka, Article 10.
87. Constitution of Sri Lanka, Article 14(a).
88. Constitution of Sri Lanka, Article 14(b).
89. Constitution of Sri Lanka, Article 14(c).
90. Constitution of Sri Lanka, Article 14(e).
91. Constitution of Sri Lanka, Article 14(f).
92. Constitution of Sri Lanka, Article 14(g).
93. Constitution of Sri Lanka, Article 15; Amita Shastri. 1999. 'Estate Tamils, the Ceylon citizenship act of 1948 and Sri Lankan politics.' *Contemporary South Asia* 8.1: pp. 65–86.
94. Neil DeVotta. 2004. *Blowback: Linguistic Nationalism, Institutional Decay, and Ethnic Conflict in Sri Lanka*. Redwood City: Stanford University Press.
95. Thirteenth Amendment to the Sri Lankan Constitution.
96. The Constitution of Sri Lanka, Chapter XVII A.
97. In the distribution of allotments according to such ratios, priority will be given to persons who are displaced by the project, the landless of the District in which the project is situated and thereafter the landless of the Province.
98. Golam Wahed Choudhury. 1969. *Constitutional Development in Pakistan*. Vancouver: Publications Centre, University of British Columbia.
99. *Chaudhari Manzoor Elahi v Federation of Pakistan,* [1975] PLD 66 (Sup Ct of Pakistan).
100. Gobinda Chandra Mandal. 2007. 'Treatment of Law to the Minorities in Bangladesh: Rhetoric and Reality', in Mizanur Rahman (ed.), *Human Rights & Corruption, Dhaka, Empowerment through Law of the Common People*, p. 221. New Delhi: Vedams eBooks.
101. Article 27.
102. Article 28.
103. Article 29.
104. Article 38.
105. Article 39.
106. Article 41.
107. *A Brief Account of Human Rights Situation of the Indigenous People in Bangladesh, Assessed by Asian Indigenous Peoples Pact* 2007.
108. International Convention on the Civil and Political Rights (ICCPR), International Convention on Elimination of all forms of Racial Discrimination (CERD), The International Covenant on Economic, Social, and Cultural Rights (ICESCR), ILO Conventions 107 (Indigenous and Tribal Peoples), and the Convention on Biological Diversity CBD)—1997.
109. *Aberchai Mog v Jt. District Judge, Khagrachari* (Writ Petition No. 3285 of 2009 and WP No. 2829 of 2006) decided on 7 October 2012.
110. See Barnett R. Rubin. 'Crafting a constitution for Afghanistan.' 2004. *Journal of Democracy* 15.3: pp. 5–19.

111. See Barnett R. Rubin. 'Crafting a constitution for Afghanistan.' 2004. *Journal of Democracy* 15.3: pp. 5–19.
112. Nassim Jawad. 1992. *Afghanistan: A Nation of Minorities*. No. 92. London: Minority Rights Group International.
113. See Peter Marsden. 2001. *Afghanistan: Minorities, Conflict and the Search for Peace*. London: Minority Rights Group International.
114. Mara Malagodi. 2013. *Constitutional Nationalism and Legal Exclusion: Equality, Identity Politics and Democracy in Nepal (1990–2007)*. Oxford: Oxford University Press.
115. Krishna B. Bhattachan. 2003. 'Indigenous nationalities and minorities of Nepal.' London: Minority Rights Group International. *Retrieved October* 29: p. 2007.
116. Surendra Bhandari. 2016. *Constitutional Design and Implementation Dynamics: Federalism and Inclusive National Building in Nepal.* Kathmandu: Himal Innovative Development and research. pp. 34–39.
117. Lyonpo Sonam Tobgye, *The Constitution of Bhutan: Principle and Philosophies* (ISBN: 978-99936-658-7-8), p. 50.
118. On 1 January 1974, during a public gathering at Sisboo, His Majesty said: 'You, the citizens of Southern Bhutan must never regard yourselves as aliens, because you and your forbearers also, were born and raised in Bhutan and as such, all of you are Bhutanese […] All of us must remain united as one people and one nation and forge ahead together.'
119. See B.R. Giri. 2004. 'Bhutan: ethnic policies in the dragon kingdom.' *Asian Affairs* 35.3: pp. 353–64.
120. Spoken in eastern Bhutan.
121. Spoken in central Bhutan.
122. Spoken in southern Bhutan.
123. 'The State shall endeavour to preserve, protect and promote the cultural heritage of our country, including […] language…'
124. Vishal Arora. 2014. 'Bhutan's Human Rights Record Defies "Happiness" Claim,' The Diplomat, April 25. http://thediplomat.com/2014/04/bhutans-human-rights-record-defies-happiness-claim/, accessed 19 July 2017.
125. See, for example, Hussain, Monirul. *Religious Minorities in South Asia: Selected Essays on Post-colonial Situations*. Manak Publ., 2002.
126. WOODWARD, CA. *Citizenship Laws in Bangladesh, Burma, Sri Lanka, Thailand and Maldives* (1976): 216–17.
127. *See* Maniku, Hassan Ahmed. 1986. 'Conversion of Maldives to Islam', *Journal of the Royal Asiatic Society Sri Lanka Branch* 31: 72–81.

SECTION B
HUMAN RIGHTS

12

Comparing Fundamental Social Rights in the European and the Indian Union

Jörg Luther

I Introduction

Social rights are considered traditionally weak rights. They are more close to national state directives than to judicial enforcement. Civil rights watching is more developed than social rights watching. Social rights regard private and public powers and subsidies governed by a principle of subsidiarity. Their implementation and costs in multilevel governance changes from place to place and from time to time. They are perceived as younger rights and rights under the stress of globalization. Their comparison is still less developed.

In order to promote a new Indo-European dialogue, this chapter offers first a comparative contextual analysis of the argument looking at the common geo-history, the different institutional frameworks, political cultures, legal systems and economic performances and the relevant international relations (in Section II of the chapter). The next step will be an attempt to outline a common 'spirit' and concept of social rights in Europe as a thin, neither neoliberal nor socialist synthesis and as a hybridization of national legal and constitutional traditions and international law that could be compared with the Indian case (Section III). The chapter looks in a further step at the state of social rights within the European Union (EU), specially the European Social Model and the ways of Europeanization of social policies and their interaction with changing European welfare state systems (Section IV). In the following step the European Social Charter (ESC) will be compared to the South Asian Association for Regional Cooperation (SAARC) Social Charter and further opportunities of social rights protection will be explored (Section V). The final question with only partial answer is what the European and the Indian Union could learn from each other's' social rights protection experiences (Section VI).

II Comparative Contextual Analysis

Any transcontinental dialogue and comparison has to practice precaution, being aware of the asymmetries of knowledge and the dangers of romantic exoticism, magisterial arrogance or curatorial particularism.[1] The EU and the Indian Union have prima facie extremely different and far distant social rights discourses. In order to measure and prospect the circulation of legal ideas and models of social rights between both Unions, one should bear in mind various relevant contexts: (a) the common history, (b) different institutional frameworks, (c) different political cultures of democracy, (d) different legal cultures, and (e) different economical performances, (f) but common international relations.

a. The history of Eurasian migrations and Indo-European languages since the so called axial age and along the Silk Road has framed a common Eurasian cultural heritage of legal myths and ideas, including the sacredness of *jeu(o)s* (*jus*)[2] as well as the inventions of empires and the rule of law (*Rajadharma v nomos basileus*). The memory of this common legal heritage has been divided by occidentalism/orientalism and partially cancelled by experiences of colonialism, but it could still support modern cosmopolitanism as well as minority rights discourses against ongoing clashes of civilizations. The lost memory of the Indian roots of the Sinti minority in Europe is just one example, the lost memory of the European roots of the concept of nationhood another. Looking at this common history, social rights are first of all grounded on the ancient duties to take care and give hospitality to the poor, the ill and the stranger, duties that have been ruled and institutionalized prior to the Christian *caritas* and Islamic *zadak* in Hindu *Dāna* and Hebrew *tzedakah*. Already the Babylonian king Hamurabi codified its laws for the purpose 'that the strong might not injure the weak, in order to protect the widows and orphans'.[3] The ancient rule of law could have been a rule of social law.

b. The different forms of federalism in both Unions matter for social rights protection. Meanwhile the Indian Union is a sovereign national mega-state, based on a postcolonial constitution with federalism and social directives, the EU is a treaty based on a supranational federation (or confederacy) of pre-existing nation states with different constitutional cultures and welfare systems and a principle of solidarity tempered by subsidiarity. The Indian Union is centralized, but moving towards more federalism, notwithstanding strong experiences of partition and secessionism.[4] The EU is less centralized and governed by an executive federalism under a perceived German hegemony, shocked by the BREXIT referendum and an increasing north/south divide, but it is still facing further demands of accession and expectations of social federalism.[5] Sovereignty and federalism matter both for the performance and effectiveness of social rights, because federalism could stimulate solidarity among communities. Federal frameworks don't necessarily enhance social homogeneity and strong solidarity among territories, but they can promote a sufficient degree of social cohesion and support social rights related services at local and regional level, but the performance of social rights under federalism has not yet been measured with universally recognized social rights indicators. The EU might become a model for a South Asian Economic Union, but federal solidarity among rich nations could be less difficult than among countries with more poverty.

c. Even democracy and political culture matter for the protection of social rights. The imperfections of democracy could be a factor and/or a consequence of the weakness of social rights and state directives, especially if associated to a concept of capabilities.[6] India is considered the 'largest democracy of the world' with a great pluralism of languages, religions and political parties, but even still high illiteracy and some troubling 'clashes within'.[7] On the other hand, the EU is developing a proper model of 'transnational democracy'[8] and their post-authoritarian democracies are facing tendencies of post-democracy. On the one hand, the Indian concept of democracy has still the purpose of a 'socialist' and 'secular' form of state, on the other hand, democracy in the EU aims to be grounded on values of a society where 'pluralism, non-discrimination, tolerance, justice, solidarity and equality between women and men prevail' (Article 2 TEU). Both unions converge on new common ideals of 'inclusive democracy' and democratic 'responsiveness', but face new realities of plutocracy, technocracy, videocracy, etc.

d. Differences in social rights protection can be grounded in different rule of law conceptions. Social rights need specific legislation and administration and can find special judges for labour, welfare and administrative justice. The Indian law has a common law culture, integrated by oriental sources of

Hindu law and other sources, meanwhile the EU law aims to offer a European synthesis of different national legal cultures, being supported by a common historical basis of Roman law. Common law traditions could be perceived as more liberal or market friendly than social rights centred, meanwhile civil law traditions can transform the 'rule of law' in a 'rule of social law' (*sozialer Rechtsstaat*). The judicial review of legislation being practised in both unions and most EU member states, socio-economic rights can find more weak forms of political and administrative protection, for example, in more realism oriented Scandinavian legal cultures.

e. The Indian economy is still fast growing with lower-middle incomes, the locomotive of BRICS, meanwhile the high income countries of the EU, India's largest trade and investment partner, suffer more the global economic slowdown and sovereign debt crisis and the Euro-group countries have more unemployment than other EU states. Both unions are members of the WTO, but the EU is only a cooperation partner, not a member of World Bank and World Monetary Fund. The OECD recommended India to improve the macroeconomic framework, to raise employment through a more flexible labor law, to increase female economic participation and to improve health outcomes for all.[9] No specific recommendations to EU have been made, but the troika's recommendations to Greece and other countries have been found incompatible with several social rights guarantees by the European Committee of Social Rights (ECSR).[10] Meanwhile in India economic growth seems to favor poverty reduction, in the Euro-group austerity policies are suspected to harm the social rights.

f. EU–India relations are relations among soft powers with voting diasporas.[11] The EU was created in the context of larger organizations of the such as the Council of Europe, North Atlantic Treaty Organization (NATO; 1949), and Organisation for Economic Co-operation and Development (OECD; 1961) and has a special status in International Labour Organization (ILO), World Health Organization (WHO), and United Nations Educational, Scientific and Cultural Organization (UNESCO), the Indian Union is a regional power in the Asia-Pacific region, part of the Commonwealth and of the SAARC, with neighbour states that have more constitutional social rights provisions than other Asian countries. Inspired by a common interest in a new bridging multilateral order based on peace and at least a minimum of global social justice, both are committed to development cooperation and have since 2004 a strategic partnership with an annual 'local' human rights dialogue. Main areas of EU concern include poverty, caste discrimination (Dalits), violence against women, children's rights, rights of indigenous people (Adivasis) and poor prison conditions.[12] Negotiations of a 'broad-based bilateral trade and investment agreement' have been stopped when India rejected clauses for the protection of labour rights and environmental sustainability.[13] Meanwhile most EU development projects support social rights, the EU–India Agenda for Action-2020 (2016) gives only a mandate to 'explore possibilities within G20 to enhance collaboration to promote decent work, productive employment, social protection and occupational safety and health and fostering sustainable global supply and value chains'.

III The Spirit and Concept of Social Rights in European Constitutional and Legal Traditions

The common tradition of social rights protection in Europe has been today at least partially 'constitutionalized' through sources of constitutional law as well as through sources of regional international human rights law. The European tradition has a pre-Christian matrix in the concepts of *cura* and *securitas* that were grounded in stoic ideals of dignity.[14] The transformation of the religious and political duties of solidarity first in pre-modern institutions of ecclesiastical and civic social assistance and later in contemporary secular social rights was promoted mainly by cultural revolutions. Subjective rights were invented at the same time when medieval canonical law recognized that 'by natural law all things are common, which means in times of necessity they must be shared with those who need them'.[15] Italian Renaissance developed a dignity concept open for human creativity and opposed to ascetic concepts of *miseria hominis*, but only the modern constitutions outlined liberty, equality and fraternity as leading principles in human and citizen's rights.

Meanwhile the US declaration of independence declared a right to the 'pursuit of happiness', the French declaration invoked in its preamble the welfare of all (*bonheur de tous*) and added the famous definition of constitutionalism whereby a society that does not divide the powers and 'ensure' (*assurer*) the rights has no constitution at all. The duty to ensure the rights implied not a legal right to security, but a right of access to justice and to military or civil service.

Sieyes's preliminaries of the Constitution recognized furthermore a right of all citizens to share the benefits (*bienfaits*) of their 'social union'. Citizens that by force of a *malheur* were unable to satisfy their needs should be ensured the 'just rights to get help (*secours*) from their con-citizens'. Human beings would need a good public education and instruction system and the Nation would need an active control over its relations with over peoples. Nevertheless the declaration should not list all the values of a good constitution, being sufficient to establish a right of citizens to all action the state can take on their benefit.[16]

Under the Jacobin Constitution of 1793 that declared directive principles on social aid and public education (Articles 22 and 23), slavery was abolished, but Napoleon revoked that decision and the declaration of 1815 granted only free primary school (Article 11). Karl Marx observed[17] that the preamble of the constitution of 1848 transformed vindicated rights to education, labour, and to 'support of the orphan, the infirm, and the aged' into directive principles of the Second Republic (Article 8), preceded by a duty of the individual 'to ensure themselves through work the means of existence and through foresightedness (*prévoyance*) the resources for the future; they shall concur to the common well-being by helping each other like brothers and to the general order by observing moral rules and written laws that reign the society, the family and the individual.' The liberal model of social state was therefore declined any subjective public social right.[18]

During the eighteenth century, the liberal reluctance to support social rights prevailed all over Europe. Social rights became popular and constitutional commitments only through the revolutions of the last century, in Latin America through the Mexican Constitution of 1917 and in Europe after the trauma of the first world war through the Constitutions of Weimar in 1919 and of Stalin in 1937. The fundamental rights and duties provisions of the Weimar Constitution translated the general principles of social protection provided for the new International Labour Organization by the almost hated treaty of Versailles in guarantees of a 'social existence respecting human dignity for all' (*menschenwürdiges Dasein*).[19] As an alternative, corporatist and fascist regimes strengthened fundamental social duties, socialist regimes tried to realize social rights without markets.

A study carried out in 1999 for the EU pointed out that after the end of the second world war social rights have been more and more constitutionalized and protected in different forms and degrees of justiciability. With the exception of the UK—the homeland of common law hasn't a single constitutional texture but a strong tradition of social legislation highlighted by Beveridge's Report of 1942 and echoed by Franklin D. Roosevelt's freedoms 'from fear and want'—all European constitutions include at least one social right, even Germany and Austria, where at least mothers or children have social rights (and regional constitutions provide further guarantees).[20]

The constitutional entrenchment of social rights is more advanced in southern than in northern Europe, including specific subjective rights to education, health care, social security, work, rarely housing, but never food or water, sometimes a constitutional declaration of a general human right to 'a decent life and to social security' (Article 9 Cyprus) or to 'lead a life in keeping with human dignity' (Article 23 Belgium). The rights clauses have been in some cases surrogated, in others integrated by directive principles of social policy (Article 45 Ireland) and fundamental constitutional principles of state action for substantial freedom and equality (Article 3(2) Italy), for the 'personal, economic and cultural wellbeing of the individual' (Article 2(2) Sweden) or simply for the '*sozialer Rechtsstaat*' (Article 28(1) Germany), a rule of law for a social state that allows to protect even positive obligations deriving from classical liberties.[21]

The textual differences are partially compensated by further explicit or implicit general clauses that oblige most EU countries to make interpretation of laws 'in the light' of international law, including existing regional human rights instruments such as the ESC. Europe has already a common concept of social rights in the Council of Europe and EU law that includes a standard set of rights or directive principles for education, healthcare, social security, specific protection for weak categories (woman, children, elders, disabled), and for a healthy environment. This concept is open for 'new social rights' related to development, land, housing, food, water and internet., the doctrines and practices of European Constitutions have framed furthermore a common European constitutional standard on the basis of a core right of a person to get protected in its own 'social existence' and various forms of legal guarantees of social security referred to property, equality or dignity rights or principles.[22]

The degree of constitutional entrenchment of social rights is not necessarily relevant for social expenditure and redistribution, but it is much disputed to what extent the success of the 'social state' is conditioned by the force of institutions and the ethnic homogeneity of the national state. One could object that the force of institutions and the perception of homogeneity can be conditioned by religious energies and by the force of the constitution as a whole. Social justice and security are at any case purposes of the European *pactum societatis et subjectionis* that citizens agree and accept for governments.[23]

A study of the European University Institute of 2010 showed that the Charter of Fundamental Rights of the European Union (CDFEU) of 2000 has strengthened the principle of indivisibility of human rights, a principle that is binding for the Union but does not impose the homologation of the national social rights protection policies and legal cultures.[24] On the one hand, the EU law reflects the trend to take them more seriously and to promote both individual and collective complaints of social rights. On the other hand they still rely in different forms and degrees to the specific constitutional identities of the European national democracies. As long as the national systems of social security are regarded, comparative social and political research divides the welfare capitalism in Europe in three areas: the liberal, the conservative–corporatist and the social-democratic one.[25] The legal comparison presents five models of welfare in the EU countries in an geographic order of decreasing economic competitiveness:

1. the Nordic welfare, based on universal citizenship rights with collective responsibility for extensive public services for health, education and job placement, extensive public employment and unemployment insurance managed by trade unions;
2. the Anglo-Saxon welfare, based on a national health service and residual entitlements of the poor through targeted, needs-based state action with individual responsibility in conditions of equality of opportunities and self-reliance maximizing markets, deregulated labour market and decentralized labour relations;
3. the North-Western version of continental welfare, based on obligatory social insurance for workers and their families (Bismarck) and a subsidiary collective responsibility allocated in families, churches, and public corporations;
4. the Southern version of the continental model, with a lower public social protection that leaves more responsibility to family assistance and voluntary third sector aid and offers a universal health care and highly differentiated pension schemes with deficits in woman employment and more fragmented trade unions (and political parties); and
5. the Eastern versions of welfare in post-communist States with new market economies that adapted and hybridized the other models under international pressure.

These differences explain why national constitutions in Europe have not been homologated to the international instruments of social rights protection. The national concepts and catalogues of social rights and state directives are more or less thick or thin in consideration of their relation to the other categories of rights, specially civil and political rights, being more or less inspired by ideals of liberalism, conservatism, and socialism and by the national design of welfare.

Nevertheless social rights are a concept of a common European public law that has a common content. Social rights can be defined as a *species* of the *genus* 'fundamental rights' of a human person because they offer at least a minimum of international and constitutional protection and mandatory legislative implementation. They are no more presumed to be not justiciable, but they can still have weaker forms of review in the international and in the national constitutional order.[26] Social rights can be distinguished from other fundamental rights by their object, being first of all expectations and claims of positive action. The fulfilment of the duty to protect social rights is generally conditioned by a mandate of legislation and of allocation of financial resources, with general principles that command gradual development over time and prohibit unreasonable regression. The duty bearers of social rights are not exclusively the state and sub- or supranational public bodies under a principle of subsidiarity, being such rights even binding for non-state actors, especially for private powerholders like employers, land- and house-owners or parents. The rights of children and workers to get alimentation and pay are most prominent examples of fundamental social rights grounding private and civil law. Finally, even after the end of the socialist regimes in Europe, social rights are encumbered by social duties (to work, schooling etc.) that concretize the responsibilities of the social rights holder for its own happiness.[27]

If this is the common analytical frame of social rights, the common spirit of their constitutional and international guarantees relies mainly to values and fundamental principles of dignity against misery, of positive freedom and substantial equality (no discrimination and equal opportunities), of solidarity duties, inclusive citizenship, and effective access to justice.

This spirit has been strengthened by the incorporation into the CFREU of most rights of the ESC that has been ratified by all EU and Council of Europe countries except Switzerland, either in the shorter original (Turin 1961) or in the longer revised version (Strasburg 1996) and was early recognized by the EU treaties and even by the jurisprudence of the European Convention of Human Rights (ECHR).[28] Under EU and Council of Europe law, social rights can be protected both as subjective rights and objective principles, or just respected as objective principles not to be promoted without political competences. The common spirit is a thin but solid, neither neoliberal nor socialist synthesis and hybridization of national constitutional and legal traditions and regional international law, a spirit that doesn't bring happiness, but helps to reduce the unhappiness in situations of fear and want.

A recent research made by Jung, Hirschl, and Rosevear (2014) divides still sharply the constitutions of post-communist countries from those of 'Western Europe and North America'. Latin America and post-communist constitutions would represent a strong entrenchment of economic and social rights, Western Europe and North America 'share a strong norm against ESR entrenchment'.[29] A more politically correct geography should recognize that the spirit of social rights is a fundamental of the constitution of the European welfare states and of the EU, being European constitutionalism more social constitutionalism than the North American one. There are of course strong North-South and West-East divides even within EU and Council of Europe, for example, on the question whether social rights of citizens should be stronger than those of other human beings. Nevertheless, the Euro-group is promoting a 'Social Rights Pillar' that takes social rights seriously as fundamental rights, with adequate international and constitutional guarantees.

IV The State of Fundamental Social Rights in the European Union: More Virtual than Real Progress?

The EU promoted the above said common spirit of fundamental social rights, but did not fill up the gap between the ideals of social justice and the reality of social inequalities. The EU is not a 'social union', but it could not survive if it would become an 'unsocial union', especially on the actual background of the migration crisis. At any case, the performance of the EU in the field of social rights protection is still controversial and uncertain.

If we look at the CRFEU and at the competences of the Union in the field of social policies, the performance of the duty to 'respect' will be presumably higher than the performance of the duties to 'protect' and 'fulfil'. The EU recognizes the indivisibility of rights and respects most, but not all social rights, being still significantly excluded the rights to housing and to fair remuneration. The realization of all social rights, however, can be only to partially promoted at EU level, being still mainly under the responsibility of the member states and their presumptive democratic governments.

If we look at the history of EU law, the transnational integration process has produced significant welfare tools such as the European Social Fund (1957), the Social security of migrant workers (Regulation No. 1408/71), the Regional Development Fund (1975), the Committee for social dialogue (1992), the European Employment Strategy (1997), the Common Principles of 'Flexicurity' (2007) and finally the strategies of Lisbon (2000) and Europe 2020 (2010).

More than half of the Europe 2020 agenda seems to be devoted to social policies and even the other economic objectives can be conceived as social investments:

> The Digital Agenda is the EU's strategy to help digital technologies, including the internet, to deliver sustainable economic growth.
>
> The Innovation Union aims to improve conditions and access to finance for research and innovation in Europe, so that innovative ideas can be turned into products and services that create growth and jobs.
>
> Youth on the Move provides support for more than 400 000 young people each year to work, train and study abroad.

Resource efficient Europe supports a shift towards a more resource-efficient, low-carbon economy to achieve sustainable growth.

An Industrial Policy for the Globalisation Era sets out a strategy that aims to boost growth and jobs by maintaining and supporting a strong, diversified and competitive industrial base in Europe offering well-paid jobs while becoming more resource efficient.

The Agenda for New Skills and Jobs is how the Commission will help the EU reach its employment target: 75 per cent of the working-age population (20–64 years) in work by 2020.

The European Platform against Poverty and Social Exclusion is designed to help achieve the EU target of lifting at least 20 million people out of poverty and social exclusion by 2020.

The balance sheet of the state of social rights shows that the EU is no more just an agency for the coordination of social policies of different welfare systems and a partial harmonization of social legislation, but points on specific flagship missions, for example, the European Platform against Poverty and Social Exclusion. The competences regarding 'social policy for the aspects defined in this Treaty', 'common safety concerns in public health matters, for the aspects defined in this Treaty' or 'economic, social and territorial cohesion' (Articles 4, para 2, 151ff, 168, 174 TFEU) have been enlarged. The open method of coordination has strengthened the 'coordination of the employment policies of the Member States, in particular by defining guidelines for these policies' (Articles 5, para 2, 145ff. TFEU) and the 'coordination of Member States social policies' (Articles 5, para 2, 151ff. TFEU), or 'actions to support, coordinate or supplement the actions of the Member States' regarding 'protection and improvement of human health; education, vocational training, youth and sport' (Articles 6, 165, 168 TFEU).

Other areas of EU policies and activities such as consumer and environment protection, agriculture or infrastructures developed further specific social rights and principles. All areas of competences can be affected transversally by social rights insofar as the EU 'shall aim to eliminate inequalities, and to promote equality, between men and women' (Article 8 TFEU), 'take into account requirements linked to the promotion of a high level of employment, the guarantee of adequate social protection, the fight against social exclusion, and a high level of education, training and protection of human health' (Article 9 TFEU), 'take appropriate action to combat discrimination based on sex, racial or ethnic origin, religion or belief, disability, age or sexual orientation' (Article 19 TFEU). Last but not least, 'given the place occupied by services of general economic interest in the shared values', the EU shall take care that such services operate on the basis of principles and conditions, particularly economic and financial conditions, which enable them to fulfil their missions' (Article 14 TFEU). From a legal point of view, the EU prospects a 'highly competitive social market development, aiming at a full employment and social progress, and a high level of protection and improvement of the quality of the environment' (Article 3 para. 3 TEU), with increased economic and social competences. The Union shall combat social exclusion and discrimination and promote social justice and protection, gender equality as well as solidarity between generations and protection of the rights of the child. The legal design of the EU has been bettered and . Even in the political reality one can observe that EU action has increased occupational safety and health and has promoted more universal and sustainable social protection systems, inclusive labour markets, a multilevel social dialogue and a quality framework for social services of general interest.[30] This European social model has therefore been considered highly competitive when compared with social policies in the United States, Latin America, Asia, and Africa.

Nevertheless, this social model is still under construction, appears vague and inconsistent and is lacking of political consensus and support. In the context of the ambiguous principle of subsidiarity, a 'highly competitive social market economy' sounds still like 'Keynes at home and Smith abroad'. An ambivalent role has been played even by the European Court of Justice (ECJ). On the one hand, ECJ protected social rights as implications of the freedom to move and of the prohibition of discriminations for citizenship, on the other hand the judges stopped collective action of trade unions colliding with economic freedoms (Viking/Laval).[31]

The popular consensus for a European solidarity is still weak. The veto against the constitutional treaty in Netherlands and France was partially motivated by a fear to lose social protection offered by the nation, which is perceived as an enlarged family. A large scale of political actors and electors still prefer to identify social security with 'national' security that should remain in the sole responsibility of the members states. When EU faced the banking and financial crisis, political scientists highlighted the persisting asymmetry between a strong neoliberal expansion of economic freedoms backed by the judges (negative integration) and a weak commitment to social policies and market-correction left to national legislators with a more restricted budget autonomy (positive integration).[32] The discriminating acronym of PI(I)GS during the sovereign debt crisis and the asymmetric effects of austerity policies marked a further loss of confidence and increasing differences between the European welfare states, with people of northern countries anxious to pay for the debts of the poorer countries of the South.

In the European post-industrial societies, new social risks have been imposed to workers and trade union membership is decreasing all over Europe as a result of the single market.[33] The European welfare states learnt new forms of recalibration and new perspectives of 'social investment'[34]. Social rights are no more a hope for socialism, but not even a horror for neoliberalism, but what is the definite state of social rights in the EU remains a controversial question.

A recent commission staff working document for the consultation on a new 'European Pillar of Social Rights' acknowledges that unemployment is decreasing, but the risk of poverty or social exclusion affects one of four persons.[35] Europe is under demographic pressure as an ageing continent with more female workers, changing family structures, growing diversity of immigration, and rising levels of education. The 'fourth industrial revolution' takes place with increased employment and social disparities that may weigh heavily on the performance of the Euro area.

As a matter of fact, the EU represents at global level ca. 7 per cent of population, 25 per cent of gross domestic product (GDP) and 50 per cent of social expenditure of the world.[36] What we call the 'European Social Model' is made today first of all by a public social expenditure rate[37] per GOP of 28.6 per cent of all EU countries and 29.4 per cent in the Euro area with larger differences east/west than north/south (for example, France 33.7 per cent, Greece 31.6 per cent, Finland 31.2 per cent, Italy 29.8 per cent, Germany 29.0 per cent, UK 28.1 per cent; Poland 17.7 per cent, Latvia 14.4 per cent). Taking all benefits together at constant prices, the annual growth over the 2008–12 period averaged an estimated 1.7 per cent in the EU 28.[38]

OECD data[39] show that in recent years some EU countries such as Greece, Estonia, Germany, Hungary, Ireland, and the UK have experienced substantial declines in social spending, but in most EU countries social spending remains at high levels. Only if one includes the private expenditures, United States comes closed even to France, meanwhile public spending in emerging economies is lower than the OECD average of 22 per cent. In the BRICS, Russia (15.7 per cent) and Brazil (14.4 per cent) leads over China (9.1 per cent), South Africa (8.8 per cent), and India (4.6 per cent in 2007). Development matters:

If we ask for the percentages of social expenditure in the EU budget, no precise answer is given by the institutions. That does not mean that their isn't any expenditure, but the budget is based on various missions and probably any attempt to separate expenditure for economy and for social purposes could be technically hard and politically unwise.

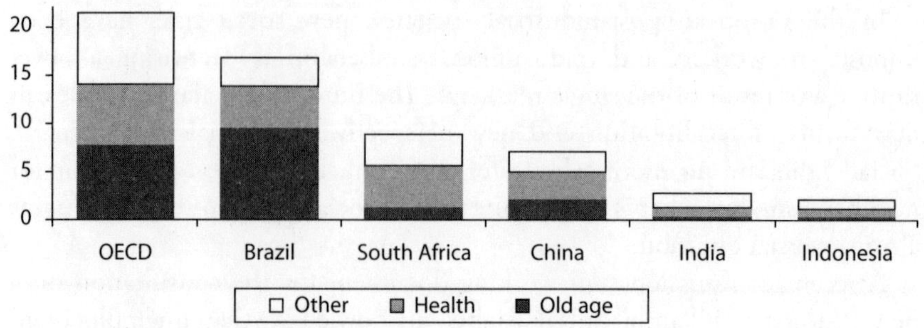

Figure 12.1 Public Social Expenditure as a Percentage of GDP in 2012 or Last Year Available
Source: Author's chart based on OECD statistics, 2016.

A global benchmarking and bench-learning for the performance of the social objectives is still under way.[40] A comparison EU–India regarding the substantial protection of social rights could be started looking at some macro data:

1. the $1.90 a day poverty headcount ratio (World Bank) was reduced in India from 31.4 per cent in 2009 to 21.3 per cent in 2011, meanwhile monetary poverty and severe material deprivation increased in EU since 2008 with 17 per cent of Europeans that live on less than 60 per cent of their country's average household income and 24 per cent at risk of poverty;[41]
2. the unemployment rate in the EU raised from 7,0 (2008) to 10.8 per cent (2013), in the Indian Union from 2.5 (2012) to 4.5 per cent (2013);[42]
3. the social security in an ageing society is conditioned by the life expectancy at birth, in the EU 80,6 (EU 28 2013) years, in India 69,89 (CIA 2012), even more increasing, and
4. the rights of the family are conditioned by the fact that more than three quarters of households in India have four or more persons, compared with one fifth in the EU 28.

V The European Social Charter Compared to the SAARC Social Charter

The European Pillar of Social Rights might be strengthened by an accession of the EU to the ESC, accession that has been already supported by both the European Parliament and the Parliamentary Assembly of the Council of Europe.[43] The ESC goes beyond the Nizza Charter (CFREU) insofar as it includes a general right to work, the right to fair remuneration, the right to be protected from poverty and social exclusion, and the right to housing. Today 19 of 28 EU member states ratified the Revised European Social Charter (RESC) of 1996, 9 states (including Germany and UK) are bound only by the 1961 Charter. Being the signing state free to make a choice of its Charter obligations, it has to added that today only France and Portugal have accepted all obligations. 14 EU member states have accepted the Additional Protocol of 1995 establishing a system of collective complaints to be examined by the ECSR. The so called Turin process within the Council of Europe aims to encourage the EU to take the ESC/RESC 'into account in the legislative process', to reinforce the dialogue between the ECSR and the Court of Justice (CJEU) and the links to the Fundamental Rights Agency (FRA), to implement 'early warning' procedures and, last but not least, to 'work towards the proposed accession of the EU to the Charter'.[44]

Now if we look at the differences between the European and the SAARC Social Charter (SAARCSC), we find first of all the purpose to 'ensure an overall and balanced social development of their peoples' (Article 1 SAARCSC) and to 'improve their standard of living and their social well-being' (preamble ESC). Being the SAARC committed to 'sustained social development' (Article 2) of developing countries (Article 2 sect. 3 ICESR), it aims not only to 'facilitate economic and social progress' (preamble RESC) but even 'to accelerate economic growth, social progress and cultural development' (preamble SAARCSC).

The SAARCSC furthermore opens with a declaration of 'principles, goals and directives' (Article 2) that imply a stronger dimension of ethical responsibility, equity, tolerance, universal respect and a human rights education 'in the context of inculcating in children intrinsic and attendant sense of duty and set of values directed towards preserving and strengthening the family, community, society and nation'.

Human dignity has not only to be 'respected' and 'protected' (Article 1 CFREU) as a 'dignity at work' (Article 26 RESC), it must be 'promoted' as well as participatory governance, social justice and solidarity (Article 2(2) vi SAARCSC) and a person must be enabled to 'realize' his or her personal dignity (xiv). A specific vulnerability of 'human rights and dignity' is recognized with regard to women and children (Article 6, 7 SAARCSC).

Poverty alleviation is the first topic of the SAARCSC (Article 3), protection against poverty and social exclusion and the last entry in the ESC (Article 30). The success of Meanwhile the Indian report is based on an absolute poverty threshold that is still lower than the World Bank indicator,[45] the right to social security and the right to social assistance in European countries are construed on the basis of a more relative concept of poverty the minimum social income through two thresholds, a collective one that amounts to 50 per cent of the country's net median equivalized household income per adult, and an individual that amounts to 40–50 per cent of the previous earnings of a person (Article 12 RESC as interpreted by the ECSR[46]). This minimum social income amounts in Norway to 1.514€, in Romania to 88€ per month.

The ESC-rights catalogue starts with the right to work and other work-related rights not included in the SAARCSC and only partially guaranteed at constitutional level in India. The right to bargain collectively and to collective action in cases of conflicts of interest are not explicitly protected by the Constitution and only half of fundamental ILO Conventions are ratified.[47]

The ESC is based furthermore on concrete undertakings of the member states for the protection of the social rights. Specially the right to health (Article 11 RESC) is protected through concrete duties of prevention, including 'the encouragement of individual responsibility in matters of health'. The SAARC Charter provides specific goals of 'population stabilization' (Article 8) and 'drug de-addiction', including a 'stabilisation in the growth of population in each country, through voluntary sustainable family planning and contraceptive methods' and prevention of 'unsustainable population changes'. Even the ESC rights can only partially invoked by migrants.

Finally, different mechanisms are provided for the implementation of the social charters. The SAARCSC distinguishes national implementation at the national level through a National Action Plan and a 'National Coordination Committee or any appropriate national mechanism as may be decided in each country' and a review through 'appropriate SAARC bodies' at the regional level (Article 10). That would neither exclude an agreement for the involvement of the SAARC Arbitration Council, nor the establishment of a specific advisory body similar to the ECSR. The independent experts of the ECSR deliver conclusions in reporting procedures and decisions on collective complaints made by organizations of employers and trade unions and NGO's with consultative status. The collective complaints procedure appears as a new form of public interest litigation, but the ECSR is not a judge and the EU has not yet embraced the position of the European parliament for a EU accession to the revised Charter. If the committee finds that the Charter has not been applied in a satisfactory manner, the Committee of Ministers shall adopt, by a majority of two-thirds of those voting, a recommendation addressed to the Contracting Party. The ECSR jurisprudence is published, but rarely quoted by courts and academic doctrine.

In conclusion, the SAARCSC is still preferring a state goal approach to the rights approach of the revised ESC, but both instruments recognize that social justice is a global problem with needs of regional protection. They come from a world of divided rights protection regimes, but they could become both more useful for the social rights protection than expected.

VI Learning Opportunities

The chapter moved from the idea that the social part of the highly competitive social market economy has to be played by fundamental social rights that are recognized and protected both at the international level as human rights and at the constitutional level either as constitutional rights or state directives. From a normative point of view, a sustainable social market economy can be reached only through an adequate protection of social rights.

The EU and the Indian Union have to bridge serious gaps between yellow ideals of happiness and a grey reality of 'weak rights' granted and protected by weakened states under the pressure of globalization. Both unions focus different economic and cultural realities of more and less developing countries, but are connected through general international human rights law and common traditions of social constitutionalism. Their human rights dialogue needs a postcolonial approach. Comparatists must be aware of sociocultural differences and asymmetries in knowledge and help institutional operators to learn from each other.

Starting from a comparative contextual analysis, the chapter remembers first the common Eurasian heritage not only of empires but even of a 'rule of social law'. Even the different forms of federalism matter for social rights protection, especially for federal solidarity and for recalibration of welfare systems. The supranational federalism of the EU might become a model for a South Asian Economic Union, but solidarity among rich nations could be less difficult than among countries with more poverty. The EU is considered to be less democratic than the biggest democracy of the world, but the imperfections of all democracies could be both a cause for and a consequence of the weakness of social rights. The different legal cultures could furthermore explain why social rights find less constitutional entrenchment in common law countries than in civil law countries. Even the economic differences are relevant: growth matters for the dimensions of poverty and financial crisis for the sustainability of social rights systems. Finally, the missing India–EU FTA is not hindering an ongoing the human rights dialogue that could even help to focus social rights. Both soft-powers could have common interests in global social justice.

The second chapter shows that there is a common 'spirit' and concept of social rights in Europe as a thin, neither neoliberal nor socialist synthesis and as a hybridization of national legal and constitutional traditions and international law discourses. The constitutional history of social rights teaches that US and Europe do not share a strong norm against ESR entrenchment in constitutions. Notwithstanding German scepticism, all European constitutions include at least one social right and all EU countries ratified the original and most (except UK and Germany) the revised ESC.

Social rights are no more presumed to be not justiciable ethics, but they can still have weaker forms of review in the international and national constitutional order. They claim for positive state action, but their realization is generally conditioned by a mandate for legislation and allocation of financial resources with a principle of gradual development over time and a prohibition of unreasonable regression. The duty bearers of social rights are not exclusively the state and sub- or supranational public bodies. Social rights imply social duties that concretize even the responsibility of the social rights holder for its own happiness. This concept relies to values and fundamental principles of dignity against misery, positive freedom, substantial equality, solidarity, inclusive citizenship and access to justice which can be construed as universal values.

The third chapter shows that the state of social fundamental rights in the EU is controversial. Aspects of progress are the growing competences and actions, even in the agenda Europe 2020, that move beyond the coordination of welfare systems by focussing social investments. Aspects of regression are increasing inequalities and poverty risks in the North/South and West/East divide. The judges play an ambiguous role in the defence of social rights, the social expenditure rate of the EU is still unavailable and the social rights pillar of the monetary and economic Union is still under construction.

The fourth chapter showed some significant differences between the ESC and the SAARC Social Charter. Both instruments reflect still ideas of a special status of social rights as rights in need of collective protection and state goals, but develop different regional solutions for the common problem of global social justice. The Europeans could learn about action plans for poverty reduction, the SAARC lawyers from ESRC 'jurisprudence'.

In conclusion, both the European and the Indian Union can learn a lot from each other and from themselves, looking at their social rights discourses as sources of virtue. Europe's social rights discourse teaches a right to hope and a duty to of politicians to promote intelligent social investments. The Indian social rights teach a duty to patience and a right to sleep that implies not only substantial health and working force recreation, but even a right to dream some progress in the realization of social rights.[48]

Notes and References

1. A. Sen. 2005. *The Argumentative Indian*, London: Penguin, p. 139ff.
2. E. Benveniste, 1973. *Indoeuropean Language and Society*, London: Faber, 379ff; critical A. Thiruvengadam, 2012. 'Excavating Constitutional Antecedents in Asia: An Essay on the Potential and Perils,' 88 *Chi-Kent. L. Rev.* 45. Available at: http://scholarship.kentlaw.iit.edu/cklawreview/vol88/iss1/5.
3. See 'The Code of Hammurabi,'http://avalon.law.yale.edu/ancient/hamframe.asp, accessed 20 July 2017.
4. M.P. Singh, 2005. 'The Constitution of India: Symbol of Unity in Diversity', 53 *Jahrbuch des öffentlichen Rechts der Gegenwart*, pp. 649–686.
5. See P. Dann, 2011. 'Federal Democracy in India and the European Union: Towards Transcontinental Comparison of Constitutional Law', pp. *Verfassung und Recht in Übersee*, 160–176.
6. A. Sen, 1999. *Development as Freedom*. New York: Knopf; M. Nussbaum, 2003. 'Capabilities as Fundamental Entitlements: Sen and Social Justice'. 9 *Feminist Economics*, 33ff.
7. M. Nussbaum, 2007. *The Clash Within*, Massachusetts: Harvard University Press.
8. Prominent J. Habermas, 2011, 'Die Krise der Europäischen Union im Lichte der Konstitutionalisierung des Völkerrechts', in: id., *Zur Verfassung Europas*, Berlin: Suhrkamp, 39ff.
9. 'OECD Economic Surveys: India 2014', DOI: 10.1787/eco_surveys-ind-2014-en, accessed 20 July 2017.
10. European Committee of Social Rights, Panhellenic Federation of Pensioners of the Public Electricity Corporation v Greece (2012), Complaint No. 79/2012.
11. S. Malhotra, 2015. *EU-India Relations: A Soft Power Approach*, http://www.eias.org/wp-content/uploads/2016/02/EU-Asia-at-a-glance-Malhotra-EU-India-Relations-A-Soft-Power-Approach-2015.pdf, accessed 20 July 2017.
12. See http://www.europarl.europa.eu/RegData/etudes/ATAG/2015/551312/EPRS_ATA(2015)551312_EN.pdf and http://www.europarl.europa.eu/RegData/etudes/STUD/2015/534987/EXPO_STU(2015)534987_EN.pdf: 'The Indian human rights situation could improve mainly through the above-mentioned domestic debates and active participation of civil society (discussed separately). Condemnations and resolutions by the European Parliament or other EU institutions may not prove particularly helpful and could even adversely affect bilateral ties. Since it is mandatory for the EU to include human rights clauses in trade agreements, the best engagement strategy for both would be to upgrade and expand dialogue, which would also provide opportunities to discuss and remove mutual misperceptions.'
13. F. Zwagemakers, 2012. *The EU's Conditionality Policy: A New Strategy to Achieve Compliance*, Milano: Giuffré 12 http://www.iai.it/sites/default/files/iaiwp1203.pd, accessed 20 July 2017.

14. T. Cicero, *De officiis*, I, 69 : '*Vacandum autem omni est animi perturbatione, cum cupiditate et metu tum etiam aegritudine et voluptate nimia et iracundia, ut tranquillitas animi et securitas adsit, quae affert cum constantiam tum etiam dignitatem.*' 'Again, we must keep ourselves free from every disturbing emotion, not only from desire and fear, but also from excessive pain and pleasure, and from anger, so that we may enjoy that calm of soul and freedom from care which bring both (moral) stability and dignity (of character).' See C. Zwierlein, 2015. 'Se-curare, sine cura, se-curitas, assecuratio: Innovationen der Sicherheitsproduktion in der Renaissance', in G. Melville, G. Vogt-Spira, and M. Breitenstein (eds.), *Sorge*, Köln: Böhlau, 109.
15. Uguccione de Pisa quoted by Van Beuren, G. 2013. 'Socio-economic Rights and a Bill of Rights: An overlooked British tradition', *Public Law*, 822. The Latin version is quoted by L. Marchettoni, 2008. Ockham e l'origine dei diritti soggettivi', *Quaderni fiorentini per la storia del pensiero giuridico moderno*, 37. Nevertheless canonical law allowed slavery over non-Christians. When the British Emancipation Act of 1833 abolished slavery and slave trade for the British Empire, exceptions were still made for the possessions of the East India Company.
16. E. Sieyes, 1789. *Préliminaire de la Constitution*, Paris : Baudouin 32–3:

    On fait que ceux des citoyens qu'un malheur fort condamne à l'impuissance de pouvoir à leur besoins, ont de justes droits aux secours de leurs Concitoyens, & c. On sait que rien n'est plus à l'espèce humain, au moral & au physique, qu'un bon système d'éducation et d'instruction publique & c. On sait qu'une Nation forme avec les autres peuples des relations d'intérêt qui méritent de sa part une surveillance. Toujours active, & c. Mais ce n'est pas dans la déclaration qu'on doit trouver la liste de tous les bien qu'une bonne Constitution peut procurer aux peuples. Il suffit ici de dire que les citoyens ont droit à tout ce que l'Etat peut faire en leur faveur.

17. K. Marx, 1851. *The Constitution of the French Republic Adopted November 4, 1848, Notes to the People No. 7, June 14, 1851* http://marx.libcom.org/works/1851/06/14.htm, accessed 20 July 2017.
18. See E. Wiederin, 2005. 'Sozialstaatlichkeit im Spannungsfeld von Eigenverantwortung und Fürsorge', 64 Veröffentlichungen der Vereinigung der Deutschen Staatsrechtslehrer (VVDStRL) 61ff.
19. Article 427: 'First. The guiding principle above enunciated that labour should not be regarded merely as a commodity or article of commerce. Second. The right of association for all lawful purposes by the employed as well as by the employers. Third. The payment to the employed of a wage adequate to maintain a reasonable standard of life as this is understood in their time and country. Fourth. The adoption of an eight hours day or a forty-eight hours week as the standard to be aimed at where it has not already been attained. Fifth. The adoption of a weekly rest of at least twenty-four hours, which should include Sunday wherever practicable. Sixth. The abolition of child labour and the imposition of

such limitations on the labour of young persons as shall permit the continuation of their education and assure their proper physical development. Seventh. The principle that men and women should receive equal remuneration for work of equal value. Eighth. The standard set by law in each country with respect to the conditions of labour should have due regard to the equitable economic treatment of all workers lawfully resident therein. Ninth. Each State should make provision for a system of inspection in which women should take part, in order to ensure the enforcement of the laws and regulations for the protection of the employed.'

20. Still sceptical C. Fabre, 2005. 'Social Rights in European Constitutions', in: G. De Burca, B. de Witte, and L. Ogertschnig (eds), *Social Rights in Europe*, Oxford: Oxford University Press, 18. In Austria an overlapping reform consensus is acknowledged by H. Schäffer, and R. Klaushofer, 2014. '*Zur Problematik sozialer Grundrechte?*' in D. Mertens, and H. Papier. 2014. *Handbuch der Grundrechte in Deutschland und Europa*, VI: Österreich, Heidelberg 3d ed., 76ff.
21. See 'European Parliament Working Paper: Fundamental Social Rights in Europe,'http://www.europarl.europa.eu/workingpapers/soci/pdf/104_en.pdf, accessed 21 July 2017.
22. E. Wiederin, 2005. '*Sozialstaatlichkeit*', 53.
23. M. Langford, 2014. 'Judicial Review in National Courts', in: R. Riedel, G. Giacca, and C. Golay (eds.), *Economic, Social, and Cultural Rights in International Law*, Oxford: Oxford University Press, 417ff.
24. University Paris Ouest Nanterre - European University Institute Social Law Working Group. 2010. *Diversity of Social Rights in Europe(S) Rights of the Poor*, Poor Rights Working Paper Series EUI LAW 07.
25. G. Esping-Andersen, 1990. *The Three Worlds of Welfare Capitalism*, Cambridge: Cambridge University Press.
26. For the constitutional level see M. Tushnet, 2008. *Weak Courts, Strong Rights. Judicial Review and Social Welfare Rights in Comparative Constitutional Law*, New Jersey: Princeton University Press, 237ff.
27. J. Waldron, 2010. 'Socioeconomic Rights and Theories of Justice,' *New York University Public Law and Legal Theory Working Papers* 245, http://lsr.nellco.org/nyu_plltwp/245, accessed 21 June 2017.
28. F. Tulkens, 2003. 'Les droits sociaux dans la jurisprudence de la nouvelle Cour européenne des droits de l'homme,' in: C. Grewe and F. Benoit-Rohmer (eds.), *Les droits sociaux ou la démolition de quelque poncifs*, Strasbourg: Presses universitaires, 117ff.
29. C. Jung, R. Hirschl, and E. Rosevear. 2014. 'Economic and Social Rights in National Constitutions'. 62 *American Journal of Comparative Law*, pp. 1043–1098. http://ssrn.com/abstract=2349680, accessed 21 June 2017.
30. D. Vaughan-Whitehead, (ed.). 2015, *The European Social Model in Crisis: Is Europe losing its soul?* Cheltenham: Edward Elgar Publications.
31. T. Kingreen, 2014. 'Epochen der Europäisierung des Sozialrechts', and Rödl, F. 3014. 'Die dialektische Entwicklung des Sozialen im Prozess der europäischen

Integration', in: P. Masuch, (ed.), *Grundlagen und Herausforderungen des Sozialstaats: Denkschrift 60 Jahre Bundessozialgericht*, Berlin: E. Schmidt, 318ff. and 539ff.; T. Hervey 2014. 'Re-Judging Social Rights in the European Union', in G. De Burca, C. Kilpatrick, and J. Scott (eds.), *Critical Legal Perspectives on Global Governance*, Oxford: Hart Publishing, 346ff.

32. F. Scharpf, 2010. 'The Asymmetry of European Integration. Or why the EU Cannot Be a "Social Market Economy"', *Socio-Economic Review*, 211ff.
33. C. Crouch, 2016. *Society and Social Change in 21st Century Europe*, London: Palgrave Macmillan.
34. A. Hemerijck, 2012. *Changing Welfare States,* Oxford: Oxford University Press.
35. Key economic, employment and social trends behind a European Pillar of Social Rights, SWD(20 16) 50; COM (2016) 127.
36. A. Cavalli, and A. Martinelli. 2015. *La società europea*, Bologna: Mulino, p. 245.
37. Expenditure for old age, sickness/healthcare, disability, family/children, housing, unemployment, survivors (widows and widowers), social exclusion not elsewhere classified.
38. http://ec.europa.eu/eurostat/tgm/.
39. http://www.oecd.org/els/soc/OECD2014-Social-Expenditure-Update-Nov2014-8pages.pdf.
40. 'The EU in the World: Living Conditions.' http://ec.europa.eu/eurostat/statistics-explained/index.php/The_EU_in_the_world_-_living_conditions. For Germany see H. Obinger, 2014. 'Deutschland im Vergleich zentraler Sozialstaatsindikatoren', in: P. Masuch (ed.), *Grundlagen*, 47ff.; L. Scruggs, C. Zimmermann, and C. Jeffords. 2013. 'Implementation of the Human Right to Social Security around the World', in: M. Lanse, (ed.). 2013. *The State of Economic and Social Human Rights*, Cambridge: Cambridge University Press, 117ff.
41. 'Close to 9 per cent of all Europeans live in severe material deprivation—they do not have the resources to own a washing machine, a car, a telephone, to heat their homes, or face unexpected expenses. 10 per cent of Europeans live in households where no one has a job. There is a wide gap in performance between the welfare systems in different EU countries—the best reduced the risk of poverty by 60 per cent, the least effective by less than 15 per cent (EU average 35 per cent).'
42. 'Statistics Explained,'http://ec.europa.eu/eurostat/statistics-explained/, accessed 21 June 2017.
43. Resolution of the European Parliament of 27 February 2014 on the situation of fundamental rights in the European Union (2012) (2013/2078(INI)); Parliamentary Assembly of the Council of Europe, Resolution of 8 December 2014 on the implementation of the Memorandum of Understanding between the Council of Europe and the European Union, at http://www.coe.int/T/DGHL/Monitoring/SocialCharter/Doc_Bruxelles_version_EN_FR_DEF.pdf, accessed 21 June 2017.
44. M. Nicoletti, 2014. *General Report*. http://www.coe.int/T/DGHL/Monitoring/SocialCharter/TurinConference/Turin-General-Report_EN.pdf. See J. Luther,

2016. 'Perspectives for an Accession of the European Union to the (Revised) European Social Charter', in: J. Luther and L. Mola (eds), *Europe's Social Rights under the Turin Process*, Napoli: Editoriale Scientifica, 135ff.

45. See 'Ministry of Statistics and Programme Implementation, SAARC Social Charter India Country Report 2014', http://www.mospi.gov.in/; G. Datt, M. Ravaillon, and R. Murgai, 2016. *Growth, Urbanization, and Poverty Reduction in India, World Bank Poverty and Equity Global Practice Group*, WPS 7568.
46. M. Mikkola, 2016. 'Minimum standards of social income in Europe', in: J. Luther and L. Mola. 2016. 6ff.
47. Not ratified: C087 - Freedom of Association and Protection of the Right to Organise Convention, 1948 (No. 87); C098 - Right to Organise and Collective Bargaining Convention, 1949 (No. 98); C138 - Minimum Age Convention, 1973 (No. 138); C182 - Worst Forms of Child Labour Convention, 1999 (No. 182); C129 - Labour Inspection (Agriculture) Convention, 1969 (No. 129).
48. SC India, *Re-Ramlila Maidan Incident Dt v Home Secretary And Ors* on 23 February, 2012.

13

Direct Complaints of Individuals against Legal Acts Adopted by the European Union

Wolfram Cremer

I Introduction

The right to file a fundamental rights complaint is provided by the legal systems of most of the Member States of the European Union (EU). By contrast, EU law does not provide the right to file a fundamental rights complaint against legal acts adopted by the EU itself, so-called EU secondary law. Of course, EU law includes the right of individuals (that is natural and legal persons) to file a complaint against the legal acts of the EU. Yet, this does not require an infringement of fundamental rights. In fact, according to Article 263 paragraph 4 of the Treaty on the Functioning of the European Union (TFEU),[1] the individual rather has to fulfil a complicated system of sophisticated admissibility requirements in order to file a complaint directly against legal acts of the EU before the EU courts. Once these requirements are met, the merits of the appeal do not depend on the applicant's individual concern or the possible infringement of subjective rights by the legal act in question. The merits of the appeal rather follow a model of objective judicial control. In other words, according to paragraph 4,

Article 263 of the TFEU, the admissibility requirements of a direct claim pose a high threshold. However, once this threshold is overcome, the merits of the appeal no longer depend on any requirements other than the objective illegality of the act.

II Structure of Paragraph 4 of Article 263 of the TFEU

Paragraph 4 of Article 263 of the TFEU says: 'Any natural or legal person may, under the conditions laid down in the first and second paragraphs, institute proceedings against an act addressed to that person or which is of direct and individual concern to them, and against a regulatory act which is of direct concern to them and does not entail implementing measures.'

According to the first variant of paragraph 4, Article 263 of the TFEU, any natural or legal person may institute proceedings against an 'act' addressed to them. In contrast, the admissibility requirements of proceedings instituted by persons not addressed by an EU act are regulated by the second and third variant of paragraph 4, Article 263 of para 4 TFEU. In opposition to the admissibility requirements of the first variant, requirements of second and third variants are significantly more complicated and—as will be demonstrated ahead—more demanding. On the one hand, the second variant requires that natural or legal persons who are not addressed by the EU act in question may only institute proceedings successfully in case the act is of 'direct and individual' concern to them. The third variant of paragraph 4, Article 263 of the TFEU, on the other hand, permits complaints by individuals against a special kind of EU acts, that is, 'regulatory acts'. Thereby, it requires the act to be of direct concern to the applicant and not to entail implementing measures. In opposition to the second variant of paragraph 4, Article 263 of the TFEU, the third variant, however, does not require an *individual* concern.

Hereinafter, the single requirement of paragraph 4, Article 263 of the TFEU will be assessed especially with regard to the interpretation within the courts' case law. Thereby, it will be demonstrated—as already indicated—that the courts have developed a system of legal protection for direct complaints of individuals which is rather unmanageable.

III Variant 1, Paragraph 4 of Article 263 of the TFEU

According to the variant 1, paragraph 4, Article 263 of the TFEU, the addressees of legal acts of the EU have a standing in court without having to meet additional requirements. The mere position as an addressee is sufficient. Furthermore, the term 'act' is to be interpreted in a broad sense. Therefore, it also includes every secondary legal acts the EU as long as it has legal effects. In practice, for example, decisions of the competition authorities of the EU, regarding antitrust proceedings or merger control are directed towards addressing single companies. Consequently, the addressed companies can institute proceedings against these acts before the EU courts. On the contrary, legal acts with an abstract and general application do not have addressees. Therefore, these acts may not be challenged according to this variant of paragraph 4, Article 263 of the TFEU. Pursuant to the EU law terminology, this especially concerns regulations and directives, which are substantial laws and framework laws, respectively.

IV Variant 2, Paragraph 4 of Article 263 of the TFEU

However, according to the second variant of paragraph 4, Article 263 of the TFEU, natural and legal persons may institute proceedings against acts, without being addressed to them, as long as these are of direct and individual concern to them. This may be the case if either someone else is addressed or the act has no addressee at all. As already indicated, the term 'act' includes all secondary legal acts of the EU, insofar as they have legal effects. While the term 'act' is interpreted (largely) unanimously, it is problematic in different respects and vastly debated how to interpret the terms 'direct concern' and 'individual concern'.

IV.1 Concern

First of all, the European Court of Justice (ECJ) rarely examines the 'concern' as an isolated requirement.[2] It rather considers it within the examination of the direct and individual concern. However, it can be learnt from the case law that a 'concern' only requires the applicant to be burdened by the act in question.

IV.2 Directness

Moreover, the requirement of directness is supposed to prevent those from instituting proceedings, who are only potentially concerned.[3] In principle, the applicant must be affected by the act ipso facto. This would not be the case, for example, if the applicant was only concerned if additional circumstances arose. Accordingly, legal acts of the EU directed towards the Member States, in principle cannot be of direct concern.[4] However, courts have made an exception, in case where the Member State is obliged to transpose the act without any discretion pursuant to EU Law.[5] Then the EU act is not only of potential concern to the person in question, but rather concerns them 'virtually automatically'.[6] In addition to that, the Union courts also assume a direct concern in cases where the Member State clearly and firmly states that, a certain measure only depends on an authorization by a Union organ.[7] The latter concern constellations in which a Member State asks—and according to EU law has to ask—the EU whether it is entitled to adopt a certain measure either favourable or burdensome for an individual. This may be illustrated by a case of state aid law. According to European state aid law every state aid given to a company by a Member State (above a certain threshold value) has to be previously authorized by the EU, more precisely by the European Commission. In such constellations, if the Member States themselves intend to give state aid to a certain company, then the granting of the state aid only depends on the Commission's authorization. In such constellations, though the Member State has clearly and firmly stated the intention that a certain measure only depended on the approval or authorization of an EU organ. However, the state aid was supposed to be granted by the Member State, not the Commission. Therefore, the refusal of the authorization by the European Commission does not directly concern the company which was supposed to receive the state aid. It is rather addressed to the Member State. Nevertheless, pursuant to the aforementioned criteria the Commission's decision is of direct concern to the company in question. The Member State had clearly and firmly stated its intention to grant state aid to a certain company in case of the Commission's authorization.[8]

IV.3 Individuality

Furthermore, the individuality criterion is being controversially debated since the European Court's fundamental decision in *Plaumann* in 1963. As a result of this overall restrictive decision direct claims of individuals against EU secondary legal acts were admitted by the Union courts only in rare exceptional cases. However, over the last 50 years, the case law was gradually shifted towards an approach focussing more on legal protection. *Grosso modo*, the Union courts' case law can be divided in five stages which will be assessed in turn.

The most restrictive early case law of the ECJ: Despite claiming not to interpret the provision on the right to institute proceedings restrictively,[9] the Court did interpret the criterion of individuality so as to provide an extensive legal protection. Thereby, the Court referred to the allegedly 'clearly restrictive wording' of Article 263, para 4 of the TFEU (formerly Article 173 para 2 EEC Treaty[10]).[11] The basis of this restrictive case law was called the *Plaumann* formula. According to this, 'persons other than those to whom a decision is addressed may only claim to be individually concerned if that decision affects them by reason of certain attributes which are peculiar to them or by reason of circumstances in which they are differentiated from all other persons and by virtue of these factors distinguishes them individually just as in the case of the person addressed.'[12] Therefore, the mere claim to be affected by a measure because of the position as a participant in competition was not sufficient to establish individuality. After all, 'a commercial activity [...] may at any time be practiced by any person'.[13] Thus, the Court did not consider (permanent) features originating from the affected person's professional activity as certain attributes in terms of the *Plaumann* formula.[14] It was rather commonly required that the number and identity of the concerned persons were ascertainable at the time of the decision.[15] Such an individualization, at the time of the decision, could especially be derived from motions brought forward before this decision was issued.[16] However, until the end of the 1970s, this orientation towards the past,[17] regarding the individualization of non-addressees only rarely[18] led to the assumption of an individual concern.

Cautious extension of the standing since the 1970s: Since the end of the 1970s the Union courts set a new course with regard to the interpretation of the 'individuality' criterion. Thereby, the Courts especially considered the participation in a procedure and procedural guarantees, significant impairment with the market or competitive position and a possible normative requirement to consider the applicant's specific interests. Each of these considerations will be assessed in turn.

Participation in the procedure and procedural guarantees: First of all, the criterion (quantitatively) which was most significant regarding the assumption of a non-addressee's individual concern by the courts was a participation in the previous administrative procedure.[19] Examples for an individualization by means of participation in a procedure can be found in state aid supervisory law,[20] anti-dumping law,[21] anti-subsidy law,[22] antitrust law,[23] and merger control.[24] Thereby, the Union courts initially applied a generous standard assuming individuality, in case the applicant was heard, their complaint initiated the investigation procedure[25] or their statements largely determined the course of the procedure. In addition, individuality was assumed even though the applicant did not participate in the procedure despite a procedural right, where he was not responsible for not participating.[26] At the same time, the courts did not require the applicants' participation in the procedure to be based on a procedural guarantee of EU primary or secondary law. In fact, the voluntary inclusion of the applicant in the procedure by the Commission was considered to be sufficient.[27] In contrast, independent interventions with the procedure or submissions independent of a procedure were not considered to be sufficient.[28] However, these guidelines were questioned or rather qualified by the Union courts in subsequent decisions. In the field of state aid law, for example, the participation in the main examination procedure was not considered to be sufficient for an individualization. The ECJ rather required the grant of state aid in question to cause a noticeable impairment of the company's market position in addition to its active participation in the procedure.[29] All in all, the court's case law regarding the participation in procedures as a prerequisite of a right to institute proceedings does not provide precise guidelines; nevertheless, in particular cases it may definitely be possible to establish an individual concern based on the participation in a procedure or the existence of procedural rights (occasionally in connection with further requirements).

Significant impairment with a market position or competitive position: In addition to participation in procedures, the Union courts in economy law contexts, on various occasions accepted a significant, noticeable or substantial impairment with the applicant's market position by the measure in question in order to establish their standing. While some of the decisions based the standing only on such significant, noticeable or substantial impairment with the market or competitive position, others demanded further cumulative preconditions.[30] In two interim orders, for example, the Court of First Instance (CFI) considered possible the admissibility in the main proceedings as the company was individualized as the 'only producer [...] in the world' or the only producer within the European Economic Area and largest supplier.[31]

Normative requirement of consideration of specific interests of the applicant: Moreover, in *Antillean Rice Mills* the CFI took into account an aspect similar to the noticeable impairment of a market position[32] in order to establish an individual concern. This was previously indicated in *Sofrimport*[33] as well as in *Piraiki-Patraiki*[34] and subsequently confirmed in *Exporteurs in Levende Varkens*. Accordingly, applicants were (also) individualized if due to specific provisions (that is, rules of EU law) a Union organ was obliged to take into account the consequences of an intended act on the position of certain persons and the applicant ranked among the latter.[35] Furthermore, this consideration of EU law provisions intended to protect the applicants' interests in the context of the disputed Union act, also characterizes the Court's reasoning regarding the criterion of individual concern in *Perrier* and *Vittel*.[36]

Restrictive countermovement of the 1990s: However, following the just outlined extension of the standing since the end of the 1970s a certain countermovement became discernible in the second half of the 1990s. Thereupon, the criterion of individual concern was partly interpreted more restrictively again.[37] Without having to elaborate on this, it can be asserted that these tendencies remained without explicit contours.

(Preliminary) rejection of the restrictive *Plaumann* formula: the CFI in *Jégo-Quéré*: Furthermore, in *Jégo-Quéré* in 2002, the CFI for the first time deviated from the *Plaumann* formula and redefined the criterion of individual concern. Accordingly, a Union measure with general application is of individual concern to a natural or legal person, if it 'affects his legal position, in a manner which is both definite and immediate, by restricting his rights or by imposing obligations on him'.[38] In addition, the number and position of other persons who are or may be similarly affected by the measure were of no relevance in this regard anymore.[39] This radical change in the case law was based on a case in which the applicant was not individually concerned according to the traditional criteria and therefore had no possibility to challenge the regulation in question. On the one hand, no national remedy was available. On the other hand, the CFI thought that neither the action for damages according to para 2, Article 340 of the TFEU[40] nor the preliminary rulings procedure according to Article 267 of the TFEU[41] were suitable or sufficient to provide effective legal protection. In doing so, the CFI referred to the opinion of Advocate General Jacobs delivered in *Unión de Pequeños Agricultores*, a case structurally similar to *Jégo-Quéré*. Therein, he recommended interpreting the criterion of individual concern more extensively than before in order to provide effective legal protection. More precisely, Advocate General Jacobs recommended a somewhat different definition of the criterion. Accordingly, a Union measure was of individual concern to the applicant 'where the measure has, or is liable to have, a substantial adverse effect on his interest'.[42]

Considering these statements and especially the CFI's definition, a resemblance with a fundamental rights complaint becomes apparent. It was merely required that the applicant was affected definitely and immediately. However, these kinds of burdens regularly also interfere with fundamental rights. Thus, in *Jégo-Quéré* the CFI paved the way for a fundamental rights complaint.

Everything remains the same or no rejection of *Plaumann*: The ECJ in *Unión de Pequeños Agricultores:* Nevertheless, the ECJ explicitly adhered to the *Plaumann* formula in *Unión de Pequeños Agricultores*.[43] It argued that it was not possible to omit the individual concern criterion in order to account for the right to legal protection.[44] This would rather require an amendment of the Treaty.[45] Furthermore, the Court stated that the TFEU (formerly EEC Treaty) created a comprehensive system of legal remedies and proceedings intended to monitor the legality of acts of Union organs. Within this system, especially according to Articles 263, 267, and 277 of the TFEU, legal protection is provided by means of cooperation with the Member States. In particular, Member States are obliged to establish within their national jurisdiction a system of legal protection and proceedings, capable of providing the observance of the right to effective judicial legal protection.[46] Following this judgment, the CFI readjusted its interpretation of the criterion of individual concern to the ECJ's course.[47]

V Variant 3, Paragraph 4 of Article 263 of the TFEU

As already indicated, since the Lisbon Treaty[48] entered into force, the strict requirements of paragraph 4, Article 263 of the TFEU are not applicable to all secondary legal acts of the EU anymore. In fact, according to the third variant of paragraph 4, Article 263 of the TFEU, natural and legal persons may challenge regulatory acts in case they are of direct concern to them and do not entail implementing measures. In contrast to the second variant of paragraph 4, Article 263 of the TFEU, the new 'special rule' for regulatory acts does not require the applicant to be concerned individually. Thus, the challenging of regulatory acts was facilitated by this rule.

Now, there is a need to delve into which kinds of legal acts can be challenged exactly. In the words of variant 3, paragraph 4, Article 263 of the TFEU: what are regulatory acts? Furthermore, what does direct concern mean in this context and what is an implementing measure?

V.1 Regulatory Acts According to the Third Variant of Paragraph 4, Article 263 of the TFEU

Since the Lisbon Treaty entered into force, the question on how to define regulatory acts according to variant 3, Article 263 paragraph 4, Article 263 of the TFEU variant 3 is a lively debated topic. Indeed, the interpretation of this requirement raises complex questions. In order to find an answer to these, it is crucial to engage with the Lisbon Treaty's new system of legal acts, as well as the norm's genesis in consideration of the European Constitution. Moreover, the findings will be analysed in correlation with the third variant of paragraph 4, Article 263 of the TFEU. At the same time, this will facilitate understanding and evaluating the subsequently described (more recent) case law of the Union courts.

The Lisbon Treaty's hierarchy regarding legal acts: In contrast to the failed European Constitution, the EU law according to the Lisbon Treaty still lacks legal acts which could be regarded as European laws and European framework laws, respectively. Whereas the Constitution Treaty[49] intended to promote the EC-Treaty's regulations and directives to European laws or framework laws,[50] the Lisbon Treaty reversed this 'relabelling'. However, it adhered to the Constitution's differentiation between legislative acts and non-legislative acts.[51] According to paragraph 3, Article 289 of the TFEU, legislative acts are those acts adopted as a result of a legislative procedure. On the one hand, there are ordinary legislative procedures according to paragraph 1, Article 289 of the TFEU, whereupon an act is proposed by the Commission and then jointly adopted by the European Parliament and the Council. On the other hand, according to paragraph 2, Article 289 of the TFEU, there are special legislative procedures whereupon an act is either adopted by the European Parliament with the participation of the Council or by the Council with the participation of the European Parliament. Both legislative procedures, however, produce legislative acts. According to paragraph 1 and 2, Article 289 of the TFEU—in this regard different from the European Constitution—these explicitly may be adopted in the form of regulations, directives or decisions. In any case, the decisive aspect in qualifying a regulation, directive or decision as a legislative act is the adoption within an (ordinary or special) legislative procedure. However, precisely because they are legislative acts pursuant to paragraph 3, Article289 of the TFEU all of these legal acts are no regulatory acts in the terms of variant 3, para 4 Article 263 of the TFEU.[52] This also applies—albeit linguistically ambiguous—to regulations, as long as they were adopted within a legislative procedure.[53]

Non-legislative acts and regulatory acts pursuant to variant 3, paragraph 4 Article 263 of the TFEU—a determination of relation, full or partial congruity? As already mentioned, the TFEU includes legislative acts on the one hand and regulatory acts on the other hand. In the context of the problem at hand, the question is whether all or any, if applicable, which non-legislative acts rank among the regulatory acts of the third variant of paragraph 4, Article 263 of the TFEU.

Overview of non-legislative acts pursuant to the Union law as amended by the Lisbon Treaty: Analysing the list of legal acts mentioned in Article 288 of the TFEU, only recommendations and opinions clearly cannot be the subject matter of an action pursuant to Article 263 of the TFEU. These have no binding force according to paragraph 5, Article 288 of the TFEU and therefore do not constitute legal acts (in a narrow sense). In comparison, it is more complicated to positively qualify all the remaining legal acts of Article 288 of the TFEU as regulatory acts according to variant 3, paragraph 4, Article 263 of the TFEU—as long as they were not adopted within a legislative procedure.

On the one hand, the TFEU corresponds to the Constitution Treaty with regard to its two-tier system (legislative/non-legislative) with its explicit hierarchy.[54] In contrast to the Constitution Treaty,[55] on the other hand, the TFEU includes regulations, directives, and decisions on both levels. Thus, regulations, directives, and decisions can be both legislative acts according to paragraph 3, Article 289 of the TFEU and non-legislative acts.

In addition, pursuant to the TFEU there are functionally different categories of *non-legislative acts* which, at this point, can and must be presented in outlines only. On the one hand, the TFEU regulates the so-called delegated legal acts as well as the so-called implementing measures more closely in Articles 290 and 291, respectively. On the other hand, there are non-legislative legal acts intended to serve the execution of certain specific provisions of the Treaties (TFEU and TEU). The latter, however, are not only regulated more closely in the section on 'the legal acts of the Union' of the TFEU—in contrast to the Constitution Treaty[56]—but they are not even mentioned at all.[57] They are non-legislative 'Treaty implementing measures'. Furthermore, another category of non-legislative acts can be identified which was also not included in the section on the legal acts of the Union and apparently completely overlooked during the negotiations on the Constitution Treaty as well as the Lisbon Treaty. Still, secondary and tertiary measures do not always depend on the transposition by the Member States, which is the constellation presumed by Article 290 of the TFEU. In fact, they are also aimed at the implementation and execution by Union organs or institutions, especially the Commission and other different agencies. Within this direct execution by the Union, the Commission, for example, adopts numerous decisions pursuant to sentence 2, paragraph 4, Article 288 of the TFEU in the context of competition law. Thereby, it especially addresses certain subjects.

In light of the four functionally different categories of non-legislative acts described, the question arises how they correspond with the three types of legal acts, which are regulations, decisions and directives. Regarding the interpretation of the third variant of paragraph 4, Article 263 of the TFEU this question does not need to be answered in detail. In fact, it suffices to indicate that in principle every type of legal act can be adopted in any one of the four categories. However, in the single case possible specifications of the delegating legal act or the authorizing Treaty or secondary law have to be considered.[58]

V.2 Regulations, Directives and Decisions as Regulatory Acts According to Variant 3, Paragraph 4 Article 263 of the TFEU

Against the background of the depicted variety of non-legislative acts it is crucial to resolve the question concerning the classification of these acts as regulatory acts pursuant to variant 3, paragraph 4, Article 263 of the TFEU. The wording may prima facie suggest that regulatory acts may only be non-legislative regulations. Nevertheless, hereinafter it will be demonstrated that and why directives and decisions may also be regulatory acts according to variant 3, paragraph 4, Article 263 of the TFEU, provided that they are non-legislative acts according to paragraph 3, Article 289 TFEU.

First of all, the wording of the norm may be emphasized in this regard. The third variant of paragraph 4, Article 263 of the TFEU does not say that the individual may institute proceedings against 'regulations' and – without having to mention every version—'*Verordnungen*', '*reglamentos*', '*regulamentos*' and '*verordeningen*', respectively. It rather says 'regulatory acts', '*Rechtsakte mit Verordnungscharakter*', '*actos reglementarios*', '*actos regulamentares*' and '*regelgevingshandelingen*'. This conceptual difference already contradicts an equalization of the terms '(non-legislative) regulations' and 'regulatory acts.' Furthermore, as already mentioned, the Lisbon Treaty establishes an explicit differentiation between legislative and non-legislative legal acts. Hence, it is even more convincing to assume a 'mere' dichotomy instead of qualifying regulatory acts as a third independent category. Therefore, in the context of the individual right to institute proceedings, regulatory acts may rather be classified as non-legislative acts. Moreover, this thesis is supported by the fact that the phenomenon of regulatory acts was launched by the Lisbon Treaty.

In addition to that, the thesis is supported by the norm's genesis. The documents available regarding the negotiations at the intergovernmental conference immediately preceding the Lisbon Treaty[59] do not shed light on the extent of the individual's right to institute proceedings. Yet, the debate within the European Convention gives information on this subject. The 'discussion circle on the Court' installed by the Praesidium of the Convention was inter alia supposed to comment on the question: 'Should the wording of the fourth paragraph of Article 230 EC concerning direct appeals by individuals against general acts of the Institutions be amended?'[60] Following a controversial debate[61] the discussion circle agreed on a version[62] differing from the third alternative of paragraph 4, Article 263 of the TFEU[63] (as well as variant 3, paragraph 4, Article III-365 of the Constitution Treaty and variant 3, paragraph 4, Article III-270 of the Draft Constitution[64]). As a consequence of a failure to agree on one variant, two alternatives were produced.[65] In particular, the subject matters of an action were not denominated as 'regulatory acts', but legal acts with general application or non-legislative legal acts. On the one hand, those who favoured the wording 'non-legislative legal acts' intended to ensure the adherence to the preceding restrictive concept regarding legislative acts (henceforth legal acts according to paragraph 3, Article 289 of the TFEU).[66] On the other hand, the term 'legal acts of general application' was supposed to include legislative acts. This applied, without exception, to legislative acts pursuant to the Draft Constitution and the European Constitution, namely, European laws and framework laws.[67] However, it would have applied to the TFEU's legislative acts as well.[68] Whereas, it is de jure not impossible for a decision according to sentence 2, paragraph 2, Article 288 of the TFEU (which is not generally applicable) to be adopted in a legislative procedure, *in praxi* it is barely imaginable.

Ultimately, the Constitutional Convention did not follow either formulation. Instead it chose the formulation 'regulatory act' which was then included in the TFEU. However, compared to the second variant of paragraph 4, Article 263 of the TFEU/paragraph 4, Article III-270 of Draft Constitution, regulatory acts are privileged. Thus, one might argue that in contrast to the 'discussion circle on the Court' the Constitutional Convention intended to change and especially to minimize the scope of the third variant. It rather intended to merely facilitate the standing vis-à-vis (European) regulations. According to the draft Constitution and the Constitution Treaty these were legal acts with general application and without exception non-legislative acts.[69] However, the published documents on the Convention's debate do not indicate why none of the discussion circle's alternatives were adopted. They neither say why the formulation 'regulatory acts' was finally selected. In any case, it is without a doubt that 'legislative legal acts' continue to follow the previous restrictive system of legal protection. Thus, these are not regulatory acts which have to be challenged according to the second alternative of paragraph 4, Article 263 of the TFEU instead.

Furthermore, it is questionable whether the Constitutional Convention also intended to exclude from the privileged standing, the (European) decisions or at least those decisions directed at addressees. According to the Draft Constitution and the EU Constitution the decision was by definition a non-legislative legal act.[70] Non-legislative directives, by the way, were seen as one of two forms of the European regulation according to the Draft Constitution and the EU Constitution.[71] The differences between the European regulation and the European decision were—as far as evident—never considered by either the Convention or its discussion circles and working groups with regard to an improved right of direct action. Even though, it was repeatedly proposed to privilege legal acts with general application, it was never discussed.[72] According to the Draft Constitution there would be decisions with general application as well as decisions in the form of specific and individual legal acts.[73]

Finally, it shall be emphasized that in case the Convention had intended to exclude (European) decisions from the privileged standing according to var 3, para 4 Article III-270 of Draft Constitution/paragraph 4, Article 263 of the TFEU, this could have been achieved unambiguously by the wording 'European regulations'. Would it have been intended to exclude decisions directed to addressees from the privileged standing, the wording could have been 'non-legislative legal acts with general application'.

Therefore, the norm's genesis clearly suggests that in addition to regulations, non-legislative decisions as well as non-legislative directives (the latter was unknown to the Draft Constitution) were possible regulatory acts. Moreover, this conclusion is further substantiated by another systematic teleological argument. The scope of application of non-legislative regulations on the one hand and the scope of application of non-legislative decisions as well as directives on the other hand, show on various occasions that Union organs may adopt regulations as well as directives/decisions according to different authorizations provided by the TFEU. For example, Article 103 of the TFEU authorizes the Council to adopt appropriate regulations or directives in order to fulfil the objectives on prohibiting anticompetitive arrangements and behaviours as well as abuse of market-dominant positions. Accordingly, in principle the Union organ has a right to freely select to act through either regulation or directive. Then, however, the admissibility of a direct complaint according to variant 3, paragraph 4, Article 263 of the TFEU cannot depend on the kind of legal act selected in the particular case.[74] A different view would render possible a 'legal abuse of form'.

Yet, the selection of either regulation or decision is only possible regarding the adoption of a legal act with general application. Regulations are, by definition, not available for the resolution of specific and individual cases. Nevertheless, it is possible to qualify specific and individual decisions as regulatory acts. Even though the just described systematic-teleological argument may not be convincing regarding specific and individual decisions, neither is the partly suggested splitting-up of (European) regulatory and non-regulatory decisions (on account of the EU Constitution).[75] Apart from the already mentioned arguments against this proposal, it would cause major difficulties in distinguishing between decisions with general application on the one hand and specific individual decisions on the other hand exclusively in the context of legal protection. In this respect, the structurally similar difficulty in distinguishing regulations and decisions according to EC Law abundantly provides illustrative material. All in all, non-legislative regulations as well as non-legislative decisions and directives may be regulatory acts according to variant 3, paragraph 4, Article 263 of the TFEU.[76] In case a legal act was adopted within a legislative procedure, however, it constitutes a legislative legal act and may only be challenged according to variant 2, paragraph 4, Article 263 of the TFEU.[77]

V.3 Case Law, Especially *Inuit Tapiriit Kanatami*

On 3 October 2013 the ECJ for the first time commented on the interpretation of the term 'regulatory acts' according to variant 3, paragraph 4, Article 263 of the TFEU in *Inuit Tapiriit Kanatmi*, a decision regarding legal remedies. Thereby, it (largely) confirmed the aforementioned position.[78]

The subject matter of the judgment was an appeal lodged by Inuit Tapiriit Kanatami and others against the decision of the CFI in Case T-18/10.[79] The case dealt with the requested annulment of Regulation (EC) No. 1007/2009 of 16 September 2009 adopted by the Parliament and the Council regarding the trade in seal products.[80] Ultimately, the CFI dismissed the case as inadmissible. The regulation in question is based on Article 95 EC Treaty (now Article 114 of the TFEU) which prohibits the placement of seal products on the market.[81] However, the regulation included an exception for seal products resulting from hunts traditionally conducted by Inuit and other indigenous communities. By means of classical interpretation methods the Court concluded that the term 'regulatory act' according to variant 3, paragraph 4, Article 263 of the TFEU meant all legal acts with general application except for legislative acts. Subsequently, it refused to affirm the existence of a regulatory act in the particular case.[82]

In its judgment regarding the applicants' appeal, the ECJ ultimately confirmed the CFI's interpretation of the term 'regulatory act' and dismissed the case as unfounded. Thereby, the ECJ based its judgment on the assumption that the interpretation of Union law norms included not only their wording, object and purpose, but also their respective context and genesis as well as the whole body of Union law.[83] Consequently, the ECJ focussed on the problem whether the regulation in question which was qualified as a legislative act according to Article 289 paragraph 3 of the TFEU could at the same time be qualified as a 'regulatory act'.[84] First, the Court stated that the term 'act' in paragraph 4, Article 263 of the TFEU included all Union acts with an authoritative legal effect. Therefore, this term included all—legislative or non-legislative—acts with general application as well as specific measures.[85] In contrast to the broadly formulated subject matters of the first and second variant of paragraph 4, Article 263 of the TFEU, the newly integrated 'regulatory act' of the third variant had to be of a more limited scope. This conclusion resulted from a contrasting juxtaposition of the second and third variant of paragraph 4, Article 263 of the TFEU: Whereas the applicant had to substantiate a direct and individual concern according to the second variant, the third variant only required the direct concern. Consequently, 'regulatory acts' could not be understood as all acts with general application, but instead had to be interpreted as a narrower category of this kind of acts. A contrary interpretation would render the differentiation of the terms 'act' and 'regulatory act' meaningless.[86] Subsequently, the ECJ referred to the former version of paragraph 4, Article 263 of the TFEU and the genesis of the latter. It establishes that the content of paragraph 4, Article III-365 of the Constitution Treaty was adopted in paragraph 4, Article 263 of the TFEU without alteration. Moreover, the preparatory work of the former revealed that legislative acts were to be excluded from the third variant's partial extension of admissibility requirements for individual actions for annulment. This was concluded from the final report of the discussion circle on the Court of Justice of 25 March 2003[87] as well as a cover note of the Praesidium of the Convention of 12 May 2003.[88]

All in all, this judgment put an end to the debate regarding the interpretation of the third variant as far as legislative acts according to paragraph 3, Article 289 of the TFEU are concerned. Insofar the judgment deserves unconditional approval due to the aforementioned reasoning.[89] Yet, there were doubts regarding Union constitutional law on account of the right to an effective remedy according to Article 47 of the Charta of Fundamental Rights of the EU.[90] Indeed, the admissibility of individual actions for the annulment of Union acts before Union courts was still very limited. To this effect, the Court, however, accurately countered that the right to an effective remedy was not violated as long as the person concerned had the opportunity to incidentally challenge the respective legislative act of the EU before a Member State court by means of a preliminary rulings procedure according to Article 267 of the TFEU.[91]

VI Direct Concern

As well as the second variant of paragraph 4, Article 263 of the TFEU, the third variant also requires the legal act to be of direct concern to the applicant. There is no reason to interpret the two variants differently in this respect. Therefore, the standards developed in order to interpret the criterion of direct concern according to the second variant (see section D. II.) are applicable when interpreting this criterion according to the third variant as well.

VII No Entailment of Implementing Measures

In addition to the criterion of direct concern, the standing of a person challenging a regulatory act pursuant to variant 3, paragraph 4, Article 263 of the TFEU requires the act not to entail implementing measures.

According to the debate at the Convention,[92] the inclusion of the additional criterion was intended to exclude individual claims against such regulatory acts that still required implementation, transposition, or executive act—especially by the Member States. Essentially, the reason for this intention was the idea that in case a legal act of the Union had to be transposed by the Member States, the individual could challenge this transposition act before the respective national courts. Within this procedure the national court could incidentally assess the legality of the Union act and—if applicable—ask the ECJ for a preliminary ruling. This restriction of the individual's standing against regulatory acts can be explained against the background of the discussions surrounding the case *Unión de Pequeños Agricultores* before the ECJ. According to Spanish law an admissible claim would have required a Member State act of transposition. In the case, however, there was no such act of transposition. Thus, a claim before the Spanish national courts would have been inadmissible. As a result, the applicant could not have achieved an incidental examination before the national courts.[93] The court ruled that in constellations like this the applicant may institute proceedings before the Union courts regardless of the entailment of implementing measures; however, this exception was restricted to these exact constellations.

Nevertheless, the question remains how to distinguish the criterion of 'no implementing measures' from the criterion of direct concern. In other words, the question is whether its incorporation is at all necessary in order to achieve the intended restriction of the standing. As just assessed, the criterion of direct concern to a large extent, prevents individuals to challenge regulatory acts that still require an act of transposition. However, at the same time it became apparent that in particular constellations the ECJ assumed the direct concern even though the Union legal act still needed transposition. This especially applies in cases in which Member States have no discretion as to the implementation or transposition. Thus, in these constellations only the criterion of 'no implementing measures' may result in the dismissal of a standing regarding 'regulatory acts'.[94]

Henceforth, the Union courts exclusively consider the specific circumstances of the individual case in order to establish whether a regulatory act entails implementing measures or not.[95] Thereby, it more or less conforms to the aforementioned position on the differentiation between the criterion of 'direct concern' and 'no implementing measures'. For example, compatibility decisions adopted by the Commission according to state aid law are in principle followed by the respective Member State's order to return the state aid. Consequently, on the basis of the aforementioned standards, the Commission's compatibility decisions entail implementing measures. Thus, actions filed against these decisions would not be admissible according to variant 3, paragraph 4, Article 263 of the TFEU.[96] In addition to that, cases regarding the classification of certain goods in the Common Customs Tariff by an implementing regulation of the Commission[97] as well as an anti-dumping implementation regulation of the Council[98] were decided accordingly.

VIII Summary

All in all, the new third variant of paragraph 4, Article 263 of the TFEU achieves an improvement of the right to file a direct claim only with regard to non-legislative acts within the scope outlined above. Beyond that, the Member States remain obliged to establish effective decentralized legal protection mechanisms in order to ensure the monitoring of the Union's legal acts which may not be challenged directly before the Union's courts.[99]

IX Conclusion

The examination has demonstrated that the system of individual claims according to paragraph 4, Article 263 of the TFEU is characterized by an exceedingly complicated regulation concept. On the one hand, the addressees of a legal act of the EU have a standing without further ado. On the other hand, in the context of norms with abstract and general application the criterion of individual concern according to variant 2, paragraph 4, Article 263 of the TFEU will be fulfilled in exceptional cases only. Therefore, individual claims against Union norms with abstract and general application will be inadmissible in most cases. Something else applies, however, to secondary legal acts of the Union which can be qualified as (non-legislative) regulatory acts. A direct claim against these acts is admissible, if it is of direct concern to the applicant and does not entail implementing measures. The pivotal criterion regarding the admissibility of a claim is the direct concern further restricted by the requirement of 'no implementing measures'. A political evaluation of such a system shall be disregarded at this point. However, it shall be emphasized that the findings do not necessarily imply gaps within the Union's legal protection system. As the ECJ proclaimed on various occasions, the Member States are obliged to design their national legal protection systems in accordance with the preliminary rulings procedure pursuant to Article 267 of the TFEU.[100]

Notes and References

1. [2012] OJ C 326/47.
2. Nevertheless, a separate examination can be found in Case C-62/70 *Bock v Commission* [1971] ECR 897, paras 4–10; Case T-86/96 *Arbeitsgemeinschaft Deutscher Luftfahrt-Unternehmen and Hapag Lloyd Fluggesellschaft v Commission* [1999] ECR II-179, paras 43–44; Case T-411/06 *Sogelma v EAR* [2008] II-02771, paras 85 sqq.
3. Cf Schwarze, 'Rechtsschutz Privater gegenüber normativen Rechtsackten im Recht der EWG' in Münch (ed.), *Staatsrecht-Völkerrecht-Europarecht* (de Gruyter 1981) 936, 972.
4. Case C-96/71 *Haegeman v Commission* [1972] ECR 1005, paragraphs 5, 8, 9, 13; Case C-92/78 *Simmenthal v Commission* [1979] ECR 777, paras 27–30; Case C-222/83 *Differdange v Commission* [1984] ECR 2889, para 12.
5. Case C-113/77 R *NTN Toyo Bearing Company v Council* [1977] ECR 1721, para 11; Case T-385/07 *FIFA v Commission* [2011] ECR II-205, para 39; Case T-55/08 *UEFA v Commission* [2011] ECR II-271, para 34; Case T-18/10 *Inuit Tapiriit Kanatami and others v Parliament and Council* [2011] ECR II-5599, para 71; Case T-262/10 *Microban International and Microban (Europe) v Commission* [2011] ECR II-7697, para 27; joined cases T-454/10 and T-482/11 *Anicav and others v Commission* (EGC, 30 May 2013); Case T-492/12 DEP *von Storch and others v ECB* (EGC, 10 December 2013); Daig, *Nichtigkeits- und Untätigkeitsklagen im Recht der Europäischen Gemeinschaften* (Nomos 1985) 11 sqq.
6. Cf *NTN Toyo Bearing Company v Council* [1977] ECR 1721, para 11; joined Cases C-41-44/70 *International Fruit Company v Commission* [1971] ECR 411, paras 23, 29.
7. Joined Cases C-106 and 107/63 *Töpfer v Commission* [1965] ECR 405, paras 555–6; *Bock* (n 2) paras 6–8; Case C-11/82 *Piraiki-Patraiki v Commission* [1985] ECR 207, paras 7–10.
8. Cf Case T-380/94 *AIUFFASS and AKT v Commission* [1996] ECR II- 2169, paras 46–7. In Case C-386/96 P *Dreyfus v Commission* [1998] ECR I-2309, paras 43–4 the ECJ summarized its case law as follows: 'for a person to be

directly concerned by a Community measure, the latter must directly affect the legal situation of the individual and leave no discretion to the addressees of that measure who are entrusted with the task of implementing it, such implementation being purely automatic and resulting from Community rules without the application of other intermediate rules(...) The same applies where the possibility for addressees not to give effect to the Community measure is purely theoretical and their intention to act in conformity with it is not in doubt(...)'.

9. Case C-25/62 *Plaumann v Commission* [1963] ECR 199, para 237.
10. Treaty Establishing the European Economic Community of 23 March 1957.
11. Case C-40/64 *Marcello Sgarlata and others v EEC Commission* [1965] ECR 215, 227. According to Thomas von Danwitz, 'Die Garantie effektiven Rechtsschutzes im Recht der Europäischen Gemeinschaft—Zur Verbesserung des Individualrechtsschutzes vor dem EuGH' [1993] NJW 1108, 1115 the requirement not to interpret the norms regarding legal protection too restrictively (at first) remained disregarded.
12. Case C-25/62 *Plaumann v Commission* [1963] ECR 199, para 238; ever since settled case law, cf Case T-2/93 *Air France v Commission* [1995] ECR II-533, para 42; Case T-221/10 *Iberdrola v Commission* (EGC, 8 March 2012) para 23; Case C-583/11 P *Inuit Tapiriit Kanatami and others v Parliament and Council* (The Court (Grand Chamber), 3 October 2013) para 72; Case C-133/12 P *Stichting Woonlinie and others v Commission* (Judgement of the Court (First Chamber), 27 February 2014) para 44; Case C-274/12 P *Telefónica v Commission* (The Court (Grand Chamber), 19 December 2013), para 46.
13. Case C-25/62 *Plaumann v Commission* [1963] ECR 199, para 107.
14. Cf Daig, *Toyo Bearing Company v Council* [1977] ECR 1721, paras 108–9; apparently dissenting Case C-6/68 *Zuckerfabrik Watenstedt v Council* [1968] ECR 409, Opinion of GA Roemer, paras 622, 629.
15. *Töpfer v Commission* [1965] ECR 405, para 556; *International Fruit Company v Commission* [1971] ECR 411, paras 16, 22; cf also Daig, *Toyo Bearing Company v Council* [1977] ECR 1721, paras 108–9.
16. *Töpfer v Commission,* para 556; *Bock v Commission* [1971] ECR 897, para 9–10. The same applies for rights awarded before the decision, cf Case C-125/06 P *Commission v Infront WM* [2008] ECR I-1451, para 72 and *Stichting Woonlinie and others v Commission,* para 46.
17. The ECJ's rigid orientation towards the past especially becomes apparent in Case C-38/64 *Getreide-Import GmbH v Commission* [1965] ECR 203, paras 212–13; also cf Wegmann, *Die Nichtigkeitsklage Privater gegen Normativakte der Europäischen Gemeinschaften* (Duncker & Humblot 1976) 141 and Daig *Toyo Bearing Company v Council* [1977] ECR 1721, para 109.
18. Examples can be found in *Töpfer v Commission* [1965] ECR 405, para 556; *Bock v Commission* [1971] ECR 897, para 10; *International Fruit Company v Commission* [1971] ECR 411, paras 16, 22 and in the 1980s Case C-1/84 *Ilford Spa v Commission* [1984] ECR 423, para 6.

19. Cf in principle Nehl, 'Wechselwirkungen zwischen verwaltungsverfahrensrechtlichem und gerichtlichem Individualrechtsschutz in der EG' in Nowak/Cremer (eds), *Individualrechtsschutz in der EG und der WTO* (Nomos 2002) 146.
20. Case C-169/84 *COFAZ v Commission* [1986] ECR 391, paras 23–4; joined Cases C-67, 68 and 70/85 *Kwekerij Gebroeders van der Kooy and others v Commission* [1988] ECR 219, paras 21–2; Case C-198/91 *Cook v Commission* [1993] ECR I-2487, para 23; Case C-225/91 *Matra SA v Commission* [1993] ECR 3203, para 17; joined Cases T-447–449/93 *AITEC v Commission* [1995] ECR II 1971, paras 35–8; Case T-49/93 *SIDE v Commission* [1995] ECR II-2501, paras 34–8.
21. Case C-264/82 *Timex v Council and Commission* [1985] ECR 849, paras 12–14.
22. Case C-191/82 *Fediol v Commission* [1983] ECR 2913, para 30.
23. Case C-26/76 *Metro v Commission* [1977] ECR 1875, para 13; Case C-210/81 *Demo-Studio v Commission* [1983] ECR 3045, para 14.
24. *Air France v Commission* [1995] ECR II-533, para 14.
25. Cf Nowak, 'Der Rechtsschutz von Beschwerdeführern im EG-Wettbewerbs- und EG-Außenhandelsrecht' [2000] EuZW 453.
26. Regarding an existing but unnoticed procedural right which would in principle not suffice in order to establish individuality, cf Case C-70/97 P *Kruidvat v Commission* [1998] ECR I-7183, paras 39, 46.
27. Cf the analysis of the judgments *Metro I*, *Timex*, *Fediol I*, *Cofaz*, *Matra* and *Cook* by Dietze, *Verfahrensbeteiligung und Klagebefugnis im EG-Recht* (Peter Lang Veriag, Frankfurt and Main 1995) 85 as well as the CFI's findings regarding the Commission's decisions adopted pursuant to paragraph 2 of Article 288 of the TFEU in[2012] OJ C326/01 in Case T-435/93 *ASPEC and others v Commission* [1995] ECR II-1281, paras 63–4 and Case T-442/93 *AAC and others v Commission* [1995] ECR II-1329, para 48.
28. Case T-585/93 *Greenpeace v Commission* [1995] ECR II-2205, para 56; joined Cases T-481/93 and T-484/93 *Vereniging van Exporteurs in Levende Varkens and others v Commission* [1995] ECR II-2941, para 59; Case T-398/94 *Kahn Scheepvaart v Commission* [1996] ECR II-477, para 42.
29. Case C-106/98 *Comité d'entreprise de la Société française de production v Commission* [2000] ECR I-3659, para 41. Cf also Case T-189/97 *Comité d'entreprise de la Société française de production v Commission* [1998] ECR II-335, para 44; Case T-86/96 *Arbeitsgemeinschaft Deutscher Luftfahrt-Unternehmen and Hapag Lloyd Fluggesellschaft v Commission* [1999] ECR II-179, para 47 sqq; cf with regard to the judgment last-mentioned the comment of Nowak/Nehl, 'EuG: Klagebefugnis in Beihilfensachen' [1999] EuZW 350. Cf regarding merger control law Case T-177/04 *easyJet v Commission* [2006] ECR II-1931, para 35.
30. Cumulative: *Timex v Council and Commission* [1985] ECR 849, paras 12–16; joined Cases T-528, 542, 543 and 546/93 *Métropole Télévision and others v Commission* [1996] ECR II-649, paras 61, 75; *Air France v Commission*

[1995] ECR II-533, paras 44–7; apparently also *Comité d'entreprise de la Société française de production* [1998] (n 29) para 44 sqq. Alternatively: Case C-358/89 *Extramet Industrie v Council* [1992] ECR I-3813, para 17; *Air France v Commission* [1995] ECR II-533, para 82; *ASPEC and others v Commission* [1995] ECR II-1281, para 69 sqq; *AAC and others v Commission* [1995] ECR II-1329, para 53; *SIDE v Commission* [1995] ECR II-2501, para 31; Case T-266/94 *Foreningen af Jernskibs-Maskinbyggerier I Danmark and others v Commission* [1996] ECR II-1399, paras 47–8; Case T-58/10 *Phoenix-Reisen and DRV v Commission* [EGC(Seventh Chamber) 11 January 2012] paras 35, 44.

31. Case T-13/99 *Pfizer Animal Health v Council* [2002] ECR II-3305, para 125; Case T-70/99 R *Alpharma v Council* [2002] ECR II-3495, para 117. Cf regarding recent more restrictive judgments Case T-120/98 *Alce v Commission* [1999] ECR II-1395, para 22; no individuality even though being largest domestic supplier Case T-11/99 *Van Parys v Commission* [1999] ECR II-2653, para 52.
32. Cf regarding the differences Waelbroek/Fosselard, 'Joined Cases T-480/93 and T-483/93, *Antillean Rice Mills NV, Trading & Shipping Co. Ter Beek BV and European Rice Brokers AVV, Alesie Curaçao NV, Guyana Investments AVV v Commission of the European Communities supported by Council of the European Union, French Republic and Italian Republic,* Judgment of 14 September 1995' [1996] CMLRev 811, 822-3.
33. Case C-152/88 *Sofrimport v Commission* [1990] ECR I-2477, para 11.
34. *Piraiki-Patraiki v Commission* [1985] ECR 207, para 31.
35. Joined Cases T-480 and 483/93 *Antillean Rice Mills NV and others v Commission* [1995] ECR II-2305, para 67; *Vereniging van Exporteurs in Levende Varkens and others v Commission* [1995] ECR II-2941, para 61. Both judgments refer to *Piraiki-Patraiki* and *Sofrimport* at the relevant places.
36. Case T-96/92 *Comité central d'entreprise de la Société générale des grandes sources and others v Commission* [1995] ECR II-1213, paras 26 sqq; Case T-12/93 R *Comité central d'entreprise de la Société anonyme Vittel and others v Commission* [1995] ECR II-1247, para 36 sqq; cf regarding the CFI's reasoning in Case T-46/06 *Galileo Lebensmittel v Commission* [2007] ECR II-93, paras 49–50.
37. Case T-47/95 *Terre Rouge Consultant SA and others v Commission* [1997] ECR II-481, paras 44–56; Case C-270/95 *Cristina Kik v Council and Commission* [1996] ECR I-1987, paras 13–15; Case T-298/94 *Roquette Frères SA v Council* [1996] ECR II-1531, paras 41–4 as well as the aforementioned restrictions regarding the standing based on a participation in the procedure. Cf regarding the allegedly anticipated conclusions within the reasoning of a merger control decision: joined Cases T-125 and 127/97 *Coca-Cola v Commission* [2000] ECR II-1733.
38. Case T-177/01 *Jégo-Quéré v Commission* [2002] ECR II-2365, para 51.
39. Case T-177/01 *Jégo-Quéré v Commission* [2002] ECR II-2365, para 51.

40. Cf Case T-177/01 *Jégo-Quéré v Commission* [2002] ECR II-2365, para 46.
41. Cf Case T-177/01 *Jégo-Quéré v Commission* [2002] ECR II-2365, para 45.
42. Case C-50/00 P *Unión de Pequeños Agricultores v Council* [2002] ECR I-6677, Opinion of AG Jacobs.
43. Case C-50/00 P *Unión de Pequeños Agricultores v Council* [2002] ECR I-6677, Opinion of AG Jacobs, paras 36–7.
44. Cf also Case C-456/13 P *T & L Sugars Limited and others v Commission* (ECJ, 28 April 2015) para 44.
45. Cf also Case C-456/13 P *T & L Sugars Limited and others v Commission* (ECJ, 28 April 2015), paras 44–5.
46. Cf also Case C-456/13 P *T & L Sugars Limited and others v Commission* (ECJ, 28 April 2015), paras 40–1; *T & L Sugars Limited* (n 44) para 49. Concerning this matter Cremer, 'Der gemeinschaftsrechtliche Grundsatz effektiven Rechtsschutzes vor mitgliedstaatlichen Gerichten' in Bruha, Nowak and Petzold (eds), *Grundrechtschutz für Unternehmen im europäischen Binnenmarkt* (Nomos 2004) 229, 234 sqq. And regarding the consequences of this view for the German administrative procedural law, 'Gemeinschaftsrecht und deutsches Verwaltungsprozessrecht—Zum dezentralen Rechtsschutz gegenüber EG-Sekundärrecht' [2004] Die Verwaltung 165, 175 sqq.
47. Cf Case T-155/02 *VVG and others v Commission* [2003] ECR II-1949, paragraphs 23, 41; Case T-94/00 *Rica Foods and others v Commission* [2002] ECR II-4677, para 50.
48. Treaty of Lisbon amending the Treaty on European Union and the Treaty establishing the European Community [2007] OJ C306/1.
49. Treaty establishing a Constitution for Europe [2004] OJ C310/1.
50. Cf Constitution Treaty [2004] OJ C310/1, Articles 1–33 paragraph 1 sub-paragraphs 2 and 3, on the one hand and EC Treaty [2002] OJ C325/33, art 249 paragraphs 2 and 3 on the other hand.
51. Cf insofar Constitution Treaty, [2004] OJ C310/1, Articles 1–33 paragraph 1 sub-paragraph 2 and 3, which qualifies European laws and European framework laws as legislative acts.
52. Cf Roer-Eide and Eliantonio, 'The Meaning of Regulatory Act Explained: Are There Any Significant Improvements for the Standing of Non-Privileged Applicants in Annulment Actions?' 14 German LJ 1851, 1857-1859; differently Everling, 'Lissabon-Vertrag regelt Dauerstreit über Nichtigkeitsklage Privater' [2010] EuZW 572, 575; idem, 'Klagerecht Privater gegen Rechtsakte der EU mit allgemeiner Geltung' [2012] EuZW 376, 378, believing that the terms regulatory act and legislative act do not exclude each other; cf also Görlitz and Kubicki, 'Rechtsakte mit 'schwierigem Charakter'' [2011] EuZW 248, 251.
53. Cf Meinhard Schröder, 'Neuerungen im Rechtsschutz der Europäischen Union durch den Vertrag von Lissabon' [2009] DÖV 61, 63–4; Wegener, 'Rechtsstaatliche Vorzüge und Mängel der Verfahren vor den Gemeinschaftsgerichten' [2008] EuR Beiheft 3, 45, 52–3; Thiele, 'Das

Rechtsschutzsystem nach dem Vertrag von Lissabon—(K)ein Schritt nach vorn?' [2010] EuR 30, 43–4; Streinz, Ohler and Herrmann, *Vertrag von Lissabon* (3rd edition, Beck München 2010) 116; Oppermann, Classen and Nettesheim, *Europarecht* (7th edition, Beck München 2016) para 61; Haratsch, Koenig and Pechstein, Europarecht (10th edition, Mohr Siebeck 2016) para 517; Hatje and Kindt, 'Der Vertrag von Lissabon—Europa endlich in guter Verfassung?' [2008] NJW 1761, 1767; differently Everling, 'Rechtsschutz in der Europäischen Union nach dem Vertrag von Lissabon' [2009] EuR Beiheft 71, 74; 'Lissabon-Vertrag regelt Dauerstreit über Nichtigkeitsklage Privater' [2010], 575; Bast, 'Handlungsformen und Rechtsschutz' in von Bogdandy and Bast, (eds), *Europäisches Verfassungsrecht* (2nd edn, Springer 2009) 557; sympathizing with the opposite view Barents, 'The Court of Justice after the Treaty of Lisbon' (2010) 47 CMLRev 709, 725.

54. Cf again Constitution Treaty [2004] OJ C310/1, Articles 1–33 paragraph 1 sub-paragraph 2 and 3, which qualifies European laws and European framework laws as legislative acts.
55. Cf Cremer, 'Der Rechtsschutz des Einzelnen gegen Sekundärrechtsakte der Union gem. Article III-270 Abs4 Konventionsentwurf' [2004] EuGRZ 577, 579–80.
56. Cf in this regard Constitution Treaty [2004] OJ C310/1, Articles 1–33 paragraph 1 sub-paragraph 2 and 3. In addition, a 'decision' was possible as an implementation instrument, which was per se a non-legislative act according to the Constitution Treaty.
57. Cf German Department for Foreign Affairs, 'Denkschrift zum Vertrag von Lissabon vom 13 Dezember 2007' (11 December 2007); http://www.auswaertiges-amt.de/cae/servlet/contentblob/358382/publicationFile/3093/Denkschrift-lissabon.pdf, accessed 21 July 2016.
58. For example, Article 109 of the TFEU [2012] OJ C326/47 limits the Council's competence to adopt regulations.
59. General Secretariat of the Council, 'European Parliament Resolution of 11 July 2007 on the convening of the Intergovernmental Conference (IGC): the European Parliament's opinion (Article 48 of the EU Treaty)' (13 July 2007); http://data.consilium.europa.eu/doc/document/ST-11626-2007-INIT/en/pdf, accessed 21 July 2016.
60. Cf the Secretariat of the European Convention, "Discussion circle' on the Court of Justice' (7 February 2003) CON 543/03; http://european-convention.europa.eu/pdf/reg/en/03/cv00/cv00543.en03.pdf, accessed 21 July 2016 and regarding the composition of the discussion circle Secretariat of the European Convention, 'Composition of the discussion circle on the Court of Justice' (14 February 2003) CON 559/03; http://european-convention.europa.eu/pdf/reg/en/03/cv00/cv00559.en03.pdf, accessed 21 July 2016.
61. Cf regarding the different proposals the Secretariat of the European Convention, 'Final report of the discussion circle on the Court of Justice' (25 March 2003) CON 636/03, para 19; http://www.europarl.europa.eu/meetdocs_all/committees/conv/20030403/03c_en.pdf, accessed 21 July 2016.

62. 'Final report of the discussion circle on the Court of Justice' (25 March 2003) CON 636/03, para 20. It said: 'Any natural or legal person may, under the same conditions, institute proceedings against an act addressed to that person or which is of direct and individual concern to him, and against an act of general appication/a regulatory act which is of direct concern to him without entailing implementing measures.'
63. The remaining changes of the final version were only editorial ones.
64. Draft Treaty establishing a Constitution for Europe [2003] OJ C 169/1.
65. On account of the formulation an act of general appication/a regulatory act these could also be understood (following a third interpretation) as cumulative requirements (an act of general application and a regulatory act); however, this interpretation was (apparently) not intended according to the 'Final report of the discussion circle on the Court of Justice', 8.
66. Cf regarding the different proposals in the 'Final report of the discussion circle on the Court of Justice', para 22.
67. This may insofar only be doubted in case of a framework law only addressed to one Member State in a single case. However, Article 1-32 paragraph 1 sub-paragraph 4 of Draft Constitution or [2003] OJ C 169/1 or Article I-33 paragraph 1 sub-paragraph 4 of Constitution Treaty implicirly [2004] OJ C310/1 implicitly state that framework laws shall be qualified as legal acts with general application.
68. The remarks on framework laws mentioned in note 67 analogically apply to directives.
69. Draft Constitution [2003] OJ C 169/1, Article 1-32 paragraph 1 sub-paragraph 4 or Constitution Treaty [2004] OJ C310/1, Article 1-33 paragraph 1 sub-paragraph 4.
70. Draft Constitution [2003] OJ C 169/1, art I-32 paragraph 1 sub-paragraph 5; Constitution Treaty [2004] OJ C310/1, art I-33 para 1 subpara 5.
71. Draft Constitution [2003] OJ C 169/1, Article I-32 paragraph 1 sub-paragraph 4 Sentence 2 Alternative. 2; Constitution Treaty [2004] OJ C310/1, Article I-33 paragraph 1 sub-paragraph 4 sentence 2 Alternative 2.
72. Fredriksen, 'Individualklagemöglichkeiten vor den Gerichten der EU nach dem Vertrag über eine Verfassung für Europa' [2005] ZEuS 99, 120–1 in contrast, noted that the question the Praesidium asked the discussion circle on the Court of Justice: 'Should the wording of the fourth paragraph of Article 230 EC concerning direct appeals by individuals against general acts of the Institutions be amended? only concerned general acts. In my opinion, on account of the depicted subsequent debate of the discussion circle, however, this question is not as significant regarding the interpretation of the term 'regulatory act' as Fredriksen claims.
73. Cf again Draft Constitution [2003] OJ C 169/1, Article I-32 paragraph 1 sub-paragraph 4.
74. Cf Christina Last,*Garantie wirksamen Rechtsschutzes gegen Maßnahmen der Europäischen Union* (Mohr Siebeck 2008) 157.
75. Cf Fredriksen, 'Individualklagemöglichkeiten vor den Gerichten der EU nach dem Vertrag über eine Verfassung für Europa', 120–1.

76. Concerning the addressees of decisions in terms of sentence 2, paragraph 4 of Article 288 of the TFEU, however, the standing according to Article 263 paragraph 4 variant 1 of the TFEU must be considered preferentially.
77. Cf Meinhard Schröder, 'Neuerungen im Rechtsschutz der Europäischen Union durch den Vertrag von Lissabon', 63–64; Hatje and Kindt, 'Der Vertrag von Lissabon—Europa endlich in guter Verfassung?', 1767; dissenting Rabe, 'Zur Metamorphose des Europäischen Verfassungsvertrag' [2007] NJW 3153, 3157; little convincing and insufficiently differentiated Pache and Rösch, 'Der Vertrag von Lissabon' [2008] NVwZ 473, 478.
78. Case C-583/11 P *Inuit Tapiriit Kanatami* (n 12); cf Cremer, 'Der EuGH bleibt sich treu—Die Nichtigkeitsklage Privater 50 Jahre nach Plaumann' [2014] ZG 82.
79. Case T-18/10 *Inuit Tapiriit Kanatami*. Cf Everling, 'Klagerecht Privater gegen Rechtsakte der EU mit allgemeiner Geltung' [2012] EuZW 376; Petzold, 'Was sind 'Rechtsakte mit Verordnungscharakter' (Article 263 Abs. 4 AEUV)?' [2012] EuR 443; Thalmann, 'Zur Auslegung von Article 263 Abs. 4 AEUV durch Rechtsprechung und Lehre' [2012] EuR 452; Streinz, 'Nichtigkeitsklage von Individuen gegen Rechtsakte mit Verordnungscharakter' [2012] JuS 472.
80. [2009] OJ L 286/36.
81. Especially Article 3 of the regulation (n 80) Cf as well Commission Regulation (EU) No 737/2010 of 10 August 2010 laying down detailed rules for the implementation of Regulation (EC) No 1007/2009 of the European Parliament and of the Council on trade in seal products [2010] OJ L 216/1.
82. T-18/10 *Inuit Tapiriit Kanatami*, para 38 sqq. For the rest, it negated an individual concern regarding the four persons it accepted as directly concerned in terms of Article 263 paragraph 4 variant 3 of TFEU [2012] OJ C326/01 in T-18/10 *Inuit Tapiriit Kanatami*, (n 5) para 88 sqq.
83. C-583/11 P *Inuit Tapiriit Kanatami*, paras 50–1.
84. However, the question was not discussed, whether irrespective of legislative acts all (and only) general acts could be qualified as regulatory acts. Cf in this regard Cremer, 'Zum Rechtsschutz des Einzelnen gegen abgeleitetes Unionsrecht nach dem Vertrag von Lissabon' [2010] DÖV 58, 61 sqq; Cremer, 'Der Rechtsschutz des Einzelnen gegen Sekundärrechtsakte der Union gem. Article III-270 Abs4 Konventionsentwurf', 579 sqq. The admissibility according to Article 263 paragraph 4 variant 3 of the TFEU [2012] OJ C326/01 was accepted for the first time in *Microban International and Microban (Europe)*.
85. C-583/11 P *Inuit Tapiriit Kanatami*, para 56.
86. Cf. regarding this systematic reasoning C-583/11 *Inuit Tapiriit Kanatami*, 57–8.
87. CONV 636/03, para 22. The Secretariat of the European Convention, 'Final report of the discussion circle on the Court of Justice' (25 March 2003) CONV 636/03, paragraph 22; http://www.europarl.europa.eu/meetdocs_all/committees/conv/20030403/03c_en.pdf, accessed 2 August 2016.

88. C-583/11 P *Inuit Tapiriit Kanatami* (n 12) para 59; referring to the Secretariat of the European Convention, 'Articles on the Court of Justice and the High Court' (12 May 2003) CONV 734/03, 20. Remarks regarding this argument Cremer, 'Der EuGH bleibt sich treu—Die Nichtigkeitsklage Privater 50 Jahre nach Plaumann', 87 sqq.
89. Critical in this regard Van Malleghem and Baeten, 'Before the law stands a gatekeeper, or, what is a 'regulatory act' in Article 263 (4) TFEU? Inuit Tapiriit Kanatami' [2014] CML Rev, 1187, 1202 sqq.
90. [2012] OJ C 326/391.
91. C-583/11 P *Inuit Tapiriit Kanatami*, para 89 sqq.
92. Cf 'Final report of the discussion circle on the Court of Justice', para 21.
93. Cf *Unión de Pequeños Agricultores*, para 26; similarly, *Microban International and Microban (Europe) v Commission,* paras 33–4. Concerning the procedural possibilities of a decentral legal protection before German administrative courts Cremer, 'Gemeinschaftsrecht und deutsches Verwaltungsprozessrecht—Zum dezentralen Rechtsschutz gegenüber EG-Sekundärrecht' [2004] Die Verwaltung 165.
94. Cf *T & L Sugars Limited*, paras 40–2, according to which the assumption of implementing measures was not called into questions by the allegedly mechanical nature of the measures taken at national level; Buchanan and Bolzonello, 'Towards a Definition of 'Implementing Measures' under Article 263, paragraph 4, TFEU' 6 EJRR 671, 675.
95. *Telefónica v Commission*, para 30; *Stichting Woonlinie and others v Commission*, para 50–1.
96. *Iberdrola v Commission*, paras 46-47; *Telefónica v Commission,* paras 35–6; *Stichting Woonlinie and others v Commission*, para 53.
97. Case T-380/11 *Palirria Souliotis AE v Commission* (ECJ (Fifth Chamber), 12 September 2013).
98. Case T-551/11 *BSI v Council* (ECJ (Seventh Chamber), 5 February 2013) paras 53–4.
99. In detail, Cremer (n 46) 171 sqq.
100. More critical regarding the effectiveness of national judicial protection than Buchanan and Bolzonello (n 94) 676; also, Albors-Llorens, 'Remedies against the EU Institutions after Lisbon: An Era of Opportunity?' *The Cambridge Law Journal*, 71(507): 534–5.

14

Sizing up the Opposition

Taking the Comparative Route to Entrench the CRPD Paradigm

Amita Dhanda

I Introduction

It is ten years since the Convention on the Rights of Persons with Disabilities (CRPD) was adopted by the United Nations (UN) amidst universal applause and loud claims of effecting a paradigm shift. The CRPD was claimed to make a paradigm shift because unlike the soft law expositions from the UN it approached the matter of disability rights from the standpoint of persons with disabilities. 'Nothing About Us without Us' was not just a battle cry it was the ruling ethic of the CRPD. At several places during the negotiations deadlocks were resolved because disabled people and their organizations would not let State Parties settle for less.[1] The need to negotiate a human rights convention in the presence and with the active participation of the stakeholders was a first in the history of the UN and the metaphor of a new era was used by several scholars to describe the Convention.[2]

The CRPD was seen to mark a paradigm shift because unlike the soft law instruments on Disability Rights,[3] the CRPD did not adopt a concessional approach towards the rights of persons with disabilities. It was thus not 'as normal and full as possible' but 'equal basis with others'. Consequently, civil–political rights which were notably absent till the Equalization Rules (when right to participation found mention) were incorporated in full measure. In fact, the CRPD brought alive the discourse of indivisibility of rights by creating categories of rights which could not be placed on either side of the divide and had to be termed hybrid.[4] The move over from paternalism was made by not just reaffirming that all persons with disabilities were persons before the law but also recognizing that persons with disabilities enjoy legal capacity on an equal basis with others in all aspects of life,[5] enjoyed both the right to liberty[6] and the right to physical and mental integrity[7] and on an equal basis with others.

Thomas Kuhn in his seminal work on paradigm shifts[8] informed how a new paradigm does not evolve from the old, rather it is born by breaking free from the old. This conceptual severance then requires its practitioners. Consequently, a new paradigm needs to create its own institutions, discourse, and acolytes; it cannot make do with those of the old.[9] Such an effort, Kuhn contends, is doomed to failure. Kuhn has his share of adherents and critics,[10] a tug of war in which I do not wish to join in this piece. Instead I rely on Kuhn to hypothesize that the CRPD can be implemented in letter and spirit only by severing all connection with the old paradigm of paternalism, protection, and support. To test this hypothesis, I draw on the methods of comparative law.

This preference needs further operationalization as there is more than one way of doing comparative law. Thus, Abel[11] is of the view that every enterprise of comparison must be driven by a purpose. Without such a purpose, the entire exercise he contends is no more than collecting different kinds of wares and putting them on display, for admiration or purchase. Abel's functional perspective towards comparative law is not universally shared. Several comparatists are of the view that comparative law contributes towards normative fecundity by providing evidence-based information on another way of doing things.[12] It has been often found that the existence of a live example in any part of the world, not only strengthens law reformers in their resolve to usher change, but also enhances people's acceptance of the reform.[13]

Whilst having an intellectual empathy with Abel's position, I do not agree with his absolute dismissal of the aggregative mode of doing comparative law. The objective of the research should determine which method is better suited. Thus, for example any virgin law making enterprise should find the second method of doing comparative law more helpful, as it brings to the aid of the lawmaker all existing ways of regulating an issue, a field, and an area. The first method of doing comparative law may be more beneficial, when the focus is on a particular issue or field, and how the problems emanating from it have been dealt elsewhere. Such an enquiry could yield data on the pervasiveness of a problem, the commonness in suggested solutions, and the reasons for success or failure. Insofar as this paper is concerned with devising strategies to maximize acceptance and diminishing dissent, Abel's method of focused study is more suitable for this piece.

Making CRPD a reality I believe requires two kinds of initiatives, one whereby there is widespread dissemination of the norms created by the Convention and the other where the opposition is converted, destroyed, or neutralized. Just as dissemination of the convention cannot happen without knowing it, its opposition cannot be won over without understanding it. This paper aims to engage with the ideas in opposition to the CRPD to assess, contrary to the Kuhnian contention, if it is possible to find a meeting ground. If such a compromise is not possible, then what steps need to be taken to make the CRPD the prevailing paradigm on disability rights?

After the adoption of the CRPD by the UN and its signature by member states the Convention came into force in May 2008, when a significantly larger number than the 20 specified in Article 45, ratified the Convention. Once the procedure for finalizing a Convention has been completed the product is binding international law. The fact of its formal adoption may be sufficient reason to undertake a study on how to make CRPD the ruling paradigm for disability human rights. Without in any way lessening the significance of formal procedures, and the legitimacy they confer on a legal instrument, there are other reasons for privileging CRPD in the disability human rights discourse.

The CRPD was drafted with the active involvement of persons with disabilities and their representative organizations. In any conversation on the rights of persons with disabilities, the primary voice has to be that of persons with disabilities. There have been claims[14] made in the name of professionals and family members by the authors of the *Lancet* personal opinion, who believed that legal text on the rights of persons with disabilities could not be settled except in the presence of their doctors and families. The authors have conflated legal and personal space. When families and doctors occupy personal space without the force of law, they do it through persuasion and affection. If these persuasive interactions cross the limits then the persons with disabilities can always access the law. However, if the families and medical professionals are ensconced in this space, by the force of law, then persons with disabilities have no escape from such protection. Without denying the reality of all-pervasive human vulnerability, I think coerced protection is oppressive and infantilizing. Insofar as a long-silenced community is asserting its right to live life on its terms, and there is enough text in the CRPD, which protects that space, I would like to carry out this exercise to find ways and means to protect this hard-won legal space. No law can really control the illegitimate exercise of power except to say, it is illegal. This determination of illegality is the only real protection that the law can provide to persons with disabilities and for this protection to be effective, it is necessary that any other has that space through personal persuasion alone and not by the force of law.

Since the purpose of this comparative study is to prevent persons with disabilities from being ambushed by arguments from forces which are not on board with regard to the CRPD, this paper shall firstly identify the spaces that need to be watched, then critically analyze the anti-CRPD arguments emanating from these spaces and lastly deliberate on possible strategies to diffuse the opposition.

II Sites of Opposition

II.1 Jurisprudence of Disability Soft Law

If the genealogy of positions is to be understood, then there is a need to understand how the question of disability rights was understood prior to the CRPD. This needs to be done to see which way of doing things continues to retain hold over the minds of people even when overtaken by the letter of the law. For all those who do not embrace the new letter the earlier book continues to occupy the mind. The preamble to the CRPD referred to all soft law instruments except the principles for the treatment of persons with mental illness (MI principles). The omission of the MI principles was deliberately done in order to signify the psychosocial community's disapproval of the principles. Non-inclusion was aimed to delegitimize the principles and support the Vancouver Resolution of the World Network of Users and Survivors of Psychiatry, which had condemned the principles because it endorsed forced treatment and partial legal capacity to persons with psychosocial disability. This condemnation notwithstanding the MI principles are the bulwark of every psychiatrist intervention in disability be it the Lancet Personal Opinion[15] or the Indian Mental Healthcare Act of 2017.[16]

The UN Enable in its Saga of the first 50 years chronologically puts down every major conceptual, legal, or programmatic intervention undertaken by the UN which has impacted on disabled persons. Whilst some of these programmatic initiatives fell by the wayside others have continued to exercise influence. The UN began its engagement with disability by needing to address the mass production of impairments by the Wars. At this juncture, the world body concentrated on rehabilitation and primarily addressed the needs of the blind and persons with physical handicap.[17] Insofar as disability was perceived in medical terms the WHO constructed triad of impairment, disability, and handicap was employed. The deficient faculty being the impairment, the inability to do the function which is ordinarily performed by the faculty being the disability, and the manner in which society treated the individual being the handicap.[18] From the 1960s, the UN shifted its attention from the impairment-centric perspective towards disability and started to pay attention to societal obstacles to the rehabilitation of persons with disabilities. From this point onwards, there was an understanding of the social model and how social attitudes produce discrimination.[19] It is of interest that the Enable narrative describes the decade in which the Declaration on the Rights of Mentally Retarded Persons and the Rights of Disabled Persons 1975 as a move over from a social to a human rights model.[20]

II.1.1 Defining disability

Both Declarations need to be noted for the perspective they adopt towards the rights of persons with mental retardation and disabilities, respectively. The Declaration on the Rights of Mentally Retarded Persons 1971 does not define mental retardation but the use of the term 'mental retardation' itself speaks to the adoption of a deficits approach. A similar outlook is found in the definition of disabled person who is described to mean 'any person unable to ensure by himself or herself, wholly or partly, the necessities of a normal individual and/or social life, as a result of deficiency, either congenital or not, in his or her physical or mental capabilities'.[21]

The MI principles operated on the premise that there were biomedical standards, which when breached caused mental illness. Consequently, principle 4 most unequivocally stated that 'a determination that a person has a mental illness shall be made in accordance with internationally accepted medical standards'.[22] In order to uphold this scientific purity the principles prohibited any diagnosis to happen due to aberration from any cultural or social expectation, or arising from membership of a religious group. The principles by making such a declaration were evidently trying to answer to the labelling critique mounted against a diagnosis of mental illness to hold that social labelling[23] will not influence medical diagnosis. Since there are no diagnostic tests other than observation and social reporting by friends and family to arrive at a determination of mental illness, the principles seemed to be setting up a claim which they could not meet in fact but could still claim to have fulfilled.[24] Thus, from the standpoint of persons with disabilities, the principles trumped their individual perception with professional expertise.[25]

The Equalization Rules in contrast to the MI principles recognized how individual impairments, social attitudes, and environment cumulatively contributed to exclusion. The functional limitations emanating from impairments, it termed disability. And the loss of opportunity which occurred due to environmental barriers and social attitudes it termed handicap.[26] The Equalization Rules ensured that the individual impairments were not the exclusive focus of attention. Yet unlike the CRPD, they still continued with the parallel approach and did not perceive social barriers as causing disability. That link gets forged in the CRPD, as disability begins to be recognized as part of human diversity.

II.1.2 Concessional approach

The above narration shows that the soft law instruments largely adopted a deficits perspective towards persons with disability. Consequent to this approach, the rights of persons with disabilities were articulated in concessional terms. Rights as juristic concepts are intended to spell the non-negotiable, something which Henry Shue holds can be demanded without embarrassment or shame.[27] In contrast, the articulation of rights for persons with disabilities begins from the premise that they cannot get it all, so there is no question of seeking an equal basis with others. They should be given as much as will allow them to function to the maximum extent possible. The Equalization Rules with their idea of preconditions for equal participation do have an opportunity linked idea of equality. Even so, Rule 4 of the Equalization Rules states 'States should ensure the provision of rehabilitation services to persons with disabilities in order for them to reach and sustain their optimum level of independence and functioning'.[28] The problem with this articulation is that it starts with a presumption of limits. All persons be they disabled or non-disabled can only attempt anything to their optimum. It is an implied condition of all effort, in making it explicit, the Equalization Rules, which are the most progressive of all the soft law instruments fall in the trap of limiting achievement for persons with disabilities.

II.1.3 Fractured articulation of rights

Whilst elaborating on the paradigm shift effected by the CRPD at the start of this piece, I had expressly mentioned that the CRPD has revived interest in the indivisibility of rights. The soft law instruments, except the Equalization Rules to a limited extent, have primarily focused on socio-economic rights. The UN's 50-year narrative is replete with references to programmatic interventions which invested in the developmental agenda[29] to make for what policy makers considered a level playing field for persons with disabilities. In contrast to this heavy-duty invocation of socio-economic rights, there is a noticeable absence of civil political rights. The absence needs to be noted as it impacts upon the bargaining capacities of persons with disabilities. From their inception socio-economic rights have been controlled by the principle of progressive realization and limited by the availability of resources, which situates them in more negotiable space within the jurisprudence of rights. The negotiability inhering within the phrases 'available resources' and 'progressive realization' has been increasingly curtailed, in order to ensure a basic minimum, but it has not been legislated out.[30] This silence has been further accentuated by the fact that though the soft law instruments effect loss of liberty with procedures, such as compulsory institutionalization in the MI principles, and loss of autonomy with guardianship in the MR Declaration and the MI principles, in neither instrument was there an explicit recognition that these procedures rob persons with disabilities of their civil-political rights. Instead the procedures were presented as interventions required in the best interests of persons with disabilities.

This normative absence in the pre-CRPD soft instruments meant that these norms were largely absent in municipal legislations. A situation which the European Charter of Human Rights[31] only partly remedied, with its few and far between decisions recognizing the civil-political rights of persons with disabilities and more especially persons with psychosocial and intellectual disabilities. The CRPD Committee would have to largely reckon with a jurisprudence of silence as it starts to initiate an empowering global discourse on the civil-political rights of persons[32] with disabilities.

This short description on the pre-CRPD law-policy situation brings home that in this period state and civil society were doing things for persons with disabilities without asking them what they desired or required. Persons with disabilities were thus objects not the subjects of rights. As a consequence, there is an evident dissonance between the non-disabled world's perception and the self- perception of persons with disabilities. This cultural imperialism was not challenged by the soft international law norms before the CRPD. The CRPD issued this clarion call and the CRPD Treaty Body (as a subsequent section will show) is valiantly monitoring the process. This history of objectification could be a barrier to the realization of the new paradigm. It may need to be reclaimed as invisibilization and oppression and called out for its objectification. The UN Enable site narrates the 50 years history in a congratulatory tone, describing milestones reached. The narrative is only defensive about the prolonged affiliation to the medical model of disability; the fact that the objectifying approach also appropriated the voice of persons with disabilities finds no expression in this official exposition.

This history needs to be remembered because whilst it may be history in the normative annals of International law, it still constitutes the belief system of several people. It may still need to be considered whether because the norms have changed now the belief system has loosened its grip.

II.2 Disability in Other Human Rights Instruments

The central argument of the paper is that the implementation of the CRPD requires both the pushing of the CRPD paradigm and an understanding of the forces which could act against it. In the previous section the pre-CRPD soft instruments were studied to highlight how both the acknowledged and not recognized history[33] could have a bearing on the present day. In this section, I focus attention on the other human rights instruments and bodies who engage with questions of disability rights. This is a matter which potentially could give rise to disputes of jurisdiction that is if there is a difference of opinion between the various human rights bodies on a matter of disability rights, then which opinion would prevail. To undertake a comprehensive survey on the disability rights contributions of all human rights bodies is beyond the scope of this piece, which is aiming to compare the other human rights instruments and its bodies with the CRPD and the CRPD Treaty Body. In what follows this piece maps the inter se relationship between the other human rights instruments and bodies and the CRPD and the CRPD Treaty Body.

This mapping was attempted at first by classifying human rights instruments and bodies as pre- and post-CRPD. A sub-classification was then made between human rights instruments, which had a disability related provision in their founding text like the CRC and Instruments which did not have such a text but which expressed concern for persons with disabilities through general guidance documents such as General Comments. General Comment No. 5 of the Committee on Social Economic and Cultural Rights or the General Recommendation 18 of the Women's Committee could be cited as illustrations. Lastly, I intended to create a category of bodies that spoke in furtherance of the CRPD and those who held otherwise. To exemplify this approach, I intended to compare the initiatives of the Human Rights Council with those of the Human Rights Committee.

Upon substantive examination, however I found the classification artificial and forced, as it tended to squeeze reality into pre-determined categories and hence failed to capture instances of institutional learning by which the CRPD paradigm was starting to become the normative frame of reference, even if it was not driving the practice of disability rights. As this realization dawned on me, I decided to revisit my rigid classifying categories which slotted various authorities on the basis of their birthing documents to categorizing them according to their outlook towards the CRPD and disability rights. The new classification has this advantage that it is not frozen in time and allows the various human rights bodies to move from one attitudinal cluster to another. This movement can be illustrated by the manner in which the Venice Commission[34] approached the matter of voting rights of persons with intellectual and psychosocial disabilities. In its first articulation of the matter the Commission demonstrated the same mechanical approach which is routinely extended to persons with intellectual and psychological disabilities where a judicial pronouncement of incompetence was seen to take care of all prejudicial imputation.[35] When the Commission was faced up with advocacy, which demonstrated the prejudicial underpinnings of its position the Commission modified its position and issued a revised interpretative declaration on the matter.[36]

On the cumulative strength of the analysis made by other scholars and the opinions expressed by the concerned human rights bodies, I suggest the following analytical categories to map the attitudes of various human rights bodies towards disability rights.

II.2.1 Conservative ableism

In the first category, I would place those human rights bodies who in accord with the soft law instruments on disability rights, most notably the MI principles, believe that a total embargo on paternalistic substitutions and forced interventions was not possible. This view also buys into the medical model of looking at disability, which speaks of inherent individual deficits which no amount of reasonable accommodation or social structuring can fix. It is not possible to create a fully equal normative structure of rights for persons with disabilities. The gap between the disabled and non-disabled world can be lessened but not closed. I term this perspective 'Conservative Ableism' as it believes that persons with disabilities have to be measured by the tape of ableism and there is no inequity or unfairness in this course of action.

To illustrate this perspective I would point to the manner in which Human Rights Committee in General Comment 35[37] has addressed the matter of mental health laws and impairment based deprivation of liberty.[38] The Committee has emphasized on 'the harm inherent in any deprivation of liberty and also the particular harms that may result in situations of involuntary hospitalization' consequently asked for outdated mental health laws to be phased out and new ones enacted observing all fair process safeguards. The Committee asks for the deprivation to be an alternative of last resort which is to be used for the shortest possible time and subjected to periodic review. And in what it possibly sees as showing that the deprivation is not targeting persons with disability, the Committee states 'The existence of a disability shall not in itself justify a deprivation of liberty but rather any deprivation of liberty must be necessary and proportionate, for the purpose of protecting the individual in question from serious harm or preventing injury to others.' In the accompanying footnote the Committee refers to two of its own decisions under the optional protocol[39] its concluding observations whilst evaluating the report of the Russian Federation[40] and Article 14(b) of the CRPD.

The CRPD reference cannot be sustained as it is neither supported by the record of negotiations surrounding the CRPD nor by the jurisprudence of the CRPD Committee. During the negotiations of Article 14 of the CRPD there were several efforts to push text which prohibited deprivation of liberty 'solely by reason of disability' or 'by reason of disability only'.[41] This formulation was resisted primarily for the reasons put forth by the Human Rights Committee. The use of the adjectives 'solely' or 'only' permits the deprivation provided some additional criteria are added to disability. Insofar as dangerous conduct whether towards self or others does not result in deprivation of liberty the addition of the adjective in no way offsets the discrimination. It was with this background that the Ad Hoc Committee decided to opt for the present formulation that 'the existence of a disability shall in no case justify a deprivation of liberty.[42] This non-discriminatory text has guided the CRPD Committee in its deliberations where the Committee has repeatedly stated in its concluding observations that impairments whether actual or perceived can in no case be used to deprive persons with disabilities of their right to liberty.[43]

In the face of such explicit evidence, the human rights committee's insistence on its interpretation can only be understood within the frame of deeply embedded visceral prejudice which is beyond reason.

II.2.2 Gradual progressivism

In this category, I place those authorities who acknowledge the need for change but prefer a gradualist approach to a dramatic makeover. This approach I see as an ideational half way house where the need for change is acknowledged and baby steps taken to effect that change. Whether this would be a permanent occupation or a transitory space cannot be predicted, but in the examples I discuss, the concerned authorities seemed to have moved both ways.

The CRPD is a late entrant in the pantheon of human rights treaties; only the International Convention for the Protection of all Persons from Enforced Disappearance was adopted later. Except for the Convention on the Rights of the Child which expressly mentioned disability as a prohibited ground of discrimination and had a dedicated Article on Children with Disabilities, no other Convention expressly referred to disability. In 1995[44] the Committee on the Convention on Economic, Social, and Cultural Rights explained this omission being prompted by 'lack of awareness' in General Comment 5. It thereupon acknowledged the policy processes happening in the UN, particularly the World Programme of Action.

As the Comment largely drew from the Standard Rules, it stayed with the idea of equality and non-discrimination in drawing out the obligations of the State towards persons with disabilities. As was noted in the case of disability rights soft law, this Comment also largely concentrated on socio-economic rights. The right to work, social security, an adequate standard of living, and physical and mental health are largely in focus. There was budding concern for civil rights with the comment speaking of the right of persons with disabilities to marry and procreate. The Comment also spoke for the right to social participation. It had a cajoling tone and a frugal approach. Thus, whilst speaking of social participation, it required governments to 'inform and educate the general public about disability. In particular, measures must be taken to dispel prejudices or superstitious beliefs against persons with disabilities'

The Comment stated what is considered right but did not dwell on next steps. Thus, it says '(b)oth the sterilization of, and the performance of an abortion on, a woman with disabilities without her prior informed consent were serious violations of Article 10(2)'. Having made the statement, it said no more. And then in the social security section, it opines '(i)nstitutionalisation of persons with disabilities, unless rendered necessary for other reasons, cannot be regarded as an adequate substitute for the social security and income-support rights of such persons'. What are the circumstances in which institutionalization could become necessary was again not dwelled on.

The General Comment No. 5 was amongst the first major articulations on disability rights by a mainstream human rights body. This was an articulation which had not severed connection from paternalism and objectification. Thus, in section F whilst speaking of physical and mental health the Comment suddenly assumed a confident superior tone to advise 'such persons should be provided with rehabilitation services' which would enable them 'to reach and sustain their optimum level of independence and functioning'. Or when referring to the role of trade unions to strengthen the right to work, the Comment again asks the organizations to be regularly consulted by governments to be effective in 'the promotion and protection of [the] economic and social interests of such persons ....'

The Committee has moved forward from this more cautious outlook and adopted the CRPD approach of saying no to deprivation of liberty on grounds of disability. In the same spirit, it has also recommended the amendment of laws which permit the complete ouster or suspension of legal capacity.[45]

As already mentioned, the CRC contained a dedicated Article on children with disabilities. The General Comment on the Article was issued by the CRC Committee only after the CRPD was adopted. The Comment in the main is an effort to read in children with disabilities in all the Articles of the CRC. Or rather to require States to report on what they have done under each of the rights for children with disabilities. It was the absence of this reporting, which caused the Ad Hoc Committee negotiating the CRPD to opt for a twin-track approach whilst settling the CRPD text. In the CRPD children had both a dedicated Article and were included in all other Articles where programmatic or legal interventions were required for them. The CRPD twin tracking was both reinforcing and advancing the CRC approach. Now with the General Comment the CRC Committee[46] has inducted the twin-track approach into the CRC, which on balance seemed like a win-win approach.

In comparison to the right to participation of the CRC, the principle of evolving capacity of the child is more ensconced in the CRPD with age and disability related support. General Comment 9 did not seem to embrace evolving capacity to the same extent, which had possibilities of dissonance between CRC and CRPD. However, some of the more recent concluding observations issued by the CRC committee and the General Comment on the best interests principle making the child's right to participation an integral part of determining best interest, and copious cross-referencing to the CRPD whilst addressing the concerns of children with disabilities seems to be closing the distance.

Unlike CRC, the Convention for the Elimination of All Forms of Discrimination against Women (CEDAW) did not have a dedicated Article on women with disabilities. This was in accord with the decision then taken to evade the intersectionality question, and to address women in essentialist terms. The decision not to see the intersections between gender, caste, region, religion, disability, and sexual orientation cost the convention hard and the number of women who found that the pure woman identity thwarted all their other identities, which for some was higher value. The CEDAW Committee made a reparative gesture in 1991 when in General Recommendation 18 it asked State Parties to provide information on the measures taken for the inclusion for disabled women and to ensure that their rights to education, employment, health services, and social security were duly protected.[47]

The CRPD in comparison followed a twin-track approach even for women with disabilities. And intersectionality is writ large in the General Comment on Women and Girls issued by the CRPD Committee insofar as the CEDAW Committee is on to several collaborative ventures and has endorsed several positions adopted by the CRPD Committee. Thus, CEDAW has adopted the CRPD position on no deprivation of liberty on the basis of impairment and other similar standards. It has also advanced the CRPD agenda by asking for a prohibition of disability-based detention including involuntary hospitalization and coercive institutionalization, whilst also asking for a repeal of the related laws.[48] The CEDAW Committee has also extended its support to the principle of free and informed consent for all health interventions[49] whilst lending its support to the demand of full implementation of Article 12 of the CRPD.[50] It does look like that CEDAW Committee would be an ally in the CRPD Committee crusade for gender justice. It is also important to note that the Special Rapporteur on Violence Against Women has in her 2012 report especially addressed the concerns of women with disabilities.[51]

A partial acknowledgement of ground level difficulties comes to the fore in the Committee Against Torture (CAT) acknowledging that there were possibilities of misuse in compulsory mental health care. Despite such admission CAT only prohibits solitary confinement and forced hospitalization when not based on medical grounds,[52] which it evidently perceived as the most egregious form of abuse. On general mental health detentions, however, the Committee was content to seek stricter scrutiny and more rigorous procedure.

The movement need not necessarily go the progressive direction is shown by the alteration of positions by the Special Rapporteur on Torture, Cruel and Inhuman Treatment. Manfred Novack the former Special Rapporteur supported an absolute ban on impairment-based deprivation of liberty including when combined with other factors such as dangerousness to self or others.[53] The Current Special Rapporteur Juan E. Méndez on the other hand, allows for the use of compulsory institutionalization as an exceptional measure, in 'emergency cases' or 'to protect the safety of the person or of others.'[54]

II.2.3 Innovative reformism

In this last category, I include both the brains and the foot soldiers of the new paradigm. These are the authorities and people who totally believe in the new paradigm and who see their role as projecting the key principles of this paradigm into other ongoing work, and make the key activities performed under the paradigm of interest to others. Innovating new solutions and forging new artefacts would be a way of achieving the above objectives.

Since the CRPD treaty body and its interpretation is the constant with whom the operation of all others is compared, the treaty body is a candidate only to the extent that it presents a unified front. Fractured verdicts, internecine rivalries and a divided house or rather a failure to present themselves as a united house would rob the treaty body of its natural candidature in this category. Excluding the first two settling down years, the CRPD Treaty Body has proven equal to the task cut out for it by the CRPD. Generally, treaty bodies issue their first General Comments on the less disputed provisions of the treaty they are shepherding. The CRPD Treaty Body possibly to send out a clear signal that it did not intend to soft pedal on the disputed questions chose to issue its first General Comment, on one of the most disputed provision of the Convention. A decision, which along with its forthright jurisprudence on all Articles where the CRPD has effected a paradigm shift[55] has made the Treaty Body stand out especially as it has had to continually keep in view the expectations of the disability community from the Committee.[56]

The Human Rights Council, a 47-member inter-governmental body which succeeded the Human Rights Commission as the apex human rights monitoring body, became operational from June 2006. The Council has emerged as one of the leading supporters of the CRPD and the CRPD Treaty Body. Thus in 2008 the Council passed a Resolution urging all concerned to act in unison to advance the rights of persons with disabilities.[57] In similar spirit the council appointed the Rapporteur on Rights of Persons with disabilities.[58] Clause (f) of the Resolution establishing the position expressly required the rapporteur '(t)o work closely with the special procedures and other human rights mechanisms of the Human Rights Council, the treaty bodies, in particular the Committee on the Rights of Persons with Disabilities, and other relevant UN agencies, programmes and funds, including the United Nations Partnership to Promote the Rights of Persons with Disabilities and the Special Envoy of the Secretary-General on Disability and Accessibility, within their respective mandates, with a view to avoiding unnecessary duplication'. The Council has backed the CRPD Committee on its interpretation of the right to liberty. States are required to undergo the Universal Periodic Review with the Council where at one place their entire human rights record is assessed. The Human Rights Council and the CRPD Treaty Body being on the same page with regard to disability rights should aid the acceptance of the new paradigm.

With all its merits, the Human Rights Council is still at the end of the day a non-specialist body on disability rights. However, in establishing a disability mandate and appointing a Rapporteur on Rights of Persons with Disabilities the Council has chosen to be informed on the disability situation by an expert who has both the experience and the expertise. The Special Rapporteur's Report on Social Protection[59] brings home how a person possessed of experience and expertise can swerve a discussion away from polarities. Thus, she informs how the CRPD has moved 'beyond traditional disability-welfare considerations towards a complex equality model that highlights the interdependence and indivisibility of all human rights.'[60] She painstakingly explains why a trade-off should not be made between social security and employment, what are disability related extra costs, and how to build a robust social protection system. What is path-breaking in the Special Rapporteur's report is that she is not adapting the concepts of the non-disabled world to the world of people with disabilities. Instead, asserting that the universal values of freedom, equality, and dignity are as much the aspiration of the disabled Catalina Devandas is creating legal and social artefacts which would assist in the realization of those values for all persons with disabilities.

A similar ideational freshness can be seen in the concept papers arising out of the OHCHR. For example, Facundo Chavez Penillas' background note[61] on international standards on the right to liberty and security of persons with disabilities was compelling deliberation on a disability neutral construction of mens rea and criminal responsibility. The paper is drawing from existing jurisprudence to ask how it can be reshaped to ensure that persons with disabilities are either incarcerated over a lifetime or let off as non-responsible beings, neither situation being CRPD compatible. The paper is not the official position paper of the OHCHR and enjoys no billing within the UN system. The only reason I am referring to the paper is to highlight the importance of discourse to effect paradigm shifts.

The encounters recorded under the three kinds of approaches are largely self-explanatory. I only wish to draw attention to the fact that the greatest amount of action is happening under the second outlook where there is a constant swing from conservatism to progress to back again. With the enactment of the CRPD and the establishment of the CRPD Committee, persons with disabilities have the opportunity to influence disability rights discourse, and as the activities of the International Disability Alliance show, they need not even be sitting inside the UN to do so.

III Constructive Dialogue between States and Treaty Bodies

The obligation to implement the CRPD primarily resides with the States. This obligation arises in two intensities, one on signature and the other on ratification. The obligation to implement the Convention, to be accountable if there is dereliction, only arise after ratification. However, the duty not to undermine the Convention or to act contrary to its provisions arises from signature. Netherlands is the 166th country which has ratified the CRPD and the optional protocol has been ratified by 89 countries.[62] The UN Enable map shows that the largest number of countries are those which have both signed and ratified the Convention, the next are countries which have signed and ratified both the Convention and the Optional Protocol, then come countries which have signed both the Convention and the Protocol, next those who have signed the Convention and lastly those who have not even signed.[63] The above narrative and the map seem to show that the Convention enjoys wide formal support. How substantial is this formal support will only be known when I analyse the concluding observations issued by the CRPD treaty body. Also, the Map does not recount how many of the countries have ratified with reservations and interpretative declarations, which makes the accession a qualified one.[64]

Be that as it may, a ratifying country is required to submit an initial report wherein the state party puts down the status of disability rights in their country within two years of ratifying the Convention. The CRPD Treaty Body, after studying the report, frames a list of issues on which there is a constructive dialogue between the State and the treaty Body, subsequent to which the concluding observations are made. These concluding observations constitute the jurisprudence of the Convention as expounded by the treaty Body. This site provides evidence on how State parties s are engaging with the CRPD and the jurisprudence of the Committee. This engagement over the years will show whether the Treaty Body will be able to carry the States with it. At present, the initial reports just show how far States need to travel to cover the CRPD distance especially in relation to the Articles, I have singled out as constituting the core of the paradigm shift. The exchange between the State Parties and the Treaty Body shows not just the agreement and disagreement between the States and the Treaty Body but also when States seem to disagree with the Treaty Body, which body of opinion do they lean towards if not agree with.

In what follows I have examined the 40 country reports that had been evaluated by the CRPD Committee till its 15th Session which concluded on 21 April 2016 to assess the extent to which States are in real agreement with the CRPD paradigm. This evaluation is not being done in relation to all Articles but three Articles which are integral part of the paradigm shift and on which counter opinions exist. I have selected Articles 1, 12, and 14 for this last comparative exercise which sets up the CRPD paradigm against the Status Reports filed by State Parties.

III.1 Article 1: Persons with Disabilities

The move over from the medical to the human rights model was amongst the most significant changes brought by the Convention. Out of the 40 countries examined[65] as many as 17[66] were practicing the medical model. Out of these 17 countries 6[67] were also called out for using derogatory language to refer to persons with disabilities whereas 4[68] countries were only referred for the use of derogatory language. New Zealand had a peculiar problem where the Google search engine spouted hate speech each time autism of intellectual disability related search was conducted.[69] In addition Spain and Hungary[70] were found to have laws that did not include all persons with disabilities and Qatar was found to create too many special regimes.[71] There was general exhortation to nearly every country to create a human rights consonant disability law and policy.

The general impression one formed after reading all the concluding observations was that whilst some countries had definitely moved out of impairments centric stage, most if not all needed to make a comprehensive survey of their laws, the procedures of participation were found wanting in most countries, which again meant that the patron-supplicant outlook prevailed and States did not think they had anything to learn from persons with disabilities and their representative organizations.

III.2 Article 12: Right to Legal Capacity

Article 12 without exception recognized the legal capacity of all persons with disabilities in all aspects of life on an equal basis with others. This one provision invalidated all laws which disqualified persons with any kind of disability who were not allowed to exercise their rights. The Article also ousted guardianship and required States to make provision for support. The Article has reservations/declarations from seven countries,[72] each of which irrespective of the language used were trying to save the system of substituted decision-making in their country.

The Treaty Body whilst making its concluding observations[73] stated the substituted decision-making was not permitted by the CRPD and hence they need to change their laws accordingly. Countries which had laws restricting legal capacity in any manner were told that such deprivation was impermissible and hence they need to modify their laws. Australia reported that it had referred the matter to its Law Commission to inquire what changes they needed to make to obtain conformity with the CRPD. The Czech Republic spoke of its system of limited guardianship and New Zealand informed it was examining supported decision-making. The Committee noted the fact but the advice remained the same. The point is that not a single country got any commendation from the Committee for making an effort. Only Austria with 55,000 persons under guardianship, half of who under total guardianship, earned the Committee's approbation for running a pilot program on supported decision-making.

III.3 Article 14: Right to Liberty

As already discussed, the controversy under this Article is that whether liberty can be denied on the basis of impairment, whether solely or along with other factors. Mental health laws and impairment driven penal detention are under the radar. The Treaty Body has expressed its opinion unequivocally and as the previous section showed has obtained a fair degree from other bodies in the UN most notably the Human Rights Council. Yet when it comes to the States and their reports the Article 12 story replays. Every state reports the existence of a mental health law or some other compulsory procedure on the strength of which persons with impairments are deprived of their liberty. On the criminal law front, the power to detain persons with impairments for indefinite periods due to an incapacity to stand trial has been reported but there is no information on how many people have in fact been detained using this power.

IV Conclusion

This piece was started with the objective of determining the support and opposition available to the new paradigm of the CRPD. I had also stated that the inquiry would help determine whether the entrenchment of paradigm would require a Kuhnian strategy or can the existing operators of the system be persuaded. The Conclusion is meant to record findings and if deemed suitable to make suggestions

In this multi-tiered comparative study one normative system was set up against the other—the CRPD against the pre-CRPD. One set of authorities pitted against the other—the Human Rights Bodies vis-à-vis the CRPD Treaty Body. And lastly the constructive dialogue between the State Parties and the CRPD Treaty Body.

Each set of comparison brings home that the old paradigm, or at least parts of it, still has adherents. The analysis also shows that with continuous engagement and advocacy the new paradigm is starting to gain ground. Herein I would specially draw attention to the growing support for the new paradigm within the human rights bodies.

The new paradigm or at least its most progressive elements seemed to show the least traction in the constructive dialogue between the Treaty Body and the State Parties. Before drawing any final conclusions from the above referred data, it is necessary to note these were initial reports of the States, which were filed before the Treaty Body had issued General Comment No. 1 and expressed its authoritative view on the mandate of the Treaty. The present analysis shows resistance. It is premature to conclude from this initial resistance that State Parties are beyond the influence of the Committee.

In the traditional classification of human rights, the right to legal capacity and the right to liberty would be categorized as civil-political rights. This classification could also explain why the Committee was not willing to acknowledge any initial efforts made on legal capacity by some State Parties. As building alliances with States is also necessary for the new paradigm to strike root, the Committee could consider using formulations which distinguishes between totally recalcitrant states and states that are starting to make the first moves. The text of the formulation would need to be so drafted that it appreciates the forward moves whilst spelling out the distance the states have still to travel. Also, the forward moves of some states could be used to show up the cussedness of the recalcitrant states. A Committee would need to strategically use its power of appreciation and condemnation to win state allies for the new paradigm.

Even as there is a case to hold back on finding total imperviousness, the fact of resistance cannot be wished away. The unequivocal stance of the Committee needs to be strengthened by the International Disability Alliance and other civil society organization by highlighting the evils of forced interventions and guardianship in such manner that it captures popular imagination. Without such awareness raising the support structure required by the new paradigm will not come up.

After all, what is the opposition to the new paradigm? The opposition in my view is a belief system, and beliefs cannot be prised open by international human rights law alone. The beneficiaries of the new system would need to come to the fore and dismantle the old piece by piece. An exclusive reliance upon authority structures, even those which favour the new paradigm, may not be enough. If this truth is accepted, possibly the most major step of entrenching the new CRPD paradigm has been taken.

Notes and References

1. Amita Dhanda. 2006. 'Legal Capacity in the Disability Rights Convention: Stranglehold of the Past or Lodestar for the Future Symposium: The United Nations Convention on the Rights of Persons with Disabilities', *Syracuse Journal of International Law and Commerce*, vol. 34: 429.
2. Arlene S. Kanter, 2006. 'The Promise and Challenge of the United Nations Convention on the Rights of Persons with Disabilities Symposium: The United Nations Convention on the Rights of Persons with Disabilities: Introduction',

Syracuse Journal of International Law and Commerce, vol. 34: 287; Rosemary Kayess and Phillip French, 2008. 'Out of Darkness into Light—Introducing the Convention on the Rights of Persons with Disabilities', *Human Rights Law Review*, vol. 8: 1; Amita Dhanda, 2008. 'Constructing a New Human Rights Lexicon: Convention on the Rights of Persons with Disabilities', *Sur-International Journal on Human Rights*, vol. 8: 43.

3. Declaration on the Rights of Mentally Retarded Persons, UNGA Res 2856 (XXVI) (20 December 1971); Declaration on the Rights of Disabled Persons, UNGA Res 3447 (XXX) (9 December 1975); Standard Rules on the Equalization of Opportunities for Persons with Disabilities, UNGA Res 48/96 (20 December 1993).
4. Dhanda, 'Constructing a New Human Rights Lexicon'.
5. Convention on the Rights of Persons with Disabilities (adopted 24 January 2007, entered into force 3 May 2008) 2515 UNTS 3 (CRPD) Article 12.
6. Convention on the Rights of Persons with Disabilities (adopted 24 January 2007, entered into force 3 May 2008) 2515 UNTS 3 (CRPD) Article 14.
7. Convention on the Rights of Persons with Disabilities (adopted 24 January 2007, entered into force 3 May 2008) 2515 UNTS 3 (CRPD) Article 17.
8. Thomas S Kuhn, 2012. *The Structure of Scientific Revolutions: 50th Anniversary Edition.* Chicago: University of Chicago Press.
9. Patricia Bizzell, 1979. 'Thomas Kuhn, Scientism, and English Studies', *College English*, vol. 40: 764.
10. D.R. McNamara. 1979. 'Paradigm Lost: Thomas Kuhn and Educational Research', *British Educational Research Journal*, vol. 5: 167.
11. Richard L Abel. 1977. 'Comparative Law and Social Theory: Modern Islamic Law.' 26 *American Journal of Comparative Law*, p. 219.
12. Jonathan Hill, 1989. 'Comparative Law, Law Reform and Legal Theory Review Article', *Oxford Journal of Legal Studies*, vol. 9: 101.
13. Jacques Vanderlinden. 2015. 'An Introduction to Comparative Law Theory and Method', *Journal of Civil Law Studies*, vol. 8: 355.
14. Melvyn Colin Freeman and others. 2015. 'Reversing Hard Won Victories in the Name of Human Rights: A Critique of the General Comment on Article 12 of the UN Convention on the Rights of Persons with Disabilities', *The Lancet Psychiatry*, vol. 2: 844.
15. Melvyn Colin Freeman and others. 2015. 'Reversing Hard Won Victories in the Name of Human Rights: A Critique of the General Comment on Article 12 of the UN Convention on the Rights of Persons with Disabilities', *The Lancet Psychiatry*, vol. 2: 844.
16. http://egazette.nic.in/WriteReadData/2017/175248.pdf.
17. The United Nations and Disabled Persons—The First Fifty Years (UN Enable-First 50 Years), 'Chapter 1: Introduction', http://www.un.org/esa/socdev/enable/dis50y01.htm, accessed 30 August 2016.
18. UN Enable—First 50 Years, 'Chapter II: What Is a Disability?', http://www.un.org/esa/socdev/enable/dis50y10.htm, accessed 30 August 2016.

19. UN Enable—First 50 Years, 'Chapter IV: The Social Welfare Perspective: 1955–1970', http://www.un.org/esa/socdev/enable/dis50y30.htm, accessed 30 August 2016.
20. UN Enable—First 50 Years, 'Chapter V: A Human Rights Approach: The 1970s', http://www.un.org/esa/socdev/enable/dis50y40.htm, accessed 30 August 2016.
21. Declaration on the Rights of Disabled Persons, UNGA Res 3447 (XXX) (9 December 1975).
22. The Protection of Persons with Mental Illness and the Improvement of Mental Health Care, UNGA Res 46/119, 17 December 1991, UN Doc A/RES/46/119.
23. T. J. Scheff, 1974. 'The Labelling Theory of Mental Illness', *American Sociological Review*, vol. 39: 444.
24. Marvin D Krohn and Ronald L Akers. 1977. 'Alternative View of the Labelling versus Psychiatric Perspectives on Societal Reaction to Mental Illness Part I: Social Control and Deviance', *Social Forces*, vol 56: 341.
25. David P Farrington. 1977. 'The Effects of Public Labelling', *British Journal of Criminology*, vol. 17: 112.
26. Standard Rules on the Equalization of Opportunities for Persons with Disabilities (UN Enable- Standard Rules), 'Introduction', http://www.un.org/esa/socdev/enable/dissre01.htm, accessed 2 September 2016.
27. Henry Shue, 1996. *Basic Rights: Subsistence, Affluence, and U.S. Foreign Policy.* New Jersey: Princeton University Press.
28. UN Enable- Standard Rules, 'Preconditions', http://www.un.org/esa/socdev/enable/dissre03.htm, accessed 2 September 2016.
29. UN Enable—First 50 Years (n 20); Standard Rules on Equalization of Opportunities for Persons with Disabilities (n 4).
30. David Bilchitz, 2002. 'Giving Socio-Economic Rights Teeth: The Minimum Core and Its Importance Note', *South African Law Journal*, vol. 119: 484; David Bilchitz, 2003. 'Towards a Reasonable Approach to the Minimum Core: Laying the Foundations for Future Socio-Economic Rights Jurisprudence', *South African Journal on Human Rights*, vol. 19: 1.
31. Peter Blanck and Eilionóir Flynn, 2016. *Routledge Handbook of Disability Law and Human Rights.* Abingdon: Routledge; Eva Brems, 2013. *Diversity and European Human Rights: Rewriting Judgments of the ECHR.* Cambridge: Cambridge University Press.
32. Persons with intellectual and psychosocial disabilities have been routinely denied their right to legal capacity and right to liberty because the very presence of the impairment makes the individual dangerous or incompetent.
33. Here, I am yet again drawing attention to the fact that the MI principles is the only soft law instrument that does not find a mention in the preamble of the CRPD and yet every mental health legislation made even after the adoption of the CRPD continues to be influenced by the MI principles.
34. The European Commission for Democracy through Law, better known as the Venice Commission, is the Council of Europe's advisory body in constitutional matters. It also provides support to new democracies on how to set up rule of law consonant systems.

35. The Venice Commission's original text stated, 'No person with a disability can be excluded from the right to vote or to stand for election on the basis of her/his physical and/or mental disability unless the deprivation of the right to vote and to be elected is imposed by an individual decision of a court of law because of proven mental disability.'
36. The modified text rejects this approach, and now states that, 'Universal suffrage is a fundamental principle of the European Electoral Heritage. People with disabilities may not be discriminated against in this regard, in conformity with Article 29 of the Convention of the United Nations on the Rights of Persons with Disabilities and the case law of the European Court of Human Rights.'
37. UN Human Rights Committee (UNHRC). 2014, 'General Comment 35: Article 9 (Liberty and security of person)'. UN Doc CCPR/C/GC/35.
38. UN Human Rights Committee (UNHRC). 2014, 'General Comment 35: Article 9 (Liberty and security of person)'. UN Doc CCPR/C/GC/35. [19].
39. *BozenaFijalkowska v Poland* CCPR/C/84/D/1061/2002 UNHRC 26 July 2005 [8.3]; *Fardon v Australia* CCPR/C/98/D/1629/2007 UNHRC 10 May 2010 [7.3].
40. UNHRC. 24 November 2009. 'Concluding observations of the Human Rights Committee: Russian Federation'. UN Doc CCPR/C/RUS/CO/6[19].
41. Ad Hoc Committee, 'Third Session: Daily summary of discussions,' 26 May 2004; 'Fifth Session, Daily summary of discussions,' 26 January 2005; 'Fifth Session, Daily summary of discussions.' 27 January 2005.
42. CRPD art 14(1)(b).
43. See CRPD/C/TUN/CO/1, para. 25; CRPD/C/ESP/CO/1, para. 36; CRPD/C/PER/CO/1, para. 29; CRPD/C/HUN/CO/1, para. 28; CRPD/C/CHN/CO/1, para. 26; CRPD/C/PRY/CO/1, para. 36; CRPD/C/SLV/CO/1, para. 32; CRPD/C/AUT/CO/1, para. 30; CRPD/C/AUS/CO/1, para. 32; CRPD/C/SWE/CO/1, para. 36; CRPD/C/AZE/CO/1, para. 29; CRPD/C/NZL/CO/1, para. 30; CRPD/C/MEX/CO/1, para. 30; CRPD/C/KOR/CO/1, para. 26; CRPD/C/DNK/CO/1, para. 37; CRPD/C/BEL/CO/1, para. 26; CRPD/C/NZL/CO/1, para. 30; CRPD/C/TKM/CO/1, para. 30(a); CRPD/C/HRV/CO/1, para. 20; CRPD/C/COK/CO/1, para. 28(a); CRPD/C/UKR/CO/1, para. 31.
44. UN Committee on Economic, Social, and Cultural Rights (UNCESCR). 1994, 'Supplement to the Report on 10th and 11th Sessions', UN Doc E/1995/22(SUPP)/4760/E.
45. UNCESCR. 12 July 2011. 'Consideration of Reports Submitted by States Parties Under Articles 16 And 17 Of the Covenant', UN Doc E/C/MDA/CO/2, para 24.
46. United Nations Committee on Rights of the Child, 27 February 2007. 'General Comment No. 9' in 'Convention on Rights of the Child', UN Doc CRC/C/GC/9.
47. UNCEDAW. 1991. 'General Comment No. 18', in 'General Recommendations Adopted by the Committee on the Elimination of Discrimination against Women', UN Doc INT/CEDAW/GEC/4729.
48. UNCEDAW. 24 July 2014. 'Concluding Observations on The Combined Fourth and Fifth Periodic Reports of India'. UN Doc CEDAW/C/IND/4-5, para 37.

49. UNCEDAW. 29 October 2013. 'Concluding Observations on The Combined Fourth and Fifth Periodic Reports of The Republic Of Moldova'. UN Doc CEDAW/C/MDA/CO/4-5, para 38(d).
50. UNCEDAW. 29 October 2013. 'Concluding Observations on The Combined Fourth and Fifth Periodic Reports of The Republic Of Moldova'. UN Doc CEDAW/C/MDA/CO/4-5, para 38(d).
51. UNGA. 3 August 2012. 'Advancement of Women: Note by the Secretary-General'. UN Doc A/67/227.
52. United Nations Sub-Committee on Prevention of Torture (UNCAT). 7 June 2010. 'Report on the visit of the Subcommittee on Prevention of Torture and Other Cruel, Inhuman or Degrading Treatment or Punishment to the Republic of Paraguay'. UN Doc CAT/OP/PRY/1, para 219–24; UNCAT. 27 November 2013. 'Report of the visit of the Subcommittee on Prevention of Torture and Other Cruel, Inhuman or Degrading Treatment or Punishment to Argentina'. UN Doc CAT/OP/ARG/1, para 94–102; UNCAT. 28 February 2014. 'Report on the visit of the Subcommittee on Prevention of Torture and Other Cruel, Inhuman or Degrading Treatment or Punishment to Kyrgyzstan'. UN Doc CAT/OP/KGZ/1, para 111–20; UNCAT. 1 February 2016. 'Report on the visit made by the Subcommittee on Prevention of Torture and Other Cruel, Inhuman or Degrading Treatment or Punishment for the purpose of providing advisory assistance to the national preventive mechanism of the Republic of Malta'. UN Doc CAT/OP/MLT/1, para 68–9.
53. UNGA. 28 July 2008. 'Torture and Other Cruel, Inhuman or Degrading Treatment Or Punishment—Note by the Secretary-General'. UN Doc A/63/175, para 64.
54. UNHRC. 1 February 2013. 'Report of the Special Rapporteur on Torture and Other Cruel, Inhuman or Degrading Treatment or Punishment', UN Doc A/HRC/22/53, para 69.
55. This aspect of the Committee's work shall be examined in the next section.
56. Herein the work of the International Disability Alliance which is an alliance of eight global and five regional networks which represents a combine of over 1,100 organizations, http://www.internationaldisabilityalliance.org/, accessed 4 September 2016). The Alliance speaks of performing two kinds of roles: one to empower its membership to hold their national governments accountable and the second to advocate for disability rights with special focus on the CRPD. This Alliance along with other civil society organizations has kept the participative element alive in the operation of the CRPD as it continually inputs into each part of the monitoring process. http://www.internationaldisabilityalliance.org/what-we-do, accessed 4 September 2016.
57. UNHRC 'Human Rights of Persons with Disabilities' UN Doc A/HRC/RES/7/9.
58. UNHRC 'Special Rapporteur on The Rights Of Persons With Disabilities' UN Doc A/HRC/RES/26/20.
59. UNGA. 2015. 'Right of Persons with Disabilities: Note by the Secretary-General', UNGA A/70/297, 7 August, reissued on 2 October 2015.

60. UNGA, 'Right of Persons with Disabilities', para 22.
61. Prepared to facilitate discussion on the right to liberty and security of person at expert meeting on 14–15 September 2016, http://www.chrusp.org/home/resources, accessed 5 September 2016.
62. UN Enable, 'The Netherlands Ratifies CRPD (total: 166)', https://www.un.org/development/desa/disabilities/news/dspd/the-netherlands-ratifies-crpd-total-166.html, accessed 1 September 2016.
63. UN Enable, CRPD and Option Protocol Signatures and Ratifications', https://www.un.org/development/desa/disabilities/wp-content/uploads/sites/15/2016/05/crpdenablemap.png, accessed 1 September 2016.
64. All the same, it is important to ask which is preferable a forthright reservation or a routine undermining even if no reservation has been entered by the country.
65. Chile, Lithuania, Portugal, Serbia, Slovakia, Thailand, Uganda, Brazil, European Union, Gabon, Kenya, Mauritius, Qatar, Ukraine, Cook Islands, Croatia, Czech Republic, Dominican Republic, Germany, Mongolia, Turkmenistan, New Zealand, Denmark, Republic of Korea, Belgium, Ecuador, Mexico, Sweden, Azerbaijan, Costa Rica, Australia, Austria, El Salvador, Paraguay, Argentina, China, Hungary, Peru, Spain, and Tunisia.
66. (CRPD/C/CHL/CO/1); (CRPD/C/ LTU /CO/1); (CRPD/C/PRT /CO/1); (CRPD/C/SVK/CO/1); (CRPD/C/ UGA/CO/1); (CRPD/C/MUS /CO/1); (CRPD/C/UKR /CO/1); (CRPD/C/CZE /CO/1); (CRPD/C/ TKM /CO/1); (CRPD/C/ KOR /CO/1); (CRPD/C/BEL /CO/1); (CRPD/C/AZE /CO/1); (CRPD/C/ CRI /CO/1); (CRPD/C/ AUT/CO/1); (CRPD/C/CHI /CO/1); (CRPD/C/ HUN /CO/1); and (CRPD/C/PER /CO/1).
67. (CRPD/C/CHL/CO/1); (CRPD/C/ LTU /CO/1); (CRPD/C/MUS /CO/1); (CRPD/C/UKR /CO/1); (CRPD/C/AZE /CO/1); and (CRPD/C/ CRI /CO/1).
68. (CRPD/C/UGA /CO/1); (CRPD/C/DOM /CO/1); (CRPD/C/ MEX/CO/1); and (CRPD/C/PER /CO/1).
69. UNCRPD. 2014. 'Concluding Observations on the Initial Report of New Zealand', UN Doc CRPD/C/NZL /CO/1.
70. UNCRPD. 2012. 'Concluding Observations on The Initial Periodic Report of Hungary, Adopted by The Committee At Its Eighth Session', UN Doc CRPD/C/HUN /CO/1; UNCRPD. 2011. 'Concluding Observations of The Committee on The Rights Of Persons With Disabilities' UN Doc CRPD/C/ESP /CO/1.
71. UNCRPD. 2015. 'Concluding Observations on The Initial Report of Qatar', UN Doc CRPD/C/QAT /CO/1.
72. Convention on The Rights of Persons With Disabilities, Declarations and Reservations by Australia, Canada, Egypt, Estonia, Georgia, Kuwait, and Netherlands.
73. (CRPD/C/CHL/CO/1); (CRPD/C/ LTU /CO/1); (CRPD/C/PRT /CO/1); (CRPD/C/SVK/CO/1); (CRPD/C/ UGA/CO/1); (CRPD/C/MUS /CO/1); (CRPD/C/UKR /CO/1); (CRPD/C/CZE /CO/1); (CRPD/C/ TKM /CO/1); (CRPD/C/ KOR /CO/1); (CRPD/C/BEL /CO/1); (CRPD/C/AZE /CO/1); (CRPD/C/ CRI /CO/1); (CRPD/C/ AUT/CO/1); (CRPD/C/CHI /CO/1); (CRPD/C/ HUN /CO/1); and (CRPD/C/PER /CO/1).

15

Disability Rights at a Crossroads

Reflections on Evolution of Public Law of Physical and Mental Disability

*Sanjay Jain**

I Introduction

All the marginalized sections of the society, namely, sexual minorities, coloured people, Dalits, etc., constitute distinct fields of enquiry in public law. However, engagement of scholars to mainstream 'Disability rights jurisprudence' as a distinct field of public law is only episodic. The main objective of this chapter is to advance a claim for the recognition of a new category in public law, that is, Physical and Mental Disability. Here, the author wants to make the phenomenon of public law exclusion of persons with disability (PWDs) a structural issue. The claim of the author to seek inclusion of PWDs in the constitutionalism and recognition of physical and mental disability as one of the distinct fields of public law is also reinforced with the entry into force of the 'United Nations [UN] convention on rights of persons with disability 2006'[1] (UNCRPD). The Constitutions in absence of sensitivity to physical and mental disability as one of the markers of diversity, exacerbate the social alienation and isolation of persons with disability, thereby reducing their human worth and treating them as less dignified and second-class citizens.

One of the main reasons for the above exclusion and marginalization is an adherence to the medical model[2] of disability, that is, by locating disability in the bodies of individuals in the institutional design of a majority of the States Constitutions around the world. Overemphasis on the medical model does not merely shift the focus away from societal barriers reflected in socio-political-economic and cultural practices, that is, the social model[3] of disability; but it also reduces PWDs as mere straws and objects of charity. In juxtaposition to this phenomenon stands the overwhelming ratifications of UNCRPD, by as many as 166 States.[4] If the same were to be more than tokenistic than the translation of this extraordinary conduct of the States in their legal order in general and Constitutions in particular is a desideratum. One of the mandates of UNCRPD is to seek equal and dignified treatment for PWDs 'at equal basis with others', a principle constituting one of the vital pillars of its substratum. The conception of equality envisaged by UNCRPD is asymmetrical in that it does not espouse formal equality rather it champions the substantive equality embracing both values of 'equality of opportunities and equality of result'. This is a paradigm shift and for its attainment, recognition of physical and mental disability as one of 'protected characteristics' and part of 'fundamental choices of human life' in Constitutionalism is imperative.

Against this backdrop, the author has to grapple with several intriguing questions touching social policy, ethics, and public law; namely, why the ratification of UNCRPD has not been translated into institutional design by these civilized states? Whether the same is merely tokenistic or it imposes obligation on the State Parties to challenge and problematize the domination of ableism in public law? Is it justified to perpetuate second class citizenship for PWDs in the institutional design, in the light of broad mandate of UN charters Universal Declaration of Human Rights (UDHR),[5] International Covenant on civil and political rights, 1966 (ICCPR),[6] International Covenant on economic social and cultural rights (ICESCR)[7] and other allied UN instruments emphasizing on recognition, protection, and enforcement of the principle of human dignity?[8] Whether 'mere conferment of privileges through affirmative action' or the 'explicit conferment of rights coupled with adequate enforcement mechanism' is in line with the mandate of UNCRPD? Whether existing notion of equality is adequate or is there a necessity to evolve a more inclusive, empowering, and reconditioned notion of substantive equality to fine tune contemporary Public law with the letter and spirit of UNCRPD?

While addressing the above questions, the author would inter alia advocate for exposition of the notion of disability equality from the standpoint of hierarchy, domination, and disadvantage by drawing from the interactive dynamics and optics of liberty, dignity, solidarity, and fraternity.

In Section II having demonstrated the need and justification for recognition of physical and mental disability as a distinct field of public law, the author would strengthen the claim based on Exclusionary Constitutionalism by empirical evidence of Constitutional expulsion of PWDs from the constitutional texts around the world in Section III. In Section IV, the author would extend the empirical enquiry to comparison of the claim that the judiciary in India is more sensitive and far less ableist than its counterpart in the US. The comparison would mainly focus on cases bearing on disability equality and reasonable accommodation. The author has chosen US and India because these are the biggest democracies with an extensive jurisprudence of opposite trajectories and particularly courts in India have drawn on doctrine of reasonable accommodation. Section V is a brief excurses on conceptualization of disability equality. It would be argued that infusion of contemporary Constitutionalism as well as judicial review with the disability equality would pave way for a more egalitarian, tolerant, just and diverse society. The crux of the arguments advanced in this chapter is the emphasis on physical and mental disability as a legitimate difference and variation in the human body rather than as a deviation from the mainstream *Anthropos*.

II Towards Evolution of Public Law of Physical and Mental Disability

While celebrating the 25th anniversary of ADA, a leading Disability Rights Activist Prof. Michael E. Waterstone laments, 'the doctrinal resting place of disability constitutional law is a bad one—under *Cleburne*, government classifications on the basis of disability are only entitled to rational basis scrutiny. Lawyers in the disability rights movement know how to count to five and have reasoned that the Supreme Court is an inhospitable place for equality claims generally.'[9]

The story is not different in other parts of the world as well and more emphasis is still laid on overcoming disability rather than on the evolution of an enabling environment. Constitutionalism is still pessimistic and neutral about societal barriers and handicapping environment around the lives of PWDs. For the perpetuation of such a state of affairs, disability deficit in political theory and constitutionalism is predominantly responsible. The author therefore seeks to make out a strong case for recognition of physical and mental disability as a distinct field of public law. To set a proper tone for the discussion, the author would briefly analyse some poignant issues:

II.1 Why Disability Must Be Addressed in the Constitutions?

Societies consist of human beings and evidently, neither all human beings are similarly situated nor do they share same traits. Thus, we come across people of different races, sexes, speaking different languages, observing diverse cultures and religions, and so on. At *pari passu,* we observe variations in mental conditions and bodily state of the human beings. With the passage of time all the societies have evolved institution of law to regulate their social, political, economic, cultural, and legal relations among one another and with the State and one of the chief ends of law has been to nurture difference and foster respect for diversity in the society. It is therefore plausible to proceed on the assumption that law, as a public institution, must serve the interests of all human beings obviously including that of PWDs. An ideal constitution must recognize 'physical and mental disability' as one of the important markers of human diversity. The schema of conferment of rights and duties in the Constitution must take cognizance of PWDs and treat them at equal basis with others.

With the overwhelming adoption of UNCRPD by almost all entire world community, the idea that people with disability are active and equal citizens[10] along with others has gained currency as one of the vital human rights standards and must reflect in the Constitutions of all the States parties by default. The outmoded view that differences arising out of physical and mental disability reduce the worth of human beings, make them incapable socio-politically and unproductive economically, does not hold ethical and moral conviction any longer. Even medical science does not provide any credible evidence that physical or mental disability by itself creates obstacles in the enjoyment of meaningful life by PWDs. It is high time therefore to abandon the deeply problematic constitutional stance of socio-political and economic exclusion of PWDs reflected in the constitutions of majority of the States. A constitution being a moral, political, and legal document must reflect the ideals of assimilation and inclusion of differences. Constitutional fostering of respect for differences helps in building an accommodative, tolerant, and inclusive society.[11] The time is ripe therefore to do away with loaded epithets like capacity, inability, mental and physical defects, etc., and adopt a more humane and enabling vocabulary to write the texts of the constitution.[12] Finally, constitution, being basic law of the land, anything expressed therein is not subject to constant change and constitutional assertions denote the principled approach of the State towards a particular issue. Long neglect of PWDs by society is an earnest issue worthy of constitutional decision and does not deserve to be left to the vagaries of partisan politics in the legislative realm. The same would also put the notion of moral reading of the Constitution in the best light.

II.2 Exclusionary Constitutionalism

With the growing movement to attach respect for differences and diversity, the much-neglected social group of PWDs began to receive some consideration in international fora with the commemoration of the International Year of Empowerment of PWDs 1981. It reached its zenith in 2006 with the adoption of UNCRPD, attracting unprecedented and overwhelming response from almost all the states. Against this backdrop, the question arises, has the International action left any significant mark on the Constitutions of member states to UNCRPD? Barring few exceptions,[13] the answer to the question is a firm 'NO'. The states still predominantly conform to the age-old idea of 'exclusion of PWDs' from the sphere of public law. The author terms this phenomenon as hegemony of ableism.

Broadly speaking, constitutionalism is a rich vein for philosophical inquiry and grapples with seminal political and philosophical questions underlying the formation of constitutions.[14] However, a vital question—should constitutions assume a particular notion of human person by assigning priority to some sections of human beings over others in the allocation of 'rights, resources, and public goods of the State', has scarcely received any serious philosophical or political considerations.[15] It is a serious philosophical deficit.

Exclusionary constitutionalism may be defined as degradation of some human beings by demeaning physical and mental variations in their bodies and isolating and alienating them from the processes of social, political, philosophical, cultural, and economic arrangements of a society. To mention some of its prominent features: (a) political exclusion of PWDs by denying them the exercise of political rights, (b) use of derogatory and humiliating language to describe physical and mental disability and PWDs by deployment of words like handicapped, physical, and mental defects, etc., (c) translating the physical and mental variations in the body as markers of incapacity, inability, incompetence, lack of productivity, human tragedy, and misfortune, (d) employing compassion, sympathy, and charity as constitutional strategies to give expressions to address PWDs and to treat physical and mental disabilities, (e) segregation of PWDs as 'a special category' worthy of exceptional treatment, (f) subjecting measures of welfare, empowerment, and even in some cases conferment of rights and their enjoyment by the PWDs to the availability of resources and, and (g) not recognizing equal status and share of PWDs over rights, resources, and public goods of State by assigning priority to the able-bodied.

In short, the raison d être of 'exclusionary constitutionalism' is to advocate the idea that physical and mental disability reduces human worth; PWDs do not fit into the notion of 'personhood' worthy of participants in the formation of constitution, and deserve less or for that matter no attention during the formation of the constitution, thereby perpetuating the 'disabling State' and blunting an overwhelming ratification of UNCRPD by the state parties.

The author would call for evolution of an inclusive theory of distributive justice and problematization of the medical based view of disability espoused by liberal philosophers like John Rawls, Ronald Dworkin, etc. 'They all treat impairments as deficiencies in the individual's capacity to convert external resources into well-being or to press external resources into the service of their chosen ends. Like expensive tastes or vaulting ambitions, impairments result in frustration and unhappiness, but because unlike most tastes and ambitions, they are involuntary, a just society must somehow compensate for the shortfall in the wellbeing that they produce'[16] Professor Anita Silver has contested this view vigorously, Characterizing PWDs as 'outliers'[17] because of their traits that make them significantly different from the 'normal' or 'typical' person, she has tried 'to develop an account that gives due consideration to people not thought to fit the models of the person presupposed by dominant moral and political theories'.[18] She views justice as a matter of engendering trust amongst people with varied characteristics, with emphasis on promotion of equal opportunity and human flourishing.[19] Similarly, the capability approach, pioneered by Amartya Sen and further developed in the context of disability by Martha Nussbaum, in particular, has made important in-roads in re-visioning a theory of social justice that takes disability seriously.[20] Constitutional designers have to redouble such efforts to dispense with devaluation of disability in the mainstream public law.

II.3 Social Vis-à-Vis Physical and Mental Disability

The author observes a strange paradox in contemporary constitutionalism in respect of diametrically opposite treatment to the social disability in contradistinction with physical and mental disability by observing the principle of 'preference in ranks'. It is possible to argue that both these disabilities are by-products of difference and are socially constructed[21] and nurtured. Both the classes experience subordination because of the prevailing social hierarchy, though it is debatable whether its degree is the same in their cases. Thus, at the level of epistemology as well as on matter of experiencing subordination, these classes appear to be similarly situated. However, there are sharp divergences in their status at the level of treatment in the constitutions in terms of significance to be attached to difference. Differences arising out of physical and mental disability, have not been thought to be worthy of being taken into account in the constitutions going right till the twentieth century. The author speculates in contending that non-representation or lack of representation of PWDs in the constitution-making processes in particular and political processes in general, in combination with the then existing standards, principles, and doctrines of law might have compounded such a remarkable exclusion of a truly marginalized section of society. The same may also be attributed to a historical accident. The idea that PWDs are 'less eligible'[22], either because of their physical incapability or mental inaptitude has also probably contributed to their exclusion from the canvass of constitutional consciousness. Differences arising out of physical and mental disability are perceived to be biological, physiological, anatomical, and psychiatric disorders, worthy of different, specific, special, clinical, paternalistic, and compassionate treatment. Even social reformers and extra-ordinarily talented philosophers join forces with the political establishment for maintaining this contingency unabashedly. The same is perceived to be neither a social menace nor necessary evil. Along with the same, religious doctrine that physical and mental disability is an outcome of misfortune, sin, or bad deeds (karma) in past births has further aggravated the ostracism of even virtual image of PWDs from the social consciousness.[23] Only in the last ten years of the twentieth century, the movement of giving constitutional expression to the human rights of PWDs and acknowledgment of their legal capacity as equal citizens has got some momentum.

On the other hand, social disability, be it owing to racial discrimination or caste discrimination or for that matter even sex discrimination, has received space in all the constitutions albeit with variations. Why? There may be a number of reasons for the same; firstly, the constitutional cognizance of social disability was imperative due to the political representation to this class. Similarly, exclusion of people on the ground of social disability is also combated for being in conflict with the ideal of human dignity, one of the bedrock principles of constitutionalism. In order to be politically correct, discrimination against citizens on the grounds of race, caste, and for that matter sex is more or less completely prohibited in all the constitutions. Its practice is viewed and perceived as anachronistic and a social evil worthy of complete abandonment and renunciation. Social disabilities have been characterized and recognized as special minorities worthy of conferment of special rights and protection.

Thus, unlike the classes of physical and mental disability, the classes of social disability have assumed sociopolitical and constitutional identity, a factor which has kept former polls apart from latter in terms of appropriation and assumption of political and constitutional space[24]. At the cost of reputation, the author emphasizes that in absence of an identity, the persons with physical and mental disability in the past as well as to a large extent even in the present are looked upon merely as the objects of charity/mercy or as victims of tragedy. To remedy this unjust state of affairs, it is imperative to recognize physical and mental disability as distinct branches of public law.

II.4 Disability-based Discrimination

There is also a fair amount of controversy whether to treat disability based discrimination at par with other prohibited grounds. According to a radical view, also advocated by critical disability studies scholars [25] till it becomes an accepted norm that disability prevention measures are to be the part of disability based discrimination as much as discrimination faced by PWDs due to denial of jobs or educational facilities, etc., the same would not have completed full circle.[26] On the other hand, there are others including parents, doctors, inter-actionalists,[27] and policy makers who take the position that 'Moral view'[28] taking precautionary measures like medication or immunization programmes to prevent disability can not necessarily be perceived as immoral and anti-disabilist because (a) to the extent these measures cover prenatal care are anterior to the birth of a human being[29]; (b) even post-birth immunization against certain impairments may not necessarily be unethical or immoral, lest it is coercive in nature[30], and (c) some impairments/ diseases may not only aggravate the health problems of PWDs but may also pose the risk of death[31]: and therefore clinical interventions are justified to promote the public policy consideration involving rights to life and human dignity. As a matter of fact, most constitutions around the world confine the scope of the disability-based discrimination regime to the post-natal physical and mental disabilities and impairments.[32] It is beyond the scope of this chapter to expand this debate any further; however, the author suggests that a special care must be taken to avoid dramatic visuals of post-disability situations in the disability prevention campaigns and programmes, so as not to unwittingly demonize PWDs being abnormal and thereby perpetuating the medical model of disability, contested and combated by disability rights movement. The author advocates the idea articulated in the UNCRPD that disability is an evolving concept and call for the adoption of the flexible stance relative to the particular disability.[33]

II.5 Is Affirmative Action Non-discrimination?

Equally it is vital to note that neither the soft lords nor the affirmative action can be perceived as equivalent to right to equal respect and concern.

Affirmative action depicts state as a offeror and PWDs as offerees, whereas, vis-à-vis ABLE BODIED persons, even the constitutional powers of the state are entrenched in respect of their fundamental freedoms and human rights. However, PWDs' entitlements depend on the discretionary powers of the state. After all, affirmative action is privilege-based and a by-product of enabling powers vested in states. This regime which is followed routinely by the states in their constitutional design is not in consonance with Article 5 of UNCRPD which inter alia lays down '1. States Parties recognize that all persons are equal before and under the law and are entitled without any discrimination to the equal protection and equal benefit of the law .... In order to promote equality and eliminate discrimination, States Parties shall take all appropriate steps to ensure that reasonable accommodation is provided ....'[34] This constitutionally unjust dichotomy therefore needs to be seriously challenged and contested from the lens of ableism and for the same evolution of public law of physical and mental disability is an imperative.

To strengthen this argument, the author backs it with empirical evidence by mapping the exclusion of persons with disabilities from the constitutions around the world in the next section.

III Mapping the Exclusion of Persons with Disabilities in the World Constitutionalism

The recognition of 'Disability' as one of the prohibited grounds of discrimination is not perceived to be an essential property of constitutionalism, if the provisions in most of the constitutions (both express and by implication) are any indication. There are very few constitutions, which have given positive expressions to the human rights of PWDs in an inclusive and empowering language. However, vis-à-vis mentally and intellectually disabled persons constitutional apathy continues unabated.[35]

The author characterizes this extraordinary exclusion of PWDs as phenomenon of hegemony of ableism,[36] or what M.J. Oliver very aptly labels as 'Politics of Disablement'.[37] The author opines that the exclusionary constitutionalism is the direct fall out of ableism and absence of emphasis on the principles of 'enabling environment' and 'human dignity' to provide appropriate and rightful space to PWDs in the frame of public law.

Keeping this perspective in mind, the vital issue how disability figures in the constitutions around the world or how constitutions echo the rights of PWDs has to be addressed. The author embarks upon this vital task with two objectives, namely, (a) to offer a narrative of extraordinary marginalization of PWDs on the constitutional canvas with the help of an ordinal framework and (b) evolution of critical doctrine of 'exclusionary constitutionalism' to expose disability deficit in contemporary Public Law standards. Neither the ordinal framework nor Critical Doctrine is scientifically accurate nor is it claimed that the twin framework can fully capture all the nuances of this rather complex subject matter; it is merely a pioneering effort to generate discussion.

To inquire and investigate the degree of sensitivity of the political institutions to physical and mental disability and PWDs, the author has undertaken an in-depth study of 195 constitutions around the world. To assess the provisions pertaining to PWDs, the framework of classification and degrees is evolved to categorize all these constitutions in two major types, namely, constitutions with and without disability inclusion provisions. The former is further subdivided into two categories constitutions with (a) direct[38] and (b) indirect disability inclusion provisions.[39] The latter is also subdivided into two types, constitutions with direct/categorical exclusion[40] of PWDs and with indirect or ambivalent exclusion.[41]

The degree of inclusion of PWDs has been assessed based on the number of provisions,[42] in a particular constitution addressing PWDs/physical and mental disability and for this purpose the Constitutions have been classified into three categories—constitutions with:

1. Marginal Disability Inclusion Provisions.[43]
2. Moderate Disability Inclusion Provisions.[44]
3. Profound Disability Inclusion Provisions.[45]

The study predominantly has employed the three variables, namely, (a) the language of the constitutions in articulating physical and mental disability/PWDs (reflecting inclusion or exclusion); (b) number of provisions in the constitutions for the same (reflecting the degree of inclusion or gravity of exclusion); and (c) adoption and ratification of UNCRPD (reflecting its impact on the constitutions). To the best of the knowledge of the author, this is the first study of its kind.[46] The author clarifies that the above framework is broad-based and some constitutions being marginal cases may not fit into the same. Neither the 'constitutional silence' nor the 'structural relationship' of provisions in the constitutions has been taken into account while undertaking the analysis. Similarly, many of the constitutions under analysis being English translations of the original, there may be some discrepancies. Furthermore, the jurisprudence evolved by the courts in this area has also not been analysed. Subject to these caveats, the author seeks indulgence of 'the Mainstream Academia'.

III.1 Major Findings

Out of 195 States, 37[47] (18.97 per cent) have constitutions with direct disability inclusion provisions. Amongst these, three States have constitutions with marginal disability inclusion provisions and the rest have constitutions with moderate disability inclusion provisions. None of the constitutions falling in this category have negative provisions. This however, does not demonstrate any significant impact of UNCRPD on these constitutions, because most of them had incorporated provisions prohibiting discrimination on the ground of disability prior to the adoption of UNCRPD. Of course, these constitutions indicate some awareness for disability rights jurisprudence.

43[48] (22.05 per cent) have constitutions with marginal disability inclusion provisions. However, even the marginal inclusion is watered down in the constitutions of 25 out of 43 States, that is, 58.13 per cent, as the same contain negative provisions;[49] 101 States[50] (51.79 per cent) have constitutions with moderate disability inclusion provisions. However, amongst these 58 states, that is, 57.42 per cent, have negative provisions; 92 states[51] (47.17 per cent) have constitutions with ambivalent disability exclusion provisions; 82 States[52] (42.05 per cent) have constitutions containing political exclusion provisions in respect of both physical and mental disability and out of these 82 States, 17 states have constitutions with indirect disability discrimination provisions, while 15 states contain direct disability discrimination provisions in their constitutions; whereas, 24.61 per cent, that is, 48 states have political exclusion provisions in respect of only persons with mental disability; whereas, 33 states[53] (16.92 per cent) even contain personal liberty exclusion provisions in respect of them in their constitutions, thereby further compounding the marginalization of this vulnerable social group. Curiously 4 states falling in this category have constitutions with direct disability inclusion provisions and 5 states have constitutions with indirect disability inclusion provisions.16 states (8.20 per cent) have constitutions expressly excluding even the mention of physical or mental disability/ PWDs in their texts.[54]

It is interesting to note that out of 195 States under study 166, that is, 85.12 per cent have ratified UNCRPD, while 89 States, that is, 45.64 per cent have ratified even the optional protocol [55] to UNCRPD. So far as merely signing of UNCRPD and its protocol is concerned, the figures are 160 and 92 respectively.[56] A close look into the reservations and declarations entered by various states reveals that mostly the states have entered reservations in respect of Article 12 dealing with legal capacity, whereas most of the states have assented to the letter and spirit of Article 5 or the notion of reasonable accommodation (hereinafter RA) unconditionally. In this light, the gravity of exclusion of persons with disability from constitutions is curious and a violation of Paragraph two[57] of Article 5 of UNCRPD by as many as 138 states by way of condoning disability-based discrimination in their constitutions is the most egregious violation of international law human rights standards. Thus, outwardly, it may appear that the community of nations have evolved a very strong regime of international legal standards to confer and recognize the 'personhood' of PWDs; however, if one looks at the legal systems inwardly, there seems to have been little change as the discriminatory provisions in the constitutions continue to dominate the world constitutional discourse unabated. This is a strange paradox and requires earnest attention from all human rights academics.

In the next section, the author further strengthens the case for revision of the ableist theory of justice by analysing judicial approaches in India and US.

IV Comparative Analysis of Judicial Approaches to Physical and Mental Disability in the US and India

In this section, the author would briefly compare the judicial approaches in the US and India vis-à-vis disability equality by focusing on the implementation and enforcement of the right of PWDs to avail RA. It will be demonstrated that the otherwise activist US Supreme Court has been subdued and legalistic in its approach in short contrast with the judiciary in India. The rationales for choosing the US for comparison with India on this aspect are manifold.

1. The Constitution of the US does not contain even a single explicit reference to physical and mental disability, whereas the Constitution of India does refer to the PWDs in a number of provisions,[58] though the emphasis is merely on affirmative action rather than on conferment of rights;
2. In the US the idea was first conceived to invoke the principle of RA to remedy disability inequality and jurisdictions all around the world, including the UN, have followed suit.
3. The text of Article 14 of the Indian Constitution and the jurisprudence evolved by the Judiciary in India has been under considerable influence of the 14th Amendment of US Constitution.
4. In the light of an inclusive and broad definition of State under Article 12 of Indian Constitution, and the evolving jurisprudence of Judiciary on the same, the scope of doctrine of State action is considerably wider in India as compared to US.
5. It is interesting to observe that Supreme Court of US has shown almost complete reluctance to imply principle of RA as a part of 14th Amendment; rather it has placed reliance on its statutory articulation

in Americans with Disability Act (ADA). On the other hand, the apex court and high courts in India have been almost categorical in recognizing the principle of RA for remedying disability inequality as a part of the open-ended principles of equality before law and equal protection of law enshrined in Article 14 of Indian Constitution, even if principle of RA is not explicitly mentioned in this article.

6. There is hardly any influence of UNCRPD on the jurisprudence in the USA in the sense that it has been scarcely alluded to by the courts there, whereas in India in many cases courts have copiously referred to UNCRPD to buttress and fructify the principle of RA as one of the integral elements of public law equality standards in India.

IV.1 Position in the US

It is alarming to find that a country championing human rights all the time does not espouse the cause of non-discrimination on the ground of physical and mental disability in its constitution. Rather judges of its apex court are not repentant about alluding to the oft-quoted uncharitable remarks by their erstwhile counterpart, 'Constitution is color blind'. As a matter of fact, the text of the US Constitution maintains stoic silence about physical and mental disability and does not regard classification of persons on the ground of physical and mental disability as 'suspect', thereby subjecting it to lowest threshold of judicial review, that is, rational basis standard.

Thus, this myopia of US Constitutionalism vis-à-vis physical and mental disability also echoes in the jurisprudence particularly of its apex court. A close look on RA jurisprudence in US demonstrates that Supreme Court has confined its application to federal administration and private sector, it has categorically refused its application in respect of the states. This goes to show that the US Supreme Court does not recognize the principle of RA as an inbuilt element of public law equality standards under 14th Amendment.[59] To elucidate this point fully the author would briefly discuss the decision of the US Supreme Court in *Board of trustees of the university of Alabama et al. v Garrett et al.*[60]

The question whether an individual with disability may sue a State for money damages in federal court by reason of the State's failure to comply with the provisions of Title I of the Americans with Disabilities Act of 1990 (ADA or Act) has been answered in the negative by the US Supreme Court in its landmark decision in *Garrett*. Respondent Patricia Garrett was a registered nurse employed as the Director of Nursing, OB/Gyn/Neonatal Services, for the University of Alabama in Birmingham Hospital. In 1994, she was diagnosed with breast cancer and subsequently underwent a lumpectomy, radiation treatment, and chemotherapy. Her treatments required her to take substantial leave from work. Upon returning to work in July 1995, she was informed by her supervisor that she would have to give up her Director's position. She then applied for and received a transfer to another, lower paying, position as a nurse manager. Aggrieved by the same, she filed a lawsuit seeking money damages against the State of Alabama under ADA. The State of Alabama moved the Federal District Court for summary judgment, claiming that the ADA exceeds Congress' authority to abrogate the State's 11th Amendment immunity.[61] The District Court agreed with petitioners. However, the above decision has been reversed by the Court of Appeals, which by relying on one of its earlier judgements, *Kimel*,[62] holds that the ADA validly abrogates the States' 11th Amendment immunity. Aggrieved by the same the petitioner, the State of Alabama moved the US Supreme Court in appeal.

Rehnquist CJ has delivered the opinion of the Court, in which O'Connor, Scalia, Kennedy, and Thomas, JJ. joined.[63] He holds that nonconsenting states are immune from such suits under the Eleventh Amendment[64] of the US Constitution. He reasons that classification on the ground of disability should be subjected to judicial review by applying neither the strict scrutiny standard nor intermediate standard as is purportingly suggested by Breyer J. in his dissenting opinion.[65] But by resorting to 'Rational basis review'. He elaborates, 'Under rational-basis review, where a group possesses "distinguishing characteristics relevant to interests the State has the authority to implement," a State's decision to act on the basis of those differences does not give rise to a constitutional violation.... Such a classification cannot run afoul of the Equal Protection Clause if there is a rational relationship between the disparity of treatment and some legitimate governmental purpose. Moreover, the State need not articulate its reasoning at the moment a particular decision is made. Rather, the burden is upon the challenging party to negative "any reasonably conceivable state of facts that could provide a rational basis for the classification."'[66]

Thus, virtually he reiterates the law laid down in *Cleburne*,[67] a case decided prior to the Vienna Declaration and Programme of Action on Human Rights 1993[68] in the instant case decided in 2001. This goes to show at one hand a complete lack of sensitivity to the international human rights law standards on rights of PWDs and on the other hand an overzealous attempt on his part to shift the focus away from constitutionalization of rights of PWDs under 14th Amendment. He federalizes the overarching congressional powers under Clauses 1 and 5 of 14th Amendment by giving primacy to the State immunity under 11th Amendment. His judgment also demonstrates the indulgence in ableism and the hierarchy of constitutional and statutory law. He observes,

'The result of *Cleburne* is that States are not required by the 14th Amendment to make special accommodations for the disabled, so long as their actions towards such individuals are rational. They could quite hard-headedly—and perhaps hardheartedly—hold to job-qualification requirements which do not make allowance for the disabled. If special accommodations for the disabled are to be required, they have to come from positive law and not through the Equal Protection Clause.'[69]

Finally, the Rehnquist C.J. opines that even if the legislative history of ADA could be interpreted to show a pattern of disability discrimination by the states, the ADA failed to abrogate the states' 11th Amendment immunity because the obligation to provide RA is not 'congruent and proportional.'[70] He states that the RA requirement of the ADA, designed to limit an employer's liability, still requires state employers to go beyond what is constitutionally required by rational basis scrutiny.[71] Under the RA standard, an employer can avoid liability by showing that the accommodation would pose an undue hardship on the operation of the business.[72] However, the majority takes the view that, even with the qualification of undue hardship standard, the RA principle is unconstitutional as it 'makes unlawful a range of alternate responses that would be reasonable but would fall short of imposing an "undue burden" upon the employer.'[73] The same leads Rehnquist CJ to hold that the ADA is not a valid abrogation of the states' 11th Amendment immunity.[74] He states that to uphold the ADA as applied to the states 'would allow Congress to rewrite the Fourteenth Amendment law laid down by this Court.'[75]

On the other hand, Kennedy J in his concurring opinion emphasizes that he agrees with the majority's finding only insofar as it holds that a private individual could not sue an unconsenting state for money damages in federal court. Whereas in his dissenting opinion Breyer J. laments that the majority opinion frustrated the very purpose of the 14th Amendment, that is, to expand the power of the federal government and to limit the power of the states. However, he does not unfortunately substantiates the same because in same breath he also holds that the standard may require a state employer to take measures that go beyond the mandates of the Equal Protection Clause.[76] Unfortunately however he justifies this expansion of congressional power under disability neutral standard, by observing, 'Of course, what is "reasonable" in the statutory sense and what is 'unreasonable' in the constitutional sense might differ. In other words, the requirement may exceed what is necessary to avoid a constitutional violation. But it is just that power—the power to require more than the minimum that § 5 grants to Congress, as this Court has repeatedly confirmed.'[77] This observation is somewhat at odds with his general finding that massive societal discrimination against disabled noted by Congress also implicates States.[78] In short, even the dissent fails in invocation of social model of disability as a substantive constitutional issue.

In *US v Georgia*[79] the interface of 14th Amendment of US Constitution and ADA has yet again surfaced with only difference that this time the claim for money damages is raised under Title II of ADA. The claim is brought by a prison inmate who is a paraplegic.

- He has alleged that the lack of accessible facilities rendered him unable to use the toilet and shower without assistance, which was often denied.
- On multiple occasions, he has injured himself in attempting to transfer from his wheelchair to the shower or toilet on his own, and,
- On several other occasions, he has been forced to sit in his own faeces and urine as prison officials have refused to assist him in cleaning up the waste.
- He has been denied physical therapy and medical treatment, and denied access to virtually all prison programs and services on account of his disability.

The US Supreme court unanimously reversed the confined judgement of the Court of Appeal based on *Garrett,* and holds that the above allegations go well beyond 8th Amendment and do amount to violations of Clause 1 of 14th Amendment and Section 12132[80] of ADA. Distinguishing the dicta in *Garrett,* the court observes that the instant case 'claims for money damages against the State under Title II were evidently based, at least in large part, on conduct that independently violated the provisions of § 1 of the 14th Amendment…' The court further adds 'While the Members of this Court have disagreed regarding the scope of Congress's "prophylactic" enforcement powers under § 5 of the 14th Amendment, no one doubts that § 5 grants Congress the power to "enforce the provisions" of the Amendment by creating private remedies against the States for *actual* violations of those provisions.' 'Section 5 authorizes Congress to create a cause of action through which the citizen may vindicate his Fourteenth Amendment rights.'[81]

IV.1.1 Analysis

The reasoning of the majority in *Garrett* clearly, demonstrates reluctance to sprinkle disability equality into 14th Amendment as an integral part of equal protection clause and precisely for this reason, there is an insistence on its part to impose obligation on the States to provide special accommodation under a positive law.[82] At the same time it finds the positive law enacted by Congress by way of ADA in excess of its legislative competence under Clause 5 of 14th Amendment vis-à-vis State's immunity under 11th Amendment. On the other hand, in *Georgia*, the Supreme Court has achieved a markedly different result not because of substantive doctrinal transformation but rather the court has been overwhelmed by the horrifying account of the atrocities faced by the vulnerable disabled prison inmate. Court is moved because of his victim image rather than by absence of application of reasonable accommodation. Moreover, *Georgia* has not been consistently followed by the lower courts.[83]

The reasoning is also problematic from the standpoint of epistemology. The above interpretation reflects the exclusionary constitutionalism and general law of non-discrimination is not expected to conform to disability equality, because the same is considered as the marker of abnormality rather than that of diversity.[84] It is submitted that irrespective of special law, the general law of non-discrimination necessitates the recognition of disability equality and therefore it constitutes the necessary though not sufficient condition for safeguarding the rights of PWDs.[85] Americans with disabilities stand on equal footing as citizens of US with their normal counter parts and therefore 14th Amendment *ex proprio vigore* has to embrace their right to be treated with equal respect and concern.[86] It is simply a constitutional rebuff to relegate them to the protection of a so-called positive law, despite the presence of an open ended 'equality regime'. The majority, by not recognizing disability as one of the markers of diversity, unduly obfuscates the mandate of the 14th Amendment merely as an able-bodied norm.[87]

The position of US Supreme Court vis-à-vis racial discrimination is strikingly different. The Court is not hesitant to combat the same by subjecting measures involving racial discrimination to the highest level of judicial review, that is, strict scrutiny review. For strengthening the same it even compromises the sensitivity on drop of a hat by asserting, 'Constitution is Colour Blind'.[88] From the perspective of UNCRPD its reasoning is tenuous as the court conflates affirmative action in reasonable accommodation, whereas, UNCRPD perceives RA as a part of the right to equality.[89]

IV.2 Position in India

Judiciary in India deserves lot of credit to incorporate disability-based discrimination as part of equality jurisprudence. It is almost a founding moment in the constitutionalism of India in the 'Ackermannian sense'.[90] By way of reverse reasoning Supreme Court has incorporated disability as one of the grounds of non-discrimination under Articles 15 and 16 of Constitution of India.[91] Of course, this incorporation has been further entrenched with India's ratification of UNCRPD.[92] However, when the post-UNCRPD decisions of the Supreme Court are examined, it is disappointing to observe any serious and consistent reverberations of the same. As a matter of fact, the pre-UNCRPD Supreme Court deserves more credit for delivering pathbreaking judgments simply in the light of the open textured language of Article 14 of Constitution of India. One of such cases is *National federation of Blind v UPSC.*[93]

The National Federation of Blind (NFB), which was established for vindication of rights of the visually challenged, filed a writ petition under Article 32 seeking a writ in the nature of mandamus directing the Union of India and the Union Public Service Commission (UPSC) to permit the blind candidates to compete for the Indian Administrative Service and the Allied Services. The petition also sought the direction to UPSC to provide them the facility of writing civil services examination either in Braille-script or with the help of a scribe. Prima facie the case manifested the demand of application of RA from NFB to UPSC.[94] This case provided the court a unique opportunity to evolve the contours of RA in India.

At any rate, the court did not explicitly ground the argument of the petitioner in any of the fundamental rights enshrined in Part III of Indian constitution. However, the court did not agree with the stand of UPSC that none of the identified posts suitable for the physically handicapped persons, and particularly for the blind, are not such which are required to be filled through competitive examination conducted by the Commission.[95] After going through the list of the posts identified as suitable for visually handicapped (blind and partially blind), the court observed, 'it is obvious that there are number of posts which are required to be filled through the civil services examination and other competitive examinations conducted by the Commission.'

However, the court frustrated the above creative reasoning by indulgence in ableism. 'We make it clear that once recruited to the lowest level of the service the visually handicapped persons shall not be entitled to claim promotion to the higher posts in the service irrespective of the physical requirements of the jobs. If in the hierarchy of promotional-posts it is found by the Government that a particular post is not suitable for the visually handicapped person he shall not have any right to claim the said post.'[96] Can this observation be justified on the ground that court was adopting a piecemeal approach in absence of any explicit constitutional or legislative mandate? One may answer the same in affirmative.

However, post the adoption of UNCRPD, Indian Supreme Court has transformed its approach by recognizing that section 33 of PWDs Act 1995 confers a substantive right to avail reservation in the public employment on persons with disability and this right is not dependent on identification of posts by the appropriate government under section 32 of the same Act.[97] By way of a huge leaf in the process of constitutionalization of human rights of PWDs, the SC has also recently extended the aforementioned right to even promotions.[98] Interestingly, although the court grounded the right to avail reservations for PWDs in Article 16(1), it was an opportunity missed so far as strengthening the discourse by invoking relevant provisions of UNCRPD including Articles 5[99] and 27.[100] Moreover, the court mired the reasoning by observing, 'The principle laid down in Indra Sawhney[101] is applicable only when the State seeks to give preferential treatment in the matter of employment under State to certain classes of citizens identified to be a backward class. Article 16(4) does not disable the State from providing differential treatment (reservations) to other classes of citizens Under Article 16(1) if they otherwise deserve such treatment.'[102] The critical question that to which other rubric than 'the backward class of citizens' PWDs belongs? is not answered by the court; nor the court has provided any criterion to distinguish between 'preferential' and 'differential treatment (reservations). Pertinently, Article 16 (1) does not use the phrase 'differential treatment'. It employs the phrase, 'equality of opportunities'.

Another important judgement having a bearing on the principle of RA was handed down by the Supreme Court in *Syed Bashir-ud-din Qadri v Nazir*[103]. In this case, inter alia the court grappled with the vital question Whether Principle of RA is incorporated in the provisions of Jammu and Kashmir Persons with Disabilities (Equal Opportunities, Protection of Rights and Full Participation) Act, 1998?

The court analysed the contours of Sections 22 and 31 of to answer the aforementioned question, by observing,

> Under the said Section, the Government and local authorities are required to formulate schemes for ensuring employment of persons with disabilities. … Chapter VI of the Act makes provision for affirmative action and Section 31 thereof provides as follows: 31. Aids and appliances to persons with disabilities. The Government shall by notification make schemes to provide aids and appliances to persons with disabilities.[104]

On the strength of this language, the court read the principle of RA in its spirit in the above provisions. The court observed, 'As submitted by Mr. Gonsalves, while a person suffering from cerebral palsy may not be able to write on a blackboard, an electronic external aid could be provided which could eliminate the need for drawing a diagram and the same could be substituted by a picture on a screen, which could be projected with minimum effort.'[105]

Emphasizing on mandatory observance of reservation provision under Section 22, the Court further observed, 'It is only to be expected that the movement of a person suffering from cerebral palsy would be jerky on account of locomotor disability and that his speech would be somewhat impaired, but despite the same, the Legislature thought it fit to provide for reservation of 1 per cent of the vacancies for such persons. So long as the same did not impede the person from discharging his duties efficiently'.[106] Going into the appraisal of the appellant by the committee the court observed, 'Coupled with the above is the fact that the results achieved by him in the different classes were extremely good....'

Taking strong exception to the insensitivity shown by the High Court, the Supreme Court almost adopted a reprimanding tone, by pointing out, ' It is unfortunate that in spite of the positive aspects of the appellant's functioning as Rehbar-e-Taleem and the clear and unambiguous object of the 1998 Act, the High Court adopted a view which was not compatible therewith. The High Court has dealt with the matter mechanically, without even referring to the 1998 Act or even the provisions of Sections 22 and 27 thereof. Instead, the High Court chose a rather unusual method in assessing the appellant's capacity to function as a teacher by calling him to appear before the Court and to respond to questions put to him. The High Court appeared to be insensitive to the fact that as a victim of cerebral palsy, the appellant suffered from a slight speech disability which must have worsened on account of nervousness when asked to appear before the Court to answer questions....'[107] Accordingly, attaching latitude to the decision of the first committee of the State, the Court ordered the State to reengage the appellant on the job.[108]

It appears that the court was in agreement with the argument advanced by Mr. Gonsalves on the strength of the US cases.[109] This is evident from the following passage; 'Several other decisions on the same lines were also supplied by Mr. Gonsalves which only repeated what had been said in Kathleen Borkowski's case.'[110]

However, the court left a number of poignant questions, whether the approach of US Supreme Court is regressive or progressive in the interpretation of RA obligation under title I? Was the court not unreflective when it put premium on US decisions, as a springboard for its reasoning? Unanswered. Besides it is submitted that the tone and tenor of the arguments advanced by the counsel for the appellant was way behind the contemporary international human rights standards, set forth in UNCRPD. He did not even refer to UNCRPD and failed to seek indulgence of the court of the fact that India has already ratified the same. He could have assisted the court to frame guidelines on doctrine of RA by using Vishaka[111] framework. In the light of the same, the author submits that it was yet another ad hoc decision displaying cavalier argumentation and incohesive reasoning. The judgement hardly has any impact on advancing rights discourse.

The decision of the Bombay High Court in *Ranjit Kumar Rajak v State Bank of India*[112]. is crucial because it extended the application of obligation to provide RA in public sector to medical conditions not covered by PWDs Act 1995. It grappled with the very important question whether hardships arising out of certain medical conditions not envisaged in the PWD Act 1995 can be remedied by constitutionalizing the principle of RA vis-à-vis such medical conditions? The court answered this question in affirmative and evolved the prototype of Vishaka, to fill the legislative vacuum in this area. The Court observed, 'When the person with Disabilities Act was enacted the, 2007 UN Protocol[113] (sic)[114] was non-existent. It is in that context we have to consider these other medical disabilities. For persons with HIV, the Supreme Court has provided for reasonable accommodation.'[115] Addressing the contention of the petitioner that in absence of obligation on the employer to provide reasonable accommodation, he would be rendered unfit to be employed, the court observed, '.. it will be for the employer to place material before this Court to show the undue hardship that will be occasioned. In the absence of any statutory provision for determining the undue hardship burden, once we hold that Article 21 is attracted then in the absence of legislation, it is open to the Court to lay down some guidelines in exercise of the powers of the Court under Article 226.'[116] The court regulated the right of an employer in public sector, that is, as a State or instrumentality within the meaning of Article 12 of the Constitution of India by subjecting it to provisions of Part III of the Constitution of India read with the Directive Principles of State Policy in Part IV, particularly Article 39(a), Article 41 and the Fundamental Duties along with international conventions on right to employment. Invoking the interaction of Articles 14,16, 21, and 51(A) (g), the court constitutionalized the right to work of persons with disabilities and to safeguard the same, incorporated the remedy of reasonable accommodation. The court observed 'A person who suffers from an ailment which medical treatment can cure and is otherwise fit to discharge the duties and responsibilities of the post to which he applies, cannot be denied the right to lead a productive life, to maintain himself and his family with dignity, and strive towards excellence as enshrined under Article 51A(g). ...A policy which unreasonably deprives a person of his right to work, (within the State's economic capacity) which is now judicially recognized as a part of right to life, would apart from being violative of Article 21, would also be violative of Articles 14 and 16(1). The consequences of upholding such a policy, if any, would be that persons who at one point of time suffered from an ailment will be denied employment in State institutions. If such a citizen is not entitled to be considered fit for consideration in public employment his chance of employment in the private sector would be nil. Do we as a State condemn all such citizens to be dependent on their families who may or may not be able to support them? Do we strip them of their dignity to life by denying them a chance to be considered for employment to live a full life? The theory of RA even in the absence of municipal law must, therefore, flow from our constitutional principle of the right to life and to live it with dignity.'[117]

The Rajasthan High Court placed reliance on the above decision of the Bombay HC in *Desh Deepak Dhamija v The Union Bank of India*[118] Noting that the facts of the instant case are almost identical to that of *Rajak* except that the petitioner in this case has not yet undergone renal transplantation, the court held, 'Thus, denial of the employment to a person suffering from renal disease specially when a person on account of some ailment, does not cease to be capable of performing the normal job functions and who does not pose any threat to the interests of other persons at the workplace during his normal activities cannot be justified. The physical disability as mentioned in the "The persons with Disabilities (Equal Opportunities, Protection of Rights and Full Participation) Act, 1995" although does not include the chronic disease, cannot be treated as prohibited or unlawful. It cannot be read to say that a person suffering from chronic disease like the renal failure cannot be granted job.... In the absence of any law, the action of State must be guided by the Directive Principles[119] which governs the legislative function of the State ....'[120]

Accordingly, the court directed the bank to allow the petitioner to join the services as Probationary Officer forthwith. A careful look on both these judgments gives rise to a very important question, Should the ratio of these judgments be read that principle of RA can be extended to medical conditions not covered by PWDs Act 1995 by grounding it in fundamental right to livelihood guaranteed by Article 21 of Constitution read with right to work guaranteed by Article 39 of Directive Principles of State Policy (DPSP)?

It is submitted that the answer to this question should be given in the affirmative. The high courts, to provide remedies to the people affected by medical conditions not covered by PWDs Act, have broken new ground of judicial review. It is remarkable how they have cemented the obligation to provide the RA through a number of provisions in Part III, IV, and IV-A of Indian Constitution to fill the legislative vacuum. The author contends that the reference to the UNCRPD by both these courts was unnecessary; they should have evolved the principle of RA by referring to academic writings and its invocation in non-disability context. Equally it is asymmetrical to assume that by ratifying UNCRPD, the legislature in India has expanded the definition of physical and mental disability.[121] It would amount to the arrogation of the legislative power by the judiciary to extend the scope of the definition of physical and mental disability given in UNCRPD to cover medical conditions[122] not mentioned in PWDs Act 1995. Judicial incorporation of diseases/impairments as a part of physical and mental disability has huge implications on matters like affirmative action by way of 4 per cent reservation in employment and 5 per cent reservation in higher education in recently introduced Rights of Persons with Disabilities Act 2016, tax exemption under Section 80U of Income Tax Act, etc. Moreover, such an extension would blur the distinction carefully drawn by the legislature between disabilities and medical disorders. Disabilities not only involve activity limitations but also are socially stigmatized. On the other hand, diseases and impairments strictly relate to the health issues and do not necessarily involve social stigma. Of course, we have borderline cases like AIDS, but solution does not lie in the opinion of the author in collapsing the distinction between the physical and mental disability and the ailments.

However, subject to the above qualifications, such decisions are a welcome progress in the sense that they are extending the application of principle of RA beyond the realm of disability. The judgements are also making progress to strengthen idea that if otherwise a person is qualified, merely because of some medical condition, her work capability and job ability should not be undermined. Of course, both Bombay and Rajasthan judgments appear to have laid down the procedure for application of RA by creatively using the precedent in the Vishaka case. In both these cases lawyers need appreciation for strengthening the rights discourse by raising creative argumentation.[123] In sharp contrast to the US Supreme Court, the judiciary in India has not sought the leaning on positive law to remedy disability discrimination. However, what is disappointing is its inconsistency. For example, Madras High Court in *Surendra Mohan v State of Tamilnadu*[124] dwarfed the scope of definition of disability by overruling the legislative mandate of PWDs Act. It stipulated that persons whose eyesight is between 40–50 per cent only are eligible for appointments as judge in the judiciary. In reaching this conclusion, the learned judge delivering the judgement referred to the difficulties faced by the blind person who had been appointed as a judge in the recent past in the state of TN.[125]

It is submitted that this judgment is extremely erroneous in many respects. Firstly, the learned judge indulges in the fallacy of simple conversion, that is, to draw sweeping generalizations from discrete facts. The legislation enacted by Parliament cannot be superseded in the guise of so called experience of high court in the appointment of visually challenged judges. This process of reasoning maybe characterized as 'institutional alter ego/official bias against person with disability'.

Secondly, the learned judge also overlooked two empowering judgements of the Bombay and Rajasthan High Courts. If the principle of RA can be extended to medical conditions not covered in PWDs Act 1995, what is the justification of its non-application to protect the rights of persons with disability covered by PWDs Act 1995? In fact, the Madras High Court unwittingly introduced the American notion of qualified disability and almost mimicked the US Supreme court[126] in contracting the scope of the definition of physical and mental disability.

Finally, the court has shown complete disregard and scant respect to the well-established presumption that domestic law must be read in the light of international law lest the former is explicitly inconsistent with the latter by giving a complete go by to the significant decision of the government of India of ratification of UNCRPD in 2007. In this connection, the author would draw attention to very vital observations of the apex court in one of its recent judgments.[127] Sikri J invoked Article 27 of Vienna Convention on Law of Treaties, 1963 and Biwako Millenium Framework, 2002 to uphold international law obligations by pointing out that in the guise of internal legislation, international law cannot be violated by India and constitutionalized the principle of RA. The Court awarded the compensation of Rs 1,000,000 to Ms Jeeja Ghosh, a severely disabled person against Jet Airways by invoking the Principle of Indirect Horizontality.[128] The author hopes that, Supreme Court would take the above position of law in account while deciding the Special Leave Appeal against this rather obnoxious judgment.[129]

A close look on the jurisprudence of both the jurisdictions demonstrates that in US more cases are brought by people with ailments in comparison to India, where people with severe physical and mental disability have often knocked on the doors of the Courts. Although this observation is not fully guarded but it definitely throws light on visibility of severely disabled persons in both these jurisdictions and without doubt Indian Supreme Court and High Courts have demonstrated extraordinary activism in absence of adequate constitutional and legal architecture in comparison with the Supreme Court of the US.

V Conceptualizing Disability Equality

Conceptualizing the notion of disability equality is contingent upon articulation of the phenomenon of 'disability inequality'. This is so because equality as a distinct and moral value cannot flourish by itself. Rather, it is parasitical on other moral values like alleviation of suffering, equitable and fair distribution of resources, human dignity, empathy, etc. The point is extremely well articulated by Prof. Scanlon. 'When I say that the idea of equality plays surprisingly little role in my thinking here, I have in mind an idea of substantive equality—that it is morally important that people's lives or fates should be equal in some substantive way: equal in income, for example, or in overall welfare. This is in contrast to a merely formal notion of equal consideration, as stated for example in the principle that the comparable claims of each person deserve equal respect and should be given equal weight.'[130] Drawing on the same, the author intends to conceptualize the notion of disability equality by reconfiguring the aforementioned moral values from the perspective of Disability Rights Jurisprudence.

This approach is also preferable because the principle of egalitarianism flourishes only when standards are prescribed for similar treatment; whereas, it is not possible to evolve such standards because the idea of similarly situated is loaded and value laden, it is not objectively verifiable. It is therefore argued that the idea of treating PWDs at equal basis with others running as a thread through the UNCRPD must be understood as a clarion call for elimination of inequalities rather than for the attainment of a nebulous notion of equality. As a result, the author pioneers his ambitious project in this chapter by enlisting the main inequalities to be dispensed with from the world constitutionalism. Put briefly, following are the main sources of disability inequality:

1. Overemphasis on Medical model and almost complete neglect of social model of physical and mental disability.
2. Perpetuation of preferential treatment to social disability over physical and mental disability; physical disability over mental disability; and moderate physical and mental disability over severe physical and mental disabilities.
3. Confusing diversity resulting from divergence in physical structure of human body with deviation, that is, misconstruing distinction between diversity and deviation.
4. Occupying the bodily differences as 'abnormal', byproduct of bad luck, and insist to treat the same with charity, sympathy and paternalism.
5. Perceiving PWDs as lesser human beings by demeaning their physical and mental disability.

6. Failure to observe diversity amongst various forms of physical and mental disability.
7. Collapsing the distinction between affirmative action and rights based approach.
8. Obfuscation of the idea of non-discrimination by objecting merely to affordable discrimination by way of reasonable accommodation.
9. Failure to notice social stigma attached to physical and mental disability.
10. Depersonalization and De-politicization of PWDs in the realm of law and politics.
11. Perpetuation of the ABLEIST notions of rationality and productivity.
12. Failure to observe the adverse impact of ableist language and culture on the lives of PWDs.

The author cautions that this is merely a rudimentary inventory of insubordination sources perpetuating disability inequality and requires fair amount of refinement. Evidently, the above formulation somewhat collapses into Exclusionary Constitutionalism. Having thus, informed the discourse from the sources of inequality, the author would make an attempt to conceptualize the notion of disability equality.

The contemporary notion of equality in order to inform itself about physical and mental disability and to be sensitive to the needs and aspirations of disabled persons has to traverse beyond the Aristotelian notions of 'equality before law and equal protection of law'. Both these notions operate in the frame of formal equality and envisage an institution of law which either ignores disability diversity or downplays the potential, personhood, capacity and productivity of disabled persons. It is important therefore to reconstruct and recondition these notions by explicit incorporation of outlawing of disability-based discrimination as one of the integral elements of rule of law, that is, to espouse a substantive and multidimensional model of equality.

Professor Sandra Fredman very aptly points out that substantive equality resists capture by a single principle, whether it be dignity, equality of results, or equality of opportunity. Rather 'it should be seen as a multi-dimensional concept, consisting of four overlapping aims: the redistributive dimension (to break the cycle of disadvantage associated with status or out-groups); the recognition dimension (to promote respect for the equal dignity and worth of all, thereby redressing stigma, stereotyping, humiliation, and violence); transformative dimension (to restructure, accommodate and positively affirm different identities while maintaining a community values) and the participative dimension (to facilitate full participation in society).'[131] To this, the author would add the fifth aim, that is, INCLUSIVE dimension, (adoption of Universal design so as to make the application of RA exceptional and to remove disabling socio-economic, political, legal, and cultural structures to foster respect for PWDs).

In this connection, a three-pronged paradigm shift for evolving disability equality advocated by Prof. Sandra Fredman is worth attention to infuse substantive equality and equality of result in contemporary constitutionalism in general and to evolve the jurisprudence in jurisdictions of US and India in particular. Firstly, in contradistinction with gender and racial discrimination law, disability equality law should be asymmetrical, that is, prohibition of discrimination only against disabled people must be emphasized rather than searching for any comparator. 'It thus aims, not at neutrality, but at redressing the disadvantage experienced by a specific group'.[132] Secondly, instead of focusing on 'principle of equality as sameness', emphasis must be to make the conduct unlawful resulting the subjection of a person to detriment on the ground of their disability.[133] Thirdly, 'recognition that equality requires more than sameness ... i.e. positive duty to promote equality, or the fourth-generation equality rights, allied to substantive equality'.[134]

For the resuscitation and reconditioning of the doctrine of equality and to make it disability sensitive, emphasis must also be laid on the value of respect. To put the point philosophically, principle of RA is an instrument of fostering 'recognition respect'; the point is more elaborately spelled out by Ian Carter, 'the status of a person as a moral agent is something 'to be reckoned with' in our practical deliberations. To say that it is something 'to be reckoned with' is to say that it is a particularly high status compared to those of the various other animate and inanimate objects that we encounter in living out our lives. That particularly high status is something that 'commands respect', in the same way as that in which an authority 'commands respect'. Indeed, to respect persons '*just is* to recognize a kind of authority that they bear'.[135]

There are two approaches to accord recognition respect to people with disability. The first approach,[136] defends the criteria of social justice distributing resources to people with disabilities for eliminating discrimination, not making up for so-called natural disadvantage. Whereas, the second approach which may be characterized as redistributive or compensatory, defends, the idea that 'resources for people with disabilities must sometimes be justified on the grounds that some natural endowments pose disadvantages even in societies that do not discriminate.'[137] It is submitted that both these approaches contain grain of truths.

It is imperative to advocate a paradigm shift from the principle of less eligibility based on the notion of rationality and the repeated focus must be on the constitutional virtue of human dignity. Constitutions must substitute state of exceptions with an inclusive and sensitive state in relation to PWDs and the notion of liberal citizen founded on normality and ableism must give way to the active social citizenship. Constitutions, in order to be inclusive, must underscore the urgent need of elimination of disabling environment and unreservedly embrace the ideals of full participation, political representation, and community-based rehabilitation of PWDs. To translate the above ideals, it is essential that contemporary constitutionalism moves away from the medical model towards the social model and from an exclusionary to an inclusive, assimilative, and accommodative institutional design.

VI Conclusion

The author has argued in this chapter for recognition of physical and mental disability as a distinct field of Public Law. It has been emphasized that elimination of inequality rather than the attainment of goal of equality is a right path. It has been established that exclusion of PWDs from the domain of Constitutionalism has led to their depersonalization. The author has also empirically established his claim of egregious exclusion of PWDs in the adjudication and actual Constitutional texts.

The cases discussed above shows that RA has been deployed in India for two purposes, as an expressive instrument to add rhetorical refurbish to the reasoning and also as a substantive mechanism. The latter approach is somewhat demonstrable in the decisions of Supreme Court in NFB case and Rajasthan High Court, whereas the former is manifested in the decision of SC in Syed Bashir. The discussion also establishes that analytical foundations of reasoning of the courts vis-à-vis RA are extremely shaky. From the standpoint of comparison, the author argues that under the influence of American Jurisprudence, both Supreme Court and High courts of India have invoked Principle of Reasonable Accommodation, and at the same time their reasoning is also influenced by UNCRPD. However, even a cursory research would suggest that narrow, pedantic, medical, and ableist approach of the US Supreme court jurisprudence is in deep tension with broad, inclusive, and social model framework of UNCRPD.

It must also be borne in mind that neither the counsels nor the Supreme Court and the High courts did consider the vital issue whether application of principle of RA in Public sector is in derogation to the mandate of Article 4(4) of UNCRPD laying down, 'There shall be no restriction upon or derogation from any of the human rights and fundamental freedoms recognized or existing in any State Party to the present Convention pursuant to law, conventions, regulation or custom on the pretext that the present Convention does not recognize such rights or freedoms or that it recognizes them to a lesser extent.'[138] In the light of Constitutional framework under Indian legal order, the author hypothesizes that the principle of RA fits more in addressing disability based discrimination in Private sector than the Public sector or government departments. In the light of categorical conferment of right to equality by way of equality before law and equal protection of law under Article 14 of Constitution of India on every citizen, its scope cannot be narrowed down by reading into it the principle of reasonable accommodation, particularly in public sphere. The author opines that RA principle being an unmediated transplant from the domain of freedom of religion into disability law and policy by EEOC of the US by way of an administrative order, its unreflective application in the field of disability rights in the field of disability rights jurisprudence may create more problems than solutions. It is therefore suggested that more theorization is required to nurture its democratic conception, so that it is characterized as a justice and not simply equity strategy, applicable in a particular case of individual with disability. Indian judiciary deserves credit for reading disability discrimination as part of right to equality under Indian Constitution, whereas, US Supreme court while declaring title I of ADA as Unconstitutional vis-à-vis States as an overreach of mandate of Clause 5 of 14th Amendment and by insisting on a special law to tackle disability discrimination has let down disability rights movement. In closing, the author would quote the memorable words of Helen Keller:

> Some people see a closed door and turn away. Others see a closed door, try the knob, and if it doesn't open, they turn away. Still others see a closed door, try the knob and if it doesn't work, they find a key, and if the key doesn't fit, they turn way. A rare few see a closed door, try the knob, if it doesn't open, and they find a key and if it doesn't fit, they make one![139]

We need such enterprising constitutional designs.

Notes and References

* I acknowledge the assistance of my wife Sakshi Jain, and my students V.V. Gnanusha and Sushil Sarayu.

1. G.A. Res. 61/106, 61st Sess., U.N. Doc. A/RES/61/106, 24 January 2007. See generally Sanjay Jain. 2009. 'UN Enabled: Marching towards a New International Multicultural Human Rights Order with Special Reference to Work and Employment of Persons with disability.' *ILS Law Review*, vol. 2: 69–98.

2. See generally Barbara M. Altman, 2001. 'Disability Definitions, Models, Classification Schemes, and Applications,' in Gary L. Albrecht, Katherine D. Seelman, and Michael Bury (eds), *Handbook of Disability Studies*, pp. 97–22. New Delhi: Sage.
3. See generally Sanjay Jain. 2016. 'Contesting Ableist Constitutionalism: Some Reflections' in *R.T.M Nagpur University Research Journal* special ed. Social and Legal Dimensions of Disabilities Laws and Policies in India, pp. 61–78.
4. The figures are up to date till 30 September 2016.
5. UDHR, G.A. Res. 217A, at 25, U.N. GAOR, 3d Sess., 1st plen. Mtg. U.N. Doc. A/810, 12 December 1948.
6. ICCPR G.A. Res. 2200 (XXI), at 2, 26, U.N. Doc A/6316, 16 December 1966.
7. International Covenant on Economic, Social and Cultural Rights, G.A. Res. 2200 (XXI), at 2(2), U.N. Doc. A/6316, 16 December 1966; General Assembly resolution 2200A (XXI) of 16 December 1966 *entry into force* 3 January 1976.
8. See generally Aharon Barak, 2015. *Human Dignity: The Constitutional Value and the Constitutional Right*. Cambridge: Cambridge University Press.
9. See Michael E.Waterstone, Disability Constitutional Law available at http://www.acslaw.org/acsblog/disability-constitutional-lawlast visited on 29th September 2016. See also Michael E.Waterstone. 2014. *Disability Constitutional Law, Emory Law Journal,* vol. 63: 527.
10. See Andrew Power, Janet E. Lord, and Allison S. de Franco (eds). 2013. *Active Citizenship and Disability: Implementing the Personalisation Of Support.* Cambridge: Cambridge University Press.
11. See Ellen Frankel Paul, Fred D. Miller, Jr., and Jeffrey Paul (eds). 2011. *What Should Constitutions Do*? Cambridge: Cambridge University Press.
12. See Michael Oliver, 1994. 'Politics and Language: Understanding the Disability Discourse.' (Paper prepared for inclusion in the MA in Disability Studies Programme: Dept of Psychotherapy, University of Sheffield).
13. See, for example, the Constitution of Ecuador, 2008.
14. See Larry Alexander (ed.). 1998. *Constitutionalism: Philosophical Foundations.* Cambridge: Cambridge University Press, ibid p. 1; Christine E. J. Schwöbel, 2011. 'Chapter 1' *Global Constitutionalism in International Legal Perspective.* Leiden: Martinus Nijhoff Publishers.
15. See Elizabeth Anderson, January 1999. 'What is the point of equality?' *Ethics,* 109 (2): 287–337.
16. See David Wasserman, 1998.'Distributive Justice,' in Anita Silver, David Wasserman, and Mary B Mahwold (ed.) *Disability, Difference, Discrimination,* Maryland: Rowman and Littlefield ibid p. 173.
17. A. Silvers and L.P. Francis, 2005. 'Justice through Trust: Disability and the "Outlier Problem" in Social Contract Theory,' *Ethics*, 116, pp. 40–76; Anita Silvers and Michael Ashley Stein 2007. 'Disability and the Social Contract.' *4 U. Chi. L. Rev.* p. 1615.

18. A. Silvers and L.P. Francis, 2005. 'Justice through Trust'; Anita Silvers and Michael Ashley Stein 2007. 'Disability and the Social Contract.' Kimberley Brownlee and Adam Cureton (eds). 2009. 'Introduction' in *Disability and Disadvantage*. New York: Oxford University Press, pp. 6–7.
19. A. Silvers and L.P. Francis, 2005. 'Justice through Trust'; Anita Silvers and Michael Ashley Stein 2007. 'Disability and the Social Contract'; Kimberley Brownlee and Adam Cureton (eds.) 2009. 'Introduction'. 'Silvers argues that the main advantage of thinking of justice in this way, rather than along the model of a social contract, is that it allows us to adopt and combine three worthwhile strategies for dealing with problems of justice that arise from differences among persons; in particular, she suggests that some differences should be ignored, some mitigated, and some embraced from the point of view of justice.' See Anita Silver, 'No Talent? Beyond the Worst Off! A Diverse Theory of Justice for Disability.' In Brownlee and Cureton (eds) 2009, *Disability and Disadvantage*. New York: Oxford University Press, pp. 163–99.
20. See generally M. Nussbaum, 2006. *Frontiers of Justice: Disability, Nationality, Species Membership*. Cambridge, MA: Harvard University Press. M. Nussbaum, 2009. 'The Capabilities of People with Cognitive Disabilities.' *Metaphilosophy* 40 (3–4).
21. See Peter Berger and Thomas Luckmann, 1991. *The Social Construction of Reality: A Treatise in the Sociology of Knowledge*. New York: Anchor Books. They are acclaimed with the coinage of the notion of social construction. Patrick Kermit (2009) notes, 'One of their main points is that social interaction (and not some other form of causality) develops conventions. As these conventions are institutionalized they become something we tend to take for granted and something that also can decide the different social roles we play. Thus, social reality is socially constructed.' 'Deaf or deaf? Questioning alleged antinomies in the bioethical discourses on cochlear implantation and suggesting an alternative approach to d/Deafness,' *Scandinavian Journal of Disability Research*, 11:2, pp. 159–74, ibid at p. 162.
22. See Bernadette McSherry and Penelope Weller. 2010. *Rethinking Rights-Based Mental Health Law*. Oxford: Hart Publishers. While critically analysing the Mental Capacity Act 2005,(UK), they illustrate the operation of this principle.
23. See Linda L. Treloar PhD RN-CS GNP/ANP-C. 2000. 'Spiritual Beliefs, Response to Disability, and the Church-Part 1.' *Journal of Religion, Disability & Health*, 3(4, 2), *Journal of Religion, Disability & Health*, 4:1, 5–31; Maysaa S. Bazna Ed and Tarek A. Hatab PE. 2005. 'Disability in the Qur'an,' *Journal of Religion, Disability & Health*, 9:1, 5–27.
24. Identity politics vis-à-vis PWD must transcend the notion of a common group identity of disabled people and identity based on difference. See Bodil Ravneberg, 2009. 'Identity politics by design: users, markets and the public service provision for assistive technology in Norway,' *Scandinavian Journal of Disability Research*, 11:2, 101–15, 'It is identity politics seen as individual life politics, reconstructed through the narratives of individuals based on their experienced stigma and dependency on public services where lack of choice,

information and control prevails.' ibid at p. 102; The famous Deaf scholar notes, 'The lowercase "deaf" refers to those for whom deafness is primarily an audiological experience. It is mainly used to describe those who lost some or all of their hearing in early or late life, and who do not usually wish to have contact with signing Deaf communities, preferring to try and retain their membership of the majority society in which they were socialized. "Deaf" refers to those born Deaf or deafened in early (sometimes late) childhood, for whom the sign languages, communities and cultures of the Deaf collective represents their primary experience as essentially akin to other language minorities.' See Paddy Ladd, 2003. *Understanding Deaf Culture, In Search Of Deafhood.* Clevedon, UK: Cromwell Press Ltd. ibid at p. xvii.

25. See generally F.K. Campbell, 2009. *Contours of Ableism.* Basingstoke: Macmillan; and F. K. Campbell, 'Disability Harms Exploring Internalized Ableism?' In C. Marshall, E. Kendall, and R. Gover, 2009. *Disability: Insights from across Fields and around the World.* vol. I, 19–34. Westport, CT: Praeger Press; H.Meekosha, 2011. 'Decolonizing Disability: Thinking and Acting Globally.' *Disability & Society* 26 (6): 667–82; H.Meekosha and R. Shuttleworth. 2009. 'What's So 'critical' about Critical Disability Studies?' *Australian Journal of Human Rights* 15 (1): 47–75.
26. '... Basically, I think that prospective parents should aspire to an ideal of unconditional welcome that would oppose selection against disabilities even if they were intrinsically harmful, or inimical to well-being', n 9 id at p. 278. David Wasserman. 2013. 'Is Disability Discrimination Different?' pp. 270–8 in Deborah Hellman and Sophia Moreau (eds), *Philosophical Foundations of Discrimination Law.* Oxford: Oxford University Press; see for further analysis Adrienne Asch and David Wasserman, 2005. 'Where is the Sin in Synecdoche: Prenatal Testing and the Parent-Child Relationship', in David Wasserman, Rober Wachbroit, and Jerome Bickenbach, eds., *Quality of Life and Human Difference: Genetic Testing, Health Care, and Disability.* New York, NY: Cambridge University Press, pp. 172–216.
27. See generally Kristjana Kristiansen, Simo Vehmas, and Tom Shakespeare (eds). 2009. *Arguing About Disability: Philosophical Perspectives.* Abingdon: Routledge.
28. See Simo Vehmas and Nick Watson. 2014. 'Moral wrongs, disadvantages, and disability: a critique of critical disability studies,' *Disability & Society*, 29(4): 638–50,' The way people see things, and the language that is used to describe certain conditions, can affect how they react to them, but freeing oneself from ablest assumptions may not in some cases be enough. There may be insurmountable realities attached to some impairments where parents feel that their personal and social circumstances would not enable them to provide the child or themselves with a satisfactory life. Impairment sometimes produces practical, difficult, and ethical choices and we need more concrete viewpoints than the ideas provided through ableism, which offers very little practical moral guidance.' p. 642.
29. In many countries including India fetus does not enjoy independent legal existence; rather fetal rights are confined to issues of succession, sex selection abortion, etc.

30. See Article 25 (b) of UNCRPD, 'In particular, States Parties shall: .... (b) Provide those health services needed by persons with disabilities specifically because of their disabilities, including early identification and intervention as appropriate, and services designed to minimize and prevent further disabilities, including among children and older persons.'
31. The US Supreme Court, in one of its notorious decisions, *Buck v Bell 274 US 200 1927*, upheld the right of the 'State Colony for Epileptics and Feeble Minded' to sterilize 'mentally defective' individuals by invoking the principle of Utilitarianism and by justifying allocation of resources to 'best citizens'.
32. Even UNCRPD echoes the same in its definition of discrimination. '"Discrimination on the basis of disability" means any distinction, exclusion or restriction on the basis of disability which has the purpose or effect of impairing or nullifying the recognition, enjoyment or exercise, on an equal basis with others, of all human rights and fundamental freedoms in the political, economic, social, cultural, civil or any other field. It includes all forms of discrimination, including denial of reasonable accommodation,' see Article 2 Para 3. See Article 10: 'Right to life, remains silent on genetic science aimed at the elimination of impairment-related human diversity, and on pre-birth negative selection of foeti with identified or imputed impairment.' See generally, Rosemary Kayess and Phillip French, 2008. 'Out of Darkness into Light? Introducing the Convention on the Rights of Persons with Disabilities.' *Human Rights Law Review* 8(1): 29.
33. 'Recognizing that disability is an evolving concept and that disability results from the interaction between persons with impairments and attitudinal and environmental barriers that hinders their full and effective participation in society on an equal basis with others,' See Para (e) of Preamble of UNCRPD. See also Article 5.
34. See Paragraphs 1 and 3 of UNCRPD.
35. See generally, J. Li, W. Cheng, X. Wang, and A.M. M. Lawson (eds). 2012. *Breakthrough—The Care Dilemma: Welfare Policies for People with Intellectual and Psychiatric Disabilities and their Families*. Beijing: National Defense University Publishing House.
36. See generally F. K. Campbell. 2009. *Contours of Ableism*. Basingstoke: Macmillan, and F. K.Campbell, 2009. 'Disability Harms Exploring Internalized Ableism?' In C. Marshall, E. Kendall and R. Gover (eds). *Disability: Insights from across Fields and around the World. vol. I*, pp. 19–34. Westport, CT: Praeger Press.
37. See generally Michael Oliver and Colin Barnes. 2012. *The New Politics of Disablement*. Second Ed. London: Palgrave Macmillan; M. Oliver. 2009. *Understanding Disability from Theory To Practice*. Second edition. London: Palgrave Macmillan. Some scholars also use the coinage 'Politics of Abelism'.
38. Constitutions explicitly enlisting physical and mental disability as one of the grounds of non-discrimination in their anti-discriminatory provisions come under this category.
39. Constitutions not mentioning disability as one of the prohibited grounds in their anti-discriminatory provisions, and keeping the conception of

discrimination evolving to recognize new ground with the appendage of words like 'other status', fall under this category.

40. The author has identified three fundamental types of exclusion of PWDs in the Constitutions in this rubric (a) expressive exclusion to physical or mental disability/PWDs in the Constitutions; (b) reference to physical or mental disability/ PWDs imposing disqualifications for holding public and political offices; and (c) citing intellectual/mental disability to justify derogation on right to personal liberty and to a large extent right to property.
41. 'Ambivalent exclusion' comes into play when the Constitution in its equality clause or anti-discriminatory provision or in both does not explicitly include physical or mental disability as one of the prohibited grounds or use open textured or generic words like 'other status' to keep the notion of discrimination evolving. Ambivalence arises because the State neither takes any articulate position on the policy issue of inclusion of disability as independent head of anti-discrimination law in its basic framework of political and fundamental principles, nor it impliedly permits its officers or instrumentalities to consciously or unconsciously exclude PWDs from benefits generally available to others. The essence of 'ambivalence exclusion' lies in irresolute and vacillating stand of the State on the conferment of right to equality and non-discrimination on PWDs and the author did not associate paternalistic or negative provisions in the constitutions with the notion of ambivalence. His notion of ambivalence is exclusively collated to the notions of equality and non-discrimination. The notion of ambivalent exclusion does not collapse or conflate with the categories of marginal or moderate inclusion, because the latter are employed to denote number of provisions, the constitution has in referring or addressing PWD/physical or mental disability, that is, the analysis is quantitative rather than qualitative; whereas, examination of ambivalence of anti-discrimination clause in the constitution requires its structural analysis.
42. To assess the degree of inclusion of PWDs/physical and mental disability, Constitutions with rights conferring, programmatic, and paternalistic provisions have been taken into account, whereas Constitutions with only negative provisions, that is, provisions denying rights to PWDs or perpetuating their political exclusion have been omitted.
43. Inclusion is marginal if the constitution contains only one positive provision,[43] that is, Marginal Disability Inclusion Provision with/without negative provisions.
44. Inclusion is moderate, if the Constitution has two or more positive provisions with or without negative provisions.
45. The inclusion of PWDs is profound in the constitution, when (a) it is fully compliant with UNCRPD, (b) it does not have any disability exclusion provisions, and (c) it evolves a non-disabling and inclusive state and prefers equality-sensitive and rights-enabling provisions to affirmative action in favor of PWDs. According to assessment of this author all Constitutions under analysis fall short of these scrupulous conditions.

46. See Sanjay Jain 'Disability in the Constitutions: Critical Analysis of Exclusionary Constitutionalism', Paper presented at International Inaugural Conference on 'Rethinking the Boundaries of Public Law and Public Space' 2014, Florence, Italy (unpublished and on file with the author).
47. Amongst these, 27 states have signed and ratified, whereas 5 states have signed UNCRPD.
48. Out of these, 30 states have signed and ratified, 12 states signed UNCRPD.
49. For the purposes of this study negative provisions means and include disqualifying PWDs from holding Political and Public offices, and People with Mental and Intellectual Disability from exercising Rights to Vote, Personal Liberty and Property.
50. Out of these, 78 states have signed and ratified, 10 states signed UNCRPD.
51. Out of these, 66 states have signed and ratified, 22 states signed UNCRPD.
52. Out of these, 61 states have signed and ratified, 13 states signed UNCRPD.
53. Out of these, 24 states have signed and ratified, 6 states signed UNCRPD.
54. Out of these, 11 states have signed and ratified, and 2 states have signed UNCRPD.
55. Adopted on 13 December 2006 during the 61st session of the General Assembly by resolution A/RES/61/106 and entered into force on 3 May 2008 after it received 20th ratification. As on 26 May 2014 signed by 158 and ratified by 145 countries.
56. These figures are available on www.un.org.disabilities/documents last visited 28 July 2016. However the figures about ratifications reported in the study by the author are from 2014.
57. States Parties shall prohibit all discrimination on the basis of disability and guarantee to persons with disabilities equal and effective legal protection against discrimination on all grounds.
58. See Article 39-A (Equal Justice and Free legal aid—reference to 'other disabilities'); Article 41 (Right to work, to education and to public assistance in certain cases—reference to 'Sickness and Disablement'). These provisions are not enforceable in the Court of law being Directive Principles of State Policy. (See Article 37). See Part D of Second schedule read with Articles 125 and 221, affording special treatment to the Disability Pension received by the persons at the time of their appointments as Supreme Court and High Court judges as a part of previous service under Govt. of India or State governments. This provision is curious because till date no person with disability has been appointed on these posts; List II Seventh Schedule Entry 9. Relief of the disabled and unemployable; See Article 243-C read with Entry 26 of Eleventh Schedule (...Welfare of the handicapped and mentally retarded) See Article 243-W read with entry 9 of twelfth Schedule (Safeguarding the interests of ...the handicapped and mentally retarded). Apart from these paternalistic provisions the Constitution of India, subject to the declaration by the Court persons of unsound mind are disqualified to hold Political offices or to cast votes. See Articles 102, 191 (Disqualification for Membership) and 326 (Elections to the House of the People and to the Legislative Assemblies of States). By way of superimposition,

Supreme Court of India recognized physical and mental disability as one of the valid grounds for removal of Governor. See Para 50(ii). This ground was incorporated by the court based on the contentions of the Petitioners rather than resorting to any rationale; respondents opposed this contention. (See paras 5 and 10, respectively). *B.P. Singhal v Union of India*. In many states Leprosy cured persons are disqualified to hold membership of local and self-government bodies like panchayat and municipalities.

59. All persons born or naturalized in the US, and subject to the jurisdiction thereof, are citizens of the US and of the state wherein they reside. No state shall make or enforce any law which shall abridge the privileges or immunities of citizens of the US; nor shall any state deprive any person of life, liberty, or property, without due process of law; nor deny to any person within its jurisdiction the equal protection of the laws (14th Amendment, Section 1).

    The Congress shall have power to enforce, by appropriate legislation, the provisions of this article (14th Amendment, Section 5)
60. (99–1240) 531 U.S. 356 (2001).
61. Id. at pp. 363. Case of Milton Ash who worked as a security officer for the Alabama Department of Youth Services (Department) has been also clubbed with this case.
62. Kimel *v* State Bd. of Regents, 139 F.3d 1426. U.S.C.A.
63. Kennedy J. has filed a concurring opinion, in which O'Connor, J., joined.
64. The judicial power of the US shall not be construed to extend to any suit in law or equity, commenced or prosecuted against one of the US by citizens of another State, or by Citizens or Subjects of any Foreign State. See more http://constitution.findlaw.com/amendment11, accessed 15 September 2016.
65. With him Stevens, Souter, and Ginsburg, JJ. joined. See for his detail reasoning pp. 380 et seq.
66. Id. at pp. 368.
67. 473 U.S. 432 (1985).
68. Adopted by the World Conference on Human Rights in Vienna on 25 June 1993.
69. See pp. 368–69. Board of trustees University of Alabama *v* Garrett 121 S.Ct. 955.
70. Id. at p. 374.
71. Id. at p. 372.
72. Section 42 U.S.C. § 12111(8). Under the ADA, reasonable accommodations include, but are not limited to, making existing facilities accessible to and usable to individuals with disabilities, job restructuring, part-time work, modified work schedules, reassignment to a vacant position, modification of equipment, and the provision of qualified readers or interpreters. Id. § 12111(9)(A),(B). However, employers are not required to provide reasonable accommodations if they would cause an 'undue hardship on the operation of the business.' Id. § 12112(b)(5)(A).
73. Id. at pp. 372 *Board of trustees University of Alabama v Garrett* 121 S.Ct. 955.
74. See Board of trustees *University of Alabama v Garrett* 121 S.Ct. 955. pp. 364.

75. As a matter of fact, protection of rights of Americans with disability under 14th Amendment must stand on the higher footing than that of RA because it is inconceivable to infer from the open ended language of 14th Amendment that it merely condones affordable discrimination by way of RA vis-à-vis States consenting to the waiver of 11th Amendment immunity.
76. See pp. 387–8.
77. Id. at pp. 386–7.
78. See p. 377.
79. *546 U.S. 151 (2006).*
80. *Title II of the* ADA provides that 'no qualified individual with a disability shall, by reason of such disability, be excluded from participation in or be denied the benefits of the services, programs, or activities of a public entity, or be subjected to discrimination by any such entity.'
81. See US *v* Georgia 546 U.S. 151 (2006) Id at pp. 159.
82. There is a growing debate in the US in academia whether the principle of RA is integral to anti-discrimination under the 14th Amendment or is it a distinct and special obligation. For the former view see generally Christine Jolls, 2001. 'Antidiscrimination and Accommodation.' 115 *Harv. L. Rev.* For later approach see generally Stewart J. Schwab and Steven l. Willborn, 2002–2003. 'Reasonable accommodation of workplace Disabilities.' 44 *Wm. & Mary L. Rev.* 1197. For substantive analysis of reasonable accommodation, See generally, Michael Ashley Stein, Anita Silvers, Bradley A. Areheart, and Leslie Pickering Francis, 'Accommodating Every Body.' 81 *U. Chi. L. Rev.* 689.
83. For example, Danny Ray Meeks *v* Derrick d. Schofield, M.D. Tennessee, Nashville Division US District court No. 3: 12–mc–00035, 29 May 2012. 2012 WL 1934416.
84. See generally John J. Donohue III, 1994. 'Employment Discrimination Law in Perspective: Three Concepts of Equality,' 92 *Mich. L. Rev.* 2612; John Gardener, 1998. 'On the ground of her Sex(uality)' *OJLS Spring* vol. 18 at 167–87; Timothy Macklem. 2003. *Beyond Comparison: Sex and Discrimination.* Cambridge: Cambridge University Press.
85. Under Inclusive Constitutionalism, physical and mental disability must be perceived not only as 'an immutable characteristic' but also part of 'the fundamental choices' of one's own life. See generally John Gardener, 1998. 'On the ground of her Sex(uality)' *OJLS Spring* Vol. 18 at 167–87; Dr Sanjay Jain, 2013. 'Some reflections on Disability based discrimination and denial of Reasonable accommodation to Persons with Disability in employment', in Sarsu Thomas, (ed.) *Gender, Human Rights and Law Vol IV*, Bangalore: Centre for Women and the Law, National Law School of India University.
86. See generally Nicole S. Richter. 2002. 'The Americans with disabilities act after University of Alabama *v* Garrett: should the States be immune from suit?' *Chicago-Kent LR* 879–98.
87. See generally Shelley Tremain (ed.). 2008. *Foucault and the Government of Disability.* Ann Arbor: The University of Michigan Press; Fiona Kumari

Campbell. 2009. *Contours of Ableism*. Basingstoke: Macmillan; Elizabeth Emens and Michael Ashley Stein (eds). 2013. *Disability and Equality Law*. Farnham: Ashgate; Leslie P Francis and Anita Silver (eds). 2000. *Americans with Disabilites—Exploring implications of the Law for Individuals and Institutions*. Abingdon: Routledge; Anita Silver, David Wasserman, and Mary B Mahwold, (eds). 1998. *Disability, Difference, Discrimination—Perspectives in Bioethics and Public Policy*. Lanham, MD: Rowman and Littlefield.

88. Per Justice Harlan in his famous dissent in *Plessy v Ferguson,* 163 U.S. 537.
89. See Article 5 of UNCRPD.
90. See generally Bruce Ackerman, 1993. *We the People—Vol. 1 Foundations*. MA: Harvard University Press.
91. Articles 15 and 16 incorporates the principle of Non-discrimination vis-à-vis citizens of India, but compromises it with the words, ' Only on the ground of...' See generally, Tarunabh Khaitan, April–June 2008.'Beyond Reasonableness—A Rigorous Standard of Review for Article 15 Infringement.' *Journal of the Indian Law Institute*, 50(2): 177–208.
92. India signed it on 30 March 2007 and ratified on 1 October 2007 but has not signed or ratified the optional protocol.
93. MANU/SC/0299/1993.
94. However, it is not clear from the judgment whether any such contention was raised on behalf of NFB.
95. See para 13.
96. See para 13.
97. See *Govt. of India through Secretary and Anr. v Ravi Prakash Gupta* and Anr. MANU/SC/0445/2010 cited with approval in *Union of India v National federation for blind* MANU/SC/1025/2013, paras 27–39.
98. *Rajeev Kumar Gupta v Union of India* MANU/SC/0718/2016. On the strength of this Judgment State of Gujarat purported to equate economically backward class of citizens as worthy of 'differential treatment' under Article 16(1). The Gujarat High Court rightly rebuffed this argument. However, the court also stated that citizens falling under economic backward class do not constitute a homogenous group. Does the Gujarat HC read Rajeev Kumar Gupta as an authority for the proposition that PWDs constitute a homogenous group is a moot question. *Dayaram Khemkaran Verma v State of Gujarat* MANU/GJ/1412/2016 paras 29.21 and 29.22.
99. This article deals with 'Equality and non-discrimination' and lays down that denial of RA to PWDs amounts to disability-based discrimination and denial of right to equality.
100. This Article recognizes 'right to work and employment.'
101. *Indra Sawhney v Union of India* AIR 1993 SC 447.
102. *Rajeev Kumar Gupta v Union of India* MANU/SC/0718/2016 Id at para 21.
103. MANU/SC/0158/2010.
104. See paras 29–30.
105. See para 31.

106. See para 32.
107. See para 35.
108. See para 36.
109. He sought support for this claim by placing reliance on one of the judgments of the appellate circuit court in the US, *Kathleen Borkowski v Valley Central School District*. In that case, the Court of Appeals set aside the order of the District Court in favor of the School by observing, 'Can a teacher with disabilities, whose disabilities directly affect her capacity to perform her job, insist that her employer provide a teacher's aide as a form of RA under Section 504 of the Rehabilitation Act, 29 U.S.C. § 794? That question is at the heart of this appeal from the entry by the United States District Court for the Southern District of New York (Charles L. Brieant, Judge) of summary judgment for the defendant Valley Central School District ('the School District'). We acknowledge that, on a proper factual showing, the answer may prove to be 'no.' But because we believe that issues of material fact have not been resolved, we vacate the entry of judgment in favor of the School District and remand the matter for further proceedings consistent with this opinion' See paras 16–17.
110. See para 17. Author submits that no substantial observation is cited in the instant case from the *Kathleen Borkowski* judgment. In paras 16 and 17, the court merely articulated the question before the court of Appeal along with facts and with due respect to the court, the question was also not properly cited.
111. *Vishaka and others v State of Rajasthan and others* (1997) 6 SCC 24.
112. MANU/MH/452/2009.
113. The cavalier approach of the court in citing UNCRPD is incredible.
114. The author is curious to find the reference to the '2007 UN Protocol'. Probably Bombay HC meant 'Optional Protocol to UNCRPD'. However, India has neither signed it nor ratified it. The same muddles the reasoning of the Court lest it is clarified that probably Bombay HC wanted to invoke UNCRPD 2006 in general and Article 5 of this convention in particular.
115. See para 25. MANU/MH/452/2009.
116. See para 25. MANU/MH/452/2009.
117. See para 27. MANU/MH/452/2009.
118. MANU/RH/063/2015.
119. In the light of Article 37, it is indubitable that directive principles are fundamental in the governance of the Nation, however it is insightful to refer these principles to fill the legislative gap or to remedy the absence of the legislation. However, the subject matter of the legislation must be covered by the principles and policy enshrined in Part IV. See generally Professor Mahendra Pal Singh, 2003. 'The Statics and the Dynamics of the Fundamental Rights and the Directives Principles—A Human Rights Perspective.' *5 SCC (Jour) 1*; Mahendra Pal Singh, 2014. 'A Theory of Constitutional Rights for India.' *8 SCC J-25*.
120. See para 22 MANU/RH/063/2015.
121. Incorporation of an international conventions into an Indian legal order is contingent upon enactment of legislation under Article 253 of the Constitution of India.

122. See Anita Silvers, 1998. 'Formal Justice,' ID at pp. 76–80 in Anita Silver, David Wasserman and Mary B Mahwold (eds). *Disability, Difference, Discrimination: Perspectives in Bioethics and Public Policy*, Lanham, MD: Rowman and Littlefield.
123. See also *Patel Suleman Gaibi v The State of Maharashtra* 2014 Bombay High Court; *Akhilesh Kumar v University Grants Commission & Ors.* 2014 ; *Tushar Keshaorao Deshmukh v Union of India 2010*; *Lalit and Ors. v Govt. of NCT and Anr.* 2010.
124. MANU/TN/1225/2015.
125. See paras 24, 25, 33–5 for detailed reasoning.
126. See *Sutton v United Air Lines, Inc.* (97–1943) 527 U.S. 471 (1999); *Murphy v United Parcel Service, Inc.* (97–1992) 527 U.S. 516 (1999); *Albertsons, Inc. v Kirkingburg* (98–591) 527 U.S. 555 (1999).
127. See *Jeeja Ghosh and another v Union of India and others*, 2016 Indlaw SC 381.
128. See paras 13, 40 to 48 for detail reasoning.
129. Supreme Court has rightly stayed this judgment of the Chennai High Court while admitting Special Leave Petition under Article 136 of the Constitution of India.
130. See T.M. Scanlon, 2003. 'The diversity of objections to inequality' in T.M. Scanlon, *The Difficulty of Tolerance: Essays in Political Philosophy*. Cambridge: Cambridge University Press, Id. at p. 202.
131. See Sandra Fredman, 2011. *Discrimination Law* (2nd edition) Oxford: Oxford University Press)155–6. See Chapter One for a detailed analysis of substantive equality.
132. See Sandra Fredman, 2013. 'Disability Equality: a challenge to the existing Anti-discrimination paradigm?', in Elizabeth Emens and Michael Ashley Stein, (eds). 2013. *Disability and Equality Law*. Farnham: Ashgate. Id at 135.
133. Id. at p. 136.
134. Id. at p. 136.
135. Ian Carter. 2013 'Are Toleration and Respect Compatible?' *Journal of Applied Philosophy* Special Issue: *Toleration and Respect*, 30(3): 195–208, Id. at pp. 197. Generally see Stephen Darwall, 1977. 'Two kinds of respect', *Ethics 88,1*: pp. 36–49, p. 40; Colin Bird, 2004. 'Status, identity, and respect,' *Political Theory 32, 2*: pp. 207–32, pp. 211–20.
136. Elizabeth Anderson, 1999. 'What is the point of equality?', *Ethics* 109: pp. 287–337, p. 289. Thomas Pogge, 2002. 'Can the capabilities approach be justified?', *Philosophical Topics* 30: pp. 167–228.
137. Linda Barkley, May 2010. 'Disability, respect, and justice.' *Journal of Applied Philosophy*. 27, 2, pp. 154–71.
138. See UNCRPD.
139. Cited by Sikri J. in *Jeeja Ghosh and another v Union of India and others*, 2016 Indlaw SC 381.

16

Three Models of Affirmative Action through the Lens of Separation of Powers

South Africa, Canada, and India

Arpita Sarkar

I Introduction

There has been much debate about the constitutionality of affirmative action. Many issues have been repeatedly raised that do not question the constitutionality of this principle of substantive equality; instead they criticize the implementation of this principle. Such questions have sought to argue that while the principle itself may be constitutional and just, the various laws and rules through which it is sought to be implemented are too problematic and foster injustice.[1] Such questions then go onto question the constitutionality of the principle inductively;[2] that is, they argue that a principle that has passed the initial theoretical test of constitutionality, but cannot be implemented properly, is practically unconstitutional.

This chapter intends to expose the fallacy of this line of questioning and criticism. It shows that equality jurisprudence has developed empirically. Thus there is no dissociation between the theoretical idea itself and its practical implementation. The chapter shows that the various tests of constitutionality have evolved to assess not only the principle as an a priori idea, but also its various practical manifestations. It highlights the different procedural practices under the constitutions that have been created for different practical assessments required in identifying who to include and who to exclude from affirmative action entitlements. By comparing the three jurisdictions of India, South Africa, and Canada, the chapter shows that all these three countries that are fighting historical injustices towards certain sections of their people have built robust institutional mechanisms for proper implementation of affirmative action and its effective judicial review.

In certain jurisdictions like India and Canada, the constitutionality of an affirmative action scheme can be challenged on its own merit devoid of any challenge on the eligibility of targeted beneficiary communities.[3] In South Africa, however, affirmative action schemes are intrinsically connected to the targeted beneficiaries.

As to the organ of the state that is best equipped to identify persons or communities for affirmative action program, it depends largely on the nature of the separation of powers between judiciary, executive, and the legislature under different constitutional set-ups. History and social structure also play a significant role in conferring authority on different organs of the state for implementation of this objective.

The first section of this work aims at studying the judicial model in South Africa where the judiciary takes the leading role in identifying communities eligible for affirmative action. The second section explores the legislative model of Canada where the designated communities are explicitly mentioned in enacted laws and are implemented verbatim without further deliberations. The third section deals with the role played by the executive organ of the state in India in identifying designated groups for affirmative actions.

The study of the three models of affirmative action from the perspective of identification of designated groups, is not conducted with the objective of claiming the superiority of one model over the others. Rather, it aims at showing how history, structure of the constitutional set-up of societies, and constitutional practices encourage different institutional mechanisms for implementation of affirmative action programs. In the same way as the objectives behind affirmative action vary with countries, the constitutional mechanism for identification of communities for affirmative action too, vary with jurisdictions. Along with debate on constitutionality of affirmative action therefore, the constitutional set up for identification of communities for affirmative action too, deserve attention and serious contemplation to develop a holistic understanding of affirmative action practices across jurisdictions.

II Judiciary Model For Identification of Communities and Persons for Affirmative Action Programmes: The South African Example

The institutionalized regulation of human relations on racial lines had resulted in social, political and economic inequalities in South Africa, which continue to the present times. Legal, systematic, and official nature of segregation (or Apartheid as it is called) existed even after independence from the British. Therefore, there was a need for equally rigorous measure to bring equality among people in South Africa.

Affirmative action in South Africa significantly differs from that in India or Canada in one respect. South Africans see entitlements under affirmative action as a share drawn out from a larger common pie. This understanding views affirmative action entitlements reducing the size of the quantum of the pie. In other words, for the purpose of affirmative action, South Africans confine themselves to understanding socio-economic resources as finite and singular. Thus, any affirmative action is seen as drawing out of finite resources for purposes that are intended to benefit few and not for common benefit of all. Resultantly, despite the legislature's direction for eligibility for affirmative action that covers majority of the population, the judiciary subsequently steps in to adjudicate upon eligibility for affirmative action on a case-by-case basis. Thus, the eventual decision-maker as to who can be beneficiaries of affirmative action is not the legislature or the executive, but the judiciary.

The vesting of power unto the judiciary is a result of South African history. The Republic of South Africa with Westminster parliamentary sovereignty was established as a dominion under Britain in 1910.[4] For the next forty years, the White-only parliament abused the principle of sovereignty of parliament to turn colonial dispossessions into legislative apartheid which validated racial disaggregation.[5] The parliamentary sovereignty also carried with it, the principle of non-interference by the judiciary which prohibited judiciary from striking down legislations violating rights. Subsequently, the Republican Constitution of 1961 and the Tricameral Constitution of 1980 also persisted non-interference by judiciary in invalidating legislations violating rights. Hence, the struggle for equal rights and liberation took the form of armed struggle which subsequently resulted in negotiations among the then existing White government and the members of liberation movement in 1991.[6] This negotiation process resulted in the 'Interim Constitution'. Eventually, the Constitution of Republic of South Africa, 1996, was validated by the Constitutional Court of South Africa in two stages to ensure adherence to the constitutional principles agreed upon at the first stage.[7]

Thus, the judiciary in South Africa transformed from a passive body to being the major player in certifying and implementing the provisions of the Constitution of 1996 including its 'Bill of Rights' of which affirmative action constitute a significant component.[8]

II.1 The Constitutional and Legislative Basis for Affirmative Action in South Africa

The Constitution of South Africa,provides for the equality before law in Section 9.[9] Section 9(3) of the Constitution explicitly enumerates grounds for non-discrimination under section 9(3). Section 9(2) in contrast does not mention persons or communities who are disadvantaged by discriminations and are entitled for legislative and other measures for furtherance of equality. Constitutionality of every affirmative action claim in South Africa is strongly entwined with the persons or communities who claim entitlement under affirmative action. Therefore, when affirmative action programmes are upheld in the court of law, legitimacy of such schemes depend to a significant degree on the persons availing such schemes despite being eligible for affirmative action.

The affirmative action clause in South African Constitution mentions legislations as one of the significant means for implementation of affirmative action by the state. These legislations in South Africa clearly mention the intended beneficiaries. The Employment Equity Act is considered as one of the major instruments of affirmative action in South Africa. Explicit mention through legislative provisions of the groups of persons become important particularly in the light of the fact that Constitution of South Africa through its provisions do not provide for a list or category of such persons but mentions a broad category of persons 'disadvantaged by unfair discriminations'.[10]

Employment Equity Act, 1998, provides for a definition of disadvantaged communities for the purpose of employment. The Act defines the beneficiaries of affirmative action as 'designated group'.[11] The designated group for the purpose of this Act are Black people, women of all races, and persons with disabilities. 'Black people' for the purpose of this Act appears in the definition clause and means African, 'coloured', and people of Indian origin who are citizens of the Republic of South Africa by birth, descent, or naturalization before 27 April 1994.[12] Black people also include those African, 'coloured', and people of Indian origin who were entitled to acquire citizenship prior to the due date but have been precluded from doing so because of the apartheid policy.[13] Black people further include South Africans of Chinese origin for the purpose of Employment Equity Act and Black Based Economic

Empowerment (BBEE) programme.[14] In effect, persons or group of beneficiaries of affirmative action comprise of the majority of the population.

Persons with disabilities for the purpose of Employment Equity Act include those persons with long-term or recurring mental or physical impairment which substantially limits their prospects of entering into or advancement of employment.[15] The Broad Based Black Economic Empowerment Amendment Act (B-BBEEAA) of 2013 provides for a narrower and targeted form of representation of people from Black community for the purpose of building the economy of the country and includes women, worker, youth, persons with disabilities, and people from rural areas, within the definition of Black community for the purpose of this Act.[16] An important objective of the BBBEEA also involves attaining an equitable representation of Black people at different levels of work forces.[17] This Act, therefore, can be read along with the Employment Equity Act, as instruments for identification of disadvantaged groups for the purpose of affirmative action.

However, in spite of comprehensive mention of persons and communities eligible for affirmative action under the Employment Equity Act and the BBBEE Act, the legality and validity of affirmative action availed by certain individuals from these designated groups are challenged before the court of law. There might be two reasons behind this practice. First, despite being mentioned in the legislation, the designated group covers majority of the population due to the inclusiveness of the categories. Therefore, it becomes imperative for the judiciary to further adjudicate upon individual entitlement to affirmative action. Second, in the absence of quota systems, often competing claims arise from within different designated groups. In such situation, the judiciary is compelled to grant relief to the more vulnerable individuals in need of affirmative action protection on the basis of their dominant identities. The judiciary in South Africa has accordingly developed a contextual jurisprudence on affirmative action which distinguishes South Africa from other jurisdictions where affirmative action claims are challenged before the court of law.

II.2 Claiming Legitimacy for the Judicial Model for Affirmative Action in South Africa

It might appear that parliamentary sovereignty during the apartheid regime was responsible for the abstinence of courts from implementing rights or striking down legislations that violated rights. Even after judicial review of legislations was introduced by the constitution, there was scepticism regarding the role of the judiciary. This is because the constitution after coming into force did not abolish the apartheid judiciary. Rather, it reposed trust in the judiciary to be mending its way to be a rights upholding institution.[18] This faith by the Constitutional Republic can be best reflected on the fact that judicial review of legislations were permitted from the lower to the highest level of judiciary including the high courts and the Supreme Court of Appeal thereby reflecting acceptance of plurality of opinion among existing judges of the apartheid regime.[19] However, there were apprehensions regarding the role that a judiciary still comprising white judges from the apartheid period, shall play with respect to rights based legislations. To put simply, the absence of any lustration laws post establishment of constitutional democracy raised doubts of bias against the judiciary.

This scepticism was eased with time due to the significant role played by the constitutional court at both the stages of drafting and certification of the constitution of 1996, ensuring its adherence to constitutional principles. The decision of *S v Makwanyane*[20] serves as one such example during the period of the interim constitution which provided assurance to the republic to place trust in the judiciary.[21] This is one such case through which the constitutional court declared its allegiance to the democratic principles which were agreed upon as part of the Constitution of South Africa.

Sachs J., in his concurring opinion in *Van Heerden* case[22], also mentioned judicial restraint.[23] He opined that in cases of both, promotion of equality under section 9(2) and prevention of unfair discriminations under section 9(3), courts must show due restraint from interfering with measures taken on this issue. According to Sachs J., the court should not be an arbitrator to decide on whether such measures could have been less intrusive etc.[24] However, he was still of the opinion that when the courts feel that such measures are introduced to unfairly and disproportionately burden the interest of the advantaged sections of the community, then the court must interfere.[25] Also, in South Africa, the same standard of scrutiny is not applied by the judiciary for all race-based classifications.[26] This is regardless of whether such classification aims at advancing discrimination or preventing it.[27] Thus, the judiciary reserves the power to review affirmative action claims despite acknowledging the necessity of exercising judicial restraint.

II.3 *Minister of Finance, The Political Office Bearers Pension Fund v Frederik Jacobus Van Heerden* 2004 (6) SA 121 (CC): The Landmark Judgment

Van Heerden decision is not the only decision on affirmative action in South Africa. The judiciary decided on affirmative action claims even under the Interim Constitution.[28] Under the Constitution of 1996 as well, affirmative action has been adjudicated upon by the Constitutional Court as well as the lower judiciary including the labour court and the Supreme Court of Appeal.[29] The *Van Heerden* decision still remains a landmark in the legal history of affirmative action cases in South Africa. The court in this case laid down that any scheme under section 9(2) of the constitution, shall be conferred with the presumption of constitutionality.

The constitutional court, in *Van Heerden*, laid down the three steps test to identify the situations in which a claim for discrimination has to be tested under section 9(2) which provides for affirmative action. For the other circumstances, according to the court, the discriminations claim has to be tested under section 9(3) which provides for grounds of discrimination.[30] The test under section 9(2) consists of assessment at the first step on whether the measure in question targets persons or categories of persons who are disadvantaged by unfair discriminations. The second step requires testing whether the measure in question protects or advances the interests of such categories of persons. And finally, in the third stage, it is required to be proved that such measures indeed promote the achievement of equality.[31] This test in itself requires the courts to make comprehensive assessment on who the disadvantaged persons or communities are.

However, the Court stated that section 9(2) does not require every person entitled to remedial scheme to show that they come from disadvantaged groups. It is sufficient to show that an overwhelming majority of members favoured under the scheme had been disadvantaged by unfair exclusions.[32]

Thus, in South Africa, courts scrutinize different forms of disadvantages on a case-by-case basis to decipher whether a person belongs to a disadvantaged community. This includes, besides enumerated grounds, even new patterns of discrimination which emerge in society. In the words of the Court in the *Van Heerden* decision:

> [27.] This substantive notion of equality recognises that besides uneven race, class and gender attributes of our society, there are other levels and forms of social differentiation and systematic under- privilege, which still persist. The Constitution enjoins us to dismantle them and to prevent the creation of new patterns of disadvantage. It is therefore incumbent on courts to scrutinise in each equality claim the situation of the complainants in society; their history and vulnerability; the history, nature and purpose of the discriminatory practice and whether it ameliorates or adds to group disadvantage in real life context, in order to determine its fairness or otherwise in the light of the values of our Constitution.

The courts in South Africa, therefore, are simultaneously responsible for ensuring that systematic patterns of discrimination are dismantled through affirmative action while at the same time, new patterns of discrimination are not created. Therefore, effectively, the courts being the final arbiter guarantee that the distribution of finite and singular socio-economic resources is balanced between the advantaged and disadvantaged communities. Identity alone, therefore, does not make disadvantaged communities entitled to affirmative action. On the basis of facts and circumstances, the courts decide who will avail affirmative action in a given situation.

III The Legislature for Identification of Vulnerable Communities for Affirmative Action: Canadian Model

Canada is a common law country (except for Quebec region which practiSes civil law system). Common law countries are capable of evolving new judicial doctrines over time in response to change in social values and societal structure.[33] However, in Canada, protection and advancement of disadvantaged communities did not get much attention from the judiciary. Lepofsky claims that the concept of equality rights gained prominence only lately between 1960–81 (the period before the enactment of the Canadian Charter and the Canadian Human Rights Act).[34] The initiative to protect minorities against discrimination was made by provincial legislatures followed by the federal Parliament. Positive effort was made by the legislature to take over the responsibility of minority protections from the hands of the judiciary because of the failure of the judiciary to acknowledge and address issues of discrimination.[35]

Even the agencies and administrative tribunals which were vested with the responsibility to address the then newly recognised problems of discrimination on the basis of age, gender, marital status etc. were authorised by the expanded legislative mandates.

The Canadian Bill of Rights, which was enacted by the federal Parliament in 1960 was meant to guarantee civil liberties against infringement by the federal parliament. This Bill, through Section 1, provided for equality before law without discrimination on the basis of colour, religion, sex, race, or national origin. The Bill was meant to prevail over all the federal statutes except those which by its provisions, exempt itself from the reach of the Bill.[36] The Supreme Court was authorised to implement the Bill of Rights to strike down discriminatory federal laws which were not in adherence with the Bill of Rights. However, instead of using Bill of Rights as a tool, the Supreme Court was of the opinion that it must show deference to the Acts of Parliament.[37] Hence, the discriminatory statutes were not struck down by the court but were harmoniously read into the Charter's provisions. Thus, legislature remained the only effective organ of the state that not only implemented affirmative action programmes, it made explicit provisions to mention who are to be included as entitled beneficiaries in such schemes.

Occupational inequality in employment faced by women, disabled persons, population of natives, and visible minorities in Canada prompted affirmative action programmes in the employment sector after the enactment of the Charter.[38] The commitment of the Charter of Rights and Freedom, to equality rights, confers obligation upon the state to ensure representation of disadvantaged groups in the employment sector. The affirmative action programme in Canada aims at reducing inequality in employment and as a consequence also intends to affect promotion, career development, recruitment, and hiring.[39] One of the major aims behind affirmative action in employment sectors has been to increase the representation of under-represented groups of people which gave rise to the concept of 'employment equity'.[40]

In Canada, affirmative action is synonymous with 'Employment Equity' though the legislature has made other laws on affirmative action. The courts have merely shown deference to the lead taken by the legislature, which remained the only branch of state in Canada to take this initiative. The legislature has made efforts in phases, to introduce affirmative action with detailed provisions. Hence, with passage of time, the legislature in Canada has emerged as the leading organ of the state for identifying communities for affirmative actions, too, while at the same time making equitable schemes for these communities in furtherance of substantive equality.

III.1 Constitutional Provisions for Affirmative Actions in Canada

The Canadian Charter of Rights and Freedoms, 1982, is the Bill of Rights entrenched in the Constitution of Canada. This Bill of Rights, through Section 15 guarantees equality to every person, either as negative right of non-discrimination or as positive right of affirmative action.

Prior to the entrenchment of this Charter in the Constitution, the basic freedoms of the people were dependent upon the legislature through enactment of federal and state laws. With the Charter coming into force, the rights and freedom enunciated in it were given the status of constitutional rights which are justiciable in the court of law. The rights guaranteed in the Charter are implemented through legislations enacted by competent bodies while the courts of law guarantee interpretation of the rights mentioned in the legislation in adherence with the Charter.

The right to equality under the Charter is also guaranteed through legislations and not directly by the Charter. Even the entitled communities for affirmative actions in Canadian system are also mentioned through legislations.

The Charter makes a broad provision that upholds the constitutionality of laws, programmes, or activities which aims at 'amelioration of conditions of disadvantaged groups' on certain grounds.[41] While 'laws' are enacted by the parliament, mention of 'programmes' and 'activities', in the equality clause authorize the executive branch of the state and even the private employers to implement affirmative action.

III.2 The Definitions of Designated Groups under Affirmative Action Laws in Canada

The Employment Equity Act of 1995 was enacted with the purpose of ensuring that no person is denied the opportunity of employment for reasons not related to ability.[42] This Act specifically mentions the sections of communities that are to be made eligible for affirmative action. The 'aboriginal peoples' comprise one of the designated groups under this Act and includes Indian, Inuit, and Metis.[43] The 'members of visible minorities' are defined as peoples other than aboriginal peoples who are non-Caucasian in race and non-white in colour.[44] Finally, the Act defines 'persons with disabilities' as persons who consider themselves disadvantaged by reason of their impairment; those persons who believe that their employer or potential employers are likely to consider them disadvantaged for the purpose of their employment because of the impairment and also includes those persons whose functional limitations owing to disability have been accommodated in their current workplace.[45]

Though the definition of 'aboriginal peoples' under the Employment Equity Act appears to be identity based, there are several layers of overlap in the identities of people described under this phrase. This issue becomes important since affirmative action under the Charter is based on identity.

According to Jeremy Webber, there are three cultural divisions of aboriginal people in Canada.[46] The first group, according to Webber, comprises the First Nations who are known as the Indian Peoples under the Constitutional Act, 1982.[47] The second group comprises the Inuit who were formerly known as the Eskimos. The third group comprise of Metis who are primarily the descendants of union between fur traders (who were especially French Canadian traders) and Aboriginal women.[48]

Communities based on identity appear to be neat and distinct and yet there are contested claims of identity among all the three groups. The controversy surrounding the definition of Metis stems from the fact that uncontested identity of Metis is conferred upon those people who can trace their roots in Red River valley in Manitoba and have developed a national identity surrounding the Red River Rebellion in late nineteenth century.[49] But there are other people who also refer to themselves as Metis because they can trace their identities to communities formed through 'analogous experience of intercultural contact'.[50] There is yet another set of people who refer to themselves as Metis because of their mixed heritage.[51]

Similarly, there have been several controversies surrounding the identity of 'First Nation' or 'Indians' too since often a person can identify with dual identity of Metis and at the same time have affiliation with the First Nation.[52] Therefore, the identity status among the three groups is blurred. However, unlike the Constitutional Court of South Africa, the Canadian Supreme Court has not developed an asymmetric level of analysis on the basis of the identity of the claimant. This is to say, that the Canadian Supreme Court neither takes into account multiple identities of a person nor sits in assessment of the dominant identity of a person with multiple identities, to determine entitlement in affirmative action. In this matter, the Supreme Court of Canada accord deference to legislature which enacts affirmative action laws.

III.3 The Nature and Functioning of Affirmative Action Legislations in Canada

The Employment Equity Act, 1995, prohibits imposition of quota on employers. Section 33(1) of the Act states that the Commission or the Tribunal established under the Act shall not impose quota system on the employer. Under Section 33(2), the Act further defines quota as 'requirement to hire or promote a fixed and arbitrary number of persons during a given period'. The Canadian government has made an attempt[53] to clarify the functioning of the Employment Equity Act. In the absence of quota system in Canada, the clarity on identity of persons become imperative for availing affirmative action.

The government of Canada mentions that the employment institutions aim at setting recruitment targets to close the gap of under-representations and developing a workforce that better reflects the diversity of communities in Canadian society.[54]

The Rosalie Abella Commission Report of 1984[55] emphasizes upon the functioning of the Employment Equity Act since the Act itself was a follow-up to this Report presented by Judge Rosalie Silberman Abella.[56] As per the Commission, the designated group comprise women, aboriginal peoples, persons with disabilities, and visible minorities who are non-Caucasian in race and non-white in colour, and comprise 60 per cent of the population.[57] These are the same groups of people who find mention in the Employment Equity Act.

Since the Canadian system of affirmative action does not have a quota system, competing claims within the four categories from the designated group appears inevitable. The members of the designated group themselves have raised this issue which finds mention in the Rosie Abella Commission Report. The Commission records the concern as:

> ...Their economic histories are different, their social and cultural context are different, their concerns are different and the particular solutions required by each group are widely disparate. Some therefore felt that it minimized the significance of each of their unique concerns to be combined with three other group.
>
> This concern also derived from a sense that they would be competing for opportunities with the other groups rather than with the general community.[58]

But the government of Canada clarifies this issue by stating that though certain positions are left open only to designated groups, filling up of the same also depends on the representation of each of the four groups within the designated group on a case basis, and the group which is more under-represented gets the job.[59] This aspect of affirmative action in Canada draws similarity with the approach of the Constitutional Court of South Africa where affirmative action claims are decided on a case-by-case basis. The similarity of this approach in both the jurisdictions might be attributed to the absence of a quota system which specifies certain number of seats for each designated group.

III.4 Reemphasizing Legislature as Leading Organ of State for Identification of Designated Communities in Canada

The *Alberta v Cunningham*[60] decision by the Supreme Court of Canada in 2011 concerned constitutional challenge to a provision of the Metis Settlements Act of Alberta.[61] The Act provided for settlement lands to eight Metis communities in the province but prohibited status Indians from becoming members of the Metis settlement. Though the members were also members of the Metis communities, they were at the same time entitled to be registered under the Indian Act. This is not an unusual practice in Canada owing to multiple identities of aboriginal peoples as has been mentioned in the earlier section of this chapter. The claimants in this case, though belonging to both communities, opted to be registered under the Indian Act in order to avail medical benefits available under the Act.

As a consequence, they were de-registered by the Registrar of the Metis Settlement Land registry, from the Metis Settlement Act as was prescribed in its provisions. Interestingly, the claimants moved the Supreme Court for violation of Section 15(1) and not Section 15(2).

The Court held that the Act was enacted under Section 15(2) which is a complete provision in itself. Section 15(1) cannot be invoked in this case. The object of this Act, the Court opined, was to promote and preserve Metis identity self-governance and culture by creating a land base for Metis. The Metis community, unlike its Indian counterpart, lacks reserves on which they could strengthen and nurture their identity, culture, and self-governance. The Metis community also lack the benefits availed by the Indian communities under the Indian Act. Therefore, inclusion of self-registered Indians within the Metis community under this Act will result in dilution of Metis identity and consequently dilute the objective of the Act.[62]

The Alberta case serves as an example that re-emphasizes upon court's deference to legislature on identification of communities entitled for affirmative action in Canada. Unlike the South African courts which take into account the most dominant identity of persons from disadvantaged groups,[63] Canadian judiciary adheres strictly to the provisions of the law and does not consider borderline cases through its interpretations.

Therefore, extension of rights under Section 15 ultimately depends on competent legislative bodies with specific mention of the entitled communities through the law. The judiciary on the other hand decides on the constitutionality of laws themselves on the ground of protection of right to equality.

IV The Executive Model for Notification of Designated Communities: The Indian Case

Affirmative action in India, from the perspective of identification of entitled communities, is heavily dependent on the role of the executive branch of the state with the Legislature playing peripheral role in notifications of disadvantaged groups. The schemes initiated for affirmative action in India do not define the communities in particular who are entitled for affirmative action. They are rather available mandatorily, to all communities notified by the President of Republic through Orders which may subsequently be amended by Act of Parliament, as Schedule Castes (SCs) and Schedule Tribes (STs). Affirmative action is also available to all those communities enlisted as the 'Other Backward Classes' (OBC) by the appropriate government. Unlike South Africa and Canada, the eligibility for availing affirmative action in India cannot be adjudicated before the court of law on a case by case basis. One's identity associated with a community enlisted or notified for affirmative action makes a person eligible despite one's social condition. This is true for persons belonging to SC and ST communities. For availing affirmative action as an OBC, however, one must not fall into the category of 'creamy layer.'[64] The Indian judiciary has decided status of persons in situations where, for example, a person of SC origin and practice had a parent practising Islam religion[65] or when a person of SC origin whose ancestor converted to Christianity reconverted to Hinduism.[66] In other situations, the Indian Supreme Court has also directed the methodology for deciding 'inadequacy of representation' of SC and ST communities for the purpose of Article 16(4-A) of the Constitution.[67] However, in none of these situations the judiciary has decided upon the eligibility of a community for affirmative action. Rather, the judiciary has decided upon the membership of persons with communities or the representation of members from communities that are already entitled to affirmative action through notifications. Hence, identification of communities in Indian context is premised primarily on the decisions of the Executive.

In the Indian context, affirmative action schemes are restricted to only those communities that are notified or enlisted. Hence, these procedures for identification of these communities comprise a serious constitutional practice which is implemented by the Executive because of conferment of authority on this organ by the Constitution itself.

IV.1 Major Provisions on Affirmative Action under the Indian Constitution

Affirmative action is mostly discussed under Articles 14, 15, and 16 of the Constitution. The 'backward classes' mentioned in these Articles for the purpose of affirmative action consist of the SC, ST, and the Other Backward Classes (OBCs)as three different sets of communities. The procedures for notification of communities for the purpose of affirmative action are also different for SCs and STs on the one hand and the OBCs on the other hand. Affirmative action in India is usually implemented through Executive orders.[68] While the Executive orders themselves face challenges in the court of law, the procedure for identification of disadvantaged groups for the purpose of affirmative action pose parallel line of challenges in the Indian context.

The definition and procedure of notification of SCs and STs are mentioned in the Constitution itself and these communities are required to be notified by the President of the Republic. SCs has been described in the Constitution of India through Article 341 as those castes, races, or tribes, or parts within the caste, race, or tribe that are deemed by the President through public notification after consultation with the Governor.[69] Such notified communities can be excluded and new communities can be included under the list of SCs by Parliament only through an enacted law. Notifications once made cannot be merely varied by subsequent notifications.[70] Similarly, Article 342 of the Constitution defines STs.

The Constitution of India also directs setting up of national commissions for the SCs and STs, through its provisions[71]. Initially, the Constitution through Article 338[72] provided for a constitutional post for a Special Officer for SCs and STs. However, through the 65th Constitutional Amendment in 1992, the Constitution directed setting up of National Commission for SCs. A similar Commission has been set up for STs under Article 338-A, through 89th Amendment of the Constitution in 2003.

Various clauses in Article 338 show that it is constitutionally mandated that the National Commission shall be set up by the President of the Republic. The members of the Commission including its chairperson shall be appointed by the President. Further, the Commission shall submit its reports to the President of the Republic. The Union and the State governments shall have to consult the commission for policy matters related to these communities.

Except for clause 10 which appears only in Article 338, Article 338-A provides for similar provisions for STs. With respect to clause 10 of Article 338, the "other backward classes" mentioned in the clause includes the socially and educationally backward classes that are identified by the President on the basis of reports of the Commission under Article 340(1).[73]

IV.2 Procedure for Notification of SCs and STs

The notification of SC and ST communities are enumerated in the Constitution (Scheduled Caste) Order, 1950[74] and the Constitution (Scheduled Tribe) Order 1950,[75] respectively, by the President of the Republic. Inclusion in and exclusion from the lists for both SC and ST communities follow rigorous procedure with limited role of the legislature.

The communities that are entitled for affirmative action under these two categories are notified in the Orders and these two lists are exhaustive. The communities whose names do not appear in the lists cannot claim for reservation even though the claiming community might belong to the same caste but belong to different sub-castes. The President of the Republic, is authorized to limit the notification to parts or groups within the castes, races, and tribes while specifying castes, races, and tribes in the notifications. Further, the President can specify castes, races, and tribes or parts thereof not for the entire state but parts of the state where he is satisfied that the examination of social and economic backwardness of the races, castes, or tribes justifies such specification.[76] The same procedure is followed for STs.

As for the procedure by which communities get included in and excluded from the two lists, after the two 1950 President Orders came into force, any subsequent addition, modification or deletion of communities from the lists can be made only by law enacted by the Parliament.[77] The state government/ Union Territory administrations begins the process by making a proposal for inclusion in/exclusion from communities with ethnographic data as support. The proposal is made to the Registrar General of India (RGI) for her/his comments. If the proposal is agreeable to the RGI, then it is sent to the specific National Commission. If it is not agreeable by the RGI, then the report is sent back to the state government/Union Territory administrations for reconsideration that might present it back to the RGI after modifications. If the modified proposal is still not agreeable by RGI, then the state government might reject the proposal.[78]

Once the proposal reaches the specific national commission according to the category (whether claim is made for SC/ST), it might be rejected by the National Commission with approval of Minister for Social Justice and Empowerment. But, if the proposal is agreeable by National Commission, then it is introduced as a Bill for consideration and passing before the Parliament as required by Articles 341(2) and 342(2) of the constitution. Once the Bill is passed by both the House of the Parliament and President gives assent, the list stands amended.[79]

The subsequent amendments made to the President's Orders and various reports by the Ministry of Social Justice and Empowerment reflect that there has not only been inclusion but exclusions of communities too through this procedure.[80] Also, reports on the procedure for inclusion and exclusion of communities reflect that a significant number of claims for inclusion are rejected by the Registrar General of India at the first stage itself.[81] Thus, the procedure reflects a rigorous procedural scrutiny exercised at every stage before a SC or a ST community is notified in the Orders.

IV.3 Subsequent Shift of Power to the Legislature under Constitutional Provision

It was felt throughout the years that it was not enough to make provisions for reservation at the stage of appointment alone. This led to the Constitution (Seventy-Seventh) Amendment Act, 1995 whereby clause (4-A) was added to Article 16. Clause (4-A) authorises the State to make provision for affirmative action in matters of promotion in public employment. This provision is applicable for the SC and ST communities. It does not extend to the OBCs. However, what becomes a matter of concern with this provision, from the separation of powers perspective, is the phrase: ".....which, in the opinion of the State, are not adequately represented in the service under the State".[82]

Thus, there was a shift from entitlement through notification to entitlement through discretion of the State for the SC and ST communities for reservation in promotion. Insertion of Article 16(4-A) and Article 16(4-B) in the Constitution was challenged before the Supreme Court of India in the case of *M. Nagaraj v Union of India*[83] on several grounds.

Kapadia J. writing for the majority in *M. Nagaraj* decision, held that in every case of providing affirmative action in promotion for SC or ST candidate, the State has to show, through quantifiable data, the compelling reasons of backwardness and inadequacy of representation of the community to which the candidate seeking promotion under affirmative action belongs. This, coupled with the factor of overall efficiency in administration mandated under Article 335 of the Constitution and also ensuring that the limit of affirmative action does not exceed 50% of the total seats available, will validate the provision on reservation in promotion.[84] The Court further added that Article 16(4-A) is an enabling provision and there is no compulsion on the State to provide for affirmative action in promotion.[85]

Another apprehension with leaving the decision of identifying communities entitled to affirmative action to the local government, was expressed in the Constituent Assembly.[86] In the words of Muniswamy Pillai:

> .....I am grateful to the Drafting Committee and also the Chairman of that Committee for bringing the second portion of it very clear, that in future, after the declaration by the President as to who will be the Schedule Castes, and where there is need for including any other class or to exclude anybody or any communities from the list of Schedule Castes that must be by the word of Parliament. I feel grateful to him for bringing in this clause, because I know as a matter of fact, when Harijans [Scheduled Castes] behave independently or asserting their right on some matter, the Ministers of provinces not only take note and actions against those members but they bring the community to which that particular individual belongs; and thereby not only the individual, but also the community that comes under that category of Scheduled Castes are harassed. By this provision, I think the danger is removed.[87]

With this shift of power in favour of the local government through insertion of Article 16(4-A), the apprehension expressed in the Constituent Assembly appears to be valid. The President's Orders for the SC and ST communities are homogenous notifications under the Constitution. However, with a shift in authority and procedure for deciphering entitlement to reservation in promotion among notified communities on individual basis, a tacit attempt is also made to shift from community based entitlement to sub-community based entitlement through individual candidate's membership in a caste and independent examinations of backwardness of those castes by the state each time reservation for promotion is sought.

IV.4 Historical Background and Constitutional Provisions for Notification of 'Other Backward Classes'

Other Backward Classes (OBCs) become entitled to affirmative action on different grounds other than the SCs and STs. Unlike the SCs and STs, the Constituent Assembly witnessed serious debates on the definition of OBCs.[88] Some members of the Assembly strongly felt that providing reservation to backward classes other than SCs will seriously jeopardise the prospects of SCs in getting reservation in government services.[89] Some other members expressed serious doubts on the vagueness and ambiguity associated with the term 'backward' in the context of Indian society.[90] However, some members like Shri K.M. Munshi argued that every community which are really backward should be availed with reservation. The definition and scope of the word 'backward' cannot be restricted and confined to particular community.[91] Instead of restricting the definition of 'backward' to the lowest social, economic and political layer of the society, Shri K.M. Munshi, asserted that the safety associated with the word 'backward' is that it is comprehensive and inclusive and covers all those communities who are in need of protection under the constitution.[92]

Though Shri T.T. Krishnamachari, another member of the Constituent Assembly, stated that the term 'backward' has to be interpreted by some supreme authority, Dr Ambedkar made clarifications regarding the authority that is supposed to interpret the term 'backward'.[93] He stated: 'Somebody asked me: "What is a backward community?" Well, I think anyone who reads the language of the draft itself will find that we have left it to be determined by each local Government. A backward community is a community which is backward in the opinion of the Government. My honourable friend Mr T.T. Krishnamachari asked me whether this rule will be justifiable. It is rather difficult to give a dogmatic answer. Personally, I think it would be a justiciable matter. If the local Government included in this category of reservations such a large number of seats; I think one could very well go to the Federal court and the Supreme Court and say that the reservation is of such a magnitude that the rule regarding equality of opportunity has been destroyed and the court will then come to the conclusion whether the local Government or State Government has acted in a reasonable and prudent manner.'[94] Thus

OBCs consist of more comprehensive list of communities to include all the backward communities that need the protection of the Constitution.

IV.5 Legislative Provisions on 'Other Backward Classes'

In 1993, a permanent statutory body was set up under the National Commission for Backward Classes Act, 1993 (NCBC Act) to address the issues of OBCs as constitutional mandate. The provisions of this Act might indicate that the Central Government which consists of the legislature too, are more involved in the procedure for identification of OBCs as compared to the SC and ST Commissions. However, Article 340 of the Constitution reveals that with the amendment of the Constitution and the enactment of the legislation, identification of communities for the OBCs are not solely left on the local government as was ensured in the Constituent Assembly.

The NCBC Act might help in ascertain the involvement of legislature. But prior to that, it is pertinent to highlight the definition of 'backward classes' under this Act. As per section 2(a): 'backward classes' mean such backward classes of citizens other than the SCs and the STs as may be specified by the Central Government in the lists." The list, under this Act is defined in section 2(c) which states:

> 'list' means lists prepared by the Government of India from time to time for the purpose of making provision for the reservation of appointments or posts in favour of backward classes of citizens which, in the opinion of that Government, are not adequately represented in the services under the Government of India and any local or other authority within the territory of India or under the control of Government of India.

Instead of the President of the Republic, as is the case for National Commissions for Scheduled Castes and Scheduled Tribes, the Central Government appoints the members of the Backward Class Commission. However, a composition of the members of the Commission shall reveal that it is not under the control of the Central Government once it is constituted. Section 3(1) provides that the Central Government shall constitute the body of the commission. Section 3(2) provides that Central government shall nominate the Chairperson who is or has been a Judge of the Supreme Court or the High Courts. The Commission shall also comprise of one social scientist and two persons who have special knowledge in the matters related to backward classes. Finally, the Commission requires a Member secretary who has been an officer with the Central Government.

The requirement of the Chairman to be a judge of an appellate court shows that commission is to be headed by a member of the judiciary. While the three other members that is, a social scientist and two persons with special knowledge about backward classes are to be appointed on the basis of their involvement with backward class issues, the member secretary is required to be an officer of the Central Government. Officers of Central Government are civil servants and are not members of political parties.

Section 9 of the Act through clause 1, confers upon the Commission, the authority to examine requests for inclusion in the list. The Commission has also been conferred with the authority to hear complaints about over inclusion or under inclusion of backward classes from the list and advise the Central Government from time to time. Section 9(2) provides that the advise of the Commission shall be ordinarily binding on the government.

This means that the government needs to furnish reasons for its disagreement with the commission in case it holds contrary views to that of the Commission. In one such case, *Ram Singh v Union of India*[95], the Supreme Court of India struck down the inclusion of *Jat* community from the list of backward classes holding that since the of the Commission had advised against inclusion of the community in the list of OBCs after examining their case, the inclusion of the community in the list by Central Government is unconstitutional since the Parliament failed to show sufficient reasons to act contrary to the advice of the Commission.[96]

At present, the Backward Class commission lists is drawn by Central Government which comprise of individual state lists.[97] However, initially when the Mandal Commission was sought to be implemented through Government Order by reserving 27 per cent seats in government services, the list of OBC comprised of those communities whose names appeared both in the list of the respective state government and the recommendation of the Mandal commission.

Thus, the involvement of the Executive, in identification of SC, ST, and OBCs, for affirmative action, is evident. The level of involvement of the Executive for each community might differ. Nevertheless, this is the main organ of the State in India that identifies entitle communities through rigorous process whereas judiciary serves as check for procedural compliance and legislature makes laws for the beneficiaries identified by the Executive.

V Conclusion

Affirmative action programmes have been introduced in some of the democratic constitutions of the world as an element of fundamental right for those communities whose oppression has not been results of natural outcomes but has been consequences of social construct.

It is true that there are affluent classes in every backward community that avail affirmative action. However, discrimination has been strongly identity based and the constitutions through affirmative action does not aim at eradicating economic wants alone. It primarily aims at abolishing discrimination on the basis of identity. Despite widespread economic diversity among oppressed groups therefore, the Constitution of India for example, recognises different categories of communities as homogenous single units based on social identities. There are claims in all the jurisdictions that form part of this study, that affirmative action under constitutions provide for vague provisions and wide discretionary power to the State to frame affirmative action programmes according to their electoral convenience. It is also claimed that identity based affirmative action fails to reach out to those among backward communities who are really deserving of it.

This study intends to establish that affirmative action are not consequences of theoretical concern for equality. In all the three jurisdictions—South Africa, Canada and India, identification of communities for affirmative action has either been mentioned in the constitution itself or has evolved as a legal practice.

It is true that the level of details on the functioning of affirmative action vary with jurisdictions. However, since the adoption of their constitutions, each jurisdiction has developed a distinct and consistent procedure of identification of communities for affirmative action programme under the separation of powers doctrine. In each jurisdiction, one organ of the State has taken the lead for identifying persons or communities to be made eligible for affirmative action. The emergence of a leading organ of the State in different jurisdictions has been either a consequence of constitutional provisions or historical and general constitutional set-up in the jurisdiction.

The Indian Constitution for example, provides for detailed unambiguous division of authorities among the different organs of the State and independent commissions, for the purpose for implementation of affirmative action including inclusion into and exclusion from lists of entitled communities for affirmative action. Other jurisdictions like South Africa and Canada do not find such detailed conferment of authority in their Constitution and Charter respectively. In all three jurisdictions, Canada, India and South Africa, the marginalized sections comprise of the majority of the population. Yet, in South Africa, the designated groups comprise a comprehensive list who are made eligible for affirmative action. The Court subsequently, decides competing claims between these communities on case by case basis. In Indian and Canadian jurisdictions however, the lists of designated groups are restricted by the legislature wherein not all the marginalized communities are made eligible for affirmative action. The Court of law does not subsequently adjudicate upon eligibility for affirmative action among designated groups though the Court may decide by virtue of descent or origin, whether a person belongs to an already notified or designated community.

This study does not aim at claiming superiority of one model of affirmative action over the others. In fact, the study of these three jurisdictions has revealed that all the three States face counter claims of fallacy in implementing affirmative action. For example, arguing stagnancy in notification of the President Orders for SCs and STs in India, there has been a shift of power in the hands of the legislature through a constitutional amendment, to determine in each case of affirmative action claim even from the extremely backward communities, their backwardness and inadequate representation of their community. Also, if limited judicial review is permitted on the 'satisfaction of the President' on rejection of mercy petitions and imposition of President's rule in the provinces under Article 356 of the Indian Constitution, then it can be argued as to why should there be no judicial review, even if limited, on President's notifications under Articles 341 and 342 of the Constitution. It may be noted that unlike the requirement of 'satisfaction of the President' in case of mercy petitions or exercise of power under Article 356, notification through President's Order does not require 'satisfaction of the President' which in turn does not leave scope for judicial review. Rather, notification by the President of entitled communities is preceded by rigorous scrutiny by the National Commissions which are constitutional bodies consisting of experts in the field.

As for Canada and South Africa, non- discrimination has been very actively dealt with in both jurisdictions whereas affirmative action cases before the courts in both the jurisdiction have been rare. The case by case scrutiny by judiciary in South Africa and reluctance of the executive and the judiciary in Canada, have resulted in very slow implementation of affirmative action. On the basis of cases available at hand however, one can decipher the procedure of identification of entitled communities for affirmative action in both jurisdictions despite the fact that neither the Constitution of South Africa nor the Canadian Charter confer authority on a distinct organ of the State to identify communities for affirmative action.

Notes and References

1. Mark A. Drumbl and John D.R. Craig. 1997. 'Affirmative Action in Question: A Coherent Theory for Section 15(2)', *Review of Constitutional Studies,* 4(1): 80–123.

2. J. L. Pretorious. 2010. 'Fairness in Transformation: A Critique of the Constitutional Court's Affirmative Action Jurisprudence', 26 *South African Journal on Human Rights*, pp. 536–570.
3. *Ram Kumar Gijroya v Delhi Sub. Service Selection*: Civil Appeal No. 1691 of 2016; The main issue in this case was whether a person who appears for a government examination under 'disadvantage group' category, can submit his/ her certificate of disadvantaged group after the last date mentioned in the government advertisement. This case did not concern itself about identifying disadvantaged groups but remained confined to the single question of whether a certificate can be submitted after the last date mentioned by the government.
4. Wessel le Roux. 2013. 'Descriptive Overview of South African Constitution and Constitutional Court' in Oscar Vilhena, Upendra Baxi, and Frans Vijeon (eds), *Transformative Constitutionalism: Comparing the apex courts of Brazil, India and South Africa*, (Pretoria: PULP) 139.
5. Wessel le Roux, 'Descriptive Overview of South African Constitution and Constitutional Court', 140.
6. Wessel le Roux, 'Descriptive Overview of South African Constitution and Constitutional Court', 141.
7. Wessel le Roux, 'Descriptive Overview of South African Constitution and Constitutional Court', 142.
8. Wessel le Roux, 'Descriptive Overview of South African Constitution and Constitutional Court', 142.
9. Section 9 (1)Everyone is equal before the law and has the right to equal protection and benefit of the law.

   (2) Equality includes the full and equal enjoyment of all rights and freedoms. To promote the achievement of equality, legislative and other measures designed to protect or advance persons, or categories of persons, disadvantaged by unfair discrimination may be taken.

   (3) The state may not unfairly discriminate directly or indirectly against anyone on one or more grounds, including race, gender, sex, pregnancy, marital status, ethnic or social origin, colour, sexual orientation, age, disability, religion, conscience, belief, culture, language and birth.
10. The Constitution of The Republic of South Africa 1996, s 9(2).
11. The Employment Equity (Amendment) Act 2014, s 1.
12. The Employment Equity (Amendment) Act 2014, s 1.
13. Mpfariseni Budeli, 'Employment Equity and Affirmative Action in South Africa: A Review of the Jurisprudence of the Courts since 1994' (Twenty Years of South African Constitutionalism), New York Law School 14 November 2014 14,
14. Mpfariseni Budeli, 'Employment Equity and Affirmative Action in South Africa'. See *Chinese Association of South Africa v The Minister of Labour* 59251/ 2007, http://www.saflii.org/za/cases/ZAGPHC/2008/174.pdf, accessed 15 March 2016.
15. Mpfariseni Budeli, 'Employment Equity and Affirmative Action in South Africa', 13.

16. The Broad Based Black Employment Equity Amendment Act 2013, s 1(c).
17. The Broad Based Black Employment Equity Amendment Act 2013, s 1(c).
18. Wessel le Roux, 'Descriptive Overview of South African Constitution and Constitutional Court'.
19. Wessel le Roux, 'Descriptive Overview of South African Constitution and Constitutional Court'.
20. 1995 (3) SA 391 (CC). In this case, the Constitutional Court of South Africa held that capital punishment is inconsistent with the human rights principles that are expressed in the interim constitution of South Africa.
21. Wessel le Roux, 'Descriptive Overview of South African Constitution and Constitutional Court'.
22. *Minister of Finance, The Political Office Bearers Pension Fund v Frederik Jacobus Van Heerden* (2004) 6 SA 121 (CC).
23. *Minister of Finance, The Political Office Bearers Pension Fund v Frederik Jacobus Van Heerden* (2004) 6 SA 121 (CC). (Sachs J.).
24. *Minister of Finance, The Political Office Bearers Pension Fund v Frederik Jacobus Van Heerden* (2004) 6 SA 121 (CC), (Sachs J.).
25. *Minister of Finance, The Political Office Bearers Pension Fund v Frederik Jacobus Van Heerden* (2004) 6 SA 121 (CC), (Sachs J.).
26. Saras Jagwanth. 2004. 'Affirmative Action in a Transformative Context: The South African Experience'. 36(3) *Connecticut Law Review* pp. 725–46, p. 734.
27. Saras Jagwanth, 2004. 'Affirmative Action in a Transformative Context'.
28. See, for example, *Public Servants Association of South Africa v Minister of Justice and Others* 1997 (3) SA 925 (T).
29. See for example, *Pretoria City Council v Walker* 1998 (2) SA 363 (CC).
30. *Minister of Finance, The Political Office Bearers Pension Fund v Frederik Jacobus Van Heerden* (2004) 6 SA 121 (CC), (Moseneke J.).
31. *Minister of Finance, The Political Office Bearers Pension Fund v Frederik Jacobus Van Heerden* (2004) 6 SA 121 (CC), (Moseneke J.).
32. *Minister of Finance, The Political Office Bearers Pension Fund v Frederik Jacobus Van Heerden* (2004) 6 SA 121 (CC), (Moseneke J.).
33. M. David Lepofsky, 1992. 'The Canadian Judicial Approach to Equality Rights: Freedom Ride or Rollercoaster?', *National Journal of Constitutional Law*, vol. 1: 1–408 esp. 317.
34. M. David Lepofsky. 1992. 'The Canadian Judicial Approach to Equality Rights'.
35. M. David Lepofsky, 'The Canadian Judicial Approach to Equality Rights'. 319.
36. The Canadian Bill of Rights 1960 S.C. 1960, c. 44, s. 2.
37. See, for example, *Curr v R.* [1972] SCR 889 (Laskin J.).
38. Carol Agocs, 1986. 'Affirmative Action, Canadian Style: A Reconnaisance', *Canadian Public Policy*, 12(1): 148–62, esp. 149.
39. Carol Agocs, 1986. 'Affirmative Action, Canadian Style'.
40. Supra 38, 150.
41. The Canadian Charter of Rights and Freedom 1982, s. 15(2).

42. Employment Equity Act 1995, s 2, http://laws-lois.justice.gc.ca/eng/acts/E-5.401/page-1.html, accessed 9 December 2015.
43. Employment Equity Act 1995, s. 3.
44. Employment Equity Act 1995, s. 3.
45. Employment Equity Act 1995, s. 3.
46. Jeremy Webber, 2015. *The Constitution of Canada: A Contextual Analysis*, Oxford and Portland, OR: Hart Publishing, p. 226.
47. Jeremy Webber, 2015. *The Constitution of Canada: A Contextual Analysis.*
48. Jeremy Webber, 2015. *The Constitution of Canada: A Contextual Analysis.*
49. Jeremy Webber, *The Constitution of Canada*, 227.
50. Jeremy Webber, *The Constitution of Canada*, 227.
51. Jeremy Webber, *The Constitution of Canada*, 227.
52. Jeremy Webber, *The Constitution of Canada*, 227.
53. Employment Equity–Myths and Reality, http://www.labour.gc.ca/eng/standards_equity/eq/pubs_eq/myths.shtml, accessed 9 December, 2015.
54. Frequently Asked questions in government services http://jobs-emplois.gc.ca/centres/faq-eng.htm, 10 December 2015.
55. Minister of Supply and Services Canada, 1984. *Equality in Employment: A Royal Commission Report.* 17 http://www.bakerlaw.ca/wp-content/uploads/Rosie-Abella-1984-Equality-in-Employment.pdf, 23 December 2015.
56. John Hucker. 1999. 'Affirmative Action Canadian Style: Reflections on Canada's Employment Equity Law' in Titia Loenen and Peter R. Rodrigues (eds), *Non-Discrimination Law: Comparative Perspectives.* Leiden: Martinus Nijhoff Publishers. p. 266.
57. Minister of Supply and Services Canada, 1984. *Equality in Employment: A Royal Commission Report.*
58. Minister of Supply and Services Canada, 1984. *Equality in Employment: A Royal Commission Report.*
59. Frequently Asked questions in government services http://jobs-emplois.gc.ca/centres/faq-eng.htm, 10 December 2015.
60. *Alberta (Aboriginal Affairs and Northern Development) v Cunningham* [2011] 2 SCR 670.
61. Peter W. Hogg, 2014. *Constitutional Law of Canada: 2014 Student Edition.* Scarborough, ON: Carswell. pp. 55–6.
62. *Alberta (Aboriginal Affairs and Northern Development) v Cunningham* [2011] 2 SCR 670.
63. In South Africa, each disadvantaged group is considered as a bearer of different histories of marginalization and oppression. For example, discrimination affects men differently from women. In *President of Republic of South Africa v Hugo*: 1997 (6) BCLR 708 (CC), Goldstone J. opined that:

    'Each case, therefore, will require a careful and thorough understanding of the impact of the discriminatory action upon the particular people concerned to determine whether its overall impact is one which furthers the constitutional goal of equality or not. A classification which is unfair in one context may not necessarily be unfair in a different context.'

64. This is a term used for those members of 'Other Backward Class' communities who cannot avail affirmative action by virtue of being wealthier and having better educational qualifications. The characteristics of creamy layer has been mentioned in *Ashok Kumar Thakur v Union of India* (2008) 6 SCC 1.
65. *Mohammad Sadique v Darbara Singh:* Civil Appeal No. 4870 of 2015.
66. *K.P. Manu v Chairman, Scrutiny Committee for Verification of Community Certificate:* Civil Appeal no. 7065 of 2008.
67. *Uttar Pradesh Power Corporation v Rajesh Kumar and Ors.*: (2012) 7 SCC 1.
68. M.P. Singh, 1994. 'Are Articles 15(4) and 16(4) Fundamental Rights?' 3 *Supreme Court Cases* (Journal) 33.
69. The Constitution of India, 1950, Article 341(1).
70. The Constitution of India, 1950, Article 341(2).
71. The Constitution of India, 1950, As. 338 and 338A.
73. Mahendra Pal Singh, *V.N. Shukla's Constitution of India* (12th edition, Eastern Book Company 2013) 998.
74. The Constitution (Scheduled Caste) Order, 1950 http://lawmin.nic.in/ld/subord/rule3a.htm, 7 December 2015.
75. The Constitution (Scheduled Tribe) Order, 1950 http://lawmin.nic.in/legislative/election/volume%201/rules%20&%20order%20under%20constitution/the%20constitution%20(scheduled%20tribes)%20order,%201950.pdf, 7 December 2015.
76. Mahendra P. Singh, 2013. *V.N. Shukla's Constitution of India* (12th Edition) Delhi: Eastern Book Company. pp. 1002–3.
77. Press Information Bureau, Government of India Ministry of Social Justice and Empowerment, *Inclusion into SC List* (2015) http://pib.nic.in/newsite/PrintRelease.aspx?relid=115783 14 January 2016. For example, the 'Marati' community was excluded from the list of Scheduled Tribes of Kerala vide the Scheduled Castes and Scheduled Tribes Orders (Amendment) Act, 2002 [No. 10 of 2003] dated 7th January 2003.
78. The Constitution (Schedule Caste) Amendment Order, 2014 9.
79. The Constitution (Schedule Caste) Amendment Order, 2014 9.
80. The Constitution (Scheduled Castes) Order (Amendment) Bill, 2012: Twenty Eighth Report, Standing Committee on Social Justice and Empowerment (2011–2012) Fifteenth Lok Sabha, 11.
81. The Constitution (Scheduled Castes) Order (Amendment) Bill, 17.
82. The Constitution of India 1950, A. 16(4-A).
83. [2006] 8 SCC 212: AIR 2007 SC 71.
84. [2006] 8 SCC 212: AIR 2007 SC 71.
85. This point has been reemphasized upon in *Suresh Chandra Gautam v State of Uttar Pradesh* Writ Petition 690 of 2015 decided on 11 March 2016.
86. See *E.V. Chinnaiah v State of Andhra Pradesh* (2005) 1 SCC 394.

87. Supra 86 (Hegde J).
88. See generally Jayant Lakshmikant Aparajit, 1992. *Equality and Compensatory Discrimination under the Indian Constitution.* Nagpur: Dattsons. pp.149–68.
89. See H.J. Khandekar, Constituent Assembly of India (vol. VII). 691–2.
90. See Mohammad Ismail Saheb, Constituent Assembly of India (vol. VII) 692–3.
91. K.M. Munshi, Constituent Assembly of India (vol. VII) 696–7.
92. K.M. Munshi, Constituent Assembly of India (vol. VII) 696–7.
93. Jayant Lakshmikant Aparajit, *Equality and Compensatory Discrimination under the Indian Constitution*, 159.
94. Dr B.R. Ambedkar, Constituent Assembly of India (vol. VII) 700–2.
95. Writ Petition Civil No. 274 of 2014.
96. Writ Petition Civil No. 274 of 2014.
97. National Commission for Backward Classes, *Central List of OBCs*, http://www.ncbc.nic.in/User_Panel/CentralListStateView.aspx 15 March 2016.

SECTION C

ENVIRONMENTAL LAW

17

The Chances of a National Sustainability Strategy for a Balanced and Stable Development

The Example of India

Michael von Hauff

I Introduction

A commitment was made by the international community of nations in 1997 to develop national sustainability strategies by the year 2002. The World Summit of Sustainable Development (WSSD) convened in Johannesburg in 2002 and pressed once again those nations that had not developed a national sustainability strategy to do so and honour their commitment (Hauff, Chandran, Saraswati 2013). A sustainability strategy, according to Agenda 21, develops and implements sustainable development as a collaborative, participative, and comprehensive process: 'A strategy should build upon and harmonize the various sectoral economic, social and environmental policies and plans that are operating in the country.' (UNCED 1992, Chapter 8.7).

In contrast to Germany and other countries, India initially did not have a separate document and there is no separate process in the context of a national sustainability strategy. India rather attempted to incorporate a conceptual framework for sustainable development directly into an existing national development planning document and to merge the existing strategies, for example, an integrated water resource management plan into the existing water policy and statutes (Hauff, Mistri 2016). In 2005, the National Rural Employment Guarantee Act was passed. This public works programme is also known as the Mahatma Gandhi National Rural Employment Guarantee Act (MGNREGA). This law guarantees hundred days of paid labour to every household in the rural areas per budget year. The law is intended to ensure that food is available to the people in rural regions. The law grants, for the first time, employment and compensation rights to the rural population of India.

The economic development of India, over the past several years, increasingly deserves attention and, in some cases, even admiration. An analysis of new trends is important in order to understand and evaluate India's current situation and future perspectives. Past analyses have primarily concentrated on the dynamic economic growth, which has increased greatly since the early 1990s—both in the national as well as the international spheres. The major focus has been on GDP and foreign trade. The overall positive economic development of India, however, is greatly hindered by several problems: poverty, pollution, inadequate energy supply, regional water stress, inequality, growing income disparity, widespread corruption, and inadequate infrastructure. It has not been possible to reduce or solve these problems satisfactorily to date (Dréze, Sen 2013). These problems may be referred to as imbalances in the context of sustainable development. However, in this respect, few other countries exhibit such a high degree of heterogeneity as India (Rothermund 2008).

The second section discusses the challenges that this paradigm presents for sustainable development. The three dimensions are contextually defined and, subsequently, the dimensions are brought together. The reason for this is that a national sustainability strategy can only be derived through a clarification of the context of the three dimensions or, the paradigm of sustainable development.

The third section classifies selected development patterns in India according to the three sustainability dimensions. This classification illustrates the extent to which Indian development corresponds to the demands of sustainable development. A brief introduction to the development of the German national sustainability strategy and the essential requirements of a national sustainability strategy is presented in the fourth section. The fifth section introduces a new method for developing a national sustainability strategy: the integrated sustainability triangle. The final chapter concludes with a presentation of several problems facing the development of a sustainability strategy for India.

II The Requirements of Sustainable Development

The challenge begins with the principle that all three dimensions of sustainable development are co-equal in rank (Hauff 2014, p. 32). In the process, it must be taken into account that the aims of sustainable development portray an ideal state. Generally, in reality there are priorities in implementation to consider regarding the three dimensions. The principle applies here that an ecological system makes it necessary to restrain economic and social actions within the limits of nature. This is made quite evident from the example of climate change. The following discussion focuses on the contextual definition of the three dimensions: the environment, economy, and society.

II.1 Ecological Sustainability

The continued survival of the human species is not ensured without the existence of certain natural states or ecological systems. Consequently, economic as well as social systems cannot be sustained on their own. Our continued existence depends on the balanced interaction of economies and society together with the ecological systems. Although there is a broad international consensus, some ecological systems, for example, the water resources in India as well as in other countries, have already partially reached a level of overconsumption that places humanity at risk. Therefore, ecological sustainability aims at the conservation of ecological systems and environmental resources. The reason for this is that ecological systems are the life support systems for all human activity. It is both a collection medium (cesspool) for anthropogenous emissions and the source of all raw materials used directly or indirectly by humans.

II.2 Economic Sustainability

The aim of economic sustainability is to strengthen economic power so as to maintain a satisfactory or desirable quality of life over time. Economic power can be strengthened by encouraging innovation, capital investment, labour productivity, and spending on research and development. However, in the context of economic sustainability, this requires a rethinking of the current production methods and consumption patterns, which are now classified as non-sustainable. A desirable living standard demands the preservation of the tangible as well as the intangible basics of life.

In the context of economic sustainability, there are divided opinions on the quantitative development of growth, but it must be noted that the measure of that growth is also being called into question (Hauff 2015, p. 113ff). A series of sustainability indicators have been developed that fundamentally differs from GDP. These do not measure the national composite income or the per capita income, that is, they are not a measure of affluence. These sustainability indicators aim at the social well-being and discussion revolves around welfare indicators or the welfare approaches such as the Index of Sustainable Economic Welfare (ISEW), the Human Development Index (HDI), or the Pressure State Response Approach of OECD. In particular, the Stiglitz study has recently received much attention in this regard (Stiglitz et al. 2009).

II.3 Social Sustainability

Although social sustainability is the subject of increasing attention, it has not been discussed or analysed for content to the same extent as the other two dimensions. Nevertheless, the idea of social sustainability, which focuses on the social cohesion of humanitarian ideals, liberty, and justice, is no less important than the other two dimensions in guaranteeing the future sustainability of a society or an economy (Hauff, Chandran, Saraswati 2013). For this reason, the term 'cohesion function' is used together with social sustainability.

One possible theoretical access to social sustainability is found in the New Institutional Economics (Hauff, Schiffer 2010, p. 1). According to this theory, it is all about the formal and informal standards and rules, which can either promote or impair the long-term cohesion of a society. An important concept in the new institutional economics is the transaction costs approach. Correspondingly, all assets have both physical as well as ownership features, although transaction costs accrue with any changes in the latter (North, Wallis 1994, pp. 611 ff). In practice, the transaction costs can vary (Scott 2006, p. 207). In the context of social sustainability, this means that a norm that promotes social cohesion is accepted by society when marginal utility (for example, safety) exceeds marginal costs (for example, the restrictions on individual rights) (Hauff, Schiffer 2010: 15).

II.4 The Relationships among the Three Dimensions

A contextual differentiation of each of the three dimensions can only describe the interrelationships among them to a limited extent. Therefore, it is essential to analyse and illustrate the complementarity of the three dimensions (Hauff 2014: 43). In the recent debate there is more discussion on the role of social capital, for example, in the preservation, accumulation, and productivity of two other kinds of capital, that is, capital in kind (real capital) and natural capital. This is evident in the areas like the stability of the law, the achievement of equal rights, and the participation (for example, civic involvement), which are categorized under social sustainability. However, environmental sustainability can also make a valuable contribution to economic sustainability—this can be illustrated by the example that clean air and clean water improve human health and increase the productivity of human capital. It may be said that the synergies springing from the complementarity of two or more kinds of capital can improve the overall quality of life.

III Selected Challenges for India in the Context of Sustainable Development

The major focus in India for sustainable development is provided by the Sustainable Development Goals, which are summarized as follows: combating poverty, education, gender equality, healthcare, environmental protection, and conservation of resources as well as global partnerships. In India, there have been a series of projects and programmes in the social area, clean-tech (clean energy, clean water, and sustainable agriculture), and human capital, all of which are designed to contribute to sustainable growth (Hauff, Chandran, Saraswati 2013: 138 ff). Progress has been noted in the area of renewable energy (especially wind energy), increases in agricultural growth to reduce rural poverty, funding for education, and expanded infrastructure to promote economic growth. The Ministry of Environment and Forests (MOEF) is responsible for the coordination of the diverse activities in support of sustainable development. In this respect, however, it must be taken into account that the projects and programmes which promote sustainable development often start at a relatively low level and, in some cases, are accompanied by a high degree of inefficiency.

In India today, the environmental, the economic, and the social dimensions diverge significantly from what is demanded for sustainable development. For this reason, examples are used to illustrate what role sustainable development can play in the stable growth of the Indian economy. As stated earlier, the macroeconomic development in India has been thoroughly positive. However, looking at the ecological sustainability, the economic sustainability, and the social sustainability there are substantial differences to what is required for the long term.

III.1 The Environmental Dimension

The overall positive macro-economic development of the last nearly twenty years has significantly contributed to the intensification of the environmental stress. An environmental crisis in India, at least in certain regions, can be observed from a study of individual environmental resources, for example, water and air and conditions have not yet reached their peak. A sufficient supply of clean water is of critical importance for agricultural production and also for the food supply. The water cycle is also a strong determinant of people's health. Consequently, water plays a critical role not only for future economic development, but also for the social development of the country (Hauff. Mistri 2016: 27).

In addition to energy production and the increasing commercial and private traffic conjestion, the industrial manufacturing sector (which generates a significant share of economic growth) is also responsible for a major share of the environmental pollution. The World Bank estimates that the annual costs incurred by India are USD 9.7 billion, which equates to 4.5 per cent of the GDP (at 1992 prices). USD 7 billion alone can be traced back to air and water pollution (USAID, 2001: 2). Indian industries produce about 36,897 million m^3 of wastewater annually, of which approximately 70.5 million m^3 are discharged daily directly and untreated into the rivers and lakes.

III.2 The Economic Dimension

An important criterion of economic sustainability is the economic strength of a country (Hauff, Chandran, Saraswati 2013: 140). This refers not only to the traditional indicators like gross domestic product (GDP), but also to the quality of economic strength. First, it is important to highlight the dynamic development of the Indian economy during the past few decades. This economic growth is not only to be attributed to the tertiary sector (service sector) alone, but also to the dynamic development of the industrial sector. The industrial sector consists of several especially strong growth sectors, which in turn have a positive impact on other sectors. But this only exacerbates the environmental problems mentioned earlier and clearly shown in the context of ecologic and economic sustainability. From an economic perspective, it must be noted that the economic growth is primarily generated by the domestic economy, although India's foreign trade has also shown positive development. This economic development has also substantially increased the average per capita income.

Despite this dynamic development, the economic strength harbours some imbalances. The fact that the secondary and tertiary sectors show greater than average rate of growth does not negate the fact that the macro-economic development still depends today to a significant degree on the primary sector. The primary sector meanwhile reflects a relatively low productivity and is, among other things, negatively impacted by climate change. Another problem is the infrastructure, which has shown a substantially lower pace of development than the overall economy. This can be said for both the energy sector as well as for the transportation infrastructure.

It is interesting to note that the tremendous dynamism in the economy is creating relatively few additional jobs in many segments of the secondary and tertiary sectors. This also explains, in part, the high percentage of approximately 80 to 90 per cent in the informal sector. This also means that the majority of the working population is living without any social security. The economic growth patterns in India identified so far have also contributed to a growing imbalance in income distribution. This leads on one hand to a relatively slow increase in buying power for the domestic demand especially among the lower-income groups.

III.3 The Social Dimension

India exhibits a series of social challenges that are problematic for social development and social cohesion. One of the best examples of these is the inequality and shortcomings in the education sector. (Hauff 2010: 259 ff). Despite very positive economic growth in the past two decades, the regional inequality between the Indian states as well as the social disparity among the population has significantly increased. (Wagner, 2009: 96). A particular challenge in India is the unequal distribution of income. According to an OECD study, gender and racial discrimination represent the major determinants of income inequality in the developing countries. (OECD, 2011: 58).

The Indian Constitution expressly names some promotional measures for disadvantaged castes, scheduled castes (SC), and scheduled tribes (ST). For example, at least 15 per cent of the student acceptance at state universities and jobs in the public sector must be provided to members of the STs. This positive discrimination was expanded by the 73rd Amendment to more disadvantaged castes whereby, an additional 27.5 per cent of the student acceptance and jobs are to be awarded to members of these castes (Azam, 2009: 1 ff.). Nevertheless, this was only partially effective in reducing the pronounced social differentiation and discrimination in India, which sometimes leads to social conflicts.

In summary, the situation in India today remains a long way off from sustainable development. This is a situation that has a long-term negative effect on the nation's environmental, economic, and social development. If, and to what degree, this will lead to social tensions cannot be determined at the present time. Of course, it is possible for India to develop a process for a national sustainability strategy. A methodical process for achieving precisely that is introduced in the fifth section. But before presenting that, it is necessary in the next section to present the German experience and several features of the national sustainable strategy of Germany. This is intended to explain some of the framework conditions for a national sustainability strategy.

IV The Implementation and Development of Germany's National Sustainability Strategy

The German government presented its first national sustainability strategy, with the title 'Perspectives for Germany', at the World Summit on Sustainable Development in Johannesburg (Hauff 2014: 225). This reflected the current generation's commitment to solving the self-inflicted problems immediately and emphasized the critical importance of change in the production and consumption structures. The sustainability strategy set down principles that addressed environmental, economic, and social dimensions. This established fundamentals that remain firmly embedded in the current version (a continuation of the first edition) of the sustainability strategy. The separate updates are notable for the fact that experts are able to bring them into the consultation process.

The originally chosen structure of the fields of action and indicators, however, is unchanged until the present. In 2006, the parliamentary Advisory Council for Sustainable Development was established by the federal government and now conducts hearings on various sustainability issues. In the next step, the Federal Statistical Office took on the monitoring tasks as an independent institution and has published two indicator reports. Beyond these steps, the federal government has based its sustainability declaration on the three dimensions of sustainability and, in this context, recognized special ecologic requirements:

> Environmental protection, economic efficiency, and social responsibility must be equally weighted so long term decisions are made in consideration of all three aspects—from a global perspective. Preserving the viability of the planet Earth is the absolute outer boundary: In this framework sense, the aim is to optimize the realization of various political goals." (Federal German Government 2008: 21).

A sustainability-based impact assessment introduced in February 2007 has become a key tool for the integration of sustainability in the political process. This document clearly shows that coordination among the individual departments of government on the overall sustainability concept is essential. Increasingly, it is now recognized that many goals can only be achieved through cooperation with the federal states and municipalities. For example, the goal of reducing land use to 30 hectares per day can only be met if the states set the appropriate planning guidance and the municipalities align their land use designations. Furthermore, in recent years it has been critically pointed out that the integration of sustainability throughout the entire political spectrum needs further enforcement. (Council of Environmental Advisors 2008, item 54).

In 2009, the federal government invited a group of international experts to audit the progress of the sustainability policies in Germany. The expert group was also tasked to formulate recommendations to promote the transition to a sustainable economy and society. The group published its findings in a report titled 'Sustainability Made in Germany'. In 2015, the expert group was reconvened in order to prepare a second progress report. In addition to specific recommendations for the individual fields of action, there were also some new general proposals. Consequently, the updates of the strategy are to be viewed not merely as a clean rinse of routine procedures.

This information of how Germany has implemented a national sustainability strategy now serves as a background to continue this chapter with an approach for developing and implementing a sustainability strategy in India.

V The Integrated Sustainability Triangle—A Method for Developing and Implementing a Sustainability Strategy

The ecological, economic, and social dimensions are to be reconciled as co-equals, in order to satisfy the needs of current and future generations (Hauff, Chandran, Saraswati 2013: 141). In the process, while people continue to interact within their social and economic systems, the long-term preservation of the natural basis of life must be ensured through sustainable consumption. Each of the three dimensions is a co-equal component for sustainable growth. Correspondingly, only when all three dimensions are taken together is a viable concept formed. On the one hand, this means that each issue is to be weighed according to its ecological, economic, and social aspects. On the other hand, as mentioned above, prioritization is by all means possible. Some topics of relevance to sustainability tend to be ecological in nature while others are more social and economic. The unique features of sustainability issues can be represented in the integrated sustainability triangle.

The integrated sustainability triangle enables systematic analysis of the interdependencies of economic, ecological, and social fields of action. This system prevents the consideration of the fields of action in isolation from one another or the undifferentiated merging of fields. Sustainable growth requires such a joint process with the participation of government, business, and society. As key actors, the responsible ministries, associations, corporations, and social organizations each have an important role to play. Each must be integrated from the start in developing a sustainability strategy and share responsibility for its implementation. In the new method, interrelationships among three dimensions are identified and respectively labelled in the interior of the triangle. The three dimensions are brought together to take an account of the growing demands of integration. The integrated sustainability triangle is differentiated into several areas to which the various subject areas of sustainable development can be assigned (see Figure 17.1). The challenge is in finding a structure that allows further operationalization.

The defined areas can be further subdivided into fields of action. In determining the fields of action, it is recommended that a manageable number be defined to ensure achievability or implementation of the sustainability strategy. Each field of action should clearly relate to the Agenda 21 Program. In addition, it is essential to fix responsibility for each field of action by assigning the implementation to one individual or organization. The next step is to coordinate and define goals for each field of action among the responsible actors. Then in a final step, define the indicators that reflect the degree of achievement. Table 17.1 shows the potential fields of action with the respective indicators that are relevant to India.

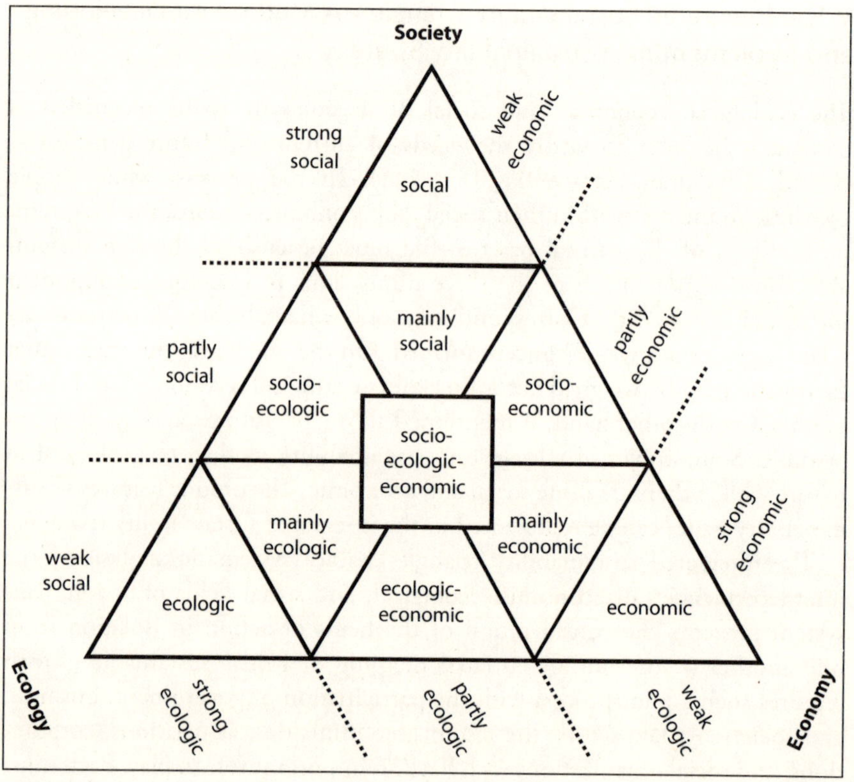

Figure 17.1 Areas of Action for Sustainable Development
Source: Author.

Table 17.1 Fields of Action and Respective Indicators for a National Sustainability Strategy for India

Field of Action	Indicators
A. Natural Basis of Life	
	Conservation Areas
	Groundwater Quality Air Quality Nitrogen Emissions Forest Areas
	Greenhouse Gas Emissions Share of Renewable Energy Compared to the Overall Energy Consumption
B. Resource Utilization	
	Energy Productivity Share of the Value of Minerals compared to the GDP
	Consumption of Exhaustible Natural Resources Loss in Power Transmission
	Efficiency of Agricultural Land Use Irrigated Farmland
	Consumption of Food Corporate Environmental Management
C. Economic Power	
	Labour Productivity GDP per Capita Global Competitiveness Index
	Gross Fixed Capital Formation
	Expenditures for Research & Development
	Access to Financial Resources
D. Performance Capability of the Society	
	Employment Rate Pay Gap between Men and Women Share of the Informal Employment Market
	Net of Social Safety Integrity with the Global Economy

(*Cont'd*)

Table 17.1 (*Cont'd*)

	Debt of the Overall Public Budget
	School Drop-Out Rates Net School Enrollment Rates Gross University Matriculation Rates Literacy Level Public Expenditures for Education
	Fertility Rate
E. Social Responsibility	
	Number of RTI Requests Phone and Internet Usage
	Development Aid Literacy Rate in Rural and Urban Regions Differences in Life Expectancy amongst Various Social Groups
	Conviction Rate
	Proportion of Women elected to the Parliament Sex Ratio at Birth Poverty Rate Consumption Share of the Poorest Quantile Income Disparities
F. Living Environment	
	Fuel Consumption of Road Transport
	Access to Electricity Access to Drinking Water
	Access to Sanitary Equipment
G. Population	
	Maternal Mortality Prevalence of Underweight Children
	Proportion of Paved Roads Proportion of Slum Population
	Corruption Indices

Source: Author's own chart based on research from Chandran et al. (2012), p. 18 f., Butola, B.S. (2013), p. 53 ff.

Figures 17.2 and 17.3 depict the fields of action and indicators in the integrated sustainability triangle.

The many areas of interaction between the fields of action are clearly shown in this graphic of fields of action and indicators. This also helps to explain why a sustainability strategy can only be implemented as an integrated process. Many approaches in the past, unfortunately, have focused only on one dimension of sustainability. Learning from experience, Agenda 21 as well as the Sustainable Development Goals take all three dimensions of sustainability into consideration (Butola, 2013: 60 f.). However, some confusion still exists at times among the relationships between the various fields of action.

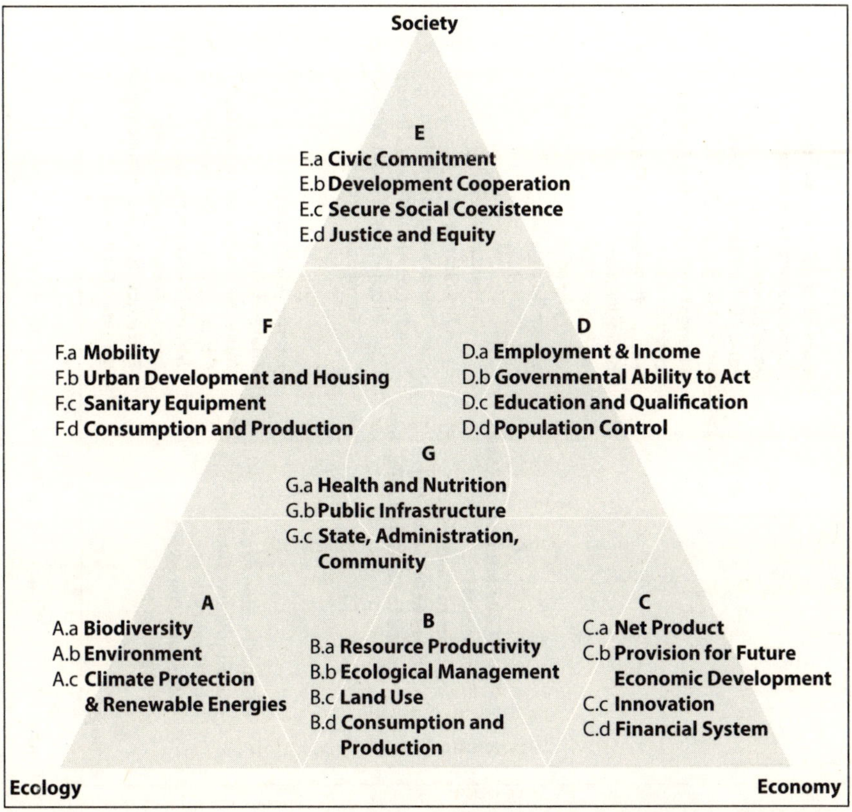

Figure 17.2 The Fields of Action in the Integrated Sustainability Triangle
Source: Author's own chart based on research from Chandran et al. (2012), p. 18 f., Butola, B.S. (2013), p. 53 ff.

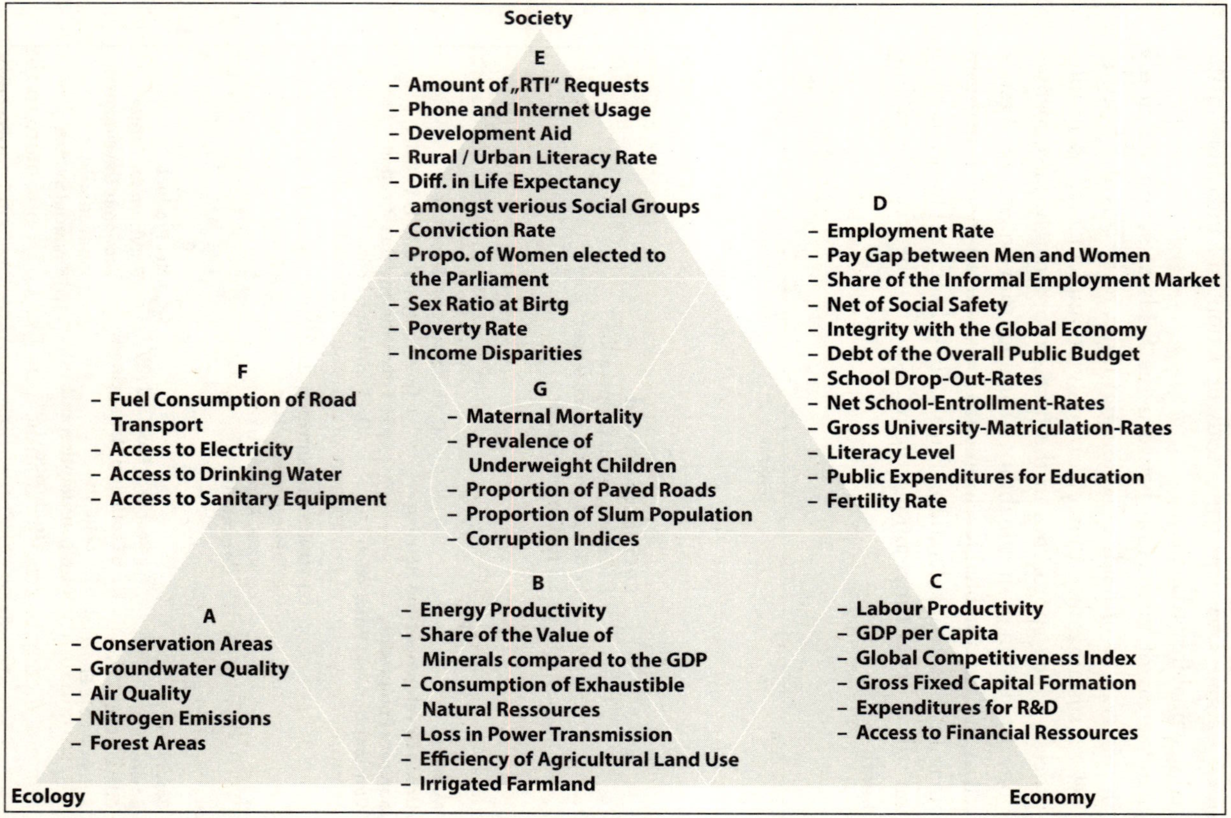

Figure 17.3 Indicators of the Integrated Sustainability Triangle
Source: Author's own chart based on research from Chandran et al. (2012), p. 18 f., Butola, B.S. (2013), p. 53 ff.

V.1 Natural Basis of Life

Land, air, and water represent basic natural resources, elementary and essential for human existence. People need the ecological systems to satisfy needs that go beyond pure survival. As mentioned above, nature provides resources and also serves as a collection pool for by-products and wastes left from consumption and production. (Brickwedde, 2010: 47). For this reason, a sustainable development policy for the preservation of our natural resources is required. The high quality of life must also be preserved for future generations (Spiellemaeckers et al. 2011: 79). This goal clearly encompasses the fields of action 'Biodiversity', 'Environmental and climate protection', and 'Renewable energies'. A more detailed look at biodiversity is provided as follows.

V.1.1 Biodiversity

Biodiversity describes the diversity of life in all of its incredible natural forms, where the number, the variety, and the evolutionary resilience are of great significance. We differentiate between genetic diversity, diversity of the species, the diversity of the ecosystems. The establishment of protected areas contributes to the preservation of biodiversity (Wolfrum 2001: 417). The wilderness conservation areas in India currently claim an area of at least 1000 hectares. This figure includes national parks, natural monuments, reserves, land conservation areas, and other areas with restricted public access. (World Bank 2014c).

In 2012, the proportion of protected areas in India to the total land area was 5.2 per cent and 14.3 per cent worldwide. In 2009, the ratio of water conservation areas to the total under state jurisdiction was 1.7 per cent in India versus 10 per cent worldwide. In 2010, India managed to increase this indicator to 5.5 per cent (The World Bank, 2014a). Both indicators reflect a gap between India and average worldwide figures, although the percentages have narrowed in recent years.

V.2 Economic Power

Economic sustainability starts with the economic strength of a country. This refers not merely to traditional indicators like GDP, but more to the quality of economic power. This includes, for example, environmentally friendly investments and innovations. A sustainable restructuring or transformation of the economy and the society depends very much on economic power (Leitch, 2006: 8 ff.). This sustainability area covers the fields of action: value creation, economic provisions for the future, and innovation.

Innovation plays a key role in the economic development of a country. In turn, the supply of human capital is an essential factor for the development of innovations (Brosch, Hauff 2009: 157). The key indicator is the expenditure on research and development (R&D). However, in the context of sustainable development, it is even more important to look at the share of the R&D budget that is distributed to innovations that can solve or reduce current social, economic, and ecological challenges, that is, sustainability problems (Chandran et al., 2012: 26.). To date, there are no relevant figures for comparison, which is why the internationally accepted indicator 'Expenditures on R&D' is used as the basis. The share of R&D expenditure of the total Indian GDP is compared with the global average in Figure 17.4.

The figures clearly show that India's R&D spending is well below the worldwide average.

V.3 Social Cohesion

The 'efficiency of the society' is an area of sustainability that addresses the socio-economic dimensions of sustainable development and, because it is highly relevant to India, it deserves a closer look. This area evaluates the improvements in equal opportunity and the elimination of discrimination.

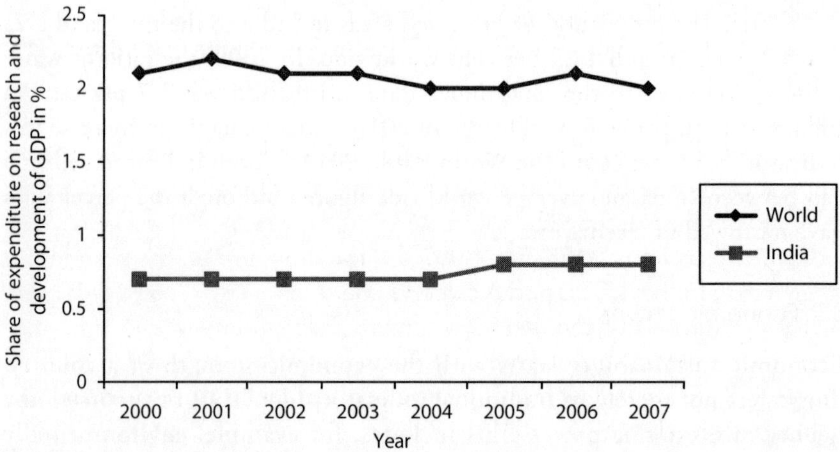

Figure 17.4 India's Expenditures for R&D in Comparison to Germany and the Global Average, 2000–7

Source: Author's own chart based on research from the World Bank (2014a): databank.worldbank.org/data, retrieved on 14 August 2014.

The assessment for this area provides information about the future development of a country and the well-being or the living standard of its citizens. (Rauschmayer et al. 2011: 19 f.). Let's take a more detailed look at the field of action called "poverty reduction."

Poverty reduction and sustainable development demand sound policy, especially, as concerns the increase in expenditures on education and the qualification of human capital (World Bank, 2000b: xiii). There is broad consensus that education and training is a prerequisite for the development of human capital and positive economic growth (Brosch, Hauff 2009: 157 f.). A World Bank study clearly confirmed the positive effect of education on the economic efficiency of a country (World Bank 2012c: 1 ff.). The limited access to education by a large percentage of the youth represents a core problem in many developing countries.

In addition to the direct costs, it is the indirect costs of education that give cause to parents who expect their children to contribute to the financial security of the family from an early age. This leads them to choose to not attend school at all or to infrequent attendance. Besides the school fees, relevant costs include, for example, classroom materials, school uniforms, transportation to school, and the opportunity cost of lost income for the family (Flammer 2009: 1 f.). The following indicators are selected for discussion subsequently: dropout rate, literacy rate, and public expenditure on education.

Poor quality of education in India is admittedly a factor in the high dropout rate. However, the opportunity costs also play a role, in particular, among the poor and increasing as they get older (Brosch, Hauff 2009: 166). The student dropout rate for the academic year 2004–5 is shown in the following chart according to grade levels and by gender.

Although the dropout rates are relatively high, some positive developments can be identified in India. In the first five years of primary school education, dropout rates have declined by half since 1980/81—from 58.7 per cent to 29 per cent. It was found that since 2002/03, the dropout rate has been lower for girls than for boys. This positive development can, perhaps, be traced back to the introduction of the free school lunch programme in 1995 (mid-day meal scheme) (Ministry of Human Resource Development 2007: XX ff.). However, there is a still a great difference between the first five years and the higher grade levels.

Figure 17.6 presents the literacy rates for people (aged 15 and above) for selected years according to gender. It can be seen that women are still disadvantaged. Yet again, a positive trend is noted in that the literacy rate for the female population is rising faster than for males. The literacy rate among males in the year 1961 was three times higher than for females. In 2001, we

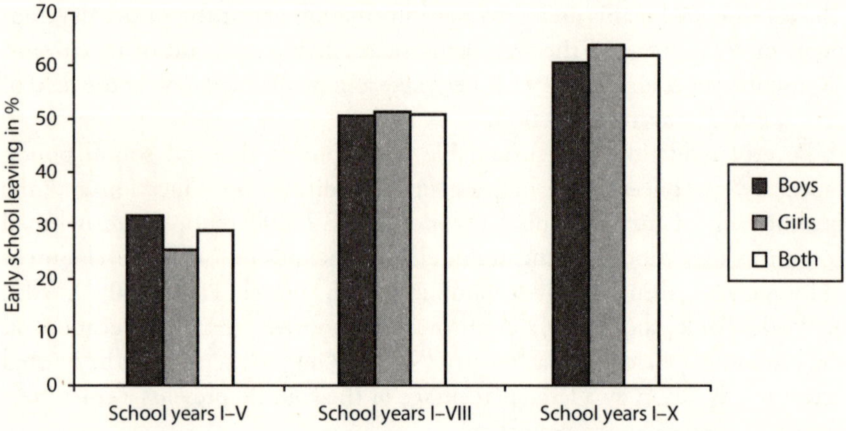

Figure 17.5 India's School Dropout Rates, 2004–5
Source: Author's own chart based on research from the Ministry of Human Resource Development (2007), p. xxi.

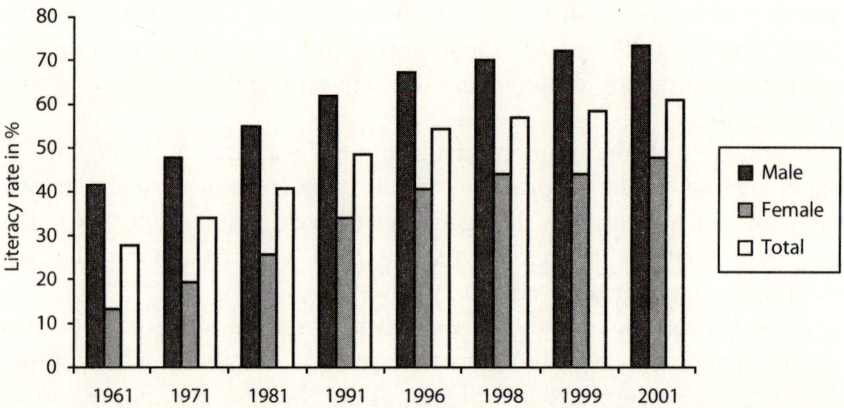

Figure 17.6 Literacy Rate of India's Adult Population, 1961–2001
Source: Author's own chart based on research from Ministry of Human Resource Development (2007), p. xxxix.

see that it was only 50 per cent higher. Yet, again we can determine that in the context of sustainable development, there is still considerable room for improvement.

The public expenditures on education are analysed in more detail in Figure 17.7 which shows the development of the Indian education budget for the period from 1990 to 2011.

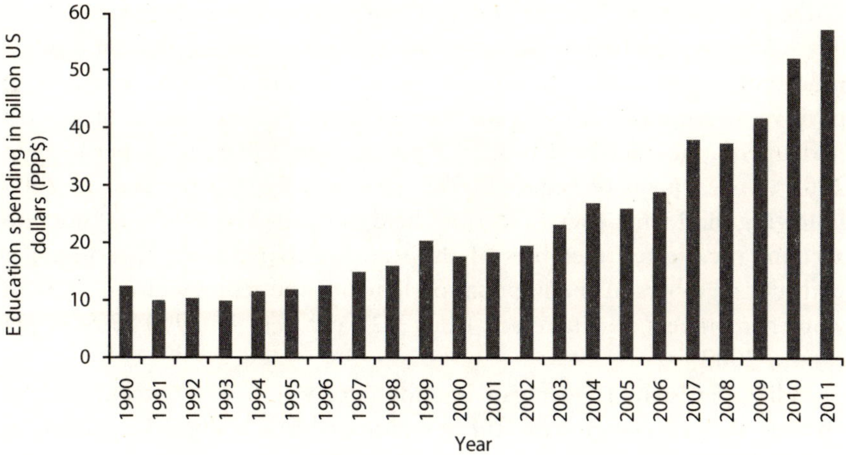

Figure 17.7 Development of the Indian Education Budget, 1990–2011
Source: Author's own chart based on research from the World Bank (2014a): databank.world-bank.org/data, retrieved on 14 August 2014.

It can readily be seen that the expenditures on education have not kept pace with the strong GDP growth. According to the Indian government's policy guidance on state education from 1986, 6 per cet of GDP is to be provided for public spending on education. In 2004, for example, spending amounted to only 3.8 per cent. In comparison to other industrializing nations, India invests significantly less per child in primary and secondary education (Brosch and Hauff 2009: 158 ff.).

The efficiency and the functioning of judicial institutions play a crucial role in maintaining social sustainability (Hauff, Chandran, Saraswati 2013: 150). An efficiently functioning judicial system in the country will ensure safe community life and will promote important human values necessary for social sustainability. The number of cases solved in relation to the total number of cases reported can very well reveal the pace at which people get justice in a country. In response to one Right To Information (RTI) query submitted in 2007, it was revealed recently that there are about 30 million cases pending in all the courts of the country. The share of the cases pending in the 21 high courts is roughly 3 million, while it is as high as 26.3 million in the subordinate courts. Out of the total crimes reported in 2009, the rate of conviction is lowest in case of crimes against women followed by the crimes against SCs and STs (Government of India 2009a). This shows a very slow-functioning judicial system and one that is incapable of giving speedy justice to the victim especially the vulnerable segments.

Despite the fact that the Indian Constitution not only grants equality to women, including universal adult franchise since the time of its independence and that it also empowers the state to adopt measures of positive discrimination to favour women, the percentage share of women parliamentarians declined from 9.7 per cent in 1991 to 9.1 per cent in 2007 (Government of India 2009b). The share is 10.3 per cent in 2009 following the 15th General Elections held in April–May 2009. Taking into account the elected members of the state legislative assemblies together with the members of the national parliament, the representation share of women members has increased from 3.28 per cent in 1990 to 6.04 per cent in 2002.

India's persistent gender gap is undoubtedly anti-development and an obstacle to inclusive growth. The sex ratio at birth is a good indicator to capture the incidence of gender gap inherent in a society, as it is a reflection of the biases favouring a male-child. Also, it can be projected to give an idea of future trends in the adult sex ratio of the country. Recently, it has been a matter of much concern because of a decline according to the latest census of India. The child sex ratio in India has dropped to 914 females for 1,000 males—the lowest since independence—based on the provisional 2011 census report (Census of India 2011). Also according to the projections given by the Population Division of United Nations Department of Economic and Social Affairs, child sex ratio in India is much lower than that of the global level (UNDES 2011).

Although there has been significant improvement in the aggregate level of economic indicators like gross domestic product, purchasing power parity, etc., there is still a massive gap between the poorest and the richest segments—of the population as mentioned before. India's recent economic development cannot be called sustainable until there is a reasonably proportionate distribution of wealth among all segments of the population. This will also help in fulfilling the objective of the sustainable development goal to eradicate poverty.

It is very important to monitor this indicator in order to evaluate the government's success in achieving its agenda of inclusive growth. The share of the poorest quintile in total consumption (consumption by the poorest fifth of the population) is a very good measure of that indicator. As seen from Figure 17.7, this share declined from 9.6 per cent in 1993–4 to 9.5 per cent in 2004–5 as measured in the rural areas. This decline was sharper in the urban areas where the ratio declined from 8 per cent to 7.3 per cent. This decrease in the share of consumption by the poorest quintile could be one of the reasons for the growing inequalities, particularly in the urban areas.

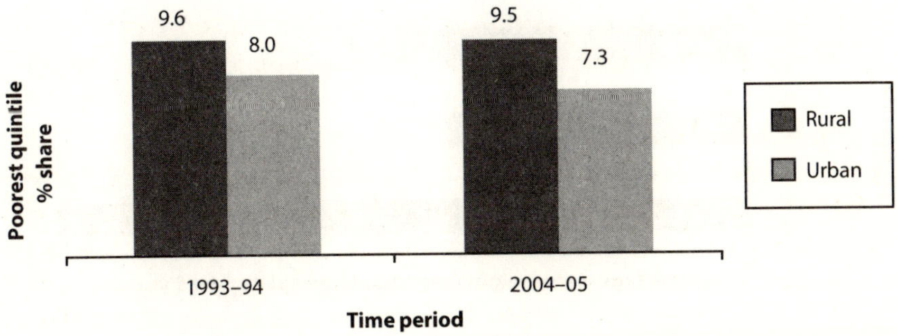

Figure 17.8 Share of National Consumption by Poorest Quintile in India (in per cent)
Source: NSSO, 1997 and 2007.

V.4 Population

Three central problems covered in the move towards sustainability are health and nutrition, public infrastructure, and governance (Hauff, Chandran, Saraswati 2013: 149). The level of health and nutrition of the population has an overall impact on the sustainable development of a country. The Millennium Development Goals have set a target for India to reduce maternal mortality ratio (MMR) to three quarters of its present level between 1990 and 2015. Incidence of deaths to women in the reproductive age group 15–49 due to pregnancy-related causes as measured by MMR has experienced a quick downturn during the period 2003–6, from 301 per 100,000 live births in 2001–3 to 254 per 100,000 live births in 2004–6, based on sample registration system data.

Statistics provided by the UN Population Division show the indicator of maternal mortality in India has improved in recent years. Statistics, being merely estimates, do not always depict the broader situation (UNDES 2011). The all-India trend of the proportion of underweight (severe and moderate) children below 3 years of age shows India is making only slow progress in eliminating the effects of malnourishment. India has a major share of underweight children in the world. According to recent National Family Health Survey (NFHS) data, it has even increased marginally, inviting a great deal of concern (Figure 17.9).

The condition of the physical infrastructure is the primary basis for the classification of slum and non-slum areas. It is a good indicator for the level of public infrastructure availability in a country. With a population of well over 1 billion people, India is the second most populous nation in the world

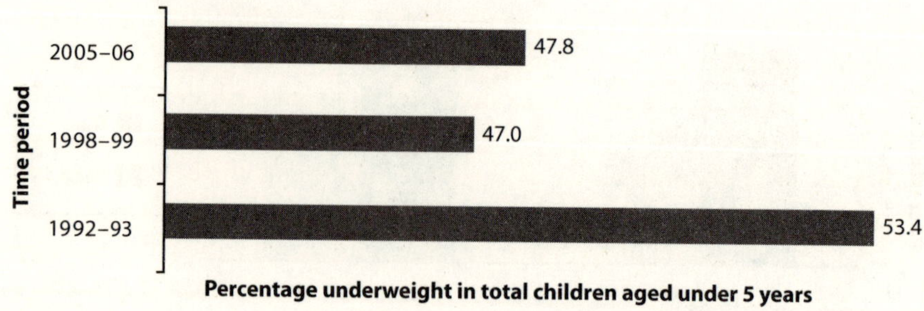

Figure 17.9 Trend in the Percentage of Moderately/Severely Underweight Children (under five years of age) in India
Source: National Family Health Survey (IIPS 2007).

and home to 63 per cent of all slum dwellers in South Asia. This amounts to 170 million people, 17 per cent of the world's slum dwellers. The expansion of India's slums is partly due to the rise in India's total population, which increased from 683 million in 1981 to 1.03 billion in 2001. This has been exacerbated by the exodus of rural peasants from the countryside seeking manual labour in India's cities.

As India continues to develop its infrastructure and compete economically with the West, it is important to achieve significant improvements in the lives of slum dwellers quickly, especially in terms of secure tenure and other community facilities. Road density is the ratio of the length of the country's total road network to the country's land area. The road network includes all roads in the country: motorways, highways, main or national roads, secondary or

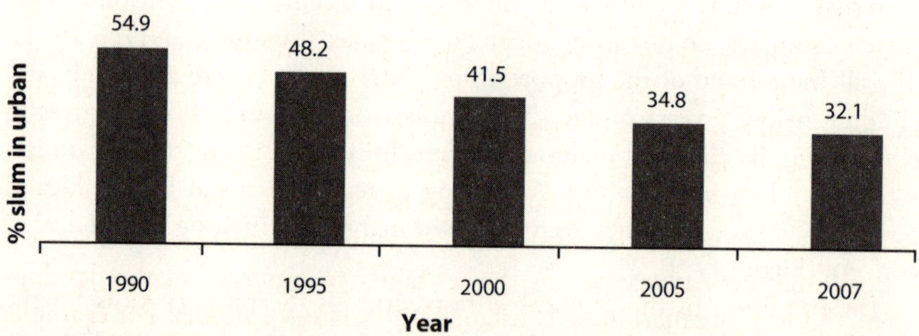

Figure 17.10 Trend in the Percentage of Urban Population Living in Slums in India
Source: United Nations, 2011.

regional roads, and other urban and rural roads. This indicator is very helpful in understanding a country's infrastructural development. As the data suggest, India has experienced a noticeable increase in the road density over the past twenty years. This is a positive indicator of economic development as it shows the level of connectivity of the local economy with the national and global economies.

Transparency is one of the most important aspects for the efficient functioning of any system and, especially, in a democracy. India at present is plagued by massive corruption scandals unprecedented in the history of the country. Common citizens in India pay bribes totaling $4bn a year and about 62 per cent of citizens polled in 'India Corruption Study' had the experience of paying a bribe or 'using a contact' to get a job done in a public office (Center for Media Studies 2008). The report also says that paying bribes has become a way of life in India.

The study done by Transparency International in 2009 proved that in private sector corruption, India ranks 85 out of the total 185 countries. India is one of the few countries besides Indonesia, Morocco, and Egypt where more than 60 per cent of the business executives included in the survey reported to have experienced pressure to pay a bribe from various key institutions (Transparency International 2009). The high incidence of corruption has a direct negative impact on the development of the country, most clearly in the economic growth. The implementation of an effective anti-corruption bill is perhaps India's most urgent need in achieving sustainable development.

VI Consideration of Restraints

In conclusion, it is necessary to ask if there are any typical 'Indian restraints' in developing and implementing a national sustainability strategy. In this respect, Mahatma Gandhi made a very poignant observation: 'The earth provides enough to satisfy everyone's need but does not provide enough to satisfy everyone's greed.' This, of course, is not a phenomenon exclusive to India, but it is applicable to India. Although globalization—in the sense of the increasing international exchange of products, services, concepts—contributes to a convergence of solutions and problems as well, there is a country-specific explanation for the restraints encountered in the development and implementation of a sustainability strategy in India. For example, when Zingel looked at the environmental problems in India, he came to the conclusion that there is a close relationship between ecological and social problems (Zingel 2009: 152).

The environmental problems in India reveal that in addition to the economic and social components, there are significant domestic and foreign considerations, security issues, and religious aspects. It is striking to note that the government of India has established and continues to develop many differentiated legislative efforts. Examples include equal opportunity laws for the various groups within the society, the development of large-scale programmes designed to solve the problems of specific segments of the population, and also the structural organization of various areas of government, for example, for financial policy, economic policy, educational policy, and even foreign trade policy.

However, when attention is focused on the implementation and control of the various policy goals, the Indian government may also be viewed as relatively weak. It is particularly evident that at the lower levels of government and administrative positions, substantially better solutions are found for the economically well-to-do and the better organized groups. This explains why the development and, especially, the implementation of a national sustainability strategy in India are faced with several fundamental obstacles.

It can be observed that the social and political heterogeneity in India exert strong pressure on the political actors to seek compromise with their social competitors Otherwise, they run the risk of political insignificance or even their own downfall (Jürgenmeyer, 2009: 85). Still, is fair to expect that at least some percentage of India's new middle class along with an increasingly powerful civic society will raise the level of awareness for sustainable development and the respective demands on the politicians will be met with a growing attentiveness in the future.

References

Azam, M. 2009. 'A Distributional Analysis of Social Group Inequality in Rural India', in: IZA DP Bonn, 2009, Heft 3973.

Brickwedde, F. 2010. 'Ökologische Nachhaltigkeit,' in: W.Krüger, (Hrsg): *Die Zukunft gibt es nur einmal*, pp. 47–60. Wiesbaden, S.: Gabler Verlag, Springer Fachmedien.

Brosch, E. and M. v. Hauff, 2009. 'Bildung und Forschung—Eine noch nicht ganz bewältigte Herausforderung', in: v. Hauff, M. (Hrsg.): *Indien—Herausforderungen und Perspektiven*, Schriften zur Wirtschaft Asiens/Economic Studies on Asia Volume 6, pp. 157–197. Marburg, S: Metropolis-Verlag.

Butola, B.S. 2013. 'Sustainable Development—An Interrogation', in: M. v. Hauff, and A. Kundu, (Hrsg.) (2013): *Imperatives of Sustainability and India's Development Path, Economic Studies on Asia Volume 12*, pp. 39–64. Marburg, S: Metropolis-Verlag.

Census of India, 2011. *Provisional Population Totals Paper 1 of 2011*. New Delhi: Registrar General and Census Commissioner of India, Government of India.

Centre for Media Studies. 2008. *TII-CMS India Corruption Study 2007 with focus on BPL Households: National Report 2008*. New Delhi: Centre for Media Studies & Transparency International India.

Chandran, D., L.R. Saraswati, and M. v. Hauff. 2012. *Requirements for the National Sustainability Strategy of India*, Kaiserslautern: Volkswirtschaftliche Diskussionsbeiträge an der Technischen Universität Kaiserslautern, Nr. 32–11.

Dalal-Clayton, and S. Bass. 2002. *Sustainable Development Strategies—a Resource Book*, London: Routledge.

Die Bundesregierung (German Government). 2002. Perspektiven für Deutschland—Unsere Strategie für eine nachhaltige Entwicklung.

Dréze, J. and A. Sen, 2013. *An Uncertain Glory: India and its Contradictions*. London: Princeton University Press.

Government of India. 2009a. *Crime in India—2009*. New Delhi: National Crime Records Bureau, Ministry of Home Affairs, Governmentt. of India.

Government of India. 2009b. *Millennium Development Goals—India Country Report 2009*. New Delhi: Central Statistical Organization, Ministry of Statistics and Programme Implementation, Governmentt. of India.

International Institut for Population Science (IIPS). 2007. *National Family Health Survey (NFHS-3), 2005–06: India: Volume II*. Mumbai: IIPS.

Jürgenmeyer, C. .2009. ‚Die indische Demokratie—eine funktionierende Anarchie', in: M. v. Hauff, (ed.): *Indien—Herausfordrungen und Perspektiven*. pp. 73–92. Marburg: Metropolis.

Leitch, Sandy. 2006. *Review of Skills: Prosperity for all in the global economy—world class skills* (Final Report). London: HM Treasury.

Ministry of Environment and Forests. 2002.: *Sustainable Development in India—Perspectives*, Paper presented at the World Summit on Sustainable Development 26 August-4 September in Johannesburg.

Ministry of Health and Family Welfare, Government of India, India, July 2007.

Ministry of Human Resource Development, Government of India (2014): Education, URL: //education.nic.in/sector.asp#stages, Stand: 14.08.2014.

North, D.C. and J.J. Wallis. 1994. 'Integrating Institutional Change and Technical Change in Economic History. A Transaction Cost Approach,' in *Journal of Institutional and Theoretical Economics*, 150, pp. 609–624.

NSSO. 2007. *Household Consumer Expenditure among Socio-Economic Groups: NSS 61st Round (July 2004–June 2005)*. New Delhi: National Sample Survey Organisation, Ministry of Statistics and Programme Implementation, Government of India.

OECD. 2011. *Divided We Stand—Why Inequality Keeps Rising*. Paris: OECD Publishing.

Planning Commission. 2008. *Eleventh Five Year Plan 2007–2012*. New Delhi: Government of India.

Rauschmayer, F., I. Omann, and Frühmann, J. (2011): *Sustainable Development: Capabilities, needs, and well-being*. New York: Routledge Studies in Ecological Economics.

Rothermund, D. 2008. *Indien: Aufstieg einer asiatischen Weltmacht*. München: C. H. Beck.

Saxena, N. C. 2002. 'Food Assistance Programmes and their Role in Alleviating Poverty and Hunger in India', paper presented at the Bhubaneswar Workshop on Food and Hunger organized by WFP on 16 May 2002.

Sachverständigenrat für Umweltfragen. 2008. *Umweltgutachten 2008—Umweltschutz im Zeichen des Klimawandels*. Berlin: Erich Schmidt Verlag.

Scott, W. R. 2006. 'Reflexionen über ein halbes Jahrhundert Organisationssoziologie', in: K. Senge and K.-U. Hellmann, (eds.): *Einführung in den Neo-Institutionalismus*, pp. 201–253. Wiesbaden: VS Verlag.

Spillemaeckers, S., L. v. Ootegem, and G.J. Westerhof. 2011. 'From individual well-being to sustainable development—A path where psychologists and economists meet', in: F. Rauschmayer, I. Omann and J. Frühmann. (Hrsg.): *Sustainable Development—Capabilities, needs, and well-being*. S. 62–82. New York: Routledge Studies in Ecological Economics.

Stiglitz, J. E., A. K, Sen, J.P. Fitoussi. 2009. Report by the Commission on the Measurement of Economic Performance and Social Progress, Paris: Commission on the Measurement of Economic Performance and Social Progress, http://ec.europa.eu/eurostat/documents/118025/118123/Fitoussi+Commission+report, accessed 26 July 2017.

Transparency International. 2009. *Global Corruption Report-2009: Corruption and the Private Sector*. Cambridge: Cambridge University Press.

UNCED. 1992. *Agenda 21*. New York.

UNDES. 2011. *World Population Prospects: The 2010 Revision*. New York: United Nations Department of Economic and Social Affairs, Population Division.

United Nations. 2011. *Millennium Development Goals Indicators*. United Nations Statistics Division Inter-agency and Expert Group, http://mdgs.un.org/unsd/mdg/Data.aspx, accessed 26 July 2017.

USAID. 2001. *Reducing Urban and Industrial Pollution in India*, Arlington.

M. v. Hauff. 2005. 'Umwelttechnischer Fortschritt aus der Sicht der neuen Wachstumstheorie.' in: S.Seiter; (ed.): *Neuere Entwicklungen in der Wachstumstheorie und der Wachstumspolitik*, pp. 211–231. Marburg: Metropolis.

M. v. Hauff. 2010. 'The relationship between justice and education: Effects on the creation of human capital in India' in: Swati Deva, (ed.): *Law and (In)Equalities—Contemporary Perspectives*, pp. 259–287.New Delhi: Eastern Book Company.

M. v. Hauff and H. Schiffer. 2010. *Soziale Nachhaltigkeit im Kontext der Neuen Institutionsökonomik*, Kaiserslautern: Volkswirtschaftliche Diskussionsbeiträge an der Technischen Universität Kaiserslautern, Nr. 30–10.

M. v. Hauff. 2014. *Nachhaltige Entwicklung—Grundlagen und Umsetzung, 2. Aufl.*, München: De Gruyter.

M. v. Hauff. 2015. *Wachstum—Die Kontroverse um nachhaltiges Wachstum*, Wiesbaden: Hessian Centre.

M. v. Hauff and A. Mistri. 2016. *Economic Development and Water Sustainability: Study from an Emerging Nation, India*, Delhi: Manak Publications.

Wagner. C. 2009. 'Aktuelle Herausforderungen für die indische Demokratie—Die unbewältigte soziale Frage', in: M. v. Hauff, (Hrsg.): *Indien—Herausforderungen und Perspektiven, Schriften zur Wirtschaft Indiens Volume 6*. S. 93–110. Marburg: Metropolis-Verlag.

Wolfrum. R. 2001. 'Biodiversität—juristische, insbesondere völkerrechtliche Aspekte ihres Schutzes', in: R. Janich, M. Gutmann, and K. Prieß (Hrsg.): *Biodiversität, Wissenschaftliche Grundlagen und gesetzliche Relevanz*, Ethics of Science and Technology Assessment, Volume 10, S. 417–443. Berlin, Heidelberg: Springer Verlag.

The World Bank. 2000. *India: Policies to Reduce Poverty and Accelerate Sustainable Development*, Report No. 19471-IN, Poverty Reduction and Economic Management Union, South Asia Region. Washington D.C.: The World Bank.

The World Bank. 2012c. *Putting Higher Education to Work—Skills and Research for Growth in East Asia*. Washington, D.C.: The World Bank.

The World Bank. 2014a. 'Terrestrial Protected Areas (% of total land area)', URL: http://data.worldbank.org/indicator/ER.LND.PTLD.ZS, accessed 14 August 2014.

The World Bank (2014b): 'World Data Bank' , URL: databank.worldbank.org/data, accessed 14 August 2014.

Zingel. W.P. 2009. 'Wirtschaft und Umwelt—Indische Lösungsansätze zu einem nicht nur indischen Problem', in: M. v. Hauff. (ed.): *Indien—Herausforderungen und Perspektiven*, pp. 133–56. Marburg: Metropolis.

18

Public Participation in Environmental Governance in India and Indonesia

Nupur Chowdhury and Arie Afriansyah

I Introduction

It is useful to begin this chapter by focusing on the differing perceptions of Environmental Impact Assessment (EIA). Technicians usually consider EIA as a management tool that scientifically explores the potential impact of a project in order to guide decision-making in terms of reducing their environmental impact.[1] For social scientists environmental impact assessment is a governance practice that includes the examination of the potential social and environmental impacts, followed by consultation with affected communities and deliberation of the future steps (including consideration of alternative pathways.[2] Regulatory specialists have concentrated on issues of regulatory compliance, optimality of regulatory burdens and economic efficiency concerns.[3] Lack of consensus has, however, not impeded the rapid proliferation of EIAs throughout jurisdictions although their substantive impact remains controversial.

In international law Principle 17 of the Rio Convention first articulated a *de minimum* version of Environmental Impact Assessment. It stated:

> Environmental impact assessment, as a national instrument, shall be undertaken for proposed activities that are likely to have a significant adverse impact on the environment and are subject to a decision of a competent national authority.

With the entry into force of the Espoo Convention in 1997, the first international agreement on EIA came into being. More than a decade later another significant milestone was established by the ICJ in the *Pulp Mills case*[4] where it held that EIA is part of the due diligence obligation under customary international law for states when they undertake projects that may cause transboundary harm. Despite these advances towards the establishment of EIA as an accepted international norm, most such espousals have shied away from elucidating the exact nature of obligation and have been content to define the contours of this exercise in procedural terms. National jurisdictions have been largely left unencumbered by international law, in designing EIA regulatory regimes to suit their own specific contexts and needs.

In some ways, a significant exception to this trend has been the European Community (EC). The EC regulatory regime has consistently harmonized EIA norms—it is referred to as Strategic Environmental Assessment (SEA)—to push towards a comprehensive cumulative assessment of national economic and industrial plans rather than review of individual projects. Despite such obvious aspiration towards the adoption of EIA in a more comprehensive manner, national practices continue to vary widely in qualitative terms.[5]

Apart from the common requirement of the EIA being as a priori submission for receiving project clearance, there is therefore wide diversity in national frameworks of EIA. Although it is difficult to simply categorize them, theorists have relied on Black's ideas on 'thick and thin proceduralism'[6] to identify and develop comparative analysis of EIA regulatory regimes.[7] This of course is of interest in terms of exploring the wide variety of institutions, legal norms, and regulatory strategies that are employed in EIA regulatory regimes across national jurisdictions. However, this kind of analysis suffers critically in offering little insight into the specificity of the EIA experience in national jurisdictions and in the significant ways in which such experiences both reflect as well as influence regulatory practice in other national jurisdictions.

More significantly, not surprisingly perhaps, there has been inordinate focus on jurisdictions like the EU or the Scandinavian countries experience in developing and implementing EIA regulatory regimes. Academic explorations of EIA regulatory regimes in developing countries from a comparative perspective have been surprisingly few. This article attempts to redress this paucity. Both India and Indonesia as large and densely populated developing countries are confronted with the challenge of bringing rapid economic development with the objective of improving the standard of living. However, the challenge is also about developing in an environmentally sustainable manner. Often a false trade-off is sought to be made between development and environmental protection. EIA regulation has emerged as a political space through which such ideas have come to be contested. And it is therefore this political space that we study in order to gain insights.

We take this opportunity to outline the contours of this exploration and the implicit aims that embed this venture.

We believe that despite the temptation to dismiss EIAs as a management tool that is structurally limited and therefore inherently incapable of making in substantive contribution towards sustainability, the EIA has emerged as a political and regulatory space in developing countries, wherein communities, individuals, civil society organizations, and even the state (sometimes quite inexplicably) have emerged as vociferous stakeholders and owners of development and not just passive recipients of state munificence that characterizes centralized economic developmental planning. Narrating national experience of the EIA and situating it in the context of national imperatives and quirks—is critical in understanding the materiality of this space. It is also important to establish this as a 'new' kind of comparative law project, a project that speaks of protest and resistance to developmental policies that are increasingly centralized and distanced from local population. Globalization and theories of transnationalism would have us believe that national jurisdictions are being increasingly erased by global currents and regulatory regimes. However the states still remain as the most accessible and legitimate democratic space in the current world. It is therefore important to explore and understand such regulatory spaces to understand the similarities of such processes across jurisdictions but also appreciate their sui generis nature. Despite their local(ity) such spaces are imbued with narratives that find resonance in many other national jurisdictions.[8] The project of comparative law is therefore also one of solidarity, empathy, and building a narrative culture of exchanging experiences rather than pursuing a homogenized best practices approach.

The chapter is divided into four sections. In the following part, we start with an overview of the historical evolution of environmental regulation in India to situate EIA within this evolution. Next we analyse key judgements on EIA specifically tracing the idea of the public and public interest that have been discussed. Most environmental clearances[9] have been legally challenged by either civil society organizations, individual members affected by such decisions or environmental activists. Therefore, in many ways, the public has always been at the centre of the legal process on environmental clearances. It is therefore interesting to trace how the public has penetrated both the conduct of the EIA as well as the judicial process on environmental clearances. The third section undertakes a similar exercise in the context of Indonesia. In the fourth section, we conclude by drawing comparisons and analysing the similarities and discontinuities between these two jurisdictions.

II India

II.1 Indian Environmental Movement: Four Phases

As a former British colony, legislations in the early part of the twentieth century were focused on the utilization of natural resources and can be generically termed as the extractive phase in Indian environmental law. The Indian Forest Act (IFA) 1927 is a good marker of the kind of legislations enacted by the colonial government. The primary aim of the IFA was to extend state ownership over forests so as to secure access to timber and other forest products. The IFA laid down the process of establishing reserved forests. The term 'reserved' refers to the exclusive control of these forests by the state. This was undertaken by taking away control community pastures and forests and denying communities their historical rights over them. The fact that IFA continues to be operative even today gives us some insight into the mindset of the forest bureaucracy. The principle of eminent domain was used as the philosophical basis for supporting the expansion of proprietary rights of the state. Interestingly, this reductive vision of the environment as a source of natural resource is also illustrated in post-independent India, by the National Forest Policy, 1952, which promoted forest conservation by way of excluding the local population.

Environmental legislations in the sense of legislations with environmental protection as the primary objective were enacted in the seventies. Indira Gandhi, the then Prime Minister of India was one of the few world leaders to participate in the Stockholm Conference in 1972, following which her government enacted the Wildlife Protection Act, 1972 (WPA). This could be termed as the second phase of environmental protection in India. Earlier the protection of wild animals was mandated under the Wild Birds and Animals Protection Act 1912, a central legislation that had attempted to regulate the time period of the hunting season and declare unlawful the hunting of certain bigger mammals. Another important legislation was the Forest Conservation Act, 1980. The objective was to stop the large-scale dereservation of reserved forests (especially by state governments) resulting in massive deforestation, by establishing the Forest Advisory Committee—an expert body—that would review applications for diversion of forest for 'non-forest' purposes and recommend necessary action to the central government and recommend necessary action to the central government. Since 'forests' as a subject matter fell within the legislative competence of state governments, here again, the Constitutional (Forty Second) Amendment Act 1976 was passed by the parliament that transferred this subject matter from the state list to the concurrent list (Seventh Schedule of the Constitution of India) thereby allowing the Union Parliament to gain legislative competence on this subject matter.

The states (federal units) were however left with a choice to adopt it with suitable amendments.[10] States were given a formative legislative role on this issue and this was recognized in the Constitution where Entry 20 under the state list (Seventh Schedule to the Constitution) specified 'Protection of Wild Animals and Birds.'[11] The WPA was enacted under Article 252 of the Constitution which empowered the federal government to enact law on a subject matter which was in the state list if two or more states gave their consent on this matter. The WPA largely followed the framework of its predecessor but with greater detail and enhanced penalties for crimes related to the poaching and killing of wildlife. Protection of wildlife through the establishment of in situ enclosures free from human habitation, species prioritization (Tiger Parks and Elephant Conservation parks) and prohibition on the killing and hunting of specific species formed the fundamental basis for the WPA.

The Water (Prevention and Control of Pollution) Act, 1974 and the Air (Prevention and Control of Pollution) Act, 1981 (WA and AA, respectively) were enacted to address industrial pollution that had become increasingly apparent in a rapidly modernizing nation. It established a licensing regime aimed at pollution control overseen by the pollution control boards who provided regulatory approval for establishing industrial units which were given licenses to pollute within specified limits. The prevention aspect has been mostly ignored because it was left to the regulatory discretion of the pollution control boards.

An interesting difference between AA and the WA is that, under the former, an area has to be notified as an air pollution control area—for the provisions of the AA to become applicable and with it the licensing regime to commence, whereas for the latter, there is a presumption of applicability unless an area is specifically notified for purposes of excluding the application of the Act. Overreliance on the regulators—in this case the Pollution Control Boards (PCBs) is also apparent in the way in which civil remedies for apprehending, reporting, and litigating against statutory offenses under the AA and the WA are difficult to access. Section 49 of the WA and Section 43 of the AA bars the Court from taking cognizance of offences under the Act unless on a complaint by the PCB or any person who has to give a notice of sixty days. Further the pollution control board may refuse to give the relevant reports of water samples tested (that are used as evidence to establish pollution) if they opine that it is against public interest.

Gas leak in the Union Carbide plant in Bhopal occurred on the night of 2 December and the ensuing death and impairment to thousands of people is the biggest industrial accident in India and shocked regulators, legislators, and the judiciary out of stupor. It exposed the lack of statutory provisions to address environmental and public harm. Occupational health and hazard was inadequate to respond to large-scale public harm and challenges to environmental safety. A lack of culture of suing for tort liability also contributed to this absence of environmental responsibility. Legislative response to this came in the form of the enactment of two critical legislations—Environment (Protection) Act, 1986 (EPA) and the Public Liability Insurance Act (PLIA), 1991. Which can be termed as the third phase of the Indian environmental protection movement.

The PLIA provided for a statutorily mandated insurance for industries that engage with hazardous activities. The EPA follows a similar framework as the WA and AA in terms of establishing a licensing regime to regulate the emission and discharge of environmental pollutants. More importantly, it empowers the central government to take measures to protect and improve the environment including the constitution of administrative bodies. Thus, the EPA is an umbrella legislation which has been used by the central government to legislate key notifications[12] establishing regulatory frameworks such as those on coastal regulation zones, hazardous waste, vehicular pollution, noise pollution, ozone depletion, and environment impact assessment. Interestingly, the EPA replicates the WA and AA in barring the court from taking cognizance of offences unless the complaint is filed by the regulator. Members of the public can only access this remedy by giving a 60-day notice to the regulator.

The judiciary reacted to the strident criticism of its failure to adequately hold the Union Carbide liable[13] for the Bhopal Gas disaster by allowing for a rapid expansion in public interest litigation on environmental issues. This judicial reaction can be split into two phases—the first phase was from 1986 to1996. This was the phase between the *Oleum Gas Leak case*[14] in which the Supreme Court (SC) formulated a standard of absolute liability for industries involved in hazardous substances and the *Vellore Citizens Welfare Forum case*. This phase also saw the adoption and application of international environmental law principles, namely, sustainable development, precautionary principle and the polluter pays principle. In this phase, the SC primarily built a discourse around environmental rights as part of the fundamental right to life and personal liberty (Article 21 of the Constitution of India). Adoption of this constitutional trope was essential since, the SC could intervene only in the case of a violation of fundamental rights (Article 21 is one the fundamental rights). Therefore, environmental violations necessarily had to be recast as violations of the fundamental right to life and liberty. However, this came at a certain cost.[15] And that cost was the false trade-off between development and environmental protection, which the court was forced to make on a large number of occasions.

This early phase effectively ended with the *Vellore Citizens welfare forum case*,[16] in which the court realized that lack of administering bodies or regulators for specific environmental problems had created a situation where its judgments were rendered unenforceable. In this particular case, the court ordered the establishment of the Loss of Ecology Authority (LOEA) to address individual compensation claims relating to the environmental damage by leather manufacturing units.[17]

The fourth phase has been characterized by an increasingly frustrated and therefore 'activist' judiciary that has taken more strident and openly critical positions vis-à-vis the executive. The *Godavarman case*[18] is emblematic in this regard. The SC expanded a writ petition filed by T.N. Godavarman challenging the felling of timber by the state government, into a continuing mandamus[19] to review all aspects of forest governance with respect to the protection of forests—specifically the issue of dereservation of forests and the use of forests for non-forest purposes.

The Indian Parliament passed the Scheduled Tribes and Other Traditional Forest Dwellers (Recognition of Forest Rights Act) (FRA) on 29 December 2006. This landmark legislation is an attempt to correct the historical wrongs of the colonial legislative architecture on forests which excluded local populations and criminalized their sustenance needs and dependence on forests. It contains fundamentally far reaching provisions that requires gram sabha consent for diversion of forest for non-forest purposes including developmental projects. Thus, the judicial response to environmental crisis has been to centralize forest administration whereas the legislature seems to be pursuing the path of subsidiarity and decentralization.

Two characteristics of the Indian environmental movement are immediately apparent from above discussion. First that it is the central government and not the states that have been instrumental in enacting legislations on environmental protection. Thus, although the subject matter competence to legislate on the protection of wild animals, forests, water are with the states; it is the central government that empowered itself to enact these legislations.

Second, environmental protection—including species protection under the WPA or water pollution control under the WA, is undertaken by the concerned government bureaucrats and regulatory bodies. Public involvement in environmental protection is little recognized within the legislative framework. In fact, legislations like the WPA, AA, and the EPA make it inordinately difficult for the public to access remedies for addressing offenses under these acts. Further although the judiciary has made access to justice easier by expanding public interest litigations on environmental matters, it has been remarkably resistant to the idea of an active public or civil society and their participatory claims to environmental decision making.[20] The FRA seems really an anomaly in this context. It is therefore not surprising that there have been reports of watering down of some of the FRA provisions.[21] In this context, the NGT Act, 2010 has also been an exception in allowing an expansive definition of 'aggrieved person', who can move court to address environmental violations.[22]

The discussion is this section is evidence of the regressive legal provisions that civil society was confronted with and which were very significant impediments to public participation. Public participation since the early days of independence was never envisaged within environmental legislations and therefore the public interest litigation movement emerged as a suitable alibi for giving the public access to legally challenge environmental decisions of the executive. The same tradition is reflected in the proliferation of legal challenges against environmental clearances (EIA regulatory process) in the National Green Tribunal. Civil society groups as well as individuals have taken advantage of the liberal provisions of the NGT Act.

II.2 Environment Impact Assessment

EIA was first mandated in 1978–9 for river valley projects. It became mandatory for other kind of projects in 1994 when the central government (Ministry of Environment and Forests (MOEF) in exercise of its power to take any measure to protect and improve the environment as provided under Section 3 of the Environment Protection Act, 1986, issued the EIA notification.[23] It introduced a process for prior environmental approval of certain kind of projects (specified in Schedule 1). The project proponents were required to submit an environmental assessment report, environmental management plan, and the details of the public hearing conducted in the vicinity of the project. The EIA process is based on the principle of positive listing, which means that the EIA is mandated only for those projects that are identified in the notification.

Post 1994, the EIA notification was amended in a big way in 2006. However, in the twelve years intervening period it underwent as many as eleven changes. Public hearing was introduced by an amendment dated April 10 1997. The State Pollution Control Board (SPCB) was given the responsibility to conduct the public hearing. Persons who could participate in the public hearing were restricted to those likely to be physically affected, or those functioning in the field of environment or the local authority wherein the project was located. Public participation was therefore restricted. It is interesting to compare this regulatory process with that of public interest litigation, wherein locus standi has been relaxed considerably to allow public spirited citizens to challenge the violation of fundamental rights, even in cases where they are not individually affected by that violation.

There has been significant decentralization of regulatory functions from the central agency (the MOEF) to State. SEIAAs were to oversee smaller-scale projects (Category 'B') and the MOEF would continue to regulate larger-scale projects (Category 'A'). Although the final regulatory approval would be decided by the MOEF or the concerned SEIAA, they in turn were to base their approvals on the recommendations of the State Expert Appraisal Committee (SEAC) and the Expert Appraisal Committee (EAC) functioning in the MOEF.

The rules for participation have since then been liberalized. The 2006 notification was reframed as the public consultation process and it includes both locally affected and 'others who have plausible stake in the environmental impacts of the project or activity'. However, in one aspect there has been regression. While earlier a public hearing panel was constituted to oversee the public hearing, post 2006, it is only the district magistrate and the representative of the SPCB, who oversee the proceedings. Earlier, members of the panel included representatives of the local bodies[24] and senior citizens nominated by the district collector. Local persons were given more ownership and qualitative control over the public hearing process through their mandatory representation in the public hearing panel.

Periodic exclusions from the list of projects requiring EIA, has become a hallmark of the EIA regulatory process. For instance in 2002, a financial limit was arbitrarily set. New projects falling within Rs 100 crores and modernization/expansion projects within Rs 50 crores were exempted from EIA. Further, the 2006 amendment also stated that public hearing may be dispensed off with if the SPCB deems that 'owing to the local situation, it is not possible to conduct a public hearing in a manner which will enable the views of the concerned local persons to be freely expressed.' The fact that public hearing is itself seen as a process that can be excluded under certain conditions, illustrates the regulatory perspective that looks at public hearing as something procedural which contributes little in substantive terms to improving the EIA process itself, and is therefore in the nature of an accommodation.

It is critical to delineate the philosophy behind public hearings conducted as part of EIA. There are four stages in the EIA process in India. First is the screening stage wherein the regulatory authority reviews the application to determine whether EIA is required to be undertaken. At this stage itself, the regulatory authority may determine that the project does not require EIA and in that case there is no requirement to the other stages—that is, scoping, public hearing, and appraisal. Second is the scoping stage is to establish the parameters or the Terms of Reference (TOR) of the EIA to be conducted. The applicant first proposes the draft TOR which is then reviewed by the Expert Appraisal Committee (EAC) before being formalized. Third is the public consultation stage, wherein the draft EIA report is provided to the general public and a public hearing is conducted at the location of the project. According to the 2006 notification:

> After completion of the public consultation, the applicant shall address all the material environmental concerns expressed during this process, and make appropriate changes in the draft EIA and Environmental Management Plan (EMP). The final EIA report, so prepared, shall be submitted by the applicant to the concerned regulatory authority for appraisal. The applicant may alternatively submit a supplementary report to draft EIA and EMP addressing all the concerns expressed during the public consultation.

There are two interesting aspects to this dictum as reproduced from the 2006 notification. First, it is left to the applicant to distill 'material concerns' from presumably immaterial ones expressed in the public consultation. Second, it is again the applicant who has to make appropriate changes in the draft EIA and EMP addressing these material concerns. Evidently, this is a clear conflict of interest, since the applicant will always tend to understate public concerns and also will not be interested in radically changing the scale of the project. Further, the report on the public consultation that is prepared by the SPCB that conducts the public hearing is not a qualitative document. It is limited to a pedantic exercise where the details of the conduct of the public hearing are reported back rather than any qualitative appraisal. Further, there is no consideration of alternatives that is required as part of this exercise of undertaking the EIA. This is significant part of the EIA process in countries like Denmark and Germany.[25] It allows for dramatic changes in the project including shifting to another physical location.

Another important aspect is that of the timing of the public hearing. Public hearing is conducted at the third stage, and therefore the public cannot input into the process of terms of reference or even in the EIA—which establishes the contours of the EIA to be conducted. They are mostly given a passive role to comment on the draft EIA report. Their concerns are left to the discretion of the applicant, and it is they who have to sift the material from what they deem to be immaterial. Further, there has to be independent first-hand vetting of the concerns expressed. Currently, a video-recording of the entire public hearing is mandatory; however, this recording is not mandatorily referred to by the EAC. It should have been possible for the public hearing to include at least one member of the regulatory body so as to ensure their concerns are duly noted and addressed. Further, at least the district magistrate or a representative of the local administration should be given a well-defined role in terms of reporting on the conduct of the EIA but also providing a qualitative report on the EIA.

What is the utility of the public hearing? Executive intent seems to provide for a constricted role for the public. Public participation is solicited to express concerns and opinions at a very late stage for any effective intervention. Public hearing is modelled so as there is a presumption in favour of the project so as to leave no space for any fundamental changes in the project scope. Public hearing is therefore only meant to rubber stamp the project. Given such a context, it is interesting to know the possibilities of having a public hearing process that is actually designed to intervene effectively in the EIA process. This would ultimately mean that public hearing may be able to trigger a veto on the project itself. We will come back to this subject in the concluding section of this article.

It is pertinent to point out some of the recent amendments made to the 2006 notification. The EIA process has undergone significant decentralization, with the more powers being given to the state-level impact assessment authority, exempting the construction of school, college, universities, hostels for education institutions, and construction of industrial sheds from requirement of environmental clearance. Projects in border areas have been given exemptions from specific regulatory obligations. Highway projects in border areas were exempted from the scoping requirement and all other linear projects were exempted from the requirement of public hearing. Although these exemptions have been subject to 'sustainable environment management' (SEM)—but this term itself is little understood and therefore its practice is especially difficult if not impossible—ultimately this will amount to an undertaking by the applicant to follow SEM without adequate review. Standardization of the TOR for preparation of the EIA report and increasing the validity of the environmental clearance from five to seven years are the other important changes initiated.[26]

Very recently, the MOEF has made a move towards decentralization.[27] Regional empowered committees have been established in the ten regional offices of the MOEF for giving approval for forest clearances upto 40 hectares. Further, SEIAA has been given more powers and District Environment Impact Assessment Authority (DEIAA) headed by the DM has been established for providing inputs on minor minerals. This decentralization has actually been accompanied by steady dismantling and dilution of regulations, and may therefore actually lead to loss of access to expertise and reduced levels of transparency. This is especially so because as per records in the last three years,[28] the maximum number of approval has been given for road projects and hydel power projects. Roads fall within 'linear projects' and are therefore exempted from a host of regulatory requirements under the EIA—including that of public hearing.[29]

II.3 Analysis of Key Judgments

The analysis of judgments have been categorized around certain specific normative aspects. First, we look at how the NGT has developed a liberalized regime of interpretation of key provisions in the NGT Act related to limitation period, 'aggrieved parties', and communication of public notice. These key procedural provisions have facilitated public access to remedies. Second, given that gram sabhas as local governance institutions have themselves filed legal challenges, we explore how their role has been redefined through judicial interpretation. Third, we look at how substantive public values have been identified by the NGT in these cases. Fourth and finally, we look at how public hearings have emerged as critical part of procedural justice in the EIA regulatory procedure. We also look at how far infirmities in the public hearing procedure have been used to overturn environmental clearances.

Who can qualify to be an 'applicant' (under Section 14 of the NGT Act) or under Section 15 can the application for relief and restitution be filed by a person who has not suffered personal injury or a 'person aggrieved' (under Section 16 of the NGT Act) so as to be competent to move the tribunal? The issue of locus standi was fundamental to the idea of the tribunal being publicly accessible. In *Wilfred J Anr v MOEF Ors*[30] the NGT discussed this issue in great detail.

The court quoted its own judgment in *Samata v Union of India*[31] in forwarding the argument that even if the applicant was not from the area where the project was to be located or even if they had not participated in the public hearing, they still had the right to challenge the environmental clearance granted on legal grounds.

It found support for a liberal and purposive construction of the provisions to allow for a liberalized regime of locus standi. This was a significant departure from the restrictive regime of limiting public remedies in the earlier environmental pollution laws. At the same time, it was recognition of the historically liberalized access regimes that allowed public interest litigation on environmental issues.

This also echoed a path-breaking judgement of the Delhi High Court in *Prafulla Samantra v Ministry of Environment & Forests & Ors*[32] that argued for an expansive interpretation of Section 11(2)(c) of the Environment Protection Act, 1986, as environmental disputes have larger public interest and therefore should not be viewed inter se and consequently allowing for narrow rules of standing.

Section 16 of the NGT Act allows a person aggrieved to move the tribunal to appeal an order within thirty days from the date on which it is communicated to him. NGT has clarified the import of the term 'communication'.

> Communication, particularly to the public, has to be by methods of mass communication, like satellite, website, newspapers etc. 'Communicated' is a strong word. It requires that sufficient knowledge of basic facts constituting the

grounds of the order should be imparted fully and effectively to the person. It is only when the content of the order is available and known to a prospective appellant that such appellant would be able to effectively exercise the right of appeal .... Mere inconvenience or the expenses incurred by the parties or by the authorities would not be a ground to adopt a different approach. (Para 55)

This strengthens procedural rights by rejecting public authorities from taking the defense of expenses or inconvenience as grounds for their inability to communicate. In effect, this strengthens the right to public information.

Understanding and empathizing with the life patterns of those affected by environmental clearances has been the hallmark of the NGT's jurisprudence on environmental impact assessment and also reflects to some extent that the SCs rethink on this issue.

In *Samatha v State of AP*,[33] the Supreme Court stated:

Agriculture is the only source of livelihood for Scheduled Tribes apart, from collection and sale of minor forest produce to supplement their income. Land is their most natural and valuable asset and imperishable endowment from which the tribals derive their sustenance, social status, economic and social equality...... (Para 10)

In *M.P. Patil v Union of India*,[34] the NGT stated:

In the framework of Indian economy, there is a relation between poverty and environment. Poverty and degraded environment are closely inter-related, especially where people depend primarily on natural resources based on their immediate environment for their livelihood. Restoring natural systems and improving natural resource management practices at the grass root level are central to a strategy to eliminate poverty. (Para 69).

Similarly in *Antarsingh Patel and Ors. v UOI*, the NGT recognized that:

It is no longer resintegra that the benefits of developmental activities must go to the local people and their quality of life must improve instead of driving them to a disadvantageous position. Depriving them of the facilities which they were already enjoying, but are likely to be deprived of due to the proposed Hydro Electric project would be contrary to the law. Citizens are at the centre of development and as such all efforts are required to be made to avoid any hardships to the affected persons. (Para 15).

It marks a significant departure from the early reductive utilitarian approach of the Supreme Court.[35] In this context, the Gram Sabha has emerged as a vociferous public voice representing the issues and needs of local populace increasing facing the threat of dispossession of livelihoods.

Underlining this role of the gram sabha in *Orissa Mining Corporation Ltd. v MOEF and Ors*,[36] the Supreme Court had ruled that the religious rights of individuals and communities to be determined by the gram sabha would have to be protected and therefore the decision of the gram sabha would have to be considered before the MOEF grants environmental approvals for developmental projects in forests or scheduled areas.

The Panchayat (Extension to Schedule Areas) Act, 1996 includes specific provisions that empower gram panchayats significantly by making their recommendation mandatory prior to the grant of prospecting and mining lease for minor minerals in schedule areas. Similarly, the *Orissa Mining* case, the court the purpose of the Forest Rights Act was to empower communities to participate in the conservation and sustainable use of forest. A gram sabha is tasked with initiating the process of determining the individual and community claims to forest rights. Relying on the PESA provision coupled with Section 13 of the Forest Rights Act,

> Gram Sabha has an obligation to safeguard and preserve the traditions and customs of the schedule tribes and other forest dwellers, their cultural identity, community resources, etc. (Para 64).

This became the basis for upholding the right of the gram sabha to examine whether the proposed mining area would affect their religious rights.

Further, to ensure independent proceedings of the gram sabha deliberating on this specific matter, the court ordered that a judicial officer nominated by the chief justice of Orissa would be an observer to the proceedings and sign the minutes of the proceedings.

Taken together, the court essentially upheld the right of the gram sabha to consider non-developmental objectives in their deliberations over a project. And while not recognizing the absolute right to veto, the court did make a clear that the MOEF has to take this into consideration while arriving at any decision to give clearance.

In *Gram Panchayat Navlakh Umbre v Union of India and Ors*,[37] the gram sabha of several villages affected by the power project passed a resolution opposing the project on account of environmental concerns. Despite this, the EAC granted environmental clearance. The court first established that the EAC ignored blatant procedural violations by the project proponent, wherein the Terms of Reference for the conduct of the EIA was drafted and approved by the EAC after the EIA had already been conducted. Further, despite the gram sabha making many representations to the regulatory authorities for addressing their reservations, they were not given a fair hearing. It is important appreciate that despite the lack of avenues for interaction between the regulator and the public in the EIA regulatory process, the gram panchayat in this case took *suo moto* initiative to directly make representations to the regulators. This also illustrates the lack of faith in the public hearing process—over which the applicant exercises inordinate qualitative control. Further, in their legal challenge, the petitioners argued

> *the proposed project should be shifted to an alternative industrial site and ought not be established in the proposed site at village Navlakh Umbre. Consequential reliefs have been sought, inter alia for conducting a comprehensive study, a fresh public hearing and a restraint on undertaking any activity pertaining to the project.* (Para 14)

The petitioners were clearly making the case for consideration of the alternative as part of the regulatory pathway.

EIA is a notification under the Environmental Protection Act 1986. As was discussed in Part 2, the provisions in the EPA on cognizance of offences is similar to those under the WA and AA. It makes it inordinately difficult to access this remedy. Despite this the gram panchayat Navlakh Umbre issued a notice to the petitioners under Section 19(b) of the EPA, following which a criminal complaint was filed—following which arrest orders were issued by the judicial magistrate for the applicant and the members of the SEAC and the SEIAA. These orders were quashed by a division bench of the Bombay High Court.

More fundamentally the court established:

> *Among the fundamental principles of environmental governance are principles that foster access to information; access to justice to the community which is liable to be affected and governance based on rule of law. Access to information, particularly to impoverished and marginalized communities, which populate our rural landscape is of vital importance. Communities must have access to all information in order to be satisfied that a proposed project meets standards of safety; that the site upon which the project is to be located is environmentally conducive and that the project will not result in a destruction of the natural habitat. Denial of information is the surest way to deprive rural communities of human rights and leads to a sense of alienation. Access to information is a source of empowerment. Participatory decision making must hence be an ingredient of environmental governance in a true sense of the term. Merely observing the forms of participation without the substance is to negate fundamental human rights*" (Para 25).

Evidently, there are two aspects that the court is clear about. First, the EIA as a regulatory process is not a strictly scientific process that looks at the potential environmental impact of projects and ways and means to mitigate that impact; more fundamentally, it is a political process that requires negotiation and balancing of certain public values. It is precisely this is recognition that allows the court to open up this 'expert-driven' process to judicial scrutiny on both procedural as well as substantive grounds. Admittedly, balance between environment and development is a false trade-off—and it reiterates the rather utilitarian and reductionist formulation of the principle of sustainable development—as was embraced by the Supreme Court. However, the recognition that it is a political process is imperative to developing methodologies for ensuring public participation. The requirements of public participation will therefore not rely on instrumental justifications of improving the EIA, but on the larger question of environmental justice.

Hazira Macchimar Samiti v Union of India and Ors[38] is a recent case wherein a fisherman's cooperative had challenged the environmental clearance granted Adani-Hajaria Port Pvt. Ltd (AHPPL). The petitioners alleged that the port construction would jeopardize their safe and proper access to sea water and would prevent their fishing activities thereby compromising their livelihood. They also alleged that AHPPL had violated the compliance conditions to the environmental clearance granted earlier by causing massive destruction of mangroves. The clearance was bad in law as it was based on the MOEF Office Memorandum of 3 November 2009 that allowed for ex post facto clearance. The public hearing process stood completely circumvented.

The NGT factually established that there was considerable destruction of the mangroves in the area owing to the port construction activities and most of it was undertaken without obtaining EC or CRZ clearance. Interestingly, the NGT recorded that:

> [It] is evident from records that the Tribunal had to spend a lot of time to get such information from MOEF and only after coercive actions, such information was placed on record by MOEF. (Para 12).

It is a clear indictment of the regulatory body. One can imagine if the Tribunal is finding it difficult to obtain information, the public access to information (other than summary EIA reports, clearances granted, and EC meeting minutes) is precarious.

A penalty of Rs 25 Crore was imposed on AHPPL. It was levied for restoration of the mouth of the creek and it was restrained from narrowing the access and the EC was set aside. The petitioner's litigation costs of Rs 2 lakh was also charged to the AHPPL.

It is evident from the preceding discussion; historically, public participation in environmental regulation has to a large extent been circumscribed by legislation in India. Newer legislations like the Forest Rights Act are important legislative interventions that have opened up spaces for greater public deliberation in environmental decision-making. Concomitantly gram sabhas have become more active in passing formal resolutions and communication them to the regulators and more importantly willing to intervene through litigation. All Courts—the Supreme Court, high court, and National Green Tribunals have consistently sought to qualitatively improve the space for public consultation by ensuring procedural rights for the public and upholding transparency and accountability of regulators. Nevertheless, there is still reticence amongst the judiciary to recognize the public right to refuse a specific kind of development project.

III Indonesia

III.1 History of Indonesian Environmental Law

Being colonized by the Dutch, the civil law tradition has heavily influenced Indonesia's system of law.[39] In addition, it consisted of large number of ethnic groups. The Indonesian legal system has also been pluralized by the existence of *HukumAdat* (customary/community law) and some aspects of Islamic Law/*shariah*.[40] This influence and pluralistic nature of law also applies to environmental law in Indonesia.

Environmental reference is expressly written in Indonesia's constitution (*Undang-UndangDasar 1945* / UUD 1945) in Article 33(3), states that:

> The land and the waters as well as the natural riches therein are to be controlled by the state and to be utilized to the greatest benefit of the people.

This acknowledgement of the Constitution's environmental protection may be argued to be far-fetched as it was not the main intention of the drafters of the constitution.[41] Nevertheless, with such control by the state of the natural resources, it is safe to assume the responsibility of Indonesia to the preservation of its natural environment.

After going through four amendments, UUD 1945 as it stands today has two new provisions that refer to environmental protection. The first provision is the new inserted of Article 34(4), states that:

> The organization of the national economy shall be based on economic democracy that upholds the principles of solidarity and efficiency along with fairness,

sustainability, keeping the environment in perspective, self-sufficiency, and by maintaining the balance between progress and with the unity of the national economy.

The second reference to the environment as a part of the basic human rights of the Indonesian people. Article 28H(1) states that: 'Every person shall have the rights to live in physical and spiritual prosperity, to have a home and to enjoy a good and healthy environment, and shall have the right to obtain medical care.

The national implementing regulation of environmental protection in Indonesia was firstly introduced in the Law No. 4 of 1982 on Environmental Management (EMA 1982). The introduction of this law was also celebrated as Indonesia joined the world's concern regarding the environment as illustrated in the United Nations Conference on the Human Environment in 1982. The EMA 1982 was also applauded for successfully incorporating international environmental concepts to domestic law such as sustainable development, intergenerational equity, environmental impact assessment, and the polluter-pays principle. The EMA 1982 was then amended twice in 1997 and 2009.[42]

III.2 Environmental Impact Assessment in Indonesia

Analisis Mengenai Dampak Lingkungan (AMDAL) is Indonesia's environmental impact assessment (EIA) system.[43] It is an instrument to maintain natural resource and environmental programmes.[44] This assessment is referred to as Environmental Impact Assessment.[45] AMDAL was introduced into Indonesia largely as a donor-driven environmental safeguard during the primetime of President Suharto's administration of the 'New Order' era—a time of not only increasing foreign support and investment but also a time of worldwide environmental awakening following the debate on environment, development, and the 'limits to growth'.[46] In contrast to EIA in the United States where the term 'impact' is associated with negative effect, AMDAL in Indonesia can also carry a positive implication.[47]

In Indonesia a project that is likely to impact the environment is legally required to undertake an AMDAL as the main environmental requirement.[48] There are huge numbers of regulations and legislation related to or governing environmental management and protection in Indonesia. These regulations and legislation may be classified into five categories, namely: (a) General Environmental Legislation (GEL); (b) Sector Environmental Legislation (SEL); (c) Ratified Environmental Convention (REC); (d) Provincial Environmental Legislation (PEL); and (e) Local Environmental Legislation (LEL). GEL refers to legislation which has been accompanied by implementing regulations governing environmental management in general and covers all sectors.[49]

For instance, Law No. 23 of 1997 regarding Environmental Management (frequently referred to as the Environmental Management Act or EMA 1997) is 'the basis for the evaluation and adjustment of all laws that contain applicable environmental provisions, namely laws concerning irrigation, mining and energy, forestry, conservation of biological resources and its ecosystem, industry, settlement, spatial management, land use, etc.' EMA 1997 contains a number of important provisions on environmental management, including the obligation to prepare an Environmental Impact Analysis (EIA/AMDAL) for any planned business/activity that has large and significant impact to the environment (embodied in Article 15).[50]

Subsequently, AMDAL was specifically mandated by the newly approved Environmental Protection and Management Law No. 32 of 2009 (EMA 2009) dated 8 September 2009 replacing Law No. 23 of 1997 on Environmental Management.[51] This is the most current environmental protection and management law, and was derived from the amendment of two previous laws, Law No. 23 of 1997 on Environmental Management, and Law No. 4 of 1982 on Principles of Environmental Management.[52]

The Indonesian government imposes a 'positive list' for a project and/or activity that requires AMDAL according to the type, scale, and location of activity through the Ministry of Environment Regulation No. 11 of 2006. The type of activity and scale of projects that require a full AMDAL process are defined in Minister of Environment Regulation No. 11 of 2006 covering the following sectors: (1) defence, (2) agriculture, (3) fishery, (4) forestry, (5) transportation, (6) satellite technology, (7) industry, (8) public work, (9) energy and mineral resources, (10) tourism, (11) nuclear development, (12) hazardous waste processing, and (13) genetic engineering. Any project and/or activity located at the border or inside a protected area, irrespective of type or scale, requires an AMDAL.[53]

Projects that are considered to have no potential significant impacts and are not listed are obliged to apply for an environmental management and monitoring (EMMP) called UKL–UPL.[54] It stands for Environmental Management Effort or *Upaya Pengelolaan Lingkungan* (UKL) and Environmental Monitoring Effort or *Upaya Pemantauan Lingkungan* (UPL) documents.[55] This kind of project and/or activity is considered as a micro or small project.[56]

The Ministry of Environment Regulation No. 08 of 2006 provides the latest guidance on the AMDAL process.[57] The process includes preparation of an Environmental Impact Assessment (*Analisis Dampak Lingkungan* [ANDAL]), an Environmental Monitoring Document (*Rencana Pemantauan*

Lingkungan Hidup [RPL]), and an Environmental Management Document (*Rencana Pengelolaan Lingkungan Hidup* [RKL]).[58] The AMDAL process has no provision for public review, except provision for the participation of NGOs as community representatives on AMDAL review committees.[59] The format of the AMDAL documentation (consisting of ANDAL, RKL, RPL, and Executive Summary/*Ringkasan Eksekutif* documents) is described in the Minister of Environment Regulation No. 08 of 2006. Section 2.1 b. 'Alternatives Studied in AMDAL'.[60]

The completed ANDAL, RKL, and RPL are submitted to the local governor/regent who then establishes an appraisal commission with membership coming from the Environment Impact Control Agency (*Badan Pengendalian Dampak Lingkungan* [BAPEDAL]; the subsidiary agency of the Ministry of Environment) and inviting submission from relevant technical agencies, representatives from affected communities, business experts, and environmental organizations. The commission then makes a recommendation to the governor/regent.[61] The BAPEDAL's tasks include the implementation of the national environmental policy, preparation of guidelines on environmental impact management, coordination of EIA processes, monitoring and management of waste discharge, promotion of environmental awareness, and settlement of environmental disputes.[62]

Once the AMDAL is approved, the applicant is granted an Environment Permit (Ijin Lingkungan) by the governor or regent. Both the governor/regent and the BAPEDAL then monitor the permit holder for compliance. If the permit conditions are violated, administrative sanctions can be imposed including suspension or revocation of the permit. Continuing to operate without an environment permit then becomes a criminal offence under the EMA 2009 and carries a potential fifteen-year prison sentence or a maximum fine up to Rp 3 billion.[63]

III.3 Relevant Cases of AMDAL Enforcement

The AMDAL in Indonesia has been the main requirement for activities that has negative potential to the environment. The importance of this requirement has been upheld in both courts—administrative and criminal courts. For those activities committed by companies, which operated without AMDAL, were given penal sentences. The first case was that of PT Power.

Steel Mandiri is an iron and steel smelting company, located in Tangerang, Banten. Based on citizens' report, in it's production process, PT Power Steel Mandiri fabricates waste in the form of sludge. Later on, the Tangerang Environment Management Agency (*Badan Pengelolaan Lingkungan Hidup*

Daerah Kabupaten Tangerang) inspected PT Power Steel Mandiri activity, and found out that PT Power Steel Mandiri has no AMDAL. In this case, the Tangerang Environment Management Agency found the indication of exceeding environmental quality standard, which is regulated in Law No. 32 of 2009 as well. The court and high court found the defendant guilty as charged.[64]

The second case shows that AMDAL is the main requirement for a company to get plantation permit since the operation have impacts on the environment. The omission to stop the pollution caused by the company had led to the penal responsibility of the operators of the company. PT. MekarsariAlam Lestari is a company running a business in the sector of plantation. It means that this company is obliged to have a Plantation Permit (*Izin Usaha Perkebunan*[IUP]). From an environmental perspective, the principal piece of supporting evidence that must be submitted with the IUP application is an AMDAL. However PT. Mekarsari Alam Lestari operated without any AMDAL and IUP. Besides that, some fires occurred in the forest that belongs to PT. Mekarsari Alam Lestari several times in 2008 until 2009. Moreover, PT. Mekarsari Alam Lestari did not try to extinguish the fire when the wildfire occurred. For that reason, the president of PT. Mekarsari Alam Lestari and manager of PT. Mekarsari Alam Lestari was sentenced to six months in prison for causing pollution. The court of appeal stated that PT. Mekarsari Alam Lestari had violated the provision under Law No. 23 of 2009.[65]

In the administrative court, the enforcement of AMDAL as a tool to protect the environment has been quite different. This is because the court has considered the lack of scientific evidence as a reason to reject lawsuits filed by environmentalist NGOs in requiring AMDAL for high-risk activities. Several NGOs in Indonesia filed a lawsuit to the administrative court for license issuing of transgenic Bt DP 5690B cotton by the minister of agriculture. 'Monagro Kimia', a subsidiary company of Monsanto in Indonesia, produces this transgenic cotton that called NUCOTN35B. The plaintiffs demand cancellation of it because they assumed that the license was issued without any prior AMDAL. For that reason, they thought that the release of this license violates the precautionary principle. The minister of agriculture, however, considers the activity of Monagro Kimia as the activity that is not obliged to have AMDAL. The administrative court agreed with the minister of agriculture's opinion, therefore the administrative court rejected the plaintiff's lawsuit. In accordance with the fact that the minister of agriculture has already made an announcement to the public about this license, and has asked for opinions of the experts, who said that transgenic cotton is not dangerous, then the administrative court concluded that there is no violation of precautionary principle in this case.[66]

In addition, the administrative court rejected the executive order to stop the reclamation of Jakarta north shore. Despite appeal an effort by the ministry of the environment, the court decision finally affirmed that a minister's decision cannot overrule the licence that is based on the higher law, the Presidential Decree. In 2003, The minister of environment issued the Minister of Environment Regulation No. 14 of 2003 on Impropriety Reclamation and Revitalization Planning in North Shore Jakarta/*Pantai Utara Jakarta*. This regulation was with regard to AMDAL, which showed that the activity of reclamation of Jakarta's northern shore could have a negative effect for the environment. Previously, there were six companies who wished to conduct reclamation in North Shore Jakarta: Bakti Era Mulia, Taman Harapan Indah, Manggal Krida Yudha, Pelabuhan Indonesia II, Pembangunan Jaya Ancol, and Jakarta Propertindo. Towards Minister of Environment Regulation No. 14 of 2003, those six companies filed a lawsuit to the administrative court in Jakarta. They requested the court to examine the license-issuing authority of the minister of environment in issuing this license. The administrative court then stated that there was indication of the minister of environment for abusing the power in issuing Minister of Environment Regulation No. 14 of 2003. Therefore, the court concluded that Minister of Environment Regulation No. 14 of 2003 was invalid.[67]

Interestingly, the administrative court enforces the requirement of AMDAL in a case of licence operation given by the local government. This licence was given to the company without the fulfilment of AMDAL. In 2008, Head of Unified Licensing Service Agency (*Kepala Kantor Pelayanan Perizinan Terpadu*) in Pati Regency, Central Java issued Head of Unified Licensing Service Agency Regulation No. 540/052/2008 on expansion of PT. Semen Gresik (Persero) Tbk industrial area, located in Sukolilo. Afterwards WALHI, an NGO in Indonesia concerned with environment-related matters, filed a lawsuit in the administrative court. The plaintiff assumed that Head of Unified Licensing Service Agency Regulation No. 540/052/2008 had violated the provision in Law No. 23 of 1997 and Minister of Environment Regulation No. 11 of 2006, since the AMDAL had not been approved when the defendant issued the Head of Unified Licensing Service Agency Regulation No. 540/052/2008. In other words, Head of Unified Licensing Service Agency Regulation No. 540/052/2008 was issued without any prior AMDAL, whereas activity of PT. Semen Gresik was considered as an activity that required an AMDAL. The judges found out that the defendant had violated the provision in Law No. 23 of 1997 and Minister of Environment Regulation No. 11 of 2006, and agreed with the plaintiff's opinion. After that, the defendant filed a lawsuit to the administrative court of appeal, and revoked the suspension of sentence. But then, the supreme administrative court affirmed the decision of the administrative court.[68]

From the cases above, it can be concluded that the upholding of AMDAL as a tool to protect the environment has been variably consistent within the court. Despite the decision of the local government, the lawsuit to uphold AMDAL should go to the administrative court or even district court if there is an indication of criminal misconduct. These courts will always assess the issues before them against the central regulations and not against the local regulations. Nevertheless, this practice of the Court arguably is movement towards positive ends.

IV Conclusion

Despite the differing legal systems, there are many similarities between the Indian and Indonesian EIA regulatory regimes. Both the Indonesian and the Indian EIA regulatory regime follow the principle of positive listing. To some extent, this ensures clarity about the kind of activities that require EIA and regulatory clearance. This also makes it easier to identify and therefore apprehend violators. Regulators in both countries are under the operational control of their parent ministry. Thus, despite including external experts within the regulatory process, the potential for executive intervention in the regulatory process is quite high and therefore at times may vitiate the regulatory process. As is evident like for instance in the *Hazira Macchimar Samiti case* and the *Transgenic Cotton case* wherein the executive intervention was aimed at circumventing the EIA process.

A unique aspect of the EIA regulatory regime in the Indonesian context is the use of criminal code to address environmental violations relating to EIA. The criminal code is used concomitantly with imposition of hefty financial penalties. This has been influential and an important part of the strategy of deterrence. Further crimes draw public attention and media coverage and therefore their impact is further heightened, unlike in India, where financial penalties and cancellation of clearance is what is provided in the notification. Financial penalties were only recently enhanced under the NGT Act. The courts have come in since then to peg the financial penalty at a percentage of the project costs.[69] However, the lack of criminal liability and the focus on financial penalty has meant that there is a tendency to accept illegal project developments as fait accompli and then regularize them through payment of fines. Given the number of EIA violations, financial penalty and even cancellation of project approvals do not seem to have an adequate deterrence effect.

Another point of comparison is the nature of the adjudicatory body. Given that environmental disputes especially those relating to EIAs require some technical expertise, does having a specialized adjudicatory mechanism makes a substantive difference? To some extent, the NGT in India, being a specialized tribunal has enabled it to not only undertake a procedural review but also a substantive review of environmental clearances–especially clear cases of non-application of mind. In Indonesia, the courts—both civil and administrative have stuck to a procedural review which has arguably, in some instances, hampered the environmental cause.

Public involvement in both countries is legislatively constrained. Within the EIA regulatory process, it is scheduled at a stage which is already quite late in the process to make any effective intervention. Further, unlike jurisdictions like Europe and the Scandinavian countries, the EIA process does not specifically consider alternatives. This is an important aspect that is missing in the EIA process in both Indonesia and India. Despite the constrains, citizens have shown remarkable grit and imagination in using new and innovative ways like gram sabha resolutions in India and citizens' reports in Indonesia to draw attention to specific projects and environmental violations. In this endeavour they have largely found judicial support through clarifying procedural rights of the citizens and expanding the regulator's obligations towards transparency and accountability. This has not been an easy exercise for the court. Indonesia's history of martial rule and the unitary administration has meant that the judiciary has been cautious in directly challenging administrative actions even when they were illegal. In India, the judiciary has often been charged with excessive activism, and violating the separation of powers principle that is embedded within the Indian Constitution. Specifically in the context of EIA, the executive has argued that the EIA regulatory regime is expert-driven and therefore should not be open to judicial interference. Despite this, the judiciary has shown great foresight in responding to public challenges to the EIA regulatory regime.

The use of the term 'foresight' is deliberate. Since there is an explicit admission in the context of India that the EIA regulatory regime is the space through which fundamental ideas of the nature, contours, and shape of economic development are contested in developing countries like India and Indonesia, it is critical to create justification and spaces in which citizens can and should actively participate in shaping the imagination of their nations.

It is in this context, that such an academic project assumes importance, as it allows us to closely study developments within comparable jurisdictions. Prima facie, these jurisdictions are comparable. As large developing countries with a specific history of colonization, regulatory spheres in these jurisdictions face similar impulses and imperatives. This also then becomes a project of solidarity that explores the contours of how such regulatory spaces—in this instance the EIA regulation—have developed—and in an era of globalization despite the trend towards greater harmonization, such spaces have retained their sui generis dynamics that are embedded within democratic public movements for greater transparency, accountability, and voice in governance.

Notes and References

* We wish to thank Ira Indriani Tri Oetami, research assistant, Faculty of Law, Universitas Indonesia and Eshani Singh, BALLB student (Batch of 2012), Jindal Global Law School for their research assistance.

1. R. Goodland, and B. Sadler. 1996, 'The Analysis of Environmental Sustainability: From Concepts to Applications', *International Journal of Sustainable Development*, vol. 3, pp. 2–21.
2. C.B. Griffin. 1999. 'Watershed Councils: An Emerging Form of Public Participation in Natural Resource Management.' *Journal of the American Water Resources Association* vol. 35, p. 505; Carl Bruch. 2002. *The New "Public": The Globalization of Public Participation* (2nd edition), Environmental Law Institute.
3. Paola Gazzola. 2013. 'Reflecting on mainstreaming through environmental appraisal in times of financial crisis—From "greening" to "pricing"', *Environmental Impact Assessment Review* vol. 41, p. 21; D Annandale and R Taplin. 2003. 'Is environmental impact assessment regulation a "burden" to private firms?', *Environmental Impact Assessment Review*, 23(3): 383; Tim Snell and Richard Cowell. 2006. 'Scoping in environmental impact assessment: balancing precaution and efficiency?', *Environmental Impact Assessment Review*, 26(4): 359.
4. *Pulp Mills on the River Uruguay (Argentina v Uruguay)*, Judgment, I.C.J. Reports 2010, p. 14. For a detailed analysis see Xiaoqin Zhu and Jinlong He. 2013. 'International Court of Justice's Impact on International Environmental Law: Focusing on the Pulp Mills Case', *Yearbook of International Environmental Law* 23: 106–30.
5. A. Barker and C. Wood. 1999. 'An evaluation of EIA system performance in eight EU countries', *Environmental Impact Assessment Review*, 19(4), 387–404.
6. Julia Black, 2000,' Proceduralizing Regulation: Part I', *Oxford Journal of Legal Studies*, vol. 20, p. 597.
7. Margherita Pieraccini, 2015. 'Rethinking Participation in Environmental Decision-Making: Epistemologies of Marine Conservation in South-East England,' *Journal Environmental Law*. vol. 27, pp. 45–67.
8. This argument is shaped by impulses similar to that espoused by Pierre Legrand. See, Pierre Legrand. 2006. 'On the Singularity of Law', *Harvard International Law Journal*, vol. 47, p. 517.
9. Regulatory process involving EIA and granting of approval.

10. Given that some states already had their own wildlife protection laws—for instance; Bengal Rhinoceros Preservation Act, 1932 (Ben.8 of 1932); the U.P. by the Wild Birds and Animals Protection (U.P. Amendment) Act, 1934 (U.P. 13 of 1934), and in its application to the C.P. by the Wild Birds and Animals Protection (C.P. Amendment) Act, 1935 (C.P. 27 of 1935); Ajmer by the Wild Birds and Animals Protection (Ajmer Amendment) Act, 1954 (Ajmer 4 of 1954).
11. This Entry was later amended by the Constitutional (Forty Second) Amendment Act 1976 which transferred the subject matter competence from the State to the Concurrent list (Entry 17B) thus enabling the Central Government to frame laws.
12. A notification is an executive order passed by a Government Department on any issue and is applicable to the general public. The competence of the executive to pass a notification is always based on a statutory provision.
13. See Jamie Cassels. 1993. *The Uncertain Promise of Law: Lessons From Bhopal*, Toronto: University of Toronto Press; Upendra Baxi. 2010. 'Writing about Impunity and Environment: The "Silver Jubilee" of the Bhopal Catastrophe,' *Journal of Human Rights and the Environment*, vol. 23 and Upendra Baxi. 2016. 'Human Rights Responsibility of Multinational Corporations, Political Ecology of Injustice: Learning from Bhopal Thirty Plus?', *Business and Human Rights Journal*, vol. 1, pp 21–40 doi:10.1017/bhj.2015.7
14. *M C Mehta v Union of India* (1987) 1 SCC 395 ('Oleum Gas Leak case').
15. For a detailed discussion on this please refer to Nupur Chowdhury. 2014. 'From judicial activism to adventurism—the Godavarman case in the Supreme Court of India [online].' *Asia Pacific Journal of Environmental Law*, Vol. 17, p. 177–89.
16. *Vellore Citizens' Welfare Forum v Union of India*. 1996. 5 SCC 647.
17. Recently the Madras High Court ordered the winding up of the LOEA and transfer of all pending cases to the National Green Tribunal, *Vellore Citizens Welfare Forums v Union of India*. 2016. SCC OnLine Mad 1881.
18. (WP 202/1995) CDJ 2005 SC 713.
19. Another case in which the Court explored this remedy was *Union of India v Sushil Kumar Modi* [1997] INSC 68 (24 January 1997).
20. See for instance the rejection of expertise of petitioners and an overreliance on 'scientific experts' and legal experts (amicus curiae)—*Narmada Bachao Andolan v Union Of India And Others* on 18 October 2000 and in *G.Sundarrajan v Union Of India & Ors* on 6 May 2013.
21. Kumar Sambhav Shrivastava. 2014. 'Ministers mount pressure to dilute Forest Rights Act', *Down to Earth*, http://www.downtoearth.org.in/news/ministers-mount-pressure-to-dilute-forest-rights-act-46325. Also see, Times News Network, 'Fears that govt watering down forest Act wrong', 30 January 2016, http://timesofindia.indiatimes.com/city/mumbai/Fears-that-govt-watering-down-forest-Act-wrong/articleshow/50776875.cms and Oommen C. Kurian. 2015. 'Implementing the Forest Rights Act', Oxfam India Policy Brief No. 15,

https://www.oxfamindia.org/sites/default/files/PB-implementing-forest-rights-act-lack-of-political-will-261115-en.pdf.
22. See, for instance, Wilfred J. Anr. (M.A. No. 182 of 2014 & M.A. No. 239 of 2014), judgment of the NGT Principal Bench (discussing in detail the purpose and expanse of the term 'aggrieved person' under the NGT Act).
23. Environment Impact Assessment Notification S.O.60 (E), dated 27 January 1994. http://envfor.nic.in/legis/eia/so-60(e).html.
24. Local bodies in the urban areas are municipalities and in rural areas are Panchayats.
24. Per Christensen, Lone Kørnøv and Eskild Holm Nielsen. 2005. 'EIA as Regulation: Does it Work?', *Journal of Environmental Planning and Management*, (48): pp. 393–412; A.Barker and C. Wood. 1999. 'An evaluation of EIA system performance in eight EU countries.' *Environmental Impact Assessment Review*, vol. 19, pp. 387–404; W. Wende 2002. 'Evaluation of the effectiveness and quality of environmental impact assessment in the Federal Republic of Germany,' *Impact Assessment and Project Appraisal*, 20(2): pp. 93–9 and C. Wood. 2003. *Environmental Impact Assessment. A Comparative Review, 2nd edn.* Edinburgh: Prentice Hall.
26. Rajya Sabha Unstarred Question No. 1134, Answered by Prakash Javdekar, Amendment to Environment Impact Assessment Notification, answered on 30 July 2015.
27. Rajya Sabha Unstarred Question No. 2326, Answered by Anil Madhav Dave, Environmental clearance to projects in Himachal Pradesh, answered on 8 August 2016.
28. Rajya Sabha Unstarred Question No. 2326, Answered by Anil Madhav Dave, Environmental clearance to projects in Himachal Pradesh, answered on 8 August 2016.
29. Deepak K. Dash, 'Javadekar eases green norms for linear projects', Times News Network, 1 January 2015, http://timesofindia.indiatimes.com/home/environment/pollution/Javadekar-eases-green-norms-for-linear-projects/articleshow/45712548.cms, accessed 27 July 2017.
30. Original Application No. 74 of 2014. Principal Bench of the NGT, New Delhi, Judgement delivered on 17 July 2014.
31. (2014) 1 All India NGT Reporter (South Zone).
32. (2009) 159 DLT 604.
33. (1997) 8 SCC 191.
34. *M.P. Patil v Union of India*, Appeal No. 12/2012, Judgment delivered on 13 March 2014 (New Delhi, Principle Bench, NGT).
35. Nupur Chowdhury. 2016. 'Sustainable Development as Environmental Justice,' *Economic and Political Weekly*, Vol. LI, Nos 26 and 27, 25 June 2016, pp. 84–92.
36. Writ Petition (Civil) No. 180 of 2011. Judgment of the Supreme Court of India on 18 April 2013.
37. (2012) 114 (5) Bom LR 2695.
38. Appeal No. 79 of 2013, National Green Tribunal, January 8, 2016.

39. Laode M. Syarif. 2010. 'Current Development of Indonesian Environmental Law,' *IUCN Academy of Environmental Law* e-Journal, Issue 1, p. 1.
40. Laode M. Syarif. 2010. 'Current Development of Indonesian Environmental Law,' *IUCN Academy of Environmental Law* e-Journal, Issue 1, p. 2.
41. Laode M. Syarif. 2010. 'Current Development of Indonesian Environmental Law,' *IUCN Academy of Environmental Law* e-Journal, Issue 1, p. 3.
42. Laode M. Syarif. 2010. 'Current Development of Indonesian Environmental Law,' *IUCN Academy of Environmental Law* e-Journal, Issue 1, p. 5–8.
43. World Bank. December 2006. *AMDAL Reform and Decentralization Opportunities for Innovation in Indonesia*, p. 10.
44. Sjaiful Bahri and Achmad Suryana, 1997. *Indonesia's Environmental Rules and Regulations Relating to Agricultural Investment: A Review*, p. 2. Bogor: ACIAR Indonesia Research Project Working Paper.
45. Takdir Rahmadi. 2014. *Hukum Lingkungan di Indonesia* (Environmental Law in Indonesia), p. 92 (1st edition) Cet. 4, Jakarta: Raja Grafindo Persada.
46. World Bank, 2006, p. 10.
47. Rahmadi, 2014, p. 92.
48. Karlheinz Spitz and Yahya Husin, 'The AMDAL Process and the Equator Principles: Common themes and apparent differences,' (paper presented in 'Mining Indonesia 2009 Conference: Unlocking Mineral Potential,' Jakarta 14–16 October 2009), p. 4.
49. USAID. 2008. *Environmental Compliance and Enforcement in Indonesia Rapid Assessment*, p. 7.
50. USAID. 2008. *Environmental Compliance and Enforcement in Indonesia Rapid Assessment*, p. 7–8.
51. Article 22 of EMA 2009. Spitz and Yahya Husin, p. 4.
52. PT Perusahaan Listrik Negara. July 2013. *Environmental Impact Assessment*. p. 9.
53. Spitz and Yahya Husin, 2009, p. 4.
54. Ary Sudijanto, 'Indonesia EIA System in Transboundary context,' (workshop on Environmental Impact Assessment in a Transboundary Context in Eastern Asia, Seoul, Republic of Korea, 13–15 June 2012), p. 10.
55. Spitz and Yahya Husin, 2009, p. 4.
56. Sudijanto, 2012, p. 10.
57. Spitz and Yahya Husin, 2009, p. 4.
58. Wildlife Conservation Society. October 2010. *Oil Palm, Biodiversity and Indonesian Law*, p. 11.
59. M.J. Philips, et. al., 'Review of environmental impact assessment and monitoring in aquaculture in Asia-Pacific', (Rome: FAO Fisheries and Aquaculture Technical Paper. No. 527), p. 212.
60. Spitz and Yahya Husin, 2009, p. 5.
61. Wildlife Conservation Society, 2010, p. 11.
62. Philips, M.J. et al., p. 212.
63. Wildlife Conservation Society, 2010, p. 11.

64. District Court, No. 87/Pid/2012/PT.BTN: PT Power Steel Mandiri Case. Maradona, 'Penegakan Hukum Lingkungan: Administrasidan Pidana' (Enforcement of Environmental Law: Administrative and Criminal) in Laode M. Syarif and Andri G. Wibisana (ed.), *Hukum Lingkungan Teori, Legislasidan Studi Kasus*, (Theories, Legislations, and Cases Study in Environmental Law) (The Asia Foundation), p. 517.
65. http://simkara.pt-pekanbaru.go.id/files_pidana/81c650caac28cdefce4de5ddc18befa0/No_235_Pid.pdf, accessed 13 August 2016.
66. Administrative Court, No. 71/G.TUN/2001/PTUN-JKT: Transgenic Cotton Case. Laode M. Syarif, Maskun, dan Birkah Latif, 'Evolusi Kebijakandan Prinsip-prinsip Lingkungan Global' (Policy Evolution and Global Environmental Principles), in Laode M. Syarif and Andri G. Wibisana (ed.). *Hukum Lingkungan Teori, Legislasidan Studi Kasus*, (Theories, Legislations, and Cases Study in Environmental Law) (The Asia Foundation), pp. 92–3.
67. Administrative Court, No. 75/G.TUN/2003/PTUN-JKT: '*Pantai Utara Jakarta*' /North Shore Jakarta Reclamation Case. Lilik Pudjiastuti, "Instrumen Hukum Lingkungan Nasional: Perencanaan, Dokumen Lingkungandan Perizinan" (National Instrument of Environmental Law: Planning, Environmental Documents and Licensing) in Laode M. Syarif and Andri G. Wibisana (ed.). *Hukum Lingkungan Teori, Legislasi, dan Studi Kasus*, (Theories, Legislations, and Cases Study in Environmental Law) (The Asia Foundation), pp. 143–4.
68. Administrative Court, No. 103 K/TUN/2010: PT. Semen Gresik (Persero) Tbk Case, http://putusan.mahkamahagung.go.id/putusan/downloadpdf/c67659860fe438929104736ca3787421/pdf, accessed 10 August 2016.
69. Usually it is 5 per cent of the project cost–see *S P Muthuraman v Union of India*, ORIGINAL APPLICATION NO. 37 OF 2015 and 213 of 2014, NGT Principal Bench, judgment dated 7 July 2015.

19

Environmental Courts and Tribunals

A Comparative Analysis of Australia's LEC and India's NGT

Usha Tandon

I Introduction

Australia had taken a lead in creating Environmental Court, way back in 1980, when, the Land and Environment Court (LEC)[1] was established in its state of New South Wales (NSW). India has established its first Environmental Court, National Green Tribunal (NGT) in 2010 at the national level. Since the late 1960s, widespread public awareness of environmental issues has resulted in a growing number of movements that aim to confront environmental degradation.[2] Environmental Courts and Tribunals (ECT) are rapidly growing throughout the world and are becoming important phenomena of twenty-first century Environmental Law.[3] The amazing growth of ECT worldwide is quite interesting, as there are no international treaties or conventions specifically requiring the states to create Special Environmental Courts. Principle 10 of Rio Declaration of 1992 is often quoted to suggest the creation of ECT, which in fact talks about 'effective access to justice and administrative proceedings ....'[4] Since there is no true international framework as yet in this regard, ECT developments have taken various forms at different national levels. This chapter provides a comparative critical analysis of Australia's LEC and India's NGT in terms of historical background, important statutory provisions, and the functioning of NSW's LEC and India's NGT.

II Historical Background

In New South Wales, prior to the establishment of the LEC, in 1980, planning and land matters were dealt with by a range of different tribunals and courts.[5] Valuation, compulsory acquisition, and land matters were dealt with by a Land and Valuation Court, Valuation Boards of Review, and the Supreme Court (for title issues). Building, subdivision, and development matters were dealt with by the Local Government Appeals Tribunal. Civil (equitable) enforcement and judicial review of both government and tribunal decisions were undertaken by the Supreme Court of New South Wales. Criminal enforcement was undertaken in the Local Court and the District Court of NSW. With the enactment of the New South Wales Planning and Environment Commission Act 1974, it was perceived that there was a need to integrate land-use planning and environmental assessment and appraisal techniques.[6]

Two main objectives are cited for the creation of NSW's LEC: One, rationalization, and two, specialization.[7] When environmental matters were broadly dealt with by a range of different courts, tribunals or boards, the whole of an environmental dispute was not resolved in one place. There was a desire to have a 'one-stop shop' for environmental, planning, and land matters. The establishment of the LEC allowed all of these diverse jurisdictions to be rationalized into one court.[8] The other objective of setting up the court was specialization. The court personnel, judges, and assessors who were to be appointed to the court needed to have knowledge and expertise in the jurisdiction. The belief was that a specialist court would better understand the science and the environmentally relevant knowledge, and ensure that decisions are scientifically and environmentally literate. It was thought that the court would be more able to deliver consistency in decision-making; that there would be a decrease in the delays because of a better understanding of the characteristics of environmental disputes, and the urgency in which they need to be treated; and also, very importantly, it would facilitate the development of environmental law policies and principles.[9]

The concerns for establishing Environmental Courts in India originated from the proactive judiciary, around thirty years back,[10] when in 1986,[11] the Supreme Court of India expressed difficulty in solving techno-science disputes handling environmental litigation. The Apex Court observed that in as much as environment cases involve assessment of scientific data, it was desirable to set up environment courts on a regional basis with a professional Judge and two experts, keeping in view the expertise required for such adjudication.[12] In 2000, the Supreme Court of India speaking through Justice Jagannath Rao[13] in *A.P. Pollution Control Board v Prof M. V Nayadu*[14] directed the Law Commission of India to seriously study the need for having Environmental Courts in India. When, in 2003, Justice Jagannath Rao became the Chairman of the Law Commission of India[15] the very first report that came out during his regime was on 'Proposal to Constitute Environmental Courts'.[16] The Law Commission recommended for the constitution of state-level environmental courts[17].

Before the National Green Tribunal Act was passed by the Governement of India, Parliament in 1995 enacted the National Environment Tribunal Act (NETA),[18] the main objective of which was to provide for the establishment of a National Environment Tribunal for effective and expeditious disposal of cases arising from accidents occurring while handling any hazardous substance, with a view to giving relief and compensation for damages to persons, property, and the environment. However, this Tribunal never saw the light of the day and was ultimately repealed with the passing of National Green Tribunal Act in June 2010. India's NGT was established on 18 October 2010 and became functional from 5 May 2011,[19] with New Delhi selected as the site for the principal bench, later followed by four zonal benches in Chennai, Pune, Bhopal, and Kolkata.[20]

III LEC Act, 1979, and NGT Act, 2010

III.1 Overview of Statutory Provisions

III.1.1 Title and objectives

New South Wales's legislation is entitled 'Land and Environment Court Act',[21] whereas Indian legislation is termed as the 'National Green Tribunal Act'.[22] Accordingly, the LEC operates in NSW and NGT operates in India.

The objective of NSW'LEC is to constitute the LEC and to make provision with respect to its jurisdiction.[23] The LEC of NSW was established in 1980 as a superior court of record, replacing the Local Government Appeals Tribunal, the Land and Valuation Court, the Clean Waters Appeal Board, and the Valuation Boards of Review. In addition, certain jurisdictions formerly exercised by the district court were also transferred to the new court.[24]

The NGT was established, as stated above, on 18 October 2010 and started functioning from 5 May 2011. The Indian Act provides for the establishment of a NGT for the effective and expeditious disposal of cases relating to environmental protection and conservation of forests and other natural resources including enforcement of any legal right relating to the environment and giving relief and compensation for damages to persons and property and for matters connected therewith.[25]

III.1.2 Composition

NSW'LEC is composed of judges, commissioners and other officers of the court. LEC is constituted as a superior court of record having a seal of its own.[26] The court consists of the chief judge appointed by the governor and such other judges as may be appointed by the governor from time to time.[27] The governor may also appoint Commissioner[28] of the Court[29] who may be a full-time or part-time Commissioner.[30] A registrar, an assistant registrar, and such other officers of the court as may be necessary for the proper administration of the Act may also be employed.[31] All proceedings in the court are heard and disposed of before a single judge who constitutes the court.[32] It also prescribes for the hearing and disposal of proceedings before one or more commissioners or other officers of the court[33] with respect to specified matters.

A person is qualified for appointment as a judge of LEC if s/he is not more than 70 years of age and holds the judicial office of this state or of the Commonwealth or is an Australian lawyer of at least seven years' standing.[34] The amended version of the Act also provides for Supreme Court judges to act as LEC judges with a few exceptions.[35] No qualification of chief judge has been prescribed. A person is qualified to be appointed as a commissioner if the person has suitable qualifications and experience in town or country planning, environmental planning or architecture, engineering, surveying, building construction;[36] special knowledge and experience in the administration of local government or town planning, in environmental science or matters relating to the protection of the environment and environmental assessment, in the law and practice of land valuation, in the management of natural resources or the administration and management of Crown lands, lands acquired under the Closer Settlement Acts and other lands of the Crown, in urban design or heritage; or has suitable knowledge of matters concerning land rights for Aborigines and qualifications and experience suitable for the determination of disputes involving Aborigines also make a person qualified to be appointed as a commissioner.[37] An Australian lawyer is also qualified to be appointed as a commissioner.[38] The commissioner holds office for a term of seven years and is eligible for reappointment.[39] The Act also provides for the disqualification of commissioner[40] provision for the acting chief judge[41] and acting judges.[42] No disqualification for judges has been prescribed.

India's NGT consists of a full-time chairperson,[43] ten to twenty full-time judicial members, and ten to twenty full-time expert members.[44] The chairperson of the Tribunal has been vested with the power to invite any one or more persons having specialized knowledge and experience in a particular case before the Tribunal to assist the Tribunal in that case.[45] The chairperson, judicial members, and expert members of the Tribunal are appointed by the central government.[46] The chairperson is appointed by the central government in consultation with the chief justice of India.[47] The judicial members and expert members of the Tribunal are appointed on the recommendations of such a selection committee and in such manner as may be prescribed.[48] Only a judge of SC of India or CJ of HC is eligible to be appointed as the chairperson or a judicial member.[49] A person who is or has been a judge of the high court is also qualified to be appointed as a judicial member of the Tribunal.[50] A person is qualified for appointment as an expert member if he has a degree in Master of Science (in physical sciences or life sciences) with a Doctorate degree or Master of Engineering or Master of Technology and has an experience of fifteen years in the relevant field including five years of practical experience in the field of environment and forests including pollution control, hazardous substance management, environment impact assessment, climate change management, and biological diversity management in a reputed national-level institution.[51] A person having administrative experience of fifteen years including experience of five years in dealing with environmental matters in the central or a state government or in a reputed national- or state-level institution is also eligible for being appointed as an expert member of the Tribunal.[52]

The chairperson or the judicial member, if he was a judge of Supreme Court, holds office for a term of five years[53] or up to seventy years of age whichever is earlier.[54] The chairperson or the judicial member, if he was the chief justice of high court, holds office for a term of five years or up to sixty-seven years of age whichever is earlier.[55] Similarly, the judicial member, if he was the judge of the high court, holds office for a term of five years or up to sixty-seven years of age whichever is earlier. The expert member holds office for a term of five years or up to sixty-five years of age whichever is earlier.[56] The chairperson, judicial member, and expert member are not eligible for reappointment.[57] To avoid conflict of interest, it is included explicitly in the Act that the chairperson, judicial members and expert members of the tribunal shall not hold any other office during their tenure.[58] In addition, for a period of two years from the date on which they cease to hold office, they cannot accept any employment in or connected with the management or administration of, any person who has been a party to a proceeding before the tribunal.[59] Their appointment by the central government or state government, however, has been saved by the statute.

The central government may, in consultation with the chief justice of India, remove the chairperson or judicial member from office on certain specified grounds which include inter alia abuse of his position as to render his continuance in office prejudicial to the public interest.[60] The chairperson or judicial member can be removed from office by an order made by the central government after an inquiry made by a judge of the Supreme Court in which such chairperson or judicial member has been informed of the charges against him and given a reasonable opportunity of being heard in respect of those charges.[61] The expert member may also be removed from his office by an order of the central government on the same grounds on which the chairperson or judicial member may be removed.[62] The Act provides that the number of expert members shall, in hearing an application or appeal, be equal to the number of judicial members hearing such application or appeal.[63]

III.1.3 Jurisdiction

NSW's LEC has been given a wide jurisdiction in relation to environmental planning and land matters. The jurisdiction is made exclusive, and hence, no other court or tribunal could exercise the jurisdiction given to the LEC. Under Part 3 of the Act, the jurisdiction of the court is divided into eight classes of proceedings.[64] Classes 4, 5, and 8 of Part 3 give original jurisdiction to LEC with respect to environmental planning protection and civil enforcement; environmental planning and protection summary criminal enforcement; and mining matters. Classes 1, 2, 3, 6, and 7 confer appellate jurisdiction on LEC with respect to environmental planning and protection appeals; local government and miscellaneous appeals and applications; land tenure, valuation, rating, and compensation matters; appeals by defendants from convictions relating to environmental offences imposed by magistrates in the local court; and appeals from magistrates in respect of environmental prosecutions which previously would have been heard by the Supreme Court of New South Wales.

Each one of these classes refers to a host of legislations with specific sections of the legislation. These classes provide jurisdiction to LEC with respect to more than fifty legislations.[65] The court also has jurisdiction to hear and dispose of the matter relating to the claim for compensation in compulsory acquisition of land.[66]

India's NGT deals with environmental matters and not with planning and land matters. Planning and land matters are dealt with by civil courts.

Chapter III of the NGT Act deals with jurisdiction and powers of the Tribunal. Section 14 of the Act prescribes original jurisdiction to the tribunal, Section 16 provides appellate jurisdiction to the tribunal, and Sections 15 and 17 deal with the powers of the tribunal to order for the relief and compensation to the victims of pollution and restitution of environment. The Act provides only civil jurisdiction to the tribunal. An interesting thing with respect to the original jurisdiction of NGT is the language in which it is drafted which states that the tribunal shall have jurisdiction over all civil cases where a substantial question relating to environment is involved and such question arises out of the implementation of the enactments specified in Schedule I of the Act. Schedule I of the Act contains only seven enactments.[67] The Schedule does not even include all modern environmental law statutes. For instance, the Wild Life Act[68] has been excluded. In India, there are more than two-hundred legislations having a direct or indirect bearing on the environment, which has been totally excluded from the purview of the Act. Thus to this extent, the present legislation has a myopic operation by providing a limited jurisdiction.[69]

The Act gives jurisdiction to the Tribunal to hear the disputes relating to the enforcement of any legal right relating to the environment.[70] Under its appellate jurisdiction,[71] the Tribunal can hear an appeal from any direction, order or decision made by the Appellate Authority under the Water Act, Water Cess Act, and Air Act. It can also hear an appeal from any order passed by the State Government under the Water Act, Forest Act as well as from any direction issued by the State Pollution Control Board under the Water Act, order by the NBA or SBB under the Biological Diversity Act.[72]

The Tribunal has been vested with jurisdiction and power to provide relief and compensation to the victims of pollution and other environmental damage arising under those seven enactments; for restitution of damaged property and for restitution of the degraded environment.[73] The Tribunal while passing any order or decision or award, apply the principles of sustainable development, the precautionary principle and the polluter pays principle.[74] The decisions of the Tribunal are taken by majority.[75] If there is a difference in opinion among the members hearing a matter and the opinion is equally divided, then the chairperson hears the matter and decides, provided he has not heard such a matter earlier.[76] However, where the chairperson himself has heard such matter along with other members of the tribunal, and if there is a difference in opinion among the members and the opinion is equally divided, then in such cases, he shall refer the matter to other members of the tribunal who shall hear such application or appeal and decide.[77]

An appeal from the award, decision or order of the tribunal lies with the Supreme Court of India.[78] The aggrieved person may file the appeal within a period of thirty days from the date on which the order or decision or direction or determination is communicated to him. The period can be extended by the tribunal to sixty days in the case of sufficient cause.[79]

III.1.4 Penalty

Under India's NGT Act, if a person fails to comply with any order or award or decision of the Tribunal, he is punishable with imprisonment for a term which may extend to three years, or with fine which may extend to ten crore rupees, or with both.[80] If the failure or contravention continues, the Tribunal may impose an additional fine which may extend to twenty-five-thousand rupees for every day during which such failure or contravention continues after conviction for the first such failure or contravention.[81] In case, a company fails to comply with any order or award or a decision of the tribunal then such a company is punished with a fine which may extend to twenty-five-crore rupees, and in case the failure or contravention continues, with an additional fine which may extend to one lakh rupees for every day during which such failure or contravention continues after conviction for the first such failure or contravention.[82] Special provision[83] for the penalty is made for the government department if it fails to comply with any order, award, or decision of the tribunal. The head of the department is deemed to be guilty of such failures and is liable to be proceeded against for having committed an offence under the Act and punished accordingly. New South Wales' LEC Act does not contain any provision for a penalty for failure to comply with its orders.

III.2 Critical Comparative Analysis of Statutory Provisions

To settle environmental disputes, the state of NSW has established a specialized court, whereas India has established a Tribunal which is a quasi-judicial body. All proceedings before NGT are deemed to be judicial proceedings and the Tribunal is deemed to be a civil court.[84] Being a tribunal, NGT has the same powers as are vested in a civil court under the Code of Civil Procedure, 1908,[85] but is not bound by procedure laid down under the Code of Civil Procedure, 1908,[86] and is guided by principles of natural justice.[87] It has the power to regulate its own procedure.[88] It is also not bound by the rules of evidence.[89]

New South Wales' LEC is a specialist court, established as a superior court of record.[90] New South Wales has established specialized courts for a population of 7.5 million,[91] whereas, India has created one Tribunal for a population of 1,336 million.[92] This centralized forum at the national level is criticized as a misfit for a vast country like India, due to its inaccessibility to the majority of people. The decision to set up specialized environmental courts in India was motivated by none else than green courts like the LEC of New South Wales. However, in the process of setting up the specialized Tribunal, the virtues of that legislation could not be preserved.[93] It may further be noted that Supreme Court of India speaking through Chief Justice Bhagwati (as he then was) in the oleum gas leak case[94] had ruled for the regional-level environmental courts in the country, the Law Commission of India in its 186th Report recommended for the constitution of state-level environmental courts, but the Government of India has established Green Tribunal at the national level with different places of sitting for the large and populous developing country.

The Green Tribunal takes away the jurisdiction of Civil Courts to entertain the appeal or settle environmental disputes.[95] It needs to be emphasized that there are around six-hundred district courts in India[96] whose jurisdiction to settle disputes, entertain appeals in environmental matters, as well as to entertain a claim for relief and compensation has been barred by the Act. The NGT has its headquarters in Delhi and four regional benches at Bhopal, Calcutta, Pune, and Chennai. It is structurally and functionally inadequate to satisfy people's needs in a vast country[97] like India. Due to lack of access, thousands of grievances related to environmental issues do not reach the adjudicatory mechanism at all. This is an unprecedented situation in the history of environmental justice in the country. This is also antithetical to the concept of 'just, quick, and cheap' judicial remedy offered by the LEC in New South Wales, Australia.[98]

The NGT Act gives only civil jurisdiction to the Tribunal. The Tribunal does not have criminal jurisdiction to prosecute for environmental crimes. With respect to civil cases, the jurisdiction of the Tribunal is where a substantial question relating to environment is involved (which specifically includes enforcement of any legal right relating to the environment) and such question arises out of the implementation of the enactments specified in Schedule I. The 'substantial question relating to environment' as defined in the Act[99] includes two types of questions. First, it includes an instance where there is a direct violation of a specific statutory environmental obligation by a person by which the community at large is affected or the gravity of the damage to the environment is substantial or the damage to the public health is broadly measurable. Second, it includes an instance where the environmental consequences relate to a specific activity or a point source of pollution. Schedule

I of the Act lists only seven statutes,[100] namely, the Water Act, Water Cess Act, Air Act, Forest Act, Environment Protection Act, Public Insurance Act, and Biological Diversity Act. One wonders as to why the Wild Life (Protection) Act, 1972, is not included in Schedule I of the Act. The Tiwari Committee Report[101] had listed around twenty central enactments, besides many state enactments related to the environment, which did not find any place in Schedule I to give jurisdiction to the Tribunal. The major flaw of the legislation is demonstrated in making the 'substantial question relating to the environment arising out of the implementation of those specified seven statues. Schedule I to the Act referring to only seven legislations is absolutely unwarranted and should be deleted. Section 14 needs to be amended to entertain cases involving enforcement of any legal or constitutional right relating to the environment. The right may arise from the Constitution of India, from any environmental statute directly or indirectly protecting the environment or it may arise from any tort action. It may be noted that in India, the modern Environmental Law, including those seven statutes is operated on criminal justice administration which stipulates a deterrent theory of punishment. They do not legislate legal rights relating to the environment, rather create environmental offenses against those who violate the legal right relating to the environment. Therefore, the NGT Act with respect to original civil jurisdiction is not in consonance with the legislative scheme of specified seven legislations.

The original jurisdiction of the Tribunal under the NGT Act could have been with respect to offences committed under those listed legislations. But, sadly, the Tribunal does not have criminal jurisdiction to prosecute offenders under the specified Acts. Reference in this regard may be made to *Bichhri case*[102] wherein the Apex Court through Justice B.P. Jeevan Reddy has suggested for the establishment of environmental courts having criminal jurisdiction.

New South Wales' LEC's jurisdiction is quite wide. It has a civil jurisdiction to deal with a range of different civil disputes concerning trees and mining; has the equitable jurisdiction of a court of chancery; and can issue equitable injunctions and declarations in civil enforcement actions.[103] It has the prerogative powers of a superior court, able to judicially review government action and subordinate legislation.[104] It also has criminal enforcement jurisdiction and can impose criminal penalties including fine and imprisonment.[105] It has an appellate jurisdiction. Appeals from the local court in relation to environmental crime go to the LEC.[106] It also has a tribunal-type function to review on the merits of the decisions of government in relation to environmental matters and make a fresh decision.[107]

IV Critical Analysis of the Functioning of LEC and NGT

This part critically examines the functioning of NSW's environmental court and India's Green Tribunal[108] in terms of independence and impartiality; speedy and efficacious justice, technical expertise; credibility and powers to enforce the orders passed by LEC and NGT.

IV.1 Independence and Impartiality

One of the essential components of a system of good environmental justice and governance is the existence of an independent and impartial adjudicator.[109] Independence not only requires independence from the legislative and executive branches of government but also independence from all influences external to the ECT which might lead it to decide cases otherwise than on the legal and factual merits. Independence is particularly apposite to specialized ECTs, as these types of fora deal with environmental and planning disputes where there is a high potential for significant external pressures.[110] In the case of NSW's LEC, establishing an environment court, as a court, rather than as an organ of the executive arm of government, and as a superior court of record, rather than an inferior court or tribunal, evidence and enhances its independence.[111] Closely related to the principle of independence is the requirement that a decision-maker be impartial. Impartiality also requires decision-makers to alert themselves to and to neutralize, as far as possible, personal predilections or prejudices or any extraneous considerations that might pervert their judgment.[112]

India's NGT has been progressive in its approach towards environmental protection in general and the rights of marginalized people in particular. The NGT has not only come down heavily against microstructures but has also challenged the big corporate sectors and the central and state governments for not following environmental regulations.[113] It has even issued warrants against high-profile government authorities like the commissioner of Delhi Police and environment minister of Odisha. It has repeatedly rejected the views of its nominal master, the Ministry of Environment Forests & Climate Change.[114] The judicial members coupled with technical expertise have exponentially strengthened the environmental protection regime in the country.[115]

IV.2 Speedy and Efficacious Justice

The overriding purpose of an ECT is to facilitate the just, quick, and cheap resolution of proceedings. The purpose of much environmental litigation is to prevent or mitigate harm to the environment. Delay in the final determination of the proceedings defers making of an order preventing or mitigating that environmental harm. The NSW's LEC provides an instructive example of case management. The court rules and practice of the NSW's LEC deal differentially with various types of cases that come before the court. Processes used include directions hearings before judges, commissioners or registrars to set timelines in the particular proceedings for filing of applications, documents and evidence, document and information exchange between the parties, interlocutory applications, and the final hearing; case management conferences; ADR processes such as conciliation conferences or mediations; and case review by the court to assure appropriate handling and timing of the case and ensure that deadlines are met and filed documents are complete. Case management include a clear, comprehensive, and current court website providing all necessary information for parties; electronic filing and processing capability; teleconferencing and video-conferencing capability for hearings and taking evidence; and computer data management systems that track the status, progress, and deadlines for each case and provide regular reports on individual cases and overall caseload.

Since its functioning in May 2011, India's NGT has been successfully upholding its mandate as a 'fast-track Court' for effective and expeditious disposal of cases relating to environmental protection and conservation.[116] The majority of the matters before NGT relate to environmental clearance and pollution.[117] The number of cases received since the establishment of NGT until 31 January 2015 is 7,768. In the written response to a question in the Lok Sabha, the union environment minister Prakash Javadekar said the number of cases disposed of until January 31 is 5,167 and the number of cases pending is 2,601.[118] It has been successful in speedy and effective settlement of environmental matters. NGT is much more regular in scheduling hearings, typically with time gaps of two to three weeks between two consecutive hearings. Perhaps, this promptness in deliberating over cases is reflected in the increasing number of cases being settled by NGT. This has also created optimism in the community regarding decisions of an environmental dispute.[119] The Act prescribes[120] thirty days for challenging an order under the Tribunal's appellate jurisdiction, the state's six months on disputes of substantial questions related to environment,[121] and five years for seeking compensation and relief.[122]

Coming to case management, the NGT website is still improving with time. The website does provide for e-filing but it has not taken off as yet. Largely the filing remains cumbersome with six sets of documents to be filed every time something new is filed. The website does try to provide all the orders of the case but it seems to get lost while doing so. The website needs substantial improvements. The NGT courtrooms do not have the facility of teleconferencing and video-conferencing as of today.[123]

IV.3 Technical Expertise

Environmental issues and legal and policy responses demand special knowledge and expertise. New South Wales' LEC's lay commissioners have knowledge and experience in environmental matters. They do not need a master's degree, but in fact many do. They are drawn from the local government, town, country and environmental planning, environmental science, arboriculture, horticulture, land valuation, architecture, engineering, surveying, management of natural resources, aboriginal land rights and disputes involving aborigines, which is one of our jurisdictions, urban design and heritage, and law. The NGT Act considers higher degrees in science, engineering, technology, and experience in Administration only as technical qualifications. It has also gone one step ahead and mentioned that degrees should be from a reputed national-level institution. There is no provision for environmental academicians who have been proactive in the field of environment protection. In its current form, the NGT Act mainly facilitates backdoor entry for retired bureaucrats.

IV.4 Credibility

New South Wales' LEC has upheld the rule of law, and that, in turn, promoted public trust and confidence in the rule of law and in the court system.[124] The number of cases being instituted at India's NGT each year is phenomenally increasing. The number of cases filed has increased from just 548 in 2012 to 3,116 in 2013 to 2,348 in the first three months of 2014.[125] This reflects a growing trust people have in NGT for resolving increasing environmental crisis. The NGT targets to dispose of cases within six months. It has been broadly successful in achieving this aim, though there have been some high-profile cases where NGT has not been able to deliver on time. It is gaining credibility and is being accepted by both industry groups and non-government organizations (NGOs) focusing on environmental protection.

IV.5 Enforcement Powers

New South Wales' LEC enforces the law through statutory notices including penalty notices (on-the-spot fines) and stops work notices; civil proceedings including court orders granting injunctions or a court declaration of a breach of the law; and criminal prosecutions imposing sentences for fines and imprisonment. If a person fails to comply with a notice, the Environment Protection Authority (EPA) may take the action required to mitigate or prevent harm to the environment and recover the costs by issuing a compliance cost notice to the person responsible.[126]

The NGT has largely been successful in implementing its orders, which usually relate to staying environmental clearances. The regional green tribunals seem even more active and aggressive than the NCT in Delhi, as the regional judges are fearless and have no ambition for national positions.[127] The NGT Act stipulates the powers vested in the Tribunal to enforce its orders including jail terms and fines amounting to crores. But it is clearly evident that there is hardly any use of such powers to enforce the directions. Given the present composition of the NGT, it is very difficult on its part to monitor its directions in each and every case. In order to implement NGT's directions effectively, it is necessary to make the implementation process more efficient through the marshalling of agencies responsible for the control of pollution, such as local government bodies and pollution control boards. It is also highly advisable to keep the petitioner involved in the monitoring of court directions. Courts and the NGT should lay down strict conditions for the implementation of environmental judgments, identify the executive agency responsible for carrying them out, and ensure the accountability of the agency if it fails to follow directions.[128]

V Conclusion

New South Wales' LEC has been functioning for the last thirty-five years, whereas India's NGT is hardly five years old, and hence the comparative analysis of this ECT has necessarily to be seen in the context of this time gap period. In the words of Brian J Preston, 'The Land and Environment Court is now long established over thirty years and is undoubtedly a model of a successful environment court.'[129] However, the functioning of NSW's LEC in the initial years is more relevant to draw meaningful comparisons with India's NGT.

In the initial years, NSW's LEC has a discordant image and operated in a climate of quite trenchant, often misconceived, criticisms about its role, leading its first chief judge to declare the Court was a 'fragile bastion'.[130] Majority of the cases before LEC related to Class 1 of its jurisdiction, categorized as the court's merit review jurisdiction, to hear appeals from decisions of a council in relation to development applications, where the court had the power to review the material in issue and substitute its decision for that of the original decision-maker. These appeals were complete hearings or 'de novo' hearings where the court assessed the merits of the development application.[131] The tension between the court and councils[132] arose where the court reviewed and overturned administrative decisions of councils. Those opposing merit review criticized that it is a waste of public and private funds for the court to conduct a review of an administrative decision and, in effect, replace it with another administrative decision.[133]

This tension forced the NSW Government to appoint a Working Party to review the jurisdiction of the LEC.[134] Its main task was to review the role of the court in determining development applications and to look at the potential for an increased use of alternative dispute resolution. The report of the Working Party, chaired by the Jerrold Cripps QC,[135] a former chief judge of the court, recommended that the merit review of council determination of development applications by the court should continue.[136] In its opinion, the court in its Class 1 jurisdiction is the most appropriate forum for such review because the court is not affected by the political considerations which often weigh heavily upon council when determining a development application and it comprises experts with experience in determination of development applications and related issues. It also called for the reform of the current framework of the court on increasing the role of alternative dispute resolution.[137]

India's NGT, in its short period of five years of functioning, has emerged as a powerful and effective quasi-judicial body, adjudicating environmental disputes in the country. The current chairperson of India's NGT, Justice Swatanter Kumar,[138] has ushered a new era in the history of India's Greening Justice playing a proactive role in protecting and enhancing the environment. The period after his appointment has seen a noticeable change exemplifying the independence and impartiality of NGT. The NGT under his robust leadership has fearlessly applied the green law for the union government, state governments, pollution control boards, big corporate bodies, big spiritual leaders, etc. India's NGT is flying high expanding its wings to reach the prestigious and powerful jurisdiction relating to Public Interest Litigation (PIL)[139] and *suo moto* powers.[140]

Like NSW's LEC, India's NGT, however, is also experiencing some teething problems in these initial years. The very success of the NGT has been a cause of anxiety for powerful interests, specifically the MEF&CC, state governments (such as the chief minister of Meghalaya) and also the concerns of the high courts.[141] With a view to clip its wings, MEF&CC, on 29 August 2014, constituted a high-level committee to review environmental laws under the chairmanship of former Cabinet Secretary T.S.R.

Subramanian. The Committee submitted its report to the central government in less than three months[142] suggesting Parliament to enact an umbrella legislation known as the Environmental Laws (Management) Act,(ELMA) that would constitute the National Environment Management Authority (NEMA) at the Centre and State Environment Management Authority (SEMA)[143] in states to deal with applications for clearances and permissions under environment-related laws.[144] To hear appeals against the decision of NEMA or SEMA, it proposed the creation of an appellate tribunal, to be constituted by the Government of India presided over by a retired judge of the high court with two senior officers of the rank of additional secretary to the Government of India.[145] The role of NGT was proposed to be limited only to the judicial review of the decisions of the appellate boards.[146] The MEF&CC would have the powers to issue directions to NEMA and SEMA in all matters.[147] It proposed to ban the jurisdiction of NGT stating, 'The decisions of the Government, NEMA or SEMA shall not be questioned before nor enquired in to by any court or tribunal either *suo moto* or at any ones behest on any ground what so ever'.[148]

The report has been criticized aiming to defang the National Green Tribunal.[149] The Parliamentary Standing Committee on Science and Technology, fortunately, after reviewing the HLC report, has rejected it. The PSC has instead recommended that the government should constitute a new committee to review the laws, noting that the three-month period given to the HLC for reviewing six environmental Acts was 'too short' and that 'there was no cogent reason for hurrying through with the report without comprehensive, meaningful and wider consultations with all the stakeholders'.[150]

To sum up, it may be said that NSW's LEC, which has now been long established over thirty years, has achieved a high standard for environmental adjudication especially under the dynamic leadership of its current chief judge who seems to be extremely efficient—administratively, judicially, as well as academically. Not resting, however, on LEC's laurels, he believes in adaptive management to continuously monitor its performance to meet the environmental challenges of the future.[151]

India's NGT though amazingly successful is also facing some real challenges. It deserves the support of various stakeholders especially the MEF&CC and needs to be improved and strengthened with better infrastructure, the appointment of office staff, case management facilities for efficient delivery of green justice. The jurisdiction of India's NGT needs to be widened and not limited to those seven legislations named in the Schedule.[152] At the same time, however, it needs to evolve some internal system for checks and balances for efficient and transparent delivery of justice.[153]

Notes and References

1. In Australia Environmental Courts are also established in three other States, namely, Queensland: Planning and Environmental Court established under Local Government (Planning and Environmental) Act, 1990 (Repealed), then under Integrated Planning Act, 1997 (Repealed) and now working under Sustainable Planning Act, 2009. http://www.courts.qld.gov.au/courts/planning-and-environment-court; Victorian Civil and Administrative Tribunal established under Victorian Civil and Administrative Tribunal Act, 1998 has jurisdiction to hear disputes relating to Planning and Environment Act, 1987. https://www.vcat.vic.gov.au/adv/disputes/planning-and-environment; South Australian Environment, Resource and Development Court established under South Australian Environment, Resource and Development Court Act, 1993. http://www.courts.sa.gov.au/OurCourts/ERDCourt/Pages/default.aspx.
2. Kurukulasriya Lal and Kristen A Powel. 2010. 'History of Environmental Courts and UNEP's Role.' *Journal of Court Innovation*, vol. 3, p. 269.
3. As of January, 2016, the number of ECT has grown to 1,200 in 44 countries. See George Pring and Catherine Pring. 2009. *Greening Justice: Creating and improving Environmental Courts and Tribunals.* Washington, D.C.: The Access Initiative.
4. UNCED, *Rio Declaration on Environment and Development*, 1992, Principle 10, para 2. http://www.unep.org/documents.multilingual/default.asp?documentid=78&articleid=1163.
5. History, http://www.lec.justice.nsw.gov.au/Pages/about/history.aspx, accessed 15 February 2017.
6. *A Practitioner's Guide to Land and Environment Court of NSW* (1st edition) NSW Young Lawyers and Environmental Law Policy, 2009.
7. Brian Preston. 2012. 'Environmental Courts and Tribunals: Improving Access to Justice and Protection of the Environment around the World.' *Pace Environmental Law Review*, 29(2): 602–4, http://digitalcommons.pace.edu/pelr/vol29/iss2/10. Brian J. Preston is the Chief Judge of the Land and Environment Court of New South Wales since November 2005.
8. Id. at 605. Subsequently, the legislature has added jurisdiction to the Land and Environment Court.
9. Id. at 605. Subsequently, the legislature has added jurisdiction to the Land and Environment Court.
10. Some of the authors claim that a report of 1980 of the Government of India, set up to review the existing environmental legislation and to recommend legislative measures and administrative machinery for environmental protection, recommended for the constitution of environment courts in all District Head Quarters, and the appointment of experts to assist the Court. For instance, see U. Sankar, 'Laws and Institutions Relating to Environmental Protection in India', p. 16 Available at http://www.mse.ac.in/pub/op_sankar.pdf, accessed 16 June 2016. However the present author after having carefully read this 49

pages report did not find any recommendation of this sort. See Department. of Science and Technology, Government of India, *The Report of Committee for Recommending Legislative Measures and Administrative Machinery For Ensuring Environmental Protection* (September 1980). This report is popularily known as Tiwari Committee Report as it was set up under the Chairmanship of N.D. Tiwari, then Deputy Chairman of Planning Commission of India.

11. *M.C. Mehta v Union of India,* 1986 (2) SCC 176 at 202.
12. *M.C. Mehta v Union of India,* 1986 (2) SCC 176 at 202. See also, *Indian Council for Enviro- Legal Action v Union of India*, 1996 (3) SCC 212.
13. Justice Jagannath Rao retired on 1 December 2000. This was his last judgment before his retirement from the Supreme Court of India.
14. Decided on 1 December 2000 reported in (2001) 2 SCC 62. See also, *A.P. Pollution Control Board v Prof M.V Nayadu,* AIR1999 SC 812.
15. Seventeenth Law Commission of India, 2003-2006.
16. Law Commission of India, Government of India, *186*th *Report on Proposal to Constitute Environmental Courts*, September 2003.
17. Id. at 142.
18. Act No. 27 of 1995.
19. Ministry of Environment and Forests (MOEF), Government of India, Notification, 5 May 2011, SO 1003 E. (The Ministry has now been renamed as Ministry of Environment, Forests, and Climate Change (MEF&CC)).
20. Ministry of Environment and Forests (MOEF), Government of India, Notification, 17 August 2011, SO 1908 E.
21. Land and Environment Court Act (LEC Act), 1979, No. 204 (NSW).
22. National Green Tribunal Act (NGT Act), 2010, No. 19 (India).
23. LEC Act, Supra n 21, Preamble.
24. Young Lawyers, *A Practitioner's Guide to Land and Environment Court of NSW,* 1.
25. NGT Act, 2010, Preamble.
26. LEC Act, 1979 No. 204 (NSW), Section 5.
27. LEC Act, 1979 No. 204, Section 7.
28. Though the word is used in singular, but reading of the whole Act implies for plurality of Commissioners.
29. LEC Act, 1979, No. 204, Section 12.
30. LEC Act, 1979, No. 204, Section 12 (2A).
31. Under the Public Sector Employment and Management Act, 2002, LEC Act, 1979, No. 204, Section 15.
32. LEC Act, 1979, No. 204, Section 6 (1).
33. LEC Act, 1979 No. 204 (NSW), Section 6 (2).
34. LEC Act, 1979, No. 204, Section 8 (2).
35. LEC Act, 1979 No. 204 (NSW), Section 11A.
36. LEC Act, 1979, No. 204, Section 12 (2).
37. LEC Act, 1979, No. 204, Section 12 (2).
38. LEC Act, 1979 No. 204 (NSW), Section 12 AA.
39. LEC Act, 1979, No. 204, Schedule I.

40. LEC Act, 1979, No. 204, Section 14 Disqualification of Commissioners (1) Where a Commissioner: (a) has a pecuniary interest, direct or indirect, in a matter which is the subject of proceedings before the Court, or (b) is a member, officer, employee or servant of a public or local authority that is a party to any proceedings before the Court, being proceedings in respect of which the Commissioner is exercising any functions conferred or imposed on the Commissioner by or under this Act or the rules, then: (c) the Commissioner shall inform the Chief Judge that the Commissioner has such an interest or is such a member, officer, employee or servant, and (d) the Commissioner shall thereupon cease to exercise those functions in relation to the proceedings.
41. LEC Act, 1979 No. 204 (NSW), Section 10.
42. LEC Act, 1979, No. 204, Section 11.
43. Justice Lokeshwar Singh Panta was its founding Chairperson. Currently Justice Swatanter Kumar holds this position since December 2012.
44. NGT Act, 2010, No. 19, Section 4.
45. NGT Act, 2010 (Act no. 19 of 2010), Section 4 (2). This power has not been invoked so far.
46. NGT Act, 2010, No. 19, Section 6 (1).
47. NGT Act, 2010 (Act no. 19 of 2010) Section 6 (2).
48. NGT Act, 2010, No. 19, Section 6 (3).
49. NGT Act, 2010, No. 19, Section 5 (i).
50. NGT Act, 2010 (Act no. 19 of 2010), Section 5 (I) Proviso.
51. NGT Act, 2010, No. 19, Section 5 (2 a).
52. NGT Act, 2010, No. 19, Section 5 (2 b).
53. NGT Act, 2010 (Act no. 19 of 2010), Section 7, first para.
54. NGT Act, 2010, No. 19, Section 7 first Proviso.
55. NGT Act, 2010, No. 19, Section 7 second Proviso.
56. NGT Act, 2010 (Act no. 19 of 2010), Section 7 third Proviso.
57. NGT Act, 2010, No. 19, Section 7, first para.
58. NGT Act, 2010, No. 19, Section 5 (3).
59. NGT Act, 2010, No. 19, Section 5 (4).
60. NGT Act, 2010, No. 19, Section 11 (1).
61. NGT Act, 2010, No. 19, Section 10 (2).
62. NGT Act, 2010, No. 19, Section 10 (5).
63. NGT Act, 2010, No. 19, Section 4 (4C).
64. LEC Act, 1979, No. 204, Sections 16 to 21C.
65. The main legislative instruments which grant the Court jurisdiction to hear and dispose of proceedings and or appeals are: *Environmental Planning & Assessment Act 1979 (NSW), Local Government Act 1993 (NSW), Protection of the Environment Operations Act 1997 (NSW), Heritage Act 1977 (NSW), Threatened Species Conservation Act 1995 (NSW), Native Vegetation Act 2003 (NSW), Contaminated Land Management Act 1997 (NSW), Roads Act 1993 (NSW), Land Acquisition (Just Terms Compensation) Act 1991 (NSW), Trees (Disputes Between Neighbours) Act 2006 (NSW), Noxious Weeds Act 1993*

(NSW), Water Management Act 2000 (NSW), Environmentally Hazardous Chemicals Act 1985 (NSW), Fisheries Management Act 1994 (NSW), Pesticides Act 1999 (NSW), Forestry and National Park Estate Act 1998 (NSW), Pipelines Act 1967 (NSW), National Parks and Wildlife Act 1974 (NSW), and *Aboriginal Land Rights Act 1983 (NSW).*

In addition, there are a plethora of environmental planning instruments under the *Environmental Planning and Assessment Act 1979* (NSW) (EP&A Act) that regulate various planning and environmental matters.

For instance, See Section 20 Class 4—environmental planning and protection and development contract civil enforcement.

(1) The Court has jurisdiction (referred to in this Act as "Class 4" of its jurisdiction) to hear and dispose of the following:

(a) proceedings under section 44 or 153 of the *Heritage Act 1977*,

(aa) proceedings under section 282 of the *Fisheries Management Act 1994*,

(b) proceedings referred to in section 35 of the *Environmental Planning and Assessment Act 1979*,

(ba) proceedings under section 10 of the *Uranium Mining and Nuclear Facilities (Prohibitions) Act 1986*,

(bb) proceedings under section 18 of the *Ozone Protection Act 1989*,

(c) proceedings under section 123 of the *Environmental Planning and Assessment Act 1979*,

(ca) proceedings under section 57 of the *Environmentally Hazardous Chemicals Act 1985*,

(caa) proceedings under Division 6 of Part 3, Part 7 and section 96 of the Co*ntaminated Land Management Act 1997*,

(cb) proceedings under section 96 of the *Pesticides Act 1999*,

(cbb) proceedings under section 108 of the *Pesticides Act 1999*,

(cc) proceedings under section 32 of the *Forestry and National Park Estate Act 1998*,

(cd) proceedings under section 60B of the *Pipelines Act 1967*,

(ce) proceedings referred to in section 69G of the *National Parks and Wildlife Act 1974*,

(cf) proceedings under section 91H of the *National Parks and Wildlife Act 1974*,

(cg) proceedings under section 176A of the *National Parks and Wildlife Act 1974*,

(cga) proceedings under sections 127L and 127O of the *Threatened Species Conservation Act 1995*,

(ch) proceedings under section 27 of the *Wilderness Act 1987*,

(ci) proceedings under Part 8.4 of the *Protection of the Environment Operations Act 1997*,

(cia) proceedings under sections 247 and 307 of the *Protection of the Environment Operations Act 1997*, (cj) proceedings that have been transferred to the Court under section 149B of the *Civil Procedure Act 2005* (*transferred civil proceedings*),

(cja) proceedings under section 100H of the *Rural Fires Act 1997*,

(ck) proceedings under section 147 of the *Threatened Species Conservation Act 1995*,

(cl), (cm) (Repealed)

(cn) proceedings under clauses 15–18 of Schedule 2 to the *Rural Lands Protection Act 1998*,

(d) proceedings under sections 673 and 674 of the *Local Government Act 1993*,

(da) applications under section 17 of the *Restricted Premises Act 1943*,

(db) proceedings under section 15D of the *Mine Subsidence Compensation Act 1961*,

(dc) proceedings under section 30 of the *Swimming Pools Act 1992*,

(dd) proceedings under Division 5 of Part 7 of the *Aboriginal Land Rights Act 1983*,

(de) proceedings under section 41 of the *Native Vegetation Act 2003*,

(df) (Repealed)

(df1) proceedings under sections 335 and 336 of the *Water Management Act 2000*,

(dg) proceedings under the *Nature Conservation Trust Act 2001*,

(dh) proceedings under section 57 or 60 of the *Plantations and Reafforestation Act 1999*,

(e) proceedings referred to in subsection (2).

(3) For the purposes of subsection (2), a planning or environmental law is:

(a) any of the following Acts or provisions:
Aboriginal Land Rights Act 1983 (other than Division 5 of Part 7), *Biological Control Act 1985*, *Coastal Protection Act 1979*, *Contaminated Land Management Act 1997*, *Environmental Planning and Assessment Act 1979*, *Environmentally Hazardous Chemicals Act 1985*, *Forestry and National Park Estate Act 1998*, *Heritage Act 1977*, Part 2 of Chapter 6, Chapter 7 or Chapter 15 of the *Local Government Act 1993*, Schedule 3 to the *Miscellaneous Acts (Planning) Repeal and Amendment Act 1979*, *National Parks and Wildlife Act 1974*, *Native Vegetation Act 2003*, Part 5 of the *Olympic Co-ordination Authority Act 1995*, *Ozone Protection Act 1989*, *Pesticides Act 1999*, *Plantations and Reafforestation Act 1999*, *Protection of the Environment Administration Act 1991*, *Protection of the Environment Operations Act 1997*, *Rural Fires Act 1997*, *Threatened Species Conservation Act 1995*, *Trees (Disputes Between Neighbours) Act 2006*, *Uranium Mining and Nuclear Facilities (Prohibitions) Act 1986*, *Waste Avoidance and Resource Recovery Act 2001*, *Waste Recycling and Processing Corporation Act 2001*, or

(b) any statutory instrument made or having effect thereunder or made for the purposes thereof, including any deemed environmental planning instrument within the meaning of the *Environmental Planning and Assessment Act 1979*. Also see legislations under Class 5 and Class 8.

66. Under Land Acquisition (Just Terms Compensation) Act, 1991 or any other Act. LEC Act, 1979, No. 204, Section 24.
67. NGT Act, 2010 (Act No. 19 of 2010), Schedule I [See sections 14(1), 15(1), 17(1)(a), 17(2), 19(4) (j) and 34(1)].
    1. The Water (Prevention and Control of Pollution) Act, 1974; (Water Act).
    2. The Water (Prevention and Control of Pollution) Cess Act, 1977.
    3. The Forest (Conservation) Act, 1980 (hereinafter Forest Act).
    4. The Air (Prevention and Control of Pollution) Act, 1981 (Air Act).
    5. The Environment (Protection) Act, 1986 (EPA).
    6. The Public Liability Insurance Act, 1991.
    7. The Biological Diversity Act, 2002.
68. Wildlife (Protection) Act, 1972.
69. C.M. Jariwala. 2010. 'National Green Tribunal: Whether(In)Justice?', *Delhi Law Review* 1.
70. NGT Act, 2010, Section 14 (1).
71. NGT Act, 2010, No. 19, Section 16.
72. A critical analysis of Section 16 bringing out its legislative flaws was provided by the author in India-Australia Workshop on 'Role of Specialist Environmental Law Courts for the Resolution of Environmental Disputes,' organized by Faculty of Law, University of Delhi in association with Australia India Institute, Melbourne, 1-2 February, 2011.
73. NGT Act, 2010, No. 19, Section 15 (1).
74. NGT Act, 2010, No. 19, Section 20.
75. NGT Act, 2010, No. 19, Section 21.
76. NGT Act, 2010, No. 19, Section 21 first Proviso.
77. NGT Act, 2010, No. 19, Section 21 second proviso.
78. NGT Act, 2010, No. 19, Section 22.
79. NGT Act, 2010, No. 19, Section 16 Proviso.
80. NGT Act, 2010, No. 19, Section 26.
81. NGT Act, 2010, No. 19, Section 26.
82. NGT Act, 2010, No. 19, Section 26 Proviso.
83. NGT Act, 2010, No. 19, Section 28.
84. NGT Act, 2010, No. 19, Section 19 (5).
85. NGT Act, 2010, No. 19, Section 19 (4).
86. NGT Act, 2010, No. 19, Section 19 (1).
87. NGT Act, 2010, No. 19, Section 19 (1).
88. NGT Act, 2010, No. 19, Section 19 (2).
89. NGT Act, 2010, No. 19, Section 19 (3).
90. For knowing the judicial hierarchy in Australia, See Brian J. Preston. 2012. 'Judicial Specialization Through Environment Courts: A Case Study of the Land and Environment Court of New South Wales.' *Pace Environmental Law Review*, 29(2): 2–3, http://digitalcommons.pace.edu/cgi/viewcontent.cgi?article=1700&context=pelr.

91. http://stat.abs.gov.au/itt/r.jsp?databyregion#/.
92. 'Population of India 2017', http://www.indiaonlinepages.com/population/india-current-population.html.
93. Kaleeswaram Raj. 2014. 'Decentralizing Environmental Justice', *Economic & Political Weekly*, 49(48), http://www.epw.in/journal/2014/48/web-exclusives/decentralising-environmental-justice.html.
94. *M.C. Mehta v UOI* 1986 (2) SCC 176.
95. NGT Act, 2010, No. 19, Section 29.
96. See http://ecourts.gov.in/index.php.
97. Kaleeswaram Raj, *M.C. Mehta v UOI* 1986 (2) SCC 176.
98. Kaleeswaram Raj, *M.C. Mehta v UOI* 1986 (2) SCC 176.
99. NGT Act, 2010, No. 19, Section 2 (m).
100. See Wildlife (Protection) Act, 1972.
101. See Department.of Science and Technology, Government of India, *The Report of Committee for Recommending Legislative Measures and Administrative Machinery For Ensuring Environmental Protection*, Annexure 12.
102. *Indian Council for Enviro-Legal v UOI* AIR 1996 SC 1446.
103. Brian J. Preston, http://stat.abs.gov.au/itt/r.jsp?databyregion#/, esp. p. 5.
104. Brian J. Preston, http://stat.abs.gov.au/itt/r.jsp?databyregion#/, esp. p. 5.
105. Brian J. Preston, http://stat.abs.gov.au/itt/r.jsp?databyregion#/, esp. p. 5.
106. Brian J. Preston, http://stat.abs.gov.au/itt/r.jsp?databyregion#/, esp. p. 5.
107. Brian J. Preston, http://stat.abs.gov.au/itt/r.jsp?databyregion#/, esp. p. 5.
108. Drawing upon examples from multiple jurisdictions, Brian J. Preston identifies twelve characteristics required for an environmental court or tribunal to operate successfully in practice. See Brian J Preston, 2014, 'Characteristics of Successful Environmental Courts and Tribunals', *Journal of Environmental*, vol. 26, p. 365 wherein he identifies and elaborates 12 key characteristics, in this regard, that include, Status and Authority; Independent from Government and Impartial; Comprehensive and Centralized Jurisdiction; Judges and Members are Knowledgeable and Competent; Operates as a Multi-Door Court House; Provides Access to Scientific and Technical Expertise; Facilitates Access to Justice; Achieves Just, Quick and Cheap Resolution of Disputes; Responsive to Environmental Problems and Relevant; Develops Environmental Jurisprudence; Underlying Ethos and Mission and Flexible, Innovative and Provides Value Adding Function.
109. See Gordon Walker. 2012. *Environmental Justice: Concepts, Evidence and Politics.* Abingdon: Routledge, pp. 48–9, cited by Brian J. Preston Id. at 369.
110. The independence and impartiality of ECT judges or decision-makers can be enabled by institutional arrangements and rules concerning selection of judges or decision-makers on the basis of appropriate qualifications; long-term tenure and security of tenure; procedural and substantive protection against the removal of judges; the means of fixing and reviewing reasonable remuneration and other conditions of service; the publishing of reasons for decisions made; and sufficient resources to maintain a functioning ECT. Such institutional arrangements and rules are intended to guarantee that judges will be free from

extraneous pressures and be independent of all authority except that of the law. George Pring and Catherine Pring. 2009. *Greening Justice: Creating and Improving Environmental Courts and Tribunals.* Washington D.C.: The Access Initiative, 75 in Brian J. Preston Id. at 370

111. Brian J. Preston, http://stat.abs.gov.au/itt/r.jsp?databyregion#/, esp. p. 613.
112. Brian J. Preston, http://stat.abs.gov.au/itt/r.jsp?databyregion#/, esp. 370.
113. See *Jeet Singh Kanwar v Union of India* Appeal No. 10 of 2011 (T) dated 16 April 2013; *Adivasi Majdoor Kisan Ekta Sangthan v Ministry of Environment and Forests* Appeal Number 3 of 2011 (T) (NEAA No. 26 of 2009) dated 20-4-2012. Id. at 194.
114. Armin Rosencranz and Geetanjoy Sahu. 2014. 'Assessing the National Green Tribunal After Four Years.' *Journal of Indian Law and Society*, vol 5, p. 191 and 192.
115. Armin Rosencranz and Geetanjoy Sahu. 2014. 'Assessing the National Green Tribunal After Four Years', *Journal of Indian Law and Society*, vol. 5., pp. 191–200.
116. The number of judgments pronounced by NGT May-Dec, 2011, 36; January--December, 2012, 91; January-December, 2013, 164; January-December, 2014 362 and for the one and a half month January-February, 15, 169. CEL on National Green Tribunal, http://www.wwfindia.org/about_wwf/enablers/cel/national_green_tribunal/.
117. Category-wise judgments adjudicated by NGT (from May 2011until February 2015: Environmental Clearance-119 (26 per cent); Forest Clearance 09 (2 per cent); Pollution 148 (32 per cent); Mining 24 (5 per cent); Forest conservation 12 (3 per cent); Limitation 23 (5 per cent); CRZ 20 (4 per cent); Cutting of Trees 20 (4 per cent); Illegal Construction 09 (2 per cent); Miscellaneous 76 (17 per cent).
118. PTI March 3, 2015, http://articles.economictimes.indiatimes.com/2015-03-03/news/59725502_1_national-green-tribunal-wildlife-crime-control-bureau-lok-sabha, accessed 3 July 1016.
119. Yukti Chowdhury, 2014. 'Tribunal on trial.' *Down to Earth*, http://www.downtoearth.org.in/coverage/tribunal-on-trial-47400, accessed 27 July 2017.
120. NGT Act, 2010, No. 19, Section 16.
121. NGT Act, 2010, No. 19, Section 14(3).
122. NGT Act, 2010, No. 19, Section 15(3).
123. Information sought from advocates appearing before NGT.
124. Brian J Preston, *Supra* n 91 at 614.
125. Yukti Choudhary, 'Tribunal on Trial', http://www.downtoearth.org.in/coverage/tribunal-on-trial-47400#1.
126. Protection of the Environment Operations Act 1997 (NSW), Section 101.
127. Armin Rosencranz and Geetanjoy Sahu. 'Assessing the National Green Tribunal After Four Years', 200.
128. Armin Rosencranz and Geetanjoy Sahu, 'Assessing the National Green Tribunal After Four Years', 195.

129. Brian J. Preston, http://stat.abs.gov.au/itt/r.jsp?databyregion#/, esp. 617.
130. Patricia Ryan. 2002. 'Court of Hope and False Expectations: Land and Environment Court 21 years on', *Journal of Environmental Law*, 14(3): 301.
131. LEC Act, 1979, No. 204, Section 39(2).
132. Councils are bodies established under the Local Government Act 1993 (NSW) (LGA). Each Council constitutes a statutory corporation.
133. The Court's Class 1 jurisdiction is usually exercised by a Commissioner. Commissioners are technical experts processing specialist knowledge and expertise.
134. Paul Lalich and Scott Neilson. 2001. 'Review of the Land and Environment Courts Jurisdiction: Review of Issues Relating to the Working Party Review and Reform of the Court', *Local Government Law Journal*, 49(51), https://www.allens.com.au/pubs/pdf/env/lecjaug01.pdf.
135. Jerrold Cripps was appointed as one of the foundation judges of the Court on 18 August 1980. He was appointed Chief Judge on 3 June 1985 and served until 1 April 1992, when he was appointed to the NSW Court of Appeal, http://www.lec.justice.nsw.gov.au/Documents/Announcements/31122015The%20Hon%20Jerrold%20Sydney%20Cripps%20QC.pdf.
136. Paul Lalich and Scott Neilson, 'Review of the Land and Environment Courts Jurisdiction, 52.
137. NGT Act, 2010, No. 19, Section 5 (3).
138. A former judge of Supreme Court of India, he is the second Chairperson of NGT, after Justice Lokeshwar Singh Panta, appointed on 20 December 2012 following a turbulent phase fraught with resignations by expert members, judges, and acting Chairperson due to the lack of infrastructure and facilities.
139. See, for instance, 'NGT to Hear PIL Challenging Environmental Clearance to Amravati.' *The Quint*. 11 March 2016. https://www.thequint.com/hot-wire/2016/03/11/ngt-to-hear-pil-challenging-environmental-clearance-to-amravati, accessed 27 July 2017.
140. See for instance *Tribunal on its own Motion v Secretary, Ministry of Environment and Forests*, NGT Judgment, 4 April 2014; *Tribunal on its own Motion v Government of NCT*, Delhi, NGT Order, 19 June 2015.
141. Gitanjali Nain Gill, 2015. 'Environmental Justice in India: The National Green Tribunal and Expert Members.' *Transnational Environmental Law* at 29. Available on CJO 2015 DOI:10.1017/S2047102515000278
142. Ministry of Environment, Forest and Climate Change (MEF&CC), Government of India, *Report of High Level Committee to review various Acts,* November 2014.
143. *Report of High Level Committee to review various Acts*, para 8.2, p. 62.
144. The NEMA and SEMA, when established under ELMA, shall replace Central Pollution Board and State Pollution Boards. *Report of High Level Committee to review various Acts*, para 8.2 (v) p. 63.
145. *Report of High Level Committee to review various Acts.* para 8.7, p. 64.

146. *Report of High Level Committee to review various Acts.* para 8.8, p. 65.
147. *Report of High Level Committee to review various Acts.* Sec 6.2 of Proposed ELMA, p. 71.
148. *Report of High Level Committee to review various Acts.* Sec 15 of proposed ELMA, p. 75.
149. Ritwick Dutta, Manoj Misra, and Himanshu Thakkar. 2015. 'The High-Level Committee Report on Environmental Law: A Recipe for Climate Disaster and Silencing People's Voice.' p. 7. www.ercindia.org/files/erc_desk/HLC%20 Report.pdf.
150. Srestha Banerjee. 2015. 'Parliamentary Standing Committee Rejects TSR Subramanian Report on Environmental Laws.' http://www.downtoearth.org.in/news/parliamentary-standing-committee-rejects-tsr-subramanian-report-on-environmental-laws-50577, accessed 27 July 2017.
151. Brian J. Preston, http://stat.abs.gov.au/itt/r.jsp?databyregion#/, esp. p. 618.
152. Wildlife (Protection) Act, 1972.
153. See Chandra Bhushan. 2014. 'NGT Must be Strengthened', http://www.downtoearth.org.in/coverage/tribunal-on-trial-47400. For an excellent insight into the internal decision-making processes of the five benches of the NGT, see Gitanjali Nain Gill, 'Environmental Justice in India: The National Green Tribunal and Expert Members.'

Index

About the Editor and Contributors

Editor

Mahendra Pal Singh is currently chancellor at the Central University of Haryana, India. He is former vice chancellor at WBNUJS, Kolkata. He is also chairperson at the Delhi Judicial Academy and is professor of law and head and dean at the University of Delhi. He is currently chair of the Centre for Comparative Law at National Law University, Delhi, as visiting professor.

Contributors

Arie Afriansyah is lecturer at the Faculty of Law, Universitas Indonesia. He is also the chairman of Djokosoetono Research Center Faculty of Law Universitas Indonesia, editor-in-chief of *Indonesia Law Review*, and senior associate editor for the *Indonesian Journal of International Law*. He obtained his bachelor's degree in law (*Sarjana Hukum*/S.H.) in 2003 from Universitas Indonesia. He became Master of International Law (MIL) in 2006 from the University of Sydney Law School, Australia, and PhD in law from the University of Otago, New Zealand, in 2013.

P. Ishwara Bhat is currently vice chancellor of West Bengal National University of Juridical Sciences (WBNUJS), Kolkata. An expert in constitutional law, and a Fulbright Nehru scholar, he possesses rich pedagogical experience, having taught courses and guided PhD students since 1979. He has handled research projects on multifarious subjects, such as language rights, multiculturalism, and law of non-profit organizations. He obtained LLD for his thesis on NPO law in 2016. His publications include several authored books and edited works, comparative studies, as well as more than hundred research articles in legal journals of international and national repute.

Maxim Bönnemann is a research fellow at Humboldt University, Berlin. He has been a visiting researcher at National Law University, Delhi, in 2015 and at the Centre for Policy Research, Delhi, in 2017.

Aratrika Choudhuri is currently a student of third year pursuing BA LLB (Honours) at WBNUJS, Kolkata.

Salmoli Choudhuri is an incoming doctoral candidate in the Department of History at the University of Cambridge, UK, and would be working on Rabindranath Tagore's legal and political thought. She is currently pursuing an MPhil in Modern South Asian Studies at Cambridge, has previously studied law at Oxford and Delhi, and has also taught legal history for a brief while to undergraduate students in Delhi. Her research interests range from history of legal and political ideas to modern Bengali culture and society.

Nupur Chowdhury is assistant professor at the Centre for the Study of Law and Governance, Jawaharlal Nehru University, New Delhi. Her current research interest includes evolving jurisprudence on environmental risk regulation in India and the design regulatory institutions (environment and public health) in a federal polity. She teaches courses on law, technology and development, constitutional law, and research methodology. She has been a member of the IUCN Commission on Environmental Law since 2010 and blogs at https://indiaenvirolegal.wordpress.com/.

Jill Cottrell taught law for 40 years at universities in Nigeria, the UK, and Hong Kong. She studied at the London School of Economics, UK, and Yale University, USA. She began a new career as an advisor on constitution-making not long before theoretical retirement, and has advised in, or on, the constitutions of, for example, East Timor, Iraq, Somalia, and Nepal. She now lives in Kenya where she works pro bono for an NGO, Katiba Institute, that supports the implementation process of the country's constitution through public interest litigation, publication, civic education, and public engagement of various kinds.

Wolfram Cremer is a German scientist who holds a chair for public law and European law at the Ruhr-University Bochum, Germany. Furthermore, he is scientific director of the Institute for Educational Research and Education Law, as well as director of the Institute for Mining and Energy Law in Bochum. Moreover, he is co-founder of the new Indo-German student exchange cooperation between Ruhr-University and National Law University, Delhi. His main areas of research are educational law, German constitutional law, and European Union law with special focus on economic law and fundamental rights and freedoms.

Philipp Dann is professor at Humboldt University, Berlin, where he holds the chair for public and comparative law. He has written widely on issues of law and development as well as on the law of the European Union and of international organizations. He is the editor-in-chief of the quarterly journal *Verfassung und Recht in Übersee* or *Law and politics in Africa, Asia and Latin America* that focuses on issues of public law in the Global South.

Swati Deva is a teaching fellow at the Faculty of Business, Hong Kong Polytechnic University. Before moving to Hong Kong in 2005, Swati taught in the National Law Institute University, Bhopal, and worked as a solicitor in Fox Mandal & Company, New Delhi. She received her LLB degree from Meerut University, Master of Business Laws from National Law School University, Bengaluru, and LLM from the University of London.

Amita Dhanda is professor of law at the National Academy of Legal Studies and Research, Hyderabad. She also heads the Centre for Disability Studies at the university. She has substantive interest in the field of public law and human rights with special reference to disability rights. Her doctoral thesis critically appraising the laws relating to the mentally ill was a pioneering effort at evaluating the human rights conformity of mental health laws in the country. The thesis was later brought out as a book entitled *Legal Order and Mental Disorder* (2000).

Yash Ghai taught law for 40 years at the universities of East Africa (Tanzania), Warwick, and Hong Kong, with shorter periods at Yale and Harvard Law Schools, USA, and the Universities of Singapore, Melbourne, Toronto, and the South Pacific. His research interests include constitutionalism and human rights, ethnic conflicts, sociology of law, and autonomy. He has published extensively on public law; his books include *Public Law and Political Change in Kenya: A Study of the Legal Framework of Government from Colonial Times to the Present* (1970) and *Hong Kong's New Constitutional Order: The Resumption of Chinese Sovereignty and the Basic Law* (1997), with many others edited or jointly edited particularly on issues of human rights, ethnicity, and autonomy.

Tanja Herklotz is a researcher and PhD candidate at the Chair for Public and Comparative Law at Humboldt University, Berlin. She holds an LLM degree from the School of Oriental and African Studies, University of London. She has conducted research in Delhi, Mumbai, and Bengaluru.

Michael von Hauff is full professor of economics and economic policy at the Technical University of Kaiserslautern, Germany. He studied economics at the Augusta State University, Georgia, USA, and at the Universities of Stuttgart and Constance, Germany. He received his PhD in 1977. In 2003, he was guest lecturer at the Nanyang Technological University, Singapore, and since 2004 he has been visiting professor at the Institute of Economics, Yangon, Myanmar. Moreover, he is a member of several national and international organizations including the European Academy of Sciences and Arts. In 2009, he was awarded the German Environmental Prize for his scientific achievements in favour of the topic of sustainable development.

Ridwanul Hoque is professor of law in the University of Dhaka, Bangladesh. He has held visiting positions at Cornell, Melbourne, and La Trobe Law Schools. He published a book titled *Judicial Activism in Bangladesh: A Golden Mean Approach* (2011) and many law review papers and book chapters in the USA, UK, Australia, Singapore, and India. Professor Hoque's areas of interest are constitutional law and theory, comparative constitutional law, and human rights of vulnerable people. He has taught public law courses seasonally at La Trobe University, Australia, and National Law University, Delhi.

Sanjay Jain is associate professor at the ILS Law College, Pune. He has been teaching since 20 years. He is the coordinator of the Centre for Public Law and Equal Opportunity cum enabling cell, and director of the research centre affiliated to the ILS Law College at Savitribai Phule Pune University, Pune. He is a 'disability rights activist'. His areas of specialization are disability rights jurisprudence, comparative constitutional law, legal theory, and international trade law. His doctoral thesis is on 'Feminism and Constitutional Law'. He has published a number of books and articles, prominent among which is *Basic Structure Constitutionalism: Revisiting Kesavananda Bharati*, co-edited with Sathya Narayan in 2011.

George Katrougalos is professor of Public Law at Democritus University of Thrace, and Alternate Minister of Foreign Affairs, Greece. He has been visiting scholar at the Law School of New York University (2007 and 2012), as Emile Noel Fellow and senior Emile Noel Fellow, respectively, and at Roskilde University (1994–5), as a fellow of the Danish Academy of Science. He has been legal advisor to the minister of education (1994, 1997–2002), to the Greek Mission at the United Nations (2000–3), and member of the committee of experts advising the Ministry of Foreign Affairs on the drafting of the European Constitution.

Markus Kotzur holds the chair for European law and public international law at Hamburg University, Germany, and is managing director of the Institute for European Integration at the Europa-kolleg Hamburg, where he also signs responsible for the Master Programme 'European and European Legal Studies'. Among others, Kotzur co-edits the *Archiv des Völkerrechts*, has co-authored academic books as well as commentaries, and extensively published on matters of European Union law, European constitutional law, and public international law. Guest lectures and study visits took him inter alia to Brazil, Hong Kong, Hungary, India, Italy, Japan, Poland, Russia, Spain, Switzerland, and USA.

Jörg Luther is full professor of Institutions of Public Law at the University of Eastern Piedmont, Italy, with courses on constitutional and comparative law at the University of Turin, Italy. As a member of the Academic Network on the European Social Charter, he recently published 'Europe's Social Rights under the "Turin Process"' in *Editoriale Scientifica*, Napoli, 2016.

Mihir Naniwadekar graduated from the National Law School of India University, Bengaluru, and is an advocate practising at the Bombay High Court. He specializes in taxation, company law, and commercial law. From 2017, he will be pursuing a PhD in law at the University of New South Wales, Sydney, with his research focusing on remedies for breaches of duties by directors, agents, trustees, and other fiduciaries.

Arpita Sarkar is senior research associate at Jindal Global Law School in O.P. Jindal Global University, Sonipat, Haryana. She has done her BA LLB from WBNUJS, Kolkata and LLM from Central European University, Budapest, Hungary. She teaches law at Jindal Global Law School.

Usha Tandon is professor and head at the Campus Law Centre, University of Delhi. With 28 years of teaching experience, she is a world-renowned scholar for her work on human development focusing on environmental protection and women empowerment. She has numerous research publications to her credit and has presented her research work at various national and international platforms in various countries including USA, UK, France, Germany, Netherlands, China, Singapore, South Korea, Malaysia, Bhutan, and Nepal. Her most recent research work includes her contribution as an expert for the upcoming World Bank's Project *Enabling the Business of Agriculture: 2017 Report.*

Moiz Tundawala is a doctoral candidate in the Department of Law at the London School of Economics and Political Science, UK, and is working on the nature of constituent power in India's constitutional tradition. He has previously studied law in London and Kolkata, and has taught comparative constitutional thought, legal and political philosophy, and law and religion in Kolkata, Delhi, and London. His research engagements are usually situated in the intersection of constitutional and political thought, legal theory, and intellectual history.

Umakanth Varottil is associate professor at the Faculty of Law, National University of Singapore. He specializes in corporate law and governance, mergers and acquisitions, and cross-border investments. While his work is generally comparative in nature, he focuses particularly on India and Singapore. He has co-authored two books on Singapore law and practice, published articles in international journals, and founded the Indian Corporate Law blog. Prior to his foray into academia, Umakanth was a partner at a pre-eminent law firm in India.

Qianfan Zhang is professor of constitutional law at Peking University Law School, China. He has a doctorate in governmental theory and studied law at the University of Maryland, USA. Later he pursued his postdoctoral studies at the University of California, USA and has worked at several universities in China before moving to Peking University. His multiple publications include *Constitutional System in the West* and *The Constitution of China: A Contextual Analysis* (2012). His research field includes constitutional jurisprudence, comparative constitutional law, Chinese Constitution, and principles of constitutionalism.